South Asia, the British Empire, and the Rise of Classical Legal Thought

'Chaudhry's "South Asia" is a brilliant rereading of the legal history of nineteenth-century India under British rule. Chaudhry shows that both before and after the shift from Company to Crown in 1857, the legal consciousness informing the creation of new law changed continuously in ways that were as important or more important than changes in legal substance. A highly original and deeply researched investigation of the way law did and didn't travel from the metropole and was transformed in the process. An important contribution to jurisprudence as well as to comparative law and critical legal history.'

—Duncan Kennedy, Carter Professor of General Jurisprudence, Emeritus, Harvard Law School

'What was law in colonial India? In this brilliant work of historical ontology, Faisal Chaudhry retells the history of Britain's India as a revealing case study of the global expansion of law's empire. Bringing together an extraordinary array of sources, from socio-legal theory and the philosophy of jurisprudence to everyday case law, Chaudhry deftly connects the theory and practice of law in colonial South Asia to the globalization of classical legal thought. More than a legal history, this book offers a new history of modern legality. It will be essential reading for historians of South Asia, for historians of the British Empire, and for all readers interested in the history of law and jurisprudence in the modern world.'

—Robert Travers, Professor of History, Cornell University

'In this theoretically rigorous and historically grounded study, Faisal Chaudhry convincingly shows how the rule of laws about landed property under Company Raj was transformed into a new normative conception of the law itself after the inauguration of Crown Raj in 1858. He skilfully places colonial India in the wider context of the global evolution of classical legal thought. He has brilliant chapters on the making of the new law of contract and jurisprudential innovation on marriages in the 1860s and 1870s. The redefinition of sovereignty in a more unitary direction can be seen to be matched by the establishment of a qualitatively new legal regime during these decades.'

—Sugata Bose, Gardiner Professor of Oceanic History and Affairs, Harvard University

South Asia, the British Empire, and the Rise of Classical Legal Thought

Towards a Historical Ontology of the Law

FAISAL CHAUDHRY

Great Clarendon Street, Oxford, OX2 6DP,
United Kingdom

Oxford University Press is a department of the University of Oxford.
It furthers the University's objective of excellence in research, scholarship,
and education by publishing worldwide. Oxford is a registered trade mark of
Oxford University Press in the UK and in certain other countries

© Faisal Chaudhry 2024

The moral rights of the author have been asserted

All rights reserved. No part of this publication may be reproduced, stored in
a retrieval system, or transmitted, in any form or by any means, without the
prior permission in writing of Oxford University Press, or as expressly permitted
by law, by licence or under terms agreed with the appropriate reprographics
rights organization. Enquiries concerning reproduction outside the scope of the
above should be sent to the Rights Department, Oxford University Press, at the
address above

You must not circulate this work in any other form
and you must impose this same condition on any acquirer

Published in the United States of America by Oxford University Press
198 Madison Avenue, New York, NY 10016, United States of America

British Library Cataloguing in Publication Data

Data available

Library of Congress Control Number: 2024932391

ISBN 978-0-19-891648-2

DOI: 10.1093/oso/9780198916482.001.0001

The maps presented in this publication hold historical significance and hence these maps do not claim to depict the present political boundaries of post-Independence India or its international borders. For accurate and up-to-date information on India's current internal and international boundaries, please refer to the political map of India issued by the Survey of India (polmap-eng-11012021.jpg (5903×6853) (surveyofindia.gov.in).

For my beloved parents,

Iqbal and Surraya Chaudhry,

for always giving themselves for ours.

Acknowledgements

The customary nature of the thanks that are extended upon the completion of any significant project is likely always to belie how far, wide, or deep they actually go. My own must first be made to those who helped guide this book from its earliest incarnation, my principal advisers during the course of graduate study at Harvard University: Professors Sugata Bose and Duncan Kennedy. In all the time during and since, Professor Bose has proved a model—both intellectually and as a person—of calm, reassurance, and constructive critique whenever it has been needed. In its foundational concern with property relations in the agrarian countryside, its subsequently unfolding thematic breadth, and its constant sympathy for the many pieces of the subcontinent's always transnationally situated mosaic, his own work has provided a sterling example. As for Professor Kennedy, my intellectual debt to him will be obvious to anyone who reads even a few pages of the book. His encouragement for the project and his keen sense of principled, critical, and solidaristic engagement has always meant that whatever influences I was soaking up from his writings, which proved so endlessly illuminating, rarely, if ever, appeared as any foreboding shadow over our relationship. In this respect, the Duncan Kennedy who appears in the footnotes of the book is a presence completely distinct from (and never imposed on) the one who it has been a treasure to get to know and who, before I ever really knew him, was already there to provide steadfast support. It is hard to say which version of Duncan has been more important. So, I can only say I am equally thankful for both, and hope that—if nothing else—this book will be understood to intersect with the towering legacy he has (and should, in years to come, be ever further appreciated for having) left to the understanding of law and legal thought, present and past. Of course, thanks also go to the staff at Oxford University Press who have watched over the project, including Prasun Chatterjee, Nandini Ganguli, Barun Sarkar, Natasha Sarkar, and Meghali Banerjee.

Further debts, first accrued in the early course of my working on the project, or otherwise, are owed to various others who proved sources of pedagogical guidance. This has included Asad Ahmed, Charles Donahue, the late (and dearly missed) Lani Guinier, Ayesha Jalal (who inspired my original interest in the study of South Asia), Cemal Kafadar, Mary Lewis, Bhavani Raman, Sunil Sharma, Wheeler Thackston, and Robert Travers. In the case of many of these debts, like that which I owe to Professor Travers, it would be inaccurate to suggest that they have accrued only early on rather than on an ongoing basis.

In later parts of the book's trajectory of development there are obviously other institutions and individuals to whom I owe thanks for assisting with intellectual and material support. In Philadelphia this included the Departments of History and South Asia Studies at the University of Pennsylvania and people like Daud Ali, Lisa Mitchell, Projit Mukharji, Deven Patel, Terenjit Sevea, Pushkar Sohoni, Ramya Sreenivasan, and Tyler Williams. At Penn, life was also immeasurably enriched by the amazingly sharp graduate students and others then connected to the area studies programme, especially Sugra Bibi, Baishakh Chakrabarti, Jawan Shir Rasikh, and Sudev Sheth. Among various others were Anannya Bohidar, Brian Cannon, Michael Collins, Divya Kumar Das, Samana Gururaja, Darakhshan Khan, and Pooja Nayak. In Tucson it included the University of Arizona and individuals like Richard Eaton, Mark Miller, Robert A. Williams (for never failing to live up to the example he strikes on the page and for always living his intellect and politics), and Nathan Dunn (for his soft-spoken roar and ever-restless and -incisive mind). In Dayton it included the University of Dayton and colleagues like Ericka Curran, Simanti Dasgupta, Shelley Inglis, Haimanti Roy, Andrea Seielstad (for her steadfast support and for never losing her fight), Dalindyebo Shabalala, Jamie Small, Andrew Strauss, Julie E. Zink, and Pamela Izvănariu (for her relentless devotion to academic excellence, a personal courage that keeps revealing new dimensions, and, most of all, the immanence of her example). Finally, it includes the University of Massachusetts School of Law and Department of History at the University of Massachusetts Dartmouth and colleagues like Ronit Amit, Hillary Farber, Geoffrey McDonald, Richard Peltz-Steele, and Lisa Owens, and Danya Reda (for her inspiring fortitude in the face of merciless odds and with special thanks for her and Nicholas Frayn's lasting friendship, which is remembered as it is experienced).

Befitting a project on South Asia, thanks also goes to those who I first encountered based on their own presence in or mutual crossings through the subcontinent; the many that could be listed under this heading include the late Yunus Jaffery, Farhat Hasan, Upal Chakrabarti (for that most refreshing of things, intellectual companionship for its own sake rather than professionalization), Rohit De, and Mitra Sharafi (who even as peers were always hubs of South Asian legal studies for all comers). Of course, this is to say nothing of the staff and personnel at the various archives and research institutions in India that welcomed me, including the National Archives of India, the Nehru Memorial Library, and the Indian Law Institute.

Beyond official institutional homes, the research and writing of this book was also supported or otherwise made possible along the way by various other entities, including the Department of History and South Asia Institute at Harvard University, the Fulbright Foundation, the British Library (with special thanks to the librarians in the Asian & African Studies Reading Room), Columbia University Law School's Center for the Study of Law and Culture (with thanks to Kendall Thomas), the American Council of Learned Societies, the Mellon Foundation, and the Max Planck Institute for Legal History and Legal Theory (with thanks to Stefan Vogenauer and Jean-Philippe Dequen). I must also extend gratitude to *Modern Asian Studies*, *The Law and History Review*, and *The Journal of the Economic and Social History of the Orient*, in which journals either pieces or preliminary versions of aspects of the argumentative contents of chapters four, six, and nine have previously appeared.

Among those who have been connected to the book at one time or another in virtue not so much of shared affiliation to the same institutional homes, but simply shared affiliation, are various friends—old, lasting, and new—who bear mentioning. These include Aaron Bartley, Foqia Khan (for having watched out and her deep knowledge of Pakistan), David Lee, Miles Rodriguez, Nahed Samour, Marjan Wardaki, Ramsi Woodcock, and Jill Zimmerman (for conversation and silence). As they will surely know, it also includes Roshan Iqbal and Razak Khan. To Razak special gratitude is owed: for seeing and sustaining the project in every phase, for faith in its uncharacteristic aspects and innumerable practical suggestions about working in and on South Asia, for never letting his own painstakingness as a historian who loves the archives diminish his fluency in matters of theory and the politics of the present, and for navigating spaces of elite academia (and, hence, among many of South Asia's elite) without ever egoistically asserting his own subaltern bona fides, despite what a mockery they could so easily make of others inhabiting such spaces and seeking to theorize about such matters.

Finally, as goes without saying most of all, thanks enough cannot be given to my family, whether for the duration of a lifetime or from whatever point within: Basit, Saima, Kavita, Samir, Inaya, Jamil, the Zahids, Sarah, Safiya, and my dear and precious parents, Iqbal and Surraya. To all, I express appreciation for putting up with the project while endowing me with love, encouragement, support, and, most of all, awareness that if I say no more or even if I said nothing at all it would make no difference to their always still being ready with more. Appropriately enough, therefore, I will let this last observation be the last observation—absolving me, as it does, of trying to elaborate any further on what is, in any case, ineffable.

Contents

List of Maps — xv
Note on Transliteration, Terminology, and Abbreviations — xix

Introduction: Paths to 'the Law' — 1

PART I: THE LEGAL HISTORY OF COLONIAL RULE IN THE SOUTH ASIAN SUBCONTINENT AND THE ONTOLOGIZATION OF 'THE LAW': THE PROBLEM AND A PROPOSED ANALYTICAL FRAMEWORK

1. The History of British Colonial Rule in South Asia as a History of Legal Development — 29
   1.1 Introduction: The Problem of the Duality of Law and the (Colonial) State — 29
   1.2 Law in the Self-Conception of Early Colonial Rule — 33
   1.3 Crown Rule and the Rise of a Legislative State — 40
   1.4 From Scientific Legislation to a Science of the Law — 43
   1.5 The Rise of Classical Legal Thought and its Globalization — 53
   1.6 The Law as a Social/Institutional Fact — 60
   1.7 The Problem of Self-Reflexivity in the Study of South Asian 'Legalities' — 65
   1.8 Social Constructionism and the Ontology of the Legal in Colonial India — 69

2. Beyond Law and History: Naturalization and its Limits in Jurisprudential Inquiry — 79
   2.1 Introduction: Questioning Law's Nature, Naturalizing the Law — 79
   2.2 The Sociological Problem of Formal versus Living Law — 85
   2.3 The Anthropological Problem of State versus Non-State Law — 88
   2.4 The Philosophical Problem of the Law's Positivism versus Normativity — 93
   2.5 The Socio-Legal Theoretical Problem of the Law's Facticity versus Validity/Legitimacy — 106

3. Denaturalizing the Law: Historical Ontology as a Method/A
   Method for Historical Ontology 121
   3.1 Introduction 121
   3.2 The Problems of Law and Language 122
   3.3 Making the Law: Ontologization versus Reification 132
   3.4 Discourse of the Law versus Discourse about the Law 136
   3.5 Ontologization and the Operative Quality of Doctrinal
       Discourse 140
   3.6 Ontologization and the Administrable Quality of Doctrinal
       Discourse 144
   3.7 Ontologization and Discourse about the Law 147
   3.8 Ontologization and Ideology in the Globalization of
       Classical Legal Thought 152
   3.9 Re-Diagramming the Plan of Parts II and III 155

PART II: LAWS AND THE LAND: PROPERTY
AND REVENUE IN THE DISCOURSE OF THE
COMPANY'S INDIA FROM 1757 TO 1857

4. From Plassey to the Permanent Settlement in the
   Company's Bengal: Property, Constitution, and a
   Historical Ontology of the Laws 161
   4.1 Introduction 161
   4.2 The Context of the Company's Advent to Power in Bengal 174
   4.3 Asiatic Despotism as a Form of Political Constitution and an
       Ontology of the Laws 179
   4.4 Sound Laws, Secure Property: Public-Sphere Discourse
       in Bengal from 1757 to 1772 188
   4.5 Property in the Land's Rent as the Basis for the Doctrinal
       Discourse of Revenue Administration after 1772 195
   4.6 Property, Constitutionism, and Political Economy after
       Hastings' Tax Farming Scheme of 1772 200
   4.7 A Distinction without a Difference? (Private) Property in
       Rent versus (Sovereign) Property in the Land Revenue
       in Phillip Francis' Plan of 1776 205
   4.8 Property in Rent as the Definitive Form of Indian Property in
       Land: Shore's Opposition to Grant Reconsidered 211
   4.9 Shore, Cornwallis, and the Duration of Permanency 217
   4.10 The Relationship between Constitutionism and Property's
        Discourses in Early Colonial Bengal 219

5. Beyond the Permanent Settlement: Property Discourse
   and Non-*Zamindari* Revenue Systems 221
   5.1 Introduction 221
   5.2 The *Raiyatwari* System of Revenue Settlement in Madras 223
   5.3 The Discourse of *Raiyatwari* Right and the Persistence
       of Property in Rent 226
   5.4 *Raiyatwari* Entitlement as Mere Lease Right? 230
   5.5 *In'am* Privileges and the Problem of Administering Rights
       without Duties 236
   5.6 Munro's Minute on 'Altamgha *Inams*': Alienating Private
       Property or Public Revenue? 239
   5.7 *In'am* Rights and the Company's Ontology of the Laws 246
   5.8 Coda: Utilitarianism, the Ricardian Law of Rent, and
       the Ontology of the Legal 254

PART III: THE LAW AND ITS BASIC ELEMENTS: RIGHTS AS REALMS AND THE WILL OF JURIDICAL PERSONS IN THE DISCOURSE OF CLASSICAL LEGAL THOUGHT IN THE CROWN'S INDIA FROM 1857 TO C.1920

6. Crown Rule and the Legalization of Property: Rights as
   Realms of Proprietary Interest 267
   6.1 Introduction 267
   6.2 The Shifting Institutional Context of the Administration
       of Justice 275
   6.3 The Shifting Political Economy of Crown Rule and
       the Recognition of New Forms of 'Proprietary' Right 278
   6.4 Legalizing Property: Baden-Powell between Revisionism
       and Classical Legal Thought 288
   6.5 Legal Ontologization and the Operativeness and
       Administrability of the Discourse of 'Proprietary Right' 300
   6.6 Rights as Proprietary Realms and Making Sense of Discourse
       about Contract(ualism) 302

7. The Private and the Public Will in the Indian Contract Act 315
   7.1 Introduction 315
   7.2 Contracts before the Contract Act 319
   7.3 The Genesis and Reception of the Indian Contract Act 330
   7.4 Reading *The Indian Contract Act of 1872* 339
   7.5 Contractual Collectivism and the Expansion of the Public Law 364

8. From Contract to the Nascent Anthropological Discourse
   about Status ... 371
   8.1 Introduction ... 371
   8.2 Status and the Law of Domestic Relations ... 374
   8.3 The Two Faces of Status in Maine's *Ancient Law* ... 377
   8.4 Legal Ontologization and the Gap between the
       Ordinary-Language and Doctrinal Discourse of Status ... 383
   8.5 The Status of the Post-Annexation Punjab ... 385
   8.6 Status in Discourse about the Customary Law in the Punjab ... 393
   8.7 From Discourse about Status as (Social) Role/Identity to
       (Ascriptive) Identity as Status ... 401
   8.8 The Status of the Personal Law (Part I): The Emergence of 'the
       Personal Law' and the Muslim and Hindu Law as its Main
       Subsystems ... 407
   8.9 Status as an Operative/Administrable Concept versus
       Taxonomic Heading ... 419

9. The Restitution of Conjugal Rights and the Nature of
   Marriage: Constituting the Subsystems of the (Religious)
   Personal Law as a Law of Status ... 425
   9.1 Introduction ... 425
   9.2 The Conjugal Family in Late-Colonial South Asia ... 427
   9.3 The Status of the Personal Law (Part II): Anglo-Muslim
       and Anglo-Hindu Law as Place-Holders for the
       Law of Status ... 430
   9.4 Conjugal Restitution and Parsi Spouses in the
       Perozeboye Case and its Aftermath ... 435
   9.5 Purely a Civil Contract? The Nature of Marriage
       among 'Muhammadans' ... 446
   9.6 The Contractual Nature of (Muslim) Marriage and Law
       in the Politics of Communitarian Identity Symbols ... 463
   9.7 Making Doctrinal Sense of the 'Sacramental' Nature of
       (Hindu) Marriage ... 468
   9.8 A Conclusion: A Note on the Instrumental Function
       of the Law (of Conjugal Restitution) ... 481

Conclusion ... 489

Bibliography ... 499
Index ... 529

Maps

1 Historical Map 1 of East India Company Presidencies on eve of Transfer of Power, 1856 — xvi
2 Historical Map 2 of British India and Princely States, 1906 — xvii
3 Historical Map 3 of Colonial Subcontinent's Commodity Economy, 1906 — xviii

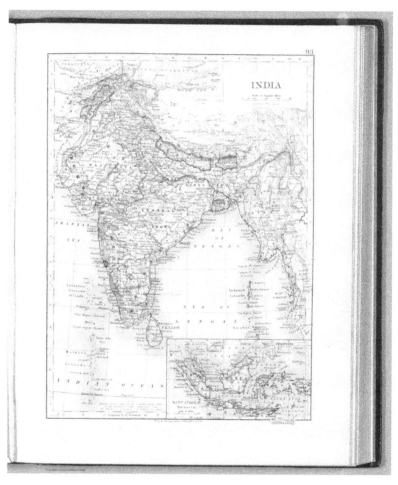

Map 1 Historical Map 1 of East India Company Presidencies on Eve of Transfer of Power, 1856 (J. H. Colton, Courtesy of the David Rumsey Map Collection, David Rumsey Map Center, Stanford Libraries)

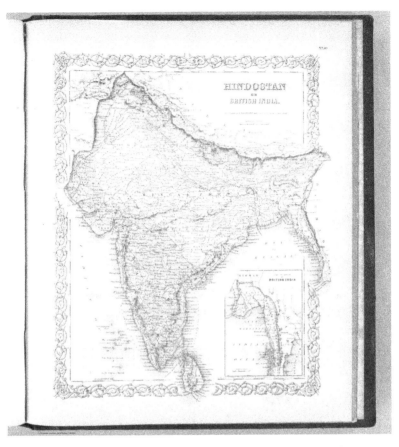

Map 2 Historical Map 2 of British India and Princely States, 1906 (W. & A. K. Johnston Limited, Courtesy of the David Rumsey Map Collection, David Rumsey Map Center, Stanford Libraries)

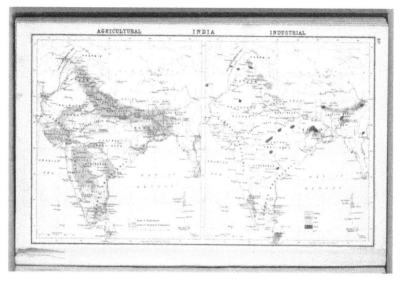

Map 3 Historical Map 3 of Colonial Subcontinent's Commodity Economy, 1906 (George Newnes, Limited, Courtesy of the David Rumsey Map Collection, David Rumsey Map Center, Stanford Libraries)

Note on Transliteration, Terminology, and Abbreviations

At various points this book uses words of administrative and juridical import during both pre-colonial and colonial times in the history of the South Asian subcontinent, including ones that were incorporated into South Asian language traditions from Arabic and Persian. Given the focus of the book on law and legal change under British colonial rule, in all but a small number of cases I have eschewed using the Library of Congress or other standard Romanization systems to more exactingly transliterate non-English words. Instead, I have usually deferred to the conventional modes of transliteration—shorn of diacritic marks, save for ain (ʿ) and hamza (ʾ), word terminal silent h's from the Persian, and markers for the Arabic *ta marbuta*—one finds in that part of the broader historiography that tends to be less attentive to these matters than scholarship focused on language and literary cultures. (For example, instead of *zamīndār* I have simply used *zamindar*; instead of *sharīʿa* I have simply used *shariʿa*; etc.) I have generally followed the same practice for subcontinental language terms of juridical and administrative import without any connection to the lexicons of Arabic and Persian. In all references to works by others, I have preserved whatever transliteration choices their authors have made.

Throughout I have used a mix of terms besides just *South Asia* to reflect the geographical domain of the book's titular focus. Of course, all of these terms—*South Asia, India, subcontinent, South Asian/Indian subcontinent*, etc.—are historically contingent and contested. For presentation's sake, I have erred on the side of varying the prose as appropriate and not getting too detained by the significant imperfections all of these terms harbour or on such grounds ruling any out. At the same time, as possible, I have also actively sought to prevent the imposing shadow of modern national borders and their own claims on lexical choice from being cast over the book. Oftentimes, therefore, I have preferred modes of reference that eschew overlap with current names of national states, even at whatever other cost of convenience/familiarity/anachronism. Finally, at various points in the presentation I use my own neologism of *Britain's India* to refer to the subcontinent instead of *British India*. This choice is intentional, sometimes being driven by the most innocuous of needs to vary the prose (and avoid overreliance on *colonial India*). At others it is driven by the aim of making joint reference, whether to the period of rule by the East India Company and the Crown in Parliament or, after 1857, to both British India and the princely states, where I have preferred to be ambiguous about whether any given statement is meant to point to British India alone (since that term, properly applied, would exclude the areas under indirect princely administration). Nothing about this neologism is meant to suggest that 'India' somehow uniquely belonged to Britain, should the reader's sensitivity make them so wonder.

The following abbreviations are used in the text:

ILR   Indian Law Reports
IOR   India Office Records
MIA   Moore's Indian Appeals
NAI   National Archives of India

Introduction
Paths to 'the Law'

Whatever opinion in short may be formed of Menu and his laws, in a country happily enlightened by found philosophy and the only true revelation, it must be remembered, that those laws are actually revered, as the word of the Most High, by nations of great importance to the political and commercial interests of Europe.

William Jones, 1796[1]

A law, they say, is a command of a particular kind ... [I]t imposes on those subjects an obligation or duty and threatens a penalty (or sanction) in the event of disobedience. The power vested in particular members of the community of drawing down the sanction on neglects or breaches of the duty is called a Right. Now, without the most violent forcing of language, it is impossible to apply these terms ... to the customary law under which the Indian village-communities have lived for centuries.

Henry Maine, 1871[2]

Few questions concerning human society have been asked with such persistence and answered by serious thinkers in so many diverse, strange, and even paradoxical ways as the question 'What is law?' Even if we confine our attention to the legal theory of the last 150 years ... we shall find a situation not paralleled in any other subject ... No vast literature is dedicated to answering the

---

[1] 'Preface', William Jones, *Institutes of Hindu Law: or, the Ordinances of Menu, according to the Gloss of Cullúca. Comprising the Indian System of Duties, Religious and Civil* (Calcutta: Printed by the Order of the Government, 1796), xvi.

[2] Henry Maine, *Village-Communities in the East and West; Six Lectures Delivered at Oxford*, 2nd edn. (London: J. Murray, 1872), 67–68.

questions, 'What is chemistry?' or 'What is the medicine?', as it is to the question 'What is law?'

H. L. A. Hart, 1961[3]

This book started from an interest in more closely examining the legal history of the eighteenth- and nineteenth-century South Asian subcontinent on its own terms and, thus, outside the contradictory ways in which its juridical past was digested under colonial rule. In its inception the book was informed by the significant outpouring of scholarship on law and colonialism that followed in the wake of the growing interest in language and discourse theory among historians, anthropologists, and other scholars of South Asia that started in the 1980s. My initial plan was to deepen earlier scholarship through a more sustained engagement with the pre-colonial past of Indo-Islamic juristic tradition in North India and its particular conceptualization of the relationship between law, religion, morality, and custom as sources of 'normativity'. With the latter concept—of normativity—in tow, it seemed that it would be possible to keep in check the tendency to presuppose a hard and fast dichotomy between British and Indian forms of law and legal system. It also seemed possible to thereby avoid epistemological difficulties of the very kind that scholars of law and colonialism had so forcefully shown to have effectively enabled the Raj's officials to sap Hindu, Islamic, and customary norms of their fluidity in the first place—namely, by recasting their selective absorption into the colonial state's legal regime as a form of cultural preservation.

Along the way, however, it became more and more difficult to locate a point of historical departure that did not demand I give more sustained consideration to issues that initially seemed of importance mainly in order to define my object of study before moving on to the main line of enquiry. As these seemingly preliminary questions revealed themselves to be anything but, very early within the research and writing process I found myself moving towards a destination that would leave me with one foot firmly planted in the territory of jurisprudence and legal theory. At the same time, the much greater difficulty these once preliminary

---

[3] H. L. A. Hart, *The Concept of Law* (New York: Oxford University Press, 1961), 1.

questions ended up harbouring also meant that so too did I find my other foot starting to shift. As a result, it soon became evident that the empirical focus of the book would have to be recalibrated as well, given the need to concentrate on the colonial state's rule of/by law rather than using it simply as a foil for justifying the type of study—of some aspect of the subcontinent's own independent juridical past—that was really needed instead.

Of course, recalibrating empirical focus did not come without some cost; as just noted, it meant eschewing an emerging state of the scholarly art that could be heard calling, in effect, to prioritize the task of developing a more complete picture of native juridical life on its own terms, whether before the advent of the colonial state or simply beyond its purview. Without detracting from the obvious importance of such a priority, which in recent years has commanded ever more sophisticated attention,[4] to my own eyes it nonetheless appeared (and has continued to appear) that better understanding colonial legal discourse on *its* own terms must be just as important, even notwithstanding the tendency that emerged, by now long since, to assume that enough ink had been spilled on inspecting colonial discourse of *any* kind. Indeed, it even appeared that it might be *more* important insofar as the law's modern spectre was liable to hang over any effort to properly grapple with the nature of juridical life before (or simply beyond) the coming of the West—no matter how otherwise accomplished such efforts might be and regardless of whether they were based on a general scepticism about applying modernity's categories to the past[5] or, in opposite

---

[4] For works focused on pre-colonial 'law' (or colonial transitions), see Nandini Chatterjee, *Negotiating Mughal Law: A Family of Landlords across Three Indian Empires* (New York: Cambridge University Press, 2020), Farhat Hasan, *Paper, Performance, and the State: Social Change and Political Culture in Mughal India* (New York: Cambridge University Press, 2021), and Robert Travers, *Empires of Complaints: Mughal Law and the Making of British India, 1765-1793* (New York: Cambridge University Press, 2022). For works, each in their own way, seeking to look beyond the horizon of colonial rigidification of native traditions and to their inner creativity, see e.g. Mitra Sharafi, *Law and Identity in Colonial South Asia: Parsi Legal Culture, 1772-1947* (New York: Cambridge University Press, 2014), Julia Stephens, *Governing Islam: Law, Empire, and Secularism in Modern South Asia* (New York: Cambridge University Press, 2018), and Elizabeth Lhost, *Everyday Islamic Law and the Making of Modern South Asia* (Chapel Hill, NC: University of North Carolina Press, 2022).

[5] See e.g. Wael Hallaq, *The Impossible State: Islam, Politics, and Modernity's Moral Predicament* (New York: Columbia University Press, 2014). From the very outset, Hallaq makes known his explicit opposition to imposing the modern notion of state on our understanding of what he

fashion, an embrace of those categories by redefining their conceptual borders.[6]

To my own eyes, therefore, what seemed most urgently needed was a way to explore anew how British domination in the subcontinent seemed both to defy and embody a rule of the law's own. In this respect, the larger explanatory journey the book needed to chart its course towards would have to involve better historicizing 'the law' not so much as a category or even an object of thought but as something that during the colonial period became more and more like a real concrete object in its own right. As it happened, the first step in my own way of doing so came to involve reckoning with what seemed to be a much starker difference between the

instead insists on identifying as 'Islamic governance' before the nineteenth century. In fact, this opposition is what underlies the very thesis of the book, according to which any notion of an *Islamic state* in today's world is simply a contradiction in terms (and, thus, literally speaking 'impossible'). Yet Hallaq never quite extends the same scepticism to the law as its own kind of uniquely modern construct. To be sure, in *The Impossible State*, as in earlier work, we find Hallaq trying to minimize the distortion the modern notion of law would seem to impose on our understanding of the pre-nineteenth century 'sharīʿa', not the least because of its centrality to his notion of 'Islamic governance'. When faced with the need to elaborate on pre-nineteenth-century sharīʿa Hallaq, thus, tends to invoke the concept of law either in inverted commas or by inserting some relevant qualifier, as when calling it a 'moral law' (see e.g. ibid., xi). At the same time, it is equally clear that Hallaq neither quite wants to nor ever proves able to sever the sharīʿa-Islamic *law* equivalence in whatever way he strives to do for the eqivalence between the (modern) state and (pre-nineteenth-century) Islamic governance, even despite how this plain inconsistency tends to undermine *The Impossible State*'s entire enterprise.

[6] In this vein, one might further consider Chatterjee's *Negotiating Mughal Law*, which is by all rights a groundbreaking work in the study of the subcontinent's early-modern legal past. To its great credit, Chatterjee's study is unsurpassed in its legal theoretical fluency even as it retains the sophistication of a work by a historian steeped in Mughal social and political history rather than just the empire's narrowly legal history of evolving judicial and administrative institutions. In confronting the problem of anachronism, in sharp contrast to Hallaq, Chatterjee opts to take the notion of law at face value in trying to reconstruct the Mughal past, and instead builds on an array of novel/uncharacteristic working definitions of the concept. See e.g. ibid., 4 (describing the book's conception of law as 'a specialized language used by common people, with the help of low-brow specialists to record, assert and dispute claims, to articulate popular expectations of the state, of peers and of betters, and ... to make striking statements of self-description', even despite not being 'conflatable with institutions or rules/norms'), 10 (contrasting 'sharīʿa-as-law' with other sources of norms yielding a 'broader sense of the "right path"'), 13 (describing law as 'more than jurisprudence, but as a mode of communication which shared and reoriented the juridical lexicon' and 'a specific trajectory of cosmopolitanism in the Indo-Persianate and Indo-Islamic world'), 72 (contrasting 'an abstract body of law in the sense of doctrine' with 'emanations from royal grace' that did not need/seek to justify themselves according to such law), 236 (suggesting an equation between '[t]he "law"' and 'a sense of right—both objective (what should be) and subjective (somebody's right)' of a kind that is expressed with particular force through documentation).

legal history of early and late colonial rule than the scholarship typically suggested as existing.[7]

In rough parallel with the transfer of power from the East India Company to the Crown after the rebellion of 1857, therefore, it instead started to appear that there was an important transition that had taken place in the legal history of colonial rule that could not be accounted for solely or even mainly in terms of the intensification of processes of codification, positivist legislation, or so-called legal transplantation that were in place already from the inception of British paramountcy in the eighteenth century. On the contrary, in the approximate interim between the advent of Company and Crown rule, it seemed more accurate to say that a fundamental shift had taken place from an overriding focus on 'laws' to one on 'the law' (whether of the 'customary', 'sacred', or 'personal' variety or, for that matter, of a kind that could be modified according to labels like 'the public' and 'the private' for the purposes of diagramming the parts within the whole or ones designating further sub-parts therein where the law 'of contract', 'of property', 'of the family', and so on nested).

Slowly but surely, then, in travelling the path I found the book taking, it seemed that it was this shift more than any from pre-colonial/non-Western varieties of normativity to colonial/Westernizing forms of legality that demanded further exploration. Assessing the modern subcontinent's history of legal change from such a standpoint, the increasingly clear emergence after the mid-nineteenth century of 'the law' as a supposedly self-contained and purportedly infinite system for normatively reclassifying the facts of the social world appeared to follow only in the wake of a formative period under early colonial rule that was quite different. With the Company's advent to power in the late eighteenth century, whether as residing in native tradition or elsewhere, it was 'the laws' that factored into the administration of justice—considered as one of the defining features of sovereignty in its most apparent sense as a practical, everyday affair—that made for the key watchword. On this implicit understanding of ruling authority, in sharp contrast to the mainstream of the Anglo-common-law world at roughly the same time—and,

---

[7] Emphasis should here be placed on *legal* history. That is, I do not mean to suggest that historians of modern South Asia in general have failed to see important and even stark differences across this both real and heuristic dividing line.

in the larger argument, the Western world at large—legality's key domain seemed to run orthogonal to, more than congruent with the other principal domain—of tax administration—in which sovereignty was made practically manifest. Standing as both consequence and cause of this unique feature of the subcontinent's development there seemed to be another as well. For with an only piecemeal conception of legal normativity based on administering justice according to sound laws rather than any conception of a distinctly *legal* kind of right in general, there also seemed to be less appearance of any inheritance the period of Company rule left to colonial posterity as a basis on which to rest a conception of the law, writ large.

Insofar as this state of affairs started changing in the subcontinent only roughly in parallel with the transfer of power in 1858, it also became evident that alongside the focus on the emergence of the law two other concerns would have to be central to the book as well. First, it was clear there could be no revisiting of the colonial rule *of/by* law without also revisiting property's oft-cited own rule in the subcontinent. Even just confining oneself to the period after the transfer of power, this is because the history of Crown Raj plainly involved a marked expansion in the recognition of landed entitlements. In the process, new holders of subordinate or so-called proprietary tenure came to be added to the ranks of those made 'legible' to the colonial state, to borrow James Scott's oft-quoted turn of phrase[8]—their composition no longer confined to those the Company originally anointed as the subcontinent's 'true proprietors' for the purposes of administering the taxation of land revenues. Of course, in

---

[8] See generally, James C. Scott, *Seeing Like a State: How Certain Schemes to Improve the Human Condition Have Failed* (New Haven, CT: Yale University Press, 1998). Scott does not offer any single definition of 'legibility' so much as he extends the term's intuitive meaning. As he puts it early on, for example,

> [t]he more I examined these efforts at sedentarization, the more I came to see them as a state's attempt to make a society legible, *to arrange the population in ways that simplified the classic state functions of taxation, conscription, and prevention of rebellion.* Having begun to think in these terms, I began to see legibility as a central problem in statecraft. *The premodern state was, in many crucial respects, partially blind*; it knew precious little about its subjects, their wealth, their landholdings and yields, their location, their very identity. It lacked anything like a detailed 'map' of its terrain and its people. It lacked, for the most part, a measure, a metric, that would allow it to 'translate' what it knew into a common standard necessary for a synoptic view. As a result, its interventions were often crude and self-defeating. Ibid., 2 (emphasis added).

broadening to consider the antecedents to this later period in the earlier era of the East India Company's raj, the necessity of revisiting the story of property's rule in the colonial subcontinent becomes all the more pronounced. Here, as the reader will see in the coming pages, my own focus is on the centrality of the identity between land and its rent-cum-surplus and what I call the 'shadow' conception this made for of property-as-rent in legal and political economic thinking.

In both respects, then, the story of property's rule in the colonial subcontinent that I tell in the book has not only turned out to differ in important ways from the long-standing historical literature on South Asia in particular; but it also demands keeping in mind that whatever points of overlap it bears to newer scholarship on other parts of the world that has emphasized the constitutive role of empire in the making of modern property law, care is still needed to attend to relevant specificities. In the case of the subcontinent—as distinct, especially, from the Americas or Oceania—the most apparent difference is surely to be found in the absence of the same kind of imperative of dispossession underlying what Brenda Bhandar has recently called the 'racial regimes of ownership' that were characteristic of the settler colonies.[9]

As for the second concern that it became evident would have to be central to the book alongside of its focus on the emergence of the law, it involved the need to look for patterns beyond South Asia. More specifically, this has necessitated considering how the history of legal change in the colonial subcontinent connected with what legal historians and theoreticians of other parts of the world have called the first globalization of law and the rise of an identifiably 'classical' style of legal thought after 1850.[10] Accordingly, any story of the law's emergence under the Crown's rule could not be told separately from trying to understand how the advent of

---

[9] Brenna Bhandar, *Colonial Lives of Property: Law, Land, and Racial Regimes of Ownership* (Durham, NC: Duke University Press, 2018). In a similar vein/with similar sympathies, see also Robert Nichols, *Theft is Property! Dispossession and Critical Theory* (Durham, NC: Duke University Press, 2020). Of course, emphasizing 'newer' scholarship on the settler colonies is not to suggest that a concern with dispossession or even its constitutive role in law and political culture is missing in past literature or its own extensions. See, e.g., Robert A. Williams, *The American Indian in Western Legal Thought: The Discourses of Conquest* (New York: Oxford University Press, 1992) and Robert A. Williams, *Savage Anxieties: The Invention of Western Civilization* (New York: Palgrave Macmillan, 2012).

[10] Duncan Kennedy, 'Three Globalizations of Law and Legal Thought', in *The New Law and Economic Development. A Critical Appraisal*, eds. David Trubek and Alvaro Santos (New York: Cambridge University Press, 2006), 19–73.

classical legal thought affected and was affected by so important a part of the modern common-law world as the subcontinent. Indeed, just as the history of British India has scarce been considered by historians of classical legal thought (to say nothing of scholars of legal theory and jurisprudence), the history of classical legal thought has scarcely, if ever, been considered by historians of South Asia.

Of course, the additional strands of concern that it was evident the book would have to address were not necessarily separate from one another. Just as a conception of the property right commensurate with a generalized notion of legal right seemed missing under the Company's rule, under the Crown's the globalizing influence of classical legal thought was made manifest by all sides of the late-nineteenth-century debate on agrarian policy, including figures both British and Indian alike and even apart from the way it was embodied not only in the stalwarts of utilitarianism and analytical jurisprudence, such as Sir Frederick Pollock and James Fitzjames Stephen, but also their adversaries like Henry Maine and his various administrator-disciples.

Put differently, in terms of the epigraphs quoted at the outset of this introduction, what was needed instead was a way to explore the possibility of a marked discontinuity rather than essential seamlessness between the thoughts expressed by William Jones and Henry Maine—separated as they were by a near century, inclusive of the divide between Company and Crown rule. For rather than simply reflecting a typically orientalist tendency to minimize the integrity of the Indian juridical past as the source of only lesser or outright dubious kinds of—sacred or customary—law, Jones and Maine would appear to be better understood as being at fundamental odds over how, in effect, to answer the question H. L. A. Hart poses in such nakedly simple terms at the end of the third epigraph. That is, namely, the question of 'what is law?'

* * *

Against the backdrop of the explanatory agenda of the book, the evolution of which I have summarized above, in the chapters that follow I take up the legal history of colonial rule in the South Asian subcontinent from what is, broadly speaking, a genealogical perspective. In this respect, the book may be all the more of a departure from the emerging state of the art in the study of law and history, which by the present is now several iterations into a seemingly inevitable response of scholarly qualification to or outright backlash against the so-called linguistic turn in the humanities and humanistic social sciences, not to mention its close cousins, post-colonialism and post-structuralism. At the same time, consistent with the nature of the enterprise—and argument—my own perspective is one that makes the book still quite different from the outpouring of scholarship on law and history, whether of South Asia or elsewhere, that followed more directly in the wake of the linguistic turn making its way into these realms of enquiry starting in the 1980s. The book, thus, hardly purports to champion any simple reversion to a monolithically conceived and always dominant colonial discourse as the be-all and end-all of legal modernity in the subcontinent—if, that is, such an image of earlier scholarship has ever been more than a caricature in the first place.

Of course, this is not to say that my debt to/sympathy with more proximally post-linguistic turn scholarship fails to leave an explicit mark on the book in other ways. Clearly, no attempt is being made to hide the book's embrace of the thematic of knowledge and its relationship to power that was at the centre of so much work in the heyday of post-structuralism's rise, including on law and empire and especially as pertaining to the subcontinent. In fact, even the book's subtitle is meant to do the opposite of obscure the influence of Michel Foucault, whose concern with 'how objects constitute themselves in discourse' was the inciting force behind my trying here to elaborate what Ian Hacking was calling the much needed field of 'historical ontology' already amidst the new and highly public front in the culture war that opened up around 'postmodernism' (and 'relativism', among other bogeys) in the 1990s.[11] As with the book's departure from the current state of the art in the study of law and empire through insisting that a focus on colonial legal discursivity in the subcontinent remains necessary on its own terms, then, the embrace of the thematic of juristic knowledge and power—rather than its reframing in whatever distinct and ostensibly more culturally interactive terms—is deliberate.[12]

---

[11] Ian Hacking, *Historical Ontology* (Cambridge, MA: Harvard University Press, 2004), 98.

[12] For two exemplary recent works in this vein, see e.g. Kris Manjapra, *Age of Entanglement: German and Indian Intellectuals across Empire* (Cambridge, MA: Harvard University Press, 2014) and Projit Bihari Mukharji, *Doctoring Traditions: Ayurveda, Small Technologies, and Braided Sciences* (Chicago, IL: University of Chicago Press, 2016).

In part this is because I believe it is plausible and even undeniable to see 'the law' as a product/'invention' of modernity, especially in the more ominous rather than laudatory (and Western exceptionalist) sense of the latter term, connoting an era of ideologico-discursive ventriloquization, false necessity, formalist equalitarian fictions, and so on. However, in at least equal part it is also because past scholarship consistent with my own commitment to sceptically regard the hero story of modernity came to be seen as (or condemned for amateurism for) encroaching upon the territory of 'proper' philosophy in a way that actually proves well-suited for my own purposes. After all, the book is meant to be more than—or, at any rate, something different from—simply a work about the history of modern South Asia. This, moreover, is not just on grounds of the titular concern with ontology but also because as a work on law-in-history the book is intended to engage—and to craft a method for engaging—questions that are central to philosophical jurisprudence.

As for what does make the book's approach to colonial legal discursivity unique, it will hopefully become more evident in the pages that follow. For now, however, it is enough to note that in reading Foucault's concern about the constitution of objects through Hacking's notion of historical ontology the book is choosing a conduit into the world of social facts that has always been situated at some remove from the more common means by which Foucault has been interpolated into historical enquiry. On one level, this is simply because Hacking's has inevitably been an effort to adapt Foucault to a more conventional philosophical orientation, given his own station as a philosopher most easily identified with the analytical rather than continental tradition. Yet, at another level, it is because Hacking is more open to seeing advantages in and a principled basis for distinguishing between enquiring into the constitution of objects and enquiring into the constitution of the subject/subjectivity.

Accordingly, seeing that Foucault's concern was more characteristically with the 'truth through which we constitute *ourselves* as objects of knowledge,'[13] Hacking describes his own as being with 'generaliz[ing to] examine all manner of constitutings';[14] for Hacking, in other words,

---

[13] Hacking, *Historical Ontology*, 2 (quoting Michel Foucault, 'What is Enlightenment?' In *The Foucault Reader*, ed. Paul Rabinow (New York: Pantheon, 1984)).
[14] Ibid., 4.

'constitutings' beyond that of the self are not only possible but pervasive. Even while acknowledging 'the difficult distinction between object and idea',[15] he nonetheless observes that just because it is often the latter more than the former that historical analysis is *really* addressed to, this does not mean that demonstrating the contingency of a phenomenon is simply the same as collapsing subject and object.[16] To elaborate the point, he offers a series of examples introduced through an entreaty that we

> [n]otice how important it is to answer the question 'The social construction of what?' For in this example [concerning the social construction of the woman refugee], X does not refer directly to individual women refugees. No, the X refers first of all to the woman refugee as a kind of person, the classification itself, and the matrix within which the classification works. In consequence of being so classified, individual women and their experiences of themselves are changed by being so classified. This sounds very complicated. But the logical point is simple. Women in flight are the product of social conditions in their homelands. It would be stupid to talk about social construction in that context, because social circumstances so manifestly provoke the fear of staying home and the hope of succor in another land. But since, in Canada, *woman refugee* may seem a straightforward and rather inevitable way of classifying some people, there is indeed a point to claiming that the classification is far from inevitable ... In my example, the concept of the woman refugee seems inevitable, once you have the practices of nationality, immigration, citizenship, and women in flight who have arrived in your country begging asylum. The author of a book on the social construction of women refugees is saying no, the concept, and the matrix of rules, practices, and material infrastructure in which it is embedded, are not inevitable at all.[17]

By way of rounding out the point, Hacking proceeds to a further example, observing that we also

---

[15] See Ian Hacking, *The Social Construction of What* (Cambridge: Harvard University Press, 1999), 14.
[16] Ibid., 1–35.
[17] Ibid., 11–12.

do not find books on the social construction of banks, the fiscal system, cheques, money, dollar bills, bills of lading, contracts, tort, the Federal Reserve, or the British monarchy. These are all contractual or institutional objects, and no one doubts that contracts and institutions are the result of historical events and social processes. Hence no one urges that they are socially constructed ... Since the Federal Reserve is so obviously the upshot of contingent arrangements, a book titled *The Social Construction of the Federal Reserve* would likely be silly; we would suspect someone was trying to cash in on the cachet of 'social construction.' But we can imagine a startling work, *The Social Construction of the Economy*. Every day we read that the economy is up or down, and we are supposed to be moved to fear or elation. Yet this splendid icon, the economy was hard to find on the front pages of newspapers even forty years ago. Why are we so unquestioning about this very idea, 'the economy'? ... [Afterall, i]t is not the economy of [, say,] Sweden in the year 2000 that one argues is a social construction (obviously it is that ...) ... Instead, that seemingly inevitable and unavoidable idea, *the economy*, may be argued to be a social construct.[18]

At the same time, whatever reasoned basis he gives for pursuing 'constitutings' of various kinds beyond that of the self under the banner of historical ontology, Hacking does not provide any hard and fast set of rules, much less blueprint, for doing so. As a result, pursuing a historical ontology of *the law*, in particular—and, more than that, pursuing it simultaneously as a way of facing Hart's epigraphic distillation of jurisprudence's essential question—has involved not just following but formulating the approach the book uses. With that task taken up across the first three chapters comprising part I, parts II and III subsequently turn to operationalizing the approach. It is there, then, in the last six chapters, that the book's overall purpose becomes to assemble a new picture of the historical development of legal modernity in the subcontinent during its long nineteenth century of colonial rule. To do so, whether within or across the chapters of parts II and III, the presentation generally oscillates between tracing what I distinguish in part I as discourse *of* and *about* law as two key sites of discursive constitution. More specifically, in these six

[18] Ibid., 13.

chapters it is discourse of and about (the law of) property, contract, and status—as the three key constituents of the private-law core of the law writ large—that mark the stopping points along the way of the substantive historical path the book carves.

If, as per the overarching argument of parts II and III, it was only really after 1850 or so that 'the law' emerged as its own distinct entity—or, as per Hacking's above entreaty, if the *idea* of 'the law' as its own distinct entity emerged only then—it remains important to distinguish *that* this may have been so from *how* it came to be so. For while the transfer of power from Company to Crown in 1858 is hardly wanting for attributions of importance—being a standard dividing line for all kinds of historiographical purposes—what really matters is to account for what followed, with regard both to its internal dynamics and to its relationship to the path dependencies inherited from the era preceding it. Therefore, lest the reader assume that the book's focus must really fall predominantly on the latter side of the mid-nineteenth-century dividing line on which both the rise of classical legal thought and the transfer of power in the subcontinent co-occurred, it is worth emphasizing that the treatment of the era of Company rule before 1858 is no mere prelude to the main discussion.

On the contrary, in training attention on the Company's efforts to restructure the land-revenue demand, part II is meant to provide the narrative and analytical foundation for the story that follows in part III. So too is it meant to set out the very different historical foundation—in the mutually constitutive institutional and discursive structures of the property right—that late-nineteenth-century legal change in British India inherited as compared to its counterparts in the Anglo-common-law mainstream. In so doing, part II diagrams the distinct point of departure from which classical legal thought commenced its rise in the late-colonial subcontinent as compared to much of the West and how it thus doubled as an engine for what I call belated ontologization in the former, more than a half-century after the law's notional emergence in the latter enabled it to play whatever determining role it is usually regarded as having played in bringing about a new era of self-sustaining economic growth and politics of rights-based liberty.

Insofar as the above is worth stating explicitly up front, it is because my ability to pursue the historical ontological approach I take is less comprehensive than I might have liked due to limitations of space and the reader's attention. With respect to the era of Company rule these limitations have required that the book remain focused on the forms of contemplation that surrounded landed power as these took shape in the name of property. Necessarily, therefore, I have devoted much less attention to other forms of contemplation that were relevant to constituting the ontology of the legal that was characteristic of the first century of formal colonial rule. The need to eschew exhaustiveness in the execution of my approach has further meant that even with respect to the period after the transfer of power, I have restricted attention to the so-called private law side of the integral legal object that emerged under Crown rule and its accompanying role within the story of the rise of classical legal thought.

Consequently, at the risk of falling into the very kind of anachronism the book is aimed at avoiding, the so-called public law side of the story is one I effectively leave aside. Yet if this is a choice connected to considerations of manageability, these are hardly the only ones justifying it. For it was, after all, the constitution of the subsystems for normatively ordering the relations of *private* juridical individuals that made for the core of the law writ large—whether in Britain's India and other parts of the colonial Afro-Asian world amidst the rise of classical legal thought in the second half of the nineteenth century or the most celebrated parts of the West starting at least a half-century earlier.

* * *

As for the more specific contents of what follows, the first of part I's three chapters sketches the nature, dimensions, and importance of the main problem the book addresses. To do so it considers how the history of British domination in the subcontinent has proven liable to be conflated with a history of legal development by situating discussion of colonial rule within the context of what Austrian jurist and political philosopher Hans Kelsen called the problem—or, for him, the pseudo-problem—of the duality of law and the state. In chapter one I also connect my examination of Kelsen, as well as my discussion of scholarship on law and history in modern South Asia, to the book's titular concerns with ontology and the rise of classical legal thought.

With much of chapter one taken up with diagramming the limits of how the law and its historicity has been grappled with in historical scholarship, chapter two extends the effort by considering the tendency to naturalize the law—as an ostensibly self-contained system of rational ordering according to norms—in other areas of learned discussion. To do so, I consider four further versions of the naturalizing tendency as they have appeared, most characteristically, in sociology, anthropology, philosophy, and socio-legal theory. The chapter thus proceeds through detailing how the law's naturalization has followed as a matter of course in sociological efforts to grapple with the problem of formal versus living law, anthropological efforts to grapple with the problem of state versus non-state law, philosophical jurisprudential efforts to grapple with the problem of law's positivism versus normativity, and socio-legal theoretical efforts to grapple with the problem of law's facticity versus validity/legitimacy.

In the light of the first two chapters, the third then closes part I of the book by turning from diagnosis and critique to proposing another way forward. Here, more specifically, I outline the key features of what I call a historical ontological approach to jurisprudence, including to the great question we saw Hart so succinctly putting at its centre in the above epigraph. Chapter three thus introduces the most important elements of a conceptual vocabulary upon which a historical ontological approach can be built—with the sparsity of these elements generally increasing their explanatory power, both with respect to the colonial subcontinent and, as it could equally be deployed, beyond as well. Through the first pair of concepts developed in this chapter, I thus distinguish between *doctrinal discourse* capable of being used to verbalize propositions *of* the law and *ordinary-language discourse* that can be used to articulate propositions *about* the law. With each emanating from its own characteristic venues of production—for the first, those connected to administration and scientizing juristic speculation and, for the second, those connected to the public sphere—the respective contribution they made to constituting the law as a distinct kind of object, or what in the book I also call the law's *ontologization*, unfolded at distinct discursive sites. Of course, this is not to say that there was some kind of impermeable barrier between these sites; nor is it to say that terms and concepts native to doctrinal discourse could not pass by osmosis into the venues of ordinary-language discourse and vice versa. It is, however, to call for greater attention to the full spectrum of ways that the law and its constituents can be invoked, all of which are clearly not simply or even mainly ones linked to technical, adjudicatory reasoning. After explicating the notion of ontologization, chapter three then turns to the second key pair of elements the book offers as part of the conceptual vocabulary of a historical ontological approach to jurisprudence. As I explain, these follow from the distinction I make in the chapter between doctrinal discourse's qualities of *operativeness* and *administrability*.

Having set out the purposes behind and contours of historical ontology as a method for jurisprudentially reckoning with the law, part II of the book moves to its historical discussion proper, commencing with the period of Company rule in the subcontinent from 1757 to 1858. With the first of part II's subsequent pair of chapters, I also commence the book's treatment of its overarching concern with Britain's so-called rule of property in the subcontinent. Accordingly, chapter four considers how and why discourse about property in the incipient colonial public sphere, the circulation of which followed from the Company's rise to power in Bengal, came to focus less on absolute dominion over landed space than it did on a notion of absolute security in the proprietor's control over (some portion of) land's rent, considered as the monetizable value of its produce over and above cost. At the same time, chapter four also considers how the Company's unique brand of talk about rendering property 'absolute' was translated—already in the lead-up to Governor Charles Cornwallis' permanent settlement with Bengal's zamindars—into an equally unique species of doctrinal discourse. For even the quite limited concept of property that Company raj made prominent was given actual doctrinal shape less in its capacity as a right over land's rent than as a duty to meet the colonial state's revenue demand.

In starting to make good on the book's aim of putting the conceptual vocabulary developed in part I to work, chapter four ultimately argues that underlying the unique form that property talk took under early colonial rule within the venues of doctrinal and ordinary-language discourse was more than simply the Company state's founding political economy of land-revenue extraction. On the contrary, so too did it follow from the colonial state's precociously modern emphasis on entitlement to value in the abstract, which was built—rather paradoxically—on a characteristically early-modern imagery in which property remained largely external to legality. In this regard, the intellectual stamp of classical political economy on the Company's property discourse was both licensed by and consonant with an older mode of discourse about the forms of constitution that 'political society' could be thought to take. Asiatic despotism as well as those of its agonistic constitutional forms that were endlessly extolled for the virtue of being less abjectly discretionary (or simply less vice-ridden), like monarchicalism and republicanism, were thus more alike than they were different with respect to the implicit ontologies according to which they arranged the alignment between sovereignty, land control, and practices of adjudicatory rectification. For in such *constitutionist* outlooks, as I call them in the pages that follow, the most discernible shape that a distinctly legal normativity took appeared in the guise of the laws that factored into the administration of justice.[19] Therefore, even notwithstanding the much-lauded connection between a sound administration of justice and an overall climate of 'law and order' commensurate with securing material wealth, the Company's constitutionist discourse was simply not predicated on making the property right in particular the basis for a distinctly legal kind of right in general in the way that was becoming emblematic of juridical modernity in the Anglo-common-law mainstream already by the late eighteenth century. With property remaining extrinsic to legality, then, it was an ontology of 'the laws' more than any of 'the law' that the Company advanced.

In the remaining chapter of part II, I extend the above line of discussion by looking at the non-*zamindari* forms of revenue settlement that came to dominate most of the rest of the areas that came under the Company's direct rule amidst its early passage from trader to sovereign. Accordingly, chapter five begins with a discussion of the *raiyatwari* system of settlement in Madras in which it was the ostensible cultivator of the soil upon whom the right to property and, more importantly, the attendant duty of revenue payment was conferred. Here I place particular emphasis on how the *raiyatwari* system proved congruent with its *zamindari* counterpart in Bengal in virtue of the way it was premised on a similar discourse about property in land's rent as well as a similar way of translating the latter idea into doctrinal terms. The bulk of the chapter then goes on to consider the difficulty the early-colonial state encountered in squaring

---

[19] As I explain in chapter four, I use 'constitutionism' intentionally for the sake of distinguishing it from the notion of 'constitutionalism' as it has come to be used by historians of early-modern political thought.

this rule of property in land's rent with pre-colonial practices of gifting control over land absent any revenue demand through institutions like the Mughal/Persianate *in'am* (granting certain kinds of land revenue-free). In the light of the preceding discussion comprising part II, chapter five concludes with a reconsideration of the supposed ideological break with Company rule's past that was represented by the ascent of Ricardian rent theory within the ranks of colonial administration after 1820.

With chapter six, part III commences the book's turn to the period after 1858, when the Company was dissolved and ruling power over British India was officially transferred to the Crown-in-Parliament. Focusing on the venues of doctrinal discourse, the chapter situates the more full-bodied doctrinalization of the property right under the Crown's raj within a larger context that saw the colonial state's founding political economy of surplus extraction through the land tax shifting amidst increasing volatility in various parts of the subcontinent's agrarian countryside. Within the legal domain, the earliest notable emblem of this shift came in the form of the Bengal Rent Act of 1859, with it also being evident in work by administrator intellectuals like Baden Henry Baden-Powell's *The Land Systems of British India*. The first in a series of new legislative measures geared towards expanding the range of 'proprietary' entitlements rendered legible to the colonial state, like its later counterparts the 1859 act functioned to incorporate lower and newly powerful strata of the agrarian hierarchy within administrative reach. As I argue in the chapter, against this backdrop the late-colonial subcontinent witnessed the gradual internalization of property into the ontology of the legal, with its proliferating array of landed entitlements underwriting a doctrinal notion of proprietary right that was finally becoming more commensurate with a notion of legal right in general. In this respect, the spate of agrarian special legislation that unfolded across the second half of the nineteenth century (and beyond) to recognize new forms of 'proprietary right' in the subcontinent also set the stage for the legal history of colonial rule to begin more fully converging with that of the wider Anglo-common-law world.

It is here, moreover, that the book's other major titular concern beyond historical ontology becomes more central to the story it tells. For it was hardly unrelated that across the second half of the nineteenth century there took place a parallel unfolding of what scholars of Anglo-American legal history have called the rise and globalization of classical legal thought. While classical legal thought's influence in the Anglo-common-law mainstream perhaps was made most clearly manifest through a commitment to legal scientism, in the subcontinent it carried the more fundamental imprimatur of a shift in the ontology of the social world of late-colonial times. 'The law' rather than 'the laws' (factoring into the administration of justice) thus increasingly became a key watchword of this era. At the same time, even as this shift proved a particular signal of ontologization in the subcontinent, as elsewhere in the common-law world so too did the growing ubiquity of 'the law' in the Crown's India witness its significance as a watchword come to be ever further reimagined in terms of a perfectly integral unicity of logically infinitely generative rules animated by the normative first principle of facilitating the will of some one or other juridical individual inside of some one or other realm of their own 'absolute' proprietary holding.

Overall, then, chapter six serves both as a bridge between parts two and three—insofar as it continues the story of the colonial rule of property—and as the entry point into the final three chapters of the book. For there, in the remainder of part III, I continue to pursue the twofold story of ontologization and classical legal thought's rise through considering the other key dimensions along which the new ideal of the law as an ostensibly self-contained and perfectly integral system of rational ordering—in effect, as a kind of concrete abstraction—was built up. Accordingly, the distinction between ordinary-language discourse (about the law) and (the) doctrinal discourse (of the law) that the book develops in part I remains one I actively seek to make good on in these final chapters.

In zeroing in on the doctrinal discourse of contract as it developed in the lead-up to and aftermath of 1872, chapter seven thus stands in overall juxtaposition to the discussion of discourse about contractualism in the colonial public sphere with which chapter six concludes. More specifically, in chapter seven I argue that as in so much of the rest of the world, in the subcontinent as well the doctrinal concept of contract in classical legal thought steadily displaced the property right at the core of the law's ontology. In its opening section, therefore, the chapter begins with a consideration of the most prominent antecedent moments in the emergence of the law of contract in the period preceding the passage of the Indian Contract Act of 1872. In subsequent sections, the chapter then turns to the Contract Act itself, first situating it in relation to the legislative council debates that took place before 1872 as well as the often-contentious commentarial reaction with which it was greeted immediately thereafter. The lion's share of my attention to the Act, however, comes through providing a close reading of its contents, with an eye towards establishing how the vision of contractual entitlement set out in its pages was undergirded by the so-called will theory upon which classical legal thought, in general, was premised. As my reading emphasizes, the classical conception of contract was not simply about prioritizing party intention and thereby extolling the virtues of the voluntarism of the private individual. Rather, the will theory also served as a crucial mechanism for elevating the public will of the state, considered as a juridical individual in its own right, which proved every bit as central to the doctrinal conception of contract in classical legal thought as its private counterpart. This meant that at the very centre of the 'private law' core of 'the law' writ large in classical legal thought there was an animating principle devoted to more than just ostensibly 'freeing' the atomized individual of laissez faire ideology to engage in instrumentally rational action in the market; so too was contractual individualism about legitimizing the regulatory impulses of the state, especially as it was taking on the proportions of its national, territorial bureaucratic version, including in its more specifically colonial incarnation. In thus emphasizing the law's commitments in theory rather than simply the magnitude of the distance between its rules and social practice, chapter seven also touches on the implications of the book's rewriting of the legal history of British rule in the subcontinent for our understanding of the relationship between ideology and actuality.

With chapter seven's focus on the will as a second foundational element of the shifting ontology of the law during late-colonial times, it leads naturally into the final two chapters of the book. For in chapters eight and nine, I complete my picture of the new ideal of the private law by looking across the internal border that separated the law of the market, consisting of property and contract, from the law of status relations within the domestic kin community. Accordingly, chapter eight begins with a consideration of the way in which classical legal thinkers understood the significance of the law of status relative to 'the law' writ large. Here, in particular, I highlight how different this understanding was from what scholars of South Asia have seen to date, through what has long been the standard view that the colonial state segregated the so-called personal law in British India into an inner realm of the cultural/religious/domestic starting from the late eighteenth century. In the main body of the chapter, I then look at the way the concept of status was taken up in ordinary-language discourse through the brand of nascent sociologico-anthropological speculation that was emerging during the era of Crown Raj, especially in the context of the Punjab after its annexation in 1849. Here, I start with the way the concept of status that Maine so famously formulated in 1861's *Ancient Law* was built atop an equivocal foundation that seems to have gone previously unnoticed within the large corpus of scholarship on his work, including by those studying South Asia. The chapter subsequently goes on to trace the broader currency that Maine's internally divided concept achieved, paying particular attention to the post-annexation Punjab and a series of legal thinkers who were involved in the redaction of the province's 'customary law', including William Rattigan, Charles Lewis Tupper, Charles Roe, and Henry Rattigan.

Among my larger purposes in chapter eight is to show how the concept of status had a very different meaning in ordinary-language discourse than that which it took on when rendered administrable through its doctrinal counterpart. As I argue in the chapter, this was due, in part, to the way that concepts were bound to undergo a process of translation when migrating between the venues of the public sphere and those of legal scientism and administration. In this respect, even in the late-nineteenth-century context of classical legal thought's rise, there were echoes of the earlier period of the Company's rule in which a noticeable gap persisted between public-sphere ideas about absolute property and their instantiation in doctrine. If this is worth highlighting in the way the chapter does, it is because the gap between the meanings that concepts tended to take on at these different sites of discourse made for an important source of variation within the object that classical legal thought was globalizing.

Consequently, in the final chapter of the book it is to this very question of variation—in the face of the uniformities that processes of globalization also necessarily wrought—that I turn. Chapter nine thus focuses on the development of one important doctrine within the larger rule regime of the law of status during late-colonial times—namely, that of the so-called restitution of conjugal rights. Through a granular examination of more than a half-century of case law in this area, the chapter demonstrates how at the colonial courts of British India, together with the Privy Council, conjugal restitution doctrine was elaborated by building upon a crucial analogy between marriage and contract. In so doing, the chapter highlights the counter-intuitive way in which arguments from the core of the law of the market were imported into the doctrinal discourse of status, including through the active participation of Indian lawyers, litigants, and judges, as they found themselves involved in marital disputes that commenced with the famed *Ardaseer Cursetjee v. Perozeboye* decisions of the 1840s and 1850s (between Parsi litigants) and that then extended out from there in disputes between Hindu and especially Muslim spouses across the next several decades.

Beyond grappling with variability amidst the tendency towards uniformity that classical legal thought's rise and globalization carried with it, my other larger purpose in this final chapter is to push for a reconsideration of the relationship between law, religion, and the notion of the personal/domestic with which they have so often been linked. While the chapter examines the evolution of one highly particularized doctrine, therefore, it does so in order to show how its overall development was indicative of the more general way that the subsystems of the personal law in British India were made to overlap with an imaginative space assigned to the law of status in classical private-law theory also only after 1850.

Indeed, it is only as the personal law was increasingly made part of 'the law' writ large that it became marginalized in the more precise way that it usually is said to have been. However, as I contend in the chapter, the marginalization of the personal law was not any strict product of a uniquely colonial rule *by* law in the subcontinent; rather, it was part of a generalized, if not unparadoxical, worldwide process. For the more the subsystems of the personal law, as species of the law of status, were integrated into the object of 'the law' writ large that was globalizing into the late-nineteenth-century subcontinent, the more could they claim, themselves, to qualify as fully and authentically 'legal' sub-components of that object—even if, as species of the law of status, they were ones that were scaled in classical legal thought only to the dimensions of norming relations within the family/domestic kin community. As a result, participants in disputes involving the subsystems of the personal law in the Crown's India found themselves uniquely incentivized to simultaneously embrace and recoil from this aspect of the rise of classical legal thought. A persistent tendency in the second half of the nineteenth century, then, witnessed Indian legal thinkers trying to prove that their own juristic traditions were every bit as systematic and ineluctably a part of 'the law' as was the contractual core of its rules for governing relations between private juridical individuals in the market.

In turning from Mainean discourse about status to the venues of doctrinal discourse, I close chapter nine by arguing that this not only led to an insistence on the 'contractual' nature of marriage within the jurisprudence of conjugal restitution but also that it noticeably politicized disputes involving the subsystems of the personal law. What such politicization ultimately meant was that the law of status became an ever more conflicted domain in the late-colonial subcontinent, with the ostensibly peripheral role it was otherwise implicitly assigned within the classical schematization of the law writ large greatly expanding in ideological import. For if in classical legal thought the law of status served as a space within which the public will of the state could most openly assert the legitimacy of its own presence directly at the centre of the law's core set of rules for governing relations between private juridical individuals, in late-colonial South Asia the law of status further became imbued with the sense that it was the key arena for fighting out a politics of communitarian identity symbols. Ever more, therefore, did claims about the irreducible legality of the personal law come to function as proxies for asserting the modernity of different traditions of socio-religious identity.

* * *

In considering the factors that charged the currents running through the domain of the personal law in British India, it is difficult to avoid alighting, even if just momentarily, on the present. Obviously, in the Muslim-majority nation states of today's South Asia—post-colonial Pakistan above all—the politics of communitarian identity symbols that attached to the old subsystems of the personal law in British India have blended seamlessly into the special role of neo-traditionalizing shariʻa consciousness as one of the motive forces enabling the supremely modernist enterprise of Islamization, especially in its most unpalatable, ominous, and retrograde aspects.[20] At the same time, now well more than

---

[20] See e.g. Ayesha Jalal, *Self and Sovereignty: Individual and Community in South Asian Islam since 1850* (New York: Routledge, 2000), 322, 567 and Faisal Devji, *Muslim Zion: Pakistan as a Political Idea* (Cambridge, MA: Harvard University Press, 2013), 232.

a half-century into the post-colonial era, with a subcontinent that has shown an undeniably marked shift to the triumph of majoritarian chauvinism in all of its major states, ongoing controversies around the Indian republic's lack of a uniform civil code have plainly made for an even more direct continuity there, with the personal law remaining as much, if not more, of a site for conducting the politics of communitarian identity symbols than it was amidst the globalization of classical legal thought. On the one hand, in such a landscape, the lingering persistence of the Muslim personal law, in particular, has obviously pushed it near to the top of the list of targets for majoritarian attack in South Asia's largest nation state, especially with the effective juridical normalization of mosque destruction, to say nothing of even more dire possibilities, having made their most overt breakthrough in recent years.[21] On the other hand, the contemporary Muslim personal law's symbolic value as a target for majoritarian attack, has, in many ways, only heightened its importance as a marker of communitarian identity for the country's biggest religious minority, its various internal fragmentations along lines of class, caste, gender, language, and region notwithstanding.

Of course, there are sure to be other present-day reverberations of the themes I have summarily touched on here in this introduction and that appear in more thoroughgoing fashion in the rest of the book as well. In fact, side by side with the ever more poisoned dynamic into which the (Muslim) personal law has been inserted, by the present day the growing institutionalization of majoritarian chauvinism in independent India has transpired squarely *within* a landscape of the rule of law that has traditionally been seen as a major distinguishing feature making the country South Asia's only state with a truly lasting liberal democratic constitutional structure. As in many other places that have seen a turn to so-called 'authoritarian/autocratic legalism' amidst the post-millennial malaise of parliamentary democracy in the age of neolberalsm (or, perhaps, its ongoing demise),[22] independent India today thus serves as a stark reminder

---

[21] See e.g. Christophe Jaffrelot, *Modi's India: Hindu Nationalism and the Rise of Ethnic Democracy* (Princeton, NJ: Princeton University Press, 2021), 428–40.

[22] See e.g. Kim Lane Schepple, 'Autocratic Legalism', *The University of Chicago Law Review* 85, no. 2 (2018): 545–83; David Trubek, Favio Sa e Silva, Marta Machado (Conveners), 'Comparative Perspectives on Autocratic Legalism: Brazil, India, and South Africa', Law & Society Association: International Research Collaborative, 2021 www.lawandsociety.org/lsair c27/; M. Mohsin Alam Bhat, Mayur Suresh, and Deepa Das Acevedo, 'Authoritarianism in

of the law's inherent equivocality and, hence, manipulability—its equally inherent formality proving as readily capable of being ventriloquized towards blatantly inegalitarian and destructive ends as of fulfilling some supposed destiny as the ultimate foundation for the only true varieties of just ordering humanity is alleged to have ever known.[23]

In this respect, today's world serves as a reminder that there may be less at stake in seeing empire's history in places like South Asia in terms of a rule *by* rather than *of* the law than it might otherwise seem. For even absent such a distinction, whether in the Anglo-common-law mainstream already from early-modern times or in the subcontinent only from late-colonial times, the emergence of the ideal of the law as an infinitely generative and perfectly integral system of rational ordering according to norms cannot be regarded in a vacuum, as if capable of being judged only as some unvarnished good gifted by colonial rule to its subjects if it is to be historically judged at all. On the contrary, as the ensuing chapters can be read to suggest, for every virtue the law might claim on behalf of its own formalism, its indeterminate and open-textured equivocality makes it more than pliable enough to serve as an instrument of whatever vice that might need to be laundered through its ontologizing, and, thus, depersonalizing discursive registers.

Indian State, Law, and Society', *Verfassung und Recht in Übersee (VRÜ) / World Comparative Law* 55 (2022): 459–77.

[23] See e.g. Duncan Kennedy, 'Legal Formality', *The Journal of Legal Studies* 2, no. 2 (1973): 351–98.

PART I

THE LEGAL HISTORY OF COLONIAL RULE IN THE SOUTH ASIAN SUBCONTINENT AND THE ONTOLOGIZATION OF 'THE LAW'

The Problem and a Proposed Analytical Framework

1
The History of British Colonial Rule in South Asia as a History of Legal Development

1.1 Introduction: The Problem of the Duality of Law and the (Colonial) State

In surveying the nearly two centuries of British rule in the South Asian subcontinent it is clear that the most basic task of colonial officialdom was to elaborate a new form of state. On the one hand, in its substantive actualization, this new form of state consisted of a novel apparatus of institutions and practices, including courts, revenue collection operations, western-style military forces, new educational policies, and the like. On the other hand, in its formal dimension the colonial state appears to have comprised a series of abstract juridical powers—namely, to legislate, to adjudicate, and to administer. Paradoxically, each of these formal powers was supposed to be the product of an instrumentality that was also their object. That is to say, even though legislation, adjudication, and administration were powers exercised over the law, it was also the law that was supposed to be the source from which these powers themselves issued. Were this not the case, not only would the foundational prerogatives of sovereignty fail to be legitimated, so too would the apparatus of institutions and practices through which the state was substantively actualized remain unmoored.

In the light of the above paradox, it can be difficult to disentangle the progression of British colonial rule in the subcontinent from the development of its constitutional-legal framework. This difficulty is doubled insofar as the state's basic constitutional powers over the law seem to have defined its lower-tier juridical powers in a way that made them structurally analogous to the legal 'rights' that the Raj was formally assigning to certain of its Indian subjects. With these observations in hand, it perhaps becomes only too clear why the history of colonial rule in the subcontinent has been so liable to appear like the historical unfolding of a particular variety of the rule of law, even if only an imperfect one according to those scholars inclined to emphasize the formal inequality separating Britain's subjects in India from its citizens in the United Kingdom.[1]

As may be apparent to some readers, the above paradox bears a close resemblance to what the famed Austrian jurist Hans Kelsen called the problem of the 'duality of law and state'.[2] According to Kelsen, given the standard assumption that law and the state are distinct kinds, philosophers and theorists have always been left to founder on asking '[i]f the State is the authority from which the legal order emanates, how can [it] be subject to this order and, like the individual, receive obligations and rights therefrom?'[3] To Kelsen, of course, the problem of 'duality' was really a 'pseudo-problem' deriving from the 'erroneous' premise on which it had too long rested. To assume dualism, he claimed, was to commit a 'fallacy of which we meet numerous examples in the history of all fields of human thought'. As such, it entails allowing '[o]ur desire for the intuitive representation of abstractions' to 'lead[] us to personify the unity of

---

[1] In this respect, it has often been said that the colonial regime was characterized by a rule *by* law more than a rule of law. See e.g. David Washbrook, 'India, 1818–1860: The Two Faces of Colonialism', in *The Oxford History of the British Empire, Vol. III, The Nineteenth Century*, ed. Andrew Porter (Oxford: Oxford University Press, 1999), 395–421 at 407–8 and Nasser Hussain, *A Jurisprudence of Emergency: Colonialism and the Rule of Law* (Ann Arbor, MI: University of Michigan Press, 2003), 7.

[2] Hans Kelsen, *General Theory of Law and State* (Cambridge, MA: Harvard University Press, 1949), 197. The duality problem should not be confused with the related, but distinct, problem that can be dated to long before Kelsen's time and having to do with the implications of the Roman law principle of *princeps legibus solutus*/the prince being above the law. See Kenneth Pennington, *The Prince and the Law: Sovereignty and Rights in the Western Legal Tradition* (Berkeley, CA: University of California Press, 1993) and more recently, touching at times on the history of modern South Asia, Kathleen Davis, *Periodization and Sovereignty: How Ideas of Feudalism and Secularization Govern the Politics of Time* (Philadelphia, PA: University of Pennsylvania Press, 2008). Even in Kelsen's own time it was this problem more than the duality problem that remained centre stage, as in the concern of Kelsen's contemporary, the famed Nazi jurist Carl Schmitt, with the 'sovereign paradox' (and the related idea of the sovereign as 'he who decides on the exception' that in our own day Giorgio Agamben has so visibly taken up). On Kelsen and Schmitt's famed debate about constitutionalism during the Weimar era see Lars Vinx, ed., *The Guardian of the Constitution: Hans Kelsen and Carl Schmitt on the Limits of Constitutional Law* (Cambridge: Cambridge University Press, 2015).

[3] Kelsen, *General Theory of Law and State*, 197.

a system, and then to hypostasize the personification'.[4] To say that 'law is created by the State' and to mean that 'law regulates its own creation', therefore, only seems problematic because 'traditional theory ... makes a superhuman being out of the State, considering it as a kind of man and simultaneously as an authority'. In this manner, Kelsen concluded, the state—being 'only a tool for the understanding of an object—becomes a separate object of knowledge, existing besides the original object'.[5] Consequently, Kelsen's approach to the duality problem turns on insisting that it is the hypostatization of the state that is the real source of difficulty. When that which was 'originally ... a way of representing the unity of a system of objects' becomes 'a new object, existing in its own right', he tells us, only then do we feel compelled to ask about 'the relationship between these two objects'.[6]

Persuasive as it may seem, the reasoning on which such a solution rests is also contingent on restricting the central insight it traffics in—about 'hypostatization'—to the 'object' of the state, alone. Presumably, for Kelsen this is because he takes the jurisprudential problem of dualism to be confined to the compass of questions about the 'auto-obligation of the state', or, in other words, to questions about the 'difficulty of conceiving of obligations and rights' as belonging to the state.[7] Yet as noted, the problem of the state's 'rights' or, equivalently, of its powers—including its fundamental 'constitutional' powers—is only one aspect of the paradox by which the law has appeared to be both the cause and effect of the colonial state in the subcontinent. This is because colonial state-building did not simply raise the spectre of the question of what legitimated the Raj's ability to legislate, adjudicate, and administer the law, if not the law itself. Rather, just as much has British state-building in the subcontinent demanded that we reckon with the seemingly vacuous tautology at the heart of the colonial state. After all, how meaningful can it be to say that the state's basic constitutional powers were irreducibly 'legal' in nature when near any and everything else that state actually undertook to do was just as readily claimed to be a part of its essentially 'legal' output—whether in the form of its more ad hoc reform initiatives, its

---

[4] Ibid., 198.
[5] Ibid.
[6] Ibid.
[7] Ibid.

more systematic construction of new institutions, or the more expansive regimes of juridified policies and practices the latter gave rise to.

Even more ominous for a solution like Kelsen's to the duality problem is the possibility of this tautology residing at the heart of not only a colonial state like the Indian but also the 'modern' liberal state more generally. If the tautology is thrown into particularly sharp relief in the history of the subcontinent, it is only because modern state-building processes are likely to seem more distant from the law's legitimating effect in a colonial context; or so is the case to the extent that processes of colonial state-building are more liable to appear as if they were imposed from above given the culturally alien idioms and more intensively exclusionary political mechanisms through which they were undertaken. As the history of colonial rule in the subcontinent makes so apparent, therefore, there is an unresolved tension in Kelsen's view, which derives from the fact that it is not just the state that has been too long objectified through hypostatization, but 'the law' as well. When Kelsen speaks his central insight—that the state was no more than its 'legal order'[8]—he too risks transforming what may be little more than an object of thought invoked to 'represent' some more disparate 'system of objects' into its own distinct entity. In so doing, like those he calls to task, Kelsen is able to evade tautology in only the most superficial of ways, naming rather than explaining the independent reality attributed to 'the legal order' in the course of lamenting the tendency to name rather than explain 'the state'.

While Kelsen's interests were philosophical in nature, the so-called duality problem—not to mention the inadequate solution Kelsen proposes for solving it—clearly has implications for humanistic thought more generally. Thus, it is not unreasonable to argue that something very much like Kelsen's blind spot about the hypostatization of 'the law' also proves true for the great many historically minded scholars who have studied the rise of the nation state and the attendant forms of social, political, and economic modernity that went with it. How much more precisely this occurs in the specific context of historical discussion of modern state-building in colonial India I discuss in the next three sections of this chapter. In the last three sections of the chapter I then begin to consider

---

[8] The tendency is pervasive throughout 'Part Two' of Kelsen's *General Theory of Law and State*. See e.g. ibid., 188–207 and 265–69.

how we might reckon with the true scope of the tendency towards hypostatization that makes the problem of duality so intractable.

1.2 Law in the Self-Conception of Early Colonial Rule

If there has obtained a baseline synonymity between the history of colonial rule in the subcontinent and its progress as a history of legal development it is not the function of analytical retrospection alone. In no small part, the overlap derives from a belief that was concurrent with colonial rule in at least some measure from its very outset. Among colonial administrators and intellectuals there was always some cognizance if not outright celebration of the supposedly unique nature of the English tradition of 'the rule of law' that the British were thought to have brought to the subcontinent. With such cognizance went the further belief that a form of authority was being imported into South Asia the likes of which its inhabitants had never previously known, given how it was based on an ethic of impersonality that privileged rule-bound certainty in the administration of justice over personal discretion. It cannot be denied, therefore, that such beliefs had always lent an imaginative dimension to historical events in Britain's India that coloured the colonial regime's practices and institutions in a very particular hue of self-conception. Accordingly, the stage had long been set for law to become an intrinsic part of the whole colonial enterprise, as a promiscuity of associations accrued around juridically tinged concepts, already, from the late eighteenth century. More specifically, one can say that an idea of 'the legal' asserted itself at what were at least three different levels of historical event that proved crucial to the advent of formal colonial rule under the East India Company. Each of these, moreover, was made evident in microcosmic form already in the immediate aftermath of the Company's earliest acquisition of de facto sovereignty when it took over as diwan of the Bengal Presidency in 1765, thus being entitled to control the province's revenues to finance its own military and commercial expansion.[9]

---

[9] Arguing that it was long before the acquisition of *diwani* that the Company's ambitions and efforts at securing sovereignty came into focus, see generally Philip J. Stern, *The*

At the first such level of event, it was through concerns about the Company's place within the Crown-in-Parliament's supposedly unitary sovereignty that the legal was confirmed as holding a special relevance to colonial rule. Such concerns required determining the nature of the Company's juridical identity amidst the transition it was making away from its role as a trading corporation. In this respect, formal colonial rule in the subcontinent brought with it a passage not just from company to sovereign but to a species of political sovereignty the precise basis of which within the structure of British national government was initially quite ambiguous. Officialdom and its thinkers would consequently have to make fresh sense of the Company's quickly expanding portfolio of activities in north-east India. Indeed, given that that transition occurred during the late eighteenth century, even determining what the colonial state in the subcontinent *was* proved difficult. For at that point in time there was simply not available the same variety of sub-sovereign legal forms that would go on to populate high imperialism's juridical menagerie of colonies, possessions, protectorates, mandate territories, and so on after the late nineteenth/early twentieth century.[10] Nor were there even available the less formalized concepts of lay imperial theorizing—about 'direct' versus 'indirect' rule—that scholar-officials would also go on to develop in the age of high imperialism. Even what juridical machinery did exist—in the form of the relatively meagre distinction between 'settler' and 'non-settler' colonies—was of little use for understanding the Company's situation.[11] Ultimately, then, the desire for

Company-State: Corporate Sovereignty and the Early Modern Foundations of the British Empire in India (New York: Oxford University Press, 2011).

[10] On the development of international law after the mid-nineteenth century see Casper Sylvest, '"Our Passion for Legality": International Law and Imperialism in Late-Nineteenth-Century Britain', *Review of International Studies* 34, no. 3 (2000): 403–23; Martti Koskenniemi, *The Gentle Civilizer Of Nations: The Rise And Fall of International Law, 1870–1960* (New York: Cambridge University Press, 2002); and Antony Anghie, *Imperialism, Sovereignty, and the Making of International Law* (New York: Cambridge University Press, 2005), chapter 2. On the distinction between protectorates and colonies and the late-nineteenth-century scramble for Africa see Andrew Fitzmaurice, *Sovereignty, Property and Empire: 1500–2000* (Cambridge: Cambridge University Press, 2014), 283–84.

[11] As Mahmood Mamdani has lucidly discussed, it was only after the scramble for Africa had come into full effect that this framework of thought matured. In the British tradition of colonial ideology, this took place most notably in the thought of Frederick Lugard, the High Commissioner of the Nigerian Protectorate. See Mahmood Mamdani, *Citizen and Subject: Contemporary Africa and the Legacy of Late Colonialism* (Princeton, NJ: Princeton University Press, 1996), 16–18.

greater Parliamentary control over the East India Company's activities stimulated an active ferment around what were actually quite novel questions about the Company's character as a chartered corporation versus ruling power. In this respect, one can say that already with Lord North's Regulating Act of 1773 and Pitt's India Act of 1784 events in the subcontinent started to become enclosed within a discernibly 'legal' kind of history.

As for the second level of event that was formative to the early history of colonial rule at which a focus on the legal became crucial, it came into view alongside concerns about the internal structure of the de facto state that was emerging under the Company's auspices, whatever its exact place within the sovereignty of the British Crown-in-Parliament. More specifically, events at this level precipitated questions about the balance of authority to be apportioned to the Company state's various 'branches' of government. Controversy first crystallized in 1773 with the establishment of a Supreme Court of Judicature at Calcutta under the Crown's seal and the creation of a new office of Governor General to supervise the Company's sovereign affairs in its new presidency. The creation of the Supreme Court extended the Company's so-called dual judiciary, which brought together its own courts with those under royal seal. More importantly, it made the forcing of the question of who held authority over the Company's affairs in Bengal inevitable. While the Court had exclusive civil and criminal jurisdiction within the Presidency town of Calcutta and general jurisdiction over all disputes involving at least one British subject, the nature of its powers beyond city limits was initially unclear. As a result, conflict between the Court and the Governor General broke out almost immediately, and though partially resolved by the early 1780s, it continued to echo with lasting overtones for many years thereafter.[12]

---

[12] The Act of Settlement of 1781 (21 Geo. III. c. 70) clarified the extent of the Court's territorial jurisdiction beyond Calcutta and its personal jurisdiction over its South Asian subjects. The Court lost its power to interfere in matters of revenue collection as well as those relating to the 'judicial functions' of the Company's own servants. The Governor General and his Council were, therefore, exempted from the Court's jurisdiction, at least in their official capacities—including as decision-makers sitting in appellate jurisdiction. In this latter role they met once per week, while using the other days to conduct 'executive' affairs. The Act of Settlement of 1781 also authorized the Governor General in Council to issue regulations for the Company's territories in Bengal outside Calcutta. See Orby Mootham, *The East India Company's Sadar Courts, 1801–1834* (London: Sweet and Maxwell, 1983), 4 and Dieter Conrad, 'Administrative Jurisdiction and the Civil Courts in the Regime of Land-Law in India', in *Our Laws, Their Lands: Land Laws and*

As historians have sometimes argued, this early battle between the Court and Governor General's Council in Bengal made for a nascent, if not full-fledged, executive-versus-judiciary rift.[13] Much the same has been seen even more starkly outside of Bengal—as in Madras, for example, where the distinctive feature of British rule is usually understood to have turned on an even more profound version of precisely the same divide. The championing of 'the district collector' as the 'central figure of the British administration' in Madras 'in place of Cornwallis's judge' in the Bengal Presidency is thus seen as the triumph of a rule by the executive over something more like a rule of law, proper, based on the supremacy of the judiciary.[14] Likewise, the decision in the Bombay Presidency to deviate from Cornwallis' path has also tended to be seen as tantamount to a victory for an alternative system of colonial administration, privileging executive expediency over the exactitude of judicial proceduralism.

At this second level of event as well, then, the history of British India came to be encased within a narrative of legal development—both retrospectively and, even if to a lesser extent, contemporaneously with the Company state's rise to formal power. Here, however, at issue has been the law's rule conceived as a proper balance of institutional powers in a Montesquieuean sense. Insofar as squabbling between courts and councils (or district judges and district collectors) has been the focus, in other words, events have been framed by a narrative of the rule of law as a means for resolving conflicts between executive and judicial power, understood as vaguely 'legal' forms of authority (or conversely as forms the authority of which gave them charge over that which was vaguely legal).

Finally, during the era of Company rule, juridically tinged concerns extended still further downward to a third level of event as well, with the early history of British rule in Bengal once more taking on microcosmic significance. Controversies and pronouncements implicating

---

Land Use in Modern Colonial Societies, eds. Jap de Moor and Dieter Rothermund (Münster: LIT, 1994),134–54 at 140–41.

[13] Robert Travers discusses the clash in something like these terms. See Robert Travers, *Ideology and Empire in Eighteenth-century India: The British in Bengal* (Cambridge: Cambridge University Press, 2007), ch. 5.

[14] See e.g. Thomas R. Metcalf, *Ideologies of the Raj* (New York: Cambridge University Press, 1995), 25.

the legal were thus part and parcel of defining colonial rule in its most immediate capacity as a form of everyday administration, regardless of how deeply the state's reach actually penetrated into subcontinental society. Simultaneous with the unfolding of events at the initial two levels discussed here, already by 1772 Governor General Warren Hastings had issued the first major proposal for reforming the Company's administration of justice. Adopted in August of that year, Hastings' 'Plan for the Administration of Justice' was soon followed by a second reform proposal issued in November of 1773.[15] Together, these measures divided up the territory of the Presidency into a number of districts, at each of which a land-revenue collector was to sit as a local civil judge alongside the continued district-level criminal jurisdiction of the Islamic *qazis* and their jurisconsults. Through the same measures of reform, Hastings also backed the initial creation of superior courts of appeal with Presidency-wide jurisdiction.[16]

It was at this third level of event that the legal was made immanent in the Company's Bengal at what we now imagine to be its most irreducible instantiation—namely, as the post hoc basis for norming intersubjective conflicts.[17] It was in this capacity, for example, that it appeared

[15] The 1772 plan is reprinted in Sir George Forrest, ed., *Historical Documents of British India: Warren Hastings*, vol. 2 (Delhi: Anmol, 1985), 290. Although it also dates from 1773, the Supreme Court at Calcutta was established by Parliament's Regulating Act of that year (under the direction of Lord North).

[16] These superior courts, dubbed the *Sadar Diwani Adalat* and the *Sadar Nizamat Adalat*, were to be respectively presided over by the Governor General and members of his council and an Indian judge assisted by the chief Muslim *qazi* and his staff. The district-, or *mofussil*-, level courts were named according to the same distinction between *diwani* and *nizamat* jurisdiction, which the Company borrowed from the nomenclature for the basic divisions of Mughal government. Despite retaining Mughal terminology, the Company's administrative divisions were novel. In the Mughal province of Bengal the *nizamat* was a branch of administration handling military and police functions relating to the general preservation of 'law and order'; the *diwani* institutions, on the other hand, handled matters such as revenue assessment and collection. Rather than a distinction about adjudicatory jurisdiction, therefore, in the Mughal context these terms spoke to the basic activities the imperial sovereign was charged with. Thus, while the provincial governor was supposed to oversee the *nizamat* he was barred from interference in *diwani* responsibilities.

[17] For example, it seems to be this sense, ultimately as a repository for rules of decision for norming disputes, that Tirthankar Roy has in mind in describing the 'common factor of imperial governance' being not 'violence' or 'collaboration', but 'legislation'. His threefold typology of such possible 'legislative project[s]' thus distinguishes 'appropriation, incorporation, and standardization'. For Roy, the colonial subcontinent fell under the second of these headings, owing to the British 'securing loyalty with the offer of juridical autonomy to communities' via 'the adoption of indigenous religious codes as civil law' as well as the third, which he contends was because of the way the colonial rule of property and contract increasingly championed 'the practice of bringing diverse legal codes into conformity' as 'incorporation failed in the presence of too

in Hastings' famed regulation mandating that '[i]n all suits regarding inheritance, marriage, caste, and other religious institutions or usages the laws of the Koran with respect to the Mahomedans and those of the Shaster with respect to the Gentoos shall invariably be adhered to'.[18] With only slight modification over the next decade,[19] the principle became the basis of the series of regulations that Governor General Cornwallis issued in May 1793. In what is now conventionally seen as a landmark event in the history of colonial rule, the so-called Cornwallis constitution ratified and extended Hastings' system of judicial administration based on 'native laws' together with the principles of justice, equity, and good conscience.[20] It also became the basis for elaborating the Company's administration of justice and asserting its sovereignty in the other Presidency areas under its early rule.[21] Claims about executive-led government aside, even in

many divisions within the society'. Tirthankar Roy, *India in the World Economy: from Antiquity to the Present* (New York: Cambridge University Press, 2012), 205–06.

[18] Under clause 23, 'Questions concerning Inheritance, Marriage, Caste' were to be 'settled agreeably to the dictates of the Koran or Shaster'—a formula later adjusted to also include all 'other religious usages, or institutions'. See Warren Hastings, 'Plan for the Administration of Justice', 15 August, 1772, reprinted in *Warren Hastings in Bengal, 1772–1774*, M. E. Monckton Jones (Oxford: Clarendon Press, 1918), 324–26.

[19] This proposal became the basis for section 27 of Regulation 11 of April 1780. In 1781 under section 93 of that year's 'Administration of Justice Regulation' the word 'succession' was added to the list of topics to be governed by the laws of the 'Koran and Shaster'. Under the influence of Elijah Impey, the Chief Justice of the Calcutta Supreme Court, section 93 was supplemented by provisions emphasizing that 'Justice, Equity and Good Conscience' were to be availed when the above sources did not furnish a clear rule of decision. All of this was further ratified by the British Parliament in the Act of Settlement of 1781 (21 Geo. III c. 70, section 17). See George Rankin, *Background to Indian Law* (Cambridge: Cambridge University Press, 1946), 9–10.

[20] Section 15 of Regulation IV of 1793 was the cognate provision, mandating that in suits regarding succession, inheritance, marriages, and caste, and all religious usages and institutions, 'the Mahomedan laws with respect to Mahomedans' and the Hindu laws with regard to Hindus, were to be considered as the general rules by which the judges were to form their decisions. It was the 'Mahomedan' and Hindu law officers who were to expound this law for the Court.

[21] Chartered Supreme Courts on the model of that in Calcutta were set up in the Madras Presidency in 1801 and Bombay in 1823. Further Acts of Parliament extended to the Presidency councils at Madras (by 39 & 40 Geo. III. c. 79 and 47 Geo. III) and Bombay (also by 47 Geo. III) the power to frame regulations concerning provincial councils and courts and concerning 'good order and government' in the Presidency capitals and their dependencies more generally. These powers were analogous to those earlier assigned to the Governor General's Council at Calcutta to issue its own regulations (under 13 Geo. III and 37 Geo. III, c. 14). In both areas, therefore, a judicial system much like Cornwallis' in Bengal was created, with relevant divisions between the district-level jurisdiction of the *mofussil* courts and the appellate jurisdiction of the *sadar* courts. Outside Bengal, however, the nomenclature was somewhat different, with the distinction being between the civil jurisdiction of the *diwani adalats* and the criminal jurisdiction of the so-called *foujdari adalats* (the latter term, roughly denoting 'military' power, being used in lieu of the term '*nizamat*').

Bombay and Madras it was a version of the Hastings-Cornwallis system, with the same deference to 'native laws', that was kept largely intact.[22] In this respect, in the Company's India it was such 'laws' that were the notional basis on which the administration of justice was supposed to be normed.[23]

* * *

While discourse about law, thus, cast a long shadow over colonial rule already from its outset, it would be a mistake to imagine that at each of these three levels of event there was a single and selfsame notion of the legal at play. If there was a connection between the development of the separate institutional 'legal' functions of state and the 'legal' rules that factored into the colonial state's administration of justice, for example, it came less through a shared phenomenon of 'the law' than it did through ideas that were normative in two different ways. At the first of these two levels of historical event, at issue was the normative force of constitutionalist theory in suggesting how best to conceive of (and divide up) governmental powers. At the level of the administration of justice, however, it was the notion of *the laws* of native tradition/society that was the focus. Whatever the specifically 'legal' variety of normativity that was implicated at the latter level, it followed from the idea that only with sound laws could there be fixed and certain 'rules of decision' for conducting dispute settlement. Alongside handling taxation, doing such justice made for one of the small number of key tasks of administration that defined sovereignty as a practical affair in this decidedly early-modern conception.

---

[22] By Regulation III of 1802 the Madras Council framed its 'code' on the basis of Cornwallis' regulations of 1793. In Bombay, after the Parliamentary acts of 1797 the Presidency Council endorsed the use of native laws, albeit in a language slightly more generalized than that of the comparable provisions in Bengal (and Madras). ('In suits regarding succession, inheritance, marriage, and caste and all religious usages and institutions, the Mahomedan laws with respect to the Mahomedans, and the Hindu laws with respect to the Hindus, are to be considered as the general rules by which the Judges are to form their decisions'.) The same provision was extended to Benares in 1799 and much of the rest of the North-Western provinces in 1800. See Herbert Cowell, *The Hindu Law: A Treatise on the Laws Administered Exclusively to Hindus by the British Courts in India*, vol. I, *The Tagore Law Lectures of 1870* (London: W. Thacker & Co., 1870), 51–54.

[23] For an important qualification to this view—or, at any rate the idea that the notional was one and the same with the actual—see Travers, *Empires of Complaints*, 251 (arguing that the narrative of Anglicization ignores the way Hastings' judicial regulations were shaped by the prior experience of modes of dispute resolution that borrowed from Persianate administrative routines and documentary forms).

Accordingly, it would be overdetermined to contend that already by the late eighteenth century the 'laws' which factored into the Company's administration of justice were part of one integral whole from which both the justification for its claim to territorial sovereignty and the would-be arrangement of its councils and courts derived. In short, there was no single and self-same continuum of 'the law' that linked together phenomena so varied as the basis for norming judicial administration, the theoretical position in virtue of which different constitutional functions could be normatively assigned to different institutions of state, and the normative meta-constitutional stance for justifying the delegation of the British Crown-in-Parliament's own sovereignty to a trading corporation. Given the available discourse of governance and attendant intellectual culture that surrounded early colonial rule, it is only through anachronism that it is plausible to maintain that 'the law' comprised one great chain of specifically legal being, as if forged from a uniform kind of normative substance.

1.3 Crown Rule and the Rise of a Legislative State

If it is fair to say that already from its outset the history of British rule in the subcontinent was being made tantamount to a history of legal development, this was true in a still only limited sense during the Company's era. As I have been suggesting, this is because there were too many different notions of 'the legal' at play within the various contexts in which considerations about the normative bases of governance arose. However, one would be much more hard-pressed to say the same for the years following the rebellion of 1857 and the subsequent transfer of power from Company to Crown the following year. After 1858 there increasingly did emerge something like a single chain of legal being in virtue of which the several levels of event just discussed became part of a joint enterprise in unfolding a shared object called by the name of the law. With the more robust form that the colonial state was taking during the second half of the nineteenth century, a marked expansion was taking place in the seeming omnipresence of a governing order that was supposed to be 'legal' in its essence. This was made most clearly manifest in the expanding body of legislation by which the colonial state formalized its interventions into the subcontinent's increasingly national polity, economy, society, and culture.[24]

After the transfer of power, in fact, the rise of the legislative state made for a fourth level of event at which a synonymity emerged between the history of Britain's India and its progression as a history of seemingly legal development. At this level, moreover, the overlap was asserted much more aggressively than at any of the others discussed above. As we have just seen, during the previous era it was mainly in elaborating the normative basis of the early colonial state's administration of justice that a notion of the legal came self-consciously into play within what historians used to call 'the official mind'.[25] In the Company's decidedly early-modern discourse, it was the 'laws' of native tradition rather than 'the law' per se that most typified *what* the legal consisted of. Only in a more tenuous way did any specific plan for or against creating a Montesquieuean separation of powers or for justifying the Raj's place within the authority structure of the Crown-in-Parliament prove necessarily connected to some particular notion of the legal. Moreover, at these levels of event the connection between law and governance was as much the product of the modern historian's reconstruction of the past in terms of the imminence of the legal as it was anything else.

Insofar as it became increasingly necessary to cloak politico-bureaucratic initiative in statutory enactment, however, something very different was taking place as the nineteenth century advanced. Fundamentally, the co-occurrence of administrative action and legislative pronouncement involved institutionalizing a form of self-consciousness

---

[24] The clamouring for a more deliberative mechanism of legislation began under the 'Utilitarian' Governor General William Bentinck. However, it was not until the Charter Act of 1853 that the sentiment was made good on. The 1853 Act expanded the number of members in the Governor General's Council—which by this time also was sitting regularly as a legislative council—from where it had been left in the Charter Act of 1833. After 1853, when sitting as a legislative council the numbers increased still further, from five (the Governor General himself, three ordinary members, and a fifth 'law member' added for the first time under Bentinck's regime) to twelve. By 1861, as the legislative output of the council began accelerating even more noticeably, the number increased to as many as twenty, now including the Viceroy (as the Governor General of India was renamed under the Crown), the Commander-in-Chief, the Governor of whatever the province in which the Council was sitting, five ordinary members, and six to twelve additional members. See George Rankin, *Background to Indian Law*, 59–76.

[25] While the locution may now sound dated, it was quite useful, at least when free of unjustifiable metaphysical baggage. See e.g. Eric Stokes, 'The Land Revenue Systems of the North-Western Provinces and the Bombay Deccan 1830–80: Ideology and the Official Mind', reprinted in *The Peasant and the Raj*, Eric Stokes (New York: Cambridge University Press, 1978), 90–118.

the very point of which was to transform anything the state did into a variety of its legal output. During the second half of the nineteenth century in Britain's India, to govern thus increasingly meant to take charge over an object called 'the law', which denoted a world-historical instrumentality that stood over and above the realms of polity, economy, and society/culture. As such, the law articulated and policed the would-be boundaries of these realms. At the same time, its supposed nature as an ostensibly distinct type of normative instrumentality meant that the law was supposed to be equally capable of exhaustively ordering the infinite array of inter-subjective transactions that took place within these various realms.

Ever more was 'the law', thus, regarded as a complex system consisting of subsegments and inner component parts making for a single and self-contained logical unicity rooted in 'rules' that covered any potential 'fact' the world might generate. This juxtaposition between early- and late-nineteenth-century British imperial governance in the subcontinent was signalled by the Raj's shift away from issuing mere 'regulations', as began to take place through the various governors' councils at the Presidency capitals already prior to the transfer of power. In noticeable contrast, under the Crown's raj the pronouncements of the new so-called legislative councils of the central and provincial governments became full-fledged Acts. In part, the novel moniker was suggestive of the advent of a form of deliberation that was more considered than the mere 'discussion confined to the seclusion of a chamber' by which the regulations of old were made.[26] Considered alongside the centralization of the judiciary under a new system of appellate High Courts and the creation of a proper apparatus for official case reporting, however, the shift from 'regulations' to 'acts' was also indicative of how thoroughly dependent the rationalization of political power was becoming upon a supposedly autonomous 'legal order'. Considered as an object distinct unto itself, the law was increasingly, by the very nature attributed to it, becoming a type of thing that could be handled independently by both the legislature and the judiciary, 'made' by the former and applied or interpreted by the latter even as it was put forth as the basis of both.[27]

---

[26] Despatch No. 44 of 10 December 1834, quoted in George Rankin, *Background to Indian Law*, 59.
[27] With the High Courts Act of 1861 Parliament scrapped the old Chartered Supreme Courts that had been set up in the capital towns of the Company's three Presidencies. The High Courts

1.4 From Scientific Legislation to a Science of the Law

Nonetheless, it would be misleading to see the law's growing ubiquity in the Crown's India as being mainly a product of a high nineteenth-century anthropological commitment to a kind of legal universalism born from the 'discovery' and othering of 'primitive society'.[28] Indeed, it would be similarly misleading to see things in terms of the rise of a legislative state. For the change that was afoot involved more than just the shift towards lawmaking[29] or the triumph of 'state law'[30] that historians of the late-nineteenth-century metropolitan and colonial worlds have both long discussed. Nor—more specifically to Britain's India—was the law's growing ubiquity simply 'tantamount' to another chapter in an uninterrupted 'story of the introduction of English law' into the subcontinent.[31] To the contrary, in the transition from early to late-nineteenth-century governance under the Raj there was something deeper at play in driving legal evolution in the face of a quickening pace of change than the state's need to resort to making the law itself rather than relying on the piecemeal casuistry of its judicial administration or the ebb and flow of organic custom in society. To see matters in the above way fails to capture how more precisely in the second half of the nineteenth century 'the

---

Act also did away with the colonial state's dual judiciary. In place of such older institutional arrangements, it established High Courts of Judicature under letters patent from the Crown in Calcutta, Madras, and Bombay. Each High Court consisted of a Chief Judge and some number of puisne judges and had original jurisdiction over admiralty issues and original and appellate jurisdiction over testamentary, intestacy, and matrimonial issues. (The High Courts had appellate jurisdiction over various other matters as well.)

[28] Adam Kuper, *The Invention of Primitive Society: Transformations of an Illusion* (New York: Routledge, 1988).

[29] See e.g. David Lieberman, *The Province of Legislation Determined: Legal Theory in Eighteenth-Century Britain* (New York: Cambridge University Press, 1989).

[30] Scholars of law and colonialism have often depicted the rise of the legislative state in terms of the triumph of 'state law'. See e.g. M. B. Hooker, *Legal Pluralism: An Introduction to Colonial and Neo-Colonial Laws* (New York: Oxford University Press, 1975); Sally Engle Merry, *Colonizing Hawai'i: the Cultural Power of Law* (Princeton, NJ: Princeton University Press, 2000); and Lauren Benton, *Law and Colonial Cultures: Legal Regimes in World History, 1400–1900* (New York: Cambridge University Press, 2002).

[31] D. H. A. Kolff, 'The Indian and British Law Machines: Some Remarks on Law and Society in British India', in *European Expansion and Law: The Encounter of European and Indigenous Law in 19th- and 20th-Century Africa and Asia*, eds. W. J. Mommsen and J. A. de Moor (New York: Oxford University Press, 1992), 201–35 at 202.

law' became the omnipresent, perfectly integrated, and ostensibly self-contained phenomenon that it is still largely purported to be today.

While the rise of legislative power was obviously key to this process, from the standpoint internal to the law itself it was of only secondary importance. This is why the period when the law was more than ever becoming a function of the colonial state was also the very same during which it was more than ever coming to be thought of as separate from the realm of the political. So is it that the late nineteenth century marks the birth of what famed British jurist A. V. Dicey dubbed the 'law of the constitution'.[32] Dicey, who had much to say about the status of the colonial legislature in the subcontinent, did not arrive by accident at such a turn of phrase, perfectly suited as it was to the new conception of the legal as an infinite and logically integral system for the rational ordering of society according to norms. On this view, the same source of normativity that dictated the institutional architecture and constitutional 'powers' that made the state a juridical actor in its own right also dictated the 'rights' (and concomitant 'duties') of the juridical persons that comprised its subject population.[33] Notwithstanding the Indian state's *colonial* character, therefore, from the middle of the nineteenth century onwards so too in the subcontinent was there increasingly asserted a version of liberal

---

[32] A. V. Dicey, *An Introduction to the Study of the Law of the Constitution* (London: Macmillan, 1885).

[33] Only on this view does Kelsen's solution to the duality problem appear self-evident, inhering in the very way he sets up the problem. This is made clear in the following passage, which suggests that we need do no more than reverse the predominant view of the direction of causality between the state and the law:

> A definition of 'the State' is made very difficult by the variety of objects which the term commonly denotes ... The situation appears simpler when the State is discussed from a purely juristic point of view. The State is then taken into consideration only as a legal phenomenon, as a juristic person ... The State as a juristic person is a personification of [the community created by a national legal order] or the national legal order constituting this community ... According to the traditional view it is not possible to comprehend the essence of a national legal order ... unless the State is presupposed as an underlying social reality. A system of norms, according to this view, possesses the unity and individuality by which it merits the name of a national legal order, just because it is in some way or other related to one State as an actual social fact ... The relation between law and the State is regarded as analogous to that between law and the individual. Law—although created by the State—is assumed to regulate the behavior of the State, conceived of as a kind of man or superman, just as law regulates the behavior of men ... State and law, according to this view, are two different objects. The duality of State and law is in fact one of the cornerstones of modern political science and jurisprudence. Kelsen, *General Theory of Law and State*, 181–82.

theory's perfect circle of legal legitimation. If the instrumentality through which the state acted and through which it authorized the actions of its subjects was the very same on the basis of which its existence was made possible in the first place, there was a seeming logical necessity to the distinction between law and the state. Especially in a place like Britain's India, it was only with the advent of this particular moment in the late nineteenth century that 'duality' presented itself as something worth puzzling over. In contrast to Kelsen's largely ahistorical way of formulating the problem, however, in actuality it derived as much from the suspect nature of making real the unreality of 'the law' in the way this occurred in the Crown's India as it did from the unreality of 'the state' itself.

In this respect, the rise of the legislative state was thus historically less important than the tendency to 'hypostasize' the law, to put Kelsen's choice of words to a use he did not, himself, anticipate. For that tendency was so thoroughgoing that rather than being just an artefact of the retrospective observer's misguided speech, the specifically legal form of ordering was increasingly transformed into an irreducible fact of how the social world was reflexively structured. In the face of this tendency, the law's obvious dependence on the state—as the font of positivist legislation—was transformed into its opposite. Accordingly, while it might be said that through statutory enactment 'the law' was made, legislation was thought to involve decisions that were moral, political, or economic—in short, of a kind involving value judgment— rather than fundamentally legal in nature. This, moreover, was no less the case under a system of parliamentary sovereignty, which was premised on an ideal that simply begged the question of where the norm of the legislature's ultimate supremacy came from if not from 'the law' itself.[34] Whereas the moral, political, and economic

---

[34] Even if they are to be considered totally distinct from theories of parliamentary sovereignty, theories of popular sovereignty elicit the same question. As to how this question—about the origins of the norm of supremacy—is specifically inflected in such contexts, the historical literature is vast. Recently, see e.g. Peter Caldwell, *Popular Sovereignty and the Crisis of German Constitutional Law: The Theory and Practice of Weimar Constitutionalism* (Durham, NC: Duke University Press, 1997); Michael Stolleis, *Public Law in Germany: 1800-1914* (New York: Berghahn Books, 2001); Pasi Ihalainen, *Agents of the People: Democracy and Popular Sovereignty in British and Swedish Parliamentary and Public Debates, 1734-1800* (Leiden: Brill 2010); James Livesey, *Making Democracy in the French Revolution* (Cambridge, MA: Harvard University Press, 2001); Mark Hulliung, *Citizens and Citoyens: Republicans and Liberals in America and France* (Cambridge, MA: Harvard University Press, 2002); Larry D. Kramer, *The People Themselves: Popular Constitutionalism and Judicial Review* (New York: Oxford, 2004) and Arthur Wilmarth, 'Elusive Foundation: John Marshall, James Wilson, and the Problem of

decision-making that undergirded legislation was about concretizing value-based preferences, group interests, or some criterion of utilitarian welfare maximization, genuinely *legal* decision-making was about fidelity to a standard of reasoned deliberation; whereas moral, political, and economically -based decisions portended the rule of man, genuinely *legal* decision-making stood at the ready to chasten personal whim and guarantee a rule of law; whereas the moral, the political, and the economic were subjective, the genuinely *legal* was objective.

Considered relative to its own internal standpoint, then, the law's emerging omnipresence was part of an ongoing process of making it an object of scrutiny, the true scope of which as an ostensibly self-contained and structurally integral whole stood waiting to be discerned. On this view, the law was a function not of the increasing power, bureaucratization, or interventionism of the state, but only of what was supposed to be a more refined ability to reveal its independence on grounds of its internal systematicity and logical unity. In this respect, Crown rule in Britain's India was infused by more than just a Benthamite discourse about the need for a proper 'science' of legislation[35] of the kind James Mill and his acolytes were championing already by the 1820s.[36] Rather, in the subcontinent, as in so much of the rest of the world, after the midpoint of the nineteenth century it was a discourse about legal scientism that was on the ascent. With ties to a more robust brand of analytical jurisprudence in the Anglophone world, after 1860 this made for an increasingly

Reconciling Popular Sovereignty and Natural Law Jurisprudence in the New Federal Republic', *George Washington Law Review* 72 (Dec. 2003): 113–93.

[35] For Mill, as for Bentham, the science of legislation was distinct from the 'field of judicature'. See, James Mill, *The History of British India*, vol. I (London: Printed for Baldwin, Cracock, and Joy, 1817), xix.
[36] Notwithstanding the attempt at 'social engineering' through abolishing *sati* and the first attempts at creating a penal code in the 1830s, most regulation under 'Utilitarian' Governor General William Bentinck concentrated on refining the institutional architecture for revenue and justice administration. It was under Bentinck, for example, that the provincial circuit and appeals courts in Bengal were abolished and replaced with Commissioners of Revenue and Circuit at each of the twenty new administrative divisions that were created. (The commissioners were to handle the duties of the former district-level judges at the provincial courts and supervise Revenue Collectors and police within their divisions.) Most of Bentinck's other important regulations were similarly aimed at bringing Bengal into closer alignment with Madras and Bombay by rolling back the Presidency's tradition of a purportedly strong division between its so-called 'executive' and 'judiciary'. See Eric Stokes, *The English Utilitarians and India* (New York: Clarendon Press, 1959), chapter 3.

audible call for a new human science of 'the law'—commensurate with its increasing naturalization as an object in its own right.

Importantly, this new discourse about legal science as an activity for the scholarly exponent of speculative jurisprudence was never very far removed from also being a renewed way of insisting on the ideal of the impartial adjudicator. In this sense, the human science of jurisprudence was simply a higher form of the practical jurisprudence of the expert in judging. In both cases, the commitment to the scientific ideal required that a form of reasoning particular to the law's own discernment be brought to bear upon it. Provided the law was seen as a relatively self-contained and internally coherent phenomenon this train of images remained plausible and even undeniable. It was on its basis, for example, that legal reason could remain largely immunized during this period from the sense that it was an exercise in discretionary judgement that necessarily had to be open to other sources of valuation, especially when the practical decision-maker was required to exceed the limit implied by the image of its exercise as the simple 'application' of rules to facts—as when dealing with cases that presented novel or complex social problems. As long as the law was its own relatively autonomous entity, legal reason could be portrayed as operating within strict constraints, even so-called hard cases being capable of being dealt with easily enough on such a view; they simply required the decision-maker to be envisioned as logically inferring an authoritative basis of decision that was already latent within the system and thus waiting to be discovered as already part and parcel of 'the law'.

Ironically, the ideal of legal scientism made its most noticeable advent into the Crown's India not through the utilitarian strand within colonial thought. Instead, it was the great adversary of neo-utilitarian, analytical jurisprudence in the Anglophone world—in the form of the historical tradition of Sir Henry Maine—that was the most visible byway of travel. If this seems paradoxical it is only because Maine made little secret of his opposition to Bentham's influence on jurisprudence, including as it was coming to be revamped after 1860 through the work of John Austin.[37] However, focusing too much on Maine's antagonism

---

[37] Austin was Bentham's leading disciple and the founding father of the British tradition of analytical jurisprudence. While some of his lectures were published in 1832 as *The Province of Jurisprudence Determined* (London: John Murray, 1861 [1832]), it was not until after his death in 1859 that he achieved real impact and lasting influence, largely through the editorial efforts of

to Austin's command theory of the law as the willed pronouncement of the sovereign misses what they more fundamentally shared.[38] In both the Austinian analytical school and the Mainean historical one there was a joint commitment to the idea that the law was a free-standing object requiring its own special modes of investigation. Accordingly, the commitment to scientism was inclusive of both the diachronic and synchronic approaches to revealing the law's holistic integrity. In the subcontinent, no less than anywhere else, therefore, scientism was shared across the divide between figures like Maine and his disciples and those who were clearly more indebted to the Austinian tradition, including both conservatives like James Fitzjames Stephen[39] and their more liberally-inclined adversaries, whether on the Viceroy's council like Courtenay Ilbert or on the British mainland like Sir Frederick Pollock.[40]

If there was something unique about colonial legal thinkers in the subcontinent who were partial to a historicist approach, it was that they drew not just on Maine but the true founder of the historical tradition as well, the great early-nineteenth-century German jurist Friedrich Carl

---

his widow. A revised edition of *Province* was issued in 1861 and a full collection of the *Lectures on Jurisprudence* appeared in 1869.

[38] Work on Maine's influence in the subcontinent has long emphasized a stark contrast with utilitarianism. See e.g. Stokes, *The English Utilitarians and India*, ch. 4; Clive Dewey, 'Images of the Indian Village Community: A Study in Anglo-Indian Ideology', *Modern Asian Studies* 6, no. 3 (1972): 291–328 at 309–10; and Metcalf, *Ideologies of the Raj*, 38, 68–73. All three focus on the opposition between the 'non-regulation' province of the Punjab where Maine's influence is seen as stoking a neo-paternalist renaissance and the more rule-bound traditions of colonial administration in the longer-standing 'regulation' territories under British rule. The opposition between Benthamite utilitarianism and Maine's influence (including through the Punjab 'tradition') has continued to be a crucial point of departure in later work as well. See e.g. Karuna Mantena, *Alibis of Empire: Henry Maine and the Ends of Liberal Imperialism* (Princeton, NJ: Princeton University Press, 2010), 19.

[39] On the relation between Stephen's conservatism and his support for Indian codification, see Sandra den Otter, 'A Legislating Empire: Victorian Political Theorists, Codes of Law, and Empire', in *Victorian Visions of Global Order: Empire and International Relations in Nineteenth-Century Political Thought*, ed. Duncan Bell (New York: Cambridge University Press, 2007), 89–113, 96. For Stephen's views on systematizing the law in the colonial subcontinent see his 'Legislation under Lord Mayo' in *The Life of the Early of Mayo—Fourth Viceroy of India*, vol. II, ed. W. W. Hunter (London: Smith, Elder & Co., 1875), 143–226.

[40] Pollock authored several important works on colonial law in British India. See Frederick Pollock and Dinshah Fardunji Mulla, *The Indian Contract Act, with a Commentary, Critical and Explanatory* (Bombay: Thacker & Company, 1905); Frederick Pollock, *The Law of Fraud, Misrepresentation and Mistake in British India* (Calcutta: Thacker & Spink, 1894); Frederick Pollock and Dinshah Fardunji Mulla, *The Indian Partnership Act: with a Commentary, Critical and Explanatory* (Calcutta: Eastern Law House, 1934).

von Savigny.[41] Given Savigny's ideas about law being equivalent to the *volksgeist*, or the spirit of the folk community, his thought found fertile ground in the subcontinent amidst the Mainean surge of interest in Indian 'custom'. Yet this particular connection should not obscure relevant others, including that which followed from how Savigny more fundamentally rooted the historicist enterprise in a view about the need for a comprehensive science of the law capable of treating its object as a coherent whole, inclusive of its several dimensions. As a result, it was not just the examination of the organic evolution of community/folk spirit over time that was vital from the standpoint of historical jurisprudence but also the discernment of the law's unicity as a logical system based on first principles.[42] This is why in his own day, despite his theory of the *volksgeist*, Savigny remained less than optimistic about the prospect of successfully codifying German law and the task of 'scientific' discernment he thought would be necessary for the enterprise to be truly successful.

Tellingly, in the subcontinent it was those who are typically identified as Maine's disciples in the Punjab—figures like Sir William Henry Rattigan, his son Henry A. B. Rattigan, and Charles Tupper—who pursued the Savignian project into its furthest reaches.[43] Their efforts to document, record, and organize the province's 'customary law' cannot meaningfully be separated from the scientizing enterprise of legal systematization. Indeed, among their ranks were individuals who proved instrumental in bringing Savigny to the wider Anglophone world. Along with other colonial administrator-intellectuals in the subcontinent, they did so not despite but because of their Indian connection, translating some of the most

---

[41] Along with Georg Friedrich Puchta, Savigny was one of the founders of German historical jurisprudence as well as a key protagonist in the rise of the related Pandectist movement within German legal thought.

[42] Savigny's most important systematizing work on Roman law was the monumental eight-volume *System des Heutigen Römischen Rechts* (published between 1840 and 1849). Like Savigny (and the larger Pandectist movement), Maine's interest in Roman law was less in the ancient tradition as such than it was in its re-analysis, abstraction, and complete re-configuration.

[43] Maine's debt to Savigny too often has been underplayed in recent decades. See e.g. George Feaver, *From Status to Contract: A Biography of Sir Henry Maine, 1822-1888* (London: Longmans, 1969). On Feaver's influence over views about the Maine-Savigny relationship see Michael H. Hoeflich, 'Savigny and His Anglo-American Disciples', *The American Journal of Comparative Law* 37, no. 1 (Winter 1989): 17–37, at 25–26. For a contrary view about Maine, and the two chapters—German and English—in historical jurisprudence, see Paul Vinogradoff, *The Teachings of Sir Henry Maine: An Inaugural Lecture Delivered in Corpus Christi College Hall on March 1, 1904* (London: Henry Frowde, 1904) and his much longer work *An Introduction to Historical Jurisprudence* (London: Oxford, 1920).

important texts within Savigny's massive corpus into English.[44] Already by 1848, for example, the Chief Justice of the Bombay Supreme Court, Thomas Erskine Perry, issued the first English version of Savigny's famed treatise on possession.[45]

Just as it is a misconception to see the analytical tradition in jurisprudence as solely positivist or neo-utilitarian given Austin's own debts to Savigny, so it is misleading to see Maine's disciples in the subcontinent solely in terms of their belief in the organic nature of custom or their anti-utilitarianism. Unlike the main centres of the Anglo-common-law world, where it was Austin who was the key conduit for German legal scientism, in late-colonial India it was Maine's acolytes who most overtly shouldered this burden.[46] Therefore, if the Mainean and Austinian traditions differed it was not in the failure of either to attribute to 'the law' the type of systematicity necessary to render it amenable to scientific investigation. Indeed, not even the administrator-intellectuals of the Punjab can be called partisans exclusively of their own particular Mainean approach. Instead, they were well aware of the possibility of productively bringing a 'scientific' method to bear on the law in more than one way. For example, as Tupper contended, it was precisely because the law was an object amenable to a logico-deductive method for examining its transcendent reality that it could not but be profitably examined through an

---

[44] Rattigan translated the second volume of Savigny's *System*, under the title *Jural Relations: or the Roman Law of Persons as Subjects of Jural Relations Being a Translation of the Second Book of Savigny's System of Modern Roman Law* (London: Wildy & Sons, 1884).

[45] Perry arrived in India in 1841 as a judge on the Bombay Supreme Court. He served as chief justice from 1847 to 1852. He also served as the president of the Indian Board of Education for a decade, with a professorship established in his name in 1855 at Bombay's Government Law School. Dedicated to 'the members of the Honorable Company's Service, Engaged in the Administration of Justice in India', Perry's translation of Savigny's 1803 *Das Recht des Besitzes* was published as *Von Savigny's Treatise on Possession: or, The Jus Possessionis of the Civil Law* (London: R. Sweet, 1848). William Holloway, a Puisne Judge on the High Court of Madras, translated the first volume of Savigny's *System*, which was originally published in Madras. See his *System of the Modern Roman Law* (Madras: J. Higginbotham, 1867). A second translation of Savigny's *Das Recht des Besitzes* was published in Calcutta, as translated by J. Kelleher. See his *Possession in the Civil Law. Abridged from the Treatise of Von Savigny, to which is added the text of the title on possession from the digest with notes* (Calcutta: Thacker, Spink & Co., 1888).

[46] Austin's relation to German legal science and to Savigny, in particular, was complicated. Even though in later life he would explicitly reject many of Savigny's ideas his experience in Germany clearly had a lasting influence on his overall intellectual development. See W. L. Morrison, *John Austin* (Palo Alto, CA: Stanford University Press, 1982), ch. 1. On the connection between Austin's method and Savigny's historicism see Wilfrid Rumble, *Doing Austin Justice: The Reception of John Austin's Philosophy of Law in Nineteenth-Century England* (New York: Continuum, 2004), 17.

empirico-inductive approach as well. To investigate the law's evolution as an organic reality in the manner Tupper preferred was thus simply another way to reveal its inner order and continuity as a system. He made as much explicit in an address on 'English Jurisprudence and Indian Studies in Law' that he delivered while Vice Chancellor of the Punjab University. As he noted,

> [a]nalytical jurisprudence and that kind of comparative jurisprudence which is its immediate offspring are indeed scientific in the same sense that Euclid is scientific or the pure political economy of Ricardo or of parts of the treatise by John Stuart Mill. Certain postulates are taken for granted, to certain terms definite meanings are annexed, and a coherent body of doctrine is built up which commands assent so long as we do not challenge its first principles. But the comparative method as described by Sir Henry Maine is scientific in the same sense that the methods of biology are scientific. Indeed, if in the passage I have quoted we substitute for 'facts, ideas, and customs' the famous words 'genera and species,' and for 'historical records' 'the geological and embryological records', we have, I think, an accurate description of a part of the actual method of biology ... I hope I have made clear the affiliation of the various studies which may be grouped under the general name of 'jurisprudence'. Analytical jurisprudence generates comparative jurisprudence of the first [and more restricted] kind [involved in comparing mature legal systems]; historical jurisprudence touched by the electric current of modern science, generates comparative jurisprudence of the second kind; and all—analytical, historical, and comparative jurisprudence—combine to form scientific jurisprudence considered as a branch of sociology.[47]

---

[47] Charles Lewis Tupper, 'English Jurisprudence and Indian Studies in Law', *Journal of the Society of Comparative Legislation* new series 3, no. 1 (1901): 84–94 at 90. As Tupper went on to note, while elaborating on the 'Tributaries of Scientific Jurisprudence':

> [A]nalytical jurisprudence is the anatomy of fully developed systems of law, while scientific jurisprudence, largely understood, is the biology of the legal institutions of mankind. Scientific jurisprudence can no more dispense with analysis than biology can dispense with the structural investigation of the existing forms of animal life ... Historical jurisprudence examines the laws of one particular country of

Indeed, the Indian Law Commission echoed much the same sentiment in its 1879 report, while touching on the dialectic of universality and particularity in the self-conception of its own efforts:

> [I]n modern times, as the freedom of judicial interpretation becomes more restricted, the reaction of the form of the law upon its substance is more extensive and deeper than in earlier days. This is the palpable danger of a complete Code. It fixes the mobile elements of the law at the moment of its creation; it may petrify them and deprive them of their capacity of growth under the care of scientific doctrine at the call of extended needs. The danger reaches its climax when the principles of a foreign system are imposed on a community of different character and habits; and the danger lies very much in the terminology. While, then, our legislature itself takes out the kernel of English judicial wisdom, it must guard against the *lex viva*, the concrete law, becoming a composition of shells and rind. As in the field of physical science every great advance in discovery is attended with some enlargement of general conceptions and some improvement of method, so in the progress of legal development under any system accepting purely rational standards, each step towards perfection involves a recognition of human relations hitherto less clearly seen, or a change of standing point from which new truths come into view.[48]

---

empire, such as that of Rome, with the object of explaining their successive acceptance or enactment and connecting them with other historical facts ... Comparative jurisprudence, in the wider sense of the term, compares the legal institutions of different countries and times for the purpose of discovering the laws of their growth. Thus both comparative jurisprudence in the narrower sense of the term, and historical jurisprudence subserve the purposes of comparative jurisprudence in the wider sense of the term, and therefore of scientific jurisprudence at large, because they provide those means of comparison upon which the progress of science depends. In this way all these kinds of jurisprudence—analytical, comparative, historical—are tributaries of the great stream which I have called scientific jurisprudence at large; and, like your five rivers before they unite in the Indus, they independently fertilise wide spaces while on their course to join that combined flood which is used, and will be more and more used as time goes on, in ever-expanding fertilisation. Ibid., 91.

[48] *Report of the Fourth Law Commission*, 1879, V/26/100/12, par. 42.

1.5 The Rise of Classical Legal Thought and its Globalization

The primacy of the adjudicator over the legislator and its foundation in the complementarity between practical and scientific jurisprudence is indicative of a wider transnational history within which the increasing interventionism of the Crown's state in the subcontinent must be situated. This involved what legal scholar Duncan Kennedy has described as the first of the three significant instances of the globalization of law and legal thought that have taken place since the second half of the nineteenth century.[49] Extending roughly from 1850 to 1914, the first globalization was inclusive of what Kennedy has called the rise of 'classical legal thought' in the Western world, as per the wider scholarly convention his own work inaugurated. While it was legal historians of the United States who were the first and most explicit in advancing this convention,[50] their underlying assertions about the nature of classical legal thought resonate with views that have been developed by English legal historians[51] and scholars of the continental legal tradition as well.[52]

---

[49] See generally Kennedy, 'Three Globalizations of Law and Legal Thought', in *The New Law and Economic Development. A Critical Appraisal*, eds. David Trubek and Alvaro Santos, 19–73 (New York: Cambridge University Press, 2006).

[50] See e.g. Morton J. Horwitz, *The Transformation of American Law, 1870–1960: The Crisis of Legal Orthodoxy* (New York: Oxford University Press, 1992); Herbert Hovenkamp, 'Law and Morals in Classical Legal Thought', *Iowa Law Review* 82 (1997): 1427–65; William Wiecek, *The Lost World of Classical Legal Thought: Law and Ideology in America, 1886–1937* (New York: Oxford University Press, 1998); Richard H. Pildes, 'Forms of Formalism', *The University of Chicago Law Review* 66, no. 3 (Summer 1999): 607–21 at 607–09; and Duncan Kennedy, *The Rise & Fall of Classical Legal Thought* (Washington, DC: Beard Books, 2006).

[51] The best-known broadly corresponding example is Patrick Atiyah, *The Rise and Fall of Freedom of Contract* (New York: Oxford University Press, 1979). However, in the context of the English legal tradition it is David Sugarman who has most carefully taken up the challenge raised by the literature on United States legal history. See David Sugarman and G. R. Rubin, 'Towards a New History of Law and Material Society in England, 1750–1914', in *Law, Economy and Society: Essays in the History of English Law, 1759–1914*, eds. G. R. Rubin and David Sugarman (Abingdon: Professional Books, 1984), 1–123 and David Sugarman, '"A Hatred of Disorder": Legal Science, Liberalism and Imperialism', in *Dangerous Supplements: Resistance and Renewal in Jurisprudence*, ed. Peter Fitzpatrick (Durham, NC: Duke University Press, 1991), 34–67.

[52] James Gordley, *The Philosophical Origins of Modern Contract Doctrine* (New York: Oxford University Press, 1991); Franz Wieacker, *A History of Private Law (with particular reference to Germany)*, Tony Weir, trans. (New York: Oxford University Press, 1995); and most recently Anna di Robilant, *The Making of Modern Property: Reinventing Roman Law in Europe and its Peripheries 1789–1950* (Cambridge: Cambridge University Press, 2023).

Importantly, classical legal thought's late-nineteenth-century and Anglophone context made it more than simply a version of 'systematizing' neo-Roman-law jurisprudence redux of the kind that had risen to prominence in the German-speaking world earlier in the century. It would, thus, be inadequate to reduce classical legal thought to a product of the inevitable delay in the propagation into the English-speaking world of the pioneering enterprise of *Konstruktionsjurisprudenz* that Pandectist thinkers like Anton Thibaut and Savigny were pursuing on the continent already in the wake of the Napoleonic code and on the basis of the pre-French-revolutionary inheritance left them by Gustav Hugo and the German Historical School of jurisprudence. Of course, this is not to deny that German legal thought was a major influence on classical legal thinkers, including leading lights like Austin.[53] However, it is to say that to view classical legal thought simply as a variation on an early-nineteenth-century continental genuine article both is insufficient as a matter of intellectual history and incurs the risk of ignoring the importance of key contextual changes that were afoot by the later part of the century; chief among these were the vast growth of the British Empire and, alongside it, the capitalist world economy. Even if classical legal thought made for an Anglicized picture of German systematization, then, it was painted on a much wider canvas than any upon which the latter's palette theretofore had been dispersed.

Despite the critique to which it would be subject by the turn of the twentieth century as a font of alleged conceptualism,[54] mechanical jurisprudence,[55] legal formalism,[56] and the like, it would also be misleading

---

[53] In addition to the citations above, see also Michael Lobban, 'Austin and the Germans', in *The Legacy of John Austin's Jurisprudence*, eds. Michael Freeman and Patricia Mundus (New York: Springer, 2012). 255–70.

[54] This term, or its German equivalent (*begriffsjurisprudenz*), is most readily associated with Rudolf von Ihering, the greatest German jurisprudential thinker of the second half of the nineteenth century. In von Ihering's view conceptual jurisprudence was to be replaced by a 'jurisprudence of interests' that would be more attuned to sociological reality. See Dennis Patterson, *A Companion to Philosophy of Law and Legal Theory* (Cambridge, MA: Wiley Blackwell, 1999), 348.

[55] Echoing von Ihering, Harvard Law Professor/Dean Roscoe Pound coined 'mechanical jurisprudence' as a term of reproach in the United States in 1908 to distinguish past tendencies in legal thought from the new brand of sociological jurisprudence he was calling for. See Roscoe Pound, 'Mechanical Jurisprudence', *Columbia Law Review* 8, no. 8 (1908): 605–23 at 608, 609–10.

[56] See e.g. Max Weber, *Economy and Society: An Outline of Interpretive Sociology, vol. II* (Guenther Roth and Claus Wittich eds., Ephraim Fischoff et al. trans. (Berkeley, CA: The University of California Press, 1978 [1921–22]), 656–57.

to equate the rise of classical legal thought with the triumph of laissez faire or even 'the freedom of contract', at least if construed in terms of the ideal of voluntarist 'individualism'. Of course, as with the influence of German Pandecticism, this is not to say there was no connection. For to deny an equivalence between classical legal thought and an ideology of laissez faire is not to contend that legal scientism's commitments to conceptual abstraction and making practical adjudication an enterprise in deductive necessity were anti-individualist.[57] Nor is it to say that the doctrinal model of contractual bilateralism (in which obligation was supposed to be based on little more than mutual assent) did not privilege a regime of formal over substantive equality between parties with unequal bargaining power. It is to say, however, that the principle of individualism underlying classical legal thought was not simply identical to the notionally private atomism of the market by the late nineteenth century, as if signifying a complete autonomy from the state.

Indeed, as much as it was the basis for rationalizing the rights of the private person in the market, individualism in classical legal thought was also the basis for rationalizing the powers of the state, considered as a public juridical person in its own right. Classical legal individualism thus underwrote the growing reach of the state into society in a way that was analogous to the manner in which legal laissez faire is thought to have underwritten the self-realization of the private individual through facilitating market action.[58] Above all, it has been Kennedy's formulation

---

[57] The ideal of deductive necessity was applicable to both the connection between rules and facts and rules and other rules (as well asso-called first principles). In the second instance, however, the derivation of the 'correct' outcome through generating a new rule proceeded by what was actually deductive *or* inductive reason. Logical inference thus connected norms to other norms by moving either down from some more abstract principle to the less abstract rule of decision *or* up from some less abstract part of the rule system to some higher-level principle, so as to then proceed back up or down from there in order to derive the ultimate rule of decision for resolving a case. Either way, logical inference between norms was necessary when there was no explicit rule for resolving a dispute. In the face of such so-called gaps in the law, reasoning remained 'legal' because it was seen as proceeding *as if* the basis for resolving the case were latent within the rule system.

[58] As the Fourth Indian Law Commission put it,

[i]n the great field of personal obligations … [t]he law … is concerned rather in facilitating than in controlling the action of individuals. But if one fails in the duty he has undertaken to another, the State intervenes, and by force compels him to perform this duty, as it would one directly imposed in the public interest, or else to render an equivalent. *Report of the Fourth Law Commission*, par. 31.

of classical legal thought that has brought this latter feature to light.[59] The emergence of the correspondence he sketches between juridical persons private and public in the legal history of the United States goes a long way towards clarifying how individual rights and state powers became analogous forms of a specifically legal *kind* of entitlement wherever classical legal thought globalized. As Kennedy explains, whether private or public, the underlying idea was that the juridical individual always had a 'power absolute' within the relevant sphere of legal interest that they were entitled to hold, howsoever circumscribed that sphere might be.[60]

What Kennedy does not emphasize, however, is that there were other important implications to this parallelism between rights and powers as well. At least in the history of the West, it proves suggestive of how the feature in virtue of which private and public entitlements shared their common legality in the classical schematization bore the mark of an earlier mode of juridical thought. As I discuss further in chapter four, this is because in the Anglo-common-law mainstream already by the late eighteenth century the conception of the essentially legal nature of rights was being given definitional substance based on the model of property as an ostensibly unitary, absolute, and physical dominion of the owner over a landed (rather than metaphorical) realm.[61] Well before the era of classical legal thought, then, it was becoming plausible in the West to think of 'the law' as a structurally integral and self-contained phenomenon unto itself because of the way its core constituent of the legal right to property bore an irreducibly *real* existence through providing for control over physical space.

One of classical legal thought's most notable—and largely unseen—achievements was thus to further abstract an equivalence in the West by which 'the right to property' had already been made synonymous

---

[59] See generally Kennedy, *The Rise & Fall of Classical Legal Thought*, ch. 2.
[60] Ibid., 2–3.
[61] It is worth emphasizing that the noted tradition of debate among historians of political ideas about the republican versus liberal/possessive individualist ethos of late seventeenth- and eighteenth-century thought in (what became) Great Britain—inclusive of its substratum of theorizing about property—is *not* what I have in mind here. For what continues to be an illuminating intervention into that debate, see J. G. A. Pocock's essays on 'Authority and Property: The Question of Liberal Origins' and 'The mobility of property and the rise of eighteenth-century sociology', reprinted in J. G. A. Pocock, *Virtue, Commerce, and History: Essays on Political Thought and History, Chiefly in the Eighteenth Century* (Cambridge: Cambridge University Press, 1985). For the canonical view of 'possessive individualism' see C. B. Macpherson, *The Political Theory of Possessive Individualism* (Oxford: Clarendon Press, 1962).

with 'property' by the early nineteenth century. Of course, as the nineteenth century progressed it cannot be denied that the increasingly intangible form that economic value in exchange was taking already was, itself, making property—as both a social institution and an economico-juridical concept—more abstract.[62] However, it would be wrong to imagine that abstraction originated solely in the logic of commodity. Rather, the originary notion of the legal right to property that was founded in the Anglo-common-law mainstream on the unitary, exclusive, and physicalist discourse of ownership was not only highly intuitive but inherently extensible as well. In this respect, as much as anything else abstraction was a function of how short a step it was from the old conception of the right to property in particular to a dawning conception of legal right in general.

On the one hand, this was obviously crucial in making sense of the proliferation of entitlements that accompanied the enfranchisement of politics and the spread of commodification during the unfolding nineteenth century. On the other, it went a long way towards rationalizing the expanding need to bureaucratically manage the free market and administratively intervene into society. When the territorial-bureaucratic national state exercised its public powers, it thus acted on the basis of entitlements that were every bit as 'legal' as the rights that authorized the permissible actions of its private inhabitants. Ultimately, this abstract conception of private rights and public powers as realms of legal interest within which their holders' respective wills were sovereign helped impel classical legal thought's globalization. Indeed, the advantages of creating a means of ideologically parsing the law's doctrinal minutiae that was not, itself, subject to the charge of liberal or conservative bias should go without saying.

* * *

Alongside the commitment to scientism and the doctrinal principle of juridical individualism, in Kennedy's view classical legal thought had a third key characteristic as well. This was its commitment to an 'exhaustive elaboration of the distinction between private and public law'. Together

---

[62] See e.g. Mary Poovey, *Genres of the Credit Economy: Mediating Value in Eighteenth- and Nineteenth-Century Britain* (Chicago, IL: University of Chicago Press, 2008).

these three traits combined to form what he calls the 'the will theory' in classical legal thought, according to which

> [t]he private law rules of the 'advanced' Western nation states were well understood as a set of rational derivations from the notion that government should protect the rights of legal persons, which meant helping them realize their wills, restrained only as necessary to permit others to do the same.[63]

As such, according to Kennedy, the will theory was an 'attempt to identify the rules that should follow from consensus in favor of the goal of individual self-realization' rather than a 'political or moral philosophy justifying this goal' or even a 'positive historical or sociological theory about how this had come to be the goal'. Because it was not anchored in any particular theoretical point of view, the will theory was highly effective in 'guid[ing] the scholarly reconceptualization, reorganization, and reform of private law rules, in what the participants understood as an apolitical rationalization project'. It did so, more specifically, by 'providing the discursive framework for the decision of hundreds or perhaps thousands of cases, throughout the industrializing West, in which labor confronted capital and small business confronted big business'. Accordingly, the ultimate effect of the will theory was to function as 'an abstract, overarching ideological formulation of the meaning of the rule of law as an essential element in a Liberal legal order'.[64]

At the same time, as Kennedy emphasizes, it also had more subtle implications, with the logic of will further undergirding key secondary characteristics of classical legal thought as well. Most important among these were two additional taxonomizing distinctions that classical thinkers routinely made. First, there is what he calls the distinction between the subjects of municipal and international law, and second, that according to which he describes the municipal law's rules for governing relations amongst private actors, themselves, being divided in two. With the latter distinction, the so-called private law was thus bisected into a law of the family, on the one hand, and a law of the market, on the other.[65]

---

[63] Kennedy, 'Three Globalizations of Law and Legal Thought', 26.
[64] Ibid., 27.
[65] Ibid., 32.

Even if of only secondary importance, both of these two distinctions clearly followed from a single core idea—namely, that the law normed behaviour by doing no more than facilitating the will of some one juridical individual or another within that individual's appropriate sphere absolute. The divide between municipal and international law, for example, was based on the idea that international law was distinguished by states being juridical individuals facilitating their own respective wills by mutually binding themselves to one another through treaties in much the same way as parties to a private contract did in municipal law. In international law, therefore, the state's legal persona was different from that which it had under municipal law, as the sole holder of public juridical personhood. Notwithstanding the parallelism between private rights and public powers, that is, in municipal law the juridical personhood of the state was not quite of the same kind as that which its subjects enjoyed. This is because state action always entailed something more than just the realization of the public juridical will, which could not be made manifest without expressly opposing the will of at least one (subset of) private actor(s). On the one hand, when attending to questions of municipal law ex post, such a consequence necessarily ensued because dispute resolution could not take place except by advancing the will of one disputant at the expense of the adverse party's own. On the other hand, when attending to questions of municipal law ex ante, the consequence necessarily ensued because prescriptive legislation/regulation could not take place except by generally empowering the holder of the public will against all private actors simultaneously or, in the alternative, by preemptively conferring rights on one subset of private actors through imposing correlative duties on some other.

Likewise, in the abstract logic of classical legal thought the distinction within municipal law between the law of the family and the law of the market was based on a deeper way of differentiating relations of contract from relations of status that turned on competing options as to which will—the private or the public—the law should facilitate. To the extent that commercial relations were contractual, in the classical ideal the law of the market was supposed to generally advance the privately willed (re)arrangement of rights and duties by otherwise competent parties. Here as well this could take place either ex ante through the operation of the general principle that mutual agreements were binding once made or ex post through settling actual contractual disputes in accord with the will of the prevailing party. To the extent that domestic relations were based on status, in the classical ideal the law was still supposed to facilitate the will, albeit in a different way. On the one hand, within the law of the family this could take place by default through facilitating the private will of the patriarch, as implied by the general refusal to allow the contractual re-arrangement of familial rights and duties. On the other, it could instead take place by advancing the public will so as to allow the state to intervene into the private space of the family in order to realign status-based domestic rights and duties in the name of 'morality', changing social mores, equity, or the like.

1.6 The Law as a Social/Institutional Fact

Though it is not a point that has been made by legal historians of the West, as I have suggested above, classical legal thought was more than just a rhetorical and attitudinal style for guiding juristic reason. It was also a way of bolstering an already extant sense in the Anglo-common-law (and continental) legal mainstream(s) that juristic reason's object of scrutiny was an actual object in itself, with a real and irreducible existence in the social world. The more 'the law' was revealed by classical legal thinkers to be a structurally integrated and relatively self-contained logical 'system', the more legality appeared to be a distinct kind of (normative) phenomenon. In this respect, that classical legal thought harboured patently metaphysical overtones is undeniable. In situating the legal history of Britain's India partly within the story of classical legal thought's rise and wider transnational diffusion we should, thus, not be surprised if we find ourselves unexpectedly breathing new life into the seemingly outdated question of whether native society 'had laws'.[66]

---

[66] As Kaius Tuori has argued, the implicitly jurisprudential question—of whether all societies really 'had' law—that was yoked to the process of European expansion and conquest was reoriented under the influence of German Romanticism, which advanced the alternative idea that law was inherent within culture. To the extent that ongoing Western expansion thus came further/instead to be buttressed by the notion that *every* society had some kind of laws, the implicitly jurisprudential question raised by the colonial encounter was also further inflected according to an evolutionist/stage theory of history. See Kaius Tuori, *Lawyers and Savages: Ancient History and Legal Realism in the Making of Legal Anthropology* (New York: Routledge, 2014), 141.

A preoccupation of colonial thinkers not just in the subcontinent but in most places where Western expansion took place, today the question is—not without justification—most likely to be regarded as the product of orientalist blinders. At the same time, such a view can obscure how the question was also a historical indicator of the depth of ingress hypostatization had made within the discursive culture of the West by the second half of the eighteenth century. In this respect, the curiosity of British and other European thinkers who sought to find some *thing* in virtue of which the conduct of the Company state's administration of justice could be rendered certain was not unrelated to the defining concern in modern philosophical jurisprudence with determining the true nature of legal normativity. To ask what kind of 'laws', if any, inhabitants of the subcontinent 'had' was, thus, not only a product of blatant Eurocentrism/the will to see native society as backward. Rather, if we listen carefully, we can also hear it resound with Kelsen's effort—a century and a half later—to reckon with the problem of the so-called duality of law and the state. As we have seen, for Kelsen that problem could only be solved by proffering the thesis that it was the law rather than the state that was the independent variable (given the idea that the state was nothing other than its legal order). In a similar way, then, reckoning with the question animating the early colonial legal encounter between the Company's raj and Indian society was premised on its own, albeit less sophisticated, version of Kelsen's independent variable thesis, which had become available in the West already by the late eighteenth century.

Of course, one obvious difference between the early orientalist search for certainty in the Company state's administration of justice and Kelsen's interrogation of the duality problem is that the former effort left its exponents unsatisfied in a way the latter evidently did not. If such a difference is telling, it is because it proves indicative of how the curiosity of early orientalists and administrator-intellectuals in the Company's India was informed by what we might call an ontology of the legal that—even if still shifting in the West in the eighteenth century—would not become properly commensurate with the administrative and economic structure of colonial rule in the subcontinent until late in the nineteenth century.[67]

---

[67] Starting from a generally later period and through a very different methodology, Teemu Ruskola has framed his investigation of the Western legal encounter with China in a related way, in order to address the question, as he puts it, of how law became such a central part of the

In Britain's India, then, an ontology of 'the law'—rather than simply an ontology of 'the laws' that factored into the administration of justice—could only truly emerge from the shadows after 1850, during a period that would be marked by the notable convergence between the transfer of power from the Company to the Crown and the global diffusion of classical legal thought.

Notwithstanding the early concern with whether South Asians had law/laws, therefore, we should not lose sight of the evident shift that took place in the metaphysical heft attributed to legal normativity between the late eighteenth and late nineteenth centuries in the colonial subcontinent. To ask about the ontology of the legal in Britain's India is, thus, to ask about a relatively plastic element in history; for it requires that we look at various factors that subjected it to reshaping. Among these were the distinct visions that informed the jurisprudential curiosity animating the eighteenth-century orientalist encounter with the subcontinent's normative traditions as well as what actually proved commensurate with the Company state's administration as it was continuing to be built during the first half of the nineteenth century, not to mention new sources of intellectual influence like classical legal thought during the era of Crown Raj. To meaningfully enquire into the ontology of the legal in Britain's India thus also requires looking at the interplay between discourse and the institutional expression of colonial rule in order to trace the gradual process by which 'the law' became much the same free-standing object in the subcontinent by the end of the nineteenth century that it was already well on the way to becoming in the metropolitan world by the second half of the eighteenth.

* * *

To look at the development of 'the law' in such a manner is not unlike examining how any complex 'institutional fact' comes into being only through certain historical processes—to borrow, for the time being, a concept drawn from the analytical/Anglo-American tradition of philosophy that has featured prominently in linguist George Lakoff's

---

'political ontology' of modernity. See Teemu Ruskola, *Legal Orientalism: China, the United States and Modern Law* (Cambridge, MA: Harvard University Press, 2013), 1.

work.[68] As Christopher Greene and John Vervaeke explain, for Lakoff institutional facts are

> facts that depend upon the way a person or culture conceptualizes the world, such as facts about marriage, business, school, or art. In Lakoff's words, 'Since institutions are products of human cognition, institutional facts must depend on human cognition.'[69]

While I will return to this issue later in the chapter, for now it is worth adding that Lakoff's concept clearly overlaps with Émile Durkheim's notion of a 'social fact'. Even though more familiar to historical and sociological thinkers, however, Durkheim's concept has not been without its own controversies, two of which in particular bear mentioning. First, there is disagreement around what Durkheim meant when he claimed that social facts are constituted by 'the beliefs, tendencies and practices of the group taken collectively'.[70] More specifically, this first controversy that has surrounded Durkheim's thinking about social facts has to do with the seemingly extra-individualist metaphysical commitments it requires—in the form of the so-called *conscience collective* that he posits.[71]

If this were all there was to the matter, there would be little occasion for putting Durkheim's ideas into further dialogue with Lakoff's notion of

---

[68] The idea is one Lakoff has discussed in greatest detail in his *Women, Fire and Dangerous Things: What Categories Reveal About the Mind* (Chicago, IL: University of Chicago Press, 1987), 170–73, 207–08. For a more recent discussion, see George Lakoff and Mark Johnson, *Philosophy in the Flesh: The Embodied Mind and its Challenge to Western Thought* (New York: Basic Books, 1999), 107.

[69] Christopher D. Greene and John Vervaeke, 'The Experience of Objects and the Objects of Experience', *Metaphor and Symbol* 12, no. 1 (1997): 3–17 at 5 (quoting Lakoff, *Women, Fire and Dangerous Things*, 170). As Greene and Vervaeke make clear, Lakoff's use of the concept of institutional facts is secondary to his larger philosophical aim in *Women, Fire and Dangerous Things* (as well as *Philosophy in the Flesh*), which is to challenge 'objectivist' views of cognition, semantics, and metaphysics with his own 'experientialist' view. However, the larger concerns involved in Lakoff's—and Greene and Vervaeke's competing—formulation need not detain us.

[70] Émile Durkheim, *The Rules of Sociological Method*, trans. W. D. Halls (New York: Free Press, 1982), 54 (noting further that 'the forms these collective states may assume when they are "refracted" through individuals are things of a different kind ... Indeed some of these ways of acting or thinking acquire, by dint of repetition, a sort of consistency which ... isolat[es] them from the particular events which reflect them. Thus they assume a shape, a tangible form peculiar to them and constitute a reality sui generis vastly distinct from the individual facts which manifest that reality'.)

[71] On the problem the notion of collective consciousness creates for the concept of social facts, see Stephen Lukes, *Emile Durkheim: His Life and Work, A Historical and Critical Study* (New York: Harper and Row, 1973), 11–15.

institutional facts. Indeed, there would not even be reason for Durkheim's direct inheritors in social theory to have so persistently—on into the present—developed new avenues for exploring the ground he was originally seeking to tread through his concept of social facts.[72] Accordingly, it is really the second source of controversy that is the more significant in clouding the utility of Durkheim's concept. More specifically, this has to do with the possibility that what he meant in proposing that certain facts are 'social' was different from what he is generally taken to have meant. That is, for Durkheim the main point did not end up being that social facts are the counterpart of natural facts, as if to have been highlighting their character as emergent phenomena produced by human sociality rather than nature. Instead, what was most significant to Durkheim in making a fact 'social' was that it entailed 'any way of acting, whether fixed or not, capable of exerting over the individual an external constraint; or: which is general over the whole of a given society whilst having an existence of its own, independent of its individual manifestations'.[73] To put the point in terms of the thought of Durkheim's counterpart in the founding of modern sociology, Max Weber, the concern here is more with 'social action' as a constraint on further individual or social action by others than it is with the accumulation of the outcomes of social action into institutional forms the seemingly independent reality of which is underwritten by the artificial unity that discursive categories necessarily impose on them as objects of thought.[74] (Compare Weber's own

---

[72] Pierre Bourdieu's notion of *habitus* is the most obvious example. See his *The Logic of Practice*, trans. Richard Nice (Palo Alto, CA: Stanford University Press, 1990). 52–53. However, other examples abound insofar as the underlying dilemma the concept of a social fact gets at concerns explaining social behaviour according to largely internalist frameworks that privilege the individual's inner beliefs and motivations as the reasons for their action versus externalist ones that treat those actions causally and the socially grounded individuals from whom they issue like any other non-agents pushed along by outside forces. To the extent that Durkheim's was an attempt to mediate this dilemma, therefore, his concept of social facts is the forerunner to many current ideas beyond Bourdieu's. Choosing at random, these include Anthony Giddens' notion of structuration, Jürgen Habermas' of communicative rationality, Niklas Luhmann's system theory, 'neo-institutionalism' in American political science and sociology, and the lineage in Marxist thought that connects György Lukács, Antonio Gramsci, and Louis Althusser (as well as their intellectual offspring).

[73] Durkheim, *The Rules of Sociological Method*, 59. Given that Durkheim discusses/defines the concept in other passages as well and that the interpretation I am presenting raises its own complex issues, the matter obviously merits greater attention than I can give it here. For another view, emphasizing the inconsistencies in what Durkheim meant by 'external' and 'constraint', see ibid., 4.

[74] For a more elaborate view of the gap between the concrete 'thingitude' Durkheim ostensibly meant to highlight through his concept of social facts and the explanatory ends towards which

way of elaborating on social action, noting that '[w]e shall speak of "action" insofar as the acting individual attaches a subjective meaning to his behavior—be it overt or covert, omission or acquiescence' and, in turn, of '[a]ction [as being] "social" insofar as its subjective meaning takes account of the behavior of others and is thereby oriented in its course.'[75])

1.7 The Problem of Self-Reflexivity in the Study of South Asian 'Legalities'

Whatever their respective limits, neither the Durkheimian concept of social facts nor Lakoff's of institutional facts has entered very prominently into historical attempts to grapple with the emergence of 'modern law', whether in the colonial or metropolitan context. Certainly, as relating to modern South Asia, the flourishing over the last four decades of research on law and colonialism in Britain's India has been otherwise focused. As Michael Anderson observed in an important early review essay, on the one hand, in the 1980s there were emerging those who brought 'political economy approaches to law in South Asia' in order to 'situate legal institutions in the context of economic, social, and sexual hierarchies'.[76] Some of the best work in this vein was done by historians of the agrarian subcontinent keen on reconsidering the relationship between the colonial ideal of the freedom of property and the actuality of the social relations of property on the ground.[77] On the other hand, there were those who began 'a vigorous reassessment of the binary oppositions frequently

---

he actually tended to use the concept see Robert Alun Jones, *The Development of Durkheim's Social Realism* (New York: Cambridge University Press, 1999).

[75] Max Weber, *Economy and Society*, vol. I., 4.
[76] Michael R. Anderson, 'Classifications and Coercions: Themes in South Asian Legal Studies in the 1980s', *South Asia Research* 10, no. 2 (November 1990): 158–77 at 161.
[77] The most important example is David Washbrook's landmark article 'Law, State and Agrarian Society in Colonial India', *Modern Asian Studies* 15, no. 3 (1981): 649–721. See also Gregory C. Kozlowski, *Muslim Endowments and Society in British India* (New York: Cambridge University Press, 1985); Nicholas Dirks, 'From Little King to Landlord: Property, Law and Gift Under the Madras Permanent Settlement', *Comparative Studies in Society and History* 28, no. 2 (April 1986): 307–33. Looking beyond the period Anderson surveys in his review, an excellent recent study bearing a clear debt to this earlier literature, especially Washbrook's article, is Rachel Sturman, *The Government of Social Life in Colonial India: Liberalism, Religious Law, and Women's Rights* (New York: Cambridge University Press, 2012).

used to characterise South Asian legalities', such as 'status/contract, tradition/modernity, East/West, law/custom, and alien/indigenous'.[78] Against the backdrop of post-structuralism's advent into history and anthropology writing based, in part, on the work of Michel Foucault and as following more directly from Edward Said's *Orientalism* and the research of the subaltern studies collective, scholarship in this second vein built on colonial discourse theory by uncovering what Anderson called a basic 'self-reflexive difficulty'. Accordingly, such writing often ended up emphasizing how 'social categories' and contrasts used to describe modern legal development in the subcontinent were the 'products of the very processes they [were] invoked to explain', having been 'actually consolidated under the auspices of colonial legal administration' in the first place.[79]

However, it would be wrong to imagine that these two scholarly tendencies were ever mutually exclusive. Rather, from the outset they were closer to complementary and even overlapping. As much as scholars reassessing the binaries that hardened divides along the juridicizable lines of caste, gender, religion, criminality, and other forms of collective identification during the colonial period,[80] those interested in the remaking of the subcontinent's political economy also highlighted the self-fulfilling prophecy—whether over the shorter or longerterm—of the juridical facilitation of new structural hierarchies based on shifting formations of class, the caste-communitarian- and gender-based ordering of emergent labour forms, and related processes like peasantization and sedentarization.[81] Insofar as these overlapping scholarly tendencies

---

[78] Anderson, 'Classifications and Coercions', 160.
[79] Ibid. See also e.g. Bernard S. Cohn, 'Law and the Colonial State in India', in *History and Power in the Study of Law: New Directions in Legal Anthropology*, eds. June Starr and Jane F. Collier (Ithaca, NY: Cornell University Press, 1989), 131–52 and Lata Mani, 'Contentious Traditions: The Debate on Sati in Colonial India', *Cultural Critique* 7 (1987): 119–56.
[80] See e.g. Lata Mani, *Contentious Traditions: The Debate on Sati in Colonial India* (Berkeley, CA: University of California Press, 1998); Anand Yang, ed., *Crime and Criminality in British India* (Tucson, AZ: University of Arizona Press, 1985); Janaki Nair, *Women and Law in Colonial India: A Social History* (New Delhi: Kali for Women in collaboration with the National Law School of India, 1996); Nicholas Dirks, *Castes of Mind: Colonialism and the Making of Modern India* (Princeton, NJ: Princeton University Press, 2001); Durba Ghosh, *Sex and the Family in Colonial India: the Making of Empire* (New York: Cambridge University Press, 2006).
[81] See e.g. Washbrook, 'Law, State and Agrarian Society in Colonial India'; Richard Saumarez-Smith, *Rule by Records: Land Registration and Village Custom in Early British Panjab* (New York: Oxford, 1996); Minoti Chakravarty-Kaul, *Common Lands and Customary Law: Institutional Change in North India over the Past Two Centuries* (Delhi: Oxford University Press, 1996); and Indrani Chatterjee, *Gender, Slavery, and Law in Colonial India* (New York: Oxford University Press, 1999).

addressed colonial legal modernization's 'self-reflexive difficulty' by focusing on the content of the law over its effects, there was reason why they shared in limiting their enquiry to how the norms of native juristic tradition were frozen, sapped of their inherent fluidity, or simply excised.[82]

Yet in so doing these tendencies generally stopped short of pursuing the self-reflexive difficulty beyond such a point—that is, to its logical end point of interrogating 'the law' under colonial rule itself. Instead, even amidst the ongoing extension of Anderson's two lines of legal historical enquiry, the law has usually been taken as given—as a kind of world-historical universal, whether through prioritizing its role as a holistic instrument for (re)making Indian economy and society or through focusing on the processes by which its presumed pre-colonial equivalent was modified or outright displaced. As a result, it is only natural that in thinking through the relationship between law and empire in Britain's India claims about curtailing, distorting, or deleting native juristic tradition have so often gone hand in hand with an emphasis on the rigidification of status group boundaries along lines of caste, class, religion, gender, and other such bases of social division/solidarity. With the lion's share of attention on the discursive constitution of various new kinds of 'legal' subjectivity, the self-reflexivity of the law, itself, has gone largely, if not entirely, unexamined.

In the process, legal discursivity has been made into something of a nondescript stand-in, whether for Foucauldian governmentality,[83] a diffusely juridical discipline through which it can be seen as partly operationalized,[84] the rise of a colonial version of Weberian legal-rational

---

[82] See e.g. Jörg Fisch, *Cheap Lives and Dear Limbs: The British Transformation of the Bengal Criminal Law, 1769–1817* (Wiesbaden: F. Steiner, 1983); Radhika Singha, *A Despotism Of Law: Crime and Justice in Early Colonial India* (Delhi: Oxford University Press, 1996); Kunjulekshmi Saradamoni, *Matriliny Transformed: Family, Law, and Ideology in Twentieth Century Travancore* (Walnut Creek, CA: Alta Mira Press, 1999); Scott Alan Kugle, 'Framed, Blamed and Renamed: The Recasting of Islamic Jurisprudence in Colonial South Asia', *Modern Asian Studies* 35, no. 2 (May 2001): 257–313; and Nandini Bhattachayya-Panda, *Appropriation and Invention of Tradition: The East India Company and Hindu Law in Early Colonial Bengal* (New York: Oxford University Press, 2008).

[83] See e.g. Graham Burchell, Colin Gordon, and Peter Miller, *The Foucault Effect: Studies in Governmentality: with Two Lectures by and an Interview with Michel Foucault* (Chicago, IL: University of Chicago Press, 1991) and David Scott, 'Colonial Governmentality', *Social Text* 43 (Autumn, 1995): 191–220.

[84] See e.g. Victor Tadros, 'Between Governance and Discipline: The Law and Michel Foucault', *Oxford Journal of Legal Studies* 18, no. 1 (Spring 1998): 75–103 at 76 (pointing out that critics of Foucault have failed to see that his intention was to equate 'juridical' discipline not with law but with a form of '*power relations* which one might call Austinian' [emphasis in original]). For a

domination,[85] what James Scott calls 'seeing like a state',[86] or simply some all-purpose ethic of codification. For example, while the latter has unquestionably been a useful rubric for illuminating the remaking of what Anderson calls Indian legalities, construed broadly enough codification becomes liable to function as a proxy for phenomena that might better be regarded as thoroughly disparate: from the Company state's sponsorship of the early orientalist efforts to extract 'native laws' from translations of sacred texts[87] to the efforts under Crown Raj to redact Indian 'custom' in the post-annexation Punjab[88] to the great upsurge in legislation that took place between 1860 and 1890.[89] In turn, codification becomes further liable to collapse important differences between the colonial state's various forms of official action and pronouncement. These include those distinguishing the Company state's early regulations from its official policy minutes and from the Raj's legislative enactments proper as well as those between different kinds of administrative casuistry; perhaps even more notably, they also include the relevant distinction there is to make between all of these forms and the varieties of public-sphere discourse that surrounded them.

More than as a social/institutional fact dependent on the particular way in which it was discursively constituted across multiple idiomizing contexts, the law under colonial rule has, thus, more often been treated as largely synonymous with the undertakings of the state, whether more specifically as its 'emissary', as Ranajit Guha famously called it, or its 'language of command', as Bernard Cohn did.[90] As a result, it has tended to

contrasting/qualifying view on whether Foucault really did intend to erect a categorial distinction between the legal and the juridical/disciplinary (as well as the relationship of both to the notion of governmentality in his late-era thought)—as opposed to envisioning them in terms of a mutually constitutive relationship—see Ben Golder and Peter Fitzpatrick, *Foucault's Law* (New York: Routledge 2009), ch. 2.

[85] Weber, *Economy and Society, vol. I*, 217–22.
[86] See, generally, Scott, *Seeing Like a State*.
[87] See e.g. Cohn, 'Law and the Colonial State' and more recently Jon E. Wilson, 'Anxieties of Distance: Codification in Early Colonial Bengal', *Modern Intellectual History* 4, no. 1 (2007): 7–23 and Bhattachayya-Panda, *Appropriation and Invention of Tradition*.
[88] See e.g. Neeladri Bhattacharya, 'Remaking Custom: The Discourse and Practice of Colonial Codification', in *Tradition, Dissent and Ideology: Essays in Honour of Romila Thapar*, eds. R. Champakalakshmi and S. Gopal (Delhi: Oxford University Press, 1996), 20–51.
[89] See e.g. Ritu Birla, *Stages of Capital: Law, Culture, and Market Governance in Late Colonial India* (Durham, NC: Duke University Press, 2009).
[90] Ranajit Guha, 'Chandra's Death', in *Subaltern Studies V*, ed. Ranajit Guha (Delhi: Oxford University Press, 1987), 135–65.

remain ensconced within the standard duality of liberal theory. Albeit here, this has followed more from its being effectively naturalized than explicitly hypostasized as the state's true basis in the way posited according to the Kelsenian perspective proper, which starts from a conception of duality not as a straightforward historical fact but as a jurisprudential problem in need of solving.

Therefore, as productive as scholarly engagement with colonial legal modernization in the subcontinent has been, historians have never directly engaged the great question of jurisprudence—about the 'true' nature of the law itself, a glimpse of which was present already amidst the early colonial encounter with the subcontinent's juristic traditions. Indeed, little attention has been given even to why the question was discernible in whatever way it was during the era of early Company rule, deriving as it did not just from orientalist tunnel vision but also a view about *what* 'the law' was supposed *to be* that was still under consolidation in the West, itself, during the late eighteenth and first half of the nineteenth centuries.

1.8 Social Constructionism and the Ontology of the Legal in Colonial India

To return full circle to the outset of the chapter, then, in discussion of the law's modernization in the colonial subcontinent the problem of duality has remained shadowy even in the face of the deep kinship it shares with what Anderson called the 'self-reflexive difficulty' that has so long garnered notice among historians and anthropologists of legal modernization in South Asia. Part of the reason why this has been so is because a full grappling with the self-reflexive difficulty would require attending to how in Britain's India—to say nothing of other parts of the (quasi-)colonial world—the law became what we now imagine it to be only after the mid-nineteenth century.

If pressing the question of self-reflexivity further is especially worthwhile in the context of legal change in modern South Asia, it is partly because the subcontinent's history of colonial rule under the British was longer than in most other areas that fell under the sway of European domination during the age of Western expansion, at least outside the Americas. Indeed, as I touched on earlier, in the case of the subcontinent it is not simply the conventional wisdom around the rise of a legislative state after 1860 that must be contended with but also the implications of what is often identified as a codifying drive that had already begun under the Company's rule from the 1770s.

In calling for greater attention to how 'the law' was distinguished as an object in its own right in the colonial subcontinent partly by calling attention to how existing historical work has failed to adequately reckon with this question, there is no denying that I still draw deep inspiration from such work, not to mention the counterpart forms of discussion that have taken place among scholars of other parts of the colonial world. Likewise, in proposing to extend the interrogation of the self-reflexive difficulty that historically minded scholars of colonial legalities have so insightfully explored to 'the law' itself, there is no denying that my concerns parallel those that have undergirded interest in the construction/emergence of other complex social/institutional facts like 'the economy'. In the study of South Asia, for example, both Manu Goswami[91] and Ritu Birla have insightfully taken up this question.[92] Outside concern with South Asia, it has been pursued to even more broad acclaim in Timothy Mitchell's work on Egypt. There, as he contends, it was not until the mid-twentieth century that any general idea of the economy came into being—contra Foucault and Karl Polyani, who respectively highlight the eighteenth and nineteenth centuries as the key moments in the making of the related phenomena they have respectively sought to account for.[93]

In tracing the emergence of the economy or related phenomena, these works each in their own way commit to 'moving beyond' merely 'discursivist framework[s]' that might otherwise incline towards

---

[91] Manu Goswami, *Producing India: from Colonial Economy to National Space* (Chicago, IL: University of Chicago Press, 2004). For Goswami, the development of the economy is just one of several consequences of the 'reconfiguration of colonial space as national space' after 1857. Ibid., 7.

[92] Ritu Birla, *Stages of Capital*. As the subtitle suggests, Birla examines the legislative institutionalization of the market and attendant processes of excluding 'vernacular' forms of capital from a realm of the 'public' that she follows a long line of scholarly tradition in arguing was constructed as the only legitimate place in which to undertake properly economic transactions.

[93] Timothy Mitchell, *Rule of Experts: Egypt, Techno-Politics, Modernity* (Los Angeles, CA: University of California Press, 2002), 3–4. As relating more closely to Foucault's particular concern with economics as a human science, see also Thomas A. Stapleford, 'Historical Epistemology and the History of Economics: Views Through the Lens of Practice', in *Including a Symposium on the Historical Epistemology of Economics (Research in the History of Economic Thought and Methodology)*, vol. 35A, eds. Luca Fiorito, Scott Scheall, and Carlos Eduardo Suprinyak (Bingley: Emerald Publishing, 2017), 113–48.

'track[ing] shifts in ideology and subjectivity' alone.[94] Mitchell, for example, describes his aim as being to show neither that the economy was just 'one more "social construction"' nor that it was 'just a new and more coherent name for economic processes that already existed'. This, as he further explains, is because whereas the first aim 'leaves' the actual 'world intact', implying that 'the object in question' was no more than 'a representation, a set of meanings, a particular way of seeing', the second fails to sufficiently take stock of how the real-world economic processes that were newly named differed from those that 'economists had always studied'.[95]

Whether they are seen as mere levels of sociological analysis or actual social phenomena, it is obviously crucial to keep in mind the imbricated nature of representation and reality—or whatever other roughly equivalent permutation of contrasting elements one might point to, be it the subjective and the objective, the ideal and the material, the discursive and the social, the conceptual and the institutional, ideas and actuality, 'words' and 'the world', and so on. Indeed, notwithstanding what is often suggested about the invasion of history and anthropology by the so-called relativist excess of 'post-modernism', most responsible historians and anthropologists interested in the theme of knowledge, power, and empire have always been well aware of as much. Already before post-structuralism's influence was approaching its height, for example, those like Cohn were formulating their concerns about colonialism's 'forms of knowledge' not just in terms of subjectivity or epistemic rupture but also processes of 'objectification'.[96] Likewise, to the extent that the focus was not on trying to reconstruct the history of Orientalism/Indology primarily as intellectual disciplines,[97] even the leading exponents of the post-structuralist linguistic turn in the history and anthropology of South Asia never maintained that colonial discourse was an autonomous causal force or, judged by its effects on subjectivity, constitutive of entirely

---

[94] Goswami, *Producing India*, 7.
[95] Mitchell, *Rule of Experts*, 4–6.
[96] For a summary, see Peter Berger, 'Theory and Ethnography in the Modern Anthropology of India', *HAU: Journal of Ethnographic Theory* 2, no. 2 (2012): 325–57 at 341.
[97] See e.g. Ronald Inden, *Imagining India* (Cambridge, MA: Basil Blackwell, 1990) and Michael Dodson, *Orientalism, Empire, and National Culture: India, 1770–1880* (New York: Palgrave Macmillan, 2007).

free-standing virtual realities.[98] This, at least, was no more the case than it has been for those who in post-structuralism/post-colonialism's wake have called for a new intellectual history of South Asia—and, indeed, a new global intellectual history—by hastening to add that any such endeavour must 'always and necessarily' be 'much more than "just" intellectual history', given the way that 'categories of thought are not just formal concepts, but ... constituted in relation to determinate objects through the mediating agency of practical activity'.[99]

Obviously, the same goes virtually by definition for work on knowledge, culture, and social communication that has been offered by critics seeking to qualify any tendency to see no world of cause and effect beyond the horizon of colonial discourse; among such critics it has been typical to emphasize that ideas, cultural idioms, and even larger traditions of knowing and believing—from 'caste' to 'Hinduism'—were always grounded in the reality of Indian society or social practice in a way others have allegedly denied by instead stressing their connection to colonial modernity.[100] Indeed, even work on the history of emotions in South Asia of the kind that draws most direct inspiration not from debates inspired by the linguistic turn so much as from the programme of conceptual history pioneered by Reinhart Kosseleck—with its analytical commitment to at least some kind of gap between the 'conceptual' and the 'social' and its apparent resemblance to the decidedly ideas-first type of Cambridge history associated with Quentin Skinner[101]—would never really deny the

---

[98] See e.g. Dirks, *Castes of Mind* and Gyan Prakash, *Bonded Histories: Genealogies of Labor and Servitude in Colonial India* (New York: Cambridge University Press, 1990).

[99] Andrew Sartori, *Bengal in Global Concept History: Culturalism in the Age of Capital* (Chicago, IL: University of Chicago Press, 2008), 233. On global intellectual history see Samuel Moyn and Andrew Sartori, eds., *Global Intellectual History* (New York: Columbia University Press, 2013).

[100] See e.g. C. A. Bayly, *Empire and Information: Intelligence Gathering and Social Communication in India, 1780–1870* (New York: Cambridge University Press, 1996), Susan Bayly, *Caste, Society and Politics in India from the Eighteenth Century to the Modern Age* (New York: Cambridge University Press, 2001), and Brian K. Pennington, *Was Hinduism Invented? Britons, Indians, and the Colonial Construction of Religion* (New York: Oxford University Press, 2005).

[101] As Kosselick puts it, '[s]ocial and conceptual histories have various velocities of change and are grounded in different repetitive structures. For this reason, the scientific terminology of social history remains directed to the history of concepts in order to ascertain experience stored linguistically. And conceptual history must continue to consult the results of social history in order to keep the difference in view between vanishing actuality and its linguistic testimony which is never to be bridged'. Reinhart Kosselick, 'Social History and Conceptual History', *International Journal of Politics, Culture, and Society* 2, no. 3 (1989): 308–25 at 324.

mutuality between the representational and the real, the conceptual and the institutional, and so on.[102]

As always, then, the rub is in how more precisely to integrate these levels of analysis/phenomena. Of course, beyond the ways its influence was made manifest or recoiled from in the history and anthropology of colonial modernity, post-structuralism writ large has engendered various other forms of response as well. Consequently, while there has been no shortage of discontent with understanding the relationship between representation and reality in 'relativist', 'culturalist', or 'post-modernist' terms,[103] at least with regard to thinking seriously about history and society such critiques tend to function, in effect, like bogeys that are belied by the dearth of real alternatives to thinking in broadly constructionist terms. Even the philosopher John Searle's portentously named 'philosophy of society' is based, ultimately, on a hair-splitting distinction between the alleged focus of his assorted adversaries on the *social construction* of reality and his own supposedly comprehensive approach to the construction of *social reality*.[104]

Indeed, more than Lakoff, it is Searle who puts the notion of institutional facts to its clearest use in the course of elaborating his so-called philosophy of society. In so doing, however, not only does he betray a near-total lack of familiarity with (or even interest in) empirical work by sociologists, anthropologists, and historians on such questions, but he also deploys a decidedly misplaced confidence in ignoring more than a century of social theory on the same. (This, moreover, is even as he maintains that institutional facts are but one subspecies of 'social facts' without ever seriously exploring the implicit debt such a turn of phrase reveals

---

[102] See e.g. Margrit Pernau, *Emotions and Modernity in Colonial India: From Balance to Fervor* (New York: Oxford University Press, 2019). As Pernau and co-author put it elsewhere, 'Emotions are never perceived as anthropological constants, but, on the contrary, as absolutely historical and contextual ... [T]hey both reflect historical transformations and bring them about'. Margrit Pernau and Helge Jordheim, 'Introduction', in *Civilizing Emotions: Concepts in Nineteenth Century Asia and Europe*, eds. Margrit Pernau, Helge Jordheim, Orit Bashkin, et al. (New York: Oxford University Press, 2015): 1–22 at 13.

[103] See e.g. Aijaz Ahmed, *In Theory: Classes, Nations, Literatures* (New York: Verso, 1992), Paul Boghossian, *Fear of Knowledge: Against Relativism and Constructivism* (New York: Clarendon Press, 2006), and Vivek Chibber, *Postcolonial Theory and the Specter of Capital* (New York: Verso, 2013).

[104] John Searle, *The Construction of Social Reality* (New York: The Free Press, 1995) and John Searle, *Making the Social World: The Structure of Human Civilization* (New York: Oxford University Press, 2010).

to thinkers like Durkheim and Weber.) By further defining institutional facts in terms of their dependence on what he calls 'collective intentionality'[105]—in philosophical parlance, roughly, the quality of aboutness that minds (or mental states) are capable of having so as to be jointly directed to some particular object of attention—Searle delivers us to a point that is, ironically, immediately adjacent to, if not entirely overlapping with, the uncredited Durkheimian notion of *conscience* collective, not to mention its difficulties as well.[106]

At whatever explanatory level Searle's account of institutional facts might be seen capable of functioning successfully, it is clearly far too general to provide any serious purchase on human history or sociological dynamics. While his intentionality-based account of institutional facts—like 'money', 'property', 'the nation state', and so on—might thus work as an internally consistent, if highly abstracted, way of describing such features of society, it remains largely sterile for the purposes of accounting for such things in the ways sociologists, anthropologists, cultural/literary studies scholars, and historians do. 'Money is money', Searle tells us, 'because the actual participants in the institution regard it as money'. This is why, he continues, 'instead of saying "observer-relative" I ... use the expression 'intentionality-relative' ... [because p]eople's attitudes are necessary to constitute something as money'.[107] Yet, clearly, this does not get us much past the ubiquitous acknowledgement that there is a trust element underlying money's various social functions (as means of payment, measure of value, etc.), which is usually made as a matter of course on the way to entering into whatever more serious form of humanistic or social scientific engagement with monetary phenomena.

Indeed, Searle's philosophy of society is not just sterile when compared to the way most serious scholars of social and historical affairs interested

---

[105] On how Franz Brentano's original predecessor idea of intentionality was taken up on the analytical/Anglo-American divide of contemporary philosophy—as opposed to how it was taken up by figures like Edmund Husserl and Martin Heidegger—see G. E. M. Anscombe, *Intention* (Oxford: Blackwell, 1957) and John Searle, *Intentionality: An Essay in the Philosophy of Mind* (New York: Cambridge University Press, 1983).
[106] See e.g. Neil Gross, 'Comment on Searle', *Anthropological Theory* 6, no. 1 (2006): 45–56. For a sense of how Searle's work has met problems from within analytical/Anglo-American philosophy proper that are not unlike those Durkheim's concept of *conscience collective* has encountered, see e.g. Michael E. Bratman, *Shared Agency: A Planning Theory of Acting Together* (New York: Oxford University Press, 2014).
[107] Searle, *Making the Social World*, 17.

in novel approaches to constructionism and wielding thick descriptions would account for the (shifting) context-dependent arrangements undergirding the intellectual-conceptual dimension of such social/institutional facts. Any account it might yield of phenomena like 'money', 'property', and 'the nation-state' simply taken on their own terms is also likely to be unilluminating as a matter of thinking seriously about society and history even when compared to the most traditional of intellectual historical approaches based on seeing ideas strictly as the products of great minds.

On the other hand, the qualification/critique of constructionism that has taken place on the basis of the so-called ontological turn among certain humanists and social scientists in recent years has likely offered the possibility of a more productive dialogue. Of course, in some areas the possibility has been more indirect than direct. In philosophy, for example, where the rise of object-oriented ontology has taken place mainly beyond the analytical/Anglo-American side of the discipline, the proximal cause of the ontological turn has come less from philosophers in the continental tradition reacting to post-structuralists within their ranks than it has from those seeking to explore and extend the legacy of thinkers like Martin Heidegger.[108] Object-oriented ontology in philosophy has thus been most clearly defined by a desire to break with post-Kantian anthropomorphism in all its forms and to do away with subjective experience as the 'correlator' of being.[109] Where post-structuralism and its discontents *have* been more directly involved in paving the way for the ontological turn, it has been along various paths of anthropological enquiry down which it has been pursued, whether in the course of re-theorizing the discipline's methodology,[110] making sense of the results of

---

[108] See e.g. Graham Harman, *Object-Oriented Ontology: A New Theory of Everything* (London: Penguin, 2018).

[109] Along with the rejection of anthropomorphism and 'correlationsim', as Steven Umbrello summarizes it, object-oriented ontology in philosophy is defined by three other characteristics: a rejection of the philosophical tendency to reductionism (by referring to an object's parts as the essence of its being or privileging its relations and effects), the notion that no object can 'attain full knowledge of other objects', and the idea that objects always remain independent of the qualities they instantiate and their relations with other objects. Steven Umbrello, 'Book Review: A Theory of Everything?' *Cultural Studies Review* 24, no. 2 (2018): 150–53 at 151.

[110] Philippe Descola, *Beyond Nature and Culture* (Chicago, IL: University of Chicago Press, 2013).

ethnographic fieldwork,[111] or facilitating the emergence of adjacent fields like animal studies.[112]

At the same time, in anthropology the ontological turn has been perhaps most noticeable for the way it has been predicated on a heightening of the commitment to relativist anti-essentialism of the kind typically associated with social constructionism. For it has entailed pushing the questioning of the nature-culture distinction ever further—all the way, in fact, to a point past that where constructionism's ostensible critique of universalism passes into its opposite, given the way it can be accused of implicitly treating nature as a uniform background against which to make assertions about the variability of culture. Construed in this way, the ontological turn in anthropology is a call for a more thoroughgoing commitment to relativization—not only of 'world views'/ epistemologies but also of 'worlds'/ontologies, themselves.[113] In one sense, then, the ontological turn involves extending the constructionist/poststructuralist agenda in anthropology to its logical end, one that demands to be reckoned with for the full range of its various complex implications. In another sense, though, the ontological turn compounds problems that are evident already in milder versions of the constructionist agenda, including those predicated on a commitment to relativism of a more purely epistemic kind.[114]

My own preference, therefore, is to draw on philosopher Ian Hacking's chastened approach to Foucault and, as noted in the Introduction, the latter's call for an enquiry into how 'objects constitute themselves in discourse'.[115] To examine how 'the law' came into being as one such object

---

[111] David Posthumus, *All My Relatives: Exploring Lakota Ontology, Belief, and Ritual* (Lincoln, NE: University of Nebraska Press, 2018).

[112] See e.g. Eduardo Viveiros de Castro, 'Exchanging Perspectives: The Transformation of Objects into Subjects in Amerindian Ontologies', *Common Knowledge* 10, no. 3: 463–84 (2004) and Luiz Costa and Carlos Fausto, 'The Return of the Animists: Recent Studies of Amazonian Ontologies', *Religion and Society* 1, no. 1: 89–109 (2010).

[113] Paolo Heywood, 'Ontological Turn, The', in *The Open Encyclopedia of Anthropology*, ed. F. Stein (2017), http://doi.org/10.29164/17ontology, 2.

[114] See e.g. David Graeber, 'Radical Alterity is Just Another Way of Saying "Reality"': A reply to Eduardo Viveiros de Castro', *HAU: Journal of Ethnographic Theory* 5, no. 2: 1–41 (2015). To those familiar with the history of modern South Asia, the dynamic of debate should be reminiscent of the disagreements that were aroused soon after the advent of post-colonial perspectives. Compare e.g. Gyan Prakash, 'Writing Post-Orientalist Histories of the Third World: Perspectives from Indian Historiography', *Comparative Studies in Society and History* 32, no. 2 (1990): 384–408 and Rosalind O'Hanlon and David Washbrook, 'Culture, Criticism, and Politics in the Third World', *Comparative Studies in Society and History* 34, no. 1 (1992): 141–67.

[115] Hacking, *Historical Ontology*, 98.

can thus be seen as a form of 'historical ontology', as Hacking calls it. In fact, it is in further situating historical ontology within the broader development of philosophy from early-modern times to the present that Hacking comes to the above words from Foucault, which he also puts into more express dialogue with the analytical/Anglo-American side of the divide within the discipline as follows:

> [i]n scholastic times, 'realism' contrasted with nominalism, while Kant made it contrast with Berkeley's idealism. In either sense we must be, to abuse Kant's words, empirical realists. There is of course a rich plethora of things around us, really existing anterior to any thought. Moreover, we cannot but sort many things as we do: we are, it seems, made to sort things much as we do. Not only translation and mutual understanding but also our sheer existence seem to depend upon this fact. But something else happens when we engage in reflective discourse. One of Foucault's projects is to understand how 'objects constitute themselves in discourse'. All our experience with immature science suggests that any chosen body of thought will define for us only some sorts of 'objects' entering into only some sorts of 'laws' falling under only some kinds of 'kinds'. About these we cannot fail to be 'nominalists', but the 'ism' is not what matters. Since most, if not all knowledge is 'immature' in this way, attempting to understand how objects constitute themselves in discourse must be a central topic, not exactly of the theory of knowledge, but of what I would now call historical ontology.[116]

If the mission of historical ontology as a form of enquiry is well-captured here, Hacking goes on to clarify its more precise analytical method in terms of the examination of words in the 'variety of types of sites' in which they appear; this, as he further explains, is because 'a concept is nothing other than a word in its sites'. On this view, to undertake historical ontological enquiry requires focusing attention on 'the sentences in which the word is actually (not potentially) used' as well as on 'those who speak those sentences', not to mention an array of related questions, like ones about the 'authority' with which they do so and 'in order to influence whom', about 'what institutional settings' within which they do so, and

[116] Ibid.

about the 'consequences' with which they do so, including those 'for the speakers', themselves.[117]

Although Hacking's method for historical ontology is thus general enough to help illuminate the conceptual/lexical underpinnings of social/institutional facts of various kinds, greater elaboration is in order if we want to arrive at a method for historical ontological enquiry into 'the law' in particular. While I will return to the details of how to do so in chapter three—the final chapter before part two of the book commences—because a historical ontological approach to the law purports to be a way of accounting for its object, it is bound to cover territory at least partially overlapping with more traditional forms of jurisprudential enquiry. Therefore, before coming back to the question of methodology to close part I, in the next chapter I consider how jurisprudential thinking—whether in the more specifically anthropological, sociological/social theoretical, or philosophical veins—has presented an array of self-limiting approaches to the law.

By *self-limiting* here I mean that such approaches have tended to take the law as a given/as a kind of world-historical universal, even while ostensibly seeking to clarify its true nature. Therefore, in turning to the limits of jurisprudential thinking, chapter two seeks both to add to the motivation for the book's historical ontological approach to the law and to echo the present chapter's central contention about how historically minded discussion of legal modernization under colonial rule has produced an ultimately similar effect—of naturalizing (or, as Kelsen might prefer, hypostatizing) the law—by leaving its duality/self-reflexivity unaddressed. In more ways than one, then, the next chapter serves as a bridge between this opening chapter and the concluding chapter of part I of the book.

---

[117] The larger passage about methodology from which the excerpt is taken is worth quoting at greater length:

> [w]hat role should social studies have in historical ontology? This is precisely the sort of methodological question that I find useless. I help myself to whatever I can, from everywhere ... Institutional history is essential, as are many other kinds of history, but the overall project is, in the end, what I can only call philosophical. Its practitioners are engaged in the analysis of concepts, but a concept is nothing other than a word in its sites. That means attending to a variety of types of sites: the sentences in which the word is actually (not potentially) used, those who speak those sentences, with what authority, in what institutional settings, in order to influence whom, with what consequences for the speakers. We first lose ourselves, as befits philosophy, in total complexity, and then escape from it by craft and skills and, among other things, philosophical reflection. Ibid., 17.

2
Beyond Law and History

Naturalization and its Limits in Jurisprudential Inquiry

2.1 Introduction: Questioning Law's Nature, Naturalizing the Law

As I argued in the last chapter, scholars of law and colonialism have generally stopped short of directly engaging the central question of jurisprudence that historical circumstance had made so evident already from the very outset of Western global expansion. Even outside the subcontinent, whether in the drive towards settlement across the Atlantic or in Afro-Asia more generally, modern imperial power confronted a similar dilemma whenever the normative worlds of non-European societies had to be reckoned with. A series of effectively synonymous questions, thus, presented themselves—about whether the colonized 'had' laws of their own; about whether the forms of political constitution they lived by involved anything more than a rule of discretion; and if social life was seen as being governed by standards embodied in textualized form or folk ways, about whether the attendant norms ultimately comprised more than just a collection of sacred injunctions, aphoristic maxims, or mere customary mores. While such questions now sound antiquated, as noted in the last chapter it is important to appreciate that they were more than just the product of Eurocentrism or a naked will to domination. Rather, they were just as much about confirming the righteousness or superiority of imperial rule and, in this respect, betrayed an anxiety/uncertainty about the nature of the unique instrument Western legal normativity supposedly comprised.

If historians surveying legal modernity from the standpoint of societies subject to (quasi-) colonial encroachment have lost hold of this great question of jurisprudential enquiry—about the nature of the legal—it is probably at least partly due to a feeling that its stakes are merely terminological. That is, to many scholars of law and history, it probably seems just as well to field other ostensibly more pressing questions—whether about jurisdictional competition and its changing circumstances, the rise of new institutional bases for dispute resolution and related forms of litigatory procedure, or the cooptation/creative reimagination of 'customary' and 'religious' norms through the intermediation of native juristic informants/agents.[1] For to the extent that the 'law-relatedness' of such questions more easily can be taken to go without saying, the great question of jurisprudence, itself, more easily can be seen as largely semantic.

Even if not entirely beside the point, questions jurisprudential are thus all too liable to be envisioned as better left to others. Therefore, before returning in the next chapter to more specifically outlining the book's historical ontological approach to legal modernity, in this chapter, rather than further situating my concerns in relation to work by historically minded observers of law and empire, I will begin by doing so in relation to several other humanistic modes of jurisprudential enquiry. Since it is obviously not possible to do so with any claim to exhaustiveness my observations will necessarily be fragmentary and prone to selection bias. Nonetheless, the discussion should remain useful for the purposes of further introducing the reader to other significant ways that law-in-modernity has been reckoned with and to begin laying out their own shared limitations, with both of these tasks being necessary to properly motivate the historical ontological approach to jurisprudence I develop here in part I (and implement in parts II and III) as an alternative.

As for the more specific extra-historical approaches to law/legal modernity that I concentrate on, these I consolidate under the headings of socio-legal theory and the philosophy of law, on the one hand, and legal anthropology and the sociology of law, on the other. Of course, from a certain angle the two entries comprising each pairing are as different

---

[1] On the gradual/emerging shift in emphasis from cooptation to creative reimagination see Faisal Chaudhry, 'Rethinking the Nineteenth-Century Domestication of the Sharī'a: Marriage and Family in the Imaginary of Classical Legal Thought and the Genealogy of (Muslim) Personal Law in Late Colonial India', *Law & History Review* 35, no. 4 (2017): 841–79 at 850–53.

from one another as each pairing, itself, is from the other, not to mention from whatever heading under which historical approaches to law and empire could be grouped. It would, then, hardly be difficult to locate significant differences within and across each heading, given the disciplinary and intellectual autonomy that both socio-legal theory and the philosophy of law as well as legal anthropology and the sociology of law have traditionally enjoyed from one another. Finally, there is also the fact that even though the first two disciplines I have consolidated under the above two headings have been generally disconnected from the contexts of the colonial/post-colonial world, the second two—meaning, the sociology and especially the anthropology of law—have obviously not been. To some extent, therefore, the ensuing discussion will have to elide these qualifiers.

Be this as it may, in grouping the various modes of non-diachronic engagement with law and legal modernity that the chapter will discuss as I have, any major differences that are concealed either within or across the headings should be belied by the deeper commonality they bespeak. This is because even as socio-legal theory, the philosophy of law, legal anthropology, and the sociology of law have embraced the great question of jurisprudence more insistently than historical modes of enquiry, each, in its own way, is still premised on naturalizing/hypostatizing what it purports to explain. In this respect, the subsequent discussion is both a departure from the last chapter's as well as an extension of it. That is, whereas in chapter one I traced the law's inadvertent naturalization/hypostatization through the historian's flight from the great question of jurisprudence, in this chapter I look at different paths into that question only to find that they end up being circumscribed, ultimately, in related ways. Indeed, more accurately put, the related limitations of these largely synchronic modes of jurisprudential accounting make them even more potent sources of hypostatization. Not only do they borrow the image of the law as a systematic logical unicity that is infinite in scope, but they also magnify that image by further emphasizing the law's identity as the pre-eminent instrument of social rationalization.

Alternatively, a differently accented way of articulating the concern of the present chapter is through asking whether it really is possible that socio-legal theory and philosophical jurisprudence as well as legal anthropology and legal sociology can take the contingency of 'the law' on the territorial-bureaucratic form of the national state for granted at the very same time as they explicitly deny it. In taking up this question in the present chapter—and offering an answer in the affirmative—I argue that, as distinct from what is the case in historical enquiry into legal modernity, in these other areas of humanistic study it has been the other half of the legacy of the late-nineteenth-century globalization of classical legal thought that has left its greatest mark. For rather than through reference to some set of generically 'legal' processes and institutions, in these other domains of enquiry the law precipitates what curiosity it does as society's purportedly master scheme of rational ordering according to norms, a deductively infinite 'system' for enveloping the world of facts by rules. Yet, in theory, this maximalist claim to self-containment that the law has asserted on its own behalf would clearly ring hollow if it was not preceded, in fact, by the growing omnipresence of the territorial-bureaucratic state over society through its effective co-extensivity with a sovereign national jurisdiction and national economy. In short, there would be little overriding or urgent need to be curious about the law in the first place if it had no claim to being the law of the national state.

Here it is imperative to note that the stance of denying the law's contingency on the national state, despite all appearances to the contrary, is just as characteristic of the exponents of a positivist philosophy of law—even of the crudest, command-of-the-sovereign kind[2]—as it is of their natural-law opponents. That is, the stance is predicated not on denying that the law is issued by the legislative organ of the state but rather on denying that the law's existence fails to be autonomous and self-contained in some relevant sense. In legal philosophical (and, in its own way, socio-legal theoretical) discussion, that sense is, namely, that of autonomy from 'politics', once the law is delivered by the legislature to the judiciary. Accordingly, even as the crude positivist would equate the law with the command of the sovereign, they would also deny—every bit as much as any natural-law theorist would—its contingency on the political state. Indeed, this goes a long way towards explaining why legal philosophical discussion remains forever animated by a desire to exorcise the

---

[2] On the distinction between crude and other forms of positivism see Irma J. Kroeze, 'Legal Positivism', in *Jurisprudence*, eds. Christopher Roederer and Darrell Moellendorf (Lansdowne, South Africa: Juta & Company, Ltd., 2004), 62–83 at 71–74.

ghost of judicial legislation, on an endless and seemingly fruitless quest to find—in one way or another—an unimpeachable basis for distinguishing a rule of law from forms of rule necessitating discretion.[3] Indeed, even if the non-positivist—whether of the natural law, Dworkinian, or assorted third way persuasions[4]—is more likely than the positivist to insist on the law's inseparability from morality/ethics, they are just as likely as the positivist to effectively defend the idea of the law's self-containment through sharing in the aim of policing the distinction between legislation and adjudication. In this respect, the constant striving to find a solution to the problem of judicial legislation in legal philosophical discussion finds its corollary in assumptions of the kind reviewed in the previous chapter that are made in legal historical discussion about the law's character as a world-historical universal.

Even beyond philosophical jurisprudence proper, in wider humanistic study the conflation of the law, legal system, and legal ordering that is common to historical enquiry is raised from a verbal artefact of the liberal state's legitimation myth to a veritable logical necessity. For whether in thinking about the modern West on its own terms or non-Western deviations from the latter's supposed standard, it is as an infinitely expandable but tightly integrated system of rational ordering, according to rules that are capable of distillation into verbal propositions, that the law is regarded. Judged from this vantage point, the national state's development into the pre-eminent unit of social community, its bureaucratization of the 'rights' and 'duties' of its subjects, and its near monopoly on arbitration appear not primarily like phenomena contingent on a path-dependent rise of new forms of institutionalized political economic and politico-bureaucratic practice. Rather, they appear like consequences of the law's own existence as a special kind of normative system.

In other words, each of the above undertakings by/processes involving the state become so many different factual predicates capable, themselves, of being subsumed under norms that are the law's own. Indeed, from the perspective of the late-nineteenth-century ideal of the law as an infinitely

---

[3] For further discussion see Faisal Chaudhry, 'The Promise and Paradox of Max Weber's Legal Sociology: The "Categories of Legal Thought" as Types of Meaningful Action and the Persistence of the Problem of Judicial Legislation', *Southern California Interdisciplinary Law Journal* 20 (2011): 249–88.

[4] See generally Roederer and Moellendorf, eds., *Jurisprudence*.

generative system for normatively reclassifying the behaviours of juridical agents, even factual developments as historically disparate as these appear less important as facts than they do on grounds of their fidelity or lack thereof to the norm system's measure of how they *ought* to have been. Thus, if the national state became the pre-eminent unit of collective life by the end of the long nineteenth century, from the perspective of the legal ideal it bequeathed to posterity, this can just as well be regarded as a function of how there were norms of the law's own according to which the state's achieving such a status was measurable as something that *ought* (or that *ought not*) to have been. Likewise, if the national state acquired an unprecedented capacity to engage in what undertakings it was increasingly pursuing so as to consolidate its pre-eminence over social life, from the naturalized perspective of the law as a self-contained system of rational ordering according to norms, this can just as well be regarded as a function of how there were norms of the law's own according to which the state's doing so was measurable as something that *ought* (or that *ought not*) to have been; indeed, to the extent that what the state *did* do with its pre-eminence was to greatly increase the elaboration of the rights *and* duties of juridical persons—so as to render them more perfectly legible, in Scott's sense of the term[5]—so too is the assumption of such rights and duties by its subjects, itself, just as well regarded as a function of how there were norms of the law's own according to which their so doing was measurable as what they *ought* (or *ought not*) to have done. Finally, to the extent that part of what the state, in its territorial-bureaucratic national form, did was to measure any or all of the above developments according to how the law said they ought (or ought not) to be (through the exercise of its own more specific capacities of legislating and adjudicating), from the perspective of the still resonant long-held nineteenth-century ideal, even this is just as well regarded as a function of how there were yet still other (constitutional) norms of the law's own according to which the state's so doing was measurable as something that it *ought* (or *ought not*) to have done.

With the law's clearly apparent contingency on the national state being the very basis for emphatically denying the same, it becomes paramount to police the boundary between legislation and adjudication. Insofar as doing so doubles as a means of hypostatizing the law by insisting on its

---

[5] See generally Scott, *Seeing Like a State* and the previous discussion of his use of the concept.

distinction in kind from politics, what we can also call the problem of judicial legislation appears and reappears both within and beyond the philosophy of law (and socio-legal theory) in a number of forms. Three of these, in particular, have proved highly intractable and therefore vital for nourishing humanistic legal study over the course of the last century or so. The first has had to do with distinguishing formal from living law; the second with accounting for the distinction between state law and non-state law as well as the counterpart distinctions between written versus unwritten law, law in the books versus law in action, and so on; and the third with asking how the law can normatively bind or, equivalently, with sorting out the relationship between the law's facticity and its normativity/validity.

While these three additional versions of the problem of judicial legislation/the need to police the boundary between law and politics can reasonably be described as making for questions that are native to the sociology of law, legal anthropology, and philosophical jurisprudence/socio-legal theory, respectively, each clearly involves a similar dilemma articulated in different terms. In the sections that follow, I thus take them up sequentially by way of pursuing the hypostatizing/naturalizing tendencies of the main extra-historical modes of jurisprudential enquiry this chapter focuses on.

2.2 The Sociological Problem of Formal versus Living Law

Underlying the first variation on the problem of judicial legislation is the observation, so vital to the origins of the sociology of law, that if formal law is a system of validity-claiming norms for governing behaviour, so too would there seem to be countless other schemes of normative ordering that do the same.[6] Among these, moreover, are ordering schemes

---

[6] On the idea of law as a scheme of normative ordering, Kelsen revealingly puts the point as follows in elaborating on the shared object and ambition of even the most radically opposed traditions in modern jurisprudence:

> [t]he theory of law which has been presented here is a juristic theory, allowance being made for the tautology. It shows the law to be a system of valid norms. Its object is norms, general and individual. It considers facts only insofar as they are in some way or other determined by norms. The statements in which our theory describes its object are therefore not statements about what is but statements about what ought to be. In this sense, it may be called a normative theory. Since about the beginning

that would seem to be more demonstratively immediate in regulating actual inter-subjective relations than formal law's own. Indeed, in making plain formal law's lack of exclusive purchase on norm(aliz)ing behaviour, the founders of the sociology of law were implicitly raising a version of the great question of jurisprudence concerning what the law really *is*. In the French intellectual tradition, this was evident already in Durkheim's way of equating the social with the 'normal' in the sense of the quantitatively regular. As the British tradition of social anthropology emerged and then went on to mature during the twentieth century a need to distinguish between the 'normal' and the 'normative' in accounting for differing schemes of social ordering would then go on to develop in a more full-fledged manner.[7]

On the one hand, then, understood in this more multilayered fashion, the formal versus living law distinction commences from trying to make best sense of the external force of compulsion in ensuring behavioural regularity among members of a social group. After all, without such enforced conformity, no social group could emerge as a mutually identifiable collective in the first place, this being why from the sociological vantage point concentrating on formal law to the exclusion of living law seemed to offer only a very incomplete picture of legal life. On the other hand, to distinguish between formal and living law in this way was to necessarily elicit the further question of whether a *true* legal order does not *really* reside elsewhere than in the realm of manifest externalization. That is, in the realm of some more irreducible internal psychological

of this century, the demand for another theory of law has been raised. A theory is asked for which describes what people actually do and not what they ought to do, just as physics describes natural phenomena. Through observation of actual social life, one can and should—it is argued—obtain a system of rules that describe the actual human behavior which presents the phenomena of law ... A sociology of law is required which describes law in terms of 'real rules,' not ought-rules or 'paper rules.' This theory of law is also spoken of as 'realistic jurisprudence.' Kelsen, *General Theory of Law and the State*, 162.

[7] On the normative versus the normal in social anthropology see e.g. Edmund Leach, *Pul Eliya: A Village in Ceylon, A Study of Land Tenure and Kinship* (Cambridge: Cambridge University Press, 1961), 296–300. In Durkheim the normal as distinct from the abnormal and/or pathological features prominently in both *The Division of Labor in Society* (New York: The Free Press, 2014 (1893)) and his *The Rules of Sociological Method* (1895). See Lukes, *Emile Durkheim: His Life and Work*, 173–78.

conviction of actually felt boundedness to the rules, which even if they could be used to describe conforming behaviour could not *really* account for it.

This is why, for example, already by 1913, the Austrian sociologist Eugen Ehrlich—often seen as the founder of the sociology of law—was calling attention to the 'inner order' behind 'human association', which he portrayed as the real source of 'living law'. Rather than any formally enumerable norms, much less any that had to have been actually enumerated by some organ of the state, for Ehrlich it was this inner order that was the real foundation of behavioural conformity and, hence, the true cause behind the regularities underpinning the possibility and persistence of human association.[8] Of course, not uncoincidentally, it was at roughly the same time that Max Weber was grounding his own sociology—including his more specifically legal sociology—in the quasi-psychological ideal types of 'meaningful action' through which he sought to account for the manner in which individuals oriented themselves to one another so as to give rise to a distinctly social level of reality in the first place.[9]

While Weber too was thus drawing attention to the inner aspect of the agent's undertakings, he was also going beyond Ehrlich by making this inner aspect into the foundational empirical correlate of the 'grounds' on which his other set of ideal types of 'domination' commanded what 'legitimacy' he argued they ultimately had to in order to lay the bases for different varieties of political constitution.[10] By correlating the forms that so-called legal rationality could take with wider authority structures in this way, Weber was also proposing an implicit solution to the key problem the living versus formal law distinction threw into relief, which had to do with the contradictory posture of acknowledging the tight relationship between formal/modern law and the territorial-bureaucratic national state while denying that it was one of necessity. In this manner,

---

[8] Eugen Ehrlich, *Fundamental Principles of the Sociology of Law*, Walter L. Moll, trans. (New Brunswick, NJ: Transaction Publishers, 2002 [1936]).

[9] Max Weber, *Economy and Society*, vol. I., 24–25 (discussing rational forms of orientation abiding means-end calculation versus values-for-their-own-sake as well as other forms of orientation based on affect, on the one hand, and the ingrained habituation to tradition, on the other).

[10] Ibid., 215–16 (discussing rational grounds of authority 'resting on a belief in the legality of enacted rules' as well as other forms grounded in 'the sanctity of immemorial traditions' as well as in charismata that rest on devotion to 'normative patterns of order revealed or ordained' by some exceptional individual).

he also demonstrated the ready way in which the formal/living law distinction could be repurposed as a means of naturalizing the law in accordance with a version of what Brian Tamanaha has called the 'evolutionary myth' of the origins/nature of law in Western thought. By positing 'an initial primordial soup in which habit and custom are dominant in the maintenance of social order, supplemented by an indistinguishable mix of religious or mystical beliefs and morality', Tamanaha thus argues, sociological thinking casts positive law as 'emerg[ing], in the haze of long forgotten yesteryear, as a *distinct* mechanism of institutionalized norm enforcement out of the customary order that prevailed in pre-political society'.[11]

2.3 The Anthropological Problem of State versus Non-State Law

Of course, the distinction between formal and living law that helped to inaugurate the sociological tradition of legal enquiry was never entirely separate from the intellectual basis on which legal anthropology itself emerged. On one level, this is borne out by sociology's overlapping origins with modern anthropology's predecessor traditions of nineteenth-century ethnology and social evolutionism. Clearly, thinkers like Henry Maine and Lewis Henry Morgan gravitated to thinking about society's distant past through kinship and custom in such a way as to have either implicitly or explicitly treated them as 'ancient' proxies for 'formal law'. On another level, as already suggested earlier, much the same is borne out by the way that later twentieth-century social anthropology eventually ran headlong into a need to complicate Durkheim's idea of the normal by splitting it off from the normative.

On yet a third level, however, the formal/living law distinction was tied to social anthropology from its inception in early-twentieth-century Britain through figures like Bronislaw Malinowski, who helped define the field around the need for a better understanding of non-state forms of legal normativity. While in many ways functionally synonymous, the

---

[11] Brian Tamanaha, *A General Jurisprudence of Law and Society* (New York: Oxford University Press, 2001), 52 (emphasis added).

parallel distinctions between formal and living law, on the one hand, and state and non-state law, on the other, differed to the extent that only the latter tended to preserve ethnology's organizing concern with explaining the reality of so-called primitive schemes of normative ordering. For example, as much is evident in Malinowski's founding text of the functionalist school of British social anthropology; its titular allusions to 'crime' and 'custom' in Trobriand society thus framed an ethnographic presentation focusing on how the relationship between these elements was governed by a larger norm of reciprocity—rather than any mere unthinking form of habit—rooted in society rather than polity.[12] Even after Malinowski—and notwithstanding the various ways British social anthropology would go on to change under structural-functionalism's influence—the concern with extra-state normative-cum-legal ordering persisted. Indeed, A. R. Radcliffe-Brown and his disciples would go on to be no less acutely focused on explaining the regulatory underpinnings of social equilibrium that made tribal and other forms of 'primitive' collective life possible.[13]

Not unlike the distinction between written and unwritten law, that between state and non-state law, which was also closely related to the formal/living law binary, built on the opposition already available within nineteenth-century evolutionist theory between law and custom. However, with ethnology maturing into/replaced by observation-based ethnography it was the 'state versus non-state law' distinction that became the most prominent in anthropology as it increasingly differentiated itself from sociology during the first several decades of the twentieth century.[14] In this context, moreover, there was firmly in place the idea

---

[12] See Bronislaw Malinowski, *Crime and Custom in Savage Society* (New York: Harcourt, 1926).

[13] Of course, one of Radcliffe-Brown's headline disagreements with Malinowski derived from his insistence that were law to be defined in terms of politically organized authority and legal sanctions it would have to be the case that not all societies had something that should be called by such a name. Yet, underneath the surface of disagreement, he was just as concerned with the regulatory underpinnings of social solidarity. See Laura Nader, *The Life of the Law: Anthropological Projects* (Berkeley, CA: University of California Press, 2002), 85–87.

[14] Tamanaha ranks the various early strands in the anthropology and sociology of law together in cementing the 'evolutionist myth' that Western legal theory has invoked to account for the origins/nature of law. Prior to the era of modern sociological and anthropological theory proper, he sees the precursor exponents of the myth as including figures from Montesquieu to Maine as well as other social evolutionists of the late nineteenth century. Tamanaha contends there was a second key myth—the 'social contract myth'—that served as the counterpart to the evolutionary myth. See Tamanaha, *A General Jurisprudence of Law and Society*, 52–71.

of 'the law' as a validity-claiming system of rational ordering according to norms that were supposed to harbour the infinite capacity to 'cover' a world of facts comprising an overlapping arena of polity, society, and economy.

As a result, when fieldwork yielded anthropological encounters with social formations devoid of long histories of organizing collective life on the basis of bureaucratized centralizing administrations, a prefabricated void, so to speak, was left where 'the law' was supposed to be. Whether through some functional equivalent ultimately attributable to the state or not, finding something to fill the void—whether exactly called by the name of the law or not—became a necessity. As with the norm of reciprocity, then, provided that 'non-state law' could plausibly be seen as capable of fulfilling the requisite function of increasing social solidarity, it could be undocumented, less than explicitly articulated, or even largely/totally unindividuated with respect to any more granular rule content. With the ethnographic method furnishing a ready way to search for and find dispute-settlement practices supervised by 'traditional' adjudicatory bodies like the Indian *panchayat*, the institutions maintaining the 'law-ways' of the Cheyenne in North America, and assorted tribunals of African custom,[15] the standing availability of such inchoate forms of 'non-state law' made 'legal pluralism' another defining watchword of the distinct tradition of the anthropology of law by the middle of the twentieth century.[16]

Notably, as fruitful as legal anthropological investigation has been, its reckoning with the problem of the law's nature has been less than explicit. Instead, falling back on the notion of legal pluralism, the focus has been on demanding parity for non-state schemes of normative ordering as much as it has been on explaining what makes state law, itself, distinctly *legal*.[17] As applied to the ethnographic present, then, the anthropological

[15] For a useful summary of this orientation written while it was still on the ascent, see Francis Snyder, 'Anthropology, Dispute Processes and Law: A Critical Introduction', in *British Journal of Law and Society* 8, no. 2 (Winter 1981): 141–80. On the anthropologist E. Adamson Hoebel and legal realist Karl Llewellyn's landmark 1944 study, *The Cheyenne Way: Conflict and Case Law in Primitive Jurisprudence* (Norman, OK: Oklahoma University Press, 1941), see Nader, *The Life of the Law*, 87–96.

[16] See e.g. William Twining, *Globalisation and Legal Theory* (London: Butterworths, 2000), 84–85.

[17] See e.g. Sally Falk-Moore's well-known handling of this issue by referring to the context in which normative orders must appear in actuality (rather than the question of which ones are legal rather than extra-legal). In this manner, she long advocated for the 'semi-autonomous

BEYOND LAW AND HISTORY: NATURALIZATION   91

search for legal pluralism has threatened to make everything law (in some at least implicit sense, if not always expressly by name, as for those in the Radcliffe-Brownian tradition). Moreover, because in the present, the 'non-state' forms of law that anthropological enquiry has documented are usually forms that are already subordinated to the state's own legal system, the concept of legal pluralism tends to affirm what it ostensibly seeks to deny—about how all law is not necessarily state law—in a way that echoes liberal theory's similar predicament (when inveighing against 'modern' law's contingency on the territorial-bureaucratic form of the national state). This difficulty partly accounts for the relative decline in the intellectual profile of the concept of legal pluralism since its heyday, from roughly the 1950s to the 1970s/80s.[18]

In fact, that we are far enough removed from that heyday is one reason why legal pluralism has been most clearly reinvigorated in recent years not among anthropologists but historians. As Lauren Benton and Richard Ross explain, it is scholars of history who have tried to divest the concept of its ties to the state/non-state law distinction in order to find a fresh way of framing questions about law and empire. Yet notwithstanding the greater novelty of legal pluralism (or some related variant) as an explanatory concept for the purposes of historical enquiry, its utility as a means of moving away from the view that the dominance of 'state law' is inevitable, unmediated, and totalizing remains limited by the same fundamental difficulty in characterizing its use in the anthropological context.[19] This

social field' in which various types of schemes for normative ordering coincide as the best unit of study. Sally Falk Moore, 'Law and Social Change: The Semi-Autonomous Social Field as an Appropriate Subject of Study' reprinted in *Law as Process: An Anthropological Approach* (Hamburg: LIT, 2000 [1978]), 54–81.

[18] Lauren Benton and Richard J. Ross, 'Empires and Legal Pluralism: Jurisdiction, Sovereignty, and Political Imagination in the Early Modern World', in *Legal Pluralism and Empires, 1500–1850*, eds. Lauren Benton and Richard J. Ross (New York: New York University Press, 2013), 1–20 at 2–3.

[19] The three problems that Benton and Ross cite as having made the traditional use of the concept problematic for historians would seem to apply, almost as acutely, to the amended version they propose for the purposes of investigating the relationship between law and empire. As they formulate them, the three—related—problems are as follows: first, that the traditional idea of legal pluralism implies, in an ahistorical manner, that state law was more monolithic and uncontested than it actually ever was; second, that it implies that the rise to dominance of state law was smooth and complete rather than partial and contested; and, third, that it underplays the complexity of the attitudes and actions through which the exponents of state law brought about whatever dominance it achieved. See ibid., 4–5. Yet, to insist on narrating history from the standpoint of legal history—by reimagining legal pluralism in terms of 'jurisdictional politics' and 'jurispractice'—carries no small likelihood of falling subject to all the same tendencies.

is because there may be only an illusory benefit in re-narrating the history of modern imperialism in terms of a competition between 'plural legal orders in empires'—whether as further emblematized by competing 'legal authorities' fighting for jurisdictional mastery, competing invocations of 'laws not for forensic advantage but as protest ideals', or 'alternative visions' of 'sovereign' or 'quasi-sovereign power' (in the sense of a 'constitutional' or overarching corporative order).

Of course, the purported benefit of re-narrating the past in such terms lies in the hope of avoiding a need to 'depend on a general definition of law'.[20] Yet to trade in what once was the anthropologist's focus on 'normative pluralism' (viz. on 'rules and norms') for a supposedly more historically sensitive attention to the above emblems of 'jurisdictional pluralism' is simply to draw on the other standard parts through which 'the law' has, metonymically, long been made to be taken for granted. On one level, doing so is simply to reintroduce a definition of the law through the back door. On another, it mistakes the fundamental problem with pluralism as a concept in legal anthropology, which was not that it inadvertently privileged 'state law'.[21] Rather, it was that insisting on distinguishing between state and non-state schemes of normative ordering was to insist on assigning 'the law' a generalized place-holder status, thus indirectly reinstating what in the last chapter I called liberal legalism's founding tautology.

For as we saw, by denying that 'the law' has had any necessary connection to the territorial-bureaucratic national state (even as its discursive and institutional ubiquity has clearly depended on the territorial-bureaucratic state's growing dominance over national society and economy), that tautology has all too easily underwritten a naturalizing/hypostatizing stance. And from the vantage point of that tautology, the law falls into place as a stand-in for anything ranging from the rationalizing normative content of the rule 'system' to the varied processes of dispute resolution that are recast as all equally ways of administering rules belonging exclusively to that system to the very basis of the state insofar as it can be attributed to the rule system as effect rather than cause.

[20] Ibid., 2, 6, 8, 6, 5.
[21] Ibid., 5.

2.4 The Philosophical Problem of the Law's Positivism versus Normativity

Further removed from concern with the societies of the non-West than either its anthropological or its sociological counterpart, while also being that much more directly engaged with the question of the law's nature, has been modern philosophical jurisprudence, which was reawakened in the mid-twentieth century with the reinvention of legal positivism. The key figures behind this eventuality were Hart, the English philosopher and Professor of Jurisprudence at Oxford,[22] and the Austrian Kelsen, who was his rough contemporary.[23] Notwithstanding the important differences between them, Hart and Kelsen cut a joint path towards delivering positivism beyond its crude, nineteenth-century command-of-the-sovereign incarnation. Accordingly, they laid the basis for its reconstruction as a philosophical view premised on denying that the law's validity had to be grounded, ultimately, in some kind of extra-legal source of value like morality or ethics, as per the contention of the main competitor tradition of natural law jurisprudence.

For both Kelsen and Hart this point is inherent in the way they absolve the law of contingency on anything other than its own rule content. In Kelsen's philosophy the law rests on what he calls a 'basic norm' (or *grundnorm*), which is hypothecated to the rule system as its ultimate foundation by those who are subject to it. Therefore, at bottom, the law's normativity becomes a function of social convention, following from a shared act of hypothetical envisioning.[24] Even more famously, in Hart's philosophy it is the so-called 'rule of recognition' that plays a similar part, serving as the basis for determining exactly what other rules autonomously belong to the legal system as its own. Whether this rule of

---

[22] See generally Hart, *The Concept of Law*.

[23] Kelsen's revision of positivism had brought him acclaim already well before his emigration to the United States in 1940. See Hans Kelsen, *The Pure Theory of Law*, Max Knight, trans. (Berkeley, CA: University of California Press, 1967). The English translation brought his original German work from 30 years earlier to a much wider audience.

[24] On the context of the wider German-speaking world of early-twentieth-century legal thought that Kelsen was connected to, including his relationship with the famed Nazi jurist Carl Schmitt, see David Dyzenhause, *Legality and Legitimacy: Carl Schmitt, Hans Kelsen, and Hermann Heller in Weimar* (New York: Clarendon Press, 1997). On Kelsen and Schmitt's famed debate on constitutional guardianship, see the recent translation by Lars Vinx, ed. *The Guardian of the Constitution: Hans Kelsen and Carl Schmitt on the Limits of Constitutional Law* (Cambridge: Cambridge University Press, 2015).

recognition is seen as an actually operative reference point for legal consciousness to puzzle over or merely one that must be attributable, in principle, to the reasoned awareness of the law's subjects, here once more the law's normativity becomes strictly a function of social conventionality.

Important differences of detail notwithstanding, Kelsen's *grundnorm* and Hart's rule of recognition both allowed positivism to divest itself of any necessary grounding in the idea of the Austinian sovereign's command. In fact, from the standpoint of its reimagining by Hart and Kelsen, positivism did not require the law to be grounded in any express/articulated set of pronouncements at all. Ironically, however, positivism's initial dominance within the renewed tradition of twentieth-century jurisprudence would go on to be undone by this very prioritization of exclusively grounding the law in the implicit normative content of its own purportedly self-contained system. By so strenuously denying that the law relied for its validity on anything outside itself, reimagined positivism thus only increased attention to the question it was trying hardest to jettison: in virtue of what did the law *really* stake its claim to its subjects' allegiance.

Ultimately, then, the reawakening of legal positivism did not simply reawaken the philosophy of law more generally. It also illuminated a corner of the question of law's nature that was related to early legal sociology's instigating concern with the efficacy of various schemes of normative ordering beyond state law in cementing collective life. Here, however, in the context of the reawakened tradition of legal philosophy, rather than a flight into questions about social solidarity, glimpsing the question of law's nature meant asking how the positive legal order generates compliance in the first place.[25] Compliance, that is, in the sense of actually felt boundedness to the law's norms[26] rather than a mere fear of its naked

---

[25] In fact, one of the major ways in which Hart departed from Kelsen was in reaching back to Austin's 'command theory of law' to criticize the positivist tendency to fail to adequately distinguish between the 'internal' and 'external' aspect of rules—corresponding roughly to the standpoint taken by an outside observer who does not, themself, feel bound by the rules versus one who 'accepts and uses' them as a 'a guide to [their own] conduct'. See Hart, *The Concept of Law*, 61. Not surprisingly, Hart's positivism has long been criticized on precisely this same basis—by pushing the question of the roots of his own notion of the 'internal aspect' of rules still further. See e.g. John Finnis, *Natural Law and Natural Rights*, 2nd edn. (New York: Oxford University Press, 2011), 12–19 and Ronald Dworkin, *Law's Empire* (Cambridge, MA: Harvard University Press, 1986).

[26] To be sure, there are different ways to understand the notion of normativity. As philosopher John Broom observes, one may distinguish two basic stances. First, there are those—like himself—who would restrict questions about normativity to ones having to do with 'oughtness' in the sense of reasons to comply with what he calls sources of 'requirements' rather than with

authority/domination or, for that matter, a true sense of civic allegiance in the light of that authority's legitimacy. (Inherited from classical sociological thinkers like Weber, the latter concepts—of authority, domination, and legitimacy—have generally gone on to become much more a part of the way socio-legal theory has grappled with the problem of the law's normativity than the way philosophical jurisprudence has.) As the legal philosopher Andrei Marmour puts it,[27] to highlight the problem of law's normativity is, thus, to ask how the law 'gives rise to reasons for action' and, relatedly, 'what kind of reasons' those are.[28]

Even as the question of law's nature has most clearly come to light in the philosophical domain, the reawakening of jurisprudence has tended to assume even more unwaveringly than legal anthropology or sociology that what the law *is*, first and last, is a largely self-contained system of rational ordering according to norms with an infinite capacity to cover

---

the purported requirements themselves; second, there are those who would equate normativity with any self-branded requirement, whether in the form of a 'norm', a 'rule', or a convention. See Oliver Lewis, 'John Broome on Rationality', *Interviews with Philosophers*, available at https://podcasts.ox.ac.uk/john-broome-rationality. See also Christine M. Korsgaard, *The Sources of Normativity: The Tanner Lectures on Human Values* (New York: Cambridge University Press, 1996). Of course, as Broome himself concedes, that these two senses of normativity could be premised on a distinction without a difference is borne out by a position other moral philosophers have long staked out. See e.g. H. A. Prichard, 'Does Moral Philosophy Rest on a Mistake?', *Mind* 21, no. 81 (1912): 21–37. Indeed, as formulated from within jurisprudence, serious investigation of the problem of law's normativity is usually premised, whether explicitly or in effect, on locating the underlying reason(s) for why the law's norms/rules/conventions *ought* to be regarded as normative, and thus deserving of deference, in the first place. See e.g. Thomas R. Kearns, 'Legal Normativity and Morality', *Western Ontario Law Review* 14 (1974): 71–104; Torben Spaak, 'Legal Positivism, Law's Normativity, and the Normative Force of Legal Justification', *Ratio Juris* 16, no. 4 (December 2003): 469–85, Sylvie Delacroix, *Legal Norms And Normativity: An Essay in Genealogy* (Portland, OR: Oxford University Press, 2006), and Maksymilian Del Mar, 'Legal Norms and Normativity', *Oxford Journal of Legal Studies* 27, no. 2 (2007): 355–72.

[27] While it is common in philosophical discourse to try to clarify the concept of normativity through reference to the concept of reasons for action (and, relatedly, that of 'oughtness'), in the wider literature other formulations obviously do come into play. See e.g. John Broome's concept of 'normative requirements', John Broome, 'Normative Requirements', *Ratio: An International Journal of Analytical Philosophy* 12, No. 4 (1999): 389–419.

[28] Andrei Marmour, 'The Nature of Law', *The Stanford Encyclopedia of Philosophy* (Fall 2008 Edition), ed. Edward N. Zalta, http://plato.stanford.edu/archives/fall2008/entries/lawphil-nature/. Marmour refers to two aspects of the normativity of the law that he maintains should come in for study amongst contemporary philosophers. It is only to the first, meriting what Marmour calls the 'explanatory task', that I am referring above. Beyond this, as he notes, a 'complete philosophical account of the normativity of law' would also require looking at what he calls a 'normative-justificatory' task of consideration as well. As he explains the relationship between these two tasks, the second would entail 'elucidating the reasons people *ought* to have for acknowledging the law's normative aspect' in the first sense.

the world of facts. Indeed, the fundamental role of this assumption in grounding jurisprudential enquiry today is evident well beyond Hart and Kelsen. It thus persists even if the law is seen as separated from morality/ethics by a boundary that is only porous—whether entirely or partially so, as per the respective views espoused under natural-law theory and Ronald Dworkin's interpretivist theory of 'law as integrity'.[29] (While it is usually regarded as the third school of modern philosophical jurisprudence requiring mention, underneath its elaborate detail Dworkinian interpretivism is very much a middle-ground position; as such, it holds as tightly as either of its counterparts to the assumption that philosophizing about law requires navigating the positivism/natural law divide.)[30]

Perhaps the most exemplary appearance of this grounding assumption comes in the work of Joseph Raz, Hart's best-known student and until his death perhaps the contemporary philosophy of law's most lauded elder statesman. Already from Raz's earliest work, 1970's *The Concept of a Legal System*—the title being a clear play on Hart's *The Concept of Law*—the key elements of his thought were well in place, remaining substantially preserved in all the years after. Lamenting what he calls the merely 'linguistic' approach to jurisprudence under which the main explanatory task is allegedly to determine 'what the word law means', Raz attempts to distinguish his own way of characterizing the object of his titular concern in this first major work.[31] For Raz, then, a 'legal system' is not systematic in the sense of its answering to society's overarching need for an ideal of 'justice' or 'law and order', nor even in the institutional sense

[29] See e.g. Dworkin, *Law's Empire*.
[30] As Scott Shapiro usefully describes it, Dworkin's way of navigating the divide is through a commitment to 'rump formalism'. To reach this conclusion, Shapiro starts from the assertion that positivism is not essentially formalist. Rather, it is simply that positivism has long been associated with formalism, where formalism itself is conceived as a commitment to the idea that legal rules are completely determinate. On this view, reawakened positivism divested itself from any formalist commitment through Hart's explicit disavowal of perfect determinacy based on his underlying belief in the open-textured nature of language. In expanding the range of the law's 'normative' content in the way he did—for example, through distinguishing the law's propositions/rules from its grounds as well as its more straightforwardly applied rules from the larger personal and political theories that adjudicators must draw on to resolve so-called hard cases—Dworkin effectively adds a measure of determinacy back into positivism. However, he does so, according to Shapiro, while consistently casting himself as an anti-positivist, even despite his real problem being merely with 'exclusive' legal positivists who believe that the law is determined not *ultimately* but *only* by social facts/conventions. Scott J. Shapiro, *Legality* (Cambridge, MA: The Belknap Press of Harvard University, 2011), 259–87.
[31] Joseph Raz, *The Concept of a Legal System: An Introduction to the Theory of Legal System* (New York: Clarendon Press, 1980 [1970]), 208, note 9.

of systematically instantiating legislative, executive, and adjudicative power in separately apportioned governmental structures and capacities. Rather, paving the way to the seemingly self-evident character of Marmour's formulation, for Raz the legal system is 'a system of reasons for actions'.[32] With jurisprudence's object of scrutiny so conceived, legal positivism touches the seemingly more rarefied air where philosophers in the analytical tradition have debated the nature of practical reason.

Ironically, despite the ostensible striving towards the actual over the theoretical, Raz's thought remains indicative of the way in which even increasingly sophisticated positivism has tended to reinstate a version of its crude command-of-the-sovereign predecessor's commitment to formalism. Of course, on one level this flies in the face of how resurgent positivism sought to conceive of itself already from its inception through purporting to have travelled a path as distant from formalism as so-called rule scepticism, situated on the opposite end of the philosophical spectrum and which Hart famously associated, to its supposed detriment, with legal realism.[33] On another level, however, the reasons to doubt the close association between formalism and resurgent positivism are only as compelling as the post-Hartian tradition's portrayal of formalism, itself, has been. And clearly, the aspect of Hart's view deriving from the depiction of rule scepticism as formalism's opposite leaves much to be desired, as can be surmised from the obvious objections there are to be made to simplistically equating legal realism with the bogey of rule scepticism in order to discredit both as philosophically incoherent.[34]

As a starting point, the conception of formalism as tantamount to a commitment to the law's determinacy[35] seems premised on a generally ill-specified underlying notion of determinacy.[36] Consider, for example,

---

[32] Ibid., 211.
[33] See Hart, *The Concept of Law*, ch. 7.
[34] On the merits of Hart's case against legal realism see Brian Leiter, 'Legal Realism and Legal Positivism Reconsidered', *Ethics* 111, no. 2 (2001): 278–301.
[35] See e.g. note 30 (discussing Shapiro's construction of formalism in such terms) and Brian Leiter, 'Legal Formalism and Legal Realism: What Is the Issue?' *Legal Theory* 16 (2010): 111–33.
[36] While the notion of formalism-as-determinism may be the dominant one in mainstream positivism, especially given its alignment with Hart's way of opposing formalism to legal realism-as-rule scepticism, it is not the only such notion available within mainstream positivism. Others offer views of formalism that are more decidedly focused on its tight connection to positivism (and that disavow any attempt to cast that connection, instead, simply as a relic of the past age of crude positivism). See e.g. Michael Stokes, 'Formalism, Realism and the Concept of Law', *Law and Philosophy* 13, no. 2 (1994): 115–59.

one of the more noteworthy efforts at cashing out such a notion. On legal philosopher Brian Leiter's view, the law's determinacy can be understood in terms of the existence of a 'class of legitimate legal reasons available for a judge to offer in support of his or her decision [so as to] justif[y] one and only one outcome either in all cases or in some significant and contested range of cases', like those that reach appellate review.[37] With this specification in mind, Leiter seeks to distinguish a more defensible species of formalist determinacy from the 'vulgar' type of old, which allegedly went hand in hand with crude positivism and which he argues hinged on the idea of 'judicial decision-making' as 'noting more than' a process of 'mechanical deduction on the model of the syllogism'.[38]

Here it is essential to keep in mind that Leiter's deeper aim in offering this more charitable interpretation of determinacy is to maintain—and really, to *strengthen*—the case against any connection between positivism (in its revitalized post-Hartian form) and formalism (in its now less vulgar conception). Yet whatever his ultimate destination, the road Leiter would have us follow is a difficult one to tread; for even his revamped notion of formalist determinacy remains question-begging, effectively assuming what it needs to prove in order to sever any connection to revitalized positivism in a way the connection between vulgar determinacy and crude positivism could not so easily be severed. After all, if the 'class of legitimate legal *reasons*' that adjudicatory decision-making can ideally be reconstructed in terms of were not simply coequal with the relevant legal rule in whatever case at hand—and instead, say, included other background reasons-cum-principles that were taken as justifying that legal rule—then there would scarcely be any difference between the vulgar and the revamped notions of formalist determinacy. That is, even in the context of vulgar formalism there would be more than enough reasons to insert into its syllogistic chains of logic, and, in turn, for the adjudicator to then be able to use to justify some 'one and only one' purportedly necessary outcome in the given case to which those reasons were 'mechanically' being applied. It would, therefore, end up being no harder—and, crucially, also no *easier*—to disentangle vulgar formalism from positivism than Leiter's more sophisticated variety would have it;

---

[37] Leiter, 'Legal Formalism and Legal Realism', 111.
[38] Ibid.

and with the difference between them thus collapsed, so, in turn, would the same fate be in store for the larger enterprise on behalf of which he sought to distinguish them in the first place.

Indeed, leaving matters here still understates the problem with Leiter's more charitable notion of formalist determinacy and the larger end towards which he means to deploy it. For even if the 'class of legitimate legal *reasons*' in terms of which adjudicatory decision-making could ideally be reconstructed *were* simply coequal with whatever relevant legal rule in a case at hand, there would still only be a difference between revamped and vulgar formalism if that rule was fully self-executing. And assuming that the rule's constituent lexical arguments and adjuncts[39] would have to be richer in semantic content than the empty algebraic x's and y's in the strings of a perfectly syllogistic logical sequence, vulgar formalism could hardly *really* be so vulgar. Plainly, it would have to avail itself at least of other linguistic and heuristic principles to give meaning to its constituent lexical arguments/adjuncts, not to mention the wider syntactic units they comprised. In turn, the distinction that was supposed to separate vulgar from revamped formalism in the first place would here once more largely collapse, again effectively vitiating the force of the case Leiter seeks to make for severing formalism of *all* kinds from the reimagined conception of positivism in the post-Hartian legal philosophical tradition.

If we make the deficiency of rejuvenated positivism's standard portrayal of formalism-as-determinacy apparent in the above manner, it also begins to appear as much like a means for effectively obscuring the deeper nature of the connection between formalism and positivism as it does anything else. Considered as a historical phenomenon, for example, rather than through any shared belief in the perfect determinacy of legal

---

[39] I am using the term 'argument' here in its standard sense in linguistics/valence theory/dependency grammar theory: namely, as an element that is necessary to complete the meaning of a predicate. More mundanely, one can say that if a predicate can generally be thought of as an expression's auxiliary and main verb elements, the arguments needed to complete the overall predicate-argument structure might include elements of both the grammatical 'subject' and grammatical 'object' of the expression (to the extent that such more informal concepts make sense for the language in which the given expression is stated). Of course, the above notion of an argument is not confined to verbal predicates. Even absent any verb element, the notion of an argument preserves a similar enough meaning as part of noun phrase predicates. As the counterpart to arguments, adjuncts are the non-necessary/dispensable elements of a predicate-argument structure. See Vilmos Ágel and Klaus Fischer, 'Dependency Grammar and Valence Theory', in *The Oxford Handbook of Linguistic Analysis*, eds. Bernd Hein and Heiko Narrog (Oxford: Oxford University Press, 2009), ch. 11.

rules, formalism's most critical link to positivism was forged through the common air of scientism they both imparted to high nineteenth-century discourse about the law. Every bit as much as positivism, then, formalism was the guarantor of the project of endowing legal nomocracy with an ever-increasing prestige as the territorial-bureaucratic national state's expanding means of administrative and discursive production made 'the law', itself, ever more ubiquitous. Suffice to say, this was a project that unilaterally depended on envisioning legal rules as an infinite source for exemplifying the Aristotelian syllogism no more than it did on envisioning the law as coequal with the command of an Austinian sovereign, let alone, as being exclusively-versus-just-ultimately dependent on the facticity of social convention.[40]

Understood instead for its ties to scientism—and, therefore, the related ideological work scientism has always done on behalf of bourgeois consciousness, whatever else it has also done more generally—formalism is best regarded as a destination that reimagined legal positivism, like its crude nineteenth-century predecessor, reaches by multiple paths. In Raz's thought, for example, the most notable such path is that which he treads—again following Hart—by insisting on the varied types of norms a true legal system comprises beyond just the prohibitive or sanctioning, including the permissive, the power-conferring, and so on. Meant, on the one hand, as a correction to crude positivism, on the other such an insistence betrays a confidence in the necessity of the world of legal norms preceding (and exhausting) the world of facts that is curiously out of step with the very critique that led to (crude) positivism's (early twentieth-century) downfall in the first place. Nonetheless, it is just such an insistence that further undergirds Raz's companion idea that the law includes rules both 'guiding ordinary individuals' and 'setting up institutions for solving disputes arising from [the rules' own] application'; as so too, in turn, does it undergird his related assertion that the criterion of a *true* legal system is that it 'exclude[s] the application of reasons ... which do not belong to the system [itself] or [that] are not recognized by it'.[41]

---

[40] On this distillation, positivism becomes an unimpeachable philosophy of law only in its 'inclusive' (and not exclusive) form. See Shapiro, *Legality*, 269.

[41] Joseph Raz, *Practical Reason and Norms* (New York: Oxford University Press, 1990 [1975]), 145.

It is hardly a coincidence that the self-contained character of the norm system should be of such paramount importance for Raz. Consistent with the naturalizing 'evolutionist myth' of the law's origins discussed earlier in the chapter, this is because it cannot but function as a way of restoring a sense of exceptionalism, effectively allowing the West's supposedly unique hallmark of the rule of law to once more be credibly understood as predicated on the strict cabining of the role of discretion in administrative decision-making. Here, then, it bears repeating that this characteristic of self-containment is not simply meant to be another name for a fidelity to a perfectly determinate (syllogistic) logic. On the contrary, understood in terms of its ideological utility, the emphasis on self-containment is indicative of the prioritization of the trope of 'certainty' in administrative decision-making that has required the law to reach only the much lower bar of non-identity with ostensibly extra-legal sources of normative evaluation. In this respect, Raz's thought echoes what has long more generally been the case for the rule of law's emblematization of Western exceptionalism, turning, as it always has, in the historical perspective, on overcoming the straw man of discretionary despotism's supposed reign elsewhere across the ages and around the world. (Of course, recurrent as it has been, this quest within legal philosophy to banish discretion also makes for a deep irony; for already decades before its reawakening, philosophical jurisprudence was beaten to the punch in this regard by Weber's legal sociology, with its dazzling account of the ideal types of 'formally rational' lawfinding in the history of the West and their role in distinguishing its 'legal-rational' mode of domination from competing, and essentially non-Western, varieties of governance rooted in non-rule-based varieties of 'charismatic' and 'traditional' authority.[42])

Hand in hand with the 'exclusionary' view of the types of reasons that go into decision-making under the law's rule, there is also Raz's insistence on the precedence of what he calls the 'formal' over the 'material' unity of a true legal system. As he elaborates, it is in virtue of the priority of formal

---

[42] With its universal analytic of juridical development culminating in the logically formally rational lawfinding of the European continent, Weber's sociology built on 'categories of legal thought' that did not simply give us old wine in new bottles. Rather, he distilled ingredients of his own Western exceptionalist concoction that still yield fresh re-combinations for thinking cross-culturally about law in our own day. On his famed 'categories of legal thought' see Chaudhry, 'The Promise and Paradox of Max Weber's Legal Sociology'.

unity that 'the problem of the identity of legal systems' must become the central preoccupation of philosophical jurisprudence.[43] Reading past the novelty of the (somewhat opaque) phrasing, Raz's focus here conceals much the same highly familiar, and even rote, concern with effectively eliminating any place for discretion. Linking the identification of a true legal system to its achieving the quality of formal unity is, in essence, a way of embedding the assumption that there must be some criteria by which to definitively determine which bases for norming the world of facts belong to the system as its own. Ultimately, then, the concern with formal unity again makes evident positivism's ongoing weddedness to the standard liberal image of law's rule as impartial and non-ideological, which formalism more generally has always been its partner in underwriting. At the same time, it also obviates the need to address the messier image that results when law's rule is instead refracted through the prism of the historically and contemporaneously constituted actuality of politics, economy, and society.

Against this backdrop, it becomes all the more telling that Raz has been unable to deny the need for grounds other than just the self-contained/relatively exclusive quality of 'true' legal systems when it comes to *truly* distinguishing them from other systems of normative ordering. Accordingly, elsewhere we find him resorting to the ostensibly commonsensical idea that what really makes a legal system a *legal* system is the 'spheres [it] regulate[s]',[44] a criterion for solving the identity problem at the supposed heart of philosophical jurisprudence that is hardly non-linguistic in character, at least in any meaningful sense of the 'linguistic' element within the historical sociology of human civilizations.[45] Suffice

---

[43] Joseph Raz, *The Authority of Law: Essays on Law and Morality* (New York: Oxford University Press, 1979), 79. (As Raz puts it while elaborating on the point: '[a] more or less clear concept of the identity of a legal system is presupposed by any investigation into its material unity', ibid., 80.)

[44] Raz, *Practical Reasons and Norms*, 150.

[45] For his own part, Raz also stakes the supposedly more-than-definitional character of his preferred exclusivity approach to the identity problem on the idea that legal statements can be identified based on their truth conditions rather than linguistic form (Raz, *The Authority of Law*, 63). In turn, this idea undergirds Raz's further claim that sufficient theories must instead commence from attending to law's normativity. Claiming that these come in two varieties, according to Raz, a first such class of sufficient theories casts 'legal standards of behaviour' as being normative only if they are justifiable by 'objective and universally valid reasons'. As for the second class, it casts 'legal standards of behaviour' as normative only if 'socially upheld as binding', regardless of their merit (ibid., 134). Suffice to say, that the norms of the legal system must, in the end according to Raz, also be distinguished by the spheres they regulate seems at odds with this

to say, by insisting on the law's so-called formal unity taking precedence over its material unity, Raz largely ignores the standard complaint that more historically and sociologically minded observers have always made against philosophical jurisprudence. For the objection is not primarily about alleging that jurisprudence is too 'abstract' in the sense of its being too abstrusely theoretical to accommodate 'the real world'. Rather, the objection is better understood as alleging that the explanatory method of jurisprudence prejudges enquiry by treating the rule system's inherently sterile self-regard as an adequate basis for understanding the fullness of its social contingency.

Of course, loudly denying that proper legal philosophy should stoop so low as to take a mere semantic/linguistic approach to understanding the law's nature based merely on definitional stipulation extends well beyond now elder statespersons of post-Hartian analytical jurisprudence like Raz. More recently, for example, Scott Shapiro has embarked on one of the most prominent new-found journeys into resetting the ship of positivism, through what he calls his 'planning theory' of law. Grounding his so-called 'plan positivism', as he also calls it, in the question of the law's nature in more explicit terms than is usually the case, Shapiro tellingly begins by asking that we recognize how 'important' it is 'to distinguish between the question of "[w]hat is law?" and the question "[w]hat is '*law*'"'. Doing so, he maintains, is necessary because '[t]he latter question [merely] concerns the meaning of the word "*law*", not the nature of the word's referent, namely, law'. On Shapiro's view, therefore, it is only the first of these questions that is non-trivial, with his elaboration of this point coming as follows:

> [i]t is nevertheless sometimes thought that the latter, semantic question is the one that preoccupies analytical jurisprudence—that legal philosophers are mainly attempting to define the word '*law*'. But this impression is mistaken. Legal philosophy is not lexicography. It is not an elaborate attempt to contribute to the Oxford English Dictionary but

---

normativity-based approach to 'the identity problem', considered as the philosophy of law's defining concern.

rather an effort to understand the nature of a social institution and its products.⁴⁶

Yet even as Shapiro makes his way into and then out from his own theory over the course of several hundred subsequent pages—navigating (and mainly keeping to) the familiar hallmark thinkers the philosophy of law usually tends to confine its focus to (e.g. Hart, Kelsen, Dworkin, and the Catholic neo-natural law theorist John Finnis)—it is hard to escape the conclusion that in the end plan positivism also, in its own way, sums to an elaborate definition of law. Of course, this may not be a problem in itself, but to the extent that it is proclaimed to be the opposite—as per the common position that is espoused by positivists like Raz and Shapiro, not to mention interpretivists like Dworkin—it leaves plan positivism no better off than those of the non-positivist counterparts the theory overtly dismisses as 'merely' linguistic.⁴⁷

If it is not immediately apparent why plan positivism can be seen as simply summing, in its own way, to a 'merely' semantic account of the law, it is very likely because Shapiro further introduces 2011's *Legality*, the major work in which he sets out his planning theory, by purporting to go all the way back to the differing ways in which the very 'nature of a thing' can be accounted for. These, he explains, come in two main varieties: a first method based on elaborating the 'identity' of a 'thing' through discerning its supposedly necessary properties and a second based on tracing the 'implication[s]' that 'follow from' a 'thing' being the kind of thing it is. Even as *Legality* adverts to operate in the tradition of analytical jurisprudence by pursuing both methods at once, it nevertheless is able to do little to extinguish the sense that the attributes the planning theory identifies as pertaining to law and/or that it traces as following by implication from law-being-law are ultimately little more than an array of *definitional* criteria.⁴⁸ Indeed, both of Shapiro's two methods of explanation—based as they are on the search for key qualities—seem to largely, if not exactly, mirror what others call the 'classical' view of categories and its larger ontological commitments, which are usually

---

⁴⁶ Shapiro, *Legality*, 7, 23–24 (emphases added).
⁴⁷ At bottom, Dworkin's famed 'semantic sting' critique of Hart and other positivists can be seen as a version of the same charge. See generally, Dworkin, *Law's Empire*.
⁴⁸ Shapiro, *Legality*, 8–12.

linked to the oversimplified understanding of category membership and, relatedly, the lexical meaning of words in terms of 'essential' properties/definitional attributes.[49]

Consider how Shapiro himself boils down plan positivism to what looks suspiciously like a definition worthy of a dictionary when he proclaims that, according to the theory, 'legal systems are institutions of *social planning* and their fundamental aim is to *compensate for the deficiencies of alternative forms of planning* in the *circumstances of legality*'.[50] The ultimately definitional character of the planning theory also surfaces in the way Shapiro substitutes the social facticity of his normative 'plans' for the 'habits of obedience' on which he says the law is made to rest in Austin's crude positivism or, alternatively, for the social-practices-cum-social-norms that he maintains Hart replaced Austin's 'habits of obedience' with in resetting the law's foundation through inaugurating his own more sophisticated brand of positivism.[51] (This result cannot be regarded as wholly surprising, given that where one disagrees, as Shapiro does, with the reasoned elaboration of another, their reasoning is bound to appear arbitrarily stipulative and 'merely semantic' rather than as if it has unlocked the true nature of the object on which definition has allegedly been imposed by stipulation. In turn, the bar is necessarily lowered for what the critic can imagine to be the 'non-semantic' reach of their own account of that same object.)

Importantly, philosophical jurisprudence's antipathy to allegedly semantic/definitional/linguistic approaches to the question of what law *is* does not simply serve as a source of confirmation bias. That is, it does not simply embed the prior assumption that the law is irreducibly characterized by its systematic and self-contained unicity, with its perfectly integral world of norms having the infinite capacity to rationally (re-) order the world of facts so as to make the latter supervene upon the former. Rather, the antipathy also buttresses the simultaneous tendency in philosophical jurisprudence towards anti-historicism—even allowing for reinvented positivism's oft-proclaimed grounding of law's normativity in something social rather than transcendent. This is because the opposition to

---

[49] See e.g. Lakoff, *Women, Fire and Dangerous Things*, 5–57 and Jean Aitchison, *Words in the Mind: An Introduction to the Mental Lexicon* (New York: Wiley Blackwell, 2012), 56–63.

[50] Shapiro, *Legality*, 171 (emphasis added).

[51] Ibid., 189.

so-called merely semantic/definitional/linguistic approaches to jurisprudence functions, in effect, as yet another basis for looking past the law's discursive and ideological dimensions. Indeed, as much is memorialized in the unflinching pride with which even so skilled a thinker as Shapiro assumes it to go without saying that the question of 'what "*law*" is' must be trivial in a way that the question of 'what law is' clearly is not (with this still being the case even if we agree to his assertion that plan positivism only concerns the latter and never stoops so low as to get bogged down in the former).

2.5 The Socio-Legal Theoretical Problem of the Law's Facticity versus Validity/Legitimacy

As much as has just been argued to be true for jurisprudence proper cannot be said to be so—at least not in quite the same way—for how the problem of the law's normativity has been taken up in the more abstractionist incarnations of socio-legal theory that fall outside the analytical/Anglo-American tradition of philosophy. With roots in nineteenth-century social thought and early-twentieth-century sociology, such varieties of intellectual speculation have always taken the law's historico-empirical aspect, and hence its discursive and ideological dimensions, more seriously than they have been taken by legal philosophers. Indeed, doing so has been a virtual necessity given the centrality of the concern with modernity and the transformations it supposedly wrought to the ongoing development of sociological thought. For two of the leading figures in contemporary social theory whom I will discuss to close this chapter, Jürgen Habermas and Niklas Luhmann, for example, integrating legal phenomena into their respective approaches to reckoning with society is based on a notion of 'modern law' the supposedly unprecedented nature of which they elaborate anew in broadly historical—or, at least, historicist—terms.

Indeed, as is well-known of Habermas, the roots of his mature thought trace back to a first major work, that was a social history of sorts. In 1962's *The Structural Transformation of the Public Sphere* he famously surveys the emergence of new spaces of bourgeois assembly and the resultant culture of public deliberation that arose in the eighteenth-century West and considers their continued evolution and eventual transformation with the advent of advertising-driven mass media and the rise of the social-welfare state.[52] Its merits or deficiencies as a history notwithstanding, in the ideal of deliberative interaction it attempts to reconstruct, Habermas' account sets the stage for the full-fledged theory of communicative rationality he would go on to elaborate by way of trying to supersede Weber's canonical sociological distillation of actor orientation into affective, traditional, value-rational, and instrumentally rational forms.[53] Of course, in its own way, so too is the mature theory of communicative action meant to provide a basis for reckoning with the evolution of the modern West. More specifically, it does so by allowing Habermas to attribute collective life to 'the capacity of actors to recognize the intersubjective validity of the different claims on which social cooperation depends' under conditions of normative pluralism.[54] In this respect, like many a predecessor, Habermas remains unabashed in characterizing (Western) modernity as historically unprecedented on the basis of an ostensibly unique 'rationality'.

Accordingly, the further extension of the theory of communicative action's companionate discourse theory of ethics into law (and politics) in Habermas' *Between Facts and Norms* comes via a step as short as its sprawling surface is dazzling. If one can summarize the animating question behind discourse ethics as asking how unconditional moral obligations can acquire force, Habermas' answer comes through elaborating a principled basis on which to foot their generalizability. It is here that his idealization of communicative rationality and public reason figures quite centrally. For the generalizability of ethico-moral obligations is staked, ultimately, on a 'dialogical principle of universalization' holding that '[a moral norm] is valid just in case the foreseeable consequences

---

[52] Jürgen Habermas, *The Structural Transformation of the Public Sphere: An Inquiry into a Category of Bourgeois Society*, Thomas Burger, trans. with the assistance of Frederick Lawrence (Cambridge, MA: MIT Press, 1989).
[53] Indeed, the entirety of the first volume of *The Theory of Communicative Action*, and no small part of the second, is taken up by Habermas' engagement, both directly and indirectly, with Weber and his ideas about rationalization and the accompanying ideal types of rationality. See, generally, Jürgen Habermas, *The Theory of Communicative Action, vol.1: Reason and the Rationalization of Society*, Thomas McCarthy, trans. (Boston, MA: Beacon Press, 1985) and Jürgen Habermas, *The Theory of Communicative Action, vol. 2: Lifeworld and System—A Critique of Functionalist Reason*, Thomas McCarthy, trans. (Boston, MA: Beacon Press, 1987).
[54] James Bohman and William Rehg, 'Jürgen Habermas', *The Stanford Encyclopedia of Philosophy* (Fall 2017 Edition), ed. Edward N. Zalta, https://plato.stanford.edu/archives/fall2017/entries/habermas/.

and side-effects of its general observance for the interests and value-orientations of each individual [can] be jointly accepted by all concerned without coercion'.[55] However, this principle, itself, depends on the prior possibility of impartial justification, which Habermas grounds in constraints inherent in linguistic pragmatics that make a particular rule or choice valid only 'if all those affected by the rule or choice could accept it in a reasonable discourse'.[56]

Against the backdrop of this overarching agenda, Habermas' further grappling with the law in *Between Facts and Norms* takes shape through attempting to provide a justificatory account of how its norms might possibly achieve legitimacy, which is critical in his eyes to the possibility of modern (bourgeois) democratic life (in the West). The law for Habermas is a/ the key instrument for reconciling the seemingly increased potential for normative conflict in societies predicated on religious pluralism and the functional differentiation of the social sphere into distinct subspheres (devoted to the market economy, bureaucratized governmental administration, and so on). As a result, for all its density and elaborate detail, Habermas' view of the law ends up hewing quite closely to traditional liberal theory. To properly fulfil its requisite instrumental role, in Habermas' account the law avails itself of a legitimacy that flows up from that of the legislative process, albeit here on grounds of legislators not simply being cogs in the representative democratic machine but as nodes of idealized deliberative communication. With this much in hand, Habermas then uses the rose-tinted lenses of idealization to survey communication and discursive production at each underlying level of political society that informs lawmaking activity as well. The overall progression thus moves, in sequence, from the communicative interactions of the citizenry in civil society, up through to what transpires in the now mass-media-constituted/mediated public sphere, and from there on into the deliberations of parliament or whatever equivalent.[57] As Habermas puts the point in his own words:

---

[55] Ibid. (quoting Jürgen Habermas, *Inclusion of the Other: Studies in Political Theory*, (Cambridge, MA: MIT Press, 1998), 42).
[56] Bohman and William Rehg, 'Jürgen Habermas'.
[57] Ibid.

if discourses ... are the site where a rational will can take shape, then the legitimacy of law ultimately depends on a communicative arrangement: as participants in rational discourses, consociates under law must be able to examine whether a contested norm meets with, or could meet with, the arrangement of all those possibly affected. Consequently, the sought-for internal relation between popular sovereignty and human rights consists in the fact that the system of rights states precisely the conditions under which the forms of communication necessary for the genesis of legitimate law can be legally institutionalized ... The normative intuitions we associate conjointly with human rights and popular sovereignty achieve their *full* effect in the system of rights only if we assume that the universality right to equal liberties may neither be imposed as a moral right that merely sets an external constraint on the sovereign legislator, nor be instrumentalized as a functional prerequisite for the legislator's aims. The co-originality of private and public autonomy first reveals itself when we decipher, in discourse-theoretic terms, the motif of self-legislation according to which the addressees of law are simultaneously the authors of their rights. The substance of human rights then resides in the formal conditions for the legal institutionalization of those discursive processes of opinion- and will-formation in which the sovereignty of the people assumes a binding character.[58]

As he subsequently turns from legislation to adjudication, Habermas' underlyingly conventional vision of the law becomes only more apparent. We thus find him even more clearly treading ground similar to that traversed by exponents of the philosophy of law proper, organizing his discussion around 'The Indeterminacy of Law and the Rationality of Adjudication'. The more specific dimensions of this 'rationality problem', as he also calls it, are highly familiar as well, demanding an explanation for how 'the application of a contingently emergent law' can 'be carried out with both internal consistency and rational external justification, so as to guarantee simultaneously *the certainty of law* and its *rightness*'.[59] While it is not possible to detail Habermas' explanation with any exhaustiveness,

---

[58] Jürgen Habermas, *Between Facts and Norms: Contributions to a Discourse Theory of Law and Democracy* (Cambridge, MA: MIT Press, 1996), 103–04.
[59] Ibid., 199 (emphasis in original).

it is telling that he summarily prefaces his line of thought through reference to 'Dworkin's theory of rights', which he describes as being 'premised on the claim that moral arguments play a role in adjudication because positive law has unavoidably absorbed a moral content'. For Habermas, in other words, Dworkinian interpretivism—and, by extension, the antagonistic strands of reawakened positivism it is so intimately tied up with—'harbors no surprise for a discourse theory' like his own, which 'start[s] with the assumption that moral reasons enter into law via the democratic procedure of legislation'.[60] No less telling is how for at least as long Dworkin has reciprocated the feeling, notwithstanding the relative silence with which the exponents of interpretivism—and, for that matter, reawakened positivism—have tended to greet the wider corpus of socio-legal theory.[61]

Indeed, it would be wrong to regard it as surprising that Habermas' legal thought has enjoyed more recognition within the philosophy of law proper than jurisprudential thinking articulated primarily in the idiom of social theory generally has. After all, even aside from his conventional framing of the so-called rationality problem, Habermas' aim is to incorporate a view of adjudication that will contribute to a normative theory capable of ultimately affirming the law's legitimacy. Consequently, there is every reason for the view of adjudication he works from, like his understanding of the law overall, to dovetail with what in the last chapter I called liberal legalism's perfect circle of legitimation.

Indeed, this aspect of Habermas' jurisprudential thinking is also highlighted in the way he sketches the connection between law and legal system. Conceived, on the one hand, in its 'narrow sense', according to Habermas, the systematicity of the law is tied up with the so-called 'rationality problem' because the legal system 'includes all interactions that are not only oriented to law, but [that] are also geared to produce new

---

[60] Habermas, *Between Facts and Norms*, 204 (noting that 'Dworkin's theory of rights is premised on the claim that moral arguments play a role in adjudication because positive law has unavoidably absorbed a moral content. This premise harbors no surprise for a discourse theory starting with the assumption that moral reasons enter into law via the democratic procedure of legislation'. Indeed, much of the rest of the main chapter on adjudication from which this passage is excerpted is devoted to Dworkin's thought as well.)

[61] See e.g. Dworkin, *Law's Empire*, 420–23. See also Eveline T. Feteres, *Fundamentals of Legal Argumentation: A Survey of Theories on the Justification of Judicial Decisions* (Amsterdam: Springer, 2017), 77–93.

law and reproduce law as law'. So understood, the legal system is institutionalized via the law's own 'self-application', making systematicity in the narrow sense blend seamlessly into liberal legalist circularity. For as Habermas explains, the 'self-application of law' occurs more specifically through 'secondary rules' of the law's own 'that constitute and confer the official powers' to legislate, adjudicate, and administer the rules that comprise the law in its primary sense of existence. In this respect, to speak narrowly of the legal system is to take it to go without saying that the law is, first and last, a relatively self-contained logical whole; as such, it hangs together on the basis of the integral cohesion between its internal parts, with the processing to which they are subject—whether originally or on an ongoing basis—by the institutions of legislation, adjudication, and administration always already unfolding in its own shadow.[62]

On the other hand, beyond the rationality problem, Habermas concurs with the wider sociological tradition by endorsing the necessity of understanding the legal system in a second, 'broad[er]' sense as well. Here, the legal system is so called because it is 'an action system' that 'includes the totality of interactions regulated by legal norms'/'all social communications that refer to law'. While ostensibly pushing beyond the narrow perspective more typical of philosophical jurisprudence, even this broader notion of the legal system for Habermas remains, in important ways, linked to the conventional understanding of the law's nature. That is, in the broad sense of systematicity the logically interconnected normative whole that is 'the law' acts, in essence, as a centre of gravity for social action beyond the realm of dispute resolution, aligning behaviour and 'stabilizing behavioral expectations' across society.[63] It is no coincidence, then, that in this broad sense Habermas' conception of systematicity should prove as highly reminiscent as it does of the so-called prediction theory of law associated with Oliver Wendall Holmes, the famed late-nineteenth-/early-twentieth-century United States Supreme Court Justice and proto-legal realist thinker, even notwithstanding its relative theoretical chastity.[64] Indeed, the focus on rendering expectations

---

[62] Habermas, *Between Facts and Norms*, 195.
[63] Ibid., 195.
[64] Of course, for Holmes the law was predictive of how courts would behave. See Oliver Wendell Holmes, 'The Path of the Law', *Harvard Law Review* 10 (1897): 457–78. While Habermas and Luhmann are, indeed, focused on social action well beyond the courtroom, there would be no 'stability of expectations' if the legal system, in the narrow sense, was not subject to

predictable, portending as it is supposed to the unique spread of social rationalization in the West, has been central to jurisprudential theory in the analytical vein at least from Jeremy Bentham's time.

Of course, within the modern sociological tradition, this broader sense of the legal system is most easily traced to Weber. Accordingly, it can hardly be surprising that its defining expectation-securing function is one that we also find structuring Habermas' way of engaging the social-theoretical corpus of Luhmann, their otherwise heated differences notwithstanding. Indeed, Habermas' thought provides a ready means for inferring how even Luhmann's underlying vision of the law, much like Habermas' own, incorporates many of the same background assumptions—about Western rationalist exceptionalism, discretion as the diametric opposite of legal nomocracy, and so on—that characterize philosophical jurisprudence proper. In Luhmann's case, this is especially notable because it is in the course of probably the most confounding of all social-theoretical departures from traditional legal philosophy that we find him still treating the law as a relatively self-contained normative instrument for rationalizing collective life/stabilizing behavioural expectations, which he also calls 'counterfactual stabilization'. (Counterfactual, that is, because as he argues, '[n]orms do not promise conduct that conforms to norms but they protect all those who are expecting such conduct' regardless of what actually does, in fact, end up occurring.)[65]

Luhmann's version of socio-legal theory, of course, is best known for the way he extends his foundational notion of autopoiesis into the study of law. By doing so, he recasts socio-legal theory as a subspecies of systems theory, the sprawling interdisciplinary enterprise in 'understand[ing] man and his environment as part of interacting systems' that was first given shape through Norbert Wiener's early post-war 'cybernetics' movement and that now commonly traces its roots all the way back to classical Greece (or one of the other familiar stops along the way, like the Italian Renaissance or the Cartesian revolution).[66] Much more overtly than

---

adjudicatory rationality so as to render it a predictable (or, as is preferred in the Weberian tradition, calculable) feature of social reality.

[65] Niklas Luhmann, *Law as a Social System* (New York: Oxford University Press, 2004), 150.
[66] Lars Skyttner, *General Systems Theory: Problems, Perspectives, Practice* (Singapore: World Scientific Publishing, 2005), 3.

Habermas, Luhmann adverts to rejecting the trappings of liberal theory, including as relating to the law. His starting point is thus to reject social and political theory's defining object of scrutiny by disavowing the understanding of 'society' as a collection of agentive persons together with their accompanying forms of social action and mental/belief states.[67] Instead, he begins from the idea that 'the central form of relationship in the social world is ... that between a social system and its environment', with the latter element, itself, comprising not any single or uniform surrounding but one that differs for each of society's specific subsystems. (That is, 'the political subsystem and *its environment*, the economic subsystem *and its environment*, the scientific system and *its environment*, the education system *and its environment*, and so on'.)[68]

With social enquiry's object of scrutiny so redefined, for Luhmann each of society's subsystems must be regarded as both 'observing' and contributing to the 'construction' of its own immediate subsystemic environment. In this respect, both the social system and its various subsystems have a self-referentially 'autopoietic' character and parallel their living (e.g. cells, brains, etc.) and psychic system counterparts. As a result, social (sub)systems have the fundamental ability to give meaning to the events that transpire within and across their boundaries, being thus further marked by a special 'communicative' aspect. Whether events originate within living, psychic, or social systems, in order to attribute to them the meanings that distinguish them as *social* events, they must first be 'communicated' so as to become bearers of meaning and thereby part of society in the first place. Demonstrating a pointed and fundamental contrast with Habermas, for Luhmann the communicative aspect does not sum, itself, to any type of rationality, some source of pragmatic constraints on how actors engage in discourse, or a basis for the inherently deliberative character of bourgeois democratic interchange. Rather, the point of focusing on 'communications' for Luhmann is that they are distinct from people, their actions, and the languages through which they

---

[67] Michael King and Chris Thornhill, *Niklas Luhmann's Theory of Politics and Law* (New York: Palgrave Macmillan, 2003), 4.
[68] Ibid., 3–4 (emphasis in original).

express themselves. As such, communications reconstitute our sense of what the most basic unit of social theoretical analysis should be.[69]

At the same time, on Luhmann's view, the law necessarily becomes 'identical to ... the legal system' in something very much like Habermas' broad sense of the term. As he puts the point, it 'is a *system of communications* which identifies itself as law and is able to distinguish between those communications which are part of itself and those which are not'.[70] The communications the law recognizes as 'belonging to the legal system' are, thus, the ones that 'count as law'.[71] Notably, that this claim is openly circular is less a bug than a feature of (Western) modernity, in Luhmann's eyes. Accordingly, he more or less accepts this open circularity as effectively unimpeachable, with it becoming a kind of datum of social life in the (legal-rational) West because it is how the social system insists on describing itself. The plainly fictitious quality such circularity imparts to the claims the law/legal system makes on its own behalf is largely, if not completely, beside the point for Luhmann. Moreover, it can be little wonder that he goes to such lengths to establish communications, themselves, as social enquiry's basic unit of analysis. The stakes of such a choice—including in the context of the legal subsystem—are best made evident in Luhmann's own words about the 'attribution of meaning', which he insists is 'an achievement of the system's communication and not an achievement of consciousness, even less a representation of external states in that consciousness'. As he further implores, it is consequently an absolute necessity to 'abandon the idea that communication is a "transfer" of preconceived meaning to another system'.[72]

Still more telling, perhaps, is how we find Luhmann making what warning he does about how to understand meaning attribution in the course of distinguishing what he calls his own preferred focus on a '*temporal* dimension as the basis of the function of law' from 'an older doctrine in sociology of law that stressed the *social* function of law using concepts like "social control" or "integration"'.[73] Indeed, the importance

---

[69] Ibid., 6, 9, 14. As King and Thornhill explain, for Luhmann '[t]he term "communication" has a very specific meaning .... [Whereas h]e defines informal exchange of views between individuals as *interaction* ... [c]ommunication is confined to the products of social systems ... [and] is a synthesis of information, utterance and understanding'. Ibid., 11.
[70] Ibid., 36.
[71] Ibid.
[72] Luhmann, *Law as a Social System*, 144, note 6.
[73] Ibid., 143.

of this so-called temporal dimension is hardwired deep inside Luhmann's theory, being implicit within his insistence on the legal system's stabilizing effect on *time-mediated* expectations.

As he puts it, with only the bare 'social relevance of law' in hand one would otherwise be left haunted by the same 'doubt' about the law's 'integrative function' that 'time and again' has been introduced into socio-legal theory—'above all, [by] the critical legal studies movement and ... other critics inspired by Marx'. Tellingly, then, it is in order to 'avoid' such doubt that Luhmann seeks to 'mov[e] the problem' away from the social/integrative function altogether. (And it is from here that we can fully understand how he reaches the above-mentioned concern with 'the attribution of meanings to communications'—in the sense of the 'maintenance of fixed meanings for repeated use, for instance the attribution of meaning to words, concepts, and true statements'—and how this results in his stark warning against seeing as 'an achievement of consciousness' what is really an achievement of 'the system's communication'.[74])

In Luhmann's rerouted path back to the law's expectation-stabilizing function we find the same characteristic of circularity that recurs in his socio-legal theory more generally. Many of the marked departures he makes from conventional wisdom thus reveal themselves eventually to be scenic roads back to something very much like the conventional wisdom. Even aside from the familiarity of the ultimate destination of 'counterfactual stabilization', we see this tendency at work in various other stops he makes along the way. For example, consider Luhmann's introduction of the 'term "coding" in contrast to the term "command"' that was

---

[74] Luhmann's warning comes not just in the course of discussing the 'maintenance of fixed meanings for repeated use' but also while distinguishing the latter variety of meaning-attribution from what he calls the 'self-binding of a communication' via 'system semantics', ibid., 144. The larger passage is worth quoting in full:

> [o]bviously, social operations take time. Even if a single communication lasts for a short moment, or not even that, when it moves from the moment at which it is invoked, it still needs to define itself in relation to time by recursive networking, that is, by relating both to past, already completed communications and to possible connections in the future. In this sense, each communication is binding time in so far as it determines the state of the system that the next communication has to assume. One has to distinguish between this and the maintenance of a fixed meaning for repeated use, for instance the attribution of meaning to words, concepts, and true statements. We call such a self-binding of a communication system semantics. Only the sedimentary deposit of semantics for further repository use leads to 'time-binding' in the narrow sense. Ibid., 143–44.

commonly associated with Bentham's elevation of the law's role in guaranteeing a security of expectations already in the early nineteenth century. On the one hand, Luhmann clearly means to be getting at something different from Benthamite-cum-Austinian positivism through his notion of the social systemic 'coding' of actions. Yet on the other, as he himself notes, both his own notion of codes and Bentham's of commands share the same essential property of being 'binary', since, as Luhmann puts it, just as coding constructs a master classification into legal/illegal '[a] command produces the difference between obedience and disobedience'. What, then, *is* the difference in what Luhmann is getting at? As it turns out, it is a rather tangential/minimal one: '[the] term "coding", in contrast to the term "command"' supposedly 'leaves open the question of the source of validity of law' in a way crude positivism supposedly does not.[75]

More fundamentally, Luhmann's recurrent tendency to end up not very far from where conventional jurisprudence begins is on display in the exceedingly familiar depiction of the exceptionalism of Western legal modernity that he leaves us with. Even as he, like Habermas, presents a more historico-empirically engaged portrait than one typically finds in the philosophy of law proper, Luhmann's remains one that is premised on a near-absolute credulity in the unique rationality of the law's supposed rule in the West as well as its centrality to the West's great (and, as he assumes, thoroughly precocious) divergence from the rest of the world. In this respect, it is premised on a second form of near-absolute credulity as well—namely, in the naturalizing evolutionist myth of the law's origins.

Indeed, in some ways Luhmann's picture ends up being even more stridently conventional than Habermas'. We thus find him jettisoning any story that would most directly attribute divergence to political economic transformation, whether born from the rise of new energy sources and industrialization in the long nineteenth-century or the rise of agrarian capitalism and the early-modern plunder of the Americas several centuries earlier. In fact, Luhmann even jettisons the much rarer version of the divergence story highlighting the economic changes of Europe's twelfth-century renaissance. While still reaching back all the way to the twelfth century, he instead offers a rewritten tale in which it is the rise of counterfactual stabilization and the birth of a superior legal rationality

[75] Ibid., 172.

that becomes the key protagonist. Consider, for example, the following sweeping passage:

> [w]ith regard to the often discussed question why the development towards modern society took place in Europe and not, for instance, in China or India, all the issues mentioned above would have to be given more emphasis. If one focuses on a comparison of Europe and China in the twelfth and thirteenth centuries, the demographic facts, the technological developments, the spread of literacy, the standard of living would all speak against Europe. Europe, however, had a developed legal culture through the achievements of Roman civil law. A large number of clerics were in fact lawyers (of canon law). In England the independent development of the common law began on these same foundations. Municipal laws were collected, codified and used as models. The struggle for sovereignty in Italian cities was fought particularly with regard to legal self-regulation. Here justiciable law was incorporated into everyday relations much more fundamentally than anywhere else in the world. When comparing these civilizations, one would find counterfactually stabilized expectations to a greater extent, even if it were still uncertain whether or not actual behaviour corresponded to these expectations. Thus it was possible to develop the social order in the face of a broader range of improbabilities if one could at least find out with what expectations one could approach the law and at what point conflicts would arise as legal conflicts which had to be decided, as a last resort, by the 'highest tribunal', namely war. In this context, monetary economy and regional diversification may seem just as important as religion, but it should not be overlooked that law gave development in Europe an important head-start, so Europe was legally prepared for higher complexity and for more improbability.[76]

This quality of Luhmann's socio-legal theory, which repeatedly finds him purporting to stand far apart from conventional wisdom only to end up just barely askew to it, is indicative of the ultimate alignment between his own hypostatizing vision of the law and that which we find at the core of so much legal philosophy proper. Indeed, as was already implicit in

[76] Ibid.

the effort to 'move' the question of the function of the law to insulate it from the kind of critique made by 'the critical legal studies movement and ... other critics inspired by Marx', Luhmann's theory seems effectively driven by the perceived inability of ordinary jurisprudential thinking to go far enough in explaining Western legal exceptionalism. Accordingly, as he repeatedly explains, his aim is to succeed where all others have allegedly failed by demonstrating how the law/legal system can be understood to have achieved true 'operative closure' (in the West).[77]

Only by doing so will the theorist be able to attribute to the law a level of self-containment greater than what is allowed by the notion of 'relative autonomy', which Luhmann sees as insufficient to solve the obvious regress problem that ideas like Kelsen's basic norm and Hart's rule of recognition leave in their wake.[78] 'Someone who understands reasoning as a reference to reasons will feel the necessity to find reasons for the reasons as well', Luhmann thus explains; and in having to undertake such a search, one will eventually have to reach for 'tenable principles' as a more fundamental class of reasons in hopes of stemming the tide of regress. As a result, when all is said and done the theorist will have to resort to something located in 'the environment of the system'—on its *outside* rather than inside—thereby shattering the ability to fully account for the faith the legal system requires holding in its own effective closure.[79] That this shattering effect most obviously ensues if the principles invoked 'carry the additional signature of "moral" [or] "ethical"' reasons means Habermasian (not to mention Dworkinian) legal thought is an obvious non-starter for Luhmann. Notably, however, the same is no less the case if the system-external reasons simply have the 'additional signature of ... "reasonable"' principles, which makes even the reawakened tradition of post-Hartian positivism little better in providing a sufficient 'theory of [juristic] argumentation' (viz. a true account of so-called 'operative closure').[80]

In Luhmann's eyes it is precisely the inadequacy of '[l]egal theories conceived in the legal system for the legal system' that yields 'the target of the concept of autopoiesis'. This is because such theories cannot handle

[77] Ibid., 312, 467.
[78] Ibid., 467, note 12.
[79] Ibid., 312.
[80] Ibid.

what in the idiom of philosophical jurisprudence proper we saw was identified as the standard problem of the law's positivism versus normativity. Given how even Hart's landmark solution must be 'paid for by the renunciation of any claim to validity by the rules of recognition', the mission of autopoietic jurisprudential theory becomes to make the law/legal system's '[v]alidity... a product of the system, [itself,] which has to be created from moment to moment'.[81] Just as we saw Habermas taking an elaborate path back to something very much like his own version of Dworkin's position, then, we see Luhmann twisting and turning his way back to his own kind of post-Hartian positivism. Taken together, their respective ways of thinking comprise two sides of the realm of socio-legal theory's most valued coin, which attributes to the law much the same total sum as philosophical jurisprudence does but now in redenominated form.

Therefore, even if, as Michael King and Chris Thornhill put it, Luhmann does not seek to 'define law as a *universally valid* system of *positive* norms' he does, nonetheless, demand we theorize it first and foremost as a 'system' (albeit now of 'communications') that is 'infinitely alterable' in scope and that appears 'as if it ha[s] no inherent ideological... content'.[82] Such being the case, '[t]he important point about Luhmann's very particular brand of positivism is that... law in modern society is, and has to be, positivist law'. While this observation is offered by King and Thornhill to qualify oversimplified conceptions of Luhmann's positivism, against the backdrop of this chapter's previous discussion it takes on a very different complexion. That is, relative to an effort to pursue the policing of the boundary between politics and law into various extra-historical corners, Luhmann's commitment to the necessary positivism of 'law in modern society' looks like it is tantamount to a way of renaturalizing the law on grounds of its already having been naturalized in the first place. After all, the reason why the image of the law in modern society must be a positivist one for Luhmann is because

> the image of law that the legal system presents to itself is a positivistic one—one of law as facts, as 'givens' produced by judges and legislators. The important theoretical implication of such self-generated positivism

---

[81] Ibid., 130.
[82] King and Thornhill, *Niklas Luhmann's Theory of Politics and Law*, 38 (emphasis added).

is not that the legal system survives in isolation from the rest of society, basing its decisions exclusively on its own previous communications, but that it exists and should continue to exist as a comprehensive autopoietic system which puts into operation legal doctrine based on a knowledge, its own knowledge, of the world *as it really is*. This is what Luhmann sees when he describes law in the process of observing its own operations and representing itself to the external world. In this light Luhmann's contribution to legal theory could well be seen as marking out the ultimate position in legal positivism—one where law becomes a free-floating unit, detached from all substantive foundations ... [even if] for Luhmann, the autopoiesis of law is in itself ... neither a good nor a bad thing.[83]

In the final analysis, then, Luhmann's socio-legal theory unapologetically restores a hard distinction between politics and the law. And in so doing, it ultimately outstrips all those other versions of speculative jurisprudential thought that are merely 'content with the internal observation and self-description of the system' and that thus have to 'do without an understanding' of what is, for him, once more a mark of the true exceptionalism of the West's 'legal system', namely that it 'creates its own world'.[84] Indeed, as King and Thornhill again let slip while trying to qualify ostensibly oversimplified views of Luhmann's positivism, '[i[f one takes a cynical perspective' subscribing to his brand of systems theory means that the

> law could well be seen as constructing a make-believe world which simplifies psychological, political, economic and other 'realities' to enable it to reject all knowledge which threatens to undermine the validity of its normative communications.

Against such a backdrop, one would have to be forgiven for concluding that the cynical view is an all but mandatory one insofar as, '[a]ccording to' none other than 'Luhmann' himself, 'such a selective vision, such partial blindness' as the law professes of itself 'is necessary and inevitable'.[85]

---

[83] Ibid., 39.
[84] Luhmann, *Law as a Social System*, 322.
[85] King and Thornhill, *Niklas Luhmann's Theory of Politics and Law*, 54. Indeed, if there is any doubt that Luhmann sees the law/legal system's self-professed blindness both as being necessary

3
Denaturalizing the Law
Historical Ontology as a Method/A Method for Historical Ontology

3.1 Introduction

If the problem of the law's naturalization along the multiple avenues of enquiry that I have considered in the first two chapters is part and parcel of its naturalization in the history of modernity more generally, including in South Asia, then what we are left with is really a species of a larger problem. Indeed, like the traditional jurisprudential problem of law's nature, the larger species of problem to which the law's naturalization belongs is as familiar as it is confounding. For it has to do with sorting out how to account for the content of the social world when the very categories through which we reckon with it function to continuously remake society in their own image.

In this closing chapter of part I, therefore, I bring together the previous discussions of the related problems of the duality, self-reflexivity, and naturalization/hypostatization of the law. More specifically, in so doing, the chapter returns to the task of detailing what a historical ontological approach to the law, as well as legal modernization under colonial rule, might look like. Before coming to the discussion of the Company's early rule of property in Bengal that launches the historical chapters of the book in part II, then, the present chapter picks up from where chapter one left off by outlining the book's distinct approach to the version of

---

and in seemingly laudatory terms, it is worth emphasizing the central role this feature takes in his narrative of the historical making of Western exceptionalist divergence. As King and Thornbill thus further note, '[t]his "blindness", he argues, is "the direct consequence of a new kind of theoretical reflexion which occurred during the 18th Century", when "European society re-organized new central problems of identity and order ... along the lines of functional differentiation"', ibid., 43 (quoting Luhmann, 'The World Society as a Social System', *International Journal of General Systems* 8, no. 8: 131–38 [1982] at 136).

South Asia, the British Empire, and the Rise of Classical Legal Thought. Faisal Chaudhry, Oxford University Press.
© Faisal Chaudhry 2024. DOI: 10.1093/oso/9780198916482.003.0004

jurisprudence's great question that is latent within the historical experience of Britain's India.

3.2 The Problems of Law and Language

Stated as above, the challenge posed by the problem of naturalization is not simply tantamount to asking whether reality can exist outside language or apart from our inner cognitive resources, even if the question of the relationship between words and the world can always be pushed so far as this limit.[1] Rather, as pertaining to properly accounting for the content of the *social* world, the larger challenge that is raised by the law's naturalization is more restricted. As such, it does not necessitate that we take a position on whether some terms/concepts—say, like those that are said to stand for natural kinds, the kinds of the hard sciences, or even certain artefactual kinds[2]—can represent the world's contents in some perfectly transparent and non-constitutive way. Instead, it only necessitates

---

[1] As partially clarified in chapter one, even apart from post-structuralism there is a long lineage of probing this limit within the Anglo-American/analytical tradition of philosophy. This, moreover, has not simply come through the work of philosophers like Richard Rorty, Nelson Goodman, and exegetes of Wittgenstein who are, to varying degrees, sometimes cast as fellow travellers with post-modernism/post-structuralism. Indeed, even beyond the many ways in which the concern animates the analytical philosophy of language proper, it surfaces recurrently as a matter of course in other subfields of philosophy. See e.g. Sandra Harding, *Objectivity and Diversity: Another Logic of Scientific Research* (Chicago, IL: University of Chicago Press, 2015) and Carrie Figdor, *Pieces of Mind: The Proper Domain of Psychological Predicates* (New York: Oxford University Press, 2018).

[2] As Hilary Putnam explains in the course of discussing his conceptual role semantics, the unique character of natural kind terms lies in the supposedly dominant role their extensions play in the determination of their meanings. Hilary Putnam, *Reality and Representation* (Cambridge, MA: MIT Press, 1988), 49. Of course, Putnam is here invoking the contrast between a word's intension versus its extension, which for the present purposes can be thought of as synonymous with the distinction between sense and reference proffered by Gottlob Frege, the figure usually credited with founding the modern analytical tradition in philosophy. The distinction speaks to the difference between the (internal cognitive) significance/meaning of a word versus what it denotes/points to in the world at large. On natural kinds more generally see Joseph Keim Campbell, Michael O'Rourke, and Matthew H. Slater, eds., *Carving Nature at its Joints: Natural Kinds in Metaphysics and Science* (Cambridge, MA: MIT Press, 2011). On 'artefactual' kinds as a close cousin of 'natural' kinds see e.g. Frank C. Keil, *Concepts, Kinds, and Cognitive Development* (Cambridge, MA: MIT Press, 1989), ch. 3 and Michael Devitt and Kim Stereiny, *Language and Reality: An Introduction to the Philosophy of Language*, 2nd edn. (Cambridge, MA: MIT Press, 1999), ch. 5. On the perilous path, more generally, from language to any wholly transparent insight into the empirical contents of the world, even for spatio-temporally bound objects see Achille C. Varzi, 'From Language to Ontology: Beware the Traps', in *The Categorization of Spatial Entities in Language and Cognition*, eds. M. Aurnague, M. Hickmann, and L. Vieu (Amsterdam: John Benjamin, 2007), 269–84.

the minimal acknowledgement that 'the law'—together with its various constituent terms/concepts such as 'contract' and 'property', as well as the more elaborate array of verbalizable propositions these constituents comprise and can go on to make—are not, themselves, words or combinations thereof of a perfectly transparent kind.[3]

In keeping with the boundaries within which I mean to confine this study's engagement with the question of the relationship between words and the world, I will generally avoid the notion of representation and instead speak of the way concepts given more tangible form in verbal discourse 'idiomize' the social world by furnishing ways to talk about it. By trading the often-fraught notion of representation for the neologistic one of idiomization, however, I do not mean to imply that the problem of the law's naturalization that nests within the larger problem of the naturalization of the contents of the social world is simply terminological. The point of striving towards denaturalization is, thus, not to demand that we police our speech so as to eliminate notions like 'property', 'contract', or, for that matter, 'the law' from our vocabulary. On the contrary, eschewing representation for idiomization serves a number of substantive purposes. First, and most basically, it allows some much-needed distance from the often artificially prosecutorial readings to which historical and humanistic scholarship labelled as being focused on social construction have come to be subject.

Second, on its very face, the trade helps us to avoid inadvertently reinstating an uninspected commitment to the representational picture of meaning and truth, which wholly apart from controversies over post-structuralism and social construction has not been without criticism even within the Anglo-American/analytical tradition of philosophy.[4] As

---

[3] By the degree to which words 'transparently' refer I have in mind the general point of contrast that Lakoff, for example, describes as distinguishing our two main types of semantic theories, whether folk or expert. Greater transparency would thus be characteristic of theories in the tradition of Frege holding that 'our linguistic expressions can be more or less faithful to the non-linguistic facts they represent' so as for words to stand capable of 'fit[ting] the world by virtue of their inherent meaning'. Lesser transparency, in contrast, would be characteristic of theories of the kind offered by Putnam and Saul Kripke, holding the relation between words and the world to be mediated by the causal force of convention—as through 'some body of people in society' whose 'domain of expertise' gives them the effective 'right to stipulate' what words 'designate'. Lakoff, *Women, Fire and Dangerous Things*, 122–23 (quoting Paul Kay, *The Role of Cognitive Schemata in Word Meaning: Hedges Revisited*, unpublished manuscript, (Department of Linguistics, University of California Berkeley, 1979), 37).

[4] George Lakoff and Mark Johnson, *Philosophy in the Flesh: The Embodied Mind and its Challenge to Western Thought* (New York: Basic Books, 1999) and Avner Baz, *When Words Are*

Avram Baz has usefully summarized, in the context of the post-Fregian philosophy of language

> [t]he prevailing conception of meaning is, importantly, representational, or as it has sometimes been put, 'descriptivist'. Those who adhere to it would not deny, of course, that we do any number of things with words other than describing, asserting, stating, or otherwise representing things as being one way or another. Nonetheless, they would insist (and presuppose in their theories and arguments) that the representational function of language is somehow primary and fundamental to it, and that there is in every (philosophically interesting) case a representational ('semantic') element to speech and thought—an 'indicative core', as [Donald] Davidson puts it ... —that may, and should, theoretically be separated from the rest of what is involved in speaking or thinking.[5]

I will return to the importance of carving out space for the non-representational potential of language towards the end of the chapter by fleshing out the role of different kinds of juridically inflected discourse in the constitution of the law while elaborating on a historical ontological approach to jurisprudence. However, for now it is enough to note that Baz's larger point in highlighting the representational theory of language as being 'first and foremost an instrument for the formation of representations, or for the expression of truth-evaluable thoughts or propositions' is to get at its underlying assumptions about meaning.[6] This is because on the representational/descriptivist view, whether at the level of words/morphemic units or larger syntactic and sentential propositions, lexical resources are seen as picking out distinct referents in the world so that in one way or another meaning can be reduced to reference.[7] Of course,

---

Called For: A Defense of Ordinary Language Philosophy (Cambridge, MA: Harvard University Press, 2012).

[5] Ibid., 17.
[6] Ibid., 18.
[7] For some of the contrasting approaches developed by linguists and philosophers—for example, through envisioning meaning in terms of the perspectives of a linguistic agent—see Akeel Bilgrami, *Belief and Meaning: The Unity and Locality of Mental Content* (Cambridge, MA: Basil Blackwell, 1992) and Noam Chomsky, *New Horizons in the Study of Language and Mind* (Cambridge: Cambridge University Press, 2000), 19–45, 164–94.

our 'prevailing conception of meaning' has come to be rooted in 'a more sophisticated story' than whatever Locke or Hume had to tell about '*how* words come to refer to items in the world' in their early 'empiricist picture of how our words and worlds relate to each other'. In its essence, however, the picture remains one that revolves around envisioning 'the world' as 'populated ... with nameable items—mental states, processes, and powers, relations, properties, etc.—that are simply waiting to be referred to or picked out by words' and that are in no way 'dependent upon the actual practice of using those words for their identity or presence'.[8]

Third, and related, therefore, eschewing representation for idiomization helps clarify what is at stake in starting from what I have called the *minimal* acknowledgement that neither 'the law' nor its verbalizable constituents makes for any perfectly transparent means of denoting the contents of the social world, much less anything akin to natural or artefactual kinds that 'carve' nature or society, as the case may be, at their joints, to borrow Plato's famed phrase.[9] For this 'minimal acknowledgement' involves more than simply a recognition of the normative as opposed to strictly descriptive orientation of the verbalizable rule content of the law to the social world it purports to denotatively reference/represent. Likewise, so too does it involve more than simply recognizing the inherently pragmatic use to which such verbalizable rule content gets put in its capacity as a collection of speech acts for rearranging the social world. (Here, it may be important to note that the point in alluding to the 'verbalizable' rule content of the law is to avoid any perception that I am suggesting that all legal norms—even within 'modern' common- and civil-law-based systems, let alone 'customary' or other historically 'non-Western' ones—are actually verbalized. Rather, the point is only that such rule content can always be given verbal form, whether in pithy rule statements or through more elaborate exposition containing some kind of underlying and ostensibly precise normative instructions. Of course, none

---

[8] Baz, *When Words Are Called For,* 17.
[9] The well-worn phrase is associated with Plato's ideas in *The Phaedrus* about the nature of universals and has played into ongoing concerns ever since, whether in metaphysics, category theory, or, more generally, attempts of all kinds styled as grappling with the relationship between science and truth. See Plato, *Plato in Twelve Volumes, vol. 9*, Harold N. Fowler, trans. (Cambridge, MA, Harvard University Press, 1925), 265d–266a.

of this is to deny that under conditions of legal modernization the tendency towards actual verbalization has intensified quite relentlessly.)

Indeed, if the only reason for taking a denaturalizing perspective on 'the law' was to remind us that its verbalizable rule content comprised a collection of speech acts for intervening into the social world, legal modernization under colonial/quasi-colonial rule would raise no real spectre of the problem of the commensurability of different norm traditions in the first place. After all, questions about the cross-cultural translatability (and discursive contingency) of 'the law' and its constituents can easily be rendered nugatory based on something like the Wittgensteinian notion Baz evokes above that *meaning is use*, which has partly underlain speech act theory ever since it was pioneered in the mid-twentieth century by J. L. Austin and Gilbert Ryle.[10] For example, in the loose field of law and language that has drawn inspiration from speech act theory there is generally scant attention paid to the problem of translation that legal modernization in the colonial/quasi-colonial world throws into such sharp relief.[11] Its moniker notwithstanding, the field instead lays claim to what titular interest it does based on emphasizing how jurisprudential thought long ago left behind the rudimentary Benthamite position that all *laws* are necessarily 'assemblages of [verbal] signs'.[12] From here, law and language's survey of the 'linguistic' aspect of legal modernity has hewn closely to the territory that Hart opened up by channelling inspiration from J. L. Austin's version of ordinary-language philosophy[13] in order to ostensibly do away with merely 'definitional' accounts of the law of the kind associated with Bentham (and John Austin) and instead proffer the

---

[10] As Marianne Constable notes, '[i]n sum, speech act analysis offers an alternative to understanding as either doctrinal and propositional or fundamentally a matter of empirical impact or even social pressure'. Marianne Constable, *Just Silences: The Limits and Possibilities of Modern Law* (Princeton, NJ: Princeton University Press, 2005), 29.

[11] For a more sustained discussion of the so-called translation problem see Chaudhry, 'Rethinking the Nineteenth-Century Domestication of the Sharī'a', 843–53.

[12] Timothy Endicott, 'Law and Language', *The Stanford Encyclopedia of Philosophy* (Summer 2016 Edition), ed. Edward N. Zalta, https://plato.stanford.edu/archives/sum2016/entries/law-language/.

[13] See J. L. Austin, *How to Do Things with Words: The William James Lectures Delivered at Harvard University in 1955* (Oxford: Clarendon Press, 1962). For a more current account of ordinary-language philosophy that is also staged as a defence of what is described as its widespread rejection in the Anglo-American/analytical tradition see Baz, *When Words Are Called For* and Oswald Hanfling, *Ordinary Language Philosophy and Ordinary Language: The Bent and Genius of Our Tongue* (New York: Routledge, 2000).

rule of recognition as the (wholly conventional) ultimate grounding of legal normativity.

On one version of the meaning is/as use idea, if the use to which (the verbalizable propositional content of) any given historically alien tradition of normativity-in-society can be seen as being put even partially converges with the use to which (the verbalizable propositional content of) the law of the modern territorial-bureaucratic national state has been, questions about the broader discursive, performative, and rhetorical aspects of the law's languages will naturally go into retreat.[14] For whatever differences are bound to exist between the varying ways that social formations in history have 'named' their systems of normativity (or the respective constituent elements comprising their more granular content), one can all too easily portray what lies beneath as being of fundamentally the same kind as 'the law' in virtue of what one can say has been done with them.

Trading representation for idiomization, on the other hand, helps us get outside of this familiar cycle of call and response by opening up to a different vista of the relationship between law and language. Drawing on an additional part of Wittgenstein's bequest to philosophy and the humanistic social sciences, the notion of idiomization points to how terms/concepts like 'the law' or 'property' are always part of context-dependent language games. Contra the default way this aspect of Wittgenstein's legacy has been taken up in the philosophy of language, to whatever extent it has been,[15] the language games that the law and its verbalizable constituents both comprise and can be channelled into appear not just at the level of the one-to-one communications by which legislators and adjudicators address those individually subject to legal doctrine through its ability, whether ex ante or ex post/legislatively or adjudicatively, to normatively refer them as individuals to a world that *ought to* be. Rather, the impact of legal discursivity extends well beyond the 'illocutionary'

---

[14] For work breaking with this tendency that takes the law's rhetorical aspect more seriously see e.g. Constable, *Just Silences*, 3, 10 and Marianne Constable, *Our Word Is Our Bond: How Legal Speech Acts* (Stanford, CA: Stanford University Press, 2014). For a more general overview, see Peter Goodrich, 'Law and Language: An Historical and Critical Introduction', *Journal of Law and Society* 11, no. 2 (1984): 173–206; Elizabeth Mertz, 'Language, Law, and Social Meanings: Linguistic/Anthropological Contributions to the Study of Law', *Law and Society Review* 26, no. 2 (1992): 413–46.

[15] See Baz, *When Words Are Called For*, 1–5.

and 'perlocutionary' dimensions of the semantics of the law's verbalizable rule content and thus well beyond the way speech act theory has traditionally staged its rebellion against narrowing the compass of meaning down to language's more immediate 'locutionary' significance.[16]

On the contrary, the language games into which means of idiomization like 'the law', '(the law of) property', '(the freedom of) contract', and so on figure operate at an additional, distinct, and broader social level as well—one where wholesale historico-cultural meaning is made, embedded, and remade. Here, at this level, rather than as referentially transparent lexical, syntactic, or even sentential instruments for picking out what must be universal in virtue of the need for social formations of all kinds to have varieties of deterrent or retributive punishment, ways of organizing social property relations, methods of memorializing binding agreement, and so on, 'the law' and its constituents have functioned more incommensurably relative to other historically alien norm traditions. Here, in other words, as idiomizations figuring into language games unfolding at the aggregate social level, 'the law' and its constituents have comprised ways of talking about the world that have been tied up with the much more contingent and latent purposes of ideologically fashioning self-assertedly 'Western' forms of economy, polity, and society.

In this respect, the deployment of such idiomizations and the way they attracted new layers of meaning the more ubiquitous they became made for a historical process the full sociality of which cannot adequately be

---

[16] On the origins of this threefold distinction, see Austin, *How to Do Things with Words*. See also Constable, *Our Word Is Our Bond*, 29 (noting that '[i]n what he characterizes as a fresh start, then, Austin points out that all (sensible) speech acts or utterances can be said to do at least three different sorts of things. They say something *locutionarily* in a vocabulary and grammar, such as presenting relevant data or naming a danger. They do something *illocutionarily* in being said, such as finding or warning. And they do something *perlocutionarily* by being said, such as confounding scholars or affecting conviction rates. Austin usually presents these as three different aspects of a given event of the issuing of an utterance, although he sometimes seems to present them as discrete acts'). On how these relatively narrow parameters of linguistic pragmatics are, themselves, cabined in the mainstream Anglo-American/analytical philosophy of language so as to subordinate even speech-act theory to the representational view of meaning/truth see Baz, *When Words Are Called For*, 17–18 (noting that '[i]n Searle, for example, every speech-act is said to include "a propositional act" that consists of "referring" to an object and "predicating" some property of it. This basic idea is subsequently developed into the idea that in every speech-act—at least every speech-act that features a "subject expression" and a "predicate expression"—"the question of the truth of the predicate expression is raised vis-à-vis the object referred to by the subject expression". The illocutionary force of the speech-act affects only "the mode in which the question of truth is raised"').

captured by methods of the kind that are most commonly associated with the dominant fields devoted to the study of language- and meaning-making, whether linguistics (including *historical* linguistics), the philosophy of language, or psychology and the cognitive sciences. This, moreover, would seem to be the case even when thinkers in such fields are oriented, in relatively heterodox fashion, to questions of pragmatics and language change or when they demand a recognition of the recurrent fuzziness of lexical categories and their character as prototypes, family resemblance headings, or conceptual metaphors more than verbal/conceptual sheathings for Platonic essences.[17] (Here, it is worth calling back to mind the contrast made in the first chapter between the historical possibilities of Hacking's way of formulating an approach to social ontology by extending Foucault's concern with the discursive constitution of objects and the historical sterility of the way Searle's philosophy of society proposes to approach institutional facts.)

To contend that we are yet to reckon with the full sociality of the language(s) of the law is not to maintain that juridical discourse *never* stands capable of picking out irreducible aspects or features of the external world. Its trafficking in a term like 'land', for instance, may be one example to the contrary. However, it is to maintain that we should not uncritically assume that so is what idiomizations like 'the law', 'property', and 'contract' must be doing. If we are to successfully adapt Hacking's call for historical ontology to the end of enquiring into the ontology of the legal, in particular, it is vital to see that the sites on which 'the law' was discursively constituted were not simply confined to venues in which juristic reason was operationalized. Nor did these sites simply vary as infinitely as the potential use contexts in which 'legal' words might appear. Rather, considered in its capacity as an emergent social/institutional fact, 'the law'—together with its constituent terms/concepts—was beheld through and, in turn, used to intervene into the social worlds of modernity via two main and reasonably distinct kinds of discourse.

---

[17] See e.g. Eve Sweetser, *From Etymology to Pragmatics: Metaphorical and Cultural Aspects of Semantic Structure* (New York: Cambridge University Press, 1990); Lakoff and Johnson, *Philosophy in the Flesh*; Jean Aitchison, *Language Change: Progress or Decay* (New York: Cambridge University Press, 2004), 55–83, 125–30; Jean Aitchison, *Words in the Mind: An Introduction to the Mental Lexicon* (New York: Wiley-Blackwell, 2012).

On the one hand, there was discourse *about* the law, which, itself, can be divided into two main forms. First under this heading, there were expert modes of discursive production in which the law was treated in whole cloth, so to speak, as part of articulating their own domain-specific propositional content. During the long nineteenth century, among these modes three gestating/metamorphosizing intellectual traditions, in particular, were especially important: those of political philosophy, reawakened already from the seventeenth century, classical political economy as it matured and then gave way to neoclassical economics, and incipient sociology-cum-anthropology. In each of these traditions of high intellectual discourse it was ever more likely to see 'the law', writ large, envisioned according to the image discussed in the first two chapters— that is, as a comprehensive 'system' of rational ordering according to rules (capable of distillation into verbal propositions). As such, 'the law' could be situated alongside 'morality', 'religion', and 'custom', as its normative others. At the same time, the above traditions of expert discourse about the law naturally dovetailed with a fourth that legal specialists, themselves, increasingly came to author wholly outside their charge as the custodians of normatively-binding doctrine and agents of discursively operationalizing juristic reason. Through this distinct form of discursive production in which juristic technicians were involved there proliferated ideas about the rule of law as the defining feature of liberalism. In turn, this helped to cast legal—as opposed to customary or sacred— normativity as a/the fundamental condition of the possibility of 'modern' polity and society, in all their supposedly unprecedented systematically rationalized incarnations.

In these several forms, such expert modes of discursive production inevitably came to subsist side by side with lay forms of the same. Discourse about the law thus included, second, the whole range of idiomizing discussion of the social and political world that could be routed through assorted rhetorical motifs and figures in the public sphere—like about the rule of law, law and order, legality versus discretion, private property, the freedom of contract, and so on. If less exacting, this second variety of discourse about the law—in the public sphere—was also that much more far-reaching.

By the closing decades of the nineteenth century, then, as made manifest whether in the public sphere or via expert traditions of knowledge production, the first collection of discursive sites on which the ontology of the legal was renegotiated were distinguished by the way they allowed the law to be constituted as an object in its own right through its invocation as an idiom of ordinary language.[18] In this respect, we must contrast discourse about the law with what, on the other hand, we can call the discourse *of* the law, which constituted its object as a systematic unicity by purporting to allow for its verbalizable constituents to be stitched together into a combinatorial infinity of new doctrinal propositions. To a first approximation, then, we can say that whereas discourse about the law constituted its object from the outside in, the law's own discourse did so from the inside out.

Far and wide around the globe, by the end of the nineteenth century it was upon this second collection of discursive sites that the most irreducible ontological stuff of legal normativity, as an ostensibly distinct phenomenon-in-the-world, came to reside. Indeed, it was based on the law's ostensibly unique discursive make-up as a relatively self-contained system of doctrinal propositions that classical legal thinkers globalized the idea that it demanded a distinct 'science' of its own commensurate with its character as a perfectly integrated totality of structure and function, not to mention a world-historical universal.

In a place like Britain's India, insisting on the unicity of the potentially infinite combinatorial output of doctrinal discourse had a second key effect as well. For it served to reorient the ontology of colonial rule away from what was its founding focus under the East India Company on the 'laws' that factored into the administration of justice, considered—in more typical early-modern fashion—as a defining feature of sovereignty as a practical affair. Simultaneously, the ontology of colonial rule was shifted towards a new focus on 'the law' through which national polity, economy, and society were to be rationalized, in the various senses of the term, under the auspices of the British Crown during the age of high imperialism.

---

[18] Following Peter L. Berger and Thomas Luckmann, we might, perhaps, also say 'objectivated'. See their classic *The Social Construction of Reality: A Treatise in the Sociology of Knowledge* (Garden City, NY: Doubleday, 1966).

3.3 Making the Law: Ontologization versus Reification

Of course, the problem of the law's naturalization is not simply 'linguistic' in nature. After all, rather than trafficking in concepts or doctrinal output with a mere air of reality, both discourse of and about the law comprise content that is meant to acquire real institutional form. Recalling Goswami's entreaty to 'mov[e] beyond … track[ing] shifts in ideology and subjectivity alone',[19] it is thus essential to recognize the continuous interplay between juridical discourse, in either of its two forms, and its actualization in the social world. Indeed, it is precisely for this reason that historical ontology holds promise as a method of jurisprudential accounting as too is it why more carefully elaborating a method for a historical ontological approach to the law through the baseline distinction between different sites of juridical discourse is important. For the distinction suggests a multiplicity of ways in which what we can call the ontologization of 'the law' has been predicated on referring to the very world it seeks to bring into being.

In the several traditions of enquiry into the law that I discussed in previous chapters, ontologization is not so much explicitly addressed as it occasionally flickers into the light from somewhere in the background. In historically minded treatment of law and empire, for example, it has long indirectly appeared in the attention given to how colonial powers rigidified pre-colonial norm traditions in the course of ostensibly trying to preserve them as a source of rules of decision within new-found systems of adjudicatory administration. In socio-legal theory and especially within Marxian-inclined approaches, on the other hand, we sometimes find an implicit or shadow concern with ontologization appearing in a more sophisticated way through repurposing the relatively well-established social theoretical concept of reification towards the ends of jurisprudence.[20]

---

[19] Goswami, *Producing India*, 7.
[20] It would take the discussion too far afield to attempt to relate what I am calling 'ontologization' to what likely remains the most sophisticated source of originary Marxian thought on law that is associated with the work of the early Soviet jurist and theoretician Evgeny Pashukanis. Without suggesting that there is either perfect (or, for my own part, any perfectly desired) overlap, there are strands enough one could pull out of Pashukanis' most important work, 1924's *The General Theory of Law and Marxism*, to do so. This is especially the case for the central strand running through the text through which Pashukanis meant to differentiate his ideas from then available forms of 'Marxist approach to the critique of law' that simply insisted

Providing what is probably the most considered attempt at doing so, Douglas Litowitz distinguishes three different uses to which the notion of reification has been put in the context of socio-legal theory.[21] According to the first, he argues that legal scholars have used reification to speak to how legislators and judges adopt stereotyped views—for example about personhood, property, and labour—and then use these to elaborate doctrine on a more granular basis. According to the second, Litowitz sees scholars invoking the concept to get at the way legal doctrine 'grants "thinghood" to ever-increasing entities, from limited liability companies to logos and phrases'. Finally, there is what he identifies as the use of the concept to channel a tendency to see the law 'as an immutable object instead of a fluid construction', especially among scholars who reflexively adopt a standpoint internal to the law. As Litowitz elaborates, here in this third guise, the notion of legal reification serves to highlight the internal standpoint's self-conscious commitment to seeing the law 'as if it were a unified whole, a thing with a definite character and essence', which makes it easier to 'gloss over the underlying conflicts that are played out within' its rule regime.[22]

On the above taxonomy, then, reification would seem to extend to the reification of 'the law' itself (as per the third use of the term) rather than just its doctrinal constituents (as per the first two uses). In this respect, the concept's explanatory reach in socio-legal theory would also seem to exceed that of the notion of rigidification in discussion of the stultifying effects of colonial legal modernization on non-Western juristic traditions, which, as we saw in the first chapter, has pressed the question of the duality of the law only so far. Yet even if reification has been refined

---

on 'demonstrating the conformity of the content of laws and legal institutions with the material intersts of the ruling class,' as distinct from engaging questions about law's 'form'/'the legal form' beyond those of content as such. See C.J. Arthur, "Introduction," in Evgeny B. Pashukanis, *Law and Marxism: A General Theory*, trans. Barbara Einhorn, C.J. Arthur, ed. (London: Pluto Press, 1989), 11. Suffice to say, to whatever extent one might read Pashukanis' endeavor as one instead insisting on the historical contingency of the law rather than its analytical (or metaphysical) universality—as is not difficult to do and as Arthur and other commentators, themselves, would seem to— there are various other strands worth tugging on as well.

[21] Douglas Litowitz, 'Reification in Law and Legal Theory', *Southern California Interdisciplinary Law Journal* 9 (1999–2000): 401–28.
[22] Ibid.: 402–03. It is Litowitz's third sense of reification that is most consonant with the more full-bodied understanding of law's historical contingency that Pashukanis would seem to deliver us to. See note 20.

into a more powerful lens than rigidification, its use in socio-legal theory has still produced only a very partial image of the law's ontologization. In part, this is simply a function of how seldom the concept has been used overall—in any of its three guises. (As Litowitz himself observes, for example, even at the height of its importance—amidst the rise of critical legal studies—the concept was invoked by name only sparingly, and hardly for the sake of theorizing its significance to law, in specific.[23])

More fundamentally, it is because in whatever ways the concept has been used to enrich jurisprudential discussion, it has remained closely tied to its original formulation in social theory by Hungarian philosopher Georg Lukács in the years after the First World War to elaborate on Marx's idea of commodity fetishism.[24] As a result, for the specifically *legal* concept of reification the priority attached to sorting out the relationship between the ideological superstructure of human society and its material base has always been both an opportunity and constraint. On the one hand, it has helped amplify the rallying cry—in one way or another—of the law's relative autonomy from naked economic interests, predicated as it has been on a view of the relationship between ideology and materiality as mutually constitutive rather than one in which the former is strictly determined by the latter. In this sense, the notion of legal reification has formed part of a bulwark against what might otherwise appear as overly reductive views of the law as purely epiphenomenal, serving to unite exponents of critical socio-legal theory and others—like E. P. Thompson, the famed Marxist chronicler of the making of the English working

---

[23] Ibid.: note 6.
[24] As Litowitz notes, each of the three main uses of the concept builds on Georg Lukács' mining of the German lexicon to highlight the notion of being 'turn[ed] into a thing'. It was this meaning that was then remade in English through a Latin neologism combining the words for 'thing' (*res*) and 'to transform' (*facere*). As Litowitz further observes, Lukács was elaborating on Marx's even earlier idea about commodity fetishism by arguing that reification was a more general version of the process of thought through which the natural and social worlds were mistaken for one another, leaving those who created and sustained the latter to imagine that their own productions were really emergent from the former and, hence, fixed and unchanging. Ibid.: 401. Marx's concern with so-called commodity fetishism and the underlying idea of the 'commodity-form', of course, was also a point of departure for Pashukanis' efforts to elaborate his own idea of the 'legal form'. For example, see Pashukanis, *Law and Marxism*, 38-41, 49, 63, 151. The same might even be said on a more attenuated basis for the notion of a 'real abstraction' that has been drawn out of Marx, most obviously by the economist and associate of the Frankfurt School, Alfred Sohn-Rethel, in elaborating on questions of epistemology. See Alfred Sohn-Rethel, *Intellectual and Manual Labour: A Critique of Epistemology* (Boston: Brill, 2021 [1978]).

class—who were thinking about histories of legality from below and from wholly outside jurisprudence.[25]

On the other hand, the priority of sorting out the base–superstructure relationship has left less room for legal reification to be fashioned into a conceptual resource for understanding the broad historical processes through which 'the law' was discursively constituted as an object in its own right. Indeed, it is no surprise that none of the main ways in which the concept has been used tend to direct attention beyond the elemental constituents (like 'labour' and 'property') of the law as a body of doctrine or its intermediate constituent output (like 'the limited liability corporation'). Missing from this perspective are not only doctrinal discourse's own larger role as a set of linguistic resources for producing and manipulating combinatorial verbal output of the norm system other than just its elemental reifications, but also any real attention to the distinct importance of discourse *about* the law, whether as emanating from extra-juristic traditions of learned expertise or ordinary-language exchange in the public sphere. Indeed, even if legal doctrine was not formulated to be part of a purportedly distinct and perfectly integrated logical system of rational ordering according to rules at either such site, the extra-doctrinal invocation of 'the law' would have remained just as crucial for bolstering its constitution as a putatively irreducible object.

Contemporary socio-legal theory has thus been missing a rigorous distinction between reification as an underlyingly subjective process and its ostensibly objective output. Accordingly, as we will see in the sections of this chapter that follow, another way in which a historical ontological approach to jurisprudence will differ from others comes from the greater emphasis it puts on the law's ontologization unfolding not only in different contexts and communities of language use but also, ultimately, on the basis of two different processes of making meaning of and in the (social) world.

Before proceeding, one caveat may be in order. Consistent with the historical focus of the argument, in the next several sections I will generally continue to use the past tense to discuss doctrinal and ordinary-language discourse and its ontologizing effect. However, this should not obscure

---

[25] See E. P. Thompson, *Whigs and Hunters: The Origin of the Black Acts* (New York: Penguin, 1975), 258–69.

the applicability of the discussion—and attendant concepts being laid out—to jurisprudentially theorizing the law in the present as well.

3.4 Discourse of the Law versus Discourse about the Law

If legal ontologization unfolded at two distinct collections of discursive sites—at one where the law's own propositions could be verbalized and another where propositions about the law could be—how much more specifically did the processes of meaning-making taking place at each respectively contribute to the law's constitution as an object in its own right? With its self-avowed concern for systematizing its object, to elaborate the discourse of the law was most visibly a function of specialized venues of administration where adjudication and conciliar or parliamentary legislative pronouncement were conducted. At the same time, the exercise of administrative rationality was closely allied with efforts taking place outside such venues to intellectually organize their output, which emerged ever more vigorously in the second half of the nineteenth century on the basis of more comprehensive judicial case reporting and treatise literature styled as scientific.

In the age of classical legal thought, then, in its *doctrinal* constitution the law became a concrete abstraction par excellence, to adapt a phrase from the French Marxist sociologist Henri Lefebvre[26] (himself adapting Hegel[27]). Even as it was supposed to be comprised by the supremely immaterial stuff of (a distinct kind of) normativity, on a more granular level the law was made up of a potentially infinite array of detailed rule statements and their ancillary verbal contents, which together were able to make for real institutional projections into the world of social action. As

---

[26] Henri Lefebvre, *The Production of Space*, D. Nicholson-Smith, trans. (Oxford: Blackwell, 1991 [1974]). Of course, Lefebvre's notion of concrete abstraction bears its own further relation/equivalence to the previously cited notion of real abstraction—as it is more commonly put, in Marxian thought. See note 24.

[27] Lukasz Stanek, 'Space as Concrete Abstraction: Hegel, Marx, and Modern Urbanism in Henri Lefebvre.' In *Space, Difference, Everyday Life: Reading Henri Lefebvre*, eds. Kanishka Goonewardena et al. (New York, Routledge, 2008), 62–80. On the particular-versus-universal/abstract-versus-concrete divide in the more philosophically conventional discussion of the Anglo-American/analytic tradition see e.g. Michael Loux, *Metaphysics: A Contemporary Introduction*, 3rd edn. (New York: Routledge, 2006), 22–24, 48–50, 98–99.

such, the law was more than just a categorical heading for collating whatever else it *actually* was that underlay the possibility of collective order, whether social practices and cultural mores, textual traditions and intellectual disciplines of juristic speculation, or organized systems of conflict mediation and dispute settlement.

Rather, like any natural or artefactual kind, the law's claim to irreducibility was staked on its identity as an interconnected array of elemental parts—comprising its major subdomains, their verbalizable rule contents and adjectival arcana, and the underlying conceptual constituents those rules operationalized. Together these made the law an integral whole, the unicity of which was borne out by the common function attributable to its elements: namely, to normatively entail any potential fact the world at large might generate. On this view, the propositions legal reason trafficked in could be seen as bearing something very much like the relationship of direct and transparent semantic reference to the external (social) world that was supposed to distinguish the high nineteenth-century conception of knowledge in the physical and (to a lesser extent) natural sciences.[28]

Indeed, as later formalized by Carl Hempel and Peter Oppenheim, in this so-called hypethetico-deductive/deductive-nomological/covering-law model of science the line between explanation and prediction all but disappears,[29] a defining feature that is clearly echoed in classical legal thought's unwavering confidence in the possibility of perfectly subsuming the world of facts by the law's norms. To say the law ruled the world was, thus, to say that it attached doctrinal discourse directly to the (social) world at large through the juridical institutions that served as its referents. This was the case, moreover, both in the event that doctrinal discourse was being used *explanatorily* to account for such institutions

---

[28] The distinction that is further developed in this section between discourse of the law and discourse about the law (as well as the contrasting processes of meaning-making to which they were respectively subject) tracks with the conflicting accounts of meaning and reference one finds respectively championed by Anglo-American/analytical philosophers who have rejected the insights of ordinary-language philosophy and those who originally proffered those insights. For an account of this conflict see Baz, *When Words Are Called For*, 9–22.

[29] Mark Blaug, *The Methodology of Economics: Or How Economists Explain* (New York: Cambridge University Press, 1992), 4–5.

in terms of the normative purposes the law had already attributed to them and *prospectively/predictively* when bringing them into being de novo.[30]

The constitutive effect of elaborating discourse *about* the law, on the other hand, was principally a function of meaning-making through venues of ordinary language use. As suggested earlier, this could take place either as part of the generalized communicative operations of the public sphere or through expert intellectual production—in areas like political economy, nascent anthropology-cum-sociology, and political/legal philosophy—when specialists in these fields needed to leave the confines of their own technical languages to invoke the law in whole cloth as an exogenous feature of the world at large. Here, however, in the venues of ordinary language use, discourse about the law needed not to be given form through chains of ostensibly strict deductive reason. On the contrary, elaborating such discourse involved invoking the law and/or its metonymic constituents (like property, contract, and so on) only in more allusive fashion, in one respect taking them for granted as already naturalized antecedent features of the external (social) world and in another as figures the meanings of which were a pragmatic function of their rhetorical use more than strict reference.

Of course, insofar as the verbal elements appearing in the discourse of the public sphere only nominally overlapped with those appearing in the venues of administration, there was always a potential for the meanings/uses of the selfsame terms to diverge in doctrinal versus ordinary-language discourse. Yet rather than hindering the discursive constitution of the law, such differences probably served to advance it, with the differing venues of discursive production playing a mutually reinforcing role. Within the public sphere, for example, ontologization followed mainly from the sheer mass of discourse about any given object of scrutiny, not the apparent unity, logical inter-connectedness, or

---

[30] As will become apparent again in the section that follows in which I elaborate on the administrable quality of doctrinal discourse, there are echoes here of Giorgio Agamben's observation that '[t]he law has a regulative character and is a "rule" not because it commands and proscribes, but because it must first of all create the sphere of its own reference in real life and *make that reference regular*'. Giorgio Agamben, *Homo Sacer: Sovereign Power and Bare Life*, Daniel Heller-Roazan, trans. (Stanford, CA: Stanford University Press, 1998), 22 (emphasis in original).

structural integrity attributed to it. More than *deduction* or even *direct reference*, then, here the watchword of ontologization was *repetition*, as the law and its constituents appeared and then reappeared, capitalizing on the tendency inherent within the production and turnover of ordinary language to reify that about which it enabled social agents to speak.[31]

Even pursuing the implications of the distinction between discourse of and about the law only so far, questions about legal consciousness start to seem misconceived, if measuring the law's immanence in society is presumed to be tantamount to asking how widespread was the awareness of its norms or about the degree to which they actually were enforced.[32] After all, considered as means of idiomizing the world, legal concepts probably found their most effective vehicle for reaching social awareness in public-sphere discourse that was free of any role in mediating juristic reason; with its sheer volume being a function of the velocity with which it turned over, discourse about the law thus seemingly stood unparalleled in its contribution to recentring the ontology of normativity onto the law and its metonymic stand-ins.

[31] As suggested at various earlier points in the text and notes of the present chapter, the well-known issues about language and the world that I am looking at through the lens of idiomization (as opposed to representation) and ontologization (as opposed to reification) have been approached from angles far and wide, including across the obviously great distance that separates social theory and allied areas of literary concern from the study of cognition and mind, modern linguistics, and the (analytical) philosophy of language. Yet even so, one should not doubt that while for most practical purposes these orientations differ to the point of being largely sealed off—and even alienated—from one another, it is hardly impossible to find compatible insights that recur across them. While few scholars working in the mind/science-adjacent fields of language study would be likely to profess any use for social or literary theory, one should hardly be surprised when one finds echoes across the chasm. Language's reifying/objectifying effect is a case in point. Consider, for example, how the underlying concerns that animate the resort (including my own) to these ideas in social theory easily dovetail with Jess Prinz's observations about words as 'perceivable entities'. Jess J. Prinz, *The Conscious Brain: How Attention Engenders Experience* (New York: Oxford University Press, 2012), 206–07.

[32] This so-called gap problem figures as prominently in contemporary sociological scholarship as it does in all sorts of historical scholarship in which the typical way the problem is construed is by juxtaposing awareness of de jure norms with the de facto patterning of social life. Marc Galanter, perhaps, is the best-known figure to have examined this problem in the context of independent India. See his *Law and Society in Modern India* (Oxford: Oxford University Press, 1989). Much the same core notion runs through a good deal of sociological work on law in the postcolonial context, especially as regards independent India, where it has probably been best developed. See generally e.g. Upendra Baxi, *Towards a Sociology of Indian Law* (New Delhi: Satvahan, 1986).

3.5 Ontologization and the Operative Quality of Doctrinal Discourse

Alongside the distinction between discourse of and about the law, there is another that was important to the shifting ontology of normativity over the course of the long and especially the late nineteenth century. On its basis, we can distinguish a first key feature of doctrinal discourse—having to do with its ostensible quality of *operativeness*[33]—that was implicit within the conception of the law in classical legal thought from a second having to do with its quality of *administrability*. On the one hand, then, the operative quality of doctrinal discourse buttressed the law's claim to ontic irreducibility by serving as the ultimate foundation for the idea that its rule content comprised a logically integral whole. Even simply in its intellectual-conceptual dimension, the law could thus be assumed to have substance and immanence in virtue of bearing a single and self-same unicity. On the other hand, the administrable quality of doctrinal discourse played its own role in buttressing the law's claim to ontic irreducibility by serving as the ultimate foundation for the idea that doctrinal discourse made for *more* than just an intellectual-conceptual phenomenon. This is because the law could not claim to comprise the unique kind of normativity it was supposed to without striving for institutional projection into the very world of facts it purported to rule.

Rather than distinguishing two basic types of juridical discourse, then, this second distinction on which a historical ontological approach to jurisprudence can be built helps enumerate two different aspects of the objectifying capacity of the discourse of the law. In Wittgensteinian terms, it makes for a way of verbalizing some of the implicit rules of the game of conceptualizing the law in the age of classical legal thought that preceded the use of the law's own rules as verbal media for making the moves in the collection of language games the law, itself, comprised.[34]

---

[33] I am borrowing the concept from Kennedy. See his *The Rise and Fall of Classical Legal Thought*, 245–55.

[34] David Egan, *The Pursuit of an Authentic Philosophy: Wittgenstein, Heidegger, and the Everyday* (New York: Oxford University Press, 2019), 15–18 and David Egan, 'Can you step in the same river twice? Wittgenstein v Heraclitus', *Aeon*, August 9, 2019, https://aeon.co/ideas/can-you-step-in-the-same-river-twice-wittgenstein-v-heraclitus.

In thinking further about the operative quality of doctrinal discourse, we can begin with how Duncan Kennedy has described its importance within classical thought: as '[a] property of some rules and principles' making for 'the ability to generate sub-rules, more concrete prescriptions that are felt to be inescapable once the abstraction is assented to'.[35] Even beyond the historical epoch of classical legal thought, then, on Kennedy's view, we can say that when a concept at a given level of abstraction within the rule system is 'operative' it implies that 'a number of more concrete sub-rules are somehow implicit' within it; in turn, it becomes 'possible to infer the existence of the more abstract whole from the concrete part and the concrete part from the abstract whole'.[36] Put another way, a constituent's being operative means that its underlying propositional content can be seen as logically entailing the propositional content of the next lower-level constituent, as if by deductive necessity and without significant intervention of discretion.

In some ways, however, my own use of the concept of operativeness diverges from Kennedy's, which is more expressly concerned with explicating legal consciousness than with legal ontologization. My own use also differs from Kennedy's insofar as it suggests that it was not just the norm system's rules that demanded to be seen as operative; instead, so too did what Kennedy tends to regard as the non-operative taxonomic headings under which the rules, proper, were grouped, like 'the law of contract', 'the law of property', 'family law', and so on. (Indeed, to emphasize the connection between operativeness and ontologization is to maintain as much already about the most important taxonomic heading of them all, 'the law' itself.)

Be these divergences as they may, it is important to see that the operative quality of doctrinal discourse should not be understood as binary, as if either present or absent. Rather, the discursive content of the law is better thought of as capable of arrangement along a continuum of operativeness. As a result, we can describe the *degree* to which any given constituent was historically operative in terms of its distance from the most immediate level at which the law purported to 'cover' the facts of the world through the application of its ultimate rule(s) of decision. The

---

[35] Kennedy, *The Rise and Fall of Classical Legal Thought*, 28.
[36] Ibid., 247.

more abstract the level at which the constituent sat, the more highly operative we can think of it as having been. Likewise, with respect to the norm system overall, its claim to bearing an integrated unicity was proportionately bolstered the more it comprised a smaller rather than larger number of most highly operative constituent abstractions. For this allowed the infinitely many potential chains of deductive inference for ultimately covering the world of facts it comprised to be traced back to a finite and hence more unitary array of constituent first principles, with these themselves understood as mere implications from 'the law' as the norm system's prime conceptual mover.[37]

Seen in this way, the different levels of operativeness at which the constituents of doctrinal discourse could be situated speak to the way the law in classical legal thought was integrated into a single and selfsame unicity in both vertical and horizontal dimensions. In the vertical dimension, integration began from the most abstract of animating values and principles that doctrinal discourse ostensibly traded in/on and that classical legal thought celebrated its scientific ability to have discerned as the law's most basic conceptual elements; among these, for example, were doctrinal concepts like 'right', 'duty', 'power', and the sovereign 'will' of a requisite holder of legal entitlement over the 'realm' that entitlement involved holding. From here vertical integration extended to the level at which the law's rule contents were schematized into its major taxonomic divisions—like, on the one side, the rules for regulating relations among private juridical individuals ('the private law') and, on the other, those for regulating relations with the public juridical individual of the state ('the public law'). Here also, at a slightly lower level of abstraction, there were the further subdivisions operating within these two halves, like that by which the private law was bifurcated into 'the law of market relations' and the 'law of status relations' or, for example, that by which the law of the market, itself, was further separated out into '(the law of) property' and '(the law of) contract' and eventually '(the law of) civil wrongs/torts' as well. The rules and sub-rules that nested under these headings then

---

[37] While it would require the exposition of more detail than I can relay here, Kennedy provides an illuminating example drawn from the post-Antebellum legal history of the United States showing how a concept of 'property right' drawn from the law of private legal relations was not only transposed into the arena of constitutional law but also made to seem like one of its own most highly operative elements. See ibid., 247–50.

came next, with the full continuum of operativeness only terminating, in a sense, at the level of (social) facticity; for in the vision of classical legal thought facticity became indistinguishable from (the law's) normativity to the extent that the self-proclaimed purpose of the latter was to remake the former in its own image, as we shall discuss further when elaborating on doctrinal discourse's quality of administrability in the next section of the chapter.

Of course, none of this is to say that a constituent such as 'the law of contract' could claim to compel the rules falling under its heading in the same way as the principle of contractual will purported to deductively necessitate the rule that a binding contract required mutual assent or, for that matter, the way the latter ostensibly necessitated an understanding of mutual assent in terms of the elements of one party's will(ingness) to make an offer and the other's to accept that offer. Nor, at the same time, is calling attention to the propositional content inhering in such headings (in virtue of their at least minimal semantic freighting) the same as maintaining that it was a propositional content of the same or even as direct a kind as was harboured by constituents of the norm system appearing at non-taxonomic levels of operativeness.

Turning further towards the other dimension of integration, only part of the significance of the operative quality of doctrinal discourse was that it minimized the law's horizontal array of most highly abstract constituents and, thus, its initial branch points for deductively covering the world of facts. Rather, operativeness also facilitated horizontal integration insofar as it led to the recurrence of those constituents across the norm system's major taxonomic (sub)domains as juristic reason pursued its purported mission of systematizing their more granular rule contents. In this respect, horizontal integration sustained and complemented integration in the other—vertical—dimension, rather than being wholly distinct from it. For the more the ontology of doctrinal discourse could be diagrammed as a skeletal arrangement of logically ordered chains in which each higher link—including the ones that demarcated different levels of taxonomic sorting—was more strongly operative than the one sitting below it, the easier it was to identify the common elements that could be affixed to those chains. Here, therefore, we are again reminded of the more precise way in which operativeness contributed to ontologization. For this came not through purporting to ground doctrinal discourse in the institutional structure of the (social) world in the way administrability did but by solidifying connections—in all directions—between the parts that ostensibly comprised the law as a free standing intellectual-conceptual whole.

3.6 Ontologization and the Administrable Quality of Doctrinal Discourse

Making for the vanishing point between the normativity of the law and the facticity of the (social) world, the administrable quality of doctrinal discourse is best explicated by proceeding in the negative, with what it was not. Accordingly, we can say that administrability made it possible to ultimately fix the meaning of doctrinal discourse in a way that was *unlike* meaning-making in the context of discourse about the law. This is because, in principle, administrability could ground the meaning of doctrinal discourse in tangible institutional referents rather than simply context-dependent usages gaining dominance, at best in an uncoordinated fashion, among those verbally trafficking in discourse about the law. Indeed, as much was the case even for those elemental verbal constituents that were nominally conserved across the discursive venues of doctrinal and ordinary language use, such as 'constitution(ality)', '(private) property', and '(the freedom of) contract', to simply name some of the more high-level examples. For to the extent that such constituents led a double life by actually factoring into self-consciously legal administration rather than just subsisting as concepts in the lexicon of ordinary-language discourse, their technical-cum-doctrinal meanings did not carry any so wide-ranging or uncontrolled an array of connotations as their incarnations in the rhetoric of extra-juristic debate and commentary. In fact, as much was true of 'the law', itself, in its semantic aspect. For its meaning *too* could be regarded as residing in the way it pointed—through a relationship of ostensibly direct reference—to the whole (social) world of facticity, the truer nature of which it proposed to pick out through norming into being (or proper shape, as the case need be).

Moreover, even beyond how administrability tied the discourse of the law to real institutional referents, its function as the ultimate facilitator of meaning-fixation in the doctrinal context was *unlike* meaning-making in the context of discourse about the law in another way as well. For the meaning of discourse about the law was generally not open to the same kind of determination through authoritative stipulation, including when it circulated in the venues of ordinary language use beyond the public sphere as such. That is, even when discourse about the law circulated within more restricted publics—like those comprised by non-juristic specialists needing to invoke the law or its constituents as features of the world at large exogenous to their own expert lexicons—it was not administrative stipulation that made the meanings of the elements so trafficked. In contrast, it was the very condition of doctrinal discourse's existence that the meaning of the propositional content it trafficked in should be ultimately capable of fixation in just such a manner, which was, after all, part of the bedrock purpose the venues of administration were meant to serve in the first place.

As social institutions in their own right, such venues found their raison d'être in authoritatively designating and re-designating doctrinal meanings in order to make administrative power workable. Rather than through a range of connotations freely ebbing and flowing into and out of existence based on the undirected use patterns of a public language,[38] in such venues meaning was a function of assigning the propositional content of verbal discourse a seemingly direct correspondence to real institutional referents in the external (social) world, including ones comprised de novo by *administering* them into being for the first time. Consequently, the ability of juristic administrators to go the last mile—that is, to go beyond merely applying the ultimate rule(s) of decision to the facts of a given case and all the way up to making doctrinal word institutional flesh in the world—was inseparable from their ability to stipulate meaning in an ostensibly categorical way.

---

[38] On the origins of the idea of a public language in Wittgenstein's rejection of the possibility of a purely private language—as in, a language that can be known only to its own speaker—see Ludwig Wittgenstein, *Philosophical Investigations*, G. E. M. Anscombe, P. M. S. Hacker, and Joachim Schulte, trans. (West Sussex, UK: Wiley-Blackwell, 2009), §§243–305. Of course, unpacking Wittgenstein's rejection/the rejection attributed to Wittgenstein of the possibility of a 'private language' makes for its own enormous literature. For a discussion see Stewart Candlish and George Wrisley, 'Private Language', *The Stanford Encyclopedia of Philosophy* (Fall 2019 Edition), Edward N. Zalta (ed.), https://plato.stanford.edu/archives/fall2019/entries/private-language/. While my own immediate purpose in invoking the notion of a public language does not necessitate wading further into the turbulent waters of this literature, it nonetheless does, here locally, tend to track with interpretations of Wittgenstein's remarks as questioning the prioritization of language's role as a vehicle for thought over communication.

In thinking about how doctrinal discourse was increasingly marked by its implicit quality of administrability it is important not to mistake our understanding of any such eventuality for three other assertions. First, it does not involve suggesting that meaning was necessarily fixed successfully within the realms of doctrinal discourse. In other words, it is necessary to guard against presuming that doctrinal discourse's purported relationship of real reference to the (social) world actually made good on the high nineteenth-century formalist commitment to a correspondence-style theory of meaning and truth, including in what we earlier saw Baz calling a representational/descriptivist guise. Rather, it is only to suggest how important the desire to ape scientific naturalism was (and has been) to the law's ontologization. More than anything, then, it was the recursive attribution of administrability to doctrinal discourse by the law's own technicians that was most significant. By implicitly proceeding *as if* administrability was one of the law's distinguishing features, juristic technicians made administrability historically central to shifting the ontology of normativity—in the period leading up to the mid-nineteenth century in the West, writ large, and then from that approximate point on in so much of the rest of the colonial/quasi-colonial world as well.

Second, and related, just because doctrinal discourse can be said to have been increasingly distinguished by the quality of administrability, this does not involve also suggesting that it actually had to be administered, let alone efficaciously so. The point is only that its underlying propositional content could be treated as if it could be institutionalized by other social institutions the very purposes of which were to assume that their own pronouncements constituted the first step—and a blueprint of sorts—for fully administering doctrinal discourse into real social being.

Third, and finally, even if the discourse of the law did go on to be administered into being, to grant as much does not involve suggesting that the resultant institutions actually had to transform the social world in any sudden, dramatic, or even appreciable way. Rather, as relating to the law's ontologization, the significance of making doctrinal word institutional flesh resided in its contribution to populating the social world with things that were ostensibly irreducible in the sense of their being demonstrably external to the subjectivity of its inhabitants. Suffice to say, the same could not be said—at least not in the same way—for the underlying propositional content of ordinary-language discourse about the law.

3.7 Ontologization and Discourse about the Law

Verbal traffic in the public sphere and other venues of extra-juristic discursive production and exchange made their own contribution to ontologizing the law in a very different way from that of doctrinal discourse. As I touched on in section four of this chapter, in these venues the processes of meaning-making through which the law's constituents asserted their undeniable presence in the (social) world were a function not of authoritative stipulation but of de facto conventions that varied with the multiplicity of their use contexts. Put, once more, in Wittgensteinian terms, not only did the language games comprised by discourse about the law prove distinct from whatever ones that could be played through making moves in the discursive medium of the law's own verbalizable rules, but because they were conducted in the distinct medium of ordinary-language discourse in the public sphere their ways of idiomizing the world through talk of the law (and its constituents) were also subject to different rules of engagement. Rather than to any demand of operativeness or administrability, discourse about the law needed to be responsive primarily to a potential for connotative plurality and sheer ubiquity.[39]

Indeed, even if its underlying propositional content was capable of referentially picking out distinct institutional features of the social world, it would have been beside the point for discourse about the law to be imagined as significant primarily for such a reason. Whether relative to the task of ontologization as such or bolstering the ideological utility of naturalizing/hypostatizing the law, what mattered most was the volume through which discourse about the law occupied the venues of ordinary language. Accordingly, at such locales what mattered was the sheer mass of allusion to the law as well as those of its constituents that nominally overlapped with the discursive elements appearing in the venues of administration, together with the rate at which such allusion turned over in ongoing debate, commentary, and reflection. The greater either variable in the equation—of mass *or* rate—was, the more the law saturated the realm of cultural representations, thereby bolstering its attendant claim to being a clearly irreducible part of the (social) world.

---

[39] See Egan, *The Pursuit of an Authentic Philosophy*.

To take a simple example, consider the notion of (the law of) contract, the circulation of which as an element within the discourse of the public sphere probably had much less to do than we tend to imagine with any precise meaning it could be given—or that it could generate in combination with other of the law's elements—for administrative purposes. Outside the venues of administration, contract asserted the law's presence in society neither insofar as it seemed to logically necessitate its own further disaggregation into a more fundamental array of constituent elements such as 'offer', 'acceptance', and 'consideration', nor, even more apparently, as any set of instructions for actually institutionalizing binding obligations between commercial agents. Whether in the public sphere, as such, or, say, for the more specialized purposes of learned ordinary-language speculation on the economic significance of stabilizing expectations in the market, discourse *about* (the law of) contract functioned more like a series of rhetorical figures, standing at the ready to be invoked for ideological uses of various kinds. Of course, at baseline, contract was tasked with metonymically standing in for the law, which itself was understood to metaphorically signify any number of nominally related ideas—from 'the rule of law' to 'law and order' to an array of formulations about historical exceptionalism (e.g. a rule of law *versus* oriental despotism; formal legal equality *versus* feudal hierarchicalism; legal rationality *versus* traditional/charismatic authority, legal normativity *versus* status, etc.).

Whatever the varying ways in which the respective meanings of these several ideas, themselves, could be construed, the semantic content of contractualist discourse in the ordinary language of the public sphere was largely, if not entirely, indifferent to technical doctrinal questions. From the standpoint of extolling the virtues of having supposedly moved from an age of status to one of free agency and contract, then, it mattered little whether courts were willing to police the so-called adequacy of consideration underlying a contract, whether contractual agreements made by minors were void rather than merely voidable, or whether it was acceptable to read an implicit fairness constraint into the explicit terms contracting parties had otherwise agreed upon. Indeed, such discourse would appear to have been equally indifferent to whether 'the law' writ large, for which contract metonymically stood, was rooted in representative parliamentary enactment as opposed to executive decree or whether judgements about its implications involved reasoning based on the strict application of deductive logic as opposed to the freer-form play of context, discretion, and ideology.

Ultimately, then, in considering the ontologizing effect of discourse about the law versus the discourse of the law, the contrasting pictures I have developed here of meaning-making in the venues of the former versus those of the latter tracks with the discussion in section two of this chapter about the dominance of descriptivist/representational theories of meaning versus their discontents in the contemporary philosophy of language.[40] That is, if in aspiring to a kind of scientific naturalism classical legal thought sponsored an ideal of doctrinal discourse as a set of resources for ultimately denoting or picking out institutional referents in the external world that it was legal normativity's very purpose to prescribe real (social) being to, ordinary-language discourse about the law marched to the beat of a different drum.

Its own contribution to fulfilling bourgeois ideology's staple aim of erecting 'the law' as a totem—and, relatedly, of sanctifying private property, the freedom of contract, the sovereignty of the nation state, and so on—did not depend on the meanings of its constituents being a purported function of their (ostensibly real) references. That task was already handled with maximum stringency by the model of 'the law' as a perfect and gapless system for rational ordering according to norms made institutional flesh in the social world that was implicit within the use of doctrinal discourse in classical legal thought. Under the prevailing division of ideological labour, discourse about the law was freed to adhere to the less artificial constraints of ordinary language in which the meanings of morphemic and other verbal constituents could fail, wander, or multiply, yet all the same still reinforce their own and, thereby, the law's totemization simply through increasing their own and, thereby, its seeming omnipresence.

Even if the relationship between the discourse of the law and discourse about the law was thus complementary—such that it was the former that provided the ultimate backstop to the law's morphemic constituents, like 'property' and 'contract', 'sovereignty'/'sovereign power' and individual

---

[40] It is worth emphasizing here that neither in general nor in the specific context of Baz's earlier cited study must the point of highlighting discontent with representationalism/descriptivism be seen as equivalent to a counter-project of formulating a grand theory of anti-descriptivism (or anti-realism, or so on). See Baz, *When Words Are Called For*, 31, 81.

'right'—it was the latter that travelled furthest and fastest, articulated as it was in the lingua franca of the public sphere. Of course, there was not any strict one-way traffic between the venues of administration and the venues of ordinary-language discourse, as if the law's key constituents originated solely in the former and then proliferated solely in the latter. On one level, this is simply because there was not necessarily any definitive fact to the matter of where a given constituent of juridical discourse originated; and even if there was this alone hardly determined where any such constituent first achieved greatest visibility so as to license its nominal reappearance across the boundary separating the discursive venues of ordinary language, with the speculative, communicative, and rhetorical purposes that were native to them, from those of administration, with their rationalizing and bureaucratizing functions.

On another level, it was because the boundary separating these two types of venues was necessarily porous, with the kinds of discourse appearing on neither of its two sides playing host only to morphemic constituents (like 'right', 'property', 'assault', 'battery', and so on). After all, the venues of administration were realms for operationalizing juristic reason, which—classical legal thought's self-conception notwithstanding—clearly involved more than just cross-referencing the law's own glossary for determining the meanings of its morphemic constituents and from there then algorithmically 'applying' the larger rule statements they figured into to 'the facts' of the world. Of necessity, in other words, operationalizing juristic reason involved drawing on concepts, semantic guidance, and additional reasoning techniques that legislators, adjudicators, and litigants could not but be at least partly ventriloquized by given their simultaneous role as individuals grounded in society. Likewise, to the extent that the constituents the law trafficked in—whether of the morphemic or otherwise more extended kind—*did* originate from extra-juristic realms of expert discursive rationality, the venues of administration had to be open to conceptual ingress from their outside before whatever was incoming could be parsed and given doctrinal form. Indeed, this was all the more the case insofar as such constituents were translated already for a first time as concepts initially intermediated via the discourses of the public sphere.

In all of these ways, then, in the context of the law's ontic accumulation, the public sphere proved just as important as a discursive space for 'constituting objects in discourse', to return to Hacking's phrase, as it did for constituting subjective consensus by mobilizing symbolic media.[41] In this respect, the view of the public sphere here offered—as a kind of vast echo chamber for maximizing nominal repetition over substantive communication, facilitating the proliferation of metaphorical associations over strictly referential meaning, and prioritizing the tropification of learned reflection over its role in deepening enlightenment in order to advance various performative, polemical, and self-aggrandizing ends—represents a significant departure from the standard way the concept has been formulated on the basis of Jürgen Habermas' work.[42]

While there is obviously no way to insist that this perspective on the public sphere, whether as concept or reality, is the only correct one to be had, much less that Habermas' is entirely or even mainly incorrect, this is also not the point. Rather, the point is to emphasize what the Habermasian view either de-emphasizes or ignores. The perspective on the public sphere this book works from in considering the ontologizing effect of discourse about the law, thus, generally eschews the vision of an ennobled realm of communicative rationality of whatever kind that is supposed to be characteristic of the emergence of true modernity.[43] Consequently, it is decidedly not in trying to recover the role of the public sphere as a purported democratic counterweight to the instrumentally rationalist ethos of the market and the state that the book is interested.

At the same time, the book's perspective on the concept and reality of the public sphere also differs from the dominant ways in which Habermas' view has been adapted to the South Asian context to date by those trying to correct for his inattention to non-bourgeois and specifically *colonial* publics, with their often more fractious than unifying dynamics. For the importance of such corrections to Habermas notwithstanding, the vision they cumulatively offer is still that of a realm of public

---

[41] See Gerard Hauser, 'Vernacular Dialogue and the Rhetoricality of Public Opinion', *Communication Monographs* 65, no. 2 (June 1998): 83–107 at 86.
[42] See Habermas, *The Structural Transformation of the Public Sphere*.
[43] This link between Habermas' earlier and later work is apparent even if not fully explicit already in *The Structural Transformation of the Public Sphere*. For only under the conditions that were institutionalized with the emergence of the public sphere in the West, as he understands it, could a categorical distinction become plausible between teleological action and the forms of purposive/instrumental rationality it is supposed to be based on and communicative action and the form of communicative rationality it is supposed to be based on. On this latter contrast, see Habermas, *The Theory of Communicative Action, vol. 1*, 75–101.

opinion and collective-will formation, even if the notions of publicity/collectivity at play are inflected in terms of building up not so much laudatory democratic solidarities as more troubling communitarian ones. (Sandria Freitag's early way of incorporating Habermas by recasting his concept in terms of clashing 'public arenas' in colonial North India comes especially to mind.)[44] Whether advancing neo-traditionalizing projects or merely intensifying pre-existing fractures within subcontinental society,[45] colonial publics have thus remained spaces of communicative rationality geared, functionally, towards inter-subjective understanding and in-group consensus.[46] Indeed, even in recent years, as focus has either shifted from colonial to vernacular publics or otherwise away from the role of publicity in forging communal fractures, the core of the Habermasian understanding—revolving around communicative rationality and the associated apparatus of discourse ethics—has remained intact in the study of modern South Asia.[47]

3.8 Ontologization and Ideology in the Globalization of Classical Legal Thought

Against the backdrop of the preceding discussion, a further way of understanding high nineteenth-century classical legal thought comes into focus. This is, namely, as an effort to maximize the law's operativeness as the rise of the territorial-bureaucratic national state was increasingly in need of administrable discourse for the purposes of making social

---

[44] Sandria Freitag, *Collective Action and Community: Public Arenas and the Emergence of Communalism in North India* (Berkeley, CA: University of California Press, 1989).

[45] See e.g. Bayly, *Empire and Information*, 351.

[46] See e.g. Douglas E. Haynes, *Rhetoric and Ritual in Colonial India: The Shaping of a Public Culture in Surat City, 1852-1928* (Berkeley, CA: University of California Press, 1991); Amir Ali, 'Evolution of the Public Sphere in India', *Economic and Political Weekly* 36, no. 26 (Jun. 30–Jul. 6, 2001): 2419–25; Veena Naregal, *Language Politics, Elites, and the Public Sphere* (London: Anthem, 2002); and Neeladri Bhattacharya, 'Notes Towards a Conception of the Colonial Public'. In *Civil Society, Public Sphere, and Citizenship: Dialogues and Perceptions*, eds. Rajeev Bhargava and Helmut Reifeld (Thousand Oaks, CA: Sage Publications, 2005), 130–58.

[47] See e.g. Dietrich Reetz, *Islam in the Public Sphere: Religious Groups in India, 1900–1947* (New Delhi: Oxford University Press, 2006), Francesca Orsini, *The Hindi Public Sphere 1920–1940: Language and Literature in the Age of Nationalism* (New York: Oxford University Press, 2009), C. A. Bayly, *Recovering Liberties: Indian Thought in the Age of Liberalism and Empire* (New York: Cambridge University Press, 2011), and Margrit Pernau, *Emotions and Modernity in Colonial India: From Balance to Fervor* (New Delhi: Oxford University Press, 2019).

relations 'legible', to again borrow James Scott's term.[48] On such a view, classical legal thought's motive force came from the imperative of unifying the verbalizable contents of the law's subdomains into highly operative vertical continuums of nesting categories, which could then, in turn, be made to seem as if they referred to the real institutional arrays in social space that they, themselves, were capable of administering into being. At the same time, on this modified view of classical legal thought, we can see why it was able to give such rigour to the idea that the law's normative force had nothing to do with discretion or the rule of man. For correct legal outcomes could be made to appear as if they followed by logical necessity from some more abstract element of doctrinal content—all the way up to the element of 'the law' itself—in virtue of being already immanent therein.

It is no wonder, then, that neither in Britain's India nor elsewhere around the world was classical legal thought a purely philosophical or even practically oriented programme of the intellect, but, instead, a larger attitudinal style, as Kennedy suggests. Moreover, because the law's claim to systematicity depended on the interconnections between its constituent parts, nothing in the classical point of view required that the full extent of its ostensible irreducibility be immediately evident. On the contrary, the classical point of view carried with it a strong sense that the law's character as an integral whole could only be discerned through scientizing discrimination, especially by those versed in juristic reasoning. Accordingly, it was as a matter of course that in the second half of the nineteenth century the task of uncovering the law's true nature by piecing together its internal order and overarching unicity spilled over beyond the territorial-bureaucratic national state's venues of administration proper. As channelled into new or newly prominent genres of doctrinal discourse pioneered by juristic specialists, a relationship of mutuality was thus forged between the increasingly dense thicket of

---

[48] See Scott, *Seeing Like a State*, 2 (asking '[h]ow did the state gradually get a handle on its subjects and their environment? Suddenly, processes as disparate as the creation of permanent last names, the standardization of weights and measures, the establishment of cadastral surveys and population registers, the invention of freehold tenure, the standardization of language and legal discourse, the design of cities, and the organization of transportation seemed comprehensible as attempts at legibility and simplification. In each case, officials took exceptionally complex, illegible, and local social practices, such as land tenure customs or naming customs, and created a standard grid whereby it could be centrally recorded and monitored'.)

sovereign pronouncement by judges and legislators through which the law was authoritatively made and remade and the flourishing forms of private and other kinds of scholarly scrutiny of the same. What resulted was a fusion between the official output of the venues of administration, with its increasingly ornate specimens of reasoned elaboration via judicial decision-making and its growing expanse of legislative enactment, and the expanding paratextual apparatus of legal treatises, textbooks, and private case-law reporters aimed at synthesizing and reshaping its more granular doctrinal content.

For its own part, so too does the perspective from ordinary-language discourse make a distinct contribution towards helping refine how we can understand high nineteenth-century classical legal thought. More specifically, it serves to remind us of classical legal thought's connection to the law's broader ideological functions, which were indexed not just to the rise of a politics focused on translating dominant interest-group agendas into formal acts of legislation or the way dispute settlement through adjudication could mask the exercise of raw political and economic power, like by privileging formal equality over substantive fairness. Rather, there was at least one other key ideological function to which ontologization was indexed as well, and in many ways, it was the most important. This involved the role of the law in helping to redefine what it meant to hold social, political, and economic power in the first place, especially in the eyes of those with larger shares of it.

Of course, this third ideological function might be thought of as overlapping with the first two or even as being indistinguishable from them. All three, in other words, could be seen as comprising aspects of a single ideological tendency that helped constitute (and, conversely, that was constituted by) the decline of older bases of coercion wherever the territorial-bureaucratic national state rose to prominence. Even so, separating out this third ideological function remains worthwhile insofar it demands we recognize the evident correspondence between the decline of older forms of coercion and the traditional problem of the law's normativity, albeit now as more specifically inflected according to the priorities of a historical ontological approach to jurisprudence.

That is, the question of how the law could elicit a feeling in its subjects of being bound cannot be disentangled from the way the law's discursive constitution as an increasingly distinct object in its own right made for a precondition to the broad shift that took place in the historical psychology of power-holding. For absent the concrete abstraction the law comprised, it is not just that modernity's agendas of sociopolitical domination and cutthroat political economic competition and monopolization would have lost the chief means of their laundering. Rather, so too would it have become exceedingly difficult for those agendas to be psychologically recast in the ways they were: namely, as less dissonant forms of role assumption vis-à-vis something that was more than just an object of consciousness because existing institutionally outside of subjectivity's baser motives.

3.9 Re-Diagramming the Plan of Parts II and III

With the small dose of additional realism that is required to appreciate the fuller range of classical legal thought's ideological functions, the potential of the historical ontological approach to the law that I have been developing in this chapter comes into more complete view. Through no more than a small number of distinctions—on the one hand, between the discourse of the law and discourse about the law and, on the other, between the operativeness and administrability of the former, both of which, themselves, contrast with the yearning towards repetition and ubiquity of the latter—we can understand legal modernization in Britain's India—to say nothing of elsewhere in the world—during the period from early Company rule to the rise of Crown Raj in a way that is both novel and responsive to an overarching question that has otherwise too easily gone unasked. Even more important, we can do so in a way that puts the historical experience of the colonial world at the centre of a jurisprudence of the law in modernity.

As for the broad contours of this way of understanding the law in modernity and how the chapters of parts II and III go on to develop them through reference to the historical experience of the subcontinent, it is worth restating some of what I have already mentioned in the introduction here in slightly different form. First, generally speaking, whether across or within the chapters of parts II and III, the reader will find the book's presentation alternating in its focus back and forth between sites of ordinary-language discourse in the (incipient) colonial public sphere and the venues of doctrinal discourse. In so doing, parts II and III of the book will argue that across the span of early and late colonial rule there took place a process by which ordinary-language and doctrinal discourse became increasingly coupled in a relationship of mutual reinforcement. As the two chapters of part II and the first of part III highlight, the most significant locus of this coupling was that which took shape with respect to property talk. However, even here the process of coupling still unfolded in a way that was significantly different from what was afoot in the central domains of the Anglo-common-law world already nearly a century before the rise and globalization of classical legal thought after 1850. In the subcontinent, on the contrary, the process of ontologizing the law commenced only from the markedly distinct starting point that the era of Company rule, starting in the second half of the eighteenth century, bequeathed to that which followed under the British Crown. Lacking the core idea of the property right, in particular, as the model for legal right, in general, late-eighteenth- and early-nineteenth-century doctrinal discourse in the Company's India was oriented less towards fashioning 'the law' into an integral unity of deductively linked verbalizable propositions than it was to an older and decidedly early-modern portrait of the ontology of the legal. In that portrait, the focus was on the role of 'sound laws' in guaranteeing 'certainty' rather than arbitrariness in the administration of justice, considered, alongside taxation, as one of the principal manifestations of sovereignty as a practical affair.

In contrast to what the voluminous scholarly literature on the colonial rule of property in the subcontinent has so often assumed,[49] property talk under the Company was, thus, less a form of the law's own talk than it was a combination of altogether extra-doctrinal and administrative discourse. In this respect, it is misleading to imagine that the early colonial discourse of 'improving' Indian society through guaranteeing the absolute 'freedom' of property constituted any sole source of theory for practice to aim at implementing (inevitably, with less than full success). In the earlier period of the Company's rule, the doctrinal core of the ontology of

---

[49] See e.g. Ranajit Guha, *A Rule of Property for Bengal: An Essay on the Idea of Permanent Settlement* (New Delhi: Orient Blackswan, 2016 [1963]) as well as the several decades of scholarship that have wrestled with its titular claim. David Washbrook's classic article is, perhaps, the best (even if an indirect) critique that also takes up matters of law directly. See Washbrook, 'Law, State and Agrarian Society in Colonial India'.

the legal was thus not comprised by 'the law' of property so much as it was by the 'laws' that factored into the administration of justice. Although it might so happen that some of those laws were seen as contributing to the security of what was doctrinally counted as property, the imaginary of the legal remained largely extrinsic to that of the proprietary under such circumstances.

Viewed in this way, there would appear to have been only a looser complementarity between ordinary-language and doctrinal discourse under the Company's rule than under the Crown's. The more the twin sites of these forms of discourse remained effectively isolated from one another early on, the less traffic there was between them of constituents that were at least nominally equivalent, with there being a correspondingly wider gap even between those like (the right to) property that did still appear in both places. Accordingly, as the final three chapters of part III demonstrate through turning from property to contract and status as the other key constituents of the law, even as the degree of complementarity between doctrinal and ordinary-language discourse increased considerably after 1850 under the influence of (impending) Crown Raj and the rise of classical legal thought, the discursive constitution of 'the law' as an object in its own right in Britain's India was destined to be less complete than it had become already before the rise of classical legal thought in the central domains of the Anglo-common-law world.

Whatever gap between law and society thus persisted in the subcontinent, it was not solely the function of some kind of failure of 'modern' or 'state' law to take root in a culture that was so different from Britain's own as the Indian. Rather, so too was the gap a function of a colonial history in which ordinary-language and doctrinal discourse had come to be effectively fused so as to make 'the law' writ large their common object only more than half a century after such an eventuality had become clearly manifest in so much of the West. In the next chapter, as I turn to the historical discussion proper of the book with part II's treatment of the Company's rule of property, I pick up many of the points developed here at the close of part I directly.

PART II
LAWS AND THE LAND

Property and Revenue in the Discourse of the Company's India from 1757 to 1857

4

From Plassey to the Permanent Settlement in the Company's Bengal

Property, Constitution, and a Historical Ontology of the Laws

4.1 Introduction

The formative years of early British rule in the subcontinent in the period after 1757 are often thought to have been characterized by a failure of the Raj's practice to live up to its lofty pronouncements, in theory, about freeing Indian property. However, closer attention to the nature of the discourse about law that surrounded the East India Company's concern with land rights is in order. The highly publicized claims regarding the need for an absolute security of property that accompanied the British rise to power in Bengal were telling in a way that is not fully captured if viewed primarily as a 'pure farce' of rhetoric on grounds of their failure to immediately subordinate land to market discipline in actuality.[1] Questions about the application of theory to practice aside, even at the level of ideas, the idiomizing function of property discourse in late-eighteenth-century South Asia took shape in a way that was different from Britain during roughly the same period.

Of course, this is not to say that in the more central domains of the common-law world there was anything like complete alignment between ordinary-language discourse about property and property's treatment in doctrinal discourse. As historian Robert Gordon notes, what is most striking to 'the backward-looking observer' of eighteenth-century England is that 'in the midst of such a lush flowering of absolute dominion talk in theoretical and political discourse English legal doctrines

---

[1] Washbrook, 'Law, State and Agrarian Society in Colonial India', 665.

South Asia, the British Empire, and the Rise of Classical Legal Thought. Faisal Chaudhry, Oxford University Press.
© Faisal Chaudhry 2024. DOI: 10.1093/oso/9780198916482.003.0005

should [have] contain[ed] so very few plausible instances of absolute dominion rights'.[2] While something similar held true in the early colonial subcontinent as well, there were two features that made the gap between absolute dominion talk and the construction given to the property right in the Company's formative schemes of administration unique.

As for the first of these features, it is rooted in the fact that in late-eighteenth-century South Asia both discourse about landed property in the incipient colonial public sphere and the doctrinal discourse of property under the Company's administration were markedly different from their counterparts in the Anglo-common-law mainstream. Talk about the importance of rendering property absolute or of freeing property into the market, thus, did not focus in the same way on the fashioning of any totalizing dominion over a landed realm through the notion of ownership.[3] Nor was it even used principally to recode conquest in terms of the highly plastic notion of occupation, which in its Lockean form figured so centrally into juridically disappearing and dispossessing native peoples in the settler colonies of the Americas already from the sixteenth century, being subsequently repurposed through more direct connection to sovereignty in the later nineteenth century for the age of so-called commercial empire and amidst the scramble for Africa.[4]

Instead, during the early years of colonial rule in Bengal property most notably emerged as an idiom of ordinary language through focusing attention on the holding of an absolute dominion over land's rent. Of course, particularly as associated with David Ricardo, the leading light of nineteenth-century British political economy, and especially as made resonant in the subcontinent through Ricardo's close associate James Mill, the economist's notion of rent[5] will be familiar to students of South Asia through historian Eric Stokes' classic study *The English Utilitarians*

---

[2] Robert W. Gordon, 'Paradoxical Property', in *Early Modern Conceptions of Property*, eds. John Brewer and Susan Staves (New York: Routledge, 1995), 96. For a similar emphasis on the reality of relationality in the common-law system of landed property see C. M. Hann, 'Introduction: The Embeddedness of Property', in *Property Relations: Renewing the Anthropological Tradition*, ed. C. M. Hann (Cambridge: Cambridge University Press, 1998), 1–47 at 8.

[3] Compare Bhandar, *Colonial Lives of Property* and 'Introduction' at note 9.

[4] See, generally, Fitzmaurice, *Sovereignty, Property and Empire*.

[5] Of course, Ricardo's conception—and the sharp distinction it allowed between rent, wages, and profits—would not become fully available until after 1815, when both he and Thomas Malthus independently developed it in its most visible form. See David Ricardo, *On the Principles of Political Economy and Taxation* (London: John Murray, 1817), ch. 2 and Thomas Malthus, *An Inquiry into the Nature and Progress of Rent* (London: John Murray, 1815).

and India (1959). For Stokes it was the Ricardian notion of differential rent—as a so-called 'unearned increment' open to being fully taxed away without harm to the prospects of economic growth—that was the key concern, especially given the ever further transformation of its radically egalitarian potential into an apologia for colonial exploitation in the years after 1820.[6]

Considered as an underpinning for a particularly colonial brand of property discourse starting from the outset of East India Company rule, the idea of rent that the present chapter highlights is not so much Ricardo's of differential rent as such, but a more basic one that pre-dated him. As such, it corresponds to a more generic notion of the monetizable value issuing from the produce of land (over and above its normal cost of production). On this view, already a century prior to Adam Smith's *The Wealth of Nations* and well before the full flowering of suspicions about landed property's connection to monopoly and wealth-siphoning, there was a clear basis for identifying land with rent in a way that made for a shadow conception of property that had the potential to cast a far less laudatory image than that which has ordinarily been drawn out from legal and economic thought for the purposes of explaining the progress of liberty and commercial prosperity in the West.[7]

Of course, this conception would not fail to gain prominence within property talk in the West, to the partial effect of casting a darkening shadow upon it there too. Even beyond Ricardo—for example, already

---

[6] It was not Ricardo who used the phrase 'unearned increment', which was popularized only much later in the nineteenth century through its association with John Stuart Mill. See John Stuart Mill, *Principles of Political Economy with Some of Their Applications to Social Philosophy* (W. J. Ashley ed., London: Longmans, Green and Co., 1909 [1848]), 817–18. Nor did Ricardo himself back any policy of taxing away the so-called unearned increment. (Even as applied to the colonial subcontinent, among the ranks of the early-nineteenth-century British political economists, it would be the elder Mill who would most vociferously back such a proposal.) Ricardo, instead, exercised his antagonism towards the landed gentry most visibly through his fealty to the new manufacturing and financial bourgeoisie. Throughout his life—and as was central to understanding his economics—the policy proposal he most overtly backed was, thus, to increase access to foreign grain, a position generally supported by the 'Manchester' lobby and that triumphed only after Ricardo's own death, with the lifting of the so-called Corn Laws in 1846. See Ricardo, *On the Principles of Political Economy*, 373–78.

[7] I explore this shadow conception of property in Faisal Chaudhry, 'Property as Rent', *St. John's Law Review* 94, no. 2 (2021): 363–438. For further consideration of how rent extraction and property concepts in the discourses of Western political economy fared in relation to Islamicate ideas about land control and surplus extraction, see, Faisal Chaudhry, 'Property and its Rule (in Late Indo-Islamicate and Early Colonial) South Asia: What's in a Name?' *Journal of the Economic and Social History of the Orient* 61 (2018): 920–75 at 944–47.

in *The Poverty of Philosophy*, his early rejoinder to the French socialist Pierre-Joseph Proudhon—Karl Marx was treating the identity of land as rent as a truism, calling '[r]ent ... property in land in its bourgeois state; that is, feudal property which has become subject to the conditions of bourgeois production'.[8] Elaborating, he even more emphatically notes as follows:

> [o]nce constituted as ground rent, ground property has in its possession only the surplus over production costs, which are determined not only by wages but also by industrial profit. It is therefore from the landowner that ground rent snatched a part of his income. Thus, there was a big lapse of time before the feudal farmer was replaced by the industrial capitalist. In Germany, for example, this transformation began only in the last third of the 18th century. It is in England alone that this relation between the industrial capitalist and the landed proprietor has been fully developed. So long as there was only M. Proudhon's *colonus*, there was no rent. The moment rent exists, the *colonus* is no longer the farmer, but the worker, the farmer's *colonus*. The abasement of the labourer, reduced to the role of a simple worker, day labourer, wage-earner, working for the industrial capitalist; the invention of the industrial capitalist, exploiting the land like any other factory; the transformation of the landed proprietor from a petty sovereign into a vulgar usurer; these are the different relations expressed by rent.[9]

As suggested earlier, however, in the colonial context this shadow conception of property based on the identity between land and rent proved especially precocious. Yet even while hiding in all the more plain sight, it has still been easy to miss. For outside those few, like Amiya Bagchi, who have made observations compatible with an appreciation of its full importance,[10] in grappling with the nature of British ideas about property

---

[8] Karl Marx, *The Poverty of Philosophy* (Marx/Engels Internet Archive, 1999 [1847]), 116.
[9] Ibid., 117–18.
[10] Contrasting the South Asian subcontinent in the early period of Company rule with England, Bagchi thus notes that

> [t]he proprietors under freehold or copyhold tenure did not hold the land *under the condition* that they had to make regular annual payments to the Crown or to some superior landlord and would have to forfeit their property if they failed to make the payment punctually. In the eighteenth century, they paid a land tax. But they paid

the tendency of scholars instead has been to pick up from the way colonial rule fixed people to land, transforming it from a substrate for fluid relations of social subordination and reciprocity into a concretized thing.[11] As Walter Neale so memorably suggested in a well-known essay, land tenure in (pre-colonial) India was directed at something inherently intangible—being organized, as in many African clan and customary systems, around ideas of 'fair shares' rather than any notion of a set and bounded 'estate' of the kind that became so prominent in England during the eighteenth century. Accordingly, the conventional wisdom about the colonial rule of property has remained that it signalled a shift away from land's inherently relational character as a basis of 'rule' and towards its inherently reified character as an object to own.[12]

> the tax because they were proprietors, and were not considered proprietors because they paid the tax. By contrast, in British India, under both the *zamindari* and the *raiyatwari* tenures, it was the prompt payment of a tax to the government every year that allowed the so-called proprietors to hold the property in land. The security of property was made subject to the superior requirement of security of public revenues from the land which after all constituted the sinews of British colonial expansion, and almost the principal *raison d'être* for maintenance of the colonial state. In an era in which revenue needs grew both for making remittances to Britain (as 'dividends' on East India Company's stock, and as expenses of the British Indian establishment in Britain) and for defraying the costs of further conquest in Asia (and even in Africa), the requirement of the security of private property in land was to be subordinated to that of the security and size of the public revenue.
>
> Amiya Kumar Bagchi, 'Land Tax, Property Rights and Peasant Insecurity in Colonial India', *The Journal of Peasant Studies* 20, no. 1 (1992): 1–49 at 5–6 (emphasis in original). As one of the few scholars of modern South Asia who has seemed to fully appreciate this point, even for Bagchi it is registered largely in passing. Observations compatible with Bagchi's insight are usually made even more fleetingly, and, like Bagchi's own, thus tend to confine their focus to a commentary on the Company's proprietors rather than its notion of property. See e.g. Jon Wilson's trenchant but vanishing description of the '[l]anded proprietor' in the Company's Bengal as existing nowhere but in the 'ledger' and denoting only 'an individual with a financial relationship with the East India Company'. Jon E. Wilson, *The Domination of Strangers: Modern Governance in Eastern India, 1780–1835* (Basingstoke: Palgrave Macmillan, 2008), 123. Stepping outside the colonial context, it is worth clarifying that one finds ideas compatible with Bagchi's insight developed in more sustained ways in the study of the origins of money and its connection to taxation. See e.g. Michael Hudson and Cornelia Wunsch, eds., *Creating Economic Order : Record-Keeping, Standardization, and the Development of Accounting in the Ancient Near East* (Bethesda, MD: CDL Press, 2004) and David Graeber, *Debt: The First 5,000 Years* (New York: Melville House, 2011). Of course, in this last connection, one can go all the way back to George Friedreich Knapp, *The State Theory of Money* (London: Macmillan, 1924).

[11] See e.g. Gregory Kozlowski, *Muslim Endowments and Society in British India*, 33; Barbara D. Metcalf and Thomas R. Metcalf, *A Concise History of Modern India* (New York: Cambridge University Press, 2006), 78.
[12] Walter Neale, 'Land is to Rule', in *Land Control and Social Structure in Indian History*, ed. R. E. Frykenberg (Madison, WI: University of Wisconsin Press, 1969), 3–15 at 4–5, 10–11.

The point here, of course, is not to deny the role of British colonial rule in recasting agrarian relations in the subcontinent and catalysing what scholars have called processes of peasantization and sedantarization through new administrative forms.[13] However, it is to insist that overlooking or simply remaining indifferent to the marked distance between property discourse in the Company's India versus the Anglo-common-law mainstream limits our understanding in important ways. Indeed, already from the second half of the eighteenth century, the colonial subcontinent's unique brand of property talk came to be situated at the very center of the debate in Bengal about who the 'true proprietors' of its soil were—whether the sovereign, its zamindar-magnates, or its ostensible cultivators (the so-called *raiyats*)—that proved so formative to structuring the Company's raj. Accordingly, the difficulty Company officialdom encountered in distinguishing any clear notion of ownership on the basis of sorting the inhabitants of agrarian society into landlords versus cultivating peasants, let alone so-called capitalist farmers, made strictly differentiating 'rent', as the return most closely associated with land, from 'profits' and 'wages' beside the point. To the contrary, it was the more basic idea of property as a flow of abstract monetizable value (above 'cost', whatever its exact components)—rather than the precise class shares into which that flow could be apportioned—that was the key point relative to the imperatives of early colonial rule. That not so much was the Company presiding over a capitalist transformation of agriculture in Bengal, as it was the case that colonial officialdom was touting itself as aiming to ostensibly bring such a form of agriculture into being, moreover, only serves to emphasize the point.

As for the more specific advantages of a public-sphere discourse focusing on proprietorship over rent, these were at least twofold. First, such a discourse allowed the Company to distinguish its own enterprise of government from those of regimes past, even as it created a 'more efficient, brutalized, and bastardized but, significantly, not dissolved' version of the pre-colonial state's political economy of surplus extraction.[14] Second, because the Company had only limited resources, especially

---

[13] See e.g. Sugata Bose and Ayesha Jalal, *Modern South Asia: History, Culture, Political Economy*, 2nd edn. (New York: Oxford University Press, 2004), 60–61 and Peter Robb, *A History of India* (New York: Palgrave, 2002), 272–73.

[14] Washbrook, 'Law, State and Agrarian Society in Colonial India', 661.

given its ongoing efforts at territorial expansion through the force of arms, a focus on entitlement over rent made the tasks of sovereign administration more manageable. After all, if property in the subcontinent was *really* a dominion over the monetizable value of agrarian produce, its guarantee required little more than committing to the proprietor's security of expectation by guaranteeing whatever subtraction was to be made therefrom.

It was from the starting point of its unique variety of absolute dominion talk, then, that the Company generated its equally unique doctrinal discourse of property. This is because insofar as it was rendered administrable and, hence, made legible to the state,[15] the already circumscribed notion of dominion over rent was restricted even further. Not only was absolute dominion talk in the public sphere thus translated, in most significant part, into an entitlement to a certainty of expectation regarding the proprietor's portion of the monetizable value issuing from the land, even this right was given definitional substance primarily through reference to the concomitant duty of revenue remittance back to the state. As a result, the administration of landed property the Company inaugurated in Bengal was marked for its way of blurring the boundary between the holding of a 'right' and the bearing of a 'duty' beyond recognition. Here, moreover, it is imperative to see that this pairing was not merely of the duty that was correlative with said right (to rent), since *that* duty necessarily had to be borne by those beyond the right holder themselves in virtue of the very definition of logical correlativity. Rather, it was an additive pairing—of a duty endowed upon the same individual, and, as such, one that notwithstanding its supplementary character soon came to overtake

---

[15] The larger relationship between Scott's notion of legibility (see 'Introduction' at note 8 and chapter 1 at note 86) and notions such as juridification or even formalization as well as the qualities of 'operativeness' and 'administrability' around which I have defined my own concept of doctrinal discourse in the previous chapter can be thought of as follows. The state formalizes social phenomena through doctrinal discourse. In so doing it creates articulable categories/propositions under which those phenomena may be administered. By rendering such phenomena administrable, they are also made legible, this being the ultimate outcome of formalization through doctrinal discourse. On this view, while juridification is one variety of doctrinal formalization, all formalization does not necessarily entail legal-doctrinal juridification. That is to say, juridification is a specific kind of formalization that involves a specific kind of doctrinal discourse, the articulable categories/normative pronouncements of which are not only administrable but also operative. However, in general, formalization requires only doctrinalization through a form of discourse the categories of which are administrable more than they are, necessarily, self-styled as operative—i.e. ostensibly connected together along vertical and horizontal dimensions of logical necessity.

the associated right as the property entitlement's true center of gravity amidst the East India Company's passage from trader to sovereign.

In this respect, the distinguishing feature of the Company's rule of property was not its preoccupation with fixing land/people to land and gridding physical space, as is so often said. Rather, it was its de-physicalizing tendency, with the object of both the designated proprietor's right and their ultimate burden comprising an equally fungible portion of the flow of value into which the irreducible stuff of land could be abstracted.

Suffice to say, this way of doctrinalizing absolute dominion talk represented a major departure from the Anglo-common-law mainstream. There, early-modern rhetoric venerating property undergirded an ostensibly absolute, unitary, and physicalist idea of right that was on the ascent at least by the mid-eighteenth century. In contrast to the Company's notion of the right to property as a basis for guaranteeing its holder an absolute security of expectation concerning the subtraction that would have to be made from the fungible flow of value comprising the land's rent, in the Anglo-common-law mainstream it was the unitary, exclusive, and physicalist idea of the property right as an entitlement over land itself that was most visible within doctrinal discourse.[16]

Amidst early colonial rule in the subcontinent even though the dominant notion of property (in land's rent) was ahead of its time in some ways—crafted as it was from the cutting edge of the upstart metropolitan discourse of (already pre-Smithian) political economy—in others it was retrograde, especially from the standpoint of the ontology of the legal it was able to support. Construed ironically, the problem was, in a sense, that the incipiently 'capitalist' overtones of the idea of dominion over the readily divisible and inherently fungible flow of value rent comprised made for a concept of juridical right that was insufficiently 'feudal' for

---

[16] On the 'physicalist' concept of the property right, see e.g. David Sugarman and Ronnie Warrington, 'Land Law, Citizenship, and the Invention of "Englishness": The Strange World of the Equity of Redemption', in *Early Modern Conceptions of Property*, eds. John Brewer and Susan Staves (New York: Routledge, 1996), 111–43; Sugarman and Rubin, 'Towards a New History of Law and Material Society in England', 28–42; Kenneth J. Vandevelde, 'The New Property of the Nineteenth Century: The Development of the Modern Concept of Property', *Buffalo Law Review* 29 (1980): 325–67; and Gregory Alexander, 'The Dead Hand and the Law of Trusts in the Nineteenth Century', *Stanford Law Review* 37, no. 5 (1985): 1189–266 at 1221. It is the later decomposition of this conception that would retrospectively be dubbed 'the disintegration of property'. See Thomas C. Grey, 'The Disintegration of Property', in *NOMOS: XXII: Property*, eds. J. Roland Pennock and John W. Chapman (New York: New York University Press, 1980), 69–85.

the purposes of sustaining the same variety of legal modernization as was then being underwritten in the West.[17] For in the central domains of the common-law world the absolute, unitary, and physicalist conception of landed right served to analytically conflate property with jurisdiction in a way that the Company's fixation on administering the duty of tax revenue payment alone clearly did not.

Of course, relative to the political economy of early colonial rule, whether precociously 'capitalist' or insufficiently 'feudal', prioritizing the duties of propertied entitlement over its concomitant rights cannot be seen as wholly surprising. Indeed, as one Home Civil Service member and past officer in the Company's army put it shortly before the transfer of power, while '[t]here are fifty different ways in which the English tax-gatherer may get at the poor man ... in India the approaches to the mud hut of the labourer are few; and the tax-gatherer must advance by them or keep away altogether'.[18] In short, the land-revenue demand had an ongoing—and even intensified—importance to the Company that it could not easily set aside, even notwithstanding its self-styled identity as an agent of 'improvement' unlike ancien régimes of the subcontinent's past. Nor do recent efforts tending to require that we partially revise previous scholarly assessments of the Company's intensification of the land-revenue demand[19] fundamentally alter this conclusion, especially insofar as they trade the previous emphasis on the supposedly increased 'appetite' for tax extraction for one that now concentrates more on the increased 'efficacy' with which a moderately heightened appetite was pursued.[20]

---

[17] The term 'feudal' should not be read to imply that Norman England was already characterized by a unitary, exclusive, and physicalist view of property. Indeed, under the Conqueror's regime of feudal property it was not land that was held so much as it was reciprocal incidents and services that were personally owed. Here, therefore, I am using 'feudal' only in the broader sense of the term according to which the system of 'estates in land' that replaced a regime of pure tenurial relations can be called 'feudal'. On the distinction between varieties of feudalism in the European context see F. L. Ganshof, *Feudalism*, Philip Grierson, trans. (Toronto: University of Toronto Press, 1964), ch. 3.

[18] John William Kaye, *The Administration of the East India Company: A History of Indian Progress* (London: Richard Bentley, 1853), 421 (quoted in Douglas M. Peers, 'Gunpowder Empires and the Garrison State: Modernity, Hybridity, and the Political Economy of Colonial India, circa 1750–1860', *Comparative Studies of South Asia, Africa and the Middle East* 27, no. 2 (2007): 245–58 at 254).

[19] The revisionist position has been associated with historians like C. A. Bayly and P. J. Marshall. For a summary, see T. Robert Travers, '"The Real Value of the Lands": The Nawabs, the British and the Land Tax in Eighteenth-Century Bengal', *Modern Asian Studies* 38, no. 3 (July 2004): 517–58 at 519–20.

[20] Douglas M. Peers, 'Gunpowder Empires and the Garrison State', 254.

Regardless, to assert that the Company's discourse of property (in rent) was not 'feudal' enough to sustain legal modernization of the kind that was transpiring in parallel in the central domains of the common-law world may still strike the reader as counter-intuitive.[21] After all, it is routine to understand the difference between modern land relations under 'capitalism' and those that were characteristic of 'feudalism' in terms of a decline in the very powers of extra-economic coercion that the lord's manorial jurisdiction once allowed over subordinates. (Indeed, this is the insight that the earlier quoted passage from Marx culminates in when we find him referencing the landed proprietor's transformation from 'petty sovreign' to 'vulgar usurer'.) However, proceeding exclusively on the basis of such an understanding makes it all too easy to miss the important difference there existed between the 'modern' concept of property in legal versus economic thought. In the central domains of the common-law

[21] To claim that the 'modern' idea of legal rights began as physicalist should not be seen as contradicted by observations one finds commonly enough made about how already by late medieval times the common law had managed to eschew Roman legal ideas about *dominion* as a direct relationship between its holder and the material substrate of the earth. See e.g. Kevin and Susan Gray, *Land Law*, 5th edn. (New York: Oxford University Press, 2007), ch. 1 (arguing that the common law has long regarded time as a fourth dimension of property). After all, one should not overestimate the degree to which the medieval conceptual system was based on denying the possibility of any 'direct ownership of land outside the *allodium* ... of the crown' and instead, as per the doctrinal discourse of the estates system, insist on the possibility of owning 'a *slice in time in the land*' alone. Ibid., 15. This view is as much the product of the modern analyst's de-physicalized understanding of the right to property as it is of any express vision on the basis of which the doctrinal discourse of the estates system was originally fashioned. Relatedly, one should also not fail to see that as an ensemble of doctrinal concepts the estates system was an instrument for moving away from parsing land control strictly in terms of the categories of tenurial relation. Limiting non-allodial title by time, as through the notion of holding an estate of fixed duration, was precipitated by a need to reckon with land control in more highly material terms than previously while still keeping intact the idea of the king as the supreme proprietor of the English realm. Here, one also must not forget that the triumph of the estates system was punctuated by various other transitions that were yet to come—like, for example, the rise of trespass and ejectment as forms of action between 1600 and 1800. These forms displaced the older real actions even as they revitalized 'a conception of an abstract right of' ostensibly 'absolute ownership'. See William Holdsworth, *An Historical Introduction to Land Law* (Oxford: Clarendon Press, 1927), 182. Likewise, it was after the triumph of the conceptual system of estates that the even more significant transition away from the notions of 'seisin' and 'disseisin' would take place, not to mention the roughly parallel decline of the distinction between legal and equitable interests in land. By the late eighteenth century, these previous moments of transition would prove themselves important prerequisites for the later revitalization of the idea of property as an ostensibly absolute (physical) dominion. Ibid., 176–88, especially at 185. Indeed, that they were helps to explain why in the twentieth century the 'reformed' common law preserved only the estates of the fee simple and term of years. Finally, of course, all of this is to say nothing of the biggest transition that was yet to come in the early-modern period with the ongoing rise of capitalism and the concomitant commodification of land, which was clearly, in its own right, a major factor in precipitating a physicalist conception of property.

world, to say nothing of its continental counterpart, the highly intuitive archetype of property as a unitary realm of landed jurisdiction was key to translating enlightenment-era natural rights discourse into an administratively viable form as an ostensibly absolute doctrinal ability to exclude. Only on the basis of this archetype was it possible to extrapolate a notion of legal right in general from the notion of the right to property, in particular.[22] For it was the archetype of an ostensibly absolute, unitary, and physical space of dominion that made it feasible to imagine that legal reason operated in a way that involved nothing more, in essence, than deciding who had 'the' right to property.[23] From the foundational deductive premise of the property right so conceived in doctrinal discourse, the casuistry of judicial administration could then, itself, be

[22] Vandevelde gives the best description of the way in which the physicalist conception of the right to property functioned as a basis for such extrapolation:
> [a]t the beginning of the nineteenth-century, property was ideally defined as absolute dominion over things. Exceptions to this definition suffused property law: instances in which the law declared property to exist even though no 'thing' was involved or the owner's dominion over the thing was not absolute. Each of these exceptions, however, was explained away. Where no 'thing' existed, one was fictionalized. Where dominion was not absolute, limitations could be camouflaged by resorting to fictions, or rationalized as inherent in the nature of the thing or the owner. The result was a perception that the concept of property rested inevitably in the nature of things and that recognition of some things as the object of property rights offered a premise from which the owner's control over that thing could be deduced with certainty. The perceived inevitability of this definition of property legitimated the concept. At the same time, the serviceability of property as a premise from which legal relations could be deduced permitted courts to use the concept to fix the boundaries of dominion between private individuals and between the individual and the state. Property law thus appeared to settle controversies while simultaneously legitimating, and even necessitating, the result. Vandevelde, 'The New Property of the Nineteenth Century', 328–29.

[23] In the English context, an instructive case in point can be found in the career of the land-law doctrine of the equity of redemption. Long-standing in the common law and originating as a measure of protection for debtors, the doctrine took on a new prominence in the second half of the seventeenth century as connected to the preservation of large fortunes in landed wealth by allowing owners who borrowed on the security of their estates to avoid their bargains in the event of an inability to meet repayment obligations. (Because they retained an equity interest, courts allowed landed owners to 'redeem' their mortgaged interest even after the lender's right to foreclose was activated.) In the context of the rising importance of absolute dominion talk, the equity to redeem started to be reconceived as an 'absolute' estate in land that the borrower held in its own right. Even as it became an increasingly important mechanism for shielding land from the free play of market forces, once the equity of redemption was cast as a unitary and absolute right to property it increasingly came to seem self-evident that the right to redeem was part of the owner's dominion. Settling such cases then became a matter of simply identifying the holder of said property right, even notwithstanding how their equity could just as well have been recast as a politically motivated subtraction from the creditor's own 'property right' to begin with. See Sugarman and Warrington, 'Land Law, Citizenship, and the Invention of "Englishness"'.

increasingly reimagined as a form of 'practical jurisprudence'. The otherwise mundane activity of settling disputes thus became nothing less than the adjudicatory deciphering of the true nature and inner order of the systematic and self-contained phenomenon in the world that went by the name of 'the law'.

Speaking broadly, then, in the West, already by the mid- to late eighteenth century this sequence of imaginative transformations was securing the ground on which to foot a conception of the law's ontologically integral unicity. For if legal right was grounded in the unquestionably *real* stuff of landed and empropertied space, then it was only appropriate that the law writ large be hypostatized as a part of the world's irreducible ontic fabric.

* * *

As for the second unique feature of the gap between discourse about property under the Company's raj and its discourse of administration, it both followed from and reinforced the first. Constituted neither by an equivalent ordinary-language discourse of absolute dominion nor the same doctrinal discourse of physicalist right-holding as in the West, property in early colonial South Asia failed to be internalized into the ontology of the legal in the way that was ongoing in the mainstream of the common-law world. Instead, under the Company, discourse about property and discourse about law overlapped mainly to the extent that an older, more circumscribed, and decidedly early-modern view of the ontology of the legal—of precisely the kind that was being displaced in the West—was recognized. On that view, the focus was on 'the laws' that factored into certain branches of sovereign administration more than it was on 'the law' considered as an autonomous and infinitely generative system for rational ordering according to norms and conceived as capable of governing all forms of inter-subjective relations, whether 'social', 'economic', or 'political'.

What thus emerged from the formative period of early British rule in the Indian subcontinent was a discourse about the rule of law as one among a limited number of forms of political constitution into which sovereign governance could be organized. The basic juxtaposition of a lawful and a despotic form of political constitution came down to whether fixed and certain 'laws' were deemed to exist that could prevent the administration of justice from becoming arbitrary. In the context of penal justice and certain aspects of inter-subjective civil relations, then, such rules of decision could be made into a symbol for a rule of law in the sense of a limitation on discretionary decision-making. According to this vision, laws were to the administration of justice as part was to whole. That is, relative to a brand of discourse about law that privileged political constitutionism over legal scientism, the ontology of the legal was necessarily circumscribed. This is because the administration of justice into which the legal directly factored was just one of several administrative tasks that defined sovereignty as a practical endeavour. As such, it was on a par with the administration of taxation, trade, or war, which did not necessarily answer to *legal* bases of normativization, while being no less legitimate for that being so.

Amidst the Company's ascent to ruling power, the administration of property in land's rent was a case in point. For along with legal administration proper the administration of the land revenue was one of the two key tasks that defined the Company's sovereignty in its Presidency areas as a day-to-day reality. As was initially the case in the Bengal Presidency, the task was sometimes left to be handled under the 'revenue jurisdiction' of civil courts; in other cases, as outside of Bengal, it could instead be left to the 'judicial function' of executive revenue officers. Relative to the constitutionist outlook, however, in neither case did it have to be seen as normatively unmoored merely because the basis of decision on which it proceeded was different from the 'laws' that made for ostensible certainty in the administration of justice proper.

* * *

In the sections of this chapter that follow, I take up these two unique features of the gap between public-sphere discourse about property and the doctrinal discourse of property in the colonial subcontinent in greater detail, considering them in reverse order. The discussion begins by looking at the two-decade period after the Battle of Plassey in 1757 and the Company's initial transition from trader to sovereign in the Bengal Presidency. More specifically, I focus on what I have been calling the discourse of early-modern 'constitutionism' that surrounded the Company's first attempts at comprehensive revenue reform under Warren Hastings' governor generalship. I then turn to the two-decade period after 1772, marked as it was by increasingly contentious debates about permanently settling the duty of land-revenue payment at a fixed rate in perpetuity on Bengal's zamindars. Here, more specifically, I reconsider the significance of the proposals for doctrinalizing the *zamindari* right to property in rent that were eventually made manifest under Governor General Cornwallis starting in 1793.

4.2 The Context of the Company's Advent to Power in Bengal

In the several decades prior to Cornwallis' famed Permanent Settlement regulations of 1793, the Company was beset by a climate of crisis as it negotiated its early passage form trader to sovereign.[24] The first step in this process took place when its armies defeated the breakaway Mughal governor of Bengal, the nawab Siraj ud-Daulah, and his French allies in 1757 at the river hamlet of Palashi. In the wake of the famed 'Battle of Plassey' the Company's military leader, Colonel Robert Clive, was catapulted to a position of prominence that led the Court of Directors in London to appoint him to the position of Governor for the province after his initial retirement to England in 1760. However, Clive's relocation back to Calcutta in 1765 was less a reward for his earlier triumph than a symbol of the Company's increasing concern with conditions in Bengal in the aftermath of Plassey. Siraj ud-Daulah's defeat had marked more a beginning than an end to turbulence, with the Company's drive for military supremacy continuing for another seven years and culminating only in 1764 with the Battle of Buxar (in contemporary Bihar). Only then did the Company achieve its definitive victory, defeating the newly allied forces of Shah Alam II, the titular Mughal Emperor, the nawab of Awadh, and Mir Qasim, the new nawab of Bengal and son of the puppet governor the Company had backed as Siraj ud-Daulah's replacement. Alongside the strains of ongoing warfare, the challenges of taking an expanded role in Bengal's internal governance very quickly embroiled the Company in controversy over its perceived culture of budgetary largesse, bribery, and

---

[24] P. J. Marshall, *The Making and Unmaking of Empires. Britain, India, and America, c. 1750–1783* (New York: Oxford University Press, 2005), ch. 7.

private profiteering by its own servants as well as other European traders operating in the countryside.

The Company's structural position in Bengal was thus such that its concern over clamping the financial siphon of corruption was bound to function as justification for further entrenching itself as overlord of the province. Prior to its victory at Buxar, aside from the profits of its business operations the Company enjoyed limited control over sources of finance internal to Bengal's economy, with its main resource consisting of rights to the revenue of some forty-odd villages it procured in increments over the course of the previous decades from land near its factory/fortification at Calcutta. Apart from the supplement provided by the revenues it drew from the so-called twenty-four *parganas* it was awarded after Plassey, the Company had to garner means of payment for the goods it was acquiring in Bengal (and other parts of the subcontinent) for the purposes of re-export on the world market through various external financial flows.[25] These included capital raised at home in Britain through joint stock offerings, direct government support from the Crown-in-Parliament, and other means of coaxing bullion out of Britain and into South Asia.

Playing on the renewed politics of dissension that broke out between the nawabs and the Mughal emperor after the defeat of their alliance at Buxar, Clive immediately sought to make a deal with the beleaguered Shah Alam II in order to bolster the Company's financial position. In exchange for guaranteeing regular payment (of 2.6 million *sicca* rupees) to the central treasury—and thereby breathing renewed life into the titular sovereignty of the emperor—the Company was recognized as diwan, or head of revenue administration, for a breakaway area comprising parts of Bengal, Bihar, and Orissa. The great promise of this arrangement for the Company was in the way it offered to limit its reliance on the importation of bullion from Britain and, thereby, to help insulate it from the increasingly vociferous accusations it faced at home about 'draining' national wealth. With the revenues of Bengal, Bihar, and Orissa, the Company had finally acquired a path to apparent financial self-sufficiency, seeming to have acquired a mechanism to fund both its so-called 'investment' in the

---

[25] The twenty-four parganas were territories administered in Mughal times as part of the port at Saptagaram (in the contemporary district of Hooghly in West Bengal). The *zamindaris* of these areas, along with other small administrative units, were conferred upon the Company in 1758 by the new British-supported nawab, Mir Jaffar.

Indian goods and raw materials it was purchasing and the expansion of its apparatus of rule.

As Douglas Peers notes, of the Mughal Empire's estimated annual revenue of 30 million pounds sterling, the Company's eighteenth-century conquests alone had secured an equivalent of 20 per cent, or nearly six million pounds sterling, for its own coffers. That sum compares to the 5.7 million pounds commanded by the Marathas and the 2.4 million pounds its other main opponent in Mysore could lay claim to.[26] Of course, other factors at play in Bengal (and beyond) would soon reveal the Company's dream of land-revenue-based self-sufficiency to be more apparent than real as new military line items continued to swell its expenditures.[27] Accordingly, one must not forget the less visible facets of the Company's financial arrangements, especially since they would become more crucial in the long run as its evolving military-fiscal state leveraged an ability to summon various kinds of debt, including through drawing on its own personnel as private creditors. (This latter factor was among those contributing to the sense—both contemporaneous with the Company's early transition to sovereign and in retrospect among historians like Holden Furber, who have perhaps too easily taken it at face value—that the Company was in thrall to privateering corruption.)[28]

Yet even if more cumulatively significant in the end, this less visible face of debt in the Company's arrangements for financing its commercial and sovereign affairs can hardly be separated from the more visible one. First, the most noteworthy periods of so-called deficit finance came only well into the nineteenth century, far removed from the heyday of post-Plassey controversy in Bengal, as the Company continued its pursuit of military conquest and territorial expansion across the subcontinent for at least a half-century after becoming the *diwan* of the eastern Presidency.[29]

[26] Douglas M. Peers, 'Gunpowder Empires and the Garrison State', 254.
[27] As Jon Wilson explains, by the middle of the 1780s 'the British exchanged geopolitical uncertainty for financial insolvency', with the Company's post-Buxar ability to draw on Bengal's land revenues encouraging the demand that it bear the costs of battle itself. By the time it signed the Peace of Mangalore in 1784 the need to pay its armies in Bombay and Madras left Calcutta in excess of three million pounds in debt to its creditors, the lion's share of which consisted of unpaid treasury orders. See Wilson, *The Domination of Strangers*, 48.
[28] Compare, generally, Holden Furber, *John Company at Work: A Study of European Expansion in India in the late Eighteenth Century* (Cambridge: Harvard University Press, 1948); Travers, ''The Real Value of the Lands', 554–57; and Peers, 'Gunpowder Empires and the Garrison State', 255–58.
[29] Ibid., 255.

Second, even with respect to the earlier period, whatever significance debt-based financing had for the Company, whether as emanating from money markets in London or from native capitalists looking for a seemingly sure bet in the subcontinent, it cannot be separated from the apparent creditworthiness its front-facing control over Bengal's land revenue depicted to the world at large.

At the same time, the changes the Company underwent after 1757 also meant that by the end of the 1760s it had evolved into 'a highly complex network of interconnected interest groups, straddling several different political systems' and making it 'vulnerable to shocks and stimuli from many different directions' at once.[30] As a result, early accusations of financial corruption naturally melded with a call from the Court of Directors in London to increase the involvement of the Company's own personnel in the collection of revenue from the *diwani* territories. Underlying the call was a mounting concern over the juxtaposition of the Company's professed role in Bengal as a commercial enterprise and its effective role as a governing authority. The growing fear that a runaway authority was mismanaging the province was only exacerbated by the terrible famine of 1770, which is thought to have taken the lives of one-fifth of Bengal's population. While the apotheosis of the famine followed from several earlier years of weak rains and failed harvests, the previous decade of warfare the Company had instigated or involved itself in clearly played its own crucial role in precipitating catastrophe.[31]

All told, then, by the middle of the 1770s the sense that the Company was in over its head had evolved into an outcry over a full-fledged crisis of governance in north-eastern India. This, moreover, entailed alarm about both the Company's governance of the territories it had won in the subcontinent and Westminster's governance of an entity to which it

---

[30] Travers, *Ideology and Empire*, 40.
[31] See Sugata Bose, *Peasant Labour and Colonial Capital: Rural Bengal Since 1770* (New York: Cambridge University Press, 1993), 14. The famine hit hardest in the eastern parts of Bengal and Bihar. As Bose emphasizes, rather than a Malthusian reverberation in the face of a population level that had become excessive, the famine was the result of a pre-existing context of relative labour deficit and, in the 1760s, low grain prices arising partly from a decline in the money supply. Moreover, the upswing in prices after the crop failures of 1768 and 1769 far exceeded what would have been commensurate with a shortfall in supply from natural factors alone. The Company's practice of stockpiling provisions for its troops, for example, contributed to a drying up of grain loans. Ultimately, rather than the forces of nature it was a crisis of 'exchange entitlements to vulnerable social groups that turned "the dearth into a famine"'. Ibid., 17–18.

was expected to continue granting juridical lifeblood through chartered monopoly even as it clearly was becoming more than a commercial enterprise. With Lord North's Regulating Act of 1773, the appointment of Warren Hastings as first Governor General of Bengal proved emblematic of both crises. It also proved indicative of Parliament's preferred way of jointly addressing them: namely, by blessing the Company in more openly asserting sub-sovereignty over its territories in South Asia at the very same time as wresting control of Indian affairs away from the Company's London-based Court of Directors.[32]

Against this backdrop, Hastings became not only a leading exponent of reorganizing the Company's administration but also increasingly a target for accusations that he embodied the old corruption. When he retired from Indian service in 1784, of course, those accusations would go on to finally overtake him, with the famed Edmund Burke leading the Parliamentary campaign to charge Hastings with high crimes and misdemeanours that resulted in his celebrated impeachment in 1787 and the beginning of his trial the next year.

Hastings' eventual acquittal in 1795 would come only after another several long years. Yet with exoneration following so soon on the heels of the new Governor General in Calcutta's issuing of the regulations mandating the Permanent Settlement and various other changes to the Company's executive and judicial institutions, an era had come to an end. By the middle of the 1790s the debate about governance in Bengal had graduated once and for all beyond the preoccupation that initially spawned it, having to do with concerns over personal corruption and the unchecked structure of Company rule. From this point on, controversy relating to the Company's government increasingly took shape through an evolving culture of public contemplation, which focused on the supposed effects of British 'improvement' on a society in the subcontinent thought to be steeped in tradition.[33]

---

[32] From this point onwards, the Company's policies in India were increasingly an extension of the Crown-in-Parliament's redoubled effort to take control over its chartered corporation. See P. J. Marshall, *Bengal: The British Bridgehead: Eastern India, 1740–1828* (New York: Cambridge University Press, 1987), 98–99.

[33] David Arnold, 'Agriculture and "Improvement" in Early Colonial India: A Pre-History of Development', *Journal of Agrarian Change* 5, no. 4 (October 2005): 505–25.

4.3 Asiatic Despotism as a Form of Political Constitution and an Ontology of the Laws

At least since the publication of Ranajit Guha's celebrated *A Rule of Property for Bengal* in 1963, the Permanent Settlement of 1793 has been made out to be a culmination of the several decades preceding it.[34] In more recent work on the intellectual landscape of early colonial Bengal, however, a more refined periodization has been offered. According to Robert Travers, in the time between 1757 and the initial attempt at revenue reform in 1772 it was less an incipiently modern ideology of free capitalist property that animated colonial officialdom than it was a 'language of the ancient Mughal constitution'.[35] Therefore, well before Hastings' great antagonist on the Governor General's Council, Phillip Francis, authored the first clear plan for settling the duty of revenue payment on the zamindars in perpetuity in 1776 the Company's ongoing efforts at transformation into a sovereign were being facilitated by a very different idiom of rule. As Travers suggests, the privileging of a language of Mughal constitution was linked to a combination of factors. These included a tendency among Company officials to regard 'their government as a form of inheritance from the Mughal empire even into the 1770s and 1780s', which was, itself, clearly underpinned by a need to 'manipulat[e] ... Mughal institutions of governance' if British rule was to succeed.

Consistent with a broader spectrum of what one might call, for lack of a better word, revisionist opinion among scholars of South Asia both

---

[34] See Guha, *A Rule of Property for Bengal*. A sizeable literature now provides a more intricate view than Guha's on the actual impact of the permanent settlement on land relations in north-eastern India. Rather than any thoroughgoing transformation in the composition of the upper levels of agrarian society, it is most conventional now to follow Ratnalekha Ray in observing that the permanent settlement brought with it, above all, was 'a great circulation of titles'. Ratnalekha Ray, *Change in Bengal Agrarian Society, 1760–1850* (New Delhi: Manohar, 1980), 252. See also, Bernard S. Cohn, 'Structural Change in Indian Rural Society, 1596–1885' in *Land Control and Social Structure in Indian History*, ed. Frykenberg, 53–121, Binay Bhushan Chaudhuri, 'Land Market in Eastern India, 1793–1940 Part II: The Changing Composition of the Landed Society', *Indian Economic & Social History Review* 12 (1975): 133–67, Rajat K. Ray and Ratnalekha Ray, 'Zamindars and Jotedars: A Study in Rural Politics in Bengal', *Modern Asian Studies* 9, no. 1 (1975): 81–102, Eric Stokes, 'Agrarian Society and the Pax Britannica in Northern India in the Early Nineteenth Century', reprinted in *The Peasant and the Raj: Studies in Agrarian Society and Peasant Rebellion in Colonial India* (New York: Cambridge University Press, 1978), 63–89, M. S. Islam, *The Permanent Settlement in Bengal: A Study of its Operation 1790–1819* (Dhaka: Bangla Academy, 1979), Marshall, *Bengal: The British Bridgehead*, 144–58, and Bose, *Peasant Labour and Colonial Capital*, 68–79.

[35] See generally, Travers, *Ideology and Empire*.

in specifics[36] and more generally,[37] Travers emphasizes how the proliferation of the language of Mughal constitution 'contributed to a wider European revaluation of cruder stereotypes of Asiatic despotism'.[38] Even if such a language/idiom was destined to recede in importance in the years immediately preceding 1793, still, during the two decades before this it remained more than just the 'ornamental aspect of imperial ideology' that historians have, at best, previously made it out to be. In fact, seen in such a manner the persistence of the language of Mughal constitution attests to the way 'that "modern" European empires had their roots in "early modern" conceptions of politics', which 'prioritized "province, lineage, and custom" as the "crucial markers of legitimacy"'. In turn, it equally proves demonstrative of how colonial ideology in the subcontinent started out being far more accommodative of native society than is commonly understood based on assumptions about the theory of oriental despotism's being the only way available for making sense of Asia's political past.[39]

There is little doubt that scholarly work like that which I have been discussing forces us to reconsider the broader intellectual currents that informed the early colonial public sphere in Bengal. Indeed, this is all the more the case insofar as the Company not only borrowed against the language of Mughal constitution but also, in building the 'culture of petitioning' undergirding its administration of justice, from key motifs and documentary forms of 'Persianate law', as Travers, himself, so strikingly has gone on to show.[40] At the same time, as much as any attempt to vet the question of the eighteenth-century transition to colonial rule in terms of pure rupture rather than continuity,[41] there is bound to be a tension in highlighting the transitory persistence of a language of

---

[36] See e.g. Wilson, *The Domination of Strangers* and Dodson, *Orientalism, Empire and National Culture*.

[37] See e.g. Joan-Pau Rubiés, 'Oriental Despotism and European Orientalism: Botero to Montesquieu', *Journal of Early Modern History* 9, nos. 1-2 (2005): 109-80.

[38] Robert Travers, 'Ideology and British expansion in Bengal, 1757-72', *The Journal of Imperial and Commonwealth History* 33, no. 1 (2005): 7-27 at 20.

[39] Travers, *Ideology and Empire*, 18.

[40] Travers, *Empires of Complaints*, 80.

[41] For a better sense of what has been a wide-ranging and often heated debate, see M. Athar Ali's not impartial, but eminently informative historiographical entry into the fray. M. Athar Ali, 'The Mughal Polity—A Critique of Revisionist Approaches', *Modern Asian Studies* 27, no. 3 (1993): 699-710.

Mughal constitution.[42] For even if it was grounded in characteristically early-modern and pre-colonial ways of thinking about politics and law, it can be made to speak to the question of transition only if simultaneously understood as some kind of product of the particular circumstances the Company faced after 1757. On the retreat of those circumstances, then, we are inevitably left wondering if we have simply deferred, or even heightened, the moment of rupture. In this respect, 1793 is liable to appear an even bigger moment of departure, with the idiom of Mughal constitution becoming one more inheritance from the past to be added to what disappeared in the face of the new-found reality of the Cornwallis regime's 'self-consciously reformist "permanent settlement"', 'elaborate code of administrative regulations', and 'rule by law'.[43]

* * *

A perhaps different, or at any rate complementary, vista can be opened on the concerns underlying recent scholarship on the period before the Permanent Settlement of 1793 if we focus more on how the language of Mughal constitution—like the language of oriental despotism—was just one instance of a broader early-modern approach to typifying the forms that political organization could take. In theories of political *constitutionism*, as I will call them—as distinct from those of modern constitutionalism—sovereignty and legality were generally set in relation to one another in the manner touched on earlier while discussing the Company's decidedly early-modern ontology of the legal. In an intellectual constellation of such a kind, neither was the main watchword 'the law', nor the main preoccupation the relation of the latter to the two triads of economy/society/polity and legislation/execution/adjudication. Instead, the main focus was on 'the laws' that laid down the basis for a sound administration of justice, which alongside various other

---

[42] As far as it is made explicit, Travers' contention is that 'the contested history of the ancient Mughal constitution cannot be used to support a theory of continuity at the level of political discourse'. At the same time, he does also note how the language of Mughal constitution 'serve[d] to blur the edges between the categories of "British" and "indigenous" politics in the eighteenth century'. Travers, *Ideology and Empire*, 250-51.

[43] See e.g. Wilson, *The Domination of Strangers*, 46 (noting that '[i]f claims about the origin of India's modern colonial state in 1793 are exaggerated, Cornwallis' new constitution involved a significant and self-conscious rupture with earlier styles of governance nonetheless'). See also Travers, 'Ideology and British expansion in Bengal', 20–21.

extra-legal administrative tasks, defined sovereignty as a practical affair. In this respect, rather than as an exponent of small state laissez faire, for example, Adam Smith was simply a political thinker in keeping with his times when declaring that 'little else is requisite to carry a state to the highest degree of opulence from the lowest barbarism' than 'peace, easy taxes, and a tolerable administration of justice'.[44]

Understood in this way, a fundamental instability characterizes political constitutionism as a conceptual framework, with the bases for distinguishing between the various forms it was predicated on theorizing being either ill-defined or illusory, at best. Even Montesquieu was hard-pressed to evade this basic problem in his canonical formulation of oriental despotism in *The Spirit of the Laws*. For the deeper understanding connecting despotism and what were supposed to be other more legitimate constitutional forms like monarchism or republicanism was thrown into sharp relief by the difficulty of trying to maintain the assertion that Asiatic states were entirely devoid of 'laws'. Of course, such a claim could always be made in the abstract, by way of stipulating a categorical difference between rulership in the West versus that in the East. The difference might even be further cashed out in terms of rulers in the West being a source of judgement constrained by 'fundamental laws' and their counterparts in the East being creatures of totalizing caprice.[45] Indeed, Montesquieu does argue as much, including by striking the tried-and-true distinction between the 'laws' that were to be found in republican or monarchical states and the mere 'mores and manners' that he saw as characteristic of despotic social formations.[46]

However, whenever such presumptive stipulation required more considered elaboration, the limited nature of the ontology of the legal that went hand in hand with the constitutionist outlook meant that assertions about Asiatic lawlessness tended to fail. In Montesquieu's case, he is left with little option but to openly contradict his own positions as needed. We thus find him repeatedly doing so—for example, in the course of discussing the activities of legislators in despotic states,[47] while trying

---

[44] Quoted in Gerald M. Meier, *Biography of a Subject: An Evolution of Development Economics* (New York: Oxford University Press, 2005), 27.
[45] Charles de Secondat Montesquieu (Baron de), *The Spirit of the Laws* (New York: Cambridge University Press, 1989 [1748]), 17–19.
[46] Ibid., 314.
[47] Ibid., 236.

to understand the nature of imperial pronouncement in China,[48] when turning attention to retaliation as a key ethic informing legal regulation under despotism,[49] and simply through the very enterprise he undertakes, given its baseline concern with determining which *laws* were 'relative to' which forms of constitution.

To be sure, Montesquieu's inconsistency in maintaining the equation between a despotic constitution and a state of lawlessness may be partly due to the fact that his conception of the 'sorts of laws' by which people are governed was broader than the particular category he most sought to deny Asiatic states—namely, that of civil laws.[50] Thus, for Montesquieu, to be lacking in civil laws was not necessarily to be devoid of all other sources of normative guidance, which also included divine right, natural right, ecclesiastical right, the right of nations, the 'general and particular' political right, the right of conquest, and domestic right within the family; rather, it was only to be devoid of the source of what he calls civil right. Likewise, it may even be that Montesquieu's inconsistency in maintaining the equation between despotism and lawlessness was partly due to the fact that it was not necessarily the existence or non-existence of laws that was, for him, always most important. Instead, we repeatedly find his real focus turning to the existence or non-existence of the underlying factors creating differences in the 'general spirit' of the laws in any given place—like climate, religion, maxims of government, and so on.[51]

Nonetheless, in the end Montesquieu's focus on 'the laws' is still diffused across too many different meanings for there to be the requisite consistency needed to deny states with a supposedly despotic constitution such norms—even of whatever particular subtype he is most keen on denying them—altogether. If we simply look at his treatment of civil laws, for example, we see that it, too, is marked by equivocation. In relation to this subtype, which he sees as naming the generative force behind what he calls civil right, he explains that it is usually 'the division of lands' that is responsible for 'swell[ing] the civil code'. Here, more specifically, his point is to clarify why despotism goes hand in hand with lawlessness—for where all lands belong to the sovereign, he suggests, there is simply no

---

[48] Ibid., 126.
[49] Ibid., 93.
[50] Ibid., 494.
[51] Ibid., 310.

need for the type of laws to which the civil codes of states with legitimate constitutions are devoted.[52] Yet no sooner does Montesquieu spell out this line of reasoning than he also concedes that despotic governments often do, in fact, have extensive civil codes. To get around the apparent inconsistency in his position and try to reinstate what he started out trying to deny to states of so-called despotic constitution he is forced to arbitrarily reclassify their civil codes as 'religious codes' in disguise. The tension, however, persists—re-emerging, for example, as he turns to the 'civil laws appropriate for putting a little liberty in despotic government'. Here we find Montesquieu reckoning with the constraints many so-called despotic states did seem to place on judging, the discretionary nature of which was supposed to be the key feature in virtue of which they were to be classified as despotic in the first place. As he is once again forced to concede, despotic states were thus evidently not devoid of normative means for 'fix[ing] what is arbitrary', as per a description he would have clearly preferred to reserve for their non-despotic counterparts alone.[53]

Ultimately, then, the very feature—of civil laws—that is most important for Montesquieu to deny to despotic states is one he is repeatedly forced to credit to all forms of constitution upon considering their various practices of administering justice.[54] The blanket condemnation of despotism for being suffused by arbitrary caprice simply falls by the wayside when the need arises for any more sustained attention to the deliberative functions of judges, viziers, and tribunals in the proverbial East. To engage in a more granular, comparativist discourse about how different societies handled the settlement or redress of disputes was thus to court the need to recognize how much more united than divided despotic and non-despotic forms appeared when viewed as different species of the same fundamental genus of political constitution. For well beyond the West, in the constraints one could find on organized administrative casuistry it was simply too hard not to see something very much like the laws

---

[52] Ibid., 292–93, 73–74.
[53] Ibid., 211.
[54] As within the longer disciplinary history of the anthropology of law, it is upon the very same types of practices—relating to the administration of dispute settlement—that distinctions between law and non-law continue to break down into our own day. See e.g. Sally Falk-Moore, ed., *Law and Anthropology: A Reader* (Malden, MA: Blackwell, 2005), 65–100.

that factored into the administration of justice that had long underlain the ontology of the legal in the early-modern perspective more generally.

Montesquieu, of course, was not unique in this regard. If it was difficult to differentiate supposedly lawless despotism from lawful monarchism or republicanism this was due to the inherent instability of the early-modern discourse of constitutionism. Much the same, for example, is made evident in the work of another leading Frenchman who proved crucial to theorizing Asiatic despotism in early-modern times, François Bernier, whose famed *Travels in the Mogul Empire* focuses specifically on the subcontinent.[55] Bernier's well-known text dates from nearly a century prior to Montesquieu's *Spirit of the Laws*, not to mention the Company's advent to official power in South Asia. Yet even so, it draws on an analytic of despotism that is remarkably similar to the ostensibly more culturally attuned language of the ancient Mughal constitution that characterized the Company's formal transition to sovereignty in Bengal during the 1760s and 1770s. On the one hand, then, we find Bernier taking pains to ground his critical commentary on politics and society in the East in the alleged absence of any 'principle of *meum* and *tuum*, relatively to land or other real possessions' in places like 'Turkey, Persia, and Hindoustan'.[56] On the other hand, like Montesquieu—and, for that matter, Company officialdom in the aftermath of the Battle of Plassey—we also find Bernier frequently relinquishing the tendency to over-simplistically denigrate subcontinental political culture and traditions of governance.

Yet even so, no more than for Montesquieu was this necessarily due to some special purchase a respect for the Mughal past commanded over Bernier's imagination. More to the point may be that such moments of restraint followed, as if by necessity, from the very nature of political constitutionalism as an analytic, requiring as it did attention to the administration of justice as one of the key endeavours that defined sovereignty under any given form of constitution as a practical affair. This made more sustained consideration of such practices of administration in the subcontinent, together with the early-modern ontology of the legal it went

---

[55] Bernier's text was originally published in Paris in 1670. After achieving wide acclaim, a first attempt at partial English translation took place in 1672. See Irving Brock, 'Preface' in *Travels in the Mogul Empire*, vol. I, François Bernier, Irving Brock, trans. (London: W. Pickering, 1826 [1670]), vii.

[56] Bernier, *Travels in the Mogul Empire*, vol. I, 263.

hand in hand with, virtually inevitable. It was, thus, bound to be difficult, if not impossible, to maintain any notion that despotic government in the subcontinent really was premised on being categorically devoid of 'laws' in light of the undeniable constraints on its administration of justice that closer attention invariably revealed.

Not surprisingly, then, Bernier altogether dispenses with any suggestion that administrative practice under the Mughals testified only, at best, to the existence of 'mores' rather than 'laws'. Instead, he simply shifts focus to other more tangential questions—asking, for instance, how good the laws governing the Mughal administration of justice really were. In the same vein, he also questions whether Mughal laws really could be properly implemented, given the lack of any full separation of institutional powers, an ironic line of attack given the failure of the French—or, for that matter, the English—constitution, itself, to live up to any such ideal. As we find him holding forth:

> [i]f it be observed that there is no reason why eastern states should not have the benefit of good laws, or why the people in the provinces may not complain of their grievances to a grand Visir; or to the King himself; I shall admit that they are not altogether destitute of good laws, which, if properly administered, would render Asia as eligible a residence as any other part of the world. But of what advantage are good laws when not observed, and when there is no possibility of enforcing their observance? Have not the provincial tyrants been nominated by the same grand Visir and by the same King, who alone have power to redress the people's wrongs? and is it not a fact that they have no means of appointing any but tyrants to rule over the provinces? either the Visir or the King has sold the place to the Governor. And even admitting that there existed a disposition to listen to a complaint, how is a poor peasant or a ruined artisan to defray the expenses of a journey to the capital, and to seek justice at one hundred and fifty or two hundred leagues from home?[57]

Indeed, at other times, rather than trying to evade the apparent existence of constraints under a despotic constitution through the evergreen

---

[57] Ibid., 267.

method of asking how much laws that might look good on paper really were enforced in practice, Bernier simply opts to concede further ground—extrapolating to allow for the presence of in-built limits at other levels of despotic administration as well. The 'Great Mogol', he thus tells us, presided over a decentralized and veritably confederal structure of governance, 'comprehend[ing] several nations' over no one of which he was 'absolute Master' and each one of which 'still retain[ed] their own peculiar chiefs or sovereign', while often paying no more than a 'trifling' amount in tribute to the central treasury.[58]

More than a century before the Company's seizure of official power created whatever imperative it did to accommodate as much as to dominate, already in Bernier we find one of the key exponents of the discourse of oriental despotism modulating its tone considerably, even absent any external/circumstantial need to do so. On one level, there can be little doubt that this was because the early-modern concept of oriental despotism represented neither any simple 'application of a category inherited from Aristotle' nor solely a 'mental scheme that blinded Europeans to the perception of the true Orient'.[59] Especially in the period before the 1790s, as Jon Wilson reminds us, in both Britain and the subcontinent elements of a shared way of construing statecraft persisted 'based on a model of familiar relations between ruler and ruled' in which it was 'as if personal familiarity was an important aspect of political conduct' and 'governance was regarded as a form of face-to-face exchange'.[60]

On another level, however, it would be misleading to imagine that the residuum of early-modern discourse about law and politics in the Company's India had to either persist or (eventually) recede. That is, it also simply may have harnessed an inner capability to extend itself in new directions and towards new ends, including ones that corresponded to the shifting imperatives of a political economy of colonial rule that was evolving at whatever different tempos it may have been either before or after the Permanent Settlement. Likewise, it would be equally misleading to see in the holdover of early-modern ideas about politics and law only either an emblem of a heretofore unacknowledged identity between ruler

[58] Ibid., 230.
[59] Rubiés, 'Oriental Despotism and European Orientalism', 109.
[60] Wilson, *The Domination of Strangers*, 1.

and ruled, so long as it persisted, or their (eventually) complete alienation from one another, once it receded.

As per the argument I have started laying out in the present section of the chapter, in addition to whatever kind of ideological/intellectual resource the discourse of oriental despotism made for as a means of easing the Company's early transition from trader to sovereign in Bengal, it carried within itself other ideological/intellectual resources as well. As we shall see in the following sections, the underlying ontology of the legal that it played host to—focusing as it did on 'the laws' that factored into the administration of justice more than 'the law' as an infinitely generative system of rational ordering according to norms—was a case in point. Accordingly, not only may the discourse of oriental despotism in the incipient colonial public sphere have proved more impactful in the long run of British rule than in whatever transitional moment wherein it was most visible, but also more pliable than its demise—even if postponed from 1757 to 1793—may otherwise be liable to suggest.

4.4 Sound Laws, Secure Property: Public-Sphere Discourse in Bengal from 1757 to 1772

If selectively dispensing with an overly reductive view of South Asia's political past was as much a product of the inability to deny the existence of an orderly administration of justice in the so-called East as it was anything else, it puts into a different light not only the thought of Bernier and Montesquieu but also the culture of public debate that began developing around the Company after 1757. It is useful here to start by considering how Luke Scrafton, the director of the Company from 1765 to 1768, entered the fray over the success or failure of early colonial efforts at formal governance in Bengal. In his *Reflections on the Government of Indostan* he thus incredulously notes as follows:

> I am amazed to see, that all the writers have asserted, that there are no laws in this country; that the land is not hereditary; and that the emperor is universal heir. I am ready to allow, there are no written institutes; no acts of parliament; and that there is no power to controul the emperor; but I must assert, that they proceed in their courts of justice

by established precedents; that the lineal succession, where there are children, is as indefeasible here as in any country, that has no check on the supreme power; and that the emperor is heir to none but his own officers, Although the Tartars, from their roving life in their own wild country where they live in tents, require few laws, and no settled police, yet they could distinguish the use of them in the countries they conquered; and accordingly, both in China and India, they made no innovation, so that the old Gentoo laws still prevail. The most immutable of these is the hereditary right to all lands, which even extends to the tenants. The lord of the manor has an uncontested right, as long as he pays the usual tax to the government; so also the tenant under him cannot be removed while he pays his lord the usual rate; and the sum at which each acre is valued, as also the taxes to the government are wrote and preserved in the county books, and can never be exceeded. These laws were wisely instituted, as barriers against oppression, and were general, except for the demesnes of the crown, which on the expulsion of the great Rajahs families, fell to the Tartar conqueror and for the Jaghire lands, which are lands bestowed by the crown out of its demesnes to the Omrahs, for the support of their forces, which, on the death of the possessor, revert to the crown; but even this regards only the lordship of the lands; for under these the right of the tenants is indefeasible.[61]

Like Bernier writing one hundred years earlier or Montesquieu writing from thousands of miles away, it was the existence of 'laws' rather than 'the law' that Scrafton was most concerned with. Moreover, even like those with an ostensibly less conciliatory attitude to the subcontinent's past, for Scrafton as well claims about lawlessness were unsustainable in the face of the evident existence of orderly 'proceedings in court' in the Mughal domain. Such facts made it painfully clear that categorically distinguishing the forms of political constitution one found in the proverbial East from those in the West was highly suspect, especially given

---

[61] Luke Scrafton, *Reflections on the Government of Indostan: with a Short Sketch of the History of Bengal, from 1739 to 1765; and an Account of the English Affairs to 1758* (London: W. Richardson and S. Clark, 1763), 26–27.

the particular importance of organized casuistry in the exaltation of England's own supposedly unique rule-of-law tradition.[62]

Even apart from his ontology of 'the laws', in other ways as well Scrafton was following the theory of oriental despotism by tapping into its highly plastic foundation of constitutionist logic more than he was reinventing or deviating from it. Like Bernier, he paid lip service to the idea that the Mughal sovereign was completely without 'check', only to then elsewhere conclude that Mughal governance was hardly totalizing in scope. There was, then, little that was new in Scrafton's idea in the above passage that sitting at some remove from the oriental imperium of the 'Great Mogul' was an order of 'Gentoo laws' remaining intact. Indeed, even above the level of the 'Gentoo' order, like Montesquieu being forced to acknowledge that 'non-cultivating' peoples had more than just social 'mores', in the afore-quoted passage we find Scrafton having to allow that 'the Tartars', whom he situates as the subcontinent's ruling political stratum, had at least a 'few laws', despite the purported fact of their living simply by 'roving' within a 'wild country'.

Much the same ends up being true for Scrafton's greatest ostensible departure from the theory of oriental despotism, which comes through his recognition of the heritability of rights under Mughal rule. Here as well, understood relative to the logic of constitutionist forms in general rather than their oriental/Asiatic variety in particular, Scrafton's remarks appear to be routine more than uniquely marked by any accommodationist tendency. In other words, to maintain that at the level of 'Gentoo' society there existed heritable claims rooted in the control of land was hardly

---

[62] The ambivalence underlying Scrafton's thought recalls the reticence his contemporary Robert Orme expressed while considering the administration of justice:
>[i]ntelligent enquirers assert that there are no written laws amongst the Indians, but that a few maxims transmitted by tradition supply the place of such a code in the discussion of civil causes; and that the ancient practice, corrected on particular occasions by the good sense of the judge, decides absolutely in criminal ones. In all cases derived from the relations of blood, the Indian is worthy to be trusted with the greatest confidence; but in cases of property, in which this relation does not exist, as a cunning subtil people they are perpetually in disputes; and for the want of a written code the justice or injustice of the decision depends on the integrity or venality of the judge. Hence the parties prefer to submit their cause to the decision of arbitrators chose by themselves, rather than to that of the officers appointed by the government.

Robert Orme, *A History of the Military Transactions of the British Nation in Indostan from 1745. To which is prefixed a Dissertation on the Establishments Made by Mahomedan Conquerors in Indostan*, vol. I (London: John Nourse, 1763), 25.

antithetical to the discourse of despotism, considered more granularly, in its capacity as a *constitutionist* idiom. To the contrary, pontificating on the East's failure to develop private property only required that the perquisites of political superiors—as distinct from social ones—be understood to have been non-heritable. It was on just such a basis that the theory of oriental despotism distinguished what to this day is still commonly portrayed as the key difference between Western and non-Western 'feudalism';[63] even in Bernier's thought, for example, it was, thus, the non-heritability of Islamicate imperial benefices that animated the claim that Mughal bureaucratic functionaries were granted only pensions and offices drawn from land rather than the same direct and sustained control over the land, itself, that European feudatories could be (and are still) said to have traditionally enjoyed.[64] Yet even as, with one hand, we find Bernier putting his finger on Crown demesnes and the mere 'Jaghire' assignments made to Mughal 'Omrahs' in order to take away from the subcontinent part of the basis for private property as an essential prerequisite to a non-despotic constitution, insofar as these exceptions prove the rule of heritability at all levels below the imperial bureaucracy, we find him with little choice but to use the other to give another part of that same basis right back.[65]

If Scrafton's *Reflections on the Government of Indostan* was unique, it was thus mainly because it was the first in a series of polemical tracts and longer works from the 1760s that were meant to contextualize the state of the Company's affairs. Other prominent entries from the period included works by Henry Vansittart, the Company's governor in Bengal from 1759 to 1764,[66] William Watts, Chief of the Company's factory at Kasimbazar,[67]

---

[63] See e.g. Ira M. Lapidus, *A History of Islamic Societies*, 2nd edn. (New York: Cambridge University Press, 2002), 123–25 and Perry Anderson, *Lineages of the Absolutist State*, 1974 (New York: Verso, 1979), 497–500.

[64] Bernier, *Travels in the Mogul Empire*, vol. I, 5.

[65] The point was a staple of discussion at the time. See e.g. Orme, *A History of the Military Transactions of the British Nation in Indostan*, vol. I, 27.

[66] Vansittart began as a writer for the Company at one of its factories in Madras in 1745 at the age of thirteen. He came under Clive's good graces and was eventually appointed to the Governor's Council at Madras, playing an important role in staving off French advances. He was eventually picked by Clive to be his replacement as Governor at Fort William in Calcutta. He also published three volumes on his time in office. See Henry Vansittart, *A Narrative of the Transactions in Bengal, from the year 1760, to the year 1764* (London: J. Newbery, 1766).

[67] Watts was a long-time inhabitant of Bengal who was appointed by Clive as the Company's representative to the Nawab's court at Murshidabad; in this capacity he played an important role in engineering Siraj ud-Daulah's downfall. His *Memoirs of the Revolution in Bengal*, appearing

John Z. Holwell, the official who oversaw the twenty-four *parganas* and who later became a member of the Council at Fort William,[68] and Robert Orme, a surgeon and member of the council at Fort Saint George in Madras,[69] among others.[70] In the culture of public-sphere debate that collected around the Company, the speculative accounts these works offered of historical events in the subcontinent leading up to its early advent to a quasi-official role as sovereign proved central. Accordingly, it would be incomplete to read these texts only as being devoted to reiterating the theory of oriental despotism, or, in a sense, only as vehicles for its displacement by a distinct theory of the ancient Mughal constitution. For the other opportunity they could not but offer was to deploy an analytic drawing on key elements of the conceptual vocabulary of constitutionism, which, as I will emphasize further below, included more than just 'the laws' thought necessary for a sound administration of justice.

Whether in the course of more specifically defending or bemoaning the Company's early performance as ruler, therefore, in these works commentators like Vansittart, Watts, Orme, and Holwell ultimately showed how porous was the line between discourse about a rule of law, on the one hand, and about a rule of despotism, on the other. With his *Memoirs of the Revolution in Bengal*, for example, Watts sought to provide a 'short and perspicuous' account of the events surrounding the fall of the province's last independent nawab, Siraj ud-Daulah. Compared

in 1760, detailed Mir Jafar's rise to power while also considering the nature of Mughal government and the Company's role in the subcontinent more generally.

[68] Born in Dublin, Holwell first made his way to the subcontinent as a surgeon in 1731. His appointment as zamindar of the twenty-four parganas came in 1751, and he served for a time as a temporary governor in 1760 before he was dismissed for his views criticizing Vansittart. He authored a number of short tracts, statements, and letters on political happenings in Bengal. Various of these were collected in two important longer works—consisting mainly of official correspondence—under the title of *India Tracts* (London: T. Becket and P.A. De Hondt, 1764) and a three-volume work called *Interesting Historical Events, Relative to the Provinces of Bengal, and the Empire of Indostan* (London: T. Becket and P. A. De Hondt, 1765 to 1771)..

[69] Orme was born in Travancore to a father who was a surgeon in the Company's employ. He returned to the subcontinent as a writer for the Company from 1743 to 1753 and then was appointed to the Madras council after a brief time in England in 1754. Of the various works written about the political upheavals of the 1760s Orme's was perhaps the most accomplished as a proper history. See his *A History of the Military Transactions of the British Nation in Indostan from 1745. To which is prefixed a Dissertation on the Establishments Made by Mahomedan Conquerors in Indostan* (London: John Nourse, 1763)..

[70] My own prompting to look anew at the writings of these figures is obviously indebted to Travers having already cleared the way. On all those mentioned in this part of the chapter, therefore, see also, generally, Travers, *Ideology and Empire*.

to the others mentioned, Watts was most likely the figure who was most derisive towards the subcontinent's past, vociferously endorsing the notion of the 'Great Mogul' not only 'as absolute Monarch'[71] but also as 'sole Possessor of Property, the single Fountain of Honour, and the sole Oracle of Justice'.[72] Yet whatever more specific features Watts attributed to the Mughal order, he also saw them to have been specified 'according to the Constitution of *Indostan*'—'if', as he hastened to add, we can agree that 'Despotism can with any propriety be stiled a Constitution'.[73]

The clearly mixed messaging notwithstanding, Watts' remarks here are really just a prelude to a chief concern that proves even more revealing. This, as he explains, is with the process by which the authority of 'the Mogul' became 'rather nominal than real', as a 'kind of anarchy' replaced the security made possible by its preceding order of political constitution. In focusing on security here, Watts draws out the key point of connection between the notion of property and a commitment to an ontology of the laws in constitutionist discourse. In contrast to the image of the property right in particular as a model of legal right in general that began emerging in the Anglo-common-law mainstream already by the time Watts was writing, for him property instead stands outside the ontology of the legal. If the esteemed status to be accorded to sound laws in virtue of their role in guaranteeing greater certainty in the administration of justice demanded further burnishing, it was, thus, because of the way they helped make the proprietor's expectations about what qualified as *their* property, itself, more certain. On this view, in other words, it was decidedly not that dominion over physical space was seen as the underlying first principle of the laws, much less in a way that equipped them with an infinitely generative power to subsume the world of facts fully under the sway of some single and selfsame system of rational ordering that they themselves seamlessly comprised.

In the conceptual lexicon of constitutionism property and sound laws subsisted side by side more than they were merged into one another. Accordingly, we find their connection drawn out in a similar fashion by

---

[71] William Watts. *Memoirs of the revolution in Bengal, Anno Dom. 1757. By which Meer Jaffeir was raised to the government of that province, together with those of Bahar and Orixa* (London: A. Millar, 1760), 1.
[72] Ibid., 5.
[73] Ibid., 1.

Holwell in his *Interesting Historical Events, Relative to the Provinces of Bengal, and the Empire of Indostan*. As the 'anarchy' that Watts wrote of as accompanying social breakdown or political turmoil was seen as threatening the security of property in the most basic sense of the term, for Holwell as well, insecurity paved the way to property's 'invasion'.[74] That here once more we find the watchword being 'property' rather than the legal 'right to property' reminds us that Holwell is another figure from the 1760s who echoed more than he dissented from Montesquieu's or Bernier's more pure version of the constitutionist theory of oriental despotism. No more than they did he suggest that the security of property derived from a 'law of property' or even property laws, per se.

To the contrary, abiding the logic of constitutionism, for Holwell the connection between the requisite security needed for property to be made absolute and the ontology of the legal lay elsewhere. Only by creating an orderly administration of justice through sound laws and avoiding a descent into brigandage and licence would the natural institution of property be secure from molestation.[75] Echoing the idea of Mughal imperium as an overlay atop a still extant ancient Hindu order, Holwell reiterates a constitutionist logic in which property is extrinsic to the laws that factored into the administration of justice, considered as one of the defining aspects of sovereignty as a practical affair. The logic is vividly on display at various points in *Interesting Historical Events*, especially as Holwell comes to the following noteworthy line of observation:

> in truth it would be almost cruelty to molest these happy people, for in this district [belonging to the Raja Gopal Singh], are the only vestiges of the beauty, purity, piety, regularity, equity and strictness of the ancient Indostan government. Here the property, as well as the liberty of the people, are inviolate, here no robberies are heard of, either private or public; the traveler, either with, or without merchandize, on his entering this district, becomes the immediate care of the government, which allots him guards without any expence, to conduct him from

---

[74] Holwell, *Interesting Historical Events*, vol. I, 18, 103, 175.
[75] This is why according to a view like Montesquieu's the criminal laws were of particular importance for rendering property secure. See Montesquieu, *The Spirit of the Laws*, 188–90.

stage to stage, and these are accountable for the safety and accommodation of his person and effects.[76]

4.5 Property in the Land's Rent as the Basis for the Doctrinal Discourse of Revenue Administration after 1772

If the culture of debate that emerged after 1757 was marked not only by a view of polity and society in the subcontinent responsive to the imperatives of negotiating empire but also a characteristically early-modern set of ideas about the relationship between sovereignty, property, and legality, public-sphere discourse in the early colonial subcontinent was also coming to be centred on a vision that was simultaneously being left behind in much of the West. To fully account for the vision's appeal under the Company's auspices, therefore, it is necessary to appreciate its continuity with the brand of absolute-dominion talk that was coming to dominate the colonial public sphere in the decades between Lord North's Regulating Act of 1773 and Cornwallis' ascendancy in the 1790s.

The wider context in which absolute-dominion talk proliferated under the Company was one marked by the ever more contentious question of settling the land-revenue demand in Bengal that culminated in the Permanent Settlement of 1793. While the argument developed in the present section thus shares an affinity with other recent work that has sought to expand the canonical story about the Permanent Settlement, it also represents a departure in other ways. This is because relative to what I have been arguing, my own interest is not in the Permanent Settlement as a categorical rupture wrought in the name of an ostensibly modernizing rule of (capitalist) property, nor even a lesser one relative to a transitional veneration of a specifically Mughal past that grew out of the fledgling Company state's need to accommodate itself to the surrounding political culture.

Instead, the present section highlights the persistence of the Company's pre-Permanent Settlement logic of constitutionism, with its ontology of the laws and conception of property as external thereto. The

---

[76] Holwell, *Interesting Historical Events, vol. I*, 198.

argument thus focuses on how even notwithstanding the definitive end the Permanent Settlement brought to the controversy that had previously raged about *who* Bengal's true proprietors were, more important was the consensus that animated the backdrop about *what* property in the subcontinent was. Whether in Bengal—or, as we will see in the next chapter, the other Presidencies where the Company pursued its revenue settlement operations—it was, thus, a dominion over land's rent more than any unitary, exclusive, and physical dominion over landed space that one and all agreed was the key object to be apportioned among the territory's proprietors. As noted in the introduction to this chapter, the concept of rent that was at the heart of this idea of propertied dominion was more generalized than the notion of a strictly Ricardian differential issuing from the fertility of the varying qualities of soil over which landlords were respectively endowed with monopoly-like juridical control. Indeed, the identity between land and *this* notion of rent made for a strand within the genealogy of abstracting rights through property concepts that not only stretches back to the seventeenth century, but that also is distinct from any that is usually emphasized on the basis of the roughly simultaneous maturation of natural rights discourse.[77]

Accordingly, if the modern idea of property/*dominium* was born in the West side by side with that of law/*ius*—as a line of thinkers stretching back from Carl Schmitt in the twentieth century to Jeremy Bentham in the nineteenth to Dominican theologians like Sylvester Mazzolini three centuries earlier have suggested[78]—then so too did it have nearly as long-lived a twin in the idea of rent. In the sixteenth century it was, thus, only a few decades after claims to land in the common law began catalysing

---

[77] See e.g. Macpherson, *The Political Theory of Possessive Individualism*; Richard Tuck, *Natural Rights Theories: Their Origin and Development* (New York: Cambridge University Press, 1979) and Annabel S. Brett, *Liberty, Right and Nature: Individual Rights in Later Scholastic Thought* (New York: Cambridge University Press, 2003). For a compatible point (and citation of supporting literature) see Lee B. Wilson, 'A "Manifest Violation" of the Rights of Englishmen: Rights Talk and the Law of Property in Early Eighteenth-Century Jamaica', *Law and History Review* 33, no. 3 (2015), 543–75 at 544, notes 3–4.

[78] Tuck, *Natural Rights Theories*, 5–7. For Bentham's declaration of property's birth with law see Jeremy Bentham, *Principles of the Civil Code (N.D.)* reprinted in *Theory of Legislation*, R. Hildreth, trans. (London: Trübner & Co., 1908), 88–218 at 113. On Schmitt's formation see his *The Nomos of the Earth in the International Law of the Jus Publicum Europaeum* (New York: Telos Press, 2003 [1950]). Of course, whether the 'modern' idea of property can really be accurately accounted for in terms of any primordial notion of dominion is a different matter, as should be evident from my own treatment of the issue/related concerns in this study, to say nothing of that of others. See e.g. di Robilant, *The Making of Modern Property*.

a transformation of the notion of the right to property—from its earlier incarnation as a narrow technical entry within the lexicon of medieval lawyers into a more abstract idea of juridical right—that the notion of rent, itself, was transformed through its connection to landed property.[79] In the process, its origins in French financial usage, as per the class of annuities known in the thirteenth century as *rente*,[80] and its more mundane usage within the common law to that point, as per the notion of purchasing land at so many years' rent, were reconstituted in terms of a still emerging tradition of classical political economy's incipient notion of an agricultural surplus.

The new-found conceptual overlap between landed property and a specifically economic notion of rent was manifest already in the pre-classical mercantilist writings of a figure like Thomas Mun. Mun, of course, is known in the history of the subcontinent as one of the early directors of the East India Company. In his *English Treasure by Foreign Trade*, published in 1628, he pushed past early mercantilist preoccupations in arguing that rather than being an end in itself the balance of trade was important primarily insofar as it reflected an increase in the total quantity of agricultural rent.[81] Even more importantly, there was the better-known William Petty—the famed pioneer of 'political arithmetick'—who three decades later more explicitly linked rent with propertied rights over land, casting the former as the defining feature of the latter. In Petty's formulation rent was revealingly conceived in terms of an extra return above the cost of production. While he thus had the intellectual wherewithal to claim that what 'we call usury' is nothing more than the 'rent' of 'Money', it was the 'Rents ... of Lands and Houses' that made for its most characteristic form.[82] Elaborating, he asked his reader to consider the following scenario:

---

[79] Clive Holmes, 'Parliament, Liberty, Taxation, and Property', in *Parliament and Liberty from the Reign of Elizabeth to the English Civil War*, J. H. Hexter, ed. (Palo Alto, CA: Stanford University Press, 1992), 122–54 at 138.
[80] Niall Ferguson, *The Ascent of Money: A Financial History of the World* (New York: The Penguin Press, 2008), 73–74.
[81] David McNally, *Political Economy and the Rise of Capitalism: A Reinterpretation* (Berkeley, CA: University of California Press, 1988), 31–32.
[82] William Petty, *A Treatise of Taxes and Contributions* (1662) reprinted in *The Economic Writings of Sir William Petty, vol. I* (Cambridge: Cambridge University Press, 1899), 1–97 at 42.

[s]uppose a man could with his own hands plant a certain scope of Land with Corn, that is, could Digg, or Plough, Harrow, Weed, Reap, Carry, home, Thresh, and Winnow so much as the Husbandry of this Land requires; and had withal Seed wherewith to sowe the same. I say, that when this man hath subducted his seed out of the proceed of the Harvest, and also, what himself had both eaten and given to others in exchange for Clothes, and other Natural necessaries; and the remainder of Corn is the natural and true Rent of the Land for that year; and the *medium* of seven years, or rather of so many years as makes up the Cycle, within which Dearths and Plenties make their revolution, doth give the ordinary Rent of the Land in Corn. But a further, though collaterall question may be, how much English money this Corn or Rent is worth? I answer, so much as the money, which another single man can save, within the same time, over and above his expence, if he imployed himself wholly to produce and make it.[83]

In this 'remarkable' passage, as David McNally calls it, Petty not only sought to 'define rent as a real magnitude ... inaugurat[ing] a line of inquiry based on a labour theory of value', but also to show that '"real rent is a surplus, not merely as it had always [previously] been considered ... a cost of production"'.[84]

At the same time, any larger striving towards a pure 'labour theory of value' notwithstanding, Petty remained less than fully 'satisfied' with such a theory, instead continually returning to 'land as a determinant of value' and making '[r]ent the central category in his analysis of economic phenomena'. For like other 'seventeenth-century theorists', it only made sense for him, too, to commence from the fact 'that land was the primary form of wealth in England and Ireland at the time', making rent naturally the 'principal' seeming 'determinant of the value of land and the basis of the prosperity of the kingdom'.[85] Whatever ambiguities there may have been in Petty's depiction of economic value, they 'reflect[ed], then, not so much the shortcomings of his theoretical equipment as the difficulty of analysing the essential features of capitalist production during the

---

[83] Ibid., 43.
[84] McNally, *Political Economy and the Rise of Capitalism*, 50 (quoting William Letwin, *The Origins of Scientific Economics* (London: Methuen and Co., 1963), 146).
[85] Ibid., 52.

transitional period in which land constituted the most important factor of production and rent the most important' form that the surplus took. Being yet to emerge 'as the central feature of the capitalist economy', on the other hand, 'profit on capital' was simply 'eclipsed by rent'.[86] It was in this act of eclipse, moreover, that rent went on to further underpin the shadow conception of property that it did in the emerging tradition of political economy, which was separate from whatever competing conception absorbed the spotlight in political philosophy through the pride of place given to dominion over territorial space in natural rights theory.

* * *

As the consensus position on the nature of property in the subcontinent from the very outset of the Company's official transition from trader to sovereign, the conception arising from the identity between land and rent was thrust out of the shadows and into the light in colonial South Asia by the material and intellectual exigencies of early colonial rule. On the one hand, this was because recasting Islamicate idioms of land control/surplus appropriation in the subcontinent[87] by identifying 'property' with an intellectually cutting-edge notion like 'rent' proved perfectly consonant with the Company's intensified political economy of revenue extraction. On the other hand, more counter-intuitively, it was because in the colonial subcontinent the identity between land and rent was more easily stripped of the less than laudable implications that *kept it* in the intellectual shadows of the late-eighteenth-century West, given how well-suited it was to the Company's generally constitutionist logic, which was already premised on keeping property extrinsic to legality.

Insofar as the ontology of the legal rested on the laws that factored into a sound administration of justice more than any notion of 'the law' writ large that could be grounded—as in the Anglo-common-law mainstream—on an absolute, unitary, and physicalist conception of rights, in the Company's India legality was neither the necessary basis of administration in general nor that of landed property in particular. Against the very different backdrop of absolute-dominion talk in the

---

[86] Ibid., 54.
[87] Chaudhry, 'Property and its Rule (in Late Indo-Islamicate and Early Colonial) South Asia', 926–40.

early colonial public sphere, then, the key locus of the doctrinal discourse of property in the subcontinent became revenue administration rather than legal administration proper.

To the extent that legal administration did deal with issues of landed wealth, it took place not so much through reference to a 'law of property' as it did on the basis of the piecemeal invocation of pre-existing native *laws* of inheritance, spousal prerogative, and the *inter vivos* transfer of and succession to shares in the context of familial and communitarian disputes. In this respect, we can say that from its outset legal modernization under conditions of early Company rule in the subcontinent was set on a very different course from that along which it had already progressed quite far in the West by the turn of the nineteenth century. With the full-scale rewriting of land control in terms of the legal entitlement to property, the Western mainstream developed the absolute, unitary, and physicalist conception of rights that made the notion of 'the law' as an objectively irreducible phenomenon imaginatively plausible. In the early colonial subcontinent, in contrast, the confluence between constitutionism and the political economy of Company rule proved a major hindrance to this taking place in any equally effective way, as I now turn to.

4.6 Property, Constitutionism, and Political Economy after Hastings' Tax Farming Scheme of 1772

Whether it made for continuity or rupture, the shift that became evident in the discursive culture of the early colonial public sphere by the mid-1770s was precipitated by a growing clamour for the Company to take direct control over its *diwani*-ship in Bengal after the ruinous famine. The first step in this direction came with the new Governor General Warren Hastings' plan to institute an expanded system of revenue collection through tax farming. Having already become widespread in Bengal during the eighteenth century as the power of the Mughal centre was dissipating,[88] the practice was initially made use of by the Company

---

[88] J. R. McLane, 'Revenue Farming and the Zamindari System in Eighteenth-century Bengal', in *Land Tenure and Peasant in South Asia*, ed. Robert Eric Frykenberg (New Delhi: Orient Longman, 1977), 20–23.

already prior to 1765.[89] However, with Hastings' plan of 1772 significant changes were introduced to the practice in not only its scope but also its structure and underlying rationale. Most importantly, the period for which territories were farmed out was extended to five years. Yet by 1775, the anti-Hastings majority on the Governor's council had come to identify the plan as a failure, criticizing the Company's servants, Hastings included, for graft and casting the tax farmers as rapacious opportunists. Such accusations only intensified the widely circulating earlier disquiet of those like William Bolts,[90] the Dutch-born merchant who moved in and out of the Company's employ, and Alexander Dow,[91] the well-known military officer turned orientalist and playwright, both of whom cast the tax farmer as a figure to be scorned already before Hastings ascended to power.

As fate would have it, Hastings' experiment with five-year farming terms ended in 1778, only a few years after it began, although this did little to quell the growing dissatisfaction that came to envelop his administration. Discontent culminated in 1784 when Britain's then prime minister, William Pitt the Younger, pushed forward a new India Act under the provisions of which a six-person Board of Control was created to oversee the Company's civil, military, and revenue affairs. In 1786, through a supplement to Pitt's earlier Act, Hastings' time in office came to its formal end, with the Marquess Cornwallis put into place as his official replacement and successor as governor general.

These events all but condemned the tax-farming system to oblivion, including by prompting a mounting intellectual attack from

---

[89] For example, Hastings' predecessor as governor from 1767 to 1769, Harry Verelst, oversaw the farming of the revenues of the Burdwan raj for three-year terms. See Travers, *Ideology and Empire*, 96.

[90] Bolts was a Dutchman engaged in private trade in Bengal. He initially arrived in Calcutta in 1759 and was hired to work for the Company soon after, moving up the ranks quickly. Along the way he became an ever more vocal critic of Company policies, especially for their negative impact on economic conditions in Bengal. See his *Considerations on Indian Affairs; Particularly Respecting the Present State of Bengal and its Dependencies*, 2nd edn. (London: J. Almon, 1772), which was published after he was expelled from India in 1768 and became one of the most prominent early condemnations of the Company's transition from trader to sovereign.

[91] Dow published two volumes of *The History of Hindostan*, in 1768 and 1772, together with translations of several Persian texts. The second volume of *The History of Hindostan* included two important addendums in the form of 'Dissertations' (one *On the Origin and Nature of Despotism in Hindostan* and another on *An Enquiry into the State of Bengal*). It was in these appendices that Dow made an explicit case against the Company for its excessive revenue demand, while also making one of the earliest pleas for permanently setting the level of that demand.

contemporaries like Thomas Law, who insisted, in effect, that the system of long leases was the opposite of a rule of property.[92] Even so, it is important not to confuse the polemic Hastings' system was met with on its demise with an accurate, much less exhaustive, reconstruction either of its relative performance or its purported *raison d'être*. At the level of its underlying rationale, rather than emblematizing the old corruption, the idea of extending the period for which territories could be farmed out was rooted in the same logic that animated Phillip Francis' first comprehensive proposal for Permanent Settlement in 1776. If this point has gone underexplored by historians,[93] it is most likely because Francis' plan set the stage for Hastings' final demise. Be this at it may, however, it should not obscure how allowing farmers to bid for five-year leases was predicated on precisely the same notion of property and its security that dominated debate in Bengal for the remainder of the century.[94]

This becomes evident when we turn to Hastings' justification for the system of extended farming terms. As he readily conceded, leasing Bengal's revenues to private contractors was only 'the most eligible' rather than the theoretically ideal option. As he also noted, however, for 'a Government constituted like that of the Company', lacking as it did the wherewithal to 'enter into the detail and minutiae of the Collections', there was little other choice. Clearly, therefore, Hastings did not fail to realize that leasing the revenue would put 'both the interest of the State and the property of the people … at the mercy of' the farmers.[95] Yet at the same time, he drew no hard and fast distinctions between the 'property of the people' that was to be entrusted to the farmers' 'mercy' and the interest they, themselves, would consequently be holding. That is, in Hastings' understanding the interest commanded by the revenue farmers under a system of extended leases was, as much as any other, a 'property' that it

---

[92] Guha discusses the recasting of Hastings' system as his 'bête noire' and a 'total and deliberate contradiction'. See Guha, *A Rule of Property for Bengal*, 9.

[93] See e.g. Marshall, *Bengal: The British Bridgehead*, 121.

[94] Perhaps most recently, Travers has emphasized how Hastings' experiment with five-year farms found its antecedents in/proved continuous with forms of *ijara*. This makes it all the more notable that he simultaneously observes how as a 'dramatic escalation of revenue farming in' Bengal, the Hastings scheme was rooted in viewing such leases 'as a way of stabilizing the Company's land revenue income' after the famine. Travers, *Empires of Complaints*, 168.

[95] Warren Hastings, 'Letter to Calcutta Committee of Revenue Consultations', 2, Range 67, vol. 54, May 14, 1772, reprinted in Mary Evelyn Monckton Jones, *Warren Hastings in Bengal* (Oxford: Clarendon Press, 1918), 266.

was incumbent upon the Company to render secure. As he explained, under a system of 'long leases' it was not just the *raiyats*—conceived ambiguously as a composite of both 'true' owners and industrious tenant farmers—who would be freed 'from being transferred every year to new landlords', thereby 'injur[ing] the cultivation and dispeopl[ing] the lands'. Rather, so too would the recipient of the tax farm 'acquire[] a permanent interest in his lands'. As a holder in his own right of the 'property of the people', the tax farmer-cum-landlord would now 'for his own sake lay out money in assisting his tenants, in improving lands already cultivated, and in clearing and cultivating waste lands'. With an absolute security of expectation, he too would be incentivized never to 'dare ... injure the rents, nor [to] encroach in one year on the profits of the next, because the future loss which must ensue from such a proceeding w[ould] be his own'.[96]

In its deeper rationale for extended tax farming, Hastings' thought leaves little doubt that he was actually the forebear of his own critics. Like them, he assumed that what property in Bengal should principally entitle its holder to was a claim on the monetizable value of land's produce. Also, like those who came after him, he assumed that what was more specifically needed in order to ensure that 'dominion' was 'absolute' was a right to a security of expectation concerning the subtraction to be made from such a 'property' by the state; only then would the tax/revenue demand be prevented from fluctuating to the point of becoming arbitrary and hence confiscatory. Importantly, this view existed separate from whatever view was simultaneously held about whom to designate as the true holders of any such brand of property, which despite the much greater attention it would receive was a conceptually secondary matter.

Already with Hastings' overhauled approach to tax farming in 1772, therefore, absolute dominion talk under British rule was being translated into the same highly circumscribed doctrinal discourse of the right to property—as an entitlement to an absolute security of expectation over a portion of land's rent—that would go on to become emblematic of the Company's administration after the Permanent Settlement. Likewise, the vision of land control embedded in Hastings' approach to tax farming also proved more akin to than different from the view espoused by the leading advocates of the Permanent Settlement insofar as

[96] Ibid., 267–68.

it, too, kept property extrinsic to the laws that factored into the administration of justice. Indeed, here—with respect to the relationship between legality and property—one would even be hard-pressed to distinguish the understanding of someone like Dow, so clearly, as we saw before, no fan of tax farming, from that of Hastings or, for that matter, either's from Montesquieu's. In none of these cases was the focus on *laws* of property, much less the law of property, so much as it was on laws that would contribute to a general climate of social order consistent with keeping property unmolested.[97]

Amidst a constitutionist discourse inflected according to the theory of oriental despotism, there was ample reason for Hastings, his critics, and anyone else operating under the Company's auspices to work from this underlying ontology. For even notwithstanding the way that property talk in the Company's incipient public sphere was doctrinalized as an entitlement to rent, it was wholly in keeping with the view from despotism to attribute to the Asiatic sovereign not landed property as such, but only a property *in* the land. Bolts' well-known indictment of the Company is instructive in this regard. In his *Considerations on Indian Affairs,* he described the Company's acquisition of '*Dewanee*' as the basis for its displacing a multiplicity of other '*Sovereigns* of a rich and potent kingdom; of the revenues of which they likewise declare themselves not only the *Collectors* but Proprietors'.[98] In a similar vein, Bolts recalls J. Z. Holwell's views on the 'subject of Dewanee' and the accompanying idea that 'the rents of the lands are the property of the Emperor'.[99]

Of course, here, Bolts' main point was to question whether it was appropriate for the Company to effectively assume the role of the subcontinent's sole proprietor by displacing the Mughal emperor. Yet in so doing he proved typical of early colonial thinkers more generally who, regardless of their views about the matter, shared in the equivocation between property *as* land and property *in* land that was inherent to the constitutionist way of envisioning *what* oriental sovereigns commanded.

---

[97] Alexander Dow, 'Plan for Restoring Bengal to its Former Prosperity', reprinted in Alexander Dow, *The History of Hindostan; Translated from the Persian. To which are Prefixed Two Dissertations,* vol. I (London: J. Walker, 1812), cxxxviii–clxiv at clvii (noting that '[p]roperty being once established, and the forms of justice to protect it delineated, public prosperity is placed on a solid foundation').
[98] William Bolts, *Considerations on Indian Affairs,* 150 (emphasis in the original).
[99] Ibid., 34.

After all, absent such equivocation, it would have been impossible for the foundational claim on which the theory of oriental despotism was built—namely, about the Asiatic sovereign being the 'sole proprietor' of the soil—to be more than a rhetorical flourish. For if not a claim over some abstraction corresponding to the monetizable value of land's productive output, in what else could the despot's 'sole proprietorship' have actually consisted? If taken as implying that the sovereign had an active footprint on every square measure of cultivated soil, let alone an active surveillance over the entirety of the remaining 'waste', the idea would, practically speaking, have been simply unintelligible.

4.7 A Distinction without a Difference? (Private) Property in Rent versus (Sovereign) Property in the Land Revenue in Phillip Francis' Plan of 1776

Of course, it was not just in the subcontinent that the great adversary of 'property' was perceived to be taxation, a quantity inherently capable of abstraction that was just as fungible as the monetizable value of the produce of land. In fact, this was all the more so where property could be abstracted not just primarily into the value of the commodities it gave rise to, as would remain the case in Bengal for some time, but also into its value as a fully generalized commodity in its own right. The worry over excessive taxation thus proved a major impetus behind the emergence of classical political economy as a distinct way of knowing, even well before Adam Smith's *The Wealth of Nations* in 1776. Obviously, in the West this concern was of more than just academic import, clearly functioning as an animating force in metropolitan politics as well. Even just a supposed excess of effort in ascertaining the proper level of taxation, let alone an excess in the actual level, was liable to attract condemnation as antithetical to property's security. It was thus hardly by accident that just as Francis was condemning the prospect of conducting a survey to better determine the 'true value of the land' in Bengal as an invasion of property, proposals to revise the English land-tax were being 'shouted down' in Westminster as 'an outrageous violation of security of property'.[100]

---

[100] See Travers, 'The Real Value of the Lands', 538.

However, what did make early colonial India stand out, especially when compared to Britain, was how fully public-sphere discourse about absolute dominion seems to have been inflected according to the conceptual accent of political economy. If in Britain it was metropolitan legal thought that retained the key role in governing property's conceptualization, under the Company's rule it was the confluence between political economy and political constitutionism that proved determinative. The mutually reinforcing relationship between them licensed a much-prolonged insistence on land and the associated agrarian order as the source from which *all* wealth flowed in the subcontinent.[101] More than just a remnant of/corresponding to a physiocratic theory of value,[102] the insistence was made manifest through a recurrent contrast between colony and metropole. As one Collector in the ceded districts of the Deccan put it, the '[l]and rent is to Indian, what the excise and customs are to English revenue'.[103]

The confluence between the decidedly early-modern discourse of political constitutionism and the, in ways, incipiently modern discourse about property as a sum of component value flows was even more evident in the back and forth around Francis' 1776 plan for Permanent Settlement. In calling for a proper survey of the lands under the Company's rule after the failure of his system of extended tax farming, Hastings emphasized the severity of the problem of unequal assessments under a despotic constitution. He thus repeatedly contrasted the nine-tenths of the land's net produce that the sovereign was said to take in the subcontinent with the mere fifth part to which the English land-tax summed.[104] Francis, for his

---

[101] For a discussion of the diversity of exactions the Company lumped together under the single heading of the land-revenue demand, see generally ibid. See also, Sudipta Sen, *Empire of Free Trade: The East India Company and the Making of the Colonial Marketplace* (Philadelphia, PA: University of Pennsylvania Press, 1998).

[102] Among Smith's major departures from Physiocracy was to assert that 'the wealth of nations' consisted of more than just the value of goods produced through the 'primary' sector of agriculture. For the Physiocrats trade and industry were, as Quesnay famously put it, sterile. See Gianni Vaggi, *The Economics of François Quesnay* (Durham, NC: Duke University Press, 1987), 42–54. For a more recent assessment of the importance of Physiocracy to the debate leading up to the Permanent Settlement, see John Albert Rorabacher, *Property, Land, Revenue, and Policy: The East India Company, c.1757–1825* (New York: Routledge, 2017), 299–362.

[103] 'Extract from Report of Principal Collector of Ceded Districts', 15 August, 1807, reprinted as 'Appendix to House of Commons', House of Commons, *The Fifth Report from the Select Committee on the Affairs of the East India Company, 1812*, vol. II, *Madras Presidency* (Madras: J. Higginbotham, 1866), 650.

[104] See e.g. Warren Hastings, 'Minute of the Governor General to the Revenue Department', November 12, 1776, reprinted in Philip Francis, *Original minutes of the Governor-General*

own part, invoked precisely the same reasoning to justify his opposition to the call for a survey, arguing that the real rate of the revenue demand was nowhere close to nine-tenths.[105] Yet for neither Hastings nor Francis was there any doubt about whether command over such flows of value constituted the essence of what property came to in the subcontinent.

Relative to this shared vision about property's nature, it becomes clear that disagreements about the identity of Bengal's true proprietors generated more heat than light. It was, thus, through little more than the force of assertion that Francis transformed Hastings' experiment with extended tax farms into its seeming opposite. That is, what was really no less a scheme for incentivizing the creation of private property (in land's rent) than Francis' own plan for Permanent Settlement was instead portrayed as a programme for sovereign ownership, their common underlying foundation in equating proprietorship with controlling rent being largely obfuscated in the process.[106]

Tellingly, Francis did not try to argue that Hastings' plan had failed to make good on channelling absolute-dominion talk into a conception focused on the security of expectation regarding the subtraction that could be made by the state from the monetizable value of the land's produce. In place of what he claimed would be the unworkable and invasive survey that his adversaries were recommending, he instead simply called for the total assessment to be set on the basis of the actual amount the Company had been able to collect during the previous three years—as opposed to the amount it had claimed was owed based on the full monetizable sum of productive output. By suggesting that the state's share was less than might otherwise be thought, Francis analytically sequestered the property his plan proposed to endow to the hands of Bengal's true proprietors from the equally fungible portion of value that was to go back to the colonial sovereign. Yet this could do only so much to obscure how on Company

---

and Council of Fort William on the settlement and collection of the revenues of Bengal: with a plan of settlement, recommended to the Court of Directors in January, 1776 (London: J. Debrett, 1782), 144.

[105] Francis, 'Minute for Revenue Department', November 29, 1776, in Francis, *Original minutes of the Governor-General and Council of Fort William*, 157.

[106] Francis, 'Plan for a Settlement of the Revenues of Bengal, Bahar, and Orixa', in Francis, *Original Minutes of the Governor-General and Council of Fort William*, 23 (accusing Hastings of supporting the sovereign's 'right to ingross the intire produce as landlord' as if he were the 'natural proprietor of the land').

officialdom's own logic of *what* property in the subcontinent consisted of, the flow back to the state could just as soon be made to appear as a form of property in its own right as could any portion he was arguing the province's so-called true proprietors should be entitled to.

Perhaps sensing as much, Francis was left demanding that as compared to the 'tenure by which' the zamindar would 'hold' his own rights, the government's claim would then become no more than a 'quit-rent'. In directing focus back onto the zamindar's dominion (over rent), Francis emphasized that its true boundaries as a claim to property might even end up being larger than their designation as a proprietor might have suggested in the first place. As he thus noted, '[i]t is not meant by these regulations to prevent the zemindar from drawing a larger rent from the constituent parts of the zemindary than its proportion of the assessment, and rendering it of more value to himself, if he improves the land it contains'. 'This', he continued,

> would be absurd and defeat the intention of the present plan [which] is only meant to fix the quit-rent of Government for every portion of land in all future sales, or transfer of property; without which, neither the actual proprietor nor the purchaser can form a determinate judgment of its value.[107]

Given the difficulty of distinguishing the drawing of a tax from the assertion of the sovereign's own claim to a property in the rent when each was as much an abstraction from land's physicality as the other, there was little reason to believe that isolating the threshold at which a taking was no more than a mere quit-rent would be any easier. As much was borne out by the outcome of Francis' repeated calls for moderating the government's demand so as to provision the zamindars with a genuine 'property'.[108] For in something of a supreme irony, his estimate of the level at which a permanent *jamma* would need to be set in order to accomplish

---

[107] Ibid., 57.
[108] Francis based his support for a principle of moderation on what he claimed was the real precedent of the subcontinent's Islamic rulers. Citing past figures for the total assessment under Akbar and of a later assessment in 1728—both of which were close to 15 million rupees—Francis suggested that the Company had wrongly assumed a higher figure demanded by Bengal's independent nawabs as the norm. See ibid., 35.

this goal ended up being significantly higher even than the notoriously excessive figure that was officially adopted under the actual Permanent Settlement of 1793.[109]

At other times in his analysis, Francis simply let the hair-splitting distinction between a sovereign tax, ostensibly genuine property, and quit-rent go into abeyance. In looking back on the distant past, for instance, he was much less keen on trying to categorically isolate the government's share of the monetizable value of land's produce from the remainder that was left to the zamindars. Here, instead, he tended to resort to the zamindars' 'possession' in explaining the basis of their long-standing role as social notables, any entitlement they simultaneously enjoyed over the flow of rent being more incidental than central to defining their exalted status.[110] Of course, there was an obvious inconsistency that characterized the view Francis developed in such moments. For when retreating into the deeper mists of history, the notion of possession he called on was really no better specified—and, therefore, also no worse—than that which the adversaries of his plan for Permanent Settlement, themselves,

---

[109] Francis' estimate of these costs summed to approximately 32 million rupees. (See Francis, Appendix IX to 'A Plan for a Settlement of the Revenues of Bengal, Bahar, and Orixa', 110.) As Marshall notes, the 1793 figure came to some 27 million rupees. This was consistent with the demand stipulated in the temporary settlements of the 1770s that those like Francis so vehemently condemned. See Marshall, *Bengal: The British Bridgehead*, 141. Of course, how high any of these figures actually were has been a subject of ongoing debate. Whereas it was once routine to assume that the Company's rule brought with it an excessive demand relative to that of precolonial times, in recent years historians have questioned such received wisdom. See Travers, 'The Real Value of the Lands', 517–21, for an overview. Marshall, for example, cautions that 'paper assessments' did not correspond to the amounts the Company 'actually collected' and that nominal increases in the demand after 1765 may have simply kept pace with prices after 1770, which had risen substantially from their lows of the 1740s. See Marshall, *Bengal: The British Bridgehead*, 142–43. Nevertheless, the figure of 27 million rupees made permanent in 1793 was 20 per cent higher than pre-1757 figures. See ibid., 141.

[110] In such moments, Francis buttressed the claim that *zamindari* control over value was merely incidental by distinguishing *zamindari* from *jagirdari* rights. As he thus noted,

[i]t is true, the forms of the royal Sunnuds, or grants, to the Zemindars, suppose them to hold of the sovereign *in capite*; but this I consider as a kind of feodal fiction, of which the sovereign in fact never pretended to avail himself as constituting a right to assume or transfer the possession. When he grants Jaguires, or lands for religious purposes, his order is addressed to the Zemindars, Chowderies, and Talookdars. The land continues to be deemed a part of the Zemindary; the sovereign only grants the revenue of it. The grantee, or *Jagheerdar*, never calls it his Zemindary or Talookdary. Mahomed Reza Cawn, in his state of Bengal, affirms that the princes have no immediate property in the lands; and that they even purchase ground to build mosques and for burying-places.

Francis, 'Note', attached to 'A Plan for a Settlement of the Revenues of Bengal, Bahar, and Orixa', 72.

drew on to make the case for the *raiyats* as Bengal's 'true proprietors', only in such moments for him to respond by reverting back to the suggestion that it was command over rent that was property's key hallmark.

* * *

Though it was voted down by the Governor General's Council, Francis' Plan of 1776 clearly set the stage for what followed. Yet as I have been suggesting, the most important way it did so was neither in its recommendation of a settlement that was permanent nor in its recommendation that settlement be undertaken with the zamindars. Instead, the most significant legacy of Francis' Plan came through the way it normalized the idea of property as an entitlement to land's rent in much the same way as Hastings' failed scheme of five-year tax farms had done. Accordingly, in the years after Francis issued his Plan, whatever disagreement ensued about the idea of a permanent *zamindari* settlement, it tended to conceal a remarkably uniform consensus. On all sides of the debate, there was shared the latent idea in classical political economy of property as abstracted into a claim to the flow of revenue that issued from land over and above cost, which had been known under the single moniker of rent well before it would more visibly go on to be differentiated by thinkers like Adam Smith into component returns for capital and labour, alongside the rent of land proper, as per what Marx would dub the 'trinity formula'.[111]

Against the backdrop of this latent identity in political economy between land and rent, the Company's focus on guaranteeing a security of expectation regarding the equally fungible, immaterial portion that could be subtracted therefrom as a way of rendering property absolute in the subcontinent becomes readily intelligible. It also serves to clarify why as this focus came to win the day, ongoing debate in Bengal led in either of two main directions. On the one hand, there were those who continued to press the question of who the province's true proprietors were by asking whether it was not really the state, rather than the zamindars, who controlled the land's rent (through the revenue demand). On the other, there were those who concentrated on how lengthy of a term for fixing the land

---

[111] Karl Marx, *Capital: A Critique of Political Economy*, Vol. 3 (New York: Penguin, 1993), 953–70.

revenue demand would be needed to if it was to be effectively 'permanent' enough to make the zamindar's entitlement 'absolutely' secure.

It was these two axes of further consideration, for example, that organized the different kinds of disagreement Cornwallis' successor and another of the main architects of the Permanent Settlement, John Shore, found himself embroiled in through the 1790s. Along the first axis, Shore thus bitterly clashed—ultimately successfully—with James Grant over the latter's lingering support for the notion that the sovereign, alone, was sole proprietor in the subcontinent; along the second, as a member of the Governor General's Council, he more amicably, though less successfully, clashed with Cornwallis over the meaning of permanency.

4.8 Property in Rent as the Definitive Form of Indian Property in Land: Shore's Opposition to Grant Reconsidered

While Shore eventually succeeded Cornwallis as governor general from 1793 to 1797, he initially rose to prominence as part of Hastings' regime, in which his acquaintance with Persian and the provincial vernacular led to his appointment as principal revenue adviser. It was on this basis that he was subsequently chosen to serve as part of the Governor General's Council in 1787, a role that made him instrumental to the implementation of the Court of Directors' 1786 order to pursue a settlement of 'the permanent and unalterable revenue of our territorial possessions in Bengal'.[112] Grant, on the other hand, came to the subcontinent in 1784, initially in a strictly personal capacity. However, by 1786 he was being asked to serve as the chief *sheristadar* or revenue accountant for the Board of Revenue at Calcutta. In this capacity, he was building on earlier work he had done for the Presidency of Madras in helping to gather revenue data for the Northern Circars, a narrow coastal strip south of Bengal comprising parts of present-day Andhra Pradesh and Odisha.

There, Grant became a proponent of the view that previous assessments of the area had underestimated the total revenue demand it could bear. Accordingly, when he came to Bengal as *sheristadar* it was a similar

---

[112] Quoted in Marshall, *Bengal: The British Bridgehead*, 122.

point of view he advanced on the Company's eastern Presidency, formalizing his thoughts in a lengthy submission to the Governor General[113] as well as 1791's *An Inquiry into the Nature of Zemindary Tenures in the Landed Property of Bengal*.[114] Drawing on pre-*diwani* revenue records, as in the context of the Northern Circars, Grant pressed the claim that estimates of the revenue the Presidency could support were distorted by various methods of concealment the zamindars had used to obscure their actual returns. In so doing, he also prompted a renaissance, of sorts, of the theory of the sole ownership of the Asiatic sovereign,[115] largely by turning the logic by which Francis deemed the government's demand no more than a quit-rent on its head. Grant thus highlighted the 'nine-tenths of the whole' of the revenue the sovereign was traditionally said to take 'for himself' to argue that it was the 'remaining tenth' left to the zamindars that was the mere shadow of property; even if not a quit-rent, it was the truly ancillary quantity, representing, at best, a 'compensation for the trouble and expence of collection'.[116] Indeed, for Grant, the sovereign's control over the rent not only made the zamindar's own holding simply a 'monthly allowance' for services rendered, but it also meant that the Asiatic ruler could be construed on the model of 'a British freeholder', here understood as a rentier above all.[117] For Grant, then, like his opponents, because property was, in the end, some portion of the abstracted,

---

[113] James Grant, 'An Historical and Comparative Analysis of the Finances of Bengal; Chronologically arranged in different periods from the Mogul Conquest to the present time—Extracted from a Political Survey of the British Dominions and Tributary Dependencies in India', reprinted as Appendix No. 4 in House of Commons, *The Fifth Report from the Select Committee on the Affairs of the East India Company, 1812*, vol. 1, *Bengal Presidency* (Madras: J. Higginbotham, 1866), 221–554.

[114] James Grant, *An Inquiry into the Nature of Zemindary Tenures in the Landed Property of Bengal, &c.* (London: J. Debrett, 1791).

[115] As Travers notes, Grant and a handful of others led a small revolt during the mid-1780s against the view of the zamindars as Bengal's true proprietors, after it had largely triumphed in the aftermath of Francis' efforts. Travers, *Ideology and Empire*, 237.

[116] Grant, *An Inquiry into the Nature of Zemindary Tenures*, vii.

[117] Ibid., 5 (noting that 'whatever may be the theoretical opinions of the Company's representatives in India, when on suspension of the ordinary functions of a Zemindar, the lands are declared *Khas*, as being put under the direct superintendence of the Khalsa [or central treasury], for the purposes of collecting the *entire* rents, by his own immediate officers, from the peasantry, in behalf of the Government ... [This] was the only principle that could justify the dismission of one Zemindar, to make room for another; to dismember the jurisdictions of some, and occasionally suspend the authority of all; to resume the entire collections of their districts for Government, with the reservation of only a small portion, about *one-tenth* of the proprietary rents, under the denomination of *Moshhaira*, as the supposed legal monthly allowance they were entitled to').

perfectly fungible value of land's produce, the distinction between holding it, moderately taxing it, and invading it was destined to be one of degree rather than kind.

Much the same comes into view when we find Grant discounting the argument for zamindar proprietorship by focusing instead on the superior property enjoyed by the *raiyats* in their own possible capacity as rent retainers. In this vein, for example, he considered situations where the sovereign's claim on the land's rent left it unappropriated, as in 'cases of allowed remissions on the Bundobust, or annual Revenue agreement, on the ground of real or pretended failure of the crops'. With there being no reason for any fee to be paid for the service of collection under such circumstances, the right to property instead vested through 'those remissions [to] be made to the *Ryots*, and not to the *Zemindars*'.[118]

* * *

For his own part, rather than focusing strictly on the historical position of the zamindars, Shore grounded his disagreement with Grant in doubts about his opponent's calculation of the total revenue demand the *diwani* territories could bear, which Grant put at some 45 million rupees.[119] In part, this was because Shore was more reticent than Grant about applying the so-called categories of the English countryside to agrarian relations in the subcontinent.[120] At the same time, it would be wrong to imagine that Shore's was a 'firm voice of dissent'[121] against the Permanent Settlement primarily with respect to its *zamindari* character and due to his sense that '[t]he relation of a zemindar to government, and of ryot to a zemindar, [is] neither that of a proprietor nor a vassal; but a compound of both'.[122] Indeed, notwithstanding his further belief that the zamindars were a 'useless, idle, oppressive race, practising every species of extortion, or countenancing it by their inactivity and ignorance', Shore still held that it was upon their ranks that the property right (to an absolute security of

---

[118] Ibid.
[119] John Shore, 'Minute respecting the Permanent Settlement of the Lands in the Bengal Provinces', 18 June 1789, reprinted as Appendix No. 1 in *The Fifth Report, vol. I, Bengal Presidency*, 127.
[120] See generally Guha, *A Rule of Property for Bengal*, ch. 6.
[121] Ibid., 187.
[122] Shore, 'Extract of Minute, 8 December 1789', reprinted in Appendix No. 5 in *The Fifth Report, vol. I, Bengal Presidency*, 601, quoted in Guha, *A Rule of Property for Bengal*, 193.

expectation in the land's rent)—and the corresponding duty of revenue payment—should be settled by 'a fixed and permanent plan'.[123]

Undoubtedly, Shore's seemingly contradictory view of the zamindars was partly due to the fact that by the 1780s enthusiasm for *zamindari* settlement needed no longer to be mainly supported by 'deep convictions about [their] historical rights' or 'by any respect for the existing generation of' those among their ranks. As P. J. Marshall explains, such niceties fell by the wayside in the face of the more hardened insistence on simply 'defin[ing] a tenure called *zamindari*' into existence that 'would involve effective proprietorship of land in return for payment of revenue for it'.[124] At the same time, for those like Shore, settling with the zamindars was not ultimately seen as an act of creating property ex nihilo. To the contrary, it required attending with open eyes to the peculiarities of an 'entire system of Eastern finance' that 'had a reference, to a form of administration' that was 'distinct from ours'.[125] On such a view, agrarian administration in the subcontinent would not be concentrated on creating property so much as on creating true proprietors capable of holding whatever variety of property—in the rent—was native to the subcontinent.

For Shore, then, it was the aim of the Company's administration to 'reduce the compound relation of a zemindar to government, and of a ryot to a zemindar, to the simple principle of landlord and tenant'.[126] By doing so, the 'two relations' that were originally combined under 'the situation of the zemindar' would be whittled down into a single role. That is, once the zamindar was no longer 'an officer of government' charged with 'protecting the peace of the country' and 'securing the subjects of the State from oppression', they would bear only a role that 'originated in the *property of the land*' for which they paid 'a portion of the rents' to the state.[127] By excising the notionally feudal remnant of the zamindar's identity as a jurisdiction holder, they would thus be made to stand forth as a private

---

[123] Shore, 'Minute respecting the Permanent Settlement of the Lands', 18 June 1789, in ibid., 130, 146.
[124] Marshall, *Bengal: The British Bridgehead*, 123.
[125] Shore, 'Minute respecting the Permanent Settlement of the Lands', 18 June 1789, in *The Fifth Report, vol. I, Bengal Presidency*, 135.
[126] Shore, 'Extract of Minute', 8 December 1789, reprinted in Appendix No. 5 in ibid., 601.
[127] Shore, 'Minute respecting the Permanent Settlement of the Lands', 18 June 1789, in ibid., 130 (emphasis added).

holder of a type of property entitlement that was uniquely suited to subcontinental agrarian circumstances.

Shore's underlying commitment to the identity between property and rent helped anchor what was otherwise a disorienting instability in his view of the zamindars. Even as he was very open in sharing his doubts about whether the colonial state really should recognize such notables as its appointed proprietors, he also actively returned to the implication that they were best suited—including on historical grounds—to the job. Smoothing out this seemingly recurrent inconsistency in Shore's thinking was the notion that what entitlement to property there was for actors like the zamindars to hold in the subcontinent was an entitlement to rent.[128] For if property was, at bottom, a claim on abstract and perfectly fungible value issuing from land's produce, determining where it was vested was not only a secondary question but also one that could scarcely be answered in categorical terms. In this respect, Shore inadvertently made clear how resilient the concept of property being doctrinalized in the early colonial subcontinent was, not to mention how different it was from its counterpart in the Anglo-common-law mainstream. The ease with which his notion of property *in* land blended with a more specific underlying idea of property in land's *rent* was a function of a tendency towards conceptual abstraction that ran directly counter to the physicalization of the right to property that was the intellectual hallmark of legal modernization in the eighteenth-century West.

So it was that Shore warned that '[a] property in the soil must not be understood to convey the same right in India as in England'.[129] For much the same reason, discounting Grant's contentions about sovereign ownership only required that he show that the state was not the *sole* proprietor,[130] which was readily possible given a notion of property as an entitlement over the monetizable value of land's produce. Conceptualizing the Mughal emperor's 'claim to a portion of the rents' as a form of sovereign proprietorship, then, posed little hazard to Shore's support for

---

[128] Ibid., 160 (describing 'the proprietary and hereditary rights of the zamindars' as a fact, even if one that was 'uncertain' in 'origin').
[129] Ibid.
[130] Ibid., 145 (noting that '[w]e have admitted the property in the soil to be vested in the zemindars; and although it should be proved, under the Mogul system, to have belonged to the sovereign, which I deem impossible, the Company ought in my opinion to relinquish it').

zamindari settlement. Consequently, he did not hesitate to concede that the state's proprietorship over a 'portion of the rents' might be so significant in degree as to 'entitle[]' it to 'the minutest information regarding the land, its produce, the rents paid by the ryots, and all transfers in their possession'.[131] Indeed, he was even ready to concede that the state's 'portion' of property could ultimately sum to the large majority of 'the rents'.[132] In the case of neither concession, however, did it affect his sense of whether the zamindars were correctly seen as having property in their own right. Whether their 'portion of the rents' came to 15 or 50 per cent of the total value that issued from the land, all the same would it be a species of the particular variety of 'property in the soil' that was endemic to the subcontinent. On Shore's view, the very different type of 'right', over abstract value, that comprised 'property in the soil' in the subcontinent—following as it did from discourse about absolute dominion in the early colonial public sphere—was such that it had to be at least partially private. For insofar as the identity between land and rent meant that the type of property latent within the Indian agrarian system was both endlessly divisible and endlessly fungible, some portion of it was bound to remain in hands other than the sovereign's own.

With this much in tow, Shore's thought was emblematic of how notwithstanding the surface of fractiousness, the discursive culture that emerged under British rule was from its very outset able to effectively cast a sheen of modernity over the Company's administration. Likewise, it also proved emblematic of how underneath the surface of disagreement, that same discursive culture was able to guarantee a measure of internal consistency to the seemingly clashing pronouncements of its own exponents where it counted most and to render the evident differences between these pronouncements and those through which property discourse was constituted in the West more than simply rhetorical. Especially insofar as it may have been more of a necessity for the Company's personnel to believe in the colonial state's new modes of legitimation than it was for those over whom it ruled, the importance of achieving such consistency must not be underestimated.

---

[131] Ibid., 160.
[132] Ibid., (further noting that '[t]he revenues of the land belong[ed] to the ruling power; which being absolute claimed and exercised the right of determining the proportion to be taken by the state').

4.9 Shore, Cornwallis, and the Duration of Permanency

What further disagreements awaited to be fought out in the wake of Shore's battles with Grant did no more than had the battles to disturb the deeper uniformity that characterized property discourse under the surface of disagreement that marked the culture of early Company rule. Principal among these further disagreements was Shore's intellectual skirmish with Governor General Cornwallis over the question of how long the 'permanent' settlement really had to last in order to make the form of dominion the colonial state was proposing to doctrinalize 'absolute'. Already in a Minute from 1789, Shore was arguing that fixing the settlement at ten years would be sufficient to fulfil the underlying purpose of permanency. As he explained, if the intention was 'to give fuller confidence to the proprietors of the soil than a ten years' lease will afford', there could be no guarantee that doing so would guarantee such an 'effect in any material degree'. Instead, he argued, 'to those who have subsisted upon annual expedients a period of ten years' would, itself, be 'a term nearly equal in estimate to perpetuity'. This was because the 'advantages of the last 3 years' of a decennial term would invariably 'depend upon their exertions during the first', which would be the truly determinative period. If there was 'neglect[] ... in the outset, few of these zemindars [would] be in possession of their lands' for even 'half the prescribed term', let alone the full ten years, and far, far fewer more than a lifetime's worth of actual perpetuity. According to Shore's estimation, therefore, even a settlement period limited to a decade needed not to be explicitly announced to the zamindars. Instead, their 'own security, without the declaration' would depend, in all cases, upon their 'exertions in the beginning of the lease'.[133]

For his own part, Cornwallis simply reversed the logic of Shore's assertions. He, thus, rhetorically asked 'if the value of permanency is to be withdrawn from the settlement now in agitation, of what avail will the power of [Shore's] arguments be to the zemindars, for whose rights he has contended?'[134] As he went on to elaborate, a 'security' limited to ten

---

[133] Shore, 'Minute on the Permanent Settlement of the Lands in Bengal; and proposed Resolutions thereon', reprinted in *The Fifth Report, vol. I, Bengal Presidency*, 567.
[134] Charles Cornwallis, Governor General's Minute, 18 September 1789, reprinted in ibid., 591.

years was no real security at all. On the contrary, rather than holding genuine property (even of whatever type native to the subcontinent), those granted such recognition would have no more than a 'property in farm for a lease of ten years, provided they will pay as good rent for it'. For Cornwallis this meant that instead of blessing such property with 'absolute' security, this amounted to rendering it subject to being 'again assessed, at whatever rent the Government of this country may, at that time, think proper to impose'. In the end, then, he quizzically asked how '[i]n any part of the world, where the value of property is known' could 'such a concession of a right of property in the soil' not just instead be 'called a cruel mockery'?[135]

Its highly contentious nature notwithstanding, this clash over the length of 'permanency' once more reveals how fundamental the deeper consensus within the discursive culture that emerged under early Company rule was about property as dominion over rent. For what Cornwallis was really arguing was that only if 'property in the soil' was made into a fixed property in the rent would it be worth calling by the name of property at all. Only then, as he put it, would it 'be worth [the landlord's] while to incentivize his tenants, who hold his farm in lease, to improve that property'. Otherwise,

> when the lord of the soil himself, the rightful owner of the land, is only to become the [revenue] farmer for a lease of ten years, and if he is then to be exposed to the demand of a new rent, which may perhaps be dictated by ignorance or rapacity, what hopes can there be,—I will not say of improvement, but of preventing desolation? will it not be his interest, during the early part of that term, to extract from the estate every possible advantage for himself; and if any future hopes of a permanent settlement are then held out, to exhibit his lands at the end of it in a state of ruin?[136]

---

[135] Ibid.
[136] Ibid.

4.10 The Relationship between Constitutionism and Property's Discourses in Early Colonial Bengal

Given how easy was the elision from property in the soil to property in its rent, by the early 1790s there was no longer any pressing intellectual reason to doctrinalize a theory of sole sovereign 'ownership'. Provided an argument could be made for the existence of some variety of private property—a task made much easier when the right to property was viewed, in its essence, as a claim to endlessly divisible and fungible quanta of value—the Company's emerging self-conception as an agent of the subcontinent's 'improvement' could be kept firmly intact and even foregrounded. In turn, it could likewise always further be imagined that the Permanent Settlement was principally about guaranteeing private rights, rather than about extracting the publicly owed duty of remittance back to the state or, for that matter, simply about the state's own claim to a property in the rent.

To whatever extent the Company was willing to admit that it was making its own claim over the non-physical and clearly non-exclusive variety of property it was rendering legible, it thus did so not in the name of some self-conceived connection between any so-called *law of* taxation and *law of* property. Rather than in terms of balancing private legal 'rights' with public legal 'powers', the state's claim over property (in the rent) was instead conceived of through reference to a conduct of revenue administration that was considered one of the basic tasks defining the state's sovereignty as a practical affair, as per the early-modern language of constitutionism and the ontology of 'the laws' that went with it. As Part II moves beyond the process of land-revenue settlement in early colonial Bengal, as we will see directly in the next chapter, matters were not fundamentally different in the other key Presidency areas the absorption of which paved the way for the Company's ongoing transition from trader to sovereign.

5
Beyond the Permanent Settlement

Property Discourse and Non-*Zamindari* Revenue Systems

5.1 Introduction

Following its ascent to power in Bengal, the Company's expansion over large parts of the remainder of the subcontinent continued for the next three decades after Cornwallis' Permanent Settlement. Through a combination of coercive diplomacy and the resort to arms it acquired effective sovereignty over the southern territories comprising its Presidency in Madras, the areas on the western coast and the Deccan plateau comprising the Presidency of Bombay, and the so-called Ceded and Conquered Provinces adjacent to Awadh, which were later renamed the North-Western Provinces. In the half-century between the Company's assumption of direct control over administration in Bengal in 1772 and the end of the primary phase of its further consolidation of territory by 1820 most of what came to be called British India was thus subsumed under a new font of centralization and the novel discourses of government attendant with its rule.[1] Much as in Bengal, elsewhere in the subcontinent as well, the discourse of the early colonial public sphere focused on land and its produce, together with 'settling' the revenue that issued from it through doctrinalizing a new system for administering the particular rights and duties the Company was most eager to render legible.

The present chapter, therefore, picks up from the last by considering the way in which the Company's particular brand of property talk informed its activities outside Bengal. While the idea of situating the duty

---

[1] With the India Act of 1784 the heads of the Presidencies centred in Bombay and at Fort St. George in Madras were styled as governors and placed under the titular authority of the Governor General at Calcutta.

South Asia, the British Empire, and the Rise of Classical Legal Thought. Faisal Chaudhry, Oxford University Press.
© Faisal Chaudhry 2024. DOI: 10.1093/oso/9780198916482.003.0006

of revenue payment directly on the ostensible cultivator of the soil became predominant in both Madras and Bombay, it was in the former that it was first implemented. There, the so-called *raiyatwari* system became the basis of a purportedly unique style of southern administration from as early as 1810. Accordingly, in the first part of the chapter I take a fresh look at Parliament's famed *Fifth Report* of 1812 on the affairs of the East India Company, which paved the way for the *raiyatwari* settlement of much of Madras. More specifically, I argue that the *raiyatwari* system was distinguished by the same feature that made administration in Bengal stand out most—namely, a doctrinal discourse of property in/as land's rent. In the second section of the chapter, I then turn to the vexing problem that was posed for such a vision of property by land held under grants of *inʿam*, which were especially common in the southern parts of the subcontinent.

Borrowed from the lexicon of Mughal rule, the category of *inʿam* was used under the Company to cover a variety of royal gifting practices by which rights to the productive value of land were conveyed absent accompanying revenue obligations.[2] First becoming prominent under the fourth of the 'great Mughals,' the emperor Jahangir (r. 1569–1627),[3] *inʿam* grants created a dilemma for colonial officialdom that would not be fully resolved until the last decades of the nineteenth century. In considering why more specifically this was the case, the chapter concentrates on Thomas Munro's fascinating 'Minute on Altamgha Inams' and the controversy from which it emerged. Written only two years after Munro assumed the governorship of Madras, the Minute was issued in response to the Supreme Court of Madras' ruling in an important case involving the inheritance of a benefice that the nawab of Arcot awarded to his former diwan. The Minute is worth considering in detail because of the way it captures the extent to which the practice of *inʿam* created an intellectual

---

[2] For a more comprehensive effort at situating *inʿam* within early-modern Indo-Islamicate land-control practices see Sudev J. Sheth, 'Revenue Farming Reconsidered: Tenurial Rights and Tenurial Duties in Early Modern India, ca. 1556–1818', *Journal of the Economic and Social History of the Orient* 61, nos. 5–6 (2018): 878–919. On the British tendency to amalgamate various types of grants under the heading of *inʿam* see Aye Ikegame, *Princely India Re-imagined: A Historical Anthropology of Mysore from 1799 to the Present* (New York: Routledge, 2013), 20.

[3] The origins of 'altamgha inams' are discussed by Irfan Habib, *The Agrarian System of Mughal India, 1556–1707* (New York: Oxford University Press, 1999), 302, 358 and W. H. Moreland, *The Agrarian System of Moslem India* (Delhi: Oriental Books, 1968 [1929]), 127.

dilemma for the Company. At issue was not simply that such grants made for a strategic problem around how to balance the Company's competing imperatives of surplus extraction and legitimation. Rather, that such a large quantity of southern society's land could be rightfully 'held' absent any duty of revenue payment created an implicit crisis of conceptualization relative to the Company's discourse of property, focused as it was on making claims to the monetizable value of the land's produce administrable as fixed and maximally 'secure' obligations of revenue payment to the state. Read as an attempt to mediate this crisis, Munro's Minute illustrates both the instability and resilience of the Company's doctrinal discourse of property. In the final section of the chapter, I conclude by considering the relationship of the discourse of property in land's rent with what historians have called the rise of the so-called Ricardian 'law' of rent in Bombay and the North-Western provinces during the 1820s and 1830s.

5.2 The *Raiyatwari* System of Revenue Settlement in Madras

While it was not until the second decade of the nineteenth century that a consensus emerged in support of *raiyatwari* settlement in Madras, attempts at directly supervising revenue administration in the southern Presidency began alongside the Permanent Settlement in Bengal. In Madras the Company's first efforts along these lines took place in two tracts under its titular control going back to the 1760s. The first, comprising the Northern Circars, consisted of a narrow column of seventeen thousand square miles along the Bay of Bengal. Spanning an area that was historically of considerable commercial prosperity, as I touched on in the last chapter, the Northern Circars made the initial context for James Grant's theory that elements within the agrarian order were systematically concealing the true revenue demand their territory could support. With large-scale zamindar-style magnates as well as 'poligar' (*palaiyakarrar*) chieftains persisting in the second half of the eighteenth century, the obstacles to asserting control over the Northern Circars were considerable. Consequently, some thirty years passed between the Company's initial acquisition of the area in 1759 and its first sustained attempt at taking charge over its administration.[4]

A similar pattern developed in the Company's other—much smaller—holding in Chingleput, where it had acquired certain areas from the nawab of Arcot in 1750 and 1763. Known simply as 'the jaghire', these areas consisted of lands adjacent to Fort St. George.[5] However, in this context as well, the Company put off asserting administrative control until the 1780s, initially opting to simply convey the areas back to the nawab on an annual lease instead. As in the Northern Circars, in the Chingleput jaghire the obstacles to penetrating the local system of communal land control, which was overseen by a class of hereditary *mirasidars*, were multifarious.[6]

With efforts to build an administration in Madras that was scarcely a decade old by the early 1790s, the next fifteen to twenty years were a period of experimentation more than uniform practice. In the wake of the so-called poligar wars between 1799 and 1805, the Company instituted a *zamindari* system in many parts of Madras, opting to settle its revenue demand upon the defeated *palaiyakarrar*.[7] In the Chingleput jaghire, on the other hand, the Company simply mandated a cumulative total that was to be collected, leaving it up to the *mirasidar* co-sharers to apportion their specific payments among themselves.[8] During these same years, the first (limited) attempt at creating a *raiyatwari* system also emerged. Its roots could be traced back to Cornwallis' appointment of Captain Alexander Read to the position of superintendent of revenue for Baramahal district, which the Company secured by the Treaty of Seringapatnam following its defeat of Tipu Sultan in the Third Anglo-Mysore war.[9] Together with the military officer Thomas Munro, Read

---

[4] Burton Stein, *Thomas Munro: The Origins of the Colonial State and His Vision of Empire* (New York: Oxford University Press, 1989), 25.
[5] *The Fifth Report*, vol. II, Madras Presidency, 36–45.
[6] Stein, *Thomas Munro*, 25.
[7] The overall extent of the *zamindari* system in Madras was not insignificant, initially covering as much as one-third of the Presidency's settled territory. By the beginning of the twentieth century estimates put the balance at closer to one-fifth, which translates to some 14,000 square miles. See Dietmar Rothermund, *Government, Landlord, and Peasant in India: Agrarian Relations under British Rule, 1865–1930* (Wiesbaden: Steiner, 1978), 115.
[8] Baden Henry Baden-Powell, *A Short Account of the Land Revenue and its Administration in British India: with a Sketch of the Land Tenures* (Oxford: Clarendon Press, 1907), 199–200.
[9] Stein, *Thomas Munro*, 37–47.

proposed that settlement in Baramahal take place directly with the cultivator and each individual be charged with paying dues directly to the colonial state in cash. On Read and Munro's view, the revenue demand would be rationalized by working with village accountants and headmen to conduct field-by-field surveys to gauge the land's actual productive capacity. Further actualizing the plan would then require recruiting such village-level personnel to train the various others who would also be needed to undertake the laborious tasks of assessing soil types and documenting localized rights claims.[10]

Although successful in some ways, the Baramahal experiment would ultimately fail to win generalized acclaim. In fact, because the rate of the assessment ended up being quite high, the fall in actual receipts that resulted from settling the district on a *raiyatwari* basis meant that by the end of his own tenure in 1799 Read's efforts came to be seen as a failure in the eyes of Madras' Board of Revenue. With Read departing South Asia for England that same year, it was Munro who was left to attempt to expand the *raiyatwari* system to other parts of Madras, like the Ceded Districts of Mysore. These comprised a territory including notable areas like Bellary, Cuddapah, and Kurnool that were first granted to the Nizam of Hyderabad in 1799 but that were taken back by the Company two years later. In the course of pursuing settlement operations in the so-called Ceded Districts Munro instituted procedures similar to those used in Baramahal, while supplementing the resultant effort at revenue assessment with an attempt to create a proper cadastral survey.[11]

Against this larger backdrop, Munro went on to become the main spokesperson for the *raiyatwari* idea. He proved up to the task, and by 1805 his communications with the Board of Revenue became an important source of inspiration for attracting newcomers to the cause. Although over the course of the subsequent decade support for expanding the *raiyatwari* system's ideal of direct cultivator settlement would remain uneven, once Munro returned to England in 1807 his

---

[10] J. T. Gwynn, 'The Madras District System and Land Revenue to 1818'. In *The Cambridge History of the British Empire*, vol. 4, *British India 1497–1858*, ed. H. H. Dowell (Cambridge: Cambridge University Press, 1940), 469 and Matthew Edney, *Mapping an Empire: The Geographical Construction of British India, 1765–1843* (Chicago, IL: University of Chicago Press, 1997), 175.
[11] Edney, *Mapping an Empire*, 175.

visibility actually increased. Upon touching down on the British mainland, he thus quickly became central to debates about the impending renewal of the Company's charter in 1813. As a result, his influence on the Parliamentary Select Committee's famed *Fifth Report* on the Company's affairs proved undeniable, with its volume on Madras becoming a de facto manifesto for extending the *raiyatwari* system throughout the rest of the Company's southern Presidency.

5.3 The Discourse of *Raiyatwari* Right and the Persistence of Property in Rent

In attending to the circumstances of Company rule in Madras in the *Fifth Report*, the Select Committee brought together extracts from correspondence, policy minutes, and other official commentary on its ongoing efforts at revenue administration in the southern parts of the subcontinent. The Company's early state-making activities in places like the Northern Circars, the Chingleput jaghire, Baramahal, and the districts ceded by the Nizam thus featured prominently, especially given the larger aim behind Parliamentary scrutiny of comparatively assessing the more inchoate experience with revenue administration in the south and the Permanent Settlement system in Bengal. Indeed, the formation of the Select Committee was undergirded by a clear dissatisfaction with the performance of the Company's governance functions in Bengal, even while the possibility of instituting a *zamindari* system throughout Madras was still very much up for debate.

At the same time, notwithstanding the implicit case the *Fifth Report* made for generalizing the *raiyatwari* system of proprietorship within Madras, it was clearly premised on much same vision of property as that which informed the Permanent Settlement. This was evident in the way advocates of *raiyatwari* settlement tended to blur their own ostensibly categorical distinction between agricultural leaseholders who merely 'farmed' the land and small 'proprietors' who had something closer to supposed ownership over it. For example, in considering the 'comparative advantages and disadvantages of Ryotwar and Zemindarry Settlements as a permanent system' for areas along the Kanara coast, then member of the Board of Revenue William Thackeray observed that even did great capitals, lodged with a few, promote improvement, more than the same capital shared among many small farmers; it would not signify, in respect to Canara and Malabar, *where they are proprietors, not farmers*. I will admit, that had I a large estate, I would rather let it out to a few rich, than to many poor farmers; not so much, because I thought that they could raise a great produce, and pay more rent, as because my rent might be more secure. But the question is, whether great *proprietors* are better than small? and I think it evident, that a number of small *proprietors*, are better in every respect, than the same land and capital, in the hands of a few great landlords.[12]

On the surface, Thackeray's point seems straightforward—namely, that the comparison between large landlords and small *farmers* with respect to the likelihood of agricultural improvement was not of much relevance to 'Canara and Malabar', where it was not small *farmers* but small *proprietors* that one found. Yet scratching the surface only slightly, it becomes apparent that Thackeray was able to so easily conclude that smallholders in these areas held true proprietorship rather than mere farming leases mainly on account of the heritable quality of the holdings, which is borne out by his avowed consternation over the tendency towards their 'minute division'. Turning the same vice even more explicitly into a virtue, Munro picked up on much the same feature to simply do away with any distinction between small proprietors and small farmers, emphasizing, instead, that the landlord and cultivator in the subcontinent were destined almost always *eventually* to become '[t]he same person, with very few exceptions'. In sharp contrast to England where the two remained 'permanently separated', as he further explained, in the subcontinent '[t]he landlord must always cultivate his own fields; and hence the collections must always be made directly from the cultivator in his quality of landlord'. Ultimately, then, there could be no 'person between the cultivator and the revenue officer, without a creation of zemindars, who must themselves in time become, either petty princes, or cultivators'.[13]

---

[12] William Thackeray, 'Extract from Report of Mr. Thackeray on Malabar, Canara and the Ceded Districts', 4 August 1807, reprinted in *The Fifth Report, vol. II, Madras Presidency*, 719 (emphasis added).
[13] 'Extract from Report of Principal Collector of the Ceded Districts Proposing a Plan for permanently settling those Districts on the Ryotwar principle', 15 August 1807, reprinted in ibid., 649–50.

Yet once moving past—or simply dispensing with—the basis of the categorical distinction between small proprietors and small farmers in the heritability of their holdings, the above line of assertion was plainly confounded by the further explanation of *why*, as Thackeray put it, the situation characterized by small proprietors would be better than that characterized by small farmers (that would arise if leasing was necessitated by ownership being instead consolidated in the hands of 'a few great landlords'). For here, the reasoning no longer depended on the heritability of the holdings of those deemed small proprietors; rather, it instead turned, once again, on the by now highly familiar notion that by remitting to the zamindars, as their fee, the extra amount of the state's revenue that would otherwise be lost to them, their property would be rendered absolutely secure.

If it was the underlying notion of property in land's rent that *really* underpinned the argument for categorically distinguishing certain kinds of interest-holders as small proprietors, however, it was no longer clear why the same could not just as well be said for small farmers on secure leases, the 'minute[]' divisibility (and heritability) of their interests notwithstanding. Ultimately, then, it would have been difficult for it *not* to become apparent that the whole sequence of reasoning really hung together on the basis of a notion of property as entitlement over rent that elided the very difference between small proprietors and small farmers that started the sequence in the first place. As one official within the revenue collectorate for the Ceded Districts tellingly emphasized:

> [t]he only matters of real importance, in a comparison of the ryotwar and zemindarry systems, are the amount of the remission to be granted, and the mode of its distribution. If the sum is in both cases equal, the direct loss to revenue, is also the same; but in the one case, the whole remission goes immediately to the ryots, by whom all land rent is produced, while in the other, it may never reach them. The zemindars will keep it from them forever, and the mootahdars for a long period of years. In the one case, the whole of it, will be immediately applied to the improvement of the country. In the other, either none, or only a small portion will be allotted to that purpose. It seems extraordinary, that it should ever have been conceived, that a country could be as much benefited by giving up a share of the public rent to a small class of zemindars

or mootahdars, who do not yet actually exist, as by giving it to the ryots, from whom all rent is derived. When the settlement of a great province is in view, the prosperity of the body of the people should be the grand object to which every thing else should be made to yield; and as it is plain that the ryots must reap infinitely more advantage from a remission granted to themselves, than from a similar one to zemindars and mootahdars, the ryotwar system, with all its supposed inconveniences, ought undoubtedly to be adopted, in preference to every other.[14]

Notably, on this view, even if the state held exclusive sway over the uncultivated waste, it would not really undercut the basis for insisting that it was the notional zamindars that were Madras' true proprietors. For as land that was not actively producing rent, waste was not really the kind of thing the control of which made sense to envision in terms of the variety of property the Company's rule was effectively premised on attributing to the subcontinent. In this respect, the existence of state-controlled waste was just as well-suited to making the case for the notional zamindar's property (in land's rent) meriting absolute security as it was for sovereign ownership of the soil.

Likewise, nor was the option of *raiyatwari* settlement, itself, at any greater disadvantage relative to such a view. For it was not any more mutually exclusive with imagining that the state could increase its revenue without disturbing the stability of expectations needed to fashion true proprietors than was Cornwallis' Permanent Settlement system in Bengal. As the unnamed revenue officer from the Ceded Districts quoted above thus went on to argue, 'by allowing the revenue to increase or diminish, according to the extent of land in cultivation' the *raiyatwari* system actually 'eases the farmer, without occasioning, on an average of years, any loss to government'. Indeed, as the same officer continued, any 'fluctuation would lessen every day, as the ryots became more wealthy, and would at last, be confined to tank lands' such that in the end 'the ryotwar system, by retaining in the hands of government all unoccupied land, [would] give[] it the power of gradually augmenting the revenue, without imposing any fresh burden upon the ryots, as long as there is an acre of waste in the country'.[15]

---

[14] Ibid., 649.
[15] Ibid., 648.

5.4 *Raiyatwari* Entitlement as Mere Lease Right?

In the years after the publication of the *Fifth Report* in 1812 and before he would be appointed as the governor of Madras in 1820, Munro returned to the province to oversee the revamping of its police and judiciary as Judicial Commissioner. At the time, the Company's Court of Directors in London had already ordered the Board of Revenue not to extend its earlier experiment with village settlements. Instead, in roughly half of the districts of Madras work was to begin immediately on instituting or renewing a *raiyatwari* system, with the same course of action to be pursued elsewhere in the Presidency after the pending expiration—in 1820—of the initial interval that had been set for using village settlements.

As *raiyatwari* rule was cemented during this period, the ways in which it was supposed to be different from the Cornwallis system in Bengal continued to be twofold. First, as per Read and Munro's early vision, a more widely deployed *raiyatwari* system would continue to build on the foundation of bypassing landlord elements in favour of settling directly with the ostensible cultivators of the soil. Second, assessment was supposed to be based on an empirically intensive field-by-field accounting of the land's productive capacity. At the same time, in contrast to the earlier support for making the assessment permanent, after 1820 the idea that *raiyatwari* settlement would entail reassessment at periodic intervals—thirty years becoming the norm in most parts of the Company's domain—emerged as a third difference of note.

Since at least the late nineteenth century there has also been a fourth key difference commonly noted as well, which has derived from seeing *raiyatwari* settlement as differing from Cornwallis' approach in Bengal on grounds of its comprising a system of mere leasehold tenure.[16] In this respect, the history of revenue settlement in Madras appears to add to the sense that the Company's commitment to freeing property was illusory; for rather than simply a gap between theory and practice, it implies that even a nominal commitment to property's rule was missing in its

---

[16] See e.g. Baden Henry Baden-Powell, *The Land Systems of British India: Being a Manual of the Land-tenures and of the Systems of Land-revenue Administration Prevailing in the Several Provinces*, vol. III (Oxford: Clarendon Press, 1892), 128–30.

southern Presidency.[17] The spread of the *raiyatwari* system, thus, would seem to have kept 'rights to private property in land... indistinct from the state's revenue rights' not only in reality but also in principle.[18]

Yet notwithstanding this view, *raiyatwari* rights were certainly no more indistinct from the state's claims on the surplus than were the entitlements assigned to zamindars in Bengal. Nor, for that matter, were they any more so than the rights assigned on a collective basis to co-sharers under the third main scheme of 'village' or *mahalwari* settlement.[19] Therefore, with respect to both the nature of the legal entitlement it doctrinalized and the method through which it did so, *raiyatwari* settlement was hardly unique, premised as it was on rendering rights legible primarily through the administration of the attendant duty of revenue payment.

Whatever the important differences between the Company's various revenue settlement systems, then, it is misleading to imagine that there was 'no coherent conceptualization of property' undergirding the form of rule they operationalized, as per what Upal Chakrabarti has usefully labelled the 'misrecognition thesis' that has been such a commonplace among scholars.[20] On the contrary, those systems all shared in the same foundational notion of property in its capacity as a doctrinal concept.[21]

---

[17] According to Washbrook, for example, the *raiyatwari* system's putative scheme of letting fields on 'an individual basis to ryots in return for annual revenue engagements' was tantamount to a resurgence of the claim to full sovereign ownership over all land; this, he suggests, came back into favour only once the conquests of 1790 to 1820 had resulted in the final defeat of the various Muslim potentates whom the Company had earlier condemned as Oriental sovereigns claiming monopoly on ownership of the soil under their purview. See Washbrook, 'Sovereignty, Property, Land and Labour in Colonial South India'. In *Constituting Modernity: Private Property in the East and West*, ed. Huri İslamoğlu-İnan (New York: I. B. Tauris, 2004), 69–99 at 87. See also David Ludden, *Peasant History in South India* (Princeton, NJ: Princeton University Press, 1985), 104, 173–74 and Dirks, *Castes of Mind*, 109.
[18] Washbrook, 'India, 1818–1860: The Two Faces of Colonialism', 407–08.
[19] *Mahalwari* settlement became most visible in the North-Western Provinces during the 1830s and entailed leaving the individualized apportionment of the total demand assessed on the village to the co-sharers constituting its empropertied members. Because payment was ultimately made through the village *lambardar*, however, practically speaking the system proved less egalitarian than it might sound. See Dharma Bhanu Srivastava, *The Province of Agra: its History and Administration* (Delhi: Concept Publishing, 1979 [1959]), 140.
[20] Upal Chakrabarti, 'The Problem of Property: Local Histories and Political-Economic Categories in British India', *Journal of the Economic and Social History of the Orient* 61, nos. 5–6 (2018): 1003–33. For an expansion of this argument see also Upal Chakrabarti, *Assembling the Local: Political Economy and Agrarian Governance in British India* (Philadelphia, PA: University of Pennsylvania Press, 2021).
[21] This is not to deny that *raiyatwari* settlement involved a greater administrative labour than the *zamindari* system. Insofar as the revenue collectorate's basic task was to assign those rights that were to be counted as the doctrinal equivalent of whatever type of property the subcontinent

While it thus may be ironic that in Madras private *raiyatwari* entitlements in land were given substance primarily as duties of payment owed by their respective holders to the state, they were no less theoretically coherent as property for this being the case and certainly no less so than the entitlements of zamindars under the Cornwallis system.

Moreover, as much as in Bengal, so too in Madras was the peculiarity of the property entitlement being defined primarily as a doctrinal duty of revenue payment destined to remain obscured. This is because in the ontology of governance following from the discursive culture surrounding the Company's transition to sovereign, the focus was neither on the individual's 'duty' to subtract (some quantum) from their property (in the rent) nor the state's own corollary *legal* 'power' over that property. Instead, surplus appropriation was legitimized in terms of the de facto task of tax administration that comprised sovereignty as a practical affair in early-modern constitutionist thought. In fact, much the same held true even where administration entailed settling conflicts through arbitration supervised under the jurisdiction of so-called revenue courts. For the mass of administrative business in such venues focused on vetting factual details about collection that had gone unrecorded through the highly imperfect system of registering property rights that the Company's revenue regime created.[22] (After all, as Matthew Edney puts it, even in South India, early revenue surveys were 'geographical, not cadastral, in character'.[23]) Only to whatever much lesser degree, if at all, did the conduct of such administration involve deciding among competing claims to legal right through evolving a jurisprudence of ownership as a doctrinal power

was thought to offer, even beyond the more involved efforts at assessment and collection in *raiyatwari* areas there were also simply more right-holders to deal with.

[22] It must not be forgotten that *raiyatwari* settlement did not entail the creation of a proper record of the individualized rights it effectively recognized. This is because any brand of property in land's rent it created was based on assigning rights not so much to the individual as to the land itself. This was consistent with the Company's primary interest, which was less to develop an exhaustive catalogue of who commanded such rights than it was to specify that a particular right attached to a particular unit of production so as to further ensure clarity about the revenue payment owed on that unit. See Rothermund, *Government, Landlord, and Peasant in India*, 41–43.

[23] Edney, *Mapping an Empire*, 174.

to exclude,[24] whether on the part of the private individual or the public person of the state.[25]

With Munro's appointment as Governor of Madras in 1820, then, whatever the outstanding differences between the *raiyatwari* and *zamindari* systems, the gap between them narrowed still further. As the work of settlement went into practical effect in South India, it soon became apparent that the oft-proclaimed moderation in the level of demand that had failed to materialize in Bengal under the Cornwallis system and that a *raiyatwari* approach was supposed to finally make good on in Madras was unlikely to materialize there either.[26] While lip service continued to be paid to the ideal of field-by-field surveying as a way of arriving at a rational assessment based on actual productivity, settlement operations in Madras proved neither resoundingly scientific nor uniform.[27] Even in places like Baramahal, where there were relatively good pre-existing surveys, assessment had been less than exact. Drawing on the expertise of local village officers, such earlier attempts had been based neither on true field-by-field enquiry nor any clearly effective effort at individualizing

---

[24] Contrast the various ways, whether implicitly or explicitly, in which the systematizing effect of adjudicating the right to property in the context of the late-eighteenth-/early- nineteenth-century Anglo-common-law mainstream has been depicted. See e.g. Vandevelde, 'The New Property of the Nineteenth Century'; Morton Horwitz, *The Transformation of American Law, 1780–1860* (Cambridge, MA: Harvard University Press, 1979), ch. 2; and Sugarman and Warrington, 'Land Law, Citizenship and the Invention of "Englishness"'.

[25] That such was the case in a context like Madras' is broadly compatible with the idea—a staple among historians—that administration in the South strongly disfavoured any separation between the magistracy and the executive. As Bhavani Raman puts the point in her study of South India under early Company rule, already prior to the judicial reforms of 1816 that institutionalized this blurring of lines, judges in Madras 'viewed their work as "determining matters of fact"... and not "matters of law" like their peers at home'. Bhavani Raman, *Document Raj: Writing and Scribes in Early Colonial South India* (Chicago, IL: University of Chicago Press, 2012), 152. At the same time, seeing matters in this way probably carries the risk of overemphasizing the degree to which arrangements initially varied under the Cornwallis system in Bengal, with its distinct cutcherry administration. At least from the standpoint of the historical ontology of the legal, it is not so much the institutionalization of a 'separation of powers' regime that matters. Rather, more to the point is the extremely limited extent to which adjudication under the Company's administration—whether in Madras or under the initial version of Cornwallis' system in Bengal—sustained an ethic of what Max Weber would call logically formal legal rationality, much less one that was specifically geared towards treating property as the cardinal deductive premise from which formal rationality was to proceed. See Max Weber, *Economy and Society, vol. I*, 656–57.

[26] Nilmani Mukherjee, *The Ryotwari System in Madras, 1792–1827* (Calcutta: Firma K. L. Mukhopadhyay, 1962), 196–97.

[27] Detailed (cadastral-style) surveying involving the demarcation of precise boundaries, the classification of soil types, a comprehensive recording of rights, and revenue assessment based on such factors was not undertaken until the 1860s. See Edney, *Mapping an Empire*, 174.

assessment according to the differing productive capacities of holdings. Consequently, they were of limited value as examples of how to apply a so-called scientific method to ongoing efforts to expand the settlement process in the name of a more generalized *raiyatwari* commitment.

Where such older experiments did not exist, the prospects for making settlement scientific proved still dimmer. In the great majority of the Presidency, therefore, even the pretence of field-by-field enquiry was difficult to maintain. For example, in the dry zone of the Tirunelveli district where settlement on a *raiyatwari* basis had not previously been attempted, sixteen years after Munro came to office near half of the cultivated fields remained unmarked, being identifiable only to local inhabitants and village officials. In the remainder of the district, where the Company's revenue settlement operations had progressed to the point of demarcating specific fields, areas so distinguished were often less units of individual cultivation than sprawling and extensive tracts. Under such conditions, the collectorate's records provided little real guidance as to which specific cultivators were responsible for which specific lands, the level of demand each relevant area of cultivation could actually bear, and even whether the revenue commensurate with any specific area's actual extent of cultivation had been paid. In such areas, as David Ludden notes, only the village official had anything approaching such knowledge.[28]

Already within the first year of Munro's governorship—when a *raiyatwari* survey was launched in Chingleput—the ideal of the scientific survey-assessment had given way, with the Board of Revenue instead backing a method of *putcut* assessment. Under this scheme, the amount to be paid by the designated *raiyat* was fixed as a sum total for all lands under their control, regardless of the differing soil types or details of cropping and production specific to individual fields. Resort to the *putcut* method thereby obviated field-by-field enquiry and any proper attempt at rationalizing estimates of productive capacity from the get-go.[29] It also allowed partisans of the *raiyatwari* idea to silently recalibrate the effective goal of the system. In the more prosperous parts of southern India under the Company's rule, where various kinds of higher rights over cultivation had deep historical roots, powerful elements in the agrarian hierarchy,

---

[28] Ludden, *Peasant History in South India*, 108.
[29] Mukherjee, *The Ryotwari System in Madras*, 145–46.

thus, were incorporated under the discourse of *raiyatwari* settlement as notional cultivators from the start.[30]

Prior to the 1860s, in fact, the *patta* document under which *raiyatwari* entitlements were granted took two different forms, either of which could be issued to persons claiming *mirasidar* status. Whereas the first type of *patta* was used to recognize low-level *mirasidars*, the other—the *samudayam patta*—was routinely granted to big *mirasidar* chiefs who commanded large numbers of cultivators as their personal tenants.[31] Regardless of whether the designated *raiyat* was a more or a less powerful land controller, however, the result was similar in obvious ways to that of landlord settlement. In this respect, a system purporting to champion cultivator rights proved distinguishable from one that was premised on recognizing *zamindari* rights in degree only, not kind.

Yet regardless of how far removed from the actual tillers of the soil the official *raiyat* ended up being, the ideal of so-called cultivator settlement informing the *raiyatwari* system did not simply go into retreat. Rather, given that it was premised on the same foundational—and peculiarly colonial—notion of property in rent as the Company's other approaches to settlement, the *raiyatwari* system involved a brand of theory that was inherently plastic. To the extent that the system was based on the same de-physicalized notion of right that the Company sought to doctrinalize elsewhere, in other words, no more than its *zamindari* counterpart did *raiyatwari* property denote any ostensible relation between persons and tangible things. In both cases, the Company's transition from trader to sovereign was marked by a similar distance from the model of right upon which legal modernity was being built in the Anglo-common-law mainstream already from the late eighteenth century. In the early colonial subcontinent, in contrast, property talk was de-physicalized and abstracted from its very inception, and this was not simply—or even mainly—insofar as it pointed to entitlements over the exchange values of discrete commodities. Instead, as I have been arguing, it was through pointing to

---

[30] See generally ibid., ch. 12.
[31] Tsukasa Mizushima, 'From Mirasidar to Pattadar: South India in the Late Nineteenth Century', *Indian Economic and Social History Review* 39, nos. 2 & 3 (2002): 259–84 at 262–63. As Mizushima notes, the contradictory nature of such a system of so-called cultivator settlement came explicitly to the fore only after 1855 when formal authorization was needed to recognize the rights of tenant-*payakaris*.

the monetizable value of agrarian produce, and in the name of political economy's most elementary idea of rent, reinscribing it as an inherently divisible and fungible quantity over and above cost that was to be seen as uniquely/preeminently issuing from land.

On the whole, then, even apart from those cases in which *raiyatwari* settlement was explicitly used to recognize dominant elements, the tendency to bypass the actual cultivator was built into the system in virtue of its very conceptual fabric. For even absent a more methodical practice of auctioning *raiyatwari* rights in the event that their holders fell into arrears in the way that was done for *zamindari* property in Bengal, the de-physicalized nature of the entitlement over rent nonetheless made *raiyatwari* property highly subject to sub-infeudation. It was thus all too readily possible for notional *raiyats* to formally reassign portions of their all too fungible property in land's rent in exchange for passing the burden of ostensible cultivation—and, in effect, the all-important duty of revenue payment that went with it—to subordinated others.

5.5 In'am Privileges and the Problem of Administering Rights without Duties

Given the de-physicalized notion of property that early advocates of *raiyatwari* shared, there was nothing in their view that determinately required the state's revenue demand to be seen as a claim to sovereign ownership. The view that Shore took in his disagreement with Grant in the context of the Permanent Settlement—arguing that *zamindari* property (in rent) should be kept distinct from the government subtraction therefrom—remained as available in Madras as it did in Bengal. It is little wonder, then, that Islamicate forms of imperial gifting—by which control over surplus was alienated free of any revenue obligation to the state and 'only taken away' after being given 'when they were to be given again'—proved so problematic for the Company.[32] Grouped by colonial

---

[32] Nicholas Dirks, *The Hollow Crown: Ethnohistory of an Indian Kingdom* (New York: Cambridge University Press, 1987), 330 (further arguing that to subject such grants to 'permanent resumption' was tantamount to 'creating ... a new political system').

officialdom under the heading of the Perso-Arabic term *in'am*, such forms of grant were especially prevalent in the South Indian context where in pre-colonial times centralizing royal authority was generally weaker than in the heartlands of Mughal North India. While the large-scale revenue immunities granted to Hindu temples were the most noteworthy example, especially in the southernmost parts of South India, it was the privileged *in'am* holdings of individuals that were greatest in total magnitude. As the colonial state's own Inam Commission estimated, in the second half of the nineteenth century some three-fifths of Madras' revenue-free lands were still held under some form of personal *in'am*.[33]

Of course, the total extent of such revenue-free holding was even more extensive prior to the Commission's work, which began only in 1858 when the colonial state was finally in a position to risk definitively alienating those whose privileges it sought to revoke. For example, David Washbrook estimates that in the early nineteenth century the percentage of land in Madras held as *in'am* varied from 12 to as much as 40 per cent in some parts of the Presidency.[34] In his well-known study of the Tamil 'little kingdom' of Pudukkottai, which emerged at the end of the seventeenth century in the area between Tanjavur and Madurai, Nicholas Dirks relays that according to Company records during the early nineteenth century a striking 70 per cent of cultivable land was classed as *in'am*.[35]

As the latter figures suggest, grants of *in'am* could not only cover lands within a given village locale, but they could also subsume many villages at once. In this respect, *in'am* gifting constituted a structural feature of the social and political organization of southern society, and the Company initially had little choice but to accept its prevalence. Accordingly, in the twenty years prior to the emergence of a consensus favouring the extension of a *raiyatwari* system throughout Madras after 1810, the Company undertook what historian Robert Frykenberg has called a 'silent' settlement in much of the Presidency by leaving pre-exiting *in'am* holdings

---

[33] Eric Stokes, 'Privileged Land Tenure in Village India in the Early Nineteenth Century', reprinted in *The Peasant and the Raj*, 46–62 at 46.
[34] Washbrook, 'Law, State and Agrarian Society in Colonial India', 657.
[35] Notably, this figure represents a significant decline from the previous half-century when, according to Dirks, 'there were at the very least another 5,000 military retainers' who were remunerated through such grants before the kingdom's war-making apparatus was gradually eliminated during the Company's initial period of 'indirect rule'. Dirks, *Castes of Mind*, 67–68.

intact.[36] It did so by classifying such areas as presumptively unsettleable, thereby pre-empting conflict with entrenched *in'amdars*, who were often petty kings or military chieftains of a kind the Company had reason to avoid antagonizing. Likewise, in the nearly one-third of Madras that was settled on a *zamindari* basis—with defeated *palaiyakarrars*—those anointed with the mantle of legal right were left free to continue making grants of *in'am* out of their newly minted property in land's rent. Ongoing additions to the total land area of the Presidency that were exempt from the state's revenue demand, therefore, went completely unchecked until at least 1803—when the Company made its first audible rumblings about taking away the power of *in'am*-style gifting from its *palaiyakarrar* partners.[37]

Yet even if the Company did undertake a so-called silent settlement in Madras by leaving large *in'amdars* intact during its early period of dominance, the revenue immunities such individuals commanded were still transformed in significant ways.[38] With *in'am* holdings left to the jurisdiction of the judiciary—with its ostensible commitment to preserving native 'laws' and 'usages'—the colonial state's policies could not but tend towards rigidification. In part, this followed from the very act of submitting *in'am*-based privileges to a discourse of legal administration that attributed their origin to 'time immemorial' and their function to the maintenance of 'traditional' caste hierarchy. In part, it also followed from—or, at any rate, was amplified by—the judicial preference to count claims of *in'am* inalienable and subject to a fixed ordering of hereditary succession.[39]

On both fronts, the gifting of control over surplus through *in'am* was sapped of its earlier dynamism, especially insofar as the proliferation of such grants in pre-colonial times can be traced to the fluctuating balance between sovereigns and subordinates during the turbulence of the eighteenth century. Accordingly, whatever reversal of its founding policy of

---

[36] Robert Eric Frykenberg, 'The Silent Settlement', in *Land Tenure and Peasant in South Asia*, 37–57.

[37] See Nicholas Dirks, 'From Little King to Landlord', *Comparative Studies in Society and History* 28, no. 2 (Apr. 1986): 307–33 at 323–24.

[38] David Washbrook, 'Economic Depression and the Making of "Traditional" Society in Colonial India 1820–1855', *Transactions of the Royal Historical Society* 6th ser., no. 3 (1993): 237–63 at 253.

[39] Ibid., 250–51.

appeasing powerful *in'amdars* the Company was hoping to effectuate after 1820, it was set in opposition to a reality of their 'traditional' rights that in no small part colonial rule had created. (Perhaps for this reason, in addition to whatever others, the process of reversal waxed and waned in its success well into the second half of the nineteenth century.)[40]

The specific reasons behind the more pronounced desire to terminate *in'am* privileges after 1820 notwithstanding, it would be wrong to imagine that it also somehow followed from the merely theoretical nature of the commitment to the Company's discourse about property in land's rent. In the next section of the chapter, I turn to elaborating on this point directly.

5.6 Munro's Minute on 'Altamgha *Inams*': Alienating Private Property or Public Revenue?

Meaning 'red seal', the term *al-tamgha* as a descriptor within the lexicon of Islamicate revenue practice dates back to at least the twelfth century. In the subcontinent the granting of *in'am-i altamgha* first became evident during Jahangir's time, as noted at the outset of the chapter, and grew more common during the subsequent reign of Shahjahan (r. 1628–58). Generally used for the purposes of conveying rights to agrarian surplus to imperial subordinates alongside full or partial exemption from the obligation to remit revenue payments back to the central treasury, from the distance of colonial-era retrospection *altamgha* grants were seen as descending hereditarily within the assignee's lineage and thus subject to escheat only when there was no heir to speak of. (They were made generally 'null and void' in 1793 by Regulation XXXVII of the Bengal Code.)[41]

---

[40] If the period from 1825 to 1850 was marked by a support for bringing *in'am* holdings back into the Company's revenue fold, this was easier said than done. Even after the *in'am* commission of 1860 was set up, the colonial state's strategy was less to confiscate the privileges of the *in'amdars* than it was to retrofit them appropriately with the doctrinal trappings of that which counted as 'true property' relative to its own administrative priorities. See e.g. Dirks, *The Hollow Crown*, 327–32.

[41] As was bluntly explained in the Regulation, this was because if the 'validity' of such 'grant[s] or alienation of Government's proportion of the produce of lands' was instead 'admitted, it is obvious that the Public Revenue would have been liable to gradual diminution'. Regulation

Notwithstanding the reasons there may be for uncertainty around how widespread the practice of making *al-tamgha* grants was,[42] such conveyances were put front and centre early on in Madras when the Supreme Court of the Presidency clashed with Munro over the alienation of a *jagir* worth 64,000 *chakrams* to one Muhammad Assim Khan, the diwan of the Nawab of Arcot and ally of the Company, Muhammad Ali Khan Wallajah.[43] Initially made in 1783, the grant was confirmed in July 1789 by a deed with all requisite proclamations about its hereditability and divisibility among Assim Khan's descendants. However, soon after Ali Khan Wallajah's death in 1795, the Company moved to 'resume' the nawab's grant to his diwan, the first of several further rounds of reversal and re-reversal of its stance over the next several years. Two years later—after the Company's initial attempt at resumption—in 1797 it reinstated the grant for the first time. However, shortly thereafter, upon further consolidating control over much of the Carnatic peninsula, it opted to attempt resumption a second time, now citing the need 'for investigation on a change of Government, according to the usage of the country on such occasions' as justification.

Yet the drama did not end there. With the second attempt at resumption still pending, in 1801 Assim Khan died, and though the diwan's will made no mention of the grant, before Ali Khan Wallajah's own earlier death in 1795, Assim Khan had made written request to Company officials seeking assurance that his gift would remain intact. By official Minute dated May 1802 his request for assurance was seemingly accepted,

---

XXXVII of 1793 ('A Regulation for re-enacting with modifications the Rules ... for trying the Validity of the Titles of persons holding or claiming a right to hold Altamgha, Jagir and other Lands exempt from the payment of public Revenue, under Grants termed Badshahi or Royal'), reprinted in C. D. Field, ed., *The Regulations of the Bengal Code: With a Chronological Table of Repeals and Amendments, an Introduction, Notes and an Index* (Calcutta: Thacker, Spink and Co., 1875), 261.

[42] The question of the prevalence—and, indeed, exact origins—of *al-tamgha* grants leaves room for uncertainty. See e.g. Henry Miers Elliot, *Supplement to the Glossary of Indian Terms* (Agra: Printed at the Secundra Orphan Press, 1845), 14–18 and Henry Miers Elliot, *Memoirs on the History, Folk-lore, and Distribution of the Races of the North Western Provinces of India: Being an Amplified Edition of the Original Supplemental Glossary of Indian Terms*, vol. 2 (London: Trubner, 1869), 4–9.

[43] As Munro noted, the by then largely obsolete denomination was valued at approximately six British pence at the time. Reprinted in A. J. Arbuthnot, *Major General Sir Thomas Munro, Governor of Madras: Selections from His Minutes and Other Official Writings*, vol. I (London: Kegan Paul, 1881), 136–63 at 136.

with the Company affirming its previous resolutions favouring the restoration of all home country (*waṭan*) *jagirs*. As a result, following Assim Khan's death in 1801, the Company reinstated the *in'am* for a second time, with all associated revenues from the territories of the underlying *jagir*—save for certain customs and other fees connected to the mineral estate—redirected towards the diwan's eldest son, Kalam-ullah.

With the lion's share of the remaining estate also passing to Kalam-ullah by the terms of his father's will, Assim Khan's other sons immediately moved to have the will set aside, arguing that their father was mentally incompetent at the time of its making. While at this first stage of suit the will withstood challenge, Kalam-ullah's brothers did prove successful in establishing that Assim Khan's personal property was to be apportioned according to the shares specified under Islamic *fiqh*-based formulas for inheritance. Emboldened, the brothers then pressed on, further bringing suit against Kalam-ullah and the Company jointly. In the second round of litigation the aim was to compel an accounting of the *jagir's* revenues and to demand their reapportionment among all of Assim Khan's children, here again on the basis of *fiqh*-based inheritance shares.

Over the Company's objection, the Supreme Court declared it a 'directly interested' party in the suit and again handed victory to Kalam-ullah's brothers. The Court's sweeping opinion built on the key claim that Assim Khan's original *in'am* constituted a form of 'property'. Consequently, the Court reasoned, not only should the grant have never been resumed in the first place but when the Company reversed that decision, as property, it should have also descended according to the same native 'laws' of Islamic inheritance that governed the distribution of Assim Khan's larger estate. In keeping with this logic, the Supreme Court appointed the collector for the district in which the lands funding the *jagir* were situated to function as the interim receiver for the associated revenues. Under this arrangement, the moneys deriving from the produce of the lands under the grant were to be reapportioned to each of the late diwan's children according to their appropriate *fiqh*-based share, rather than alone to Kalam-ullah, who, in any case, had by then effectively abandoned his role as manager of the *jagir*, leaving mounting arrears in his wake. While the Madras government 'acceded' to the course of action the Court ordered—'for no other reason but that of its being the only one by which discussion with the Supreme Court could be obviated'—for his own part, Munro could not let 'so extraordinary a decision pass without' comment.⁴⁴

It was, then, in response that in February 1822 he authored his lengthy 'Minute on Altamgha Inams', offering a wide-ranging critique of the Supreme Court's decision, which he saw as a threat to the foundation of the Company's administrative order. While Munro's objection was partly due to the feeling that the Supreme Court had encroached on the domain of politics by converting a matter of 'State policy' into a 'question ... of private right between two brothers', his more fundamental concern lay elsewhere—with the very idea that the *in'am* should be counted a form of property.⁴⁵ Accordingly, Munro highlighted the Court's sequence of assertions about the non-resumable nature of the grant and its attendant suggestion that the *jagir* was held as an inviolable legal right. Similarly alarming to Munro was the fact that in order to reach this conclusion the Court seemed to be claiming that the origins of such a property right extended all the way back to the *parvana* through which the Nawab Ali Khan Wallajah initially issued the *in'am* to Assim Khan in 1789.

According to Munro, the Court was fundamentally lacking in authority to negate the government's resumption of a grant that constituted only a non-propertied entitlement. To support his position, he summoned the by-then familiar distinction between property (in land's rent) and a mere claim to public revenue. However, in contrast to those who advanced such a distinction in the context of the debate on revenue settlement in Bengal, Munro's principal aim was not so much to categorically deny the status of property to the state's claim on perfectly fungible rental value. Instead, his main aim was to deny such status to those forms of *private* entitlement to the monetizable value of land's produce that could not be given substantive definition primarily as duties of the type the Company was *really* concerned with rendering administrable.

Against the backdrop of this more fundamental aim, Munro's case against the Supreme Court's decision quickly ran into difficulty, even though his reasoning began in a way that seemed straightforward enough given the nature of public-sphere debate in the Company's India up to

---

⁴⁴ Ibid., 139.
⁴⁵ Ibid., 145. It is primarily this aspect of the disagreement between Munro and the Court to which Burton Stein confines his attention. See Stein, *Thomas Munro*, 263.

that point in time. That is, Munro began by invoking political economy's shadow concept of property as the true owner's right to retain (some portion of) the monetizable value of land's produce. He thus asked his audience to imagine a village with a gross product of 100 per cent, with the expense of cultivation comprising 40 per cent and the rent another 20 per cent. He then proceeded to argue that the residuum of 40 per cent that was left to go back to the sovereign could not properly be counted as property (in the land's rent) because it was, instead, to be categorically distinguished as merely a public revenue. Were a village—or, for that matter, a *pargana*—with such characteristics to be subsumed under a *jagir* and then granted to some recipient like Assim Khan it would be 'the 40 only, composing the Government share, which [would be] granted'. As for the 20 per cent comprising the rent, according to Munro, it would remain where it was 'as before'—namely, 'in the hands of the owner'. Likewise, in the event of the revocation of the grant of such a hypothetical village or *pargana*, 'the property of the landlord [would] not [be] affected by the change'; instead, 'it [would be] the 40 only, composing the Government revenue or share, which [would be] affected by the resumption'. On Munro's reasoning, then, no more than if the original residuum of 40 per cent had made its way to the government treasury as 'public revenue' would its alienation into the hands of the *in'amdar* transform it into 'property'. In both scenarios, in other words, for Munro it was the 20 per cent, alone, that constituted the true owner's 'property' (in the rent).[46]

At least at first glance, Munro's repurposing of the peculiarly colonial discourse of property under the Company's rule to the effect of undermining the coherence of the Supreme Court's decision was quite deft. However, the peculiarity of that discourse also meant that his case against the Court was not without its own problems. If in its essence property in the subcontinent was no more than a perfectly fungible portion of the monetizable value of land's produce, it was hardly foolproof to insist that *this* percentage of the return constituted true property in a way in which *that* categorically did not. The more Munro insisted that the *in'am* holder had no irrevocable right (over rent), the more did he threaten to destabilize the fundamental distinction between being a 'true' holder of private property under the Company and whatever its own supposed role might

---

[46] Arbuthnot, *Major General Sir Thomas Munro, Governor of Madras*, 142.

be as a claimant in its own right to some other portion of the monetizable value of the land's produce.

For the only way Munro could minimize the resemblance between the *in'am* right of old and the type of properly modern right to property the Company claimed to be making 'absolute' was by insisting that the *in'amdar* was really a stand-in for the government as the recipient of a public revenue. Yet the more the *in'amdar* in society and the fisc in the colonial state became indistinguishable with respect to what they were entitled to, the more obvious it became that both equally could be seen as proprietors. Tellingly, then, as his Minute unfolded, Munro was left to simply double down on his initial distinction between property and public revenue, in the process making a mockery of the Company's foundation myth—based as it was on improvement through proprietorship—and its legitimation function. Accordingly, in defending a general power on the colonial government's part to resume *in'am* gifts he insisted that the 'jagirdar ceases to have any interest in the village or pargana, because he never had any property in the land' to begin with but 'merely *in* the revenue which is now resumed'.[47] To the extent that such grants were revocable, moreover, he was left elsewhere maintaining that where the underlying 'lands are held ... by ryots having' an ostensibly 'hereditary proprietary right in the whole lands of the village', even these are really 'limited to the public revenue or Government share of the produce, and do not give a foot of land'.[48]

Perhaps because relying on bald insistence was so unsatisfactory, Munro waffled back and forth on whether claims to the 'public revenue' could not also just as well be conceived as claims to a property *in* the public revenue. On reverting to the view that it was wrong to strike such an equivalence, Munro conjured a hypothetical *jagirdar* in the domain of whose grant were *raiyats* whose footprint did not extend into the proverbial waste beyond the areas they directly cultivated. He then asked what would happen in the event of the termination of such a *jagir*, claiming that it would only be the 'public revenue' that was resumed since it, alone, would have been granted to the *jagirdar* in the first place. As for the 'property'—whether that of the *raiyats* in the area of original

---

[47] Ibid. (emphasis added).
[48] Ibid., 143.

cultivation or that which would accrue to the former *jagirdar* were they to be the agent making the desert of the former waste bloom—Munro maintained that it would remain intact, since the rent would have gone undisturbed. As he explained,

> [w]hen such a jagir is resumed, no private rent is affected by the resumption. The ancient hereditary ryots pay the public revenue of their lands to Government in place of the jagirdar, and the jagirdar himself pays the public revenue of the waste lands which he may have brought into cultivation; and if he agrees to this condition, he retains possession of them with the same proprietary rights as the other landowners or ryots of the district. It is obvious, therefore, that though in rare cases of unclaimed or waste lands Government may confer a private proprietary right, it never resumes it; and that there is no foundation for the opinion that resumption is an unjust violation of private property, since the thing resumed is always public revenue—*never the landlord's rent*.[49]

That such reasoning followed from the specificity of the discursive culture of early Company rule is made evident in the way Munro addressed the argument of the Chief Justice of the Madras Supreme Court that to permit the revocation of Ali Khan Wallajah's grant to his diwan would require that it be seen as equally permissible to revoke rights to Crown lands once granted away by the 'kings and queens of England'.[50] Dismissing the analogy, Munro again invoked the distinction between property (in rent) and public revenue. '[A]lienation in England', he thus declared, 'was merely a transfer of the Crown lands to private individuals'; as such, it conveyed *only* a property in the soil 'liable to all public taxes'.[51] Even if the 'owners changed', therefore, the 'estates themselves ... like other lands of the kingdom' still bore 'all the public burdens of the time—to military service, aids, escuage, & c.' In this respect, the English 'Crown became poorer, but the nation richer' through such acts of alienation. In the subcontinent, on the other hand, making grants in *in'am* involved transferring 'away the public revenue of the lands', exempting recipients 'from

---

[49] Ibid. (emphasis added).
[50] Quoted in ibid., 147.
[51] Ibid.

military service' and 'from every kind of tax or public burden'. With the lands underlying such grants having been made 'entirely useless as a resource of the State', it was only natural that they should be revocable in a way that those in England simply were not.[52] In short, Munro was construing English royal grants in a manner completely opposite to how he was insisting grants made by sovereigns in the subcontinent had to be understood.

This position was strained even further under the weight of its own inconsistency to the extent that Munro was suggesting that there was no other choice but to envision royal grants of 'property in the soil' in England as involving the transfer of a merely secondary asset compared to what was being transferred to the in'amdar in the subcontinent.[53] After all, in the English context Munro knew well that it was neither the meagre cultivator nor even the more robust yeoman to whom such grants were being made, but mainly the great 'barons and churchmen' upon whom the country's traditional social order was thought to rest. Indeed, this is likely why he found it so difficult not to fall back into equivocation, noting later, for example, that under certain circumstances the 'alienation by an Indian prince' may be 'a transfer from the State of all public taxes on land to individuals as private property'.[54]

5.7 In'am Rights and the Company's Ontology of the Laws

Whatever the disagreement between Munro and the Madras Supreme Court concerning Ali Khan Wallajah's grant to Assim Khan, it is liable to be misleading to see it primarily as a microcosm of some structural conflict between the executive and judiciary over the meaning of a genuine rule of the law's own.[55] Nor was the disagreement between Munro and the

---

[52] Ibid., 149 (emphasis added).
[53] Ibid., 147.
[54] Ibid., 148.
[55] As noted previously, this has long remained a staple of discussion for modern historians. Stokes, for example, contrasts law and executive administration based on the canonical, but notoriously tenuous, distinction between discretionary decision and its non-latitudinarian legal foil. As he notes, 'the administration of the law was not ... to be understood as the actions of executive officers vested with discretionary powers, but solely as the operation of the judicial

Court primarily notable even just as an exemplar of some foundational conflict between the Company's theory and its practice where it came to rendering the freedom of property 'absolute'. On both fronts, the contrast with the early-nineteenth-century Anglo-common-law mainstream is instructive. For in that context if there was anything that went by the distinct name of the law of property, the rules that could be grouped under its heading were neither made operative—in the sense outlined in the closing chapter of part I—in a single venue of administration nor did they hold together in virtue of advancing allegiance to market discipline alone.

More important in assessing the disagreement between Munro and the Supreme Court, thus, may be the way it reflected a crisis of conceptualization given the confounding relationship between the Company's notion of property (in rent) and the sovereign tradition of gifting revenue immunities that was so important to the political culture of pre-colonial South Asia. At its core, this crisis of conceptualization derived from the difficulty of accommodating pre-colonial practices of gifting rights of surplus control without simultaneously imposing obligations on their claimants. In this respect, the institution of *in'am* was threateningly out of keeping with the essential aim of the Company's administration, which was hardly to reimagine claims to abstract rental value as 'property' simply for its own sake. Rather, in so doing the point was to make more clearly legible the proprietor's corresponding responsibility to deduct from their newly enumerated holding an equally fungible share of monetizable value—even as much as the lion's share—as the colonial government's taking. Doctrinally speaking, in other words, the Company's regime was predicated on giving substance to what limited array of juridical entitlements the early colonial state trafficked in not through the element of right as their defining criterion so much as the corresponding element of duty.

process in the courts'. Stokes, *The English Utilitarians and India*, 235. While such a view draws a sharp line between the polity's legal and non-legal output, in other ways it 'legalizes' the entirety of the state's functioning in the standard way that I have discussed in chapter one. That is, upon fast-forwarding to the epoch of the mature territorial-bureaucratic national state (including in its colonial incarnation) the hard and fast distinction Stokes and other historians use to characterize early Company Raj effortlessly collapses in the face of the positivist taxonomic category of 'administrative law'. At base, this is because underlying both the reinforcement and dismantling of such a distinction between the polity's legal versus executive output is the notion of 'the law' as a norm order infinitely generative in its potential to cover the world of facts.

So long as there was no urgent need to make areas under *in'am* legible to the colonial state, the question whether such grants should be counted as 'property' could be dealt with simply by leaving it unasked. After all, if *in'am*-based rights had been originally granted subject to no duty of revenue payment, by avoiding a reckoning with the practice the Company could ensure that its discourse of property remain undisturbed. Indeed, lacking as *in'am*-based claims were in the constituent element that effectively defined juridical entitlement under the Company's new order, there was ample reason to prefer keeping them out of the colonial state's spotlight—even if to the extent that they constituted bases for personal asset wealth, there was no reason, in principle, why such claims should remain isolated from the Company's administration of justice and the underlying ontology of 'the laws' it was predicated upon.

Clearly, then, as indicated by Munro's Minute, legitimizing a wide-ranging class of claims to alienated surplus that the colonial state had no hand, itself, in alienating posed a major challenge to the Company's political economy of extraction. Yet, once brought into the light, what fix could there be for the intellectual conundrum the institution of *in'am* created when—at least if analysed as a basis for provisioning rights—it was virtually indistinguishable from one of property that, under the Company, was supposed to be the key to the subcontinent's 'improvement' through its focus on entitlement to the monetizable value of land's produce? Between the two horns of this dilemma, the symbolic shadow of the ancien régime that *in'am* cast over the Company's purportedly modernizing rule of property was only the least of the ways it proved foreboding. For validating such gifts to individuals deracinated from their former bureaucratic identities on grounds of the exigencies of military expansion when the need to placate powerful elements in southern society was acute—as the Company initially did with Assim Khan's *in'am*—was one thing; doing so past the point when the Company had moved on to consolidating its role as supreme hegemon in the subcontinent was another.

* * *

Overall, in his Minute on Altamgha Inams Munro's reasoning proved emblematic of the way the Company's peculiar doctrinal discourse of property remained insulated from the conception in the Anglo-common-law mainstream—to which the Madras Supreme Court was also making overtures—of legal right as an ostensibly absolute, unitary, and physicalist dominion. On the one hand, the dispute about Assim Khan's *in'am* provided an opportune moment to inveigh against further legitimizing claims to the abstract monetizable value of the land's produce that carried with them no accompanying duty of revenue payment. This is because in arguing that the grant should be considered only a revocable right in the public revenue the consequence of Munro's position would have been to affirm the power that followed from Kalam-ullah's exclusive inheritance rather than to deny it.[56] That is, relative to the case at hand Munro's view did not function to threaten but to uphold the 'traditional' landed privilege Kalam-ullah was claiming to have inherited from the family's deceased patriarch. At the same time, in the larger argument, Munro's view obviously made it easier for the colonial state to cancel unconstrained rights of the kind that went with grants in *in'am* and instead transform them into substrates for a more legible duty of revenue payment whenever doing so might more closely coincide with its interests in making the underlying surpluses appropriable.[57]

On the other hand, the controversy over Assim Khan's *in'am* was treacherous ground—and not just because Munro was left decrying a decision that had already been made. For the Supreme Court had run together questions about what counted as property (in the land's rent) with questions about administering the intergenerational descent of family

---

[56] As Munro warned, if the Supreme Court was to 'gradually extend its jurisdiction over' the many among the 'native religious establishment and municipal servants' maintained by *in'am* grants this could 'destroy their respect for the authority of Government'. As a consequence, 'the affairs of the country' would be thrown 'into confusion. Were the Court once to begin to receive suits respecting lands assigned for the maintenance of public servants, it would be impossible for Government to realize the revenue, or to maintain good order in the country'. Even if the Court was 'not likely to interfere in such matters', the prospect of having 'no assurance' that it would not, Munro warned, was unacceptable. Arbuthnot, *Major General Sir Thomas Munro, Governor of Madras*, 140.

[57] It should be emphasized once more that there was no timeless form of tradition that the Company's initial deference to powerful *in'amdars* either embodied or advanced. Rather, in the pre-colonial context, especially amidst the flux of the eighteenth century, grants in *in'am* exemplified the baseline fluidity of relations between rulers and subordinates. Rather than forms of privilege rooted in the immemorial past the alienation of state revenues through *in'am* reflected the inherent negotiability of landed power in a political culture characterized by what Susan Rudolph has so memorably called the reciprocal performance of 'ritual sovereignty'. See Susan Rudolph, 'Presidential Address: State Formation in Asia—Prolegomenon to a Comparative Study', *The Journal of Asian Studies* 46, no. 4 (Nov. 1987): 731–46 at 740. (More recently, much the same idea has been discussed in terms of the 'layered' or 'shared' nature of sovereignty in the pre-colonial subcontinent. See e.g. Bose and Jalal, *Modern South Asia*, 83, 204, 206.) On the symbolic negotiability of *in'am* in particular see generally Dirks, 'From Little King to Landlord'.

wealth. Therefore, on its own, Munro's principal objection—to that part of the decision equating *in'am* with legitimate property—was insufficient for shielding the inheritance of Assim Khan's eldest son, Kalam-ullah, from degradation. By the terms of the Court's decision, such an outcome could only be guaranteed by arguing that Assim Khan's original grant had to be altogether excluded from administration according to the 'laws' of Islamic inheritance. This was despite the fact that under the Company's regime the applicability of those inheritance rules to the disposal of family wealth was not contingent on any prior translation/certification of such holdings as 'property'. Yet to fully engage the Supreme Court on its own terms it was necessary for Munro to do more than just set forth an alternative doctrinal basis for the eventual transformation of *in'am* into a kind of property that could be retrofitted as needed in the future with a duty of revenue payment. That is, he also had to show that Kalam-ullah's *in'amdari* right needed not be opened up to degradation through subjection to the Company's administration of the native 'laws' of Islamic inheritance.

Indeed, it was in order to meet the latter challenge that Munro inverted both of the Court's two main findings. He thus insisted that because 'the thing granted to Kalam-ullah Khan was public revenue' it could not be 'affected by the Mahomedan law of inheritance'. In doing so, however, he could not but also partially validate the Court's logic insofar as he too was joining—even if only ultimately to try to sever—the question of the applicability of the laws of native tradition to Assim Khan's grant and the question of determining the status of the *in'am* as 'property'. In a plainly circular manner, he simply buttressed this insistence through asserting that the rules of Islamic inheritance were 'applicable' only to claims obtaining 'between individuals' that 'descend[ed] … in the family' and not 'between the sovereign and the individual' whose privileges were subject to being 'resumed'.[58]

Beyond the problem of circularity, Munro's reasoning here was also beset by internal contradiction. In implicitly prioritizing the notion of control over abstract rental value over the more conventional idea of dominion over landed space he was decomposing the property right into what today we might call its separable

---

[58] Arbuthnot, *Major General Sir Thomas Munro, Governor of Madras*, 158.

incidents.⁵⁹ His case against the Supreme Court's decision, consequently, partly hinged on the idea that absent a component immunity-right against revocation, an entitlement to the monetizable value of land's produce could not really be a true property right. While this was a possibly effective way, in theory, to cast aspersion on the Court's classification of Assim Khan's *in'am* as property notwithstanding its being devoid of any concomitant duty of revenue payment, Munro was simultaneously undermining the basis for excluding such holdings from the potentially fragmenting effect of native laws of inheritance and succession.

If without the incident of immunity from revocation even a right to rental value could not be regarded as a true property entitlement under the Company's regime, what significance could a finding that something *was* property have for justifying its subjection to the colonial state's administration of justice based on 'native laws' relating to the intergenerational disposal of family wealth? Ultimately, then, Munro's demand that pre-colonial modes of sovereign gifting like *in'am* only be counted as true property rights if irrevocable served to emphasize how under the Company's regime the subjection of disputes about family wealth to 'the laws' of native inheritance and succession did not really depend on whether those disputes were rooted in 'property' claims obtaining 'between individuals' as opposed to claims on the public revenue obtaining between the 'individual and the state', as he argued in the previously quoted excerpt.⁶⁰

* * *

---

⁵⁹ A. M. Honoré, 'Ownership'. In *Oxford Essays in Jurisprudence: A Collaborative Work*, ed. Anthony Gordon Guest (Oxford: Clarendon Press, 1961), 107–47 (stating that '[o]wnership comprises the right to possess, the right to use, the right to manage, the right to the income of the thing, the right to the capital, the right to security, the rights or incidents of transmissibility and absence of term, the prohibition of harmful use, liability to execution, and the incident of residuarity: this makes eleven leading incidents. Obviously, there are alternative ways of classifying the incidents; moreover, it is fashionable to speak of ownership as if it were just a bundle of rights, in which case at least two items in the list would have to be omitted', ibid., 113). Though Honoré is often credited with the notion of property as a collection of incidents, as will be discussed in greater detail in the next chapter, the origins of decomposing the property right's 'bundle' into a multitude of separable 'sticks' in a highly visible way is best traced to late-nineteenth-century classical legal thinkers. It would go on from their to become even more visible in the mounting attacks on the formalist commitments of those thinkers that soon after would put a fine point on the end of legal thought's late-nineenth century.

⁶⁰ See note 58.

That despite his intentions to the contrary Munro should have found his reasoning still entangled in such difficulties testifies to what it means to say that property remained extrinsic to the ontology of the legal under the formative period of early colonial rule. Rendering some version of such a category administrable for revenue-settlement purposes was simply not the same as grounding legal administration proper in an objectified notion of right-cum-operative concept extrapolated from that same category. Whether landed wealth was commanded as *in'am* or through the colonial state's categories of *zamindari* or *raiyatwari* holding, the administration of its transmission or of disputes about its transmission across lines of generational descent needed not to be conducted in the name of property in order to fall within the purview of the Company's rule of 'the laws'. As a feature of casuistry under the Company's administration of justice, this marked a major departure from the Anglo-common-law mainstream, where reasoning about 'property' was fast becoming *the* way par excellence of reasoning about 'the law'. In the early colonial subcontinent, on the other hand, to administer society in the name of property involved mainly a form of rights talk focusing on the control of rent; even this, moreover, was given doctrinal instantiation not primarily as any first principle of a distinctly 'legal' brand of reason but as a means of operationalizing the juridical duty of revenue payment.

What, then, of the administration of disputes about rights to the monetizable value of land's produce of the kind that the Company was 'settling' in the name of property? After all, especially in a system like the Madras Presidency's, the process of recognizing such 'property' involved more than simply identifying a right-holder to be made into a new node of official tax obligation and then being done with the matter. Obviously, in so doing, conflicts over the entitlements being recognized were bound to arise and require adjudicatory processing, whether by way of tending to questions about the official boundaries of the propertied revenue unit, about who could properly claim status as a cultivator, or about whatever other matters like what constituted/was to be done in the event of a right-holder's failure to meet their all-important duty of payment.[61]

---

[61] The well-known Madras administrator Francis Ellis provides a good sense of the types of issues around which such early disputes centred. See e.g. 'Letter from F. W. Ellis to the Board of Revenue', Board of Revenue Consultations, 24 December 1812, cited in Raman, *Document Raj*, 182.

Of course, in Madras that such disputes were administered through the adjudicatory function of the district-level institutions of the revenue department did reflect some kind of difference from the Cornwallis system in Bengal. (This especially would have been the case before 1830, at which point the creation of the Commissioners of Revenue and Circuit brought to Bengal much the same blurring of lines between the district-level adjudicative functions of the judiciary and the executive). Yet even so, it would be misleading to imagine that property's internalization into the ontology of the legal depended on the venue in which such disputes were handled, whether in the civil courts of 'the judiciary' proper (with its general jurisdiction) or the revenue courts of the so-called 'executive' (with its special jurisdiction). In either case, the institutional site of dispute settlement was less a font of 'the law' than it was simply a means of conducting local administration. After all, it was only on such a basis that the civil judiciary in Bengal could be charged with the curious responsibility of guaranteeing property's so-called free alienability by standing watch over a system of government confiscation of *zamindari* entitlements once their respective holders had fallen into arrears and time had come to possibly auction them off. Suffice to say, in this capacity the Company state was hardly functioning as a neutral judicial umpire promoting efficiency by doing no more than refereeing the minimal rules needed to facilitate the ability of private actors to send property circulating through the market.[62]

Simply put, the internalization of property into the ontology of the legal did not turn on whether landed wealth was or was not subject to

---

[62] In recent years, some scholars have drawn on the somewhat contradictory combination of neoclassical and new institutionalist strands in economics to argue for a recasting of the early colonial state's property regime as laying the groundwork for relations that tended towards the maximization of 'efficiency' (in the welfare economics sense of the concept). See e.g. Tirthankar Roy, 'Law and Economic Change in India, 1600–1900'. In *Law and Long-Term Economic Change: A Eurasian Perspective*, eds. Debin Ma and Jan Luiten van Zanden (Stanford, CA: Stanford University Press, 2011), 115–37 and Anand V. Swamy 'Land and Law in Colonial India'. In ibid., 138–57. Even on this view, however, it would seem to be an unusual kind of institutional infrastructure/constraint the Company's early 'land market' in Bengal—based on confiscation and auction—would have constituted. For a better understanding of the economics literature informing such an approach see the seminal work of Harold Demsetz, including A. A. Alchian and H. Demsetz, 'The Property Right Paradigm', *Journal of Economic History* 33, no. 1 (Mar. 1973): 16–27. A critique of a neoclassical paradigm of Demsetz's type, though also partly an extension of it, the work of Douglass North, the founding father of the 'new institutionalism' in economics, is also important in this connection. See Douglass C. North, *Institutions, Institutional Change and Economic Performance* (New York: Cambridge University Press, 1990).

the more ardent exactitudes of judicial proceduralism. Where the adjudication of disputes was undertaken in the name of the type of property entitlement the Company's administration was primarily focused on 'settling', it mattered little to the operative ontology of the legal whether this was done by judicial courts proper or executive revenue courts. In neither of these contexts more than the other did the Company's doctrinal discourse remake the property right in particular into the basis for a distinct kind of legal right in general, much less one upon which 'the law' was supposed to stand as an infinitely generative system of rational ordering according to norms that could 'rule' any and every type of social transaction the 'world of facts' might offer up.

5.8 Coda: Utilitarianism, the Ricardian Law of Rent, and the Ontology of the Legal

While I have just argued that the conflict between Munro and the Madras Supreme Court reflected the uncompromising persistence of the Company state's formative ideology of property (in land's rent), by 1820 British colonialism in the subcontinent is usually seen to have crossed into a new era of intellectual commitments. On this view, with its primary wave of military expansion having ended after the third Anglo-Maratha War of 1817–18, the colonial state reached the brink of a new age of reformism that lasted largely uninterrupted until the great rebellion of 1857.[63] Of course, the ways in which scholars have mapped this ideological shift have been various: whether as the end of an older and less domineering, even if still reifying, orientalist approach to knowing South Asian society and culture;[64] the beginning of a more emphatic rule of colonial difference;[65] a high point in the confluence between moral reformism and evangelism in the ongoing wake of the Charter Act of

---

[63] See e.g. Metcalf, *Ideologies of the Raj*, 28–43; C. A. Bayly, *Indian Society and the Making of the British Empire* (Cambridge: Cambridge University Press, 2008 [1988]), 120–23 and Burton Stein, *A History of India*, 2nd edn. (Malden, MA: Wiley Blackwell, 2010), 216–22.

[64] See generally e.g. Metcalf, *Ideologies of the Raj*, ch. 1.

[65] See e.g. Partha Chatterjee, *The Nation and its Fragments* (Princeton, NJ: Princeton University Press, 1993), 18–25.

1813;[66] or a precursor to the high imperialism of the late nineteenth century that found its exponents increasingly speaking a language of liberal universalism.[67]

Because these various formulations have subtly adjusted rather than outright refuted historian Eric Stokes' canonical account of the triumph of utilitarian ideology in colonial India going into the 1830s, it has been easy for the accumulation of small shifts to give the impression that the older scholarly consensus has, by now, long since been left behind. Moreover, the subsequent rise of interest in replacing preoccupations of old with the so-called official mind by forging a more genuine (and globally connected) field of South Asian intellectual history has only deepened this sense.[68] For example, in recent years, scholars interested in the relationship between liberalism and empire such as C. A. Bayly and Andrew Sartori have sought to recast the several decades after 1820 as an era of vernacular liberalism characterized by native actors attempting to 'recover liberties' and forge 'universalistic particularisms' and 'parochial cosmopolitanisms'.[69]

However, with respect to the understanding of the ideological currents informing revenue settlement, there has remained a more stable—and effectively uniform—consensus in favour of Stokes' emphasis on the rise of a specifically Ricardian view of rent after 1820 as marking a crucial dividing line in the intellectual history of colonial rule.[70] This is because if—following Ricardo—rent is to be understood specifically as 'the differential advantage enjoyed by all soils of a higher quality than the last taken into cultivation,'[71] it would appear all the more plausible to see

---

[66] See e.g. Stokes, *The English Utilitarians and India*, Peter Robb, *Liberalism, Modernity and the Nation* (New York: Oxford University Press, 2007), 14–27, and Bose and Jalal, *Modern South Asia*, 62.

[67] See e.g. Uday Singh Mehta, *Liberalism and Empire: A Study in Nineteenth-Century British Liberal Thought* (Chicago, IL: University of Chicago Press, 1999).

[68] Shruti Kapila and C. A. Bayly, eds., *An Intellectual History for India* (New York: Cambridge University Press, 2010) and Moyn and Sartori, *Global Intellectual History*.

[69] C. A. Bayly, *Recovering Liberties* and Andrew Sartori, *Bengal in Global Concept History: Culturalism in the Age of Capital* (Chicago, IL: University of Chicago Press, 2008).

[70] See generally Stokes, *The English Utilitarians and India*. It is worth emphasizing that whatever critique Stokes' text has come in for—based on its being excessively focused on 'formal statement[s] of policy aims' over 'the working practice of British rule' (as Stokes, himself, came to regard his own ideas (See Stokes, 'The First Century of British Colonial Rule in India: Social Revolution or Social Stagnation?', reprinted in *The Peasant and the Raj*, 19–45 at 30))—it has left largely undisturbed Stokes' portrait of the influence of Ricardian rent theory once it came to be increasingly taken up by teachers and students alike at the Company's college at Haileybury.

[71] Stokes, *The English Utilitarians and India*, 88.

those Ricardo influenced who were within the Company's orbit—James Mill being not the least among them—as having had reason to find in his thought a novel instrument for reordering revenue policy in the way that Stokes suggests was taking place after 1820. Indeed, there are several ways in which the Ricardian idea of rent can be seen as having done so. Consider, for example, the point that the rise of Ricardian thinking signalled the final demise of the ambition to fix the state's revenue demand in perpetuity. As we have seen, for most of the period from 1790 to 1820 this made for a goal effectively shared by both the engineers of the Cornwallis system in Bengal and the *raiyatwari* system elsewhere, especially in its formative version under Munro.[72]

Likewise, a second—and even more important—way that Ricardian rent theory has continued to be seen as having reoriented the intellectual framework of revenue settlement in the subcontinent is through signalling the retreat of the earlier preoccupation with identifying the subcontinent's authentic owning class. If, as the utilitarians within the Company's ranks insisted, rent was no more than an unearned increment distinctly different from the wages of labour and profits of stock, the question of identifying the private parties who were the subcontinent's so-called true proprietors would appear to have become secondary.[73] After all, whether absorbed by zamindar notables or mixed into an overall return retained by individual *raiyats* or village clans, the portion comprising the so-called unearned increment could easily enough still be seen as *unearned*. On any such view, then, prior to the ascent of utilitarianism, one might say that there would have been good reason for concern to have focused on finding the Indian proprietor (in order to

---

[72] The idea of making a *raiyatwari* settlement permanent followed from Munro's early experience with Read in Baramahal, and it continued to inform his outlook all the way up to the time of the *Fifth Report*. See e.g. Munro, 'Principle of the Ryotwar System', Evidence Before the Select Committee of the House of Commons, 15 April 1812, reprinted in Arbuthnot, *Major General Sir Thomas Munro, Governor of Madras*, 106–08. Moreover, as noted in chapter four, in the context of debates in the period before 1793 in Bengal, the line between settling the revenue demand permanently and for decades-long periods was tenuous. Even when the partisans of *raiyatwari* settlement stopped advocating for permanency, the idea that the demand would be set for extended periods clearly echoed Shore's view, contra Cornwallis, that the duration of permanence in the context of settling with Bengal's zamindars need not, literally speaking, be permanent.

[73] For a critique of Stokes' understanding of utilitarianism and its use in the Indian context see F. Rosen, 'Eric Stokes, British Utilitarianism, and India', in *J.S. Mill's Encounter with India*, eds. Martin I. Moir, Douglas M. Peers, and Lynn Zastoupil (Toronto: University of Toronto Press, 1999), 18–33.

incentivize productivity through ostensibly limiting the state's demand upon them and ensuring them a reliability in their private expectations); after 1820 and the rise of the so-called Ricardian law of rent, however, one might equally say that there was reason for concern to have shifted to the apparent lack of any good reason for the Company *not* to tax the quantum comprising the whole of the unearned increment.[74]

To be sure, on the above narrative of ideological reorientation, it is actually 1819 rather than 1820 that becomes the true inflection point in the trajectory of revenue policy. For it was in that year that Mill was appointed to the Department of the Examiner of Correspondence at India House in London, paving the way for his becoming Office Head by 1830, thus ascending from the institution's lowest to highest ranks in little more than a decade.[75] At the same time, in the North-Western provinces—where the law of rent is usually said to have informed the colonial state's evolving outlook most explicitly—1819 was the year that Holt Mackenzie, secretary to the Governor General in Calcutta, penned his famed Memorandum on the land-revenue problems of the Ceded and Conquered provinces (as the North-Western provinces were known until the passage of the Parliamentary Act that renamed them in 1835). It was in that document that the Company's leading expert on revenue affairs first recommended that assessment in the northwest adhere to a 'net produce' criterion for resolving the theretofore irresolvable dilemma of properly quantifying the magnitude of the unearned increment.

To the extent that the Ricardian law of rent really did inaugurate a new phase in the ideology of colonial rule, the moment when Mackenzie's recommendations in the Memorandum were formally adopted through Regulation VII of 1822 takes on a milestone importance. In Regulation

---

[74] As Mill declared to the House of Commons Select Committee of 1831:

[n]ine-tenths probably of the revenue of the Government of India is derived from the rent of land, never appropriated to individuals, and always considered to be the property of government; and to me that appears to be one of the most fortunate circumstances that can occur in any country because in consequence of this the wants of the state are supplied really and truly without taxation. As far as this source goes the people of the country remain untaxed. The wants of government are supplied without any drain either upon the produce of any man's labour, or the produce of any man's capital. Quoted in Stokes, *The English Utilitarians and India*, 91.

[75] This came a year after the elder Mill's famed three-volume *The History of British India* was published, to immediate acclaim. Initially, Mill was responsible for drafting revenue dispatches to colonial India, which he continued to do until his promotion in 1830.

VII's wake much the same net produce criterion was extended beyond the North-Western provinces to other parts of the subcontinent as well. Most important among these were the former domains of the Maratha *peshwa* in the Deccan that had been newly absorbed into the Bombay Presidency in 1818. As in Madras, while in Bombay—after Mountstuart Elphinstone's appointment as Lieutenant Governor in 1819—it was also a *raiyatwari* system through which settlement was commenced, the process there was generally more steeped in the 'utilitarian deluge' then purportedly flooding the colonial subcontinent.[76]

Particularly instrumental to the policy's unfolding in the Deccan was the young revenue officer Robert Pringle, who became the key exponent of the law of rent in Bombay following his time as a pupil of Ricardo's friend and rival, the famed Thomas Malthus, while training at the Company's college at Haileybury. On arriving in the subcontinent, Pringle was appointed Superintendent of Revenue Survey and Assessment in the Bombay Deccan, a position he was given after the initial proposal to settle the Company's revenue demand in the *peshwa's* former territories at one-third of their gross produce was abandoned.[77] While at Pringle's initiative a supposedly scientific assessment procedure was, thus, extended to a core part of the Bombay Presidency as well, it was ultimately no more successful there in living up to its billing than it was in the North-Western provinces.[78]

If anything, the effort to make good on the net produce criterion was actually less successful in Bombay insofar as it had already come to be regarded as a failure by 1835. Support for Regulation VII in the North-Western provinces, on the other hand, persisted for more than a decade, with the measure being replaced only in 1833 by Regulation IX. Under the latter, Mackenzie's 'scientific' scheme for determining the net produce by a so-called aggregate-to-detail calculation was abandoned. In its place a procedure based even more overtly on guesswork was adopted instead. Through the new 'detail-to-aggregate' method, amounts that had

---

[76] Ravinder Kumar, *Western India in the Nineteenth Century: A Study in the Social History of Maharashtra* (Toronto: University of Toronto Press, 1968), ch. 3.
[77] Ibid., 86.
[78] For a description of and attempt to explain the failure in terms of the economics of information see Neeraj Hatekar, 'Information and Incentives: Pringle's Ricardian Experiment in the Nineteenth-Century Deccan Countryside', *Indian Economic and Social History Review* 33, no. 4 (1996), 437–57.

been actually paid in the past became the basis for determining a cumulative sum that was then to be individually apportioned on a per head basis among those tasked with the obligation of revenue payment. For the next nine years, it was this new method that was utilized in the northwest under R. M. Bird. (The same sequence of events was also responsible for making *mahalwari* settlement the colonial subcontinent's third main system of revenue affairs.)[79]

Notwithstanding the failure of its implementation in practice, as per the standpoint developed in this chapter, even viewed strictly for its ideological significance the Ricardian law of rent did not necessarily make for as abrupt or thoroughgoing a reorientation as scholars have tended to think. Instead, the peculiar variety of property talk that had developed already during the Company's ascent to power in the second half of the eighteenth century would seem to suggest that no more than earlier colonial thinkers did the utilitarian advocates of a more scientific doctrine of rent articulate a vision in which property was metaphorically structured as an ostensibly absolute right of physical dominion over a unitary realm of landed space. In other words, the more technical the Ricardian notion of rent as an unearned increment was, the less was it an exception to the rule about what property had come to mean in the discursive culture of the Company's raj than it was a corroboration of the same.

Accordingly, the divergence between absolute property talk in the Company's India and the mainstream of the Anglo-common-law world that had become apparent already in the back and forth over the question of who to invest with true ownership in Bengal remained firmly intact long after. However, in order to see why this was so one must appreciate how the essence of property talk amidst the Company's ontology of the laws—whether in 1780 or 1830—was not the question of *who* property's owner was but rather *what*, at least in the subcontinent, property was thought of as being. For it was only based on the implicit answer to the *what* question that the Company sought to administer 'property' into being in the first place, regardless of the identity of its designated holders, which at least from the standpoint of the historical ontology of the legal was never more than a secondary issue, whatever appearances to the contrary it took on within the colonial public sphere.

---

[79] See Srivastava, *The Province of Agra*, 118–19.

On the view that I have been developing in the last two chapters, then, if Ricardian rent theory stood out it was mainly for the way it simply inverted the balance between those who could lay claim to the perfectly fungible quantum of monetizable value upon which the Company's decidedly non-physicalist conception of property supervened. Rather than a moderate tax relative to the residuum of the land's productive value that constituted the administratively designated right-holder's 'true property', the state's demand was now unapologetically proclaimed to be the predominant item in the balance sheet. In so freeing the colonial state, in principle, from any check on its claim over the unearned increment, utilitarianism in the subcontinent left an ambiguous legacy. Equally did it thus stand capable of being interpreted as an importation of Benthamite philosophical radicalism as did it a revitalized theory of sole sovereign ownership consistent with an orientalist view of post-Islamicate India as an inherently Asiatic domain.[80]

Either way, the utilitarian influence could do little to disturb the foundational image of property in the subcontinent as a command over rent in the general rather than Ricardian sense of the concept that can be traced back to the seventeenth century. Judged from this vantage point, for a measure like Regulation VII to have theoretically left no more than a mere tenth or twentieth part of the assessment to the revenue obligee appears to be much less significant than it otherwise might seem. Of course, this is partially due to the fact that Mackenzie, like the colonial subcontinent's other leading utilitarian ideologues, faced a situation in which there was little practical ability to fully implement James Mill's position, which was inclusive of an antagonism even to would-be *peasant* property in the unearned increment. (Here one must recall that for Mill, Ricardian rent was supposed to be taxable up to its full amount *in all cases*.)

At the same time, another reason why Regulation VII's extreme position on the permissible extent of the government's taking is less outstanding than it may at first seem is because it did little to change the fact that property under the Company's raj continued to be given ultimate

---

[80] See e.g. S. Ambirajan, *Classical Political Economy and British Policy in India* (New York: Cambridge University Press, 1978). In setting out a similar argument to that of Stokes regarding the importance of Mill's emphasis on the law of rent, Ambirajan perhaps more clearly articulates its purported role in resetting revenue policy by restoring the old theory of sovereign ownership through a new lens.

definitional shape more in its capacity as a duty than as a right. Relative to property's doctrinal structure as a juridical entitlement under the Company's administration, it was largely a matter of indifference whether leaving a mere 10 to 20 per cent of the unearned increment to private hands was to be seen as a matter of practical necessity, on the one hand, or of its belonging, in theory, to its private holder as a 'property' *in* that 10 to 20 per cent, on the other. On the contrary, what really mattered was that the administrability of the lion's share of the unearned increment as a duty (of payment) was perfectly in line with the way in which property had been doctrinally instantiated by the Company ever since its advent to power in Bengal.

Therefore, if Ricardian rent doctrine 'provided … both a coherent policy for the demarcation of public and private rights in the land, and a clear criterion of assessment',[81] one must not lose sight of the fact that it did so only in keeping with the colonial state's already-established pattern of rule and, thus, only because the rights so demarcated continued to be given substance as forms of juridical entitlement mainly in relation to the corresponding obligations the Company's revenue settlement efforts were preoccupied with defining. Indeed, already well before the rise of Ricardian ideas, there had accumulated ample reason for colonial discourse to envisage property more as an inherently divisible sum of the monetizable value of land's produce than as an ostensibly indivisible dominion of persons over things, as per its portrayal within the discourses of legal modernity that were simultaneously emerging in the West. We can, in this respect, say that rather than through combining the various proverbial 'sticks' in its 'bundle', property under the Company's rule was founded on their disaggregation, with only a select few being worth the colonial state's while to make legible in the first place.

The limitations of its practical impact on assessment and collection procedures after 1820 aside, even utilitarianism's significance as an ideology merits qualification. For no more than previously did the rise of Ricardian rent theory during the Company's later period of rule lead to property's internalization into the ontology of the legal. Rather, even amidst the ascent and then heyday of utilitarian reform during the 1830s property continued to be discursively constituted on much the

---

[81] Stokes, *The English Utilitarians and India*, 92.

same footing as it had been from the time of the earliest efforts at British state-building in Bengal. In turn, the already established divergence from the underlying historical ontology of legal modernization in the Anglo-common-law mainstream continued in much the same way after 1820 as it had started out with after 1760.

If, therefore, as David Washbrook so memorably argued, the 'elaboration of a legal system' under the Company that 'treated and protected landed property as if it existed at a remove from the state' ended up being no more than 'pure farce', this was not simply because of the 'Janus faced' nature of the early colonial state.[82] For if the Company's failure to create an economic framework for implementing a truly free market was indicative of its substituting a rule *by* law for a genuine rule *of* law, it did so neither simply to shore up dominant elements in the hierarchy of agrarian society nor even just for the sake of guaranteeing an intensified version of the ancien régime's political economy of surplus extraction. We will continue to miss the full significance of the early colonial state's sweeping pronouncements about the freedom of property if we assess them only in terms of the degree to which they were implemented in the face of the vagaries or roadblocks that conditions 'on the ground' threw up 'in practice'. Instead, as per the conceptual machinery of the method of historical ontology outlined in chapter three, we would be better off appreciating how avowals *about* property's rule were made through an ordinary-language discourse of public-sphere contemplation that was relatively distinct from the discourse into which a concept like property had to be ultimately translated in order to be recast into doctrinal terms.

This being a feature of the ontology of the legal that was hardly unique to the colonial subcontinent, the genesis of 'the law' thus depended on more than just the sovereign's abiding the ostensibly law-like principles of political economy. Even in early-nineteenth-century Britain, the melding of absolute dominion talk with actually administrable doctrine was an ongoing process. As such, it was predicated on what in the Anglo-common-law mainstream, too, remained a considerable distance that would have to be traversed before a properly operative and administrable doctrinal notion of the property right could become fully abstracted into

---

[82] Washbrook, 'Law, State and Agrarian Society', 665. While it is Washbrook who has most clearly formulated this point, it remains one that is widely asserted.

the pure realm of valued interest that the 'possessive individual' could be deemed to hold absolutely, subject—ostensibly—only to its willing exchange on the market according to the generalized logic of commodity.

All told, then, in 1830 no more than in 1790 did any 'theory' of property stand—at the doctrinal level—waiting in the wings for the Company to import into its practices of administration in the subcontinent, even had it wanted to. Instead, in the first half of the nineteenth century it was only an absolute, unitary, and physicalist notion of the property right that metropolitan juridical thought had at the ready for the purposes of fashioning 'the law' writ large. However, as I have been suggesting over the course of the last two chapters, no such model of the property right made sense in a context of ongoing state-building like that which the Company was undertaking, which had little need to attempt to legalize administration in general. Indeed, even in the West, it would not be until the end of the long nineteenth century that any such project would materialize in full, notwithstanding the fact that it had started well before it did in the subcontinent given the priorities of British rule. After all, what sense would there have been in being able to recast any potential social, economic, or political transaction as being already 'covered' by 'the law' absent a significant level of bureaucratization and the need to juridically manage something more akin to an actually extant and purportedly 'free' market economy?

If the early Company state did not always turn rhetoric into reality, then, this was due to the bifurcated nature of the legally theoretical as much as it was to the constraints of the practical. For in the colonial state's founding tendency to under-juridify the property right—given its main concern with formalizing the means of revenue administration in property's name—we find a reminder that legal ideas were unfolded at more than one discursive level, a fact about 'theory' that is hardly without its own 'practical' significance.

Indeed, as I have also been suggesting over the course of the last two chapters here in part II, not the least part of this fact's significance is that the extremely limited way in which the Company juridified the property entitlement made for only a highly imperfect basis from which to extrapolate a notion of legal right in general. In turn, it can be little surprise that in the colonial subcontinent this same state of affairs had the potential to limit the basis for discursively constituting 'the law' as an ostensibly autonomous and supposedly infinitely generative system of rational ordering according to norms; of course, equally unsurprising is that it also had the potential to require the dominance of the latter ideal to await the late nineteenth century and the emergence of a new order in the wake of the transfer of power from Company to Crown.

In fact, testifying to as much is that it was only after the middle of the nineteenth century—with the proliferating recognition of new so-called proprietary rights—that the Company's characteristically early-modern ontology of 'the laws' fully began giving way to a more thoroughgoing ontology of 'the law'. As I will discuss in the next chapter, such burgeoning juridification was the product of a confluence of key changes in the political economy of colonial rule under the Crown and the rise and globalization of classical legal thought. As we will see directly as part III of the book commences, in the subcontinent among its key exponents were figures including Baden Henry Baden-Powell, Sir Frederick Pollock, Henry Maine, and numerous lesser-known Indian lawyers, judges, and—even more inadvertently—litigants.

PART III

THE LAW AND ITS BASIC ELEMENTS

Rights as Realms and the Will of Juridical Persons in the Discourse of Classical Legal Thought in the Crown's India from 1857 to c.1920

6
Crown Rule and the Legalization of Property

Rights as Realms of Proprietary Interest

6.1 Introduction

In part II, I argued that the Company's preservation of a political economy of surplus appropriation through land-revenue extraction involved breaking from the pre-colonial past neither simply through the intensification of that mechanism nor merely because of what turned out to be the rhetorical trappings with which it was surrounded. On the contrary, the intensification of the pre-colonial regime of surplus appropriation also mattered deeply to the specific course that legal modernization took in the subcontinent; indeed, this was all the more so in combination with the Company's rhetorical focus on rendering the entitlement to (some part of) the monetizable value of land's produce 'absolute,' which came to work hand in glove with a doctrinal discourse that shared in keeping the property right largely extrinsic to the ontology of the legal.

Of course, it may seem counter-intuitive to assert that a conception making property more rather than less abstract should have detained the law's discursive constitution as its own distinct object in what way was happening in the West already from the late eighteenth century. After all, parsing 'property' according to an archetypical form that was untethered from land's spatially bounded physicality would seem to have much in common with what was transpiring within the legal systems of the Anglo-common-law mainstream as they matured. Borrowing from historian Martha Howell's summary of events in the West, in other words, the more closely property was associated with a monetarily measurable value—in the discourse of the early colonial state in the subcontinent, a kind of *rental* value—the more 'movable and, thus, abstract' would it seem under the Company to have become. Indeed, this might all the more seem to be the case insofar as the Company wrought an additional abstraction from the direct materiality of land through its commitment to auctioning rental entitlements, especially in Bengal.[1] Even allowing for the fact that such a government-sponsored system for promoting alienability was not propelled by the same 'power of the market' that Howell emphasizes in the Western context, there might seem reason to think that the course of events in the Company's subcontinent recapitulated—in highly abbreviated form—the centuries-long transition that is imagined to have taken place in the West from the medieval to the modern period with respect to (the law of) property. After all, can it be doubted that already under the Company revenue settlement involved things tangible becoming 'dematerialize[d]' and made 'fungible, one for another' through the emergence of an 'abstract' notion of value?[2]

The intuitive appeal of the last question notwithstanding, there are at least two reasons why it is misleading to see the evolution of property discourse in Britain's India in such terms. First, as I have already suggested in part II, it fails to capture the precise manner in which the property right proved formative to legal modernization in the West, itself, during the late eighteenth and early nineteenth centuries. In the main centres of the Anglo-common-law world, for example, legal development did not

---

[1] The existence of such a land market in Bengal, such as it was, is among the major pieces of evidence underlying Tirthankar Roy's case for the Company's having a definitive advantage over its native rivals in consolidating its role as supreme sovereign in the subcontinent. See generally Tirthankar Roy, 'Rethinking the Origins of British India: State Formation and Military-fiscal Undertakings in an Eighteenth Century World Region', *Modern Asian Studies* 47, no. 4 (2013):1125–56.
[2] Martha C. Howell, 'The Language of Property in Early Modern Europe'. In *The Culture of Capital: Property, Cities, and Knowledge in Early Modern England*, ed. Henry S. Turner (New York: Routledge, 2002), 19. According to Howell's representative account, the dematerializing effect of commercialization was tantamount to making property 'more fully of the market'. With respect to the category of 'immovable property', in particular, she argues that dematerialization involved land coming to be treated more and more like the older legal category of property in movables. It thus became increasingly 'purchased and purchasable, capable of being mortgaged, divided, rented and leased'. Judged from the vantage point of this basic distinction available to medieval law—between movables and immovables—according to Howell, early-modern commercialization created a 'dramatic crisis of definition', leaving 'Europeans ... prisoners of old language [that was] developed during a different age' when property had another kind of social meaning. While Howell concedes that it took centuries 'before the market would render all goods conceptually fungible by means of price', on her account anything that facilitated the categorization of 'property' 'simply by *market value* rather than kind' becomes a step in the same direction. Ibid., 20–23.

simply or even mainly witness '(the law of) property' functioning as a categorical heading for grouping together various measures according to which the territorial national state ever further authorized new practices of converting land, labour, and capital into things that an owning class could claim a kind of legal monopoly over for the purposes of directing production and concentrating the gains to be won therefrom into its own hands. Nor, conversely, was the only function of '(the law of) property' to serve as a categorical heading for bringing together various measures for formally subsuming the recombination of such factors of production into new varieties of commodified output, the consumption of which presumed the ability to first securely hold them, even if only provisionally for the purposes of working them up for impending sale on the market. Rather, so too does the significance of the property right's legalization reside in the way it—in a sense—transformed the whole of the law into a law of property.[3]

As for the second reason it is misleading to understand the development of property discourse in the colonial subcontinent on Howell's model of facilitating growing 'abstraction' and 'movability', it is because the Company's administration of justice was not characterized by any very expansive attitude towards abstracting rights to commodity value in the name of property. Indeed, as was made evident in part II, the juridical form of the property entitlement the Company extrapolated from land's productive value became legible primarily in relation to the sovereign task of revenue administration. Moreover, insofar as property was consequently made administrable more as a duty than a right, it was still

---

[3] This observation should not be confused with the oft implied/expressed idea that the law always originates as a law of property given the evident way in which normative usages so often develop out of the need to manage the social relations of landed wealth. (See chapter 4 at note 78.) As compared to the fact that the English common law, say, originally derived from relations of tenure and (later) estates in land or that its substance was long 'secreted' only within the 'interstices' of the procedural forms of action that existed for protecting such interests, the role of property in the absolute, unitary, and physicalist doctrinal conception of the late eighteenth and early nineteenth centuries was something quite different. (Henry Maine, *Dissertations on Early Law and Custom* (London: John Murray, 1883), 389.) Much the same language about the 'secretion' of substance through procedure was borrowed from Maine by F. W. Maitland. (See F. W. Maitland, *Equity, also, the Forms of Action at Common Law: Two Courses of Lectures* (Cambridge: Cambridge University Press, 1909).) Indeed, on the absolute, unitary, and physicalist view, if the law's rule was a rule of property's own, this was because reasoning on the basis of property was seen as the exemplary form of reasoning on the basis of rights; and, in turn, reasoning on the basis of rights was the exemplar for rationally discerning the abstract structure and elemental basis of a form of normativity that was supposed to be uniquely legal.

not a duty of the kind that proved characteristic of incipient legal modernity in the West. That is, under the Company's regime property's obligations made neither for a substrate of political belonging in the way its attendant duties are seen to have in both liberal and republican conceptions of national community nor for the ontic converse of the legal rights (viz. powers) of the state in its capacity as a public juridical individual in its own right. Indeed, this last point further serves to emphasize that property's juridification under the Company was hardly the result of a precocious form of classical legal thought's characteristic analytical ethic of deciphering a symmetry between 'private' legal rights and 'public' legal powers in order to uncover the ostensibly parallel elements underpinning any complex legal entitlement. (Of course, as part III clarifies, it was only in the last decades of the nineteenth century that even in the West such an ethic would become explicit.)

All told, then, if the founding difference between property's modern conceptualization in Britain's India and Britain itself was to narrow, there were effectively two possible conditions under which such an outcome could ensue. On the one hand, changes in political economic circumstance might lead the way in facilitating the prevailing conception of property to be internalized into the ontology of the legal in the subcontinent in a manner not unlike how in the West even from the late eighteenth century 'absolute dominion' talk was translated into administrable form. On the other hand, the shifting circumstances might be more purely intellectual, with change thus led from within the domain of juridical discourse itself. This might occur, for example, through the evolution of property's conceptualization in doctrinal discourse so as to facilitate its internalization into the ontology of the legal through being transformed into something more like a general principle of juridical reason.

As the present chapter argues, following the great rebellion of 1857, it was shifts of both kinds that happened as circumstances of varied character conspired to push legal development in the Crown's India. Simultaneously with the colonial political economy's transition away from its earlier focus on surplus appropriation through the land tax, property discourse in the subcontinent also shifted under the increasingly global sway of classical legal thought. As in the Anglo-common-law mainstream, then, in Britain's India as well, this latter change was signalled by the rise of a new conception of the right to property as relative, disaggregable, and immaterial. At the same time, whereas in the West this change represented an evolution from an earlier doctrinal idea of the right to property as absolute, unitary, and physicalist, in the subcontinent it marked a passage away from the peculiarly colonial conception of property as an entitlement to land's rent. In contrast to the Crown's India, therefore, in the Anglo-common-law mainstream the evolving notion of the right to property in classical legal thought represented not only departure but also continuity.

Accordingly, in the West the classical view of the late nineteenth century partly reflected a waning ability—one that would fully collapse only in the early twentieth century—on the part of legal and political elites to preserve their faith in a non-political ideal of the rule of law. Especially in the context of the ever more strident attack on property's bourgeois dominion by its assorted socialist foes after Europe's year of revolutions in 1848, maintaining the fiction that rights represented simple relationships between persons and things was becoming increasingly difficult. To see property as relative, disaggregable, and immaterial—or, as per the name this view would go on to acquire as it matured and become ubiquitous in the twentieth century, to see property as a 'bundle of rights/sticks'—was thus not simply to legitimize the pervasiveness of the logic of the market.[4] Rather, just as importantly, it was to admit that property was always a relationship between persons, and that as such it was constituted through countless many rules that the judiciary, as much as the legislature, was responsible for making and remaking. From here, only a short logical step was needed to reach the further conclusion that granting or denying recognition to the proverbial sticks in property's

[4] See e.g. Thomas C. Grey, 'The Disintegration of Property'. In *Nomos XXII69*, eds. J. Roland Pennock and John W. Chapman (New York: New York University Press, 1980), Horwitz, *The Transformation of American Law 1870–1960*, ch. 5, and Gregory Alexander, *Commodity and Propriety: Competing Visions of Property in American Legal Thought, 1776–1970* (Chicago, IL: University of Chicago Press, 2008), ch. 11. While it has been common to insist that the bundle of sticks view was particular to the Anglo-American common-law tradition, comparable views were being explicitly articulated at roughly the same time among continental jurists. Anna di Robilant dubs these 'tree view' of property. See Anna di Robilant, 'Property: A Bundle of Sticks or a Tree', *Vanderbilt Law Review* 66 (2013): 869–932 and her more expansive treatment of the same topic in di Robilant, *The Making of Modern Property*. To say that the bundle of sticks view became and remains ubiquitous is not to say that it has not also been a source of discontent, with some disputing its accuracy as a picture of property's 'true' nature. For the most recent lineage of discontent see e.g. J. E. Penner, 'The "Bundle of Rights" Picture of Property', *UCLA Law Review* 43 (1996): 711–820 and Daniel B. Klein and John Robinson, 'Property: A Bundle of Rights? Prologue to the Property Symposium', *Econ Journal Watch* 8, no. 3 (Sep. 2011): 193–204.

bundle was based on an equally countlessly many acts of political choice contingently determining how and to whom to distribute society's benefits and burdens. To understand property rights, even just implicitly, as being relative or disaggregable was, consequently, as much to begin to concede that they were logically arbitrary as was saying that they were immaterial was to further accede to the commodification of everything.[5] In this respect, within the Anglo-common-law mainstream, classical legal thought's shifting view of the property right after 1860 signalled both an ascent to the high point of formalist jurisprudential abstraction and a sowing of the intellectual seeds of formalism's own (eventual) demise.

At the same time, the classical view proved more than capable in the West of sustaining the eighteenth century's founding conception of 'the law' as resting upon its own distinct elemental basis.[6] For to see the property right as disaggregable was not only to imagine that the distribution of its component parts adhered to no natural or necessary logic but also to purport to uncover the even more fundamental constituents of which legal right in general was comprised. Whatever the denaturalizing tendency of the classical view, it only deepened the ongoing ontologization of the law. For if under the absolute, unitary, and physicalist view legal right

---

[5] As Vandevelde puts the point in the context of the legal history of the United States, by the second half of the nineteenth century even though the progressive 'dephysicalization of property' had 'greatly broadened the purview of property law' it also jeopardized what supposedly made the property right so distinct. By making it so that '[a]ny valuable interest' could be 'potentially declared the object of property rights', the tendency to greater abstraction 'threatened to place the entire corpus of American law in the category of property', transforming 'practically any act' into 'either a trespass on, or a taking of, someone's property'. Ultimately, abstraction thus portended its own undoing by evacuating property of the very meaningfulness that allowed it to function as a supposedly secure basis from which to deduce legally 'correct' outcomes in the first place. Vandevelde, 'The New Property of the Nineteenth Century', 330. In the context of their discussion of the equity of redemption in England, Sugarman and Warrington reach a compatible conclusion about that doctrine's own final demise, which, as they show, took place only in tandem with a larger shift away from the exclusivity of the property right and towards the contractually willed bargain over forms of legally protected interest as the organizing principle of private law doctrine. See Sugarman and Warrington, 'Land Law, Citizenship, and the Invention of "Englishness"', 133–34.

[6] Of course, none of this is to say that the substantive legal treatment of landed property was uniform across the proverbial West, or, for that matter, even across the Anglo-common-law mainstream. For a notable recent discussion of some formative differences between how landed property was legally treated in England versus the early United States, see Claire Priest, *Credit Nation: Property Laws and Institutions in Early America* (Princeton, NJ: Princeton University Press, 2021).

could be considered an irreducibly real phenomenon because of the way its propertied archetype corresponded to an inherently material referent comprised by the landed space of the owner's absolute dominion, under the classical view ontologization still followed from a parallel formula. It was simply that now, increasingly, what instead gave the phenomenon of legal right its irreducibly real point of reference in the (social) world was the juridically institutionalized 'realm absolute' of its holder's valued property interest—regardless of how expansive or circumscribed that might be.

Suffice to say, the relative, disaggregable, and immaterial view of property did not make itself felt in quite the same way in Britain's India. While in the subcontinent as well it undergirded important changes in polity and economy, these took more specific shape in a colonial context of mounting distress for rural smallholders and tenants and an attendant shift towards exploitative credit provision as the key mechanism of surplus extraction. Accordingly, under Crown Raj the view of property in classical legal thought asserted its influence most dramatically in the form of a rolling wave of recognition of subordinate agrarian rights after the Bengal Rent Act of 1859. Moreover, in the subcontinent the view remained largely unannounced, continuously muted by a countertendency that was simultaneously developing within the discursive culture of late-colonial rule. This involved the developing ubiquity of a revisionist interpretation of the Company's era, according to which previous officials were charged with wrongly assuming that the 'English' concept of property could be made to fit land-control practices so culturally specific and varied as those that obtained in the subcontinent.

During the last decades of the nineteenth century this early version of the critique of the colonial state's rule of property from the theory-practice divide was increasingly articulated through reference to the merely 'proprietary' character of land rights in the subcontinent. There was no one who more clearly channelled this discourse of proprietary right than judge and pre-eminent expert on South Asian agrarian relations Baden Henry Baden-Powell. For example, in his 1892 masterwork, *The Land Systems of British India*, Baden-Powell observed that '[t]he first thing that will strike the student is the use of the term "proprietary right" in these pages and in Indian Revenue books generally'. This, he explained, was because the term 'does not occur in textbooks on English law or jurisprudence', instead being a neologism that in Baden-Powell's estimation had been adapted for the peculiarities of the subcontinental situation.[7]

As I further contend in the second main section of the chapter, in this revisionist narrative of the Company's rule of mere proprietary right what we are really hearing is the stifled echo of a larger revolution of ideas that was beginning to take place in the West under the influence of classical legal thought, with legal and political ideologues eventually being forced to question the coherence of the very concept of property itself. In the subcontinent, if this revolution was less than fully visible, it was because it was reoriented through a turning inward. That is, rather than making the shifting view of property explicit, even the most sophisticated of thinkers, like Baden-Powell, tended to see the reasons compelling the Raj's new-found recognition of subordinate agrarian rights in largely culturalist terms, as due to the particularities of Indian society. In the process, the colonial rule of law was inoculated against the more unforgiving critique of rights talk that was spreading within the Western legal mainstream. At the same time, supporters and opponents of the peasantry alike set the stage for an emergent form of Indian nationalism whose own mainstream would be left consistently struggling with the constraining tendencies of its rights-talking, legalist origins.

As in part II, then, the present chapter continues elaborating the book's story of the arc of property talk under colonial rule. As in chapters three and four, the presentation here also follows the general method set out in part I by moving back and forth across the boundary between ordinary-language discourse about the law—here, about its increasingly prominent new elemental basis of proprietary right—and the discourse of the law that played host to the legislative advent of a plethora of new kinds of subordinate agrarian entitlements that doctrinally instantiated a more fully legalized notion of right. Here, however, in tracing the story into the second half of the nineteenth century, after the transfer of power to the Crown, the present chapter—to say nothing of the ones in part III that follow—tracks the internalization of property's conceptualization into that of 'the law'. It does so, moreover, in the course of demonstrating how the rise of classical legal thought coincided with an ontologization of the

---

[7] Baden-Powell, *The Land Systems of British India*, vol. I, 218.

law in British India that was detained by at least a century as compared to Britain itself, given the Company's founding priority of reinscribing the subcontinent's ancien régime of surplus appropriation through the land-revenue demand in a language of property in/as rent.

6.2 The Shifting Institutional Context of the Administration of Justice

With the events of May 1857 that launched the sepoy mutiny-cum-rebellion, British rule in the subcontinent was met with its greatest—as well as a completely unexpected—shock. Notwithstanding the intensity of the force of arms with which the uprising was quashed over the next year, the colonial state's resort to terror was only the most visible of the immediate consequences it inspired. Of longer-term import was the demise of the East India Company, which was finally displaced from its commanding role over Indian governance owing to the events of 1857 (as too were the last remaining vestiges of Mughal sovereignty it had nominally preserved). With the Company's dissolution, its three main Presidencies as well as the other areas under its direct rule were brought under the sovereignty of the British Crown-in-Parliament in 1858. In the process they were also integrated into a much more substantial infrastructure of imperium. As touched on in chapter one, this meant a thoroughgoing reorganization of the institutions of central and provincial government. With the proliferation of quasi-legislative bodies and bureaucratic agencies of various kinds, together with the policies and programmes they were charged with carrying out, a notable expansion was thus under way in what Habermas might call the 'steering media' of colonial administrative power.[8]

With more specific reference to the administration of justice, the transfer of power brought the most significant overhaul of its institutional architecture since the formative years of its consolidation during the 1790s.[9] Outside revenue matters, that architecture had remained in

---

[8] See generally, Habermas, *The Theory of Communicative Action, vol. 2.*
[9] The discussion in this section closely follows Gregory Kozlowski's superb summary. See Kozlowski, *Muslim Endowments in British India*, 116–23.

place, with minor regional variations, for some seven decades, which, as we saw in chapter one, made for an overall jurisdictional pyramid that moved up from the native *amins*, to district-level *zilla* courts in major provincial cities, to the highest appellate or ʿ*adalat* courts that were divided over 'criminal' and 'civil' affairs. Of course, there was also the parallel array of Supreme Courts at the three main Presidency centres, which quickly enough came to traffic in business involving litigants of all faith communities, despite their initial reservation, in disputes involving British personnel/subjects and select minorities like Armenians.

It was these last two facets, especially, that were transformed after the rebellion. Within a half-decade after the transfer of power, already in 1862 both the Supreme Courts and the ʿ*adalat* courts were done away with, along with their rather confounding jurisdictional division of labour. In their place, the Crown established a new more unified array of chartered High Courts, with judges appointed on the final say of the British monarch. Situated at the original Presidency seats of Calcutta, Bombay, and Madras, together with Allahabad, the High Courts functioned both as appellate bodies and institutions with original jurisdiction over affairs in the locales where they were situated. Additionally, the Crown also established a series of Chief Courts at places like Lahore and Nagpur, with their justices appointed on the final say of the Viceroy of India. Finally, at the apex of the new system stood the Privy Council in London. All told, then, there was a continuous line of authority running from the lowest of *munsif* courts, which presided over rudimentary civil and criminal matters in the subcontinent, to the subordinate magistrates at the district level, who were themselves supervised by a district magistrate, up through a chain of higher-level appeal that terminated only in the Monarchy, which by royal proclamation confirmed the decisions of the Privy Councillors.

Much the same trajectory of change was advanced (and symbolized) by the 1864 decision to do away with the Hindu and Muslim assessors, who were a hallmark of the Company's founding commitment to ostensibly preserve native laws. Doing so, of course, famously catalysed official case reporting and the attendant rise of 'Anglo-Hindu' and 'Anglo-Mohammedan' law. The new appellate institutions also encouraged the rise of a 'document Raj'[10] surpassing any under the Company in virtue

---

[10] See, generally, Raman, *Document Raj*.

of their much more exacting ways of keeping case files, which could include magistrate-level decision-making, transcripts of witness testimony, and other relevant paperwork. Much the same went for the generally enhanced educational qualifications of those who staffed the ranks of the new judicial hierarchy, which tended to be less British the further down one went in the pyramid. This effect was evident starting from the level of the magistrates, a majority of whom were Indian and who now were required to have BA degrees and knowledge of English. Likewise, British—and for that matter, any Indian—members of the Indian Civil Service who served as subordinate judges were required to undertake at least some brief course of legal study in England during their training.

At the same time, at what was for the present purposes the most significant level—of the High Courts—few of the predominantly British Judges were individuals who had proceeded all the way up from the Indian Civil Service's judicial track. Rather, most of the judges on the upper tier of the judiciary were highly trained legal minds, many of whom also had practical experience in the metropole as members of the Bar. Of course, this also meant that one characteristic that Indian Civil Service personnel turned subordinate judges and the types of individuals who tended to be picked as High Court judges did have in common was their increasing distance from any familiarity with subcontinental juristic traditions.

A final key factor that pushed the transformation of the institutional architecture of the administration of justice was the emergence of a more distinct legal profession. Indeed, other than at the level of the litigants themselves, it was here that the Raj's subjects in South Asia asserted their presence most insistently within the new system. As Gregory Kozlowski notes, lawyering became 'an attractive career path for large numbers of Indians', with some one-quarter of the approximately 600 students attending Aligarh College in the three decades from 1877 to 1911 'finding their way into some branch of the legal profession'. (That number stood second only to the some 300 who entered government service.)

Individuals like these who remained in the subcontinent and did their legal training at one of British India's rising institutions of higher education completed a full range of courses—including, jurisprudence, contracts, torts, evidence, procedure, criminal law, and the study of material more specific to their immediate context like the Indian Penal Code—and were destined to become advocates or *wakils* as members of the Indian

Bar. However, even if arguably better trained than their counterparts who went to Britain, it was the latter who, as barristers, carried a more rarefied air of prestige, automatically becoming members of the Indian Bar once admitted to the Bar in England, Scotland, or Ireland.[11] This difference between those colonial subjects who were part of the more elite British-trained stratum of lawyers and those who were trained in the subcontinent was, of course, important in various ways. At the same time, the overall growth of the legal profession that both were a part of meant they jointly contributed to making the Raj's transformed apparatus for administering justice, ultimately, 'the nursery school of India's nationalist movement'.[12]

6.3 The Shifting Political Economy of Crown Rule and the Recognition of New Forms of 'Proprietary' Right

Increasing bureaucratization and its various manifestations within institutions like those of the judiciary both complemented and proved partly constitutive of developments at the economic level as well, including ones that were becoming evident already before the rebellion. By 1850, for example, commercial production of crops like cotton and jute had achieved industrial scale. During the next several years the first stages of a modern steel and iron industry also materialized.[13] Plantation production and extractive industries, on the other hand, would not take on what greater importance they did until after the transfer of power. For example, as late as 1858 there was still only a single major player, the Assam Company, involved in tea cultivation in the subcontinent; over the course of the next decade, however, the number expanded rapidly as the tea plantations of eastern India became significant magnets for private capital and, of course, migrant labour.[14] Likewise, it was only with

---

[11] Kozlowski, *Muslim Endowments in British India*, 120–21.
[12] Ibid., 119.
[13] See generally Morris D. Morris, *The Emergence of an Industrial Labour Force in India: A Study of the Bombay Cotton Mills, 1854–1947* (Berkeley, CA: University of California Press, 1965).
[14] Shyam Rungta, *The Rise of Business Corporations in India,1851–1900* (London: Cambridge University Press, 1970), ch. 5.

the westward extension of the East India Railway during the decade after its launch in Calcutta in 1855 that coal mining began to take off. (Other forms of mining, for example of gold, also increased significantly in these years.) Of course, railway construction stood in a category all on its own in terms of significance, both in its ability to attract (metropolitan) investment capital in search of guaranteed returns in the subcontinent and in its capacity as an instrument for revolutionizing the transport system on which wider commercial and industrial expansion depended.[15]

To stand watch over this critical new enterprise, in 1854 the colonial state established a railroad authority. Economically speaking, even more important was the new Public Works department that was set up by the colonial government that same year. In subsequent decades it became the key sponsor of the other handful of infrastructure projects that attracted capital and spurred economic expansion scaled to more overt-seeming ambitions of 'modern' transformation (in ways, of course, that sceptics of the economic effects of colonial rule on the subcontinent's internal development have long argued were a mixed blessing, starting already with the early nationalist critics of deindustrialization and the drain of wealth).[16] Canal construction in the Punjab was, perhaps, the most important other example, though notably it became prominent only some time later, starting in the 1880s, some two decades after the Company's dissolution.[17] All of this, of course, is to say nothing of the government's

---

[15] Dharma Kumar and Tapan Raychaudhuri, eds., *The Cambridge Economic History of India*, vol. 2: *c. 1757–c. 1970* (New York: Cambridge University Press, 1983), 737–61 and Dietmar Rothermund, *An Economic History of India: from Pre-Colonial Times to 1991*, 2nd edn. (New York: Routledge, 1993), 32–36.

[16] See e.g. Dadabhai Naoroji, *Poverty and Un-British Rule in India* (London: Swan Sonnenschein & Co.), 228–29 and Romesh Chunder Dutt, *The Economic History of India During the Victorian Age. From the Accession of Queen Victoria in 1837 to the Commencement of the Twentieth Century*, vol. II, (London: Kegan Paul, 1906), 10. Various controversies persist around the historical implications of the railroads. These include questions about whether the guarantee to investment capital was a 'drain' on the subcontinent or a return for the untold positive externalities such investment would go on to produce and about the significance of track paths being directed towards moving raw materials from the interior to coastal ports for export. See e.g. Aditya Mukherjee, 'The Return of the Colonial in Indian Economic History: The Last Phase of Colonialism in India', *Social Scientist* 36, no. 3/4: 3–44 (2007) and Dan Bogart and Latika Chaudhary, 'Railways in Colonial India: An Economic Achievement?' In *A New Economic History of Colonial India*, eds. Latika Chaudhary, Bishnupriya Gupta, Tirthankar Roy, and Anand Swamy (New York: Routledge, 2016), 140–66.

[17] Kumar and Raychaudhuri, eds., *The Cambridge Economic History of India*, 677–736 and Richard G. Fox, *Lions of the Punjab: Culture in the Making* (Berkeley, CA: University of California Press, 1985), ch. 4.

role in institutionalizing a more integrated system of all-India monetary, fiscal, and credit arrangements of the type needed for sustaining the expansion of production, marketing, and trade.[18]

Developments at the level of polity and economy were not mutually constitutive of one another simply at the level of institutions, however. Other important cyclical trends in the economy and ad hoc actions by the state began to reinforce each other by the early 1850s as well. Chief among these was the reversal of the long period of stagnation and price depression that characterized conditions in most of the subcontinent during the three decades after the Company's initial military expansion came to an end in 1820.[19] Already in the half-decade before the transfer of power a noticeable rise in the price level had become evident. The factors contributing to this price recovery were several, including the above-referenced influx of British capital for railway construction after 1853, an expanding demand for rice in the eastern parts of the subcontinent by 1852 due to British war-making in Upper Burma,[20] and changing conditions on the world market, which stoked demand for Indian cotton and jute.[21] The re-conquest of North India in the wake of the rebellion also had its own part to play, initially pushing up prices in various areas by squeezing supply and later intensifying the same effect through inflationary military spending.[22]

Especially with the last factor, which ended up proving a fiscal force significant enough to push the Company's treasury towards deficit, signs were becoming visible that the older pattern of colonial rule's political

---

[18] It was only in 1862, for instance, that an annual budget was introduced for British India as a whole. A unified paper currency was not mandated until 1861's Paper Currency Act, and it was only in 1921 that the three major Presidency Banks were consolidated into a central bank of sorts in the form of the Imperial Bank of India. See Kumar and Raychaudhuri, eds., *The Cambridge Economic History of India*, ch. 9. For a particular emphasis on this point, see Tirthankar Roy, *A Business History of India: Enterprise and the Emergence of Capitalism from 1700* (New York: Cambridge University Press, 2018), 69–125.

[19] See e.g. C. A. Bayly, *Rulers, Townsmen and Bazaars: North Indian Society in the Age of British Expansion, 1770–1870* (New York: Cambridge University Press, 1983), ch. 7 and Sumit Guha, *The Agrarian Economy of the Bombay Deccan, 1818–1941* (New York: Oxford University Press, 1985), ch. 2.

[20] Rothermund, *An Economic History of India*, 28.

[21] Jute became an important substitute for Russian flax once the flax supply was disrupted by the Crimean War in the period from 1854 to 1856. It was the United States' Civil War (1861–65) that elicited the great boom period for Indian cotton. See B. R. Tomlinson, *The Economy of Modern India, 1860–1970* (New York: Cambridge University Press, 1993), 119–20.

[22] Rothermund, *An Economic History of India*, 28.

economy was giving way. As historians of the agrarian countryside have observed, by the time of the transfer of power in 1858 a long-term decline in the importance of the land-revenue demand as a mechanism for extracting surplus from Indian agriculture was under way. More specifically, this was made manifest through the diminishing importance of the land tax relative both to the total level of agricultural output and to other available revenue sources as new forms of indirect taxation came online. While the data is not free of controversy, standard sources estimate that from 1850 to 1901 the nominal increase in collections was 25 per cent, while agricultural prices increased by as much as 80 per cent during roughly the same period. (The increase in output, itself, is estimated to have reached 20 per cent from 1869 to 1901.)[23] Likewise, already in the twelve years from 1858 to 1870 the land revenue's contribution to the state's cumulative intake fell by as much as ten points, from 50 to 40 per cent of the total.[24]

Ultimately, the retreat in the land revenue's significance that is made evident by figures like these derived from the fact that the tax rate could not just be raised overnight. The effects of such a constraint were only exacerbated by the inability of the state's demand to keep pace with the larger inflationary tendency just catalogued, which during the 1850s alone saw prices doubling in many parts of the subcontinent.[25] With the overall rise in prices continuing all the way until 1930, the disparity that had clearly developed between nominal and real revenue rates by the 1860s meant that once it started to reverse in importance, the land tax was destined never again to regain the primacy it once had.[26]

Of course, this is not to say that the land-revenue demand suddenly became insignificant, much less that it did not remain a highly visible element in the state's budgetary regime and, hence, a persistent target of agrarian protest. The gradual abeyance of the land tax was also a product of its becoming a prime target for the early/proto-nationalist critics of the economic effects of British rule, like Dadabhai Naoroji,[27] Mahadev

---

[23] The figure for the increase in agricultural prices is for the period from 1861 to 1901. See Kumar and Raychaudhuri, eds., *The Cambridge Economic History of India*, 918.
[24] Ibid., 916.
[25] Rothermund, *An Economic History of India*, 28.
[26] Ibid., 29.
[27] See generally Naoroji, *Poverty and Un-British Rule*.

Govind Ranade,[28] and Romesh Chunder Dutt,[29] among others.[30] Indeed, the intellectual deconstruction of the land tax was not uncommonly joined to a plea for reconstruction that melded with the wave of legislation that was cresting in recognition of certain subordinate agrarian rights. As Ranade thus put it, what was needed to 'lighten[]' the 'heavy hand' of the land tax and the 'dead-weight of revenue settlements, which paralyze' the 'energies' of the cultivators was 'the magic of property'.[31]

However, more directly, the colonial political economy's founding mode of surplus appropriation through the 'the state's revenue onslaught' and the attendant 'rent offensive' it continued to precipitate by landlords through the first half of the nineteenth century was eroded by the new mode of appropriation that displaced it.[32] As Sugata Bose puts it, from 1870 until the beginning of the Great Depression in 1930 it was the 'credit mechanism' that assumed 'pre-eminence in extracting the surplus'.[33] This meant that while private transfers from agriculturists remained critical, by the last thirty years of the nineteenth century they were increasingly routed through usurious interest payments to the local moneylender. While the latter figure might be a traditional intermediary in the agrarian economy who had long filled such a role, they could also be an agriculturist in their own right—such as an up-and-coming entrepreneurial peasant who had benefitted from commercialization and now saw fit to diversify into the business of making loans. Yet regardless of the moneylender's precise identity or whether it was the cultivator who was the recipient of their advances or the landlord, the underlying dynamic of the new political economy of colonial rule was set by a larger system of primary production for the world market into which the subcontinent

---

[28] See e.g. Mahadev Govind Ranade, *Essays on Indian Economics: A Collection of Essays and Speeches* (Madras: G. A. Natesan and Co., 1906).
[29] See e.g. Dutt, *The Economic History of India in the Victorian Age*.
[30] On the lasting importance of their work see Irfan Habib, 'Studying a Colonial Economy without Perceiving Colonialism', *Modern Asian Studies* 19, no. 3 (1985): 355–81. (For an updated version of the deflationary view of the early nationalist critique of the drain, de-industrialization, and the like that Habib is contesting see generally Roy, *A Business History of India*, 40–125 and Roy, *India in the World Economy*, 123–209.)
[31] M. G. Ranade, *Journal of the Poona Sarvajanik Sabha, Quarterly* IV, no. 2 (Oct. 1881): 57 (quoted in Bipan Chandra, *The Rise and Growth of Economic Nationalism in India: Economic Policies of Indian National Leadership, 1880–1905* (New Delhi: Har-Anand Publications, 2010), 368–69).
[32] Sugata Bose, *Peasant Labour and Colonial Capital*, 113.
[33] Ibid., 114.

was now more definitively being integrated under the Crown. For even if it was the South Asian moneylender who was the proximal source of usury capital, the gears that sustained the new mechanism of surplus extraction turned in the financial markets of London.[34]

In the final analysis, then, the post-1850s price recovery and the wider process of agricultural commercialization it was tied up with made for mixed results. Certainly, a net decline in the real burden of the state's land-revenue demand was not the only consequence. Alongside the sizeable number of urban intermediaries, traditional trading groups, and relatively well-to-do agriculturists who captured new opportunities for profit, there were those whose survival was more dependent on low prices for food and other basic commodities. For such individuals, increasing integration into the world market meant greater economic volatility and hence greater instability in meeting fundamental needs. As a result, periods of decline in the 1870s and the 1890s in global demand for the types of higher-value cash crops to which many small producers in the subcontinent had turned proved disastrous. In such times, crises became dramatically evident through surges of famine and other forms of agrarian distress,[35] with the tightening connection between the Indian countryside and the global economy having deeply polarizing effects. So-called 'rich peasants', whose control over land was secure and significant enough in scale to garner a surplus, tended to gain through increasing returns on their capital. Conditions for smaller-holders or subsistence agriculturists, however, continued to seriously fluctuate, both from locale to locale and over seasonal and secular—whether over the shorter or the longer term—time.[36]

---

[34] Though his focus is on Bengal, Bose's general description of the path of credit can be regarded as more widely applicable:

> Merchant capital, which originated in the arenas of high finance in the metropolis, was exchanged and forwarded by the purchasing firms through a network of commission agents to the primary producers. The peasant usually received his dadan or advance from a small trader-moneylender directly dependent on the flow of funds from above. The primary interest of the entire hierarchy of lenders, whether the borrower was contracted to sell to a particular lender or not, was to secure the crop at a low village-level price. Ibid., 123.

[35] Bose and Jalal, *Modern South Asia*, 80–83.
[36] Tirthankar Roy, 'Economic History and Modern India: Redefining the Link', *The Journal of Economic Perspectives* 16, no. 3 (2002): 109–30 at 116.

Simultaneously, with regard to legal evolution the most important consequence of this era was to set the stage for a shift away from the older context that the Company had inaugurated after 1757 through its focus on property in land's rent. Among the key arenas of change was the colonial public sphere, where a marked controversy emerged about the proverbial peasantry, exploited from above by new superiors in the agrarian hierarchy and killed in their millions by a protracted spate of famines starting in the late 1860s.[37] A mounting outcry thus ensued over the plight of the indebted at the hands of the moneylender, who took on an increasingly demonized image. Long-standing British anxieties about colonial 'improvement' leading to the mixed blessing of dissolving the immemorial bonds on which South Asian society was thought to rest were increasingly transformed into a preoccupation with the parasitic treachery of figures like the *mahajan* and *bania*. They became opportunists strictly devoted to speculation, a view that tended to obscure the possibility of their deeper roots in the practice of productive agriculture and their possible role as beneficiaries of the Crown's own policies encouraging agricultural commercialization, especially for the world market. Instead, in official eyes it was the moneylender who became the near exclusive source of ruin, whether because they stood directly behind the exploited cultivator or indirectly so where it was the indebtedness of some agrarian superior that became the more proximal cause of peasant distress. Throughout the colonial subcontinent, therefore, after 1857 a similar fear underwrote the dramatic upsurge in legislative measures to protect new classes of agrarian subordinates from their 'propertied' or moneyed superiors.[38]

It was in Bengal that the first inkling of these measures emerged with the Rent Act of 1859, which extended to a limited subsegment of the higher peasantry modest protections against increases in the payments

---

[37] For contrasting views about the relationship between environmental and economic factors in the making of late-nineteenth-century famines see Mike Davis, *Late Victorian Holocausts: El Niño Famines and the Making of the Third World* (New York: Verso, 2001) and Tirthankar Roy, *Natural Disasters and Indian History* (Oxford: Oxford University Press, 2012). See also Tamoghna Halder, 'Colonialism and the Indian Famines: A Response to Tirthankar Roy', *Developing Economics: A Critical Perspective on Development Economics*, Feb. 20, 2023, https://developingeconomics.org/2023/02/20/colonialism-and-the-indian-famines-a-response-to-tirthankar-roy/.

[38] See Hermann Kulke and Dietmar Rothermund, *A History of India*, 4th edn. (New York: Routledge, 2004), 268.

demanded of them. This regime was strengthened considerably, even if in ways still confined to the relatively more privileged ranks of agrarian society, through the Bengal Tenancy Act of 1885. Elsewhere in the subcontinent varying levels of protection for occupancy rights, rights against rent enhancement, and the like followed suit or were concurrent with these measures in Bengal. These included the milder Oudh Tenancy Act of 1868; the Punjab Tenancy Act of the same year, which was comprehensively revised in 1887 and then again in 1898 in the wake of the passage of the 1885 Act in Bengal; in Punjab, the even more important Land Alienation Act of 1901, which altogether prohibited transfers of land from statutorily designated agriculturists to statutorily designated non-agriculturists (with the intended referent of the latter term misleadingly imagined to correspond to a strictly urban rentier); the equally momentous Deccan Agriculturists' Relief Act of 1879, which followed in the wake of agrarian riots against Marwari moneylenders in and around Poona that stunned colonial officialdom; the Central Provinces Tenancy Act of 1883, which was revised so as to become British India's most comprehensive in 1898; the Malabar Tenancy Act of 1887, which was revised in 1900; the Bombay Khoti Leases Act of 1865 and provisions within the Khoti Settlement Act of 1880, both of which were substantially updated in a revised Settlement Act dating from 1904; the North-Western Provinces Tenancy Act of 1901, which built on measures passed earlier in 1873; and, through certain of its provisions, the Madras Estates Land Act of 1908.

Of course, especially where occupancy rights were involved, the recognition of such new kinds of entitlement may have simply reinstated many of the same problems that plagued the original forms of property (in rent) that had been recognized under the Company. This is because it was still higher-tier land controllers who were privileged over actual cultivators. In this respect, such recognition was both cause and consequence of whatever split became evident in the late nineteenth century between rich peasants and the disenfranchised mass of smallholders, sharecroppers, and itinerant agricultural wage labourers who fell below them; and, indeed, agrarian reform legislation did attract criticism that was, at times, reminiscent of earlier strands within the response to the Company's initial attempts at revenue settlement. After all, there were those who sought to justify the *raiyatwari* approach by arguing that it would repair the Cornwallis system's arbitrary division of 'occupancy' from 'proprietary' right[39] and its effect of making the latter into little more 'than a right to collect from the cultivators'.[40]

Yet to the extent that such a critique had been articulated as part of the experience of colonial rule already from the beginning of the nineteenth century, in its earlier more occasional incarnation the notion of 'proprietary' right was invoked primarily as a synonym for the right to property, as per one ordinary, even if secondary, meaning of the term at the time.[41] According to this earlier usage, in other words, the distinction between a mere occupancy right and a genuine 'proprietary right' was invoked polemically as part of the debate about *who* to invest with the claim to rental value that the Company was concerned with making legible in the name of property. In such debate, the question was not about whether the very concept of property was up to the task of capturing land-control practices like those in the subcontinent, let alone about whether it might be less logically coherent than was conventionally imagined.

Therefore, with the various legislative measures expanding subordinate agrarian rights after 1860, an ostensible concern over the oppression of the peasant was underwriting something quite novel. It did so, more specifically, by paving the way to a juridification of agrarian social relations far exceeding any that was previously effectuated through the Company's administration of native laws and property in rent. In this respect, as much as it was about anything else, the expanding recognition of subordinate rights was about deepening the state's administrative power—namely, by assembling under a single rubric of imagination norms that varied widely in content. Some focused on restricting the capacity to increase the ground rent demanded of subordinates; others concentrated on limiting the ability to evict or prohibiting the transfer of indebted lands; still others elaborated defining criteria for different

---

[39] 'Extract: Fort St. George Revenue Consultations: Memoir of Mr. Thackeray ... to ... Lord William Cavendish Bentinck, in favour of Ryotwar Permanent Settlements', 29 April 1806, reprinted in *The Fifth Report, vol. II, Madras Presidency*, 603.

[40] 'Extract: Fort St. George Revenue Consultations: Mr. Hodgson's Report on the Province of Dindigul, 28 March 1808', 16 August 1808, reprinted in ibid., 703.

[41] This is the predominant way in which the term is used where it appears in the Company's regulations. See e.g. Regulation I of 1793 ('A Regulation for Enacting into a Regulation certain Articles of a Proclamation'), par. VI; Regulation II of 1793 ('A Regulation for abolishing the Courts of Mal Adalat or Revenue Courts'), par. XVI; Regulation III of 1793 ('A Regulation for Re-enacting ... Rules for the Decennial Settlement of the Public Revenue'), par. XIV; Regulation VII of 1828 ('A Regulation for Amending Provisions of Regulation XV'), par. V in C. D. Field, ed., *The Regulations of the Bengal Code*.

classes of tenancy or made provision for tacitly allowing adjudicators to look to the equities of the bargains made between agrarian debtors and their creditors. However, all markedly expanded the compass of officially recognized entitlements rooted in land beyond command over the monetizable value of its produce alone. In the process, doctrinal discourse in the colonial subcontinent was finally accumulating a version of the property right better suited to serving as a model for a distinctly legal kind of right in general.

Yet as noted earlier, by the time in the late nineteenth century when this was taking place it was no longer any equivalence between propertied entitlement in land and an ostensibly unitary and physicalist realm of its holder's absolute dominion that was being struck in the Crown's India. Rather, the equivalence was with whatever immaterial realm of legal interest might be disaggregated for recognition through agrarian reform legislation and within the circumscribed boundaries of which its holder still reigned supreme, albeit now only in a way that was *relative to* other possibly competing interests that might also be/have been made legible by the state.[42] Seen in this way, the parallels with the emerging view of rights in classical legal thought are difficult to miss.

Even so, in the actual course of historical events the parallels remained occluded by the tendency to recast this shifting view of property as a necessary response to the merely 'proprietary' character of rights in the subcontinent. In tandem, there was an additional tendency to retrospectively reimagine that the relative, disaggregable, and immaterial view of the property right had been recognized all along, at least on a de facto basis, starting already during the formative period of colonial revenue settlement decades earlier. On this reimagining, Crown rule differed from the Company's mainly insofar as it involved a willingness to reckon with the subcontinent's uniquely limited species of proprietary entitlements on a de jure basis as well.

In the end, therefore, the globalizing influence of classical legal thought was neatly repackaged as testimony to the willingness of the colonial state to accommodate the infinite parochialism of South Asian society and

---

[42] Peter Robb is one of the few to take at least indirect stock of this point. See Peter Robb, 'Law and Agrarian Society in India: The Case of Bihar and the Nineteenth-Century Tenancy Debate', *Modern Asian Studies* 22, no. 2 (1988): 319–54 at 348.

culture. Indeed, even for a figure as adept at thinking about land control and tenurial relations between superiors and subordinates in the subcontinent's agrarian economy as Baden-Powell, the influence—and critical edge—of the view of rights in classical legal thought came only flickeringly into focus, as I will turn to directly.

6.4 Legalizing Property: Baden-Powell between Revisionism and Classical Legal Thought

The narrative of Indian exceptionalism that was assembling around the notion of the proprietary nature of rights in the subcontinent was spelled out by Baden-Powell not just in *Land Systems*, as I touched on at the outset of the chapter, but elsewhere in his writings as well. Already a decade earlier he was explicitly insisting on much the same line of thought, instructing officers in the Imperial Forestry Service that '[t]he Indian "proprietary right" is a thing *sui generis*', with no such 'term [being] … used in English text-books'.[43]

As the true precursor to the contemporary scholarly emphasis on the gap between colonial theory and the subcontinent's reality, this late-nineteenth-century revisionist understanding of the rule of property has too long gone unexamined; likewise, Baden-Powell's writings have too long been treated more as a secondary than a primary source.[44] While the encyclopedic *Land Systems* appeared only in 1892, by the time of its publication Baden-Powell had already had a long career as a functionary in the Crown's government. The second of fourteen children born to Oxford Professor of geometry and liberal Anglican theologian Reverend Baden Powell, Baden Henry Baden-Powell was born in 1841, sixteen years before his better-known half-brother, Robert Stephenson Baden-Powell,

---

[43] Baden Henry Baden-Powell, *A Manual of the Land Revenue Systems and Land Tenures of British India* (Calcutta: Office of the Superintendent of Government Printing, 1882), 90.

[44] Stokes is among the most candid of historians in making explicit his debt to Baden-Powell. At the same time, he also exemplifies the tendency to treat Baden-Powell mainly as a secondary source. What I am calling Baden-Powell's revisionism Stokes effectively regards as consistent with the progress of intellectual understanding by the late nineteenth century more than as a point of view indebted to larger historical changes that were afoot the world over in the legal theoretical apparatus for understanding the nature of property. See e.g. Stokes, 'The First Century of British Rule: Social Revolution or Social Stagnation', reprinted in *The Peasant and the Raj*, 31.

the founder of the Boy Scouts. Brought up partly in Ireland and educated at the St. Paul's School in London, Baden Henry entered the Indian Civil Service in 1860 and made his way to the subcontinent in 1861 at the age of twenty. He would remain there until he retired in 1889, twelve years before his death in 1901.[45] After a first decade that was spent in several different roles, including as a judge on the Punjab Small Cause Court, in 1870 Baden-Powell was appointed by the Imperial Forest Department, which had been founded in 1864, to serve as the province's Conservator of Forests. In his last decade in the subcontinent, during which he continued to be based in the Punjab, Baden-Powell served first as a Division Judge starting in 1881, then as a Commissioner of Division, and finally as a judge on the province's Chief Court.

Land Systems was, thus, a culmination of more than three decades of experience in the subcontinent, and it was from this vantage point that Baden-Powell reflected on the 'proprietary' nature of land rights in the subcontinent. As he elaborated, 'the use of such a phrase' was

> due to the feeling that we rarely acknowledge anything like a complete unfettered right vested in any one person. The interest in the soil has come to be virtually shared between two or even more *grades* ... It is true that, in many cases, only one person is called 'landlord' or 'actual proprietor' but his right is limited; the rest of the right, so to speak, is in the hands of the other grades, even though they are called 'tenants,' or by some vague title such as 'tenure-holders.' In many cases, as we have seen, this division of right is accentuated by the use of terms like 'sub-proprietor' or 'proprietor of his holding.' 'The proprietary right' seems then a natural expression for the interest held by a landlord, when that interest is not the entire 'bundle of rights' (which in the aggregate make up an absolute or complete estate) but only *some* of them, the remainder being enjoyed by other persons.[46]

Of course, in expressing this view Baden-Powell was picking up on elements of the earlier criticism of the Cornwallis system, which, as

---

[45] Little biographical detail is available about Baden Henry Baden-Powell. The family's lineage is laid out in detail at www.pinetreeweb.com/bp-family-tree-500-years.htm (accessed 13 June 2023).

[46] Baden-Powell, *The Land Systems of British India*, vol. I, 218–19.

I mentioned earlier, called attention to its way of dividing the 'occupancy' from the 'propriety' of the true owner. For Baden-Powell, however, the emphasis was now on the inherently dispersed nature of property's dominion in the subcontinent. His overall analysis was, thus, marked by the same features that distinguished the revisionist use of the idea of proprietary right during the late nineteenth century more generally.

To wit, in the above excerpt Baden-Powell's main point is not that the inferior holder's 'tenure' was proof of *theirs* being the only 'true' claim to property; nor was the main point to give the lie to the designated landlord's own. Rather, the point was that 'grades'—like possession, occupancy, possessory occupancy, and the whole further continuum of interests capable of being framed as unique to the subcontinent—could be considered 'proprietary' rights in their own regard. Even in the event that such grades were deemed 'sub-proprietary' the fundamental point was the same. For the strong suggestion was that they remained indicative of a state of affairs in which the claims of the agrarian subject in the subcontinent fell far short of 'property' in the full juridical sense of the term in English law.

In keeping with the revisionist outlook, to Baden-Powell much the same was illustrated from the very outset of the colonial state's encounter with agrarian society in South Asia. Both in surveying recent developments and in looking back on the earlier era of British rule, therefore, it was all too easy for him to look past the insistence on a notion of property as command over rent during the Company's time. In the merely 'proprietary' form of right Baden-Powell ostensibly saw before him, what he instead deciphered was the special imprimatur of a uniquely Indian social context in which land-control practices self-evidently outstripped a notion of property that was supposedly otherwise clearly applicable in the Western context. Accordingly, he retrospectively envisioned revenue settlement in the Company's India as if it had always aspired to the rule of only a limited arrangement of the sticks in property's full bundle. Noting, for example, that '[t]o say that a man is "proprietor", and that he is the "malguzar" or revenue-payer, are, in our official literature, practically synonymous', Tellingly, Baden-Powell then further remarked as follows:

> even in Madras and Bombay, where … no landlord body had grown up over the village cultivators, so that they could not be regarded as a

jointly responsible proprietary of the whole, the individual occupants were nevertheless vested ... with a definite, transferable, and heritable right, subject to the revenue demand: and this, for most practical purposes, is undistinguishable from a proprietary title.[47]

Such disavowal of a will on the Company's part to a more full-fledged rule of property was belied, however, by the deeper analytic Baden-Powell implicitly channelled in order to reach this conclusion. This is because only on its surface did the revisionist view equating 'proprietary' right with a uniquely Indian variety of fragmented authority over land follow from a knowledge of the empirical specificities of agrarian society in the subcontinent. Contrary to what administrator-intellectuals like Baden-Powell suggested, so too did it follow from what were the shifting sands beneath the edifice of property talk in the Anglo-common-law mainstream.

Apart from a few explicit references to those shifts in *Land Systems*—via Baden-Powell invoking the notion of property as a so-called bundle of sticks—the logic of classical legal thought remains largely implicit in his thinking, including in his other works. For example, 1882's *Manual of Jurisprudence for Forest Officers* opens tellingly with several chapters on 'the General Law', these, themselves, beginning with a first on 'General Notions Regarding Property'.[48] In 1893's *Course of Lectures on ... the Law of the Forest* the same approach was expanded in both scope and sophistication.[49] Read in tandem, these two works reveal both Baden-Powell's debt to the ethos of classical legal scientism and the quite different understanding of the relationship between property, right, and law that underlay his assessment of what it was that was transpiring in the Crown's India with the recognition of new types of subordinate agrarian rights. He thus commenced the *Lectures* by explaining that because forests were often yet to be made property there first needed to be clarity on what property, itself, was. This was only natural, according to Baden-Powell,

---

[47] Ibid., 287 (emphasis in the original).
[48] Baden Henry Baden-Powell, *A Manual of Jurisprudence for Forest Officers: Being a Treatise on the Forest Law and those Branches of the General Civil and Criminal Law with a Comparative Notice of the Chief Continental Laws* (Calcutta: Superintendent of Government Printing, 1882), ch. 1.
[49] Baden Henry Baden-Powell, *Forest Law: A Course of Lectures on the Principles of Civil and Criminal Law and on the Law of the Forest (Chiefly Based on the Laws in Force in British India)* (London: Bradbury, Agnew, & Co., 1893).

because in 'law, as in every other science or art, we begin with very simple and elementary conceptions', science being 'after all, only common knowledge systematized and arranged'.[50] From here he then urged that care be taken in attending to 'the variety of ways in which we speak of "property",—indicating by our phraseology certain peculiarities connected with the legal idea of ownership, which perhaps we do not very clearly apprehend'.[51] The student of the subcontinent should remain particularly vigilant, he instructed, since they were more likely to have 'heard such a phrase as—"This forest is the *property* of Government, but such and such villages or individuals have *rights in* it.'[52] However, the most elementary turn of phrase that Baden-Powell thought merited correction if the concept of property was to be cleansed of its ambiguity was that by which it could be 'used to signify both the thing owned and the right of ownership'. In this vein, he suggested that in place of the latter usage there should be made a distinction between property as 'the *subject* of the right' and ownership as '*the right* over it.'[53]

All told, then, both in *Land Systems* and Baden-Powell's other writings we see more than just a view driven by an expert knowledge of the empirical specificities of land-control practices in the subcontinent. On the contrary, his ideas closely tracked the decline of both the Company's founding idea of property in land's rent in the subcontinent and the conceptualization of the right to property as ostensibly absolute, unitary, and physicalist in the West. In the colonial and metropolitan worlds alike, each of these older respective views was now being replaced by the classical idea of the right to property—and, by extension, legal right more generally—as relative, disaggregable, and immaterial. Indeed, it was not by accident that during Baden-Powell's time in the subcontinent the meaning of 'proprietary right' was shifting precisely in the direction of these three new defining qualities. Nor was it accidental that reference to the merely proprietary nature of rights was markedly increasing in frequency in colonial discourse during the very same period, after appearing only in what more selective ways it did previously.[54] Even if

---

[50] Ibid., 6.
[51] Baden-Powell, *A Manual of Jurisprudence for Forest Officers*, 2.
[52] Ibid., 1.
[53] Ibid., 2.
[54] No less a figure than Sir Edward Coke, for example, uses the term only sparingly. A characteristic use among those ways in which it does appear in his writings occurs in Part I of his

certain aspects of that earlier usage—particularly, that by which 'proprietary right' could serve also as a synonym for 'property right'—harboured strands of original meaning that could be amplified within the discourse of Company rule,[55] the same was not the case once the concept became a proxy for bundle of sticks logic. Instead, by the early twentieth century the notion that rights represented socially relational arrangements of immaterial 'proprietary' control over their objects had passed into Anglophone discourse more generally. Well beyond the Crown's India, therefore, by the early 1900s it was becoming common for 'proprietary right' to stand for the view in classical legal thought of property interests in the law in general.

That property was relative, for example, figured prominently in the opening pages of Baden-Powell's lectures on *Forest Law* where he set out a general proposal for conceiving of rights as creations of 'the law—written, unwritten, or customary'. As he explained, whatever its form when 'the law ... declares or recognizes' a right in 'one or more persons' it does so only while thereby marking out 'a corresponding *duty* or *obligation* lying on one or more other persons'.[56] Consequently, he continued,

> not only is there always an obligation corresponding to a right (for you cannot have a *right* without someone also being *obliged* to respect it); but also these rights and obligations are (when they arise out of human dealings) in many cases *reciprocal*, i.e., not only does one person have a

---

Institutes of the Law of England: '[i]f the proprietary will sue for such subtraction of Tithes in the Ecclesiastical Court, then he shall recover but the double value by the express words of the ...' Edward Coke, *The First Part of the Institutes of the Laws of England or a Commentary Upon Littleton*, 10th edn. (London, 1703 [1628]), 159. Even by the latter half of the eighteenth century, in William Blackstone's celebrated *Commentaries on the Laws of England*—the four books of which were published between 1765 and 1769—'proprietary' appears sparingly, only some half dozen times; and when it does, it occurs most often in the context of Blackstone's discussion of the 'proprietary colonies' of North America or their 'proprietary governments'. See e.g. William Blackstone, *Commentaries on the Law of England, Book the First* (Oxford: Clarendon Press, 1765), 105 and *Commentaries on the Law of England, Book the Second*, 9th edn. (London: W. Strathan, 1783 [1765]), 257.

[55] In his six-volume *History of British India*, for example, James Mill uses the term several times in this manner—as a synonym for the right to property. (See e.g. James Mill, *A History of British India, in six volumes, vol. III*, 3rd. edn. (London, 1826 [1817]), 450. That said, even Mill uses 'proprietary' just as frequently in what was its main sense—as a descriptor for different types of colonial government (as in the distinction between 'proprietary' and 'charter').

[56] Baden-Powell, *Forest Law*, 19 (emphasis in the original).

right and the other an obligation, but *vice versa*, the person who has the obligation has also a right. If A. enters into an agreement with B. that B. shall take £1 and make a box for A.; A. has the *right* to B.'s services in making the box, and also to the box itself when finished; and B. has the *obligation* to make the box and hand it over; but then again B. has the reciprocal *right* to get £1 and A. has the *obligation* to pay it.[57]

It was through this same lens—in which all rights appeared to be constitutive of relations between persons—that Baden-Powell highlighted what he deemed to be one of the fundamental tenets of forest law. This, he explained, followed 'on the same principle [that] the owner of any property is obliged [to]'; as such, it required that the holder of a right in forest lands 'use the same in such a way as not to injure his neighbours or endanger the welfare of the whole community"'. Ultimately, then, for Baden-Powell it was not sufficient to blandly invoke the principle of *sic utere*; on the contrary, as he more emphatically reminded his audience, where '[f]orest rights' were concerned, it was in virtue of the analytical necessity of the reciprocity of rights more generally that they could only 'be exercised, within certain limits'.[58]

Similarly, Baden-Powell drew on the idea that property was disaggregable as well. As he explained in his *Manual of Jurisprudence for Forest Officers*, though 'property' (or 'ownership', as he preferred) was often spoken of 'as if it was a simple' thing, it was always internally a 'composite' of many such things—meaning, many such rights (and duties).[59] These he divided into two basic categories of rights that persons ostensibly held over things, including, first, the right of 'possession' and, second, a whole series of other 'rights enjoyed by one party on or over the property of another'.[60] Yet even with respect to the disaggregability of property, Baden-Powell still betrayed a divided consciousness about the source of his analysis. On the one hand, he pointed to the 'conflicting circumstances' of the subcontinent as being responsible for making 'the proprietary right' that was recognized by 'British law ... far from ... absolute'.[61]

---

[57] Ibid., 8.
[58] Baden-Powell, *A Manual of Jurisprudence for Forest Officers*, 104.
[59] Ibid., 26.
[60] Baden-Powell, *Forest Law*, 15.
[61] Baden-Powell, *A Manual of the Land Revenue Systems*, 90.

More specifically, he articulated much the same claim he would make in *Land Systems* about how in the subcontinent there developed unique 'strata' or 'grades' of proprietary right.[62] This, he argued, was because '[t]he native idea had not formulated such a thing as the *status* of a "proprietor"'.[63] Yet on the other hand, like classical legal thinkers more generally, he was also well-acquainted with the systematizing jurisprudence of early-nineteenth-century German thinkers like Savigny. Accordingly, his idea about the 'composite' nature of the property right the British were left recognizing in the subcontinent was staked on more than just an analysis of the historical consequences of circumstantial particularity alone. Instead, Baden-Powell openly appealed to the authority of 'the Roman lawyers' in suggesting that ownership in general could be thought of as 'the bundle of all possible rights which, together, make up an absolutely unrestrained enjoyment'.[64] A necessary implication of this insight, he advised, was that the party who was casually called 'owner' usually had 'something less than the absolute or perfectly full enjoyment of his property'. For the rights 'mak[ing] up a perfect... ownership' could just as well be 'detached and vested in other persons'.[65]

Still, it was nowhere more than in relation to the classification of subordinate tenures that Baden-Powell's thinking revealed a tension between his debt to the new logic of property in classical legal thought and his insistence that English concepts could scarce be used to describe a country to which, as he claimed, even the most basic category of 'India' could not be applied 'properly'.[66] This is because it was not just the messy empirical facts of South Asian social structure that made it so hard to distinguish proprietary from under-/sub-proprietary tenures. Rather, the difficulty was just as much a function of the bundle of sticks analytic that underlay the revisionist discourse of proprietary right itself, which continuously frustrated any effort at line drawing.

Too often, therefore, affirming the 'proprietary' character of a tenure became a hopelessly indeterminate affair. For on the one hand, doing so might involve highlighting some 'possessory' essence of the tenurial right

---

[62] Ibid., 89.
[63] Ibid., 86.
[64] Ibid., 27.
[65] Ibid., 26.
[66] Baden-Powell, *The Land Systems of British India, vol. I*, 5.

in a way that was ultimately no more than question-begging (as to what qualified as 'true' possession in the first place). On the other hand, trying to distinguish the truly 'proprietary' based on some non-possessory stick in property's bundle was just as likely to prove problematic; for invariably, doing *that* degenerated into an equally ad hoc process of selecting some other disaggregated interest in land as the one to deem the 'truly' essential.

For example, discounting the idea that in Oudh only the *taluqdars* had proprietary claims, Baden-Powell insisted that reference to the mere 'sub-tenure' of lower-tier members of the agrarian hierarchy 'do[es] not really impose any complication'. As he explained, 'under these different "sub-tenures" the landlord parted with certain individual sticks out of the bundle which together made up the totality of the enjoyment of full ownership'. Yet whether they were 'subordinat[ed] to the [rights of the] Taluqdar' or clearly non-possessory, '[s]uch separated rights' were, all the same, 'in their nature proprietary'.[67]

However, at other times when dealing with so-called sub-proprietary tenures Baden-Powell simply abandoned the logic underlying his reasoning above. Consider, for instance, his approach to sub-proprietors in Bengal. One basis that was always available for denying a genuinely proprietary character to the claims of such individuals was that they comprised no more than (de facto) rights of 'contract,' respectively binding only two parties at a time rather than empowering either against the world at large. Yet for Baden-Powell, '[t]he root of all the early tenant difficulties in Bengal' was not simply that the claims of tenants were less than fully proprietary because merely contractual. Rather, 'just as in Ireland', he explained, the problem went even deeper, having to do with 'the inability of authorities to contemplate a relation which they might call a "tenancy" if they pleased, but which was founded on *status*, not on *contract*'.[68]

The two horns of the dilemma posed by subordinate tenures were made even more visible when Baden-Powell considered the Bengal Rent Act of 1859. Of particular concern was its rule mandating that occupancy rights should be contingent on twelve years of continuous presence on

---

[67] Baden-Powell, *The Land Systems of British India, vol. II*, 237.
[68] Baden Henry Baden-Powell, 'The Permanent Settlement of Bengal', *English Historical Review* X, no. 38 (Apr. 1895): 276–93 at 290.

the land (which subsequently became the basis for debating similar measures across British India). On this matter, Baden-Powell professed that he could see nothing in the nature of legal right, itself, that negated either of the two 'case[s that could be] stated on both sides'—for or against—recognizing occupancy as a basis of genuinely proprietary tenure. Thus, he opined,

> [t]hose who favoured the landlords' view would urge that it was unfair to the Zamindars and other proprietors now saddled with the responsibility, strict and unbending, for the revenue that was to be paid in good years and bad alike, to tie their hands, and to refuse them the full benefit of their lands by creating an artificial right in the tenantry; such a rule would be to virtually deprive the landlord of the best share of his proprietary rights. If it was wise of Government to recognize the proprietary right at all, it must be wise also to recognize the full legal and logical consequences of that right ... On the other side the advocate of the tenant would reply: The new landlords confessedly owe their position to the gift of Government; why should they get all? why should not the benefits conferred be equally divided between the raiyats on the soil and the 'proprietors'?[69]

Notwithstanding his own admission, however, in the end Baden-Powell attempted to resolve the dilemma of apparent indeterminacy by again invoking the unique nature of circumstances in the subcontinent—here as the explanation for why both sides, for and against juridifying the occupancy right, seemed plausible. '[I]n truth', he thus noted, the reason that no one of these clashing positions could be 'theoretically determined' as the more correct was because 'the idea of landlord and tenant, as we conceive the terms, and the consequences which flow from it, have no natural counterpart in Indian custom'.[70]

In the light of the above, it can hardly be surprising that Baden-Powell should have emphasized the 'mysterious and unintelligible darkness' that Indian land-tenure arrangements made for in the eyes of colonial officialdom.[71] At the same time, his ambivalence about whether it was

---

[69] Baden-Powell, *The Land Systems of British India*, vol. I, 213–14.
[70] Ibid., 215.
[71] Ibid., 1.

custom/circumstance or the indeterminacy of available concepts that complicated questions about tenancy in the subcontinent never quite went away. After all, as he well knew, the more that rights were capable of being imagined as circumscribed 'realms' of legal interest which could be held 'absolutely' even without commanding full dominion over their respective substrates of landed space, the more did it make sense to see subordinate tenure-holders as commanding their own kind of property. His discussion of colonial Ajmer, with its preservation of 'the features of Rajput organization', serves as another notable example in this regard.

In the context of the first book of the second volume of *Land Systems*, which focused on the *mahalwari* revenue system of the North-Western Provinces, he stopped to reflect on the general effect that British rule was having on the area. Towards this end, he remarked on 'how inevitably changes of time and circumstance modify land-tenures, without any conscious act on the part of the authorities'.[72] However, when he went on to consider the position of the cultivator on the Rajput chief's own estate, he was left to conclude only that '[o]ut of these facts the reader may weave any theory ... which he pleases'. For 'it is only when such a state of things exists under direct English authorities that we are obliged to try and translate the facts into the language of Acts and Regulations'; and only upon doing so, 'insensibly and gradually' do such facts 'assume the features and the incidents of Western institutions'. Ultimately, he continued, '[t]hat is why the Ajmer cultivator is a member of a "proprietary community", and his brother in the next-door Rajput state is a "tenant", or whatever else we may please to call him'.[73]

If, on the one hand, Baden-Powell's attempts to attribute the difficulty of determining whether subordinate tenures were 'proprietary' or 'sub-proprietary' to the exceptionalism of South Asian traditions were unsurprising, on the other, they were equally ironic. This is because debates focusing on the peculiarity of tenant right in the subcontinent would become an important channel through which the notion of 'proprietary right' would diffuse into the Anglophone world at large. Indeed, in breaching colonial South Asia's permeable discursive boundary, that notion ever further became a ready shorthand for abbreviating the complex

[72] Baden-Powell, *The Land Systems of British India*, vol. II, 340.
[73] Ibid., 341.

series of arguments by which legal entitlements in general were coming to be regarded as relative, disaggregable, and immaterial.

Of course, controversies simultaneously raging in Ireland alone were sufficient to give the lie to Baden-Powell's suggestion that 'proprietary right' was a concept destined never to be found in 'text-books on English law or jurisprudence' outside the colonial subcontinent.[74] Already with the meagre protections set out in the first Irish Land Act of 1870 it was common to envision the custom of Ulster in terms of a tenant right that was 'of a quasi-proprietary kind' even if 'far short of a[n English] copyhold, or a right of occupancy in some points of capital importance'.[75] Ten years later, by the time that more robust protections were passed with the second Irish Land Act of 1881, the quasi-descriptor was just as easily dropped in favour of affirming that the recognition given to certain classes of tenants was, indeed, a form of 'proprietary right'[76] or simply, as per a slightly longer-standing usage, 'peasant proprietary'.[77] Notwithstanding the increasing visibility of high theoretical arguments favouring tenant right by the likes of figures from John Stuart Mill to Alfred Marshall,[78] then, the 'blueprint' for tenant right in Ireland—including the 'conservative' case for it—was drawn from the colonial subcontinent. As Peter Grey reminds us, figures like the liberal Indian administrator George Campbell—who a year before Gladstone's Irish Land Act would author the influential tract, *The Irish Land* in 1869—proved crucial in

---

[74] Ibid., 218.

[75] William Connor Morris, *The Irish Land Act: 33 and 34 Vict. Cap. 46: with a Full Commentary and Notes* (Dublin: E. Ponsonby, 1870), 39. In a similar vein, it was sometimes said that Ulster tenant right was 'semi-proprietary'. See e.g. George Campbell, *The Irish Land* (Dublin: Hodges, Foster, and Co. 1869), 154.

[76] See e.g. William Galbraith Miller, *Lectures on the Philosophy of Law* (London: Charles Griffin and Company, 1884), 125.

[77] In the Irish context, examination of the early land acts in terms of the 'peasant proprietary' were numerous. See e.g. William Leigh Bernard, *The Irish Land Question: Suggestions for the Extended Establishment of a Peasant Proprietary in Ireland* (Dublin: Hodges, Foster, & Figgis, 1880); E. O. MacDevitt, *A Manual of the Irish Land Acts of 1870 & 1881* (Dublin: Thom, 1881), 50, 62; and *The Land Act of 1881: Rent, Peasant Proprietary, and Some Observations on the Congested Districts Board, and on the Departments of Agriculture and Industry* (Dublin: John Falconer, 1903).

[78] F. M. L. Thompson, 'Changing Perceptions of Land Tenure in Britain, 1750–1914'. In *The Political Economy of British Historical Experience, 1688–1914*, Donald Winch and Patrick K. O'Brien (New York: Oxford University Press, 2002), 119–38 at 133.

transposing the new-found support for subordinate agrarian rights in the subcontinent to a very different part of Britain's empire.[79]

6.5 Legal Ontologization and the Operativeness and Administrability of the Discourse of 'Proprietary Right'

It was not just in relation to debates about the plight of the tenantry that the concept of proprietary right increasingly became a place-holder for the de-physicalized view of legal right in general among classical thinkers. Late-nineteenth-century exponents of juristic discourse made their own contribution through prominent systematizing works that helped standardize the classical view of rights within the Anglo-common-law mainstream. The colonial connection to what we still today regard as part of the jurist's common sense is thus clearly revealed in important treatises by the likes of William Markby,[80] Thomas Erskine Holland,[81] and Sir Frederick Pollock.[82] Holland, for example, invoked the concept of 'proprietary rights' in the course of explaining how entitlements to property fundamentally involved relations not between the 'Person and all outward objects, as Things' but between 'him and other people'.[83] Likewise, he refracted classical legal consciousness back through the colonial experience[84] when invoking the idea of 'degrees of proprietary right' to argue that juridical entitlements could vary widely in the incidents they conferred—ranging from 'absolute ownership to a narrowly limited power of user'.[85] In so doing, he—like the others—not only registered

---

[79] Peter Gray, 'The Peculiarities of Irish Land Tenure, 1800–1914: from Agent of Impoverishment to Agent of Pacification', in ibid., 139–64 at 154–55.

[80] Markby was a judge on the Calcutta High Court and later a reader in Indian law at Oxford. On his invocation of the notion of proprietary right see e.g. William Markby, *Lectures on Indian Law* (Calcutta: Thacker, Spink and Co., 1873) and William Markby, *Elements of Law: Considered with Reference to Principles of General Jurisprudence* (Oxford: Clarendon Press, 1871).

[81] Holland was an Oxford-trained barrister who eventually replaced William Blackstone as Vinerian Professor of law at his alma mater.

[82] See e.g. Frederic Pollock and Robert Samuel Wright, *An Essay on Possession in the Common Law* (Oxford: Clarendon Press, 1888).

[83] Thomas Erskine Holland, *The Elements of Jurisprudence*, 2nd edn. (Oxford: Clarendon Press 1882 [1880]), 140.

[84] Gray and Gray, *Land Law*, 102 (discussing the 'spectrum of propertiness' and 'the varying degrees of propertiness' of 'proprietary rights').

[85] Holland, *The Elements of Jurisprudence*, 139.

an at least implicit awareness of debates happening in distant corners of the empire, but also connected them to the 'scientific' pretensions of a brand of late-nineteenth-century jurisprudence that explicitly conducted itself as an exercise in deciphering the law's first principles and basic elements.[86]

Even in the subcontinent, neither in the specifically revisionist role it played in looking back on the Company's rule of property (in land's rent) nor in its effect of obscuring the wider influence of classical legal thought under the Crown did the discourse of proprietary right clash with the drive to abstract 'the law'. Regardless of whether new forms of subordinate agrarian entitlement were imagined to be proprietary in some way specific to the evolution of South Asian society and culture or altogether sub-proprietary, the more they were given official recognition the more did they carve diverse operative paths for the propagation of the ostensibly binding force of deductive legal reason. In turn, with such increasing operativeness went the increasing sense that to proceed from the first principle of the doctrinally proprietary was to proceed in the name of an overarching idea of right the multiple administrable forms of which distinguished a normativity that was irreducibly legal in virtue of its ability to assert a real presence in the social world.

On the one hand, then, the discourse of proprietary right could not but begin to reverse what we might, following Max Weber, call the decided lack of logically formal legal rationality characterizing the Company's administration of justice.[87] On the other hand, it also could not but represent the beginnings of the internalization of property into the ontology of the legal in the subcontinent—at least a century after a similar process was under way in the Anglo-common-law mainstream and in a manner that proved crucial to the much-detained ontologization of the law writ large. By the time in the late nineteenth century when this began to take place in the subcontinent, however—as Baden-Powell's thought so well illustrates—it was no longer in the venues of administration alone that

---

[86] Markby, Pollock, and Holland's works on general jurisprudence became widely known, being taken up directly, for example, by famed Dean of Harvard Law School Roscoe Pound. Pound adopted a notion of 'proprietary right' that borrowed heavily from Holland, especially. See e.g. Roscoe Pound, *Outlines of Lectures on Jurisprudence: Chiefly from the Analytical Standpoint*, 2nd edn. (Cambridge, MA: Harvard University Press, 1920 [1903]).

[87] See chapter 2 at note 42.

the fonts of such ontologization were to be found. Neither did intensified ontologization simply issue from other visible sources of 'social rationalization', whether as rooted in the orientalist and utilitarian encounter with South Asian society in the early colonial period or the remaking of the Crown's polity in the image of an 'ethnographic state' based on a more robust will and set of tools for counting and classifying.[88]

Rather, in Britain's India—like elsewhere in the Anglo-common-law world—it was a new kind of scientific jurisprudential thinker, imbued with an analytical consciousness indebted to classical legal thought, who became the most visible discursive sponsor of the definitive shift away from the Company's old ontology of the laws. Consisting of a mix of British and South Asian administrator-intellectuals, such thinkers made their aspiration to scientize 'the law' manifest in synthetic treatise works, comprehensive casebooks, compilations that aimed to redact the contents of the so-called living or customary law, and various other subgenres of an upstart tradition of systematizing late-nineteenth-century jurisprudential speculation.[89]

6.6 Rights as Proprietary Realms and Making Sense of Discourse about Contract(ualism)

While the shifting conception of property as a basis of legal right that Baden-Powell was drawing on remained obscured within the universe of his own thought, it was often even more so in the wider contestations surrounding what historian Peter Robb calls the 'pro-peasant resurgence' of the 1880s. For among thinkers not so meticulous as Baden-Powell it was often that much less clear whether the 'unfinished business of Indian land policy' from a century previous was being pursued through anything more than a simple rehashing of older patterns of debate about who the soil's true proprietors were.[90] Even so, that the relative, disaggregable, and

---

[88] See generally Dirks, *Castes of Mind*.

[89] See e.g. Michael H. Hoeflich, 'John Austin and Joseph Story: Two Nineteenth Century Perspectives on the Utility of Civil Law for the Common Lawyer', *American Journal of Legal History* 29, no. 1 (Jan. 1985): 36–77 and David Sugarman, 'Legal Theory, the Common Law Mind and the Making of the Textbook Tradition'. In *Legal Theory and Common Law*, ed. William Twining (New York: Basel Blackwell, 1986), 26–61.

[90] Peter Robb, *Ancient Rights and Future Comfort: Bihar, the Bengal Tenancy Act of 1885 and British Rule in India* (Richmond, Surrey: Curzon Press, 1997), 220.

immaterial view of property in classical legal thought implicitly structured the positions both for and against the rights of the proverbial peasantry cannot be doubted. Above all, it was in the lead-up to the Tenancy Act of 1885 in Bengal that this was made evident—especially among the exponents of the pro-peasant stance, to whom the bundle of sticks view of rights offered obvious advantages.

Of course, in the latter context those siding with Bengal's tenantry went so far as to insist that the real purpose of 1793's permanent settlement had always been to fix in perpetuity *both* the amount paid by zamindars to the government and that paid by *raiyats* to their zamindars.[91] Plainly, such insistence was made possible by more than just the desire to rehabilitate Cornwallis' reputation by transforming him into the original champion of *raiyatwari* 'property'. Re-reading the Governor General's limited acknowledgement that an increase in the zamindar's demand should not be so arbitrary as to constitute the *raiyat's* constructive eviction was, in other words, one but not the main—much less the only—factor that allowed the issue of the tenant's rights in Bengal to be reopened. As a matter of intellectual history, nor did it follow alone from the post-mutiny resort to custom as a vehicle for advancing a new brand of conservatism[92] or, as Andrew Sartori has illuminatingly argued more recently, a resort to custom as a vehicle for the very opposite—that is, for 'radicaliz[ing] … certain elements of *liberal* thought in their application to Indian agrarian society'.[93]

We can better appreciate why this was so by considering how in a work like C. D. Field's 1879 *Digest of the Law of Landlord and Tenant in Bengal*, as Robb notes, one of its author's basic premises was that occupancy itself comprised a kind of property.[94] Underpinning Field's thought here

---

[91] Ibid., 119.
[92] For a classic statement of the case, see e.g. Thomas Metcalf, 'The British and the Moneylender in Nineteenth-Century India', *The Journal of Modern History* 34, no. 4 (Dec. 1962): 390–97 and Thomas Metcalf, 'Laissez-Faire and Tenant Right in Mid-Nineteenth Century India', *Indian Economic and Social History Review* 1, no. 74 (Jan. 1964): 74–81.
[93] Andrew Sartori, 'A Liberal Discourse of Custom in Colonial Bengal', *Past and Present* 212, no. 1 (Aug. 2011): 163–97 at 169. The view attributing custom's ascent across the British empire in the second half of the nineteenth century to what Sartori labels a resurgent new Tory conservatism has long been a staple among historians of modern South Asia, as he notes.
[94] Robb, *Ancient Rights and Future Comfort*, 106. One might say that, stated in terms of a dichotomy between 'property' and 'occupancy' rather than by splitting the difference between them in the way Field engineered to do, Jo Guildi effectively thematizes her recent 'global history of twentieth-century property' around the struggle over 'occupancy property'. See Jo Guildi, *The*

would have been one of two probably more fundamental others: first, that the would-be occupancy entitlement comprised a bundle of (sub-)proprietary sticks in its own right or, second, that it comprised an individual proprietary stick disaggregated from the full bundle of ownership in the ostensibly clear sense of the term in the West. Importantly, these two possibilities were hardly mutually exclusive. Rather, they were iterative: the first was the product of applying to the second the same very much classical analytical ethic underlying its own production. Consequently, by the lights of neither idea did occupancy 'property' have to have any set structure, as if some one or several select (sub-)proprietary elements defined its essence, whether including a right against eviction, a right to persistent usufruct, a right against rent enhancement, a right to pass any other such right across lines of intergenerational descent, and/or whatever others.

Tellingly, much the same mindset also animated W. W. Hunter, whose own well-known support for the recognition of subordinate agrarian rights in Bengal was staked on what he called the 'ownership' that tenants held over 'cultivation'. From this perspective, any additional rights that such 'owners' might be recognized as enjoying—say, to a fixity or moderation in the payments demanded of them by their superiors—could once more easily be made to fall into place as sticks in the property of cultivation's own bundle.[95] Therefore, in all cases, the proponents of juridifying subordinate rights in 1880s Bengal—or, for that matter, anywhere else in the Crown's subcontinent during roughly the same period—were arguing something fundamentally similar. For whether the proposed landed right was one of occupancy, cultivation, or whatever else and whether it was conceived as proprietary or even sub-proprietary, the point was that it was every bit as much a (metaphorical) realm (of legal interest) held 'absolutely' by those commanding it as was the dominion (over land's rent) held by those upon whom the Company built its originary rule of property.

Long Land War: The Global Struggle for Occupancy Rights (New Haven, CT: Yale University Press, 2021), 22 and generally.

[95] Here again W. W. Hunter's 'Dissertation on Landed Property and Land Rights in Bengal' is one of the texts Robb, himself, discusses. See Robb, *Ancient Rights and Future Comfort*, 117.

Even for those who were more ambivalent about or outright hostile to tenant right in Bengal, there was often little choice but to articulate their own ideas in the same new terms of the relativized, disaggregated, and de-physicalized view of property. In Arthur Phillips' Tagore Law Lectures of 1874, for example, the bundle of sticks view was treated as if it was simply part of a background of common sense. 'Whatever the ryot has', Phillips thus opined,

> the zemindar has all the rest which is necessary to complete ownership of the land: the zemindar's right amounts to the complete ownership of the land subject to the occupancy ryot's right, and the right of the village, if any, to the occupation and cultivation of the soil, to whatever extent these rights may in any given case reach.[96]

At other times, the new logic of property in classical legal thought left its trace among those less than supportive of endorsing the claims of the tenantry in a way that requires greater effort to discern. A case in point is long-time civil service officer (and later) member of parliament Sir Charles Wingfield, who avowed in his *Observations on Land Tenures and Tenant Right in India* that 'never, in any part of India, did mere length of permissive occupancy, on payment of rent, confer any right ... to hold the land against the will of the proprietor'. Yet even Wingfield's steadfast opposition to the 1859 Rent Act's rule of twelve years' presence as the basis for conferring an occupancy right was based only in a most circuitous way on reiterating past debating points about the true identity of Bengal's proprietors. In accord with the revisionist narrative's view of the Cornwallis system, he thus granted that the effective conferral of 'proprietary rights' on only the zamindars constituted a 'wrong done to the peasant proprietors at the permanent settlement'. Yet equally did he insist that it was unacceptable in the present to endow a class of persons with a 'part property in the land' simply on the basis of 'the right of occupancy'.[97]

In elaborating on the further basis of this apparently inconsistent position, Wingfield reasoned in a manner that became even more conflicted.

---

[96] Arthur Phillips, *The Law Relating to the Land Tenures of Lower Bengal* (Calcutta: Thacker, Spink and Co., 1876), 363.
[97] Charles Wingfield, *Observations on Land Tenure and Tenant Right in India* (London: W. H. Allen & Co., 1869), 33, 34, 35.

For on the one hand, he asserted that those recognized as having a 'part property' after 1859 had to be considered an entirely different stratum than the true peasant proprietors of the past who 'possessed' not just the 'rights of occupancy' but 'a great deal more'.[98] On the other, he insisted that it was the Cornwallis system that had 'deprived the subordinate proprietors of the last remnants' of the kind of 'independent rights' that made them 'proprietors' on his view in the first place.[99] Notably, the connection between these ideas had little to do with whether or not occupancy tenants in Wingfield's own day were the progeny of the peasant proprietors of yesteryear who, as much as the zamindars, he took to be true holders of an original 'proprietary' right.

Nor was Wingfield's an attempt to forge any connection through demonstrating which 'independent rights' over and above the 'right of occupancy' would have been sufficient to warrant a recognition of 'part property'. Instead, in the face of the indeterminacy within the bundle of sticks perspective that problems of subordinate tenure raised more generally, Wingfield simply projected a false certainty. Whereas Baden-Powell equivocated and emphasized the inapplicability of English ideas to Indian reality when confronted with the same indeterminacy, Wingfield left it to implication to deny that any stick of occupancy could be considered coloured with the proprietary shading of the bundle from which it was disaggregated. So too, likewise, did he leave the denial of any possibility of considering occupancy a (sub-)proprietary bundle in its own right to go without saying.

* * *

Given the scarcely enunciated—and often obscured—presence of the classical view of rights in debates surrounding the pro-peasant resurgence in Bengal and elsewhere, it is not surprising that the second half of the nineteenth century in British India has so often been regarded as an age of both the emergence and the frustration of an ideology of contractual freedom. From one scholarly perspective it has, thus, appeared a truism that the 'faith in the freedom of contract burned too strongly' to be suspended other than on the exceptional basis of agrarian special

---

[98] Ibid., 79.
[99] Ibid., 33.

legislation.[100] From this standpoint, only in the Deccan, through the Agriculturists' Relief Act, and in the Punjab, through the Land Alienation Act, did an anti-contractualist stance come into full flower; for only such measures prohibited the alienation of property outright, making it difficult to deny that they ran counter to a pure commodity logic of exchange.[101] As for measures guaranteeing occupancy and other forms of subordinate right, on this perspective they are more easily accommodated than special legislative prohibitions on alienation; for occupancy-type rights can always be seen as first steps towards contractualizing the social relations of property, by readying them for incorporation under a logic of commodity as discrete 'proprietary' elements of the type necessary for the purposes of being eventually made subject to market exchange. In recent scholarship, for example, Sartori can be seen taking something very much like the latter path, arguing that the rise of subordinate agrarian rights in Bengal represented a pursuit of 'Lockean' ideas of the 'property-constituting capacities of labor' and, consequently, remained 'constitutively bound to practices of commodity exchange' via a tradition of 'vernacular liberalism' that diffused across the late-colonial subcontinent.[102]

However, judged from another scholarly point of view, it has equally appeared a truism that so evidently widespread a concern about the peasantry as developed after 1860 must foretell a very different story about the degree to which 'interference' with contractual freedom became

---

[100] Stokes, 'The Land Revenue Systems of the North-Western Provinces and Bombay Deccan', 105. See also Rothermund, *An Economic History of India*, 46; K. A. Manikumar, *A Colonial Economy in the Great Depression. Madras (1929-1937)* (Chennai: Orient Longman, 2003), 35 and Ian Brown, *A Colonial Economy in Crisis: Burma's Rice Cultivators and the World Depression of the 1930s* (New York: Routledge, 2005), 20–21.

[101] See e.g. Rothermund, *An Economic History of India*, 46 and Dietmar Rothermund, 'Freedom of Contract and the Problem of Land Alienation in British India', *South Asia* 3, no. 1 (1973): 57-78. Likewise, Neil Charlesworth emphasizes how it was an opposition to legislative interference in agrarian debt relations that took hold elsewhere in Bombay outside the Deccan, given what the Act was taken to have portended. See Neil Charlesworth, *Peasants and Imperial Rule: Agriculture and Agrarian Society in the Bombay Presidency, 1850-1935* (New York: Cambridge University Press, 1985), 240–47. There were other measures that limited—without imposing full prohibitions on—alienation. For example, the Land Revenue Amendment Act of 1901 in Bombay empowered the government to settle waste lands and fields through a new kind of tenure that included no right of transfer in the event of their being forfeited to the government because of default. See Chandra, *The Rise and Growth of Economic Nationalism in India*, 428–29.

[102] Andrew Sartori, *Liberalism in Empire: An Alternative History* (Oakland, CA: University of California Press, 2014), 7–8.

widespread. On this view, both the Deccan Agriculturists' Relief Act and the Punjab Land Alienation Act look more like the tip of an iceberg that included the whole litany of other legislation recognizing subordinate rights after mid-century. For even if all of these measures cannot be seen as hindering the alienation of property to the same extent, they are all still liable to appear as if they decreased the overall degree to which the relations of agrarian production were subjected to a strict market discipline.[103]

Suffice to say, the persistence of these opposing points of view is bound to remain difficult to understand unless we take better stock of the influence—whether more or less obscured—of classical legal thought on the debate about subordinate agrarian rights in the Crown's India. Like the opposing sides in that debate, contemporary historians who disagree about whether the freedom of contract really was ascendant as a norm during the latter half of the nineteenth century are operating on what are really two distinct understandings of individualism in classical legal thought. Indeed, already as part of that late-nineteenth-century debate each such understanding of individualism could, to admittedly varying degrees, be found playing a key role in structuring the output emanating from the different venues of discursive production in which the law was being ontologized.

For late-nineteenth-century opponents of tenant right (as for certain historians today) discourse *about* contract was, thus, read as an indicator of the state's asserting an express presence where it would not otherwise have been able to had the ideal of individual self-realization through the market actually been kept to. This is because in the venues of ordinary-language discourse, the 'freedom' that contract was celebrated as embodying—like the 'absoluteness' of property before it—was a stand-in for a notion of individualism that needed to mean nothing more specific than that 'the law' should stay out of supposedly voluntarist economic relations. So understood, in the context of land relations

---

[103] For example, this has long been an emphasis of Thomas Metcalf. See, generally his 'The British and the Moneylender in Nineteenth-Century India' and Metcalf and Metcalf, *A Concise History of India*, 134. See also e.g. Clive Dewey, 'The Influence of Sir Henry Maine on Agrarian Policy in India'. In *The Victorian Achievement of Sir Henry Maine: A Centennial Reappraisal*, ed. Alan Diamond (New York: Cambridge University Press, 1991), 353–75 and Peter Robb, 'Bihar, the Colonial State and Agricultural Development in India, 1880–1920', *The Indian Economic and Social History Review* 25, no. 2 (1988): 205–35.

the freedom of contract appeared (and appears) to be synonymous with a regime holding the private alienation of property interests—whether, say, through the bargained-for mutuality of an agreement for outright transfer or merely for lease—maximally sacrosanct. In turn, any hint of the 'regulatory' presence of the state's law became (and becomes) a form of 'interfering' with that freedom. Measured against such an ideal, it can be little surprise that near any resort to agrarian legislation under the Raj in order to provide for rules other than those ensuring the obligatory character of bargains once made should seem (and have been capable of being made to seem) like a violation of contractual individualism-as-tantamount to laissez faire.

The more that tenant right was opposed on a basis that ostensibly reiterated the previous era's battles over the identity of the true proprietors of the subcontinent's soil—as it was, in no small part, by Wingfield—the more it called to mind this particular sense of contractual individualism. The same was true even with regard to legislation empowering peasants against moneylenders (as distinct from legislation empowering tenants against landlords), especially when opposition was registered in the discourse of the public sphere through fixating on the interventionist character of such measures. The reception of Richard Temple's[104] *India in 1880*[105] is a useful case in point. Temple, of course, was a well-known figure, holding various positions in the colonial administration—starting in the Punjab as secretary to John Lawrence after the Anglo-Sikh wars and eventually reaching the position of governor of Bombay in 1877—before leaving the subcontinent in 1880 for England, where he was elected to parliament as a Conservative in 1885. He also proved an easy target for interrogation, given his support for using administrative power in the 1870s to attempt to curb famine and thereby to bypass market mechanisms through measures like importing rice and grain on the Government's account.[106] Accordingly, in an 1881 review of Temple's book, *The Calcutta*

---

[104] Temple started out as secretary to Lawrence after joining the Bengal Civil Service (and prior to Lawrence's ascent to the office of Viceroy for India from 1864 to 1869). Before becoming Governor of Bombay he held various other posts, including as Commissioner for the Central Provinces in the 1860s, Resident at the princely state of Hyderabad, and lieutenant governor of Bengal. These and other details of his career are given in his memoir. See Richard Temple, *Men and Events of My Time in India* (Reprint, Delhi: B. R. Publication Corporation, 1985 [1882]).
[105] Richard Temple, *India in 1880*, 3rd edn. (London: John Murray, 1881).
[106] Temple became visible in the context of the famine of 1874 in Bengal and Bihar. On this basis, he went on to feature a few years later in 1877 in attempts to deal with famine in Madras,

Review vehemently lamented its author's failure to 'say[], in clear language, whether or no the circumstances [faced by Deccan agriculturists] are a sufficient justification for [the Relief Act's] interference with the freedom of contract, or whether those circumstances are so special as to restrict the interference to that one region if it is desirable there'.[107]

It is ironic, to say the least, that decrying such measures as deviations from the brand of individualism commonly equated with contractual freedom in the public sphere should have so often advanced rather than hindered contract's ongoing doctrinalization as a general category within the ontology of the law that was emerging under the Crown's rule. For even when the focus was on contract(ual individualism) as no more than a proxy for economic laissez faire still it was a focus on a category with a nominally identical counterpart in doctrinal discourse. Indeed, with respect to the public sphere as a venue for the law's ontologization, as noted in chapter three, this suggests that it was the velocity at which a category like contract turned over within the discourse of ordinary language that was ultimately most important—the exact purpose for which it did so being much less so.

Within the all-purpose language of laissez faire, then, the idiom of the 'freedom of contact' could be celebrated as that to which the colonial state was resolving to hold without flinching, lamented as that from which it was deviating by limiting the absolute liberty with which 'proprietary' interests could be disposed of, or fretted about as that through which British 'improvement' would, once and for all, dissolve and rebuild Indian society anew.[108] Yet all the same, each mode of discursive engagement proved equally as capable a means for proliferating the seemingly

---

where he had made his way on special deputation to advise the provincial government on the crisis it was facing. On reaching Bombay to assume his post as that province's Governor in 1877 Temple was greeted by a society in the throes of similar distress. See Temple, *Men and Events of My Time in India*, 393–408, 442–56, 461–68. For Temple's views on the alleged excessiveness of government measures to curb these famines see Temple, *India in 1880*, 330–42.

[107] H. G. Keene, 'Art. I.-India in 1880', *The Calcutta Review* 73, no. 145 (1881): 1–15 at 12.

[108] See e.g. Paul Samuel Reinsch, *Colonial Administration* (New York: Macmillan, 1905), 16 (noting that '[t]hrough the rigid enforcement of contract the vast agricultural debtor class has been gradually enslaved to the money lenders and is being ousted from its ancestral holdings. As the government upholds the principle of freedom of contract and will not fix the price of grain in times of shortage, the calculating native capitalist is enabled to hold his stock of food for higher prices regardless of the fact that people may be dying of famine by the thousand in the neighborhood').

equivalent—and substantively hypostasized—element of 'contract', thereby increasing its ubiquity and bolstering the sense that it had an undeniably real presence within the new social world of colonial rule.

At the same time, it was hardly the case that relative to the doctrinal logic of classical legal thought new forms of subordinate agrarian right could be reconciled only, at best, as exceptions to contractualism, understood as privately willed self-realization through the market. On the contrary, just as important to the classical view was a second altogether different sense of the 'individualism' of contract. Returning to an earlier example, we can see this by considering Temple's response to critiques like *The Calcutta Review's* of his perspective on the Deccan Agriculturists' Relief Act. For whereas *The Review* invoked the figure of 'the freedom of contract' to demand clarification on Temple's assessment of the Act's implications for laissez faire, in his own reflections Temple completely eschewed such an idiom. However, rather than to avow an anti-contractualist stance, he did so only by way of affirming much the same set of ideological commitments as his critics—namely, to the purportedly 'progressive' force of the colonial rule of law and a notion of 'individualism' that he, too, saw as residing at its core. Accordingly, for Temple as well, by the 1880s British government in the subcontinent elicited a passage from 'patriarchal administration' and 'personal rule' to the 'now complete, substitution of the reign of law for the reign of individuals'.[109] Likewise, to him as well it was contract that was the key engine behind this movement, being (at the core of) '[t]hat great division of law which relates to mercantile affairs and to dealings between man and man'.[110]

Where Temple differed, however, was in his view about the role of the state in the development and ongoing perfection of this latter 'division' of the law under the Crown's rule. Rather than being antithetical to the spirit of contractual freedom, for Temple it was a clear necessity that the state be able to insert itself among the individual parties to the contract in its own capacity as a juridical *individual*, albeit of a public kind. On this view, when debtors and creditors were locked in dispute—as they were in the Deccan—only the state could guarantee the primacy of truly individualist values. For, as Temple noted, when 'duly executed' bonds were

---

[109] Temple, *India in 1880*, 188–89.
[110] Ibid., 180.

'manifestly given by ignorant debtors' there was far more reason to see such actors as 'victims of usurious creditors' than there was to see them as properly voluntarist contractual agents. Rather than standing in the way of the individualism of contract, then, by allowing for additional legal recourse the state was facilitating it—namely, by obviating a defect in the 'will' of some relevant private juridical person. Crucially though, the relevant act of assertion on the part of the state here came not in the form of the willed command it issued in its capacity as a positivist sovereign legislator through enacting the Deccan Agriculturists' Relief Act. Rather, the relevant act of assertion was that which came at the stage of selecting or formulating in doctrinal discourse the norm on the basis of which the state deemed itself compelled to *substitute its will* as a (public) juridical individual for that of one or both of the private parties' own. In other words, it was the act of assertion that came at the stage when the terms of the parties' deal necessitated re-norming—on those occasions prospectively contemplated by whatever the relevant legislative enactment—according to the administrable propositional content of doctrinal discourse.

In the process, alongside 'right', the notion of 'the will' was thus consistently affirmed as a second key element in the discursive constitution of 'the law' writ large, as an objective doctrinal unicity under the Crown's rule (and, as we shall see in the next chapter, of 'the law of contract' more specifically as one of its core constituent parts). For as Temple himself put it—in words that draped an older constitutionist discourse about the defects of the ancien régime in the new garb of classical legal thought—only through such an act of assertion would the state succeed in externalizing the law as 'a fixed system to which all men can steadily look'; and only on this coming to pass, he went on to explain, would the law be divested, as needed, of the subjective 'will of persons, who however able and well-meaning will be sure to differ one from the other'.[111]

All told, then, what Temple was doing, in effect, was emphasizing the unbreakable connection between the will—in its capacity as a doctrinal element that put the state at the very centre of the law of contract's individualist ethos—and the relative, disaggregable, and immaterial view of property as a model for legal right. Since such a connection did not require contractual individualism to be equated with laissez faire, a view

[111] Ibid., 189.

like Temple's was perfectly in line with those according to which the agrarian tenant's occupancy (or, for that matter, their so-called cultivation) could be seen as comprising a 'limited property' of its own.[112] In fact, the more discernible classical legal thought's abstracted idea of the property right was among those advancing or disputing the 'pro-peasant' resurgence, the more did it secure a footing for contract, itself, to be abstracted—both into a basic subdomain of legal scientific analysis and also into a basic sub-component of the law's implicit ontology. For the relative, disaggregable, and immaterial model of right naturally lent itself to the doctrinal idea of contract as a generalized relation among juridical individuals wilfully engaged in the formally mutual reassignment of the boundaries of their respective realm(s) of proprietary interest.[113]

* * *

If in the late nineteenth century the meaning of contract varied in a way not unlike the meaning of property during the early decades of Company rule, as I have suggested in part I, this illustrates how the ontology of the legal was always contingent on a balance of forces between doctrinal and ordinary-language discourse. However, this alone did not make Britain's India unique. For legal modernization under colonial rule can hardly be distinguished from legal modernization under properly liberal rule merely by differentiating the ordinary linguistic from the doctrinal as distinct registers of discourse through which the ontology of the legal was (re)constituted—the first by rendering articulable propositions about the law and the second by rendering articulable propositions of the law.

To the contrary, such a distinction was a feature of the law's development in general. Of course, this is not to say that the ontologization of legal concepts in the colonial subcontinent may not, at times, have leaned on one of these discursive registers more heavily than the other. Nor is it to say that this fact, in itself, did not make for an important difference between colonial South Asia and the Anglo-common-law mainstream,

---

[112] Baden-Powell, *The Land Systems of British India*, vol. III, 272.
[113] The very similar view about 'contracting' for property rights that has been developed by economists in the wake of Ronald Coase's landmark article on 'The Problem of Social Cost' (*Journal of Law and Economics*, vol. 3 (Oct. 1960): 1–44) may thus be less novel than is commonly thought. For a comprehensive discussion see Gary Libecap, *Contracting for Property Rights*, (New York: Cambridge University Press, 1989), 1–29.

as was so evident already with respect to the meaning of the concept of property during the Company's era.

Yet wherever the balance rested at any given moment, one thing that is for certain is that by the end of the second half of the nineteenth century the scales determining where it levelled off were coming into more equal alignment in places like the Crown's subcontinent and, for that matter, elsewhere where the rise of classical legal thought was felt. For if nothing else, classical legal thought's globalization involved the spread of an attitude by which jurists and political ideologues of most any stripe could imagine themselves to be trained on a distinct kind of normativity not primarily because it was actively ruminated upon in the public sphere nor even because it was legislated by the state but because it could be seen, with increasing vigour, as making for a perfectly integral *doctrinal* system with a purportedly infinite generative power.

On this view, it was in the very nature of 'the law' to consist of a totality of norms that logically entailed the totality of the world's facts in virtue of an internal order that, itself, made for an endlessly connected unicity of component rules and subdomains of rules operatively connected in both vertical and horizontal dimensions of doctrinal discursive space. While the registers of both doctrinal and ordinary-language discourse would, thus, continue to be important after mid-century, it was in the direction of the former more than the latter that the scale would go on most notably to tilt, including in Britain's India.

7
The Private and the Public Will in the Indian Contract Act

7.1 Introduction

In summarizing the implications of the shift towards classical legal thought's doctrinal idea of property as any realm of its holder's valued interest that the last chapter explored, we can point to its having a twofold importance in the subcontinent. First, it was consistent with the expanding range of 'proprietary' entitlements that changing circumstances increasingly forced the colonial state to recognize after 1850; second, it was indicative of the rise of a more generalizable concept of legal right in the aftermath of the dissolution of the East India Company. That said, even confining ourselves to the level of new legal imaginaries, the developing ubiquity of 'the law' as an object of discursive preoccupation during these years was not simply due to the way that property increasingly came to be understood as relative, disaggregable, and immaterial in contravention to its previously archetypical conception. As the closing section of the last chapter already started to address, also crucial to the shifting ontology of the law's rule in the subcontinent after 1850 was a new ideal of contract, considered as an overarching conceptual category with its own purported elemental basis in the juristic notion of the will.

Within the imaginary of classical legal thought, then, the juristic ideas of will and right became ever more inseparable, this being both cause and consequence of the new ideal of contract, itself, entering into an ever more direct feedback loop with the relative, disaggregable, and immaterial view of property. To fully understand why this was so it is necessary to see that while propertied entitlement was still modelled on the image of its holder's being 'absolute' over the realm of interest they commanded, nothing required the scope of any such entitlement to be maximal. Rather, the more that juridified rights proliferated, the more did the respective realms of proprietary interest they carved out come to seem not only relative but also mutually invasive. In turn, the meaning of the absoluteness of rights was defined more and more in terms of a freedom of action of the will to operate unencumbered within its requisite domain of proprietary interest, whatever the exact—and possibly quite circumscribed—scope of that domain and including to the potential effect of realigning its borders.

Overall, then, the doctrinal discourse *of* contract played a role in ontologizing 'the law' that was different from that which the increasingly audible discourse *about* contractual freedom did in the context of agrarian special legislation under Crown rule. If slogans about laissez faire dispersed the roots of contract talk far and wide over the field of emerging national consciousness, it was logically operative doctrinal concepts/principles like the will that created deeper anchor points along the surface. In this respect, the doctrinal discourse of contract offered a thicker description of the law's would-be ontology than could any ideology of contractual freedom in the public sphere. Moreover, through particularized abstractions like the will doctrinal discourse posited an ontology that was about more than only an individualist 'market ethics grounded in contractual relations' of the kind Ritu Birla has so forcefully highlighted in her study of the 'barrage of novel and foundational legal measures' enacted by the Raj after 1870.[1]

Of course, Birla's deeper concern is with the way in which post-transfer-of-power legislation like the Indian Companies Act and the Negotiable Instruments Act confined indigenous varieties of profit-making activity (what she calls 'vernacular capitalism') to a private realm of culture coded in terms of 'premodern gemeinschaft'. On this view, it may seem natural to see the corresponding economic space set up by the Raj's 'legal standardization of market practice'[2] as aspiring to a form of purely Gesellschaft relations[3] meant to coincide with a logic of atomistic 'laissez faire', as per

---

[1] Birla, *Stages of Capital*, 20–21, 4.
[2] Ibid., 25.
[3] Ibid., 23, 24. Introduced by German social thinker Ferdinand Tönnies in 1887's *Gemeinschaft und Gesellschaft* (Jose Harris and Margaret Hollis, trans. (New York: Cambridge University Press, 2001)), these terms were meant to contrast different organizational principles of social interaction. Whereas *Gemeinschaft* (lit. community) was supposed to be indicative of forms of aggregation in which the individual was oriented to the group for its own sake as a collectivity, the concept of *Gesellschaft* pointed to forms of aggregation animated by an orientation towards

the meaning the latter turn of phrase acquired in the rhetoric of the public sphere. Moreover, in the context of the study of South Asia this way of seeing things tends to build on a larger scholarly tradition interpreting colonial law reform going back to the 1770/80s as being, in essence, a dichotomizing project for separating culture from economy, the inner from the outer, the spiritual from the material, the community from the individual, and so on.

Yet it was only in a very incomplete sense that the doctrinal discourse of contract was premised on any theoretically pure commitment to atomistic individualism, whether in British India or, for that matter, elsewhere in the world of classical legal thought. This is because the new forms of commercial, industrial, and financial interaction the Raj helped legislate into being did not define the logic of contract in the law so much as they assumed it. That is, juridical institutions like the limited liability corporation, the trust, the commodity futures agreement, and the like were supposed to be manifestations of a deeper and more abstract normative phenomenon by which the law stood capable of 'covering' commercial interactions of a potentially infinite variety. In this respect, as the present chapter argues, just as foundational—if not more so—than specific enactments on negotiable instruments, trusts, etc.[4] was a measure like *The Indian Contract Act (IX) of 1872*, which set forth a framework for handling binding legal agreement in a way that was neither inherently voluntarist

---

the possibility of advancing one's own individual self-interest through social interaction. Of course, much the same contrast was struck in one way or another throughout the course of the development of early sociological theory—whether in Durkheim's counterposing of 'mechanical' and 'organic' solidarity in his *The Division of Labor in Society* or Weber's even more direct reformulation of Tönnies. For Weber this came through recasting the contrast he was building on in terms of a division between 'communal' and 'associative' forms of human 'consociation', which Weber further grounded in his own more fundamental conceptual distinction between social action based on value rationality and that based on instrumental rationality. See Weber, *Economy and Society*, vol. I, 40–41.

[4] As the Fourth Law Commission put it in 1879 while saluting the virtues of codification, though it was thought to be true that 'when legislation proceeds by special laws, more complete and minute attention is paid to the detailed provisions called for by the particular circumstances dealt with', it too 'often becomes evident through the logical development of one set of rules that it has proceeded upon an underlying conception inconsistent with the radical idea or group of ideas involved in another special law'. Leaving only the option of 'subjugat[ing] the one principle to the other either by [further] formal legislation or by a forced method of interpretation, with ... [its own] injurious consequences', as the Commission continued to explain, 'special laws' ultimately demonstrated why a true Code, in which 'such a result can hardly arise', was much better. *Report of the Fourth Law Commission*, 1879, V/26/100/12, 3 at par. 4.

nor inherently anti-statist. Instead, when judged from the vantage point of the internal doctrinal structure of the law of contract that it was devoted to elaborating, Act IX was as much an instrument for freeing the juridical person of the state and promoting the twin values of collectivism and regulation as it was for ostensibly freeing *homo economicus* and promoting autonomy and self-realization as the diametrically opposite supposed pair of values.

Insofar as the new 'scientific' understanding of binding agreement—styled as being based on 'a constant attention to uniform and expansive general principles in legislation' and making for a 'system' capable of being put to a 'true use' of 'co-ordinat[ing relevant] facts'[5]—was generated from within doctrinal discourse, collectivism and regulation were values that were complementary rather than antithetical to contract's larger imaginary. Importantly, this was not simply in the sense that the market—considered as a realm in which commercial agents came together to exchange commodity values—required some sovereign entity to enforce agreements once made or even just to determine what constituted licit values suitable for agreed exchange in the first place. Rather, as the counterpart value positions on a normative spectrum that also played host to individualism and self-determination, collectivism and regulation animated doctrinal discourse in just as fundamental a way, being part and parcel of the will in its inherently dual character as both private *and* public. This was especially the case given how—when considered on its own terms—the will proved as important to defining 'the law of contract' as 'the law of contract'—when considered alongside the notion of legal right as any realm of its holder's proprietary interest—proved to defining 'the law' writ large. In fact, one main trajectory of change during the late nineteenth century witnessed the leading lights of colonial law reform naturalizing such part-to-whole logic as a feature of a universalized history of legal evolution. Accordingly, writing in 1879, the members of the Fourth Law Commission proclaimed that the Raj was simply reinstituting the same true arrangement of the law—based on a 'comparatively few, carefully chosen' principles that were nothing less than 'the principles of human nature itself'—that ancient codification in the subcontinent

---

[5] Ibid., 4–5 at par. 7, 8.

itself had supposedly been groping towards.[6] As the Commissioners went on to note:

> [t]he law relating to immoveable property and its incidents may well admit considerable variations according to local circumstances. Landed estates are usually collected in one province and subject to one law; but even when this is not so, little or no practical inconvenience arises from a property in Bengal being held on a different tenure from one in Madras. Within the sphere of transactions variable at the will of those who engage in them, it is in the mutually dependent and ever-extending operations of commerce that a need of uniformity of law first becomes apparent; and thus the law of contracts, first in fragmentary sections and then in a systematic collection of general principles, claimed early recognition in the formation of the Indian Code.[7]

In the three main sections of the present chapter that follow, I look at the importance of this nesting cluster of concepts—of contract, right, and the will—as features of the shifting ontology of the law and its rule in the subcontinent. More specifically, in the first section, the chapter considers the pre-history of the Contract Act in controversies surrounding labour and employment relations during the early decades of the nineteenth century; in the second, it turns to the debates about the Act in the Governor General/Viceroy's Council that immediately preceded its passage in 1872; and finally, in most significant part, in its third section the chapter undertakes a close reading of the Act itself.

7.2 Contracts before the Contract Act

It has been conventional to see Act IX of 1872 as a means of transplanting existing common-law rules into British India in order to remedy the flaws of the early choice—going back to the first two decades or so after the Battle of Plassey—to use native personal laws as the rules of decisions for

---

[6] Ibid., 10 at par. 20–21.
[7] Ibid., 11 at par. 22.

disputes about contractual agreements.[8] After all, in spelling out the jurisdiction of the Company's *mufassil* courts under section seventeen of the Regulating Act of 1781, Hastings' ongoing judicial reforms did specify that 'all matters of contract and dealing between party and party' were to be administered 'in the case of Hindus by their own laws'.[9]

Alternatively, as Titas Chakraborty notes, labour historians often begin the story of colonial contract law with Bengal Regulation VII of 1819, which made it a criminal offence for labourers in Bengal, Bihar, and Orissa to violate their ostensibly binding agreements with those procuring their services. Chakraborty's own reason for highlighting this alternative genealogy is to argue that the origins of such regulation actually go back further, to at least a century earlier when already long before the advent of Company rule European merchant capital had sought to expand its coercive power over indigenous boatmen as well as their own sailors by instituting similar criminal penalties for violating employment agreements. (Even a measure like Regulation VII, according to Chakraborty, had more immediate antecedents going back in excess of a decade—in the form of the Company's otherwise seemingly unrelated measures from 1806 to empower a centralized police force.)[10]

However, much as had remained the case in Britain during the first half of the nineteenth century, the focus of these previous measures was on 'matters of contract' in the sense of a variety of otherwise disparate agreement forms—like sale, loan, bailment, and so on.[11] It was in just such a vein that Henry Colebrooke completed work on William Jones' *Digest of Hindu Law*[12] under the further descriptive subtitle of a treatise

---

[8] See e.g. R. N. Gooderson, 'English Contract Problems in Indian Code and Case Law', *Cambridge Law Journal* 16, no. 1 (1958): 67–84 at 67.

[9] 21 Geo. III *c.* 70. See also Rankin, *Background to Indian Law*, 9–10.

[10] Titas Chakraborty, 'Controlling Labor Mobility as a State Building Process: The Ascendancy of the English East India Company State in Bengal 1700-1819'. Paper presented for 'New Directions in South Asian Labor History' session of the 48th Annual Conference on South Asia, University of Wisconsin-Madison, October 18, 2019. See also Titas Chakraborty, 'Desertion of European Sailors and Soldiers in Early Eighteenth-Century Bengal,' in *A Global History of Runaways: Workers, Mobility, and Capitalism, 1600-1850*, eds. Marcus Rediker, Titas Chakraborty, and Matthias van Rossum (Oakland, CA: University of California Press, 2019), 77–95.

[11] See Rankin, *Background to Indian Law*, 89.

[12] Jones' work brought together texts in the *mitakshara* and *dayabhaga* traditions of Hindu juridical thought with commentary on them by the Hindu pandit Jagannatha Tarkapanchanana. Work on the *Digest's* two volumes eventually had to be handed over to Colebrooke, who finalized them only in 1797. (See Jagannatha Tarkapanchanana, *A Digest of Hindu Law, on Contracts and Successions*, H. T. Colebrooke, trans. (Calcutta: East India Company Press, 1801)). Overall,

'on Contracts and Successions'.[13] Much the same was true of other early works that fed into the Company's administration of Hindu and Muslim laws, including those by Francis Macnaghten,[14] his son William Hay,[15] and Thomas Strange.[16]

The conventional story of the colonial elaboration of contract law thus significantly underplays the novelty of the Contract Act; after all, the Act's content did not follow from some course of doctrinal development that had taken place in Britain centuries earlier but from one that was unfolding there only just before and even roughly simultaneously with the influence, whether nascent or overt, of classical legal thought, including in the subcontinent.[17] Likewise, therefore, the conventional story underplays how recent the emergence of contract was as a distinct heading within the taxonomy of the common law. In the mainstream of the Anglo-common-law world, even simply grouping together disparate types of binding agreements as *contracts* (for the sale of goods, for bailment, for hire, for assorted forms of service, etc.) was still relatively unheard of during the first twenty years of the nineteenth century.[18] Several

the *Digest* proved a more substantial work than the earlier *Code of Gentoo Laws* that Nathaniel Brassey Halhed delivered to Hastings in 1776 after translating and extrapolating a Persian translation made by Hindu pandits from a compilation of original Sanskrit texts on litigation.

[13] The organization of the *Digest* speaks to the context from which it emerged, which saw Company officialdom wanting to document Hindu norms on enforceable forms of agreement more than any abstracted set of first principles for a law of contract. The text thus consisted mainly of a serial description of different agreement types: 'On Loans and Payment', 'On Interest', 'On Pledges', 'On Deposits and Other Bailments', and so on.

[14] Sir Francis Workman Macnaghten, *Considerations on the Hindoo Law as it is Current in Bengal* (Serampore: Printed at the Mission Press, 1824). Macnaghten the elder's text had only a single chapter on the subject, which was devoted primarily to excerpting pronouncements quoted in Colebrooke's *Digest*.

[15] William Hay Macnaghten, *Principles and Precedents of Hindu Law: Being a Compilation of Primary Rules relative to the Doctrine of Inheritance, Contracts and Miscellaneous Subjects*, 2 vols. (Calcutta: Printed at the Baptist Mission Press, 1828). As in his companion text on the *Principles and Precedents of Moohummudan Law* (Calcutta: Printed at the Church Mission Press, 1825) from three years earlier, Macnaghten the younger made little more than titular reference to the subject of contracts.

[16] Sir Thomas Strange, *Elements of Hindu Law: Referable to British Judicature in India*, 2 vols. (London: Butterworth and Son, 1825). While he did consider more general topics such as competence and consideration, most of Strange's twelfth chapter 'On Contracts' consisted, true to its time, of a serial description of specific types of agreements that had not yet been covered in his previous chapters.

[17] See e.g. Shivprasad Swaminathan, 'Eclipsed by Orthodoxy: The Vanishing Point of Consideration and the Forgotten Ingenuity of the Indian Contract Act 1872', *Asian Journal of Comparative Law* 12, no. 1 (July 2017): 141–65.

[18] There were a handful of more generalizing works that emerged after 1790, with the publication of John Joseph Powell's *Essay Upon the Law of Contracts and Agreements*, 2 vols.

more decades would have to pass before a self-contained field of *contract* would become ubiquitous as a way of pointing to a distinct subdomain of rules for governing private juralrelations in the market and, relatedly, in its capacity as a core constituent of 'the law' writ large. As a result, in the main centres of the common-law world, between the emergence and maturation of 'the law of contract' a lengthy chronological expanse had to be traversed before the category became generalized and, in the process, more fully naturalized. This meant that in the subcontinent—where, as I highlighted in part II, it was only a more limited ontology of 'the laws' that Company rule was founded upon—the distance that would have to be traversed before contract emerged as its own distinct field would be even greater.

As in the wider Anglophone world, in the colonial subcontinent the call for a more 'scientific' approach to the law based on divining the first principles of its major subdomains like contract would have to wait until mid-century before becoming clearly audible. Still speaking tellingly in the plural, for instance, in 1853 the Second Indian Law Commission called for 'contracts', considered as one of the 'very many important

(London: J. Johnson and T. Whieldon, 1790). These followed sporadically if still consistently. See e.g. Samuel Comyn, *Treatise of the Law Relative to Contracts and Agreements Not Under Seal* (London: J. Butterworth, 1807), Edward Hobson Vitruvius Lawes, *A Practical Treatise on Pleading in Assumpsit* (London: W. Reed, 1810), Henry Thomas Colebrooke, *Treatise on Obligations and Contracts* (London: C. Roworth, 1818), Joseph Chitty, *A Practical Treatise on the Law of Contracts and Defences to Actions Thereon* (London: S. Sweet, 1826), and William Fox, *A Treatise on Simple Contract and the Action of Assumpsit* (London: V. & R. Stevens and G. S. Norton, 1842). Even among those contemporary scholars who have been most vocal about questioning whether nineteenth-century developments in contract doctrine were as novel as some would suggest, it is generally agreed that the handful of texts just cited multiplied noticeably after mid-century. What remains undisputed is that as these works multiplied, so too was it only after the mid-nineteenth century that new works on contract began to take on a more ambitious intellectual scope, not to mention coherence. This becomes clear even simply through comparing the most prominent works from the earlier part of this period—see e.g. Charles Greenstreet Addison, *A Treatise on the Law of Contract* (London: W. Benning, 1847)—to those that came a generation later. This is because the most visible examples of the later works became canonical, each going through several editions. See e.g. Steven Martin Leake, *The Elements of the Law of Contract* (London: Stevens,1867), Frederick Pollock, *The Principles of Contract at Law and in Equity: Being a Treatise on the General Principles Concerning the Validity of Agreements, with a Special View to the Comparison of Law and Equity, and with References to the Indian Contract Act, and Occasionally to Roman, American, and Continental Law* (London: Stevens, 1876), and William R. Anson, *Principles of the English Law of Contract* (Oxford: Macmillan and Co., 1879). Alongside these, eventually, various other similarly systematizing works by jurists in the United States and other lesser-known English writers also appeared.

subjects of Civil Law', to be reformulated through legislative intervention.[19] It would take another two decades and a Third Law Commission (convened in 1861) for the call to be comprehensively answered through bringing the Contract Act of 1872 to fruition. Indeed, in order to fully make good on the Act, the abstracted first principles it channelled would, themselves, have to be further linked to the still emerging idea of property as any realm of its holder's valued interest through additional legislation in the form of the Transfer of Property Act of 1882. As the Fourth Law Commission explained in 1879, only then would the rule regime that the new approach to contract was meant to undergird truly extend over 'the whole of the ground which could be profitably occupied by law relating to ... interests in property'.[20]

Yet insofar as the Contract Act emblematized the way classical legal thought was bringing the notion of will and the conception of rights as realms of proprietary interest into intimate connection, it clearly bore some relationship to pre-existing measures focused on amplifying the enforceability of bilateral agreements. Nor did the imperative to mobilize subaltern labour go into abeyance between whatever earlier point from which the history of colonial contract regulation might be seen as having commenced and 1872. On the contrary, because it remained a standing priority, in the years after the transfer of power the 'subject' of 'contracts' repeatedly became a matter of controversy. Accordingly, a sense of both the necessity of existing approaches to regulating certain kinds of bilateral relation and what they left to be doctrinally desired gave a fillip not only to discourse about contractualism but also to the work of the Third Law Commission in preparing Act IX of 1872.

7.2.1 The Workman's Breach of Contract Act of 1859

Proximal to the transfer of power and before work on the Contract Act picked up in earnest, perhaps the most notable context in which the preoccupation with contractualism became apparent involved labour unrest

---

[19] Indian Law Commission, Report of 13 December 1855, quoted in Rankin, *Background to Indian Law*, 88.
[20] *Report of the Fourth Law Commission*, 1879, V/26/100/12, 28.

in Bengal just after the 1857 rebellion. In legal historical terms this culminated in the passage of the Workman's Breach of Contract Act (VIII) of 1859 that originated through a petition filed by the masters and wardens of the Calcutta Trade Association. Pushing for the creation of a new remedy under magistracy jurisdiction, the Trade Association sought to enable employers to bring suit against workmen and servants for 'willful breach of contract' and 'desertion of services'. Although its applicability was initially restricted to Calcutta, essentially the same measure was soon extended, in one form or another, to cover much of the rest of British India as well. Already in 1859, the Act was expanded to the Punjab and Pune; by 1860 all of the Bombay Presidency went on to be included under its basic approach; it came to reach Kanpur in 1862; two years later in 1864 much of Madras and today's Assam were added; in South India, European planters succeeded in bringing Travancore on to the list of places where the basic provisions of the Act became law another year later, after securing the passage of the Criminal Breach of Contract Act of 1865; by 1873 Sindh came into the fold; and thereafter various other areas like Nagpur would continue being incorporated under a similar regime on into the early twentieth century.[21]

While clearly designed to bolster the power of capital, doctrinally speaking the Act was something of a halfway house in terms of its substantive framework for governing labour. It thus split the difference between the old rules of master and servant in the common law and classical legal thought's partiality towards reconstructing the employer-employee relationship in terms of the ostensibly mutual wills of the contracting parties. In keeping with the first of these two aspects there was the Workman's Breach of Contract Act's provisions making breach of contract by workmen and servants punishable through imprisonment for up to three months and hard labour.[22] Although the Act did shed the

---

[21] See Ian J. Kerr, 'Labour Control and Labour Legislation in Colonial India: A Tale of Two Mid-Nineteenth Century Acts', *South Asia: Journal of South Asian Studies*, XXVII, no. 1 (April 2004): 7–25 at 16–17 and Michael Anderson, 'India, 1858–1930: The Illusion of Free Labor', in *Masters, Servants, and Magistrates in Britain and the Empire, 1562-1955*, eds. Douglas Hay and Paul Craven (Chapel Hill, NC: The University of North Carolina Press, 2004), 422–54 at 431, note 52; Paul E. Baak, 'About Enslaved Ex-Slaves, Uncaptured Contract Coolies and Unfreed Freedmen: Some Notes about "Free" and "Unfree" Labour in the Context of Plantation Development in Southwest India, Early Sixteenth Century-Mid 1990s', *Modern Asian Studies* 33, no. 1 (Feb. 1999): 121–57 at 134–39.

[22] Employers were made liable only for civil damages for breaking their contracts. See Anderson, 'India, 1858–1930', 431.

punishment of lashes, in preserving other harsh penal sanctions it built on the tradition of disciplining labour through criminalization that went back to measures like those touched on at the outset of this section of the chapter as well as various others, from the Company's earliest Police Regulations to Macaulay's Draft Penal Code.[23]

Of course, even if we do not regard legal rules as simply 'irrelevant' to organizing employment relations in nineteenth-century South Asia,[24] the ongoing resort to labour regulation through criminal penalties has often made colonial rule seem like an outlier[25] compared to the away in which work was coming to be administered as a relationship of formal civil equality in the metropolitan world.[26] However, just as it is mistaken to assume that greater formal equality made labour relations in the metropole free of coercion, it would be wrong to imagine that the lingering of criminal penalties in the colonial subcontinent entirely negated the importance of the classical view of contract. As a first matter, the Workman's Breach of Contract Act applied only to employment predicated on monetary advances, which was both a concession to planter interests and a mark of the deepening of market-based mechanisms of labour exploitation.[27] Second, when compared to other sources of labour regulation

---

[23] See e.g. Ravi Ahuja, 'The Origins of Colonial Labour Policy in Late Eighteenth-Century Madras', *International Review of Social History* 44, no. 2 (Aug. 1999): 159–95.

[24] Anderson, 'India, 1858–1930', 454.

[25] See e.g. Prabhu Mohapatra, 'From Contract to Status? Or How Law Shaped Labour Relations in Colonial India, 1780-1880', in *India's Workforce: of Bondage Old and New*, eds. Jan Breman, Isabelle Guérin, and Aseem Prakash (New York: Oxford University Press, 2009), 96–125 (arguing that with the end of the drive for codification by the 1880s, the ongoing resort to criminal sanctions for breach of employment contracts both defied the Raj's more vocal commitment to modernization—as through the Contract Act of 1872—and demonstrated how it was the employment 'contract' that consequently produced 'status' during late-colonial times, thus having made for an apparent reversal of Maine's celebrated thesis about the trajectory of modernity).

[26] Of course, even outside the colonial world, it would be naïve to assume that liberal approaches to labour regulation simply involved a wholesale transition to 'free labour'. Plainly, such an ideal—of freely contracted labour—also functioned as a convenient rhetorical trope for facilitating the persistence of and ongoing resort to various non-formalized labour arrangements, other assorted types of extra-economic coercion over workers, and, perhaps most significantly, unpaid—and gendered—household work. In a host of ways, all of these forms—among others—functioned to subsidize 'modern' employment relationships based on ostensibly equal bargaining, while also sustaining social reproduction. See e.g. Robert Steinfeld, *Coercion, Contract, and Free Labour in the Nineteenth Century* (New York: Cambridge University Press, 2001) and Douglas Hay and Paul Craven, 'Introduction', in Hay and Craven, eds., *Masters, Servants, and Magistrates in Britain and the Empire*, 1–58.

[27] As Anderson notes, however, this limitation did much less than it adverted to where it came to actually limiting the Act from being used as a basis for penally sanctioning labourers. This was because effective advances through servitude and labour for wages in the

from the time like the Employers' and Workmen's Disputes Act (IX) of 1860, the Workman's Breach of Contract Act actually involved a retreat from a regime of employee censure based on criminalization.[28] Indeed, this is why most of the jobbers, sardars, and other assorted middlemen who recruited workers defended the 1859 Act's retention of some criminal penalties as a minimum necessity for advancing the freedom of contract under Indian circumstances.[29] As one agent for the Bengal–Nagpur Railway put it, allowing breach of employment duties to be punished through some form of penal sanction was only natural in the subcontinent given the 'irresponsible disregard for contractual obligations normally displayed by Indian labour'.[30] On this view, criminal penalties were simply a way of allowing the Raj—through the colonial state's own will as a legal agent—to make up for the defective private will of the labourer in the subcontinent.

The seemingly antiquated vestiges of criminalization, thus, could easily enough be remade into indicators of an incipiently modern

late-nineteenth-century subcontinent continued to be tightly bound up with the demand for credit. Therefore, the Act often became more popular among employers than were the labour-related clauses of the Penal Code. For example, in Assam, where the Penal Code's provisions were often invoked to regulate labour on tea plantations, the Workmen's Breach of Contract Act came to be resorted to even more frequently. In Madras, as well, it was used most often in the context of plantation production, including of tea, coffee, pepper, and other spices. (In Madras the Act was eventually replaced in several of its plantation districts with the Madras Planters Labour Act of 1903.) In the Punjab it was in the context of public works, and canal construction in particular, that the Act proved most relevant, with a sharp increase in offences prosecuted under it taking place between 1890 and 1920. In the North-Western Provinces the Act became a common tool for employers only amidst the uptick in wartime industrial production, with its use then slowing after 1920. See Anderson, 'India, 1858–1930', 432–35.

[28] Kerr, 'Labour Control and Labour Legislation in Colonial India', 19 (further noting that the annual reports on the administration of criminal justice in the Punjab between 1891 and 1925, for example, show that whereas anywhere from five hundred to several thousand offences were reported under the Workmen's Breach of Contract Act, under Act IX of 1860 there were often none at all).

[29] So was it that the Act 'came to be viewed by employers as an expression of the presence of a third party, the colonial government, prepared to enforce exchange in a context where employers believed Indian labourers could not be trusted to fulfil their contracts." In this way, as Kerr further argues, "[t]he colonial regime reduced uncertainty and facilitated enforcement, thus lowering transaction costs in contexts where advances frequently were necessary to purchase labour power'. Ibid., 20–21. It is worth noting that Kerr's own view was that the Act was at odds with a phenomenon of contractualism that he too perceived to have been largely equivalent to an 'ideology of classical liberalism'. As such, on his assumption, contractualism mandated that 'the state should interfere little in the labour market and in work disputes'. Ibid., 23–24.

[30] Quoted in ibid., note 59 (where Kerr also observes that submissions to this effect were commonplace).

approach to the law based on preferentially operationalizing contract's core values of collectivism and regulation over those of autonomy and self-determination. To transform the imaginary of the Act's resort to criminal penalties did not depend on assuming any inevitable gap between contractualism as a liberal ideal and the invariable need for its relaxation in administrative practice. Nor was such a possibility of making the vice of criminalization a virtue simply a hangover of what scholars of South Asia have called the romantic ideology through which British officialdom, going back to the founding of Company rule, had long venerated autocratic paternalism as most consistent with 'traditional' political culture in the subcontinent.[31] Instead, even in an example like that of the earlier-quoted Bengal-Nagpur railway agent—who was plainly not any kind of legal technician—his was a sentiment premised on channelling a form of argumentation inherent within the doctrinal discourse of contract, being essential to imaginatively reconstituting the core of the law writ large both in the subcontinent and elsewhere in the world of classical legal thought.

7.2.2 Indigo Production Contracts in Bihar: Criminalization, Specific Performance, or a Fairness-Based Standard?

Similar lessons can be gleaned from a second highly notable context in which the preoccupation with contractualism became clearly apparent in the period after the Second Law Commission and before the passage of the Contract Act in 1872. This involved the indigo economy of Bihar and the so-called Blue Mutiny of 1860, which took place only two years before Henry Maine joined the Governor General's Council of British India as Law Member and only five years before he would lead the way to completing the first draft of the Contract Act.

---

[31] It is Eric Stokes who first highlighted this so-called Romantic—and paternalist—tendency, which he contrasted with his titular radical utilitarian counterpoint as part of the Company's 'Battle of the Two Philosophies'. Whereas the latter was devoted to constructing a colonial form of administration based on English principles, according to Stokes, the former took an ostensibly more laudatory and 'romantic' view of native traditions of so-called despotic rule, including for the purposes of justifying a joinder of judicial and executive/administrative power. See generally Stokes, *The English Utilitarians and India*, 1–80.

Witnessing complaints of Bihari indigo cultivators against European planters finally boiling over, the Blue Mutiny had antecedents dating back to the 1820s. Already at that point planters had begun to call for an ability to enforce cultivation agreements against agriculturists through criminal sanctions. Subsequently, those demands were given renewed impetus as indigo prices collapsed in the 1840s and 1850s at the tail end of North India's long post-conquest economic depression.[32] In the decade before indigo unrest came to a head, depressed prices and volatility in the agrarian economy made cultivators increasingly wary of tying themselves to production agreements based on advances paid by planters. Only two years after the British had brought the wider disturbance of 1857 to a bloody end, in Bihar cultivators were renouncing their production agreements en masse, attacking indigo factories, and uprooting existing crops. It was against this backdrop that colonial officialdom again started seriously considering the planters' call for legislation to empower the Raj to punish cultivators through imprisonment and hard labour in the event of their flouting their agreements.

Maine, of course, famously opposed this call to further entangle contractualism with criminalization.[33] Yet as in the case of the Workmen's Breach of Contract Act of 1859, it would be a gross oversimplification to imagine that he, or others, did so strictly on the basis of equating the law of contract with some anti-statist logic of laissez faire. Instead, Maine marshalled support for legislating into being what was, in its own right, a highly interventionist alternative that would have allowed the provincial government to compel indigo labour through the remedy of specific performance. Even more tellingly, by the time Maine arrived in Calcutta in 1865 the climate in the Bengal legislative council had shifted considerably. His own support for enacting a civil remedy of specific performance was no longer contending chiefly with criminalization as the other

---

[32] Sandra den Otter, 'Freedom of Contract, the Market and Imperial Law-Making'. In *Critiques of Capital in Modern Britain and America: Transatlantic Exchanges 1800 to the Present Day*, eds. Mark Bevir and Frank Trentmann (New York: Palgrave Macmillan, 2002) 49–72 at 52–53.

[33] Maine had voiced his opposition already before touching down in Calcutta in 1865. See ibid. A very similar overall argument is made by den Otter on the basis of a wider discussion in her 'The Political Economy of Empire: Freedom of Contract and 'Commercial Civilization' in Colonial India'. In *Worlds of Political Economy: Knowledge and Power in the Nineteenth and Twentieth Centuries*, eds. Martin Daunton and Frank Trentmann (New York: Palgrave Macmillan, 2004), 69–94.

main option. Rather, his adversaries on the Governor General's Council were now equally drawing on the equivocal doctrinal values of contract in classical legal thought to propose draft legislation expanding the discretion of judges to look behind the terms of bargains. Enshrining a standard of 'fairness' and 'equity' as the rule of decision for conflicts between planters and cultivators, this competitor proposal was the one that proved ultimately victorious. As such, it easily beat a proposal by Maine that, even notwithstanding its break with antiquated criminalization, was effectively deemed too naked an intervention in favour of planter interests, despite its voluntarist trappings.[34]

In neither case, however, did any one of these alternatives more clearly embody the supposedly 'fixed, abstract, rational and universal rules' of 'contract law' than the other.[35] First, each equally represented a break from the old framework of master and servant doctrine, just as each equally involved moving away from regulating the planter-cultivator relationship through criminalization. Second, a standard of equity and fairness ostensibly more favourable to the cultivator was no less individualist (and also no more paternalist) than a bright line rule allowing the colonial state's judges to compel specific performance. As I will return to, this is because if the construction of contract as a generalized field within the law was predicated on a doctrinal logic of facilitating mutual agreement, in the event of conflict the state would have no choice but to select a norm that would have to be justified on the basis of curing a defect in the will of some one private individual or the other. After all, this was what it meant for the state to substitute its own will as a public juridical individual for that of some one party to the bargain rather than the other in order to resolve disputes. Either under Maine's preferred rule of specific performance or a standard of fairness, then, the justification for any given outcome would have to be similar to that which was articulated by the agent

---

[34] Den Otter, 'Freedom of Contract, the Market and Imperial Law-Making', 54–55. This is not to say that den Otter attributes such concerns, themselves, only to an equitable streak within colonial policymaking. Her own view is that 'racial considerations' about inflaming cultivators in the subcontinent against what was a largely white European array of landed interests in the indigo context proved decisive for advising against Maine's emphasis on specific performance.

[35] Ibid., 56–57. For den Otter the qualities of fixity, abstraction, and rationality define 'contract' as the basis of 'the law of the market' in a way that is taken to make any standard of fairness its diametric—and, in a sense, extra-legal—opposite.

for the Bengal–Nagpur railway in defending criminal penalties under the Workmen's Breach of Contract Act.

This point is especially worth keeping in mind as we turn to the more direct history of debate about the Contract Act of 1872. As both a framework for defining first principles and a set of resources for settling disputes between private parties, the Act necessitated that the state function as ultimate guarantor for the law of contract, and, in the larger argument, the law writ large. Rather than taking away from the sense that the law was built of legal rather than political stuff, the standing possibility of substituting the public for the private will vindicated this sense by confirming that contract rested ultimately on an ontologically distinct elemental basis.

7.3 The Genesis and Reception of the Indian Contract Act

Notwithstanding the expression of interest by the Law Commissioners in passing legislation on the broader subject of 'contracts' going back to the early 1850s, it was not until after the launch of the Third Law Commission in 1861 that work on the Contract Act officially commenced. The process began in London, from where the Law Commissioners completed a draft bill in 1866. For the next several months afterwards, members of a Parliamentary Select Committee then haggled over the draft, with it eventually reaching the Imperial/Governor- General's Legislative Council at the turn of the next year, 1867, alongside an introductory 'Statement of Objects and Reasons'. Here, W. N. Massey tellingly introduced the Act as 'a measure embodying the whole Law of Contract'[36] that would, furthermore, 'curiously and carefully ... accord with the law both as declared by Hindu and Muhammadan jurists, and also as propounded by the Courts' in Britain's India.[37] After final publication in July 1867—under the title of a 'Bill for defining the law relating to Contracts, Sale or Moveables, Indemnity and Guarantee, Bailment, Agency and Partnership'—the

---

[36] This began, tellingly, with W. N. Massey's introduction of the bill as a 'a measure embodying the whole Law of Contract'. IOR, Public and Judicial Department Records (L/P&J/), Abstract of Proceedings of the Legislative Council of the Governor-General of India, 6 December 1867, 375.
[37] Ibid., 386.

proposed Act was then forwarded to British India's provincial governments for feedback, which took the better part of the next year.[38]

From this point, the process of reaching a final version of the legislation involved resolving a number of disagreements about both the wording and substance of different provisions in the bill, especially given the distance between the Law Commissioners in London and the members of the Governor General's Council in Calcutta.[39] Progress languished for the rest of Maine's tenure as a law Member on the Council, with the draft text only making its way back to the Secretary of State for India and the Parliamentary Select Committee in London in 1870. By that point, however, the Third Law Commission's mandate had grown stale, and effective custody over the bill remained with the Imperial/Governor General's Legislative Council in the subcontinent. With Maine's departure, it was the new Law Member, Sir James Fitzjames Stephen, who became the most prominent exponent of the cause after his appointment in the summer of 1869.[40]

As a result, in the years before the Act's final passage in 1872, what further changes it underwent were owed to Fitzjames Stephen—especially the new introductory section that was added to provide definitions of basic terms.[41] Fitzjames Stephen also took the lead in pressing the case before the Law Commissioners for the changes made by the Legislative Council, despite a relationship between Calcutta and London that was steadily growing sour after 1870. True to his reputation, he did so less through offering the Commissioners carrots than by waving sticks. In

---

[38] IOR, Public and Judicial Department Records (L/P&J/), Abstract of Proceedings of the Legislative Council of the Governor-General of India, 24 February 1871, 79–80.

[39] As a previous law member of the Governor General's Council, Courtenay Ilbert, explained at the time, the most substantial bone of contention was a provision in the bill allowing a purchaser in good faith to acquire valid title over the goods they obtained (the point of this being to encourage the security of market transactions). The Select Committee vigorously objected to the principle, arguing that in the subcontinent, in particular, it would inadvertently encourage theft. See Ilbert, 'Indian Codification', *Modern Law Review* V, no. 20 (October. 1889): 347–69 at 351.

[40] Ibid., 351–52.

[41] Though Fitzjames Stephen's tenure as Law Member ended that same year, only three years after his initial appointment, in his time in the post he witnessed a resurgence of the drive towards codification. Alongside the Contract Act, under his influence the Native Marriages Act and the Indian Evidence Act were also passed in 1872, with the second coming almost entirely from Fitzjames Stephen's own hand. Under his watch substantial revisions were also made to the Criminal Procedure Code as well as the Indian Limitation Act (IX) of 1871, which was a thorough reworking of an earlier measure on the same subject from 1859. See K. J. M. Smith, *James Fitzjames Stephen: Portrait of a Victorian Rationalist* (New York: Cambridge University Press, 1988), ch. 6.

February 1870, for example, he issued a Minute expressing dismay at the Law Commission's efforts to sap the Council of the independent power it needed and that it was initially assigned. While Fitzjames Stephen's confrontational tone quickly led him to surmise that his removal from the Council would be imminent, no such outcome actually came to pass. Instead, by the end of 1870 his influence was clearly increasing, and the members of the Law Commission were left conceding that the Legislative Council was unlikely to take up any of London's recommendations on how to amend the draft.[42] By February 1871, Fitzjames Stephen was thus well placed to recommit the bill for the Council's further consideration, now in a form that would 'greatly shorten and simplify... important parts of the law'.[43]

Amidst a looming change in government in Calcutta, initial consideration of the February draft had to be put off until the summer, with the process expected to be completed only some time during the winter months of the same year.[44] This meant that from the time Fitzjames Stephen recommitted the bill it would take more than a year before it was fully approved in April 1872. While for much of this time it was inevitable that the Act would eventually be passed, the last stage of the process was not without controversy. When Fitzjames Stephen moved for final consideration of the bill on 9 April 1872, besides ongoing concerns about the Parliamentary Select Committee's reaction,[45] a good deal of discussion was necessary to address a proposed amendment by George Campbell, then Lieutenant Governor of Bengal and member of the Council.

Much as in the context of the Workmen's Breach of Contract Act or indigo production in Bihar, Campbell's amendment was indicative of the equivocality of contractualism's doctrinal logic. In his eyes 'the law of contract as laid down in the Bill' was 'altogether a very hard law', not only in its proposition that 'whatever a man had promised he must perform' but also in its refusal to allow mistakes (of fact or law) to excuse a party's performance in the event of a failure to truly understand the deal to which

---

[42] John Roach, 'James Fitzjames Stephen (1829–94)', *Journal of the Royal Asiatic Society of Great Britain and Ireland* no. 1/2 (Apr. 1956): 1–16 at 4.
[43] IOR, Abstract of Proceedings of the Legislative Council of the Governor-General of India, 24 February 1871, 79.
[44] Ibid., 80.
[45] IOR, Public and Judicial Department Records (L/P&J/), Abstract of Proceedings of the Legislative Council of the Governor-General of India, 9 April 1872, 322–84.

they had ostensibly assented.[46] Campbell thus asked whether it would be proper for the Council to 'maintain, in all its integrity and all its rigidity' a provision about performance that even if 'perfectly logical' could 'only be equitable in all causes if you supposed that all men and all women were equal'.[47] Originally, as he explained, he believed it would be best to insert into the Act an 'equitable clause to the effect that, if the Court considered that the bargain was a hard and one-sided one, it should be able to mitigate the damages to any extent to which it thought fit'. However, in light of fears about 'alarm[ing] the Council', the actual amendment he proposed was more modest, intended only to avoid 'infring[ing] the principle that a contract made must be performed' while still giving 'the Court a certain power of mitigating the practical operation of the contract'.[48] In particular, Campbell pushed to expand section sixteen of the draft Act by adding an illustrative example to its provisions on undue influence.[49] Emphasizing that the illustration should reflect the subcontinent's 'particular social context', he offered the following:

> A, a rich and powerful zamindar, induces, B, C and D, poor and ignorant ryots holding under him, to engage to grow certain produce and deliver it to him for a term of twenty years, in consideration of an inadequate price for which no independent ryot would have so engaged. A employs undue influence over B, C and D.[50]

However, Fitzjames Stephen and a majority of the other voting members of the Council sided with the zamindars and planters,[51] who argued

---

[46] Ibid., 348.
[47] Ibid., 347.
[48] Ibid., 350.
[49] In the version of the Bill that was being considered this clause read as follows:
> When a person in whom confidence is reposed by another, or who holds a real or apparent authority over that other, makes use of such confidence or authority for the purposes of obtaining an advantage over that other, which, but for such confidence or authority, he could not have obtained, then the contract would be void. Ibid.
[50] Campbell's illustration read as follows:
> A, a rich and powerful zamindar, induces, B, C and D, poor and ignorant ryots holding under him, to engage to grow certain produce and deliver it to him for a term of twenty years, in consideration of an inadequate price for which no independent ryot would have so engaged. A employs undue influence over B, C and D. Ibid., 351.
[51] See F. S. Chapman's comments on the proposal. Ibid., 354–55.

that the draft's existing treatment of undue influence was more than adequate.[52] If the aim was to seek protection for 'specific classes of agricultural contracts', they explained, Campbell would better be advised to introduce 'special legislation' on the topic.[53]

The opposition to Campbell's proposed addition has sometimes been explained in terms of a wider antagonism to law and legalism.[54] However, as with the split between Maine and the majority of the Council over the question of introducing a planter-friendly remedy of specific performance in the context of indigo production agreements in Bihar, it is more accurate to say that both sides were quite steadfastly pursuing the law's own logic, albeit in the two different directions that its inherent equivocality signposted. Even putting aside the basic consensus on most of the draft's text[55]—with one and all concurring that it 'embod[ied]' nothing less than 'the whole Law of Contract'[56]—what points of disagreement remained were often articulated in hyperbolic terms. Positions for and against Campbell's proposed changes tended to take shape through a soundbite vocabulary that was not atypical of late-nineteenth-century legalism. In this respect, it would be misleading to take at face value claims of the kind Fitzjames Stephen made alleging that Campbell wanted 'simply the passion of the Judge' to rule[57] or those made by Sir William Robinson, another member of the Legislative Council, charging Campbell with endorsing a 'loose and discretional law'. Decrying the abandonment of 'precise and certain general laws, with clear and really stringent legal penalties for their infraction' in the way Robinson did was largely a rhetorical gesture. For when it came to elaborating on

---

[52] See Major General H. W. Norman's comment. Ibid., 359.

[53] This was how one of the Council members, J. R. Bullen-Smith, articulated what proved to be the most general basis of opposition to Campbell's amendment. Ibid., 354.

[54] According to Fitzjames Stephen, such an antagonism—to 'law and lawyers'—was detectable in the Council itself. See ibid., 324. For the recapitulation of a similar idea among modern historians, see e.g. Roach, 'James Fitzjames Stephen', 10. The idea is also latent, in ways, in the more generalized view among historians of South Asia contrasting those colonial officials who supported an ostensible 'rule of law' with the partisans of 'executive government'. See e.g. Metcalf, *Ideologies of the Raj*.

[55] IOR, Abstract of Proceedings of the Legislative Council of the Governor-General of India, 9 April 1872, 347–48.

[56] See note 36.

[57] IOR, Abstract of Proceedings of the Legislative Council of the Governor-General of India, 9 April 1872, 366.

what more this meant Robinson's lament that Campbell's proposal would 'leave' the 'judicial administration' of the Act 'very much to ... equity and good conscience' amounted to little more than a boilerplate recitation of an increasingly boilerplate idea—namely, that rigid rules were preferable to more flexible standards in deciding cases.[58]

Consequently, Campbell as well as those who supported his changes tended to simply invert their opponents' aphoristic logic. According to Richard Temple, who was also a member of the Legislative Council, rather than being 'confined to local or exceptional cases' best addressed through special measures, Campbell's changes to the draft made sense because they targeted an endemic limitation on the freedom of the will that was 'felt in many Provinces of the Empire'.[59] Not only would the additions help to flesh out the draft's approach to undue influence doctrine, but they would also complement a number of its other provisions, like those making certain types of agreements void on grounds of public policy. For Temple Campbell's additions would address a general rather than special circumstance of transacting in the subcontinent that it was the very purpose of the law of contract to contemplate.[60]

Not surprisingly, his view here echoed Campbell's own reasoning, which rather than to 'abandon precise and general laws', as Robinson alleged, could be—and was by Campbell—defended as being rooted in an aim of the exact opposite kind—namely, to lay down 'the law in a clear and precise form'.[61] Similarly, Campbell turned Fitzjames Stephen's charges on their head, especially as relating to his supposed partiality to a discretionary 'rule of justice, equity, and good conscience' over a genuine rule of law. In the face of the related allegation that he would just as well see a regression back to the judicial order of the East India Company, with its absence of any 'exact law' on 'the whole subject of contracts', Campbell simply asserted that his proposed changes were instead part

---

[58] This was how W. Robinson put the point. See his comments in ibid., 358, 356.

[59] Temple estimated that such a provision might affect the types of agreements by which as many as 60 to 70 million lived (out of a total population that the 1872 census put at some 236 million). Ibid., 364.

[60] Ibid., 365.

[61] It was through achieving such clarity and precision in the form of the law rather than based on the 'merits or demerits' of its content that he claimed the real advantages of the 'Code of Napoleon, and other well-known Codes' were to be found. Ibid., 343.

of a maturation process by which the law of contract would 'gradually' continue to 'take regular shape' in a way appropriate to the subcontinent. It was thus necessary, he maintained, for the Raj to specifically avoid the developmental path of English 'equity law', which, at any rate, in Britain was 'just as much fixed law as any other law' notwithstanding its being historically 'distinct from the common law'. As he continued, if the notion of 'equity law' was even applicable to the types of changes Campbell was seeking to introduce into the bill, it was not in whatever 'primary sense of the word' those like Fitzjames Stephen meant; rather, as per the default understanding of the law in classical legal thought, it was only in the sense of arriving at a rule regime better suited to comprehensively covering binding agreement in the form it took amidst the specificities of the subcontinent.[62] Directly contrary to a rule of personalized and unsystematic casuistic 'passion', then, Campbell explained that his changes were meant to make 'the deliberate opinion of a competent Judge' more likely to result. After all, as he noted, '[i]t was not a question of fact, but of law' as to 'whether, in a certain case a contract ought to be enforced or not'. To use the provisions of the proposed Contract Act to further define exceptional conditions under which agreement was not truly mutual was, thus, clearly about perfecting, not abandoning the law.[63]

The highly stereotyped character of the debate Campbell's proposal inspired makes what otherwise might be liable to seem an exceedingly trivial matter stand out. Rather than out of any indifference, much less opposition to law and legalism, both sides were equally acting on the basis of one of the more neglected contributions of law and legalism to political modernity: namely, an ability to ventriloquize debate—whether more specifically by legislators (as was effectively the case here), judges and litigants, or self-styled commentators in the public sphere—according to highly regimented permutations of logic and rhetoric. Indeed, the same lesson runs throughout the various discussions that surrounded the Act and its interpretation even after it was officially passed into law, as I will turn to directly.

---

[62] Ibid., 346.
[63] Ibid., 366–67.

7.3.1 First Reactions to the Act and the Critique of its 'Technicality'

Immediately after the final version of the Contract Act was made official, a prominent strain of critique focusing on its excessive formalism emerged, which picked up on the spirit of the additions Campbell proposed to make to the draft bill's undue influence clause. For example, troubled by the initial series of decisions the judiciary handed down under the Act Arthur Connell argued that the 'uniformity in [its] conception of right' rendered it ill-equipped to cover a society of 'Hindoos' making up a 'living body with its own laws of unmeasured antiquity'.[64] At root, for Connell, the problem was that the Act was fundamentally a piece of 'speculative legislation' produced by the 'lucubrations of the legal mind' rather than by prioritizing a fidelity to social reality. Blaming Fitzjames Stephen and, above all, Whitley Stokes, the chairman of the Fourth Law Commission and the new Law Member on the Governor General's Council, for their worry about a slide into a discretionary rule of 'equity and good conscience', Connell substituted its opposite: a fear about rule application becoming a mechanistic devotion to the false ideal of logically deducing ostensibly necessary outcomes from exceedingly abstract premises.[65]

This way of reversing the warning that the Act was liable to become a channel for a kind of equity and good conscience-based ad hocery was evident at various other moments as well. Proffering a counter-warning against an excessively harsh formalism in the Raj's approach to contractualism was, thus, a recurrent theme in the work of the well-known civil servant and overseer of the Peasant Indebtedness Inquiry of 1895-96, Septimus Thorburn—above all in his highly influential *Musalmans and Money-lenders in the Punjab*. Allowing, on the one hand, that the Contract Act did little to regulate actual life in the countryside, Thorburn argued, on the other, that this was due to its being 'totally incomprehensible to agriculturists'. Even more notably, he alleged that the

---

[64] Arthur Knatchbull Connell, *Discontent and Danger in India* (London: C. Kegan Paul, 1880), 75. Connell was a relatively minor figure, though he did author another well-received tract following up on his first. See Arthur Knatchbull Connell, *The Economic Revolution of India and the Public Works Policy* (London: K. Paul, Trench & Co., 1883).

[65] Connell, *Discontent and Danger in India*, 71-74.

Act was an outright impediment to effective governance insofar as it was equally incomprehensible to 'about 75 per cent. of Judges' as well as 'the practising lawyers who ma[d]e their livelihood by misinterpreting' it.[66] In a later work, Thorburn extended the same line of thought, explaining that the Act had given rise to 'a whole series of varying and sometimes conflicting decisions' based on the difficulties courts inevitably ran into when trying to give meaning to its different conceptual abstractions like "consent", "ignorance", and "undue influence".[67]

With such a view at his disposal, Thorburn was able to turn the logic of his opponents on its head even more stridently than those such as Campbell or Connell. Describing an 1879 judicial decision creating a presumption of 'undue influence' when the borrower was an agriculturist and the lender a usurer as a 'ruling of heart, not of law', for example, Thorburn transformed the would-be condemnation of those like Fitzjames Stephen into a commendation.[68] Only by eschewing what he called the excessively 'technical'[69] view of the Contract Act that was being bolstered by the judiciary would a truer ideal of the law emerge. For without a 'reversion to simple equitable laws' in the immediate term, he explained, the Act's ostensible commitment to the 'freedom of contract' would go on 'benefit[ting] the rich and astute at the expense of the poor and ignorant' indefinitely.[70] It can be little wonder, then, that we find Thorburn rejoicing at thought of the 'plague of over-legislation' hitting a wall less than two decades after the Act was passed.[71]

As with much of the debate preceding the passage of the Act, whatever strains of anti-legalism it may be tempting to read into Thorburn's remarks are better understood as part of a stereotyped set of argumentative positions and counter-positions that increasingly defined what it meant to speak from within the perspective of the law in the late nineteenth

---

[66] S. S. Thorburn, *Musalmans and Money-lenders in the Punjab* (Edinburgh: W. Blackwood and Sons, 1886), 118–19.
[67] S. S. Thorburn, *The Punjab in Peace and War* (London: W. Blackwood and Sons, 1904), 249.
[68] Ibid., 250.
[69] See e.g. ibid., 249, 252 and Thorburn, *Musalmans and Moneylenders*, 131, 188. In using the idea of excessive 'technicality' as a stand-in for that of excessive formalism, Thorburn seemed to be repurposing one side of what for pre-classical legal thinkers was a contrast between technicality and liberality. See Kennedy, *The Rise & Fall of Classical Legal Thought*, xiii.
[70] Ibid.
[71] Thorburn, *The Punjab in Peace and War*, 252.

century. Indeed, in a context in which the very basis and output of the state, itself, was increasingly being redefined in terms of the self-same object of 'the law', even the notional dichotomy of old between administration based on equity and administration based on laws was fast becoming obsolete. It was now all too easy to rehabilitate the old vice of equity—once a stand-in, especially outside of the context of the English courts of equity, for a rule of discretion—as a virtue internal to the law itself. To reach 'rulings of heart, not law', as Thorburn put it, was to draw on a requisite equivocality that had to be inherent within legal rules if they were to be used to actually administer the infinite variety of factual arrangements the law now had to purport to be capable of norming in an age of ever-accelerating social commerce. What Thorburn called an excessively 'technical' view of the law was merely the other side of reading its rules as necessarily more open-textured than formalistically binary. That is, if viewed from the 'technical' perspective alone, the law's rules would invariably become mere logical abstractions classifying the sheer variety of the world's facts in terms of their consistency or inconsistency with the supposedly clear dictates of those rules on what was bound to seem like an arbitrary basis.

7.4 Reading *The Indian Contract Act of 1872*

As I have just discussed, in both the immediate lead-up to and aftermath of the passage of the Contract Act it is notable how the key contrast between fixed rules supposedly imposing certainty on decision-making and a mere rule of discretion had a way of functioning more like a trope performatively mimicked by opposing sides in a scripted back-and-forth than a genuine basis of reasoned disagreement. At the same time, it was not only during such moments of polemical debate that the rule of law's defining criteria revealed themselves to be troublingly rhetorical. Ample basis for reaching the same conclusion was endemic to the Act itself, which was internally structured, overall, as a systematized way of equivocating over key pairs of opposing values, only one side of which the private law—in its supposed capacity as an instrument for forging political economic modernity—was typically idealized as championing in the discourse of the public sphere.

According to this commonplace public sphere imaginary, the private law tradition was (and continues to be) of overriding importance in the triumph of formal democracy and market society in the West. This is because it is seen as having fostered not only a calculable certainty in economic (and social) transactions over and against the uncertainty of a rule of discretion but also freedom over paternalism, individualism over collectivism, and self-determination over statist regulation. Importantly, however, the imaginary was not just a product of an overarching framing narrative into which the private law (or even just its main subdivisions) was (or were) made to fit wholesale, as a kind of causal variable shaping society and history in its (or their) own right. Rather, it was also the product of a more granular view about the rule content of private law doctrine, according to which it was (and continues to be) held that only through particular arrangements thereof was (and is) it possible to normatively cover the infinite world of social facts so as to allow adjudicators to resolve interpretive disputes in a largely neutral and apolitical fashion.

In the remainder of the chapter, then, I offer a close examination of the doctrinal content of the Contract Act together with the broader array of commentary through which its significance was worked out under the Raj. I do so not simply by looking at the Act's various provisions in a piecemeal way. Rather, in this last main section of the chapter my focus is on the principle (or, if one likes, meta-concept) of the will that intellectually organized the Act's discursive contents into a coherent whole and, simultaneously, that the Act discursively constituted as the foundational element of 'the law of contract'. In each of these two respects, the will proved central to contractualism's role in furthering the larger shift towards a classically inflected ontology of 'the law' that was under way in the colonial subcontinent after the advent of Crown rule.

At the same time, as I will also show, because as a doctrinal concept the will was inherently dualistic, serving as a proxy for the values associated with both the private and the public, it was also deeply paradoxical. That is, it was indicative of how—at the level of doctrinal discourse—the late nineteenth century's new legal ontology was built upon giving the lie to its own preferred image—as championed in the discourse of the public sphere—of the law's rule as being, in essence, about promoting certainty over discretion, freedom/liberty over paternalism, individualism over collectivism, and self-determination over statist regulation. Indeed, the dualism of the will meant that the values of both privity *and* publicity, self-determination *and* regulation, and so on were built into the innermost doctrinal core of the law writ large that contract played such a key role in constituting, given its place, alongside of property, at the ontic centre of the ideal of the private law.

7.4.1 The Organization of the Contract Act

Perhaps what stands out most about the Contract Act in its final form is how it followed an organization that by the time of its passage was, for legal thinkers, becoming a canonical way of schematizing contract as a general doctrinal field. On this approach, it was crucial to start from a foundational distinction between contractual and non-contractual agreement. Doing so lent itself to arranging the discursive stuff of the field—whether definitions of basic terms, rule statements, examples meant to illustrate such statements, etc.—according to a series of stages leading up to and following the formation of a contractual state of relations. The making of an offer, or—as in the parlance of the Indian Contract Act, a proposal—and its acceptance were thus the prerequisites to the emergence of binding obligation, these being construed as the basic indicators of a mutual intent among the contracting parties for their respective wills to be legally bound to one another.

However, even before the Act reached its more comprehensive elaboration of doctrine, its contents were presented in microcosmic form through the small number—only ten in all—of definitions Fitzjames Stephen took pains to spell out in the new opening 'interpretation clause' that was added to the final version of the legislation. Here, 'proposal' and 'acceptance' were at the very top of the list,[72] alongside a third definition, for 'parties', that followed and elaborated on the first two by specifying that for contractual formation to be valid the proposal had to be made by

---

[72] Under the heading of the general 'interpretation clause' these were defined as follows:
(a) When one person signifies to another his willingness to do or to abstain from doing anything, with a view to obtaining the assent of that other to such act or abstinence, he is said to make a proposal. (b) When the person to whom the proposal is made signifies his assent thereto, the proposal is said to be accepted. A proposal, when accepted, becomes a promise.

a 'promisor' and accepted by a 'promisee'.[73] This initial cluster of definitions was followed by a next set of three relating to 'consideration', as the third main element—beyond proposal and acceptance—necessary for a contract to be properly formed.[74] A final cluster of three more definitions went on to round out the previous several through detailing how contractual formation could be negated in the event of 'void' and 'voidable' agreements.[75]

Overall, then, the interpretation clause distinguished itself in much the same way as the Act as a whole did: by asserting that contract was a distinct and distinctly legal phenomenon with a discernible essence that could be boiled down to a set of elements and first principles so basic as to mirror those of 'human nature itself'.[76] As Sir Frederick Pollock enviously remarked in his treatise on English contract law

> [i]t is somewhat curious that no such thing as a satisfactory definition of Contract is to be found in any of our books. The truth is that not one definition but a series of definitions is required, and this want is supplied by the interpretation clause of the Indian Contract Act (to be presently quoted) with a completeness and accuracy which in the present writer's judgment are not likely to be much improved upon for any practical purpose.[77]

---

[73] *The Indian Contract Act, 1872* (Act No. IX of 1872), 'Preliminary', §2. The definition read as follows:

    (c) The person making the proposal is called the promisor and the person accepting the proposal is called the promisee. Ibid.

[74] Under the heading of the same interpretation clause these read as follows:

    (d) When, at the desire of the promisor, the promisee or any other person has done or abstained from doing, or does or abstains from doing, or promises to do or to abstain from doing, something, such Act or abstinence or promise is called a consideration for the promise. (e) Every promise and every set of promises, forming the consideration for each other, is an agreement. (f) Promises which form the consideration or part of the consideration for each other are called reciprocal promises. Ibid.

[75] These definitions were as follows:

    (g) An agreement not enforceable by law is said to be void. (h) An agreement enforceable by law is a contract. (i) An agreement which is enforceable by law at the option of one or more of the parties thereto, but not at the option of the other or others, is a voidable contract. (j) A contract which ceases to be enforceable by law becomes void when it ceases to be enforceable. Ibid.

[76] See note 6.

[77] Pollock, *Principles of Contract at Law and in Equity*, 1. This is why in their separate treatise on the Act, Pollock and his co-author could also be found noting that though its opening section

The opening three chapters of the Act, comprising most of its first half, were devoted to further unpacking the three clusters of terms Fitzjames Stephen included for definition in the Interpretation Clause, more exhaustively elaborating formation, voidness, and voidability doctrine. The last three chapters of the first half of the Act then went on to lay out doctrine relating to the immediate post-formation stage of interaction, covering aspects of the abstract duty of parties to discharge the specific obligations they mutually willed into being through the contract. For instance, chapter four focused on 'performance' as the most basic variety of discharge. Chapters five and six, on the other hand, introduced 'breach of contract', treating it, in effect, as a kind of lapsed discharge and detailing the types of relief available to the non-breaching party.

With the first half of the Act focused on laying out the basic doctrinal constituents of contract as a generalized phenomenon, the second half was devoted to detailing a range of social transactions that were to be counted as its specific manifestations. Not unlike the early-nineteenth-century tendency to lay out the rules pertaining to various *contracts* in a serial ordering by type, therefore, the five remaining chapters of the Act addressed the contract for sale, for indemnity and guarantee, for bailment, for agency, and for partnership, respectively.

7.4.2 Contractual Formation: The Archetype of Mutualizing the Private Will

The role of formation doctrine in buttressing the idea of a distinctly legal species of willed relations followed from the assumption of so-called bilateral, promise-for-promise agreement as the paradigm. On the abstract understanding of contract as a meeting of the minds, private agreements between juristic individuals were made binding by a mutuality of the will, considered as both one of the law's foundational ontic elements and a kind of meta-principle for operationalizing legal reason. Promising fitted into this picture because more than performance it represented an act purely devoted to externalizing internal intentions, and in this respect

was merely 'an interpretation clause', it 'really declare[d] a considerable part of the substantive law'. Pollock and Mulla, *The Indian Contract Act: with a Commentary*, 11.

it could be deemed best suited to determining whether a contract had truly been willed into the world. Indeed, leading commentators in late-colonial India on the 1872 Act emphasized this point at various turns. As Calcutta High Court Justice Sir Henry Cunningham and his colleague on the Madras High Court H. H. Shephard put it:

> [a] contract consists, it has been shown in almost every instance, of reciprocal promises, and these promises are to a greater or less degree inter-dependent, so that a failure to perform on the one side generally justifies a refusal to perform on the other.[78]

Cunningham and Shephard were here inveighing against the old common-law rule under which promise-for-promise exchanges could only be enforced under exceptional circumstances by treating them as independent covenants. A failure by one party to make good on such a covenant thus did not erase what were seen as the independent rights and obligations of the other under their own covenant, a feature of the old regime that the authors of the above passage clearly saw as out of keeping with the general rubric of mutuality that had become canonized by the time they were writing.

There was a related consequence of the centrality of bilateral formation doctrine to classical legal thinkers that is worth emphasizing here as well, which involved the strenuous emphasis it necessitated on distinguishing between contract as a field of general versus special law. That is, for the law to dictate the elements required for private juridical persons to legitimately enter into a state of contractual relations was also for it to authorize the terms of the legitimately formed contract to dictate what parties could and could not do within that state of relations. This was a major factor in enabling the doctrinal discourse *of* the law (of contract) to play what key role it did in buttressing the ontologizing thrust of contractualist discourse within the public sphere. Doctrinal discourse could, in this respect, plausibly license a public sphere imaginary that continuously idealized its object as a perfectly integral and infinitely

---

[78] Sir Henry Cunningham and H. H. Shephard., 'Introduction'. In *The Indian Contract Act: No. IX of 1872, together with an Introduction and Explanatory Notes, Table of Contents, Appendix and Index*, 7th edn. (Madras: Printed at the Lawrence Asylum Press, 1894), xxvii.

generative system of rational ordering according to norms (rather than discretion) with a notional ability to cover any set of facts the world might offer up only if parties to a contract could be portrayed as engaging in a kind of special legislation among themselves.

Paradoxically, however, for exactly the same reason the doctrinal discourse *of* contract tended to undermine a key premise of rule of law ideology that discourse *about* contract in the public sphere emphasized just as insistently: namely, the notion that market freedom was tantamount to a strong separation of the private from the public. After all, the default presumption in formation doctrine that it was a 'wholly executory' or bilateral contract being formed gave the appearance—at least on its surface—of channelling the spirit of laissez faire by requiring the exchange of no more than one individually willed promise for another.[79] Likewise, by privileging the individually willed intention to be bound, 'the law of contract' gave the appearance—again, on its surface—of being fully continuous with a model of legal right as any realm of proprietary interest commanded 'exclusively' and 'absolutely' by its holder, with the two parties joined, in effect, by the logic of potential preference-satisfying trade as owners of propertized commodity values. Yet once beyond this surface, the twofold rule of norms (leading into and coming out of the agreement) that formation doctrine was devoted to celebrating demonstrated how inseparable the private and the public were in the law of contract. For if private juridical persons were free to wilfully determine how to govern their own affairs as parties to a mutual agreement, at a minimum the meeting of their minds had to take place under conditions that could only be elaborated and policed by the public will of the state, considered as a juridical individual in its own right.

As both a foundational element in the ontology of 'the law' and a meta-principle for organizing contract as a distinct field, the will had

---

[79] See Atiyah, *The Rise and Fall of Freedom of Contract*, 1–4. Atiyah distinguishes between three types of basic situations that are typically seen as generating legal liability or in which, equivalently, one can understand promises as being binding. In the first, the contract or promise can be found binding after a price has been paid. In the second, the contract or promise can be deemed binding because one party (the promisee) has acted in reliance on it so as to leave themselves in a worse position than if the promise or contract had never been made. In the third, the promise or contract will not have been paid for nor will it have been relied upon; therefore, no distinct reliance- or benefit-based reason for enforcement exists (at least initially) and liability can be said to accrue, instead, for reasons inherent within the promise itself.

a role in commingling the private and the public that came to light through formation doctrine in other ways as well. The 1872 Act's treatment of so-called unilateral formation—that is, the formation of a contract through the exchange of a promise not for another promise but for an act of performance—is a case in point. Such forms of binding agreement were dealt with in the first chapter of the Contract Act in a separate section entitled 'Acceptance by Performing Conditions, or Receiving Consideration'.[80] Here it was paramount to differentiate such unilateral agreements premised on performing (a condition) from the paradigm of their bilateral counterpart while still classifying them as binding, which was made much more readily possible on account of the inherent equivocality of the concept of the will. This is because although generally such agreements could not be enforced by the party exchanging the performance until it was completed, thus making the promisor's promise freely revocable, in some cases the promise could be enforced. These generally involved addressing the possible unfairness that could result from a regime of free revocability by allowing action in reliance on the other party's promise to suffice to render the agreement binding. Indeed, if the action was sufficient, there seemed compelling reason to allow for liability in some cases even absent *any* distinct instance of privately willed intention in the first place; that is, not only when there was no 'acceptance' via a promise by the one party but also no 'proposal' via a promise by the other.

Of course, to erase the difference between promise and performance in this way was to threaten to undermine the whole rubric of a mutual meeting of the parties' minds that allegedly made 'the law of contract' a distinct ontic domain in the first place. It was in order to reconcile this difficulty that the Contract Act selectively recast performance as a proxy for promising. So was it that the section dealing with unilateral agreement in the first chapter declared that '[p]erformance of the conditions of a proposal, *or* the acceptance of any consideration for a reciprocal promise which may be offered with a proposal, *is an acceptance* of the proposal'.[81] While this provision stopped short of outright substituting the public

---

[80] *The Indian Contract Act, 1872*, ch. 1 at §8.
[81] Ibid. (emphasis added).

for the private will, each such resort to 'objectifying' the individual's subjective intent by treating their externalized act(s) as the indicator of an ostensibly mutual state of mind was nonetheless an expressly regulatory intervention into the space of private dealing by the state rather than any mere umpiring effort by its neutral judges to facilitate what both parties wanted.

As needed, even the most high-profile commentators commended the Act for turning the basic rubric of formation as a meeting of *minds* on its head in the context of situations where the promisor's proposal made the counterparty's acceptance a function not of returning a promise but of the performance of some express condition. As Frederic Pollock and Dinshah Mulla emphasized in what quickly became the most important treatise on the Act, in such cases it was the potentially communicative character of all acts more than acts of communication as such that mattered:

> [i]t is a matter of the commonest experience that the communication of intentions may be effectively made in many other ways besides written, spoken, or signaled words. For example, the delivery of goods by their owner to a man who has offered to buy them for a certain price will be understood by every one, unless there be some indication to the contrary, to signify acceptance of that offer. No words are needed, again, to explain the intent with which a man steps into a ferry-boat or a tramcar, or drops a coin into an automatic machine. It is also possible for parties to hold communications by means of prearranged signs not being any form of cipher or secret writing, and not having in themselves any commonly understood meaning. This does not often occur in matters of business. Means of communication which a man has prescribed or authorized are generally taken as against him to be sufficient. Otherwise an unexecuted intention to communicate something, or even an unsuccessful attempt, cannot be treated as amounting to a communication; much less can a mere mental act of assent have such an effect in any case[82]

---

[82] Pollock and Mulla, *The Indian Contract Act: with a Commentary*, 25.

7.4.3 Consideration and the Duality of the Will

Given the focus on mutual promising, it might seem curious—in the way that it did in other late-nineteenth-century common law contexts—that the 1872 Act required agreements to be supported by 'consideration' in order to qualify as enforceable contracts. Defined in the Act as anything (to be) done or (to be) abstained from being done by one party on behalf of the other,[83] consideration was seemingly at odds with the emphasis on manifestation of party will through proposal and acceptance. After all, to the extent that proper formation required privately willed intention to be externalized it was not through requiring that it be materially embodied in the form of some token. Instead, notwithstanding situations of unilateral exchange and conditionality on express acts, the focus in bilateralism was on the promise itself as having an inherently communicative character capable of making manifest the internal state that was to be attributed to each party's mind.

Still, it would be wrong to view the consideration requirement simply as a hangover—or even, mainly, as an indicator—of the law of contract's deeper past. In legal historical discussion, while such a view carries a surface plausibility, it becomes less tenable on closer inspection. More specifically, it is worth stopping here momentarily to consider two different forms in which this view has come. On the one hand, according to a first—and more deflationary—version of the view, consideration is best seen as a vestige of days gone by given its character as a legal formalism. On this view, for example, the well-known principle that courts should not enquire into the adequacy of consideration[84] appears indicative of

---

[83] The full definition ran as follows:
> (d) When, at the desire of the promisor, the promisee or any other person has done or abstained from doing, or does or abstains from doing, or promises to do or to abstain from doing, something, such Act or abstinence or promise is called a consideration for the promise.

The Indian Contract Act, 1872, 'Preliminary', §2. The formulation given to consideration in this section was conceptualized somewhat differently from how it often otherwise was in the common-law world; this shows in the apparent allowance made for acts (or abstentions) of third parties being able to qualify as valid consideration. That said, too much significance should not be attributed to the Act's turn of phrase here, especially given the way it tended to be negated by interpretations that qualified the language by requiring that any such act still would have to be done 'at the desire of' the promisor. For an important early decision—by the Allahabad High Court—addressing this point, see *Durga Prasad v. Baldeo*, 3 All. 221 (1880).

[84] As Cunningham and Shephard noted, '[t]hough the law, however, insists on there being some consideration to support a contract, it does not specify how much, nor will it enquire into

how consideration was not unlike the antiquated but once widespread notion that in order for agreements to be binding they had to be memorialized through a seal. Yet this way of seeing things suffers from the obvious defect that it proves incapable of accounting for how the pride of place historically given to consideration increased in direct rather than inverse proportion to the late-nineteenth-century growth of 'the law of contract' as its own distinct doctrinal domain.

On the other hand, there is also a more laudatory view of consideration's pre-nineteenth-century past that is commonly associated with Morton Horwitz's work on the legal history of the United States. On Horwitz's view, the so-called bargain theory of consideration that triumphed amidst Anglo-America's ongoing commercial revolution in the late nineteenth century was not only typified by the principle that courts should not inspect the adequacy of consideration, but it was also part of the demise of an earlier version of the doctrine in the common law that prioritized equity over greasing the wheels of exchange.[85] Making for a greater ambivalence about the 'modern' consideration requirement than is precipitated by its more deflationary counterpart, Horwitz's view also necessitates greater attention to fully appreciate its limits. This is because the Horwitz thesis has always come with inbuilt grounds for scepticism based on questioning how much of a break the bargain theory really was from whatever preceded it during the early-modern epoch of the English moral economy's past.[86] Consequently, centring as it has on how much really changed during the late nineteenth century, the debate the Horwitz thesis has inspired has all too easily obscured other possible aspects of consideration's novelty in classical legal thought. Perhaps chief among these is the special role it played in securing a new imaginary around 'the law', with this aspect of its novelty coming not despite its technical and arcane nature as a doctrine but because of it.

From the standpoint of the law's ontologization, in other words, exactly when or to what extent adjudicators passed from rationalizing

---

the adequacy of the consideration'. Cunningham and Shephard, 'Introduction'. In *The Indian Contract, Act 1872*, xv.

[85] See e.g. Morton Horwitz, 'The Historical Foundations of Modern Contract Law', *Harvard Law Review* 87, no. 5 (1974) 917–56.
[86] See e.g. Alfred W. B. Simpson, 'The Horwitz Thesis and the History of Contracts', *The University of Chicago Law Review* 46, no. 3 (1978): 533–601.

consideration as a means of policing the equity of agreements once made to rationalizing it as a means of accelerating unbridled commerce may be less important than its growing discursive ubiquity as a formal building block of something that went by the name of 'the law of contract'.[87] In fact, the latter feature of the consideration requirement in classical legal thought also speaks to another aspect of its novelty that is otherwise too easily obscured. As I will return to, this had to do with the appearance of thoroughgoing modernity that consideration took on when seen as a necessary invention of the pronounced growth and bureaucratization of state power. In this respect, one can say that the doctrine served as a standing justification for the state—in its capacity as a juridical individual in its own right—to assert for its public will a rightful place at the very centre of relationships that were ostensibly the product of privately willed self-determination alone.

Given its confounding nature, it is not surprising that the consideration requirement attracted multiple, and not always consonant, explanations, including among commentators on the Indian Contract Act. For some its role within the Act was best understood as an equivalent for the object leading parties to come together through attempted bargaining in the first place—that is, as the very point of the exchange rather than some mere incident devoted to memorializing it.[88] To the extent that the Act itself explicitly distinguished 'lawful consideration' from a 'lawful object', for others the requirement became little more than a way of restating the need for proposal and acceptance; seen as such, it could be explained as a kind of redundancy serving to reiterate the primacy of mutual assent as the key to contractual formation.[89] On this view, the consideration

---

[87] It stands to reason that the less potentially connected adjudication was to ground-level reality in places like the subcontinent—where the gap between colonial law and South Asian society remained wide—the more practically important arcane or otherwise formalistic elements of doctrine were likely to be as an alternate basis for the possibility of the law's immanence.

[88] As Cunningham and Shephard noted, '[w]here there are reciprocal promises, it is obvious that the thing which, from the one party's point of view is the object of the promises, is, from the other party's point of view, its consideration, and *vice versa*'. Cunningham and Shephard, 'Introduction', in *The Indian Contract Act 1872*, xii.

[89] Given that section 10 of the second chapter of the Act defined contracts as agreements made by free consent, a lawful consideration, *and* a lawful object (*The Indian Contract Act of 1872*, ch. 2), in their commentary Pollock and Mulla displayed mixed feelings about such a view. For example, while wrestling with the 'extremely important proposition that a contract may be formed by the exchange of mutual promises' in a way that made each promise consideration for the other, they contemplated the implications of situations in which such a promise-cum-consideration had no intrinsic value in itself. If so, they pointed out, it would still be a

requirement was burnished with the same symbolic import that emanated from reciprocal promising: it was a doctrinal mechanism for making the autonomy of the private will manifest in the world.[90]

Regardless of whether it is seen as making for a requirement clearly distinct from or overlapping with the elements of proposal and acceptance, there is no doubt that the doctrinal discourse of consideration helped shift the law's centre of ontic gravity towards the building block of the will. Even as the ideal of legal right that could be generalized from the model of property as any realm of its holder's valued interest was moving away from its founding emphasis on the ostensibly 'absolute' way that such interests were commanded and towards a new emphasis on their role as facilitators of individual autonomy, then, it was not any simple logic of laissez faire that was being touted in classical legal thought. Likewise, if late-nineteenth-century consideration doctrine itself seemed to extol a kind of laissez faire virtue, it could not but be responsible, simultaneously, for securing a place for the state to establish its own legitimate presence at the very heart of the private law.

Indeed, the last observation is borne out in the Indian Contract Act in ways that go beyond the simple fact that its drafters chose to retain the consideration requirement. To return to the earlier mention of the Act's endorsement of the rule against enquiring into the adequacy of consideration, even notwithstanding the way it generally restricted the state from invalidating the private will of contracting parties in the face of seemingly unequal bargains it was hardly without exceptions.[91] At baseline, of course, there was the distinction between agreements based

---

possible step too far to believe that such a view was necessitated by 'logical deduction from the general notion of consideration itself' rather than simply being a function of 'a positive institution of law required by convenience of business in civilized life'. Pollock and Mulla, *The Indian Contract Act: with a Commentary*, 22.

[90] See Atiyah, *The Rise and Fall of Freedom of Contract*, 138–46. James Gordley makes a similar point while highlighting consideration's earlier origins as a common law pleading device. As he notes, 'the requirement of consideration had historically meant that the plaintiff could recover in assumpsit in a variety of disparate cases in which this seemed sensible to judges. Some of these cases were ordinary bargains or exchanges. Some were not, at least not in any ordinary sense'. Only 'with Blackstone', did 'Anglo-American treatise writers' begin to 'define and rationalize the consideration requirement' by identifying it 'with what civil lawyers called the "causa", which means a sensible reason for making a contract'. James Gordley, 'The Common Law in the Twentieth Century: Some Unfinished Business', *California Law Review* 88, no. 6 (Dec. 2000): 1815–75 at 1848–49.

[91] Among these exceptions were ones in which

on insubstantial, but still lawful, consideration and those that could be deemed outright void because based on presumptively unlawful forms. At the same time, this did not mean the state was entirely barred from probing the adequacy of what was exchanged; the Act still allowed insubstantial but lawful forms of consideration to be policed by the parallel route of adjudicators looking to whether whatever was given was insignificant enough as to cross over into being indicative of an outright lack of truly freely given consent.[92]

Conversely, even when there might seem to be no—rather than just insubstantial—consideration and, thus, no possibility of a binding, privately willed agreement in the first place, here as well the state could still point to the operation of the public will as an alternate basis for binding the two parties to one another. In *Kedarnath v. Gorie Mahomed*, for example, the Calcutta High Court considered a suit brought by one of the Municipal Commissioners of Howrah, a district adjoining Hooghly, and one of the trustees for the area's Town Hall fund against an individual who had pledged one hundred rupees towards the construction of the Hall.[93] After a significant number of pledges had been collected, the Commissioners entered into an agreement to commence construction of the facility. However, when the defendant-builder had a change of heart the plaintiffs brought suit against him claiming breach of contract. While

> [t]he consideration or object of an agreement is lawful, unless it is forbidden by law; or is of such a nature that, if permitted, it would defeat the provisions of any law; or is fraudulent; or involves or implies injury to the person or property of another or; the Court regards it as immoral, or opposed to public policy. In each of these cases, the consideration or object of an agreement is said to be unlawful. Every agreement of which the object or consideration is unlawful is void ... If any part of a single consideration for one or more objects, or any one or any part of any one of several considerations for a single object, is unlawful, the agreement is void ... Agreement made without consideration is void, unless (1) it is expressed in writing and registered under the law for the time being in force for the registration of assurances, and is made on account of natural love and affection between parties standing in a near relation to each other; or unless (2) it is a promise to compensate, wholly or in part, a person who has already voluntarily done something for the promisor, or something which the promisor was legally compellable to do; or unless (3) it is a promise, made in writing and signed by the person to be charged therewith, or by this agent generally or specially authorised in that behalf, to pay wholly or in part a debt of which the creditor might have enforced payment but for the law for the limitation of suits. In any of these cases, such an agreement is a contract.
> *The Indian Contract Act, 1872*, ch. 2 at §§23–25.

[92] Specifically, here the Act stated that inadequacy 'may be taken into account by the Court in addressing the question of whether the consent of the promisor was freely given'. Ibid., §25.

[93] *Kedarnath v. Gorie Mahomed* (1886) 14 Cal. 64.

the case turned on the seeming lack of consideration that went with a mere pledge, the Court nonetheless insisted that there was a binding contract. As it explained, '[t]he subscriber by subscribing his name says, in effect,—In consideration of your agreeing to enter into a contract to erect or yourselves erecting this building, I undertake to supply the money to pay for it up to the amount for which I subscribe my name'.[94] In the light of an obvious lack of any real bargained-for exchange by the defendant, the Court's insistence on finding consideration was all the more notable given how easily it could have reached the same result by simply sidestepping the issue and holding the agreement enforceable under other provisions of the Act—like those in its fifth chapter on 'Certain Relations Resembling Those Created by Contract'.

Being among the Act's shortest, that chapter was especially indicative of the symbolic politics of staking out a new intellectual ethos that was being played out within its pages. While the brevity of chapter five of the Act might make it seem incidental, its inclusion was anything but, being—as much as anything else—a statement affirming a place for the operation of the public juridical will within the space of private relations. What united the five titular situations the chapter contemplated was the way they symbolized the possibility of there being binding obligation between two parties even absent facts evidencing an intent on their part to be bound. In this respect, chapter five served to codify the wider late-nineteenth-century doctrine of 'quasi-contracts', which allowed for the creation of bilateral jural relations between parties through the operation of law.[95] On this reading, the chapter's brevity is best understood as a function of the ideological commitment to minimizing the prominence of non-contractual forms in a leglislative enactment that the public-sphere discourse of liberal legalism preferred to portray as a means of championing private self-determination, not to mention the ideological commitment in liberal imperialism to bringing this ideal of voluntarist

---

[94] Ibid.
[95] In the earlier of the several editions of Pollock's major treatise on contract in the common law (see Pollock, *The Principles of Contract at Law and in Equity*), the first being published in 1876, the subject tended to be excluded from the table of contents altogether. Mentions appeared explicitly, under the topic's own proper subheading as part of the lengthy first chapter on Offer and Acceptance, only with the 4th British edition of the text, which was published in 1885. (It was with the appearance of this edition that the work's title was reformatted to exclude the long subtitle that referred more specifically to *The Indian Contract Act*.)

freedom to cultural milieus—like the subcontinent's—that were generally portrayed as being devoid of the same. Therefore, in eschewing the resort to quasi-contract in favour of finding the consideration requirement to have been met, the Calcutta High Court in *Kedarnath* was simply helping to maintain the preferred imaginary of the law as a mere facilitator of private, party will.[96]

7.4.4 Extending the Public Will: Obligations *Quasi Ex Contractu*

Within the common-law tradition, quasi-contractual liability's closest ancestor was a notion of obligation based on implied promising. However, the former did not emerge out of the latter through any straightforward process of linear evolution so much as it did as a by-product of the rise of contract, itself, as a distinct field/phenomenon.[97] Absent the wider

---

[96] On this very basis and soon after the end of the colonial era one of the first of the post-independence Indian Law Commissions urged that the *Kedarnath* decision be scrapped in favour of a more straightforward approach to cases with similar facts by calling for the creation of an express reliance-focused rationale for possible binding obligation. As it noted,

[g]reat injustice is done sometimes where a promise is made which the promisor knows will be acted upon and which is in fact acted upon and then it is held that such promise is unenforceable on the ground of want of consideration. A common example of such a case is where a person agrees to pay a subscription to a charitable institution with the knowledge that a building will be constructed with the aid of the amount subscribed and the trustees of the charity incur expenditure on the faith of the fulfilment of the promise ... In India, some Judges have upheld such promises on the ground that they were supported by consideration inasmuch as the expenditure was incurred 'at the desire of the promisor', while other Judges have held that the facts did not justify the finding that the expenditure was incurred 'at the desire of the promisor' and thus the agreement being without consideration was void and unenforceable [citing *Kedarnath v. Gorie Mahomed*]. In our opinion, the former view puts considerable strain on the meaning of the expression 'at the desire of the promisor.' 'A promise, which the promisor should reasonably expect to induce action or forbearance of a definite and substantial character on the part of the promisee and which does induce such action or forbearance, is binding, if injustice can be avoided only by enforcement of the promise [citation omitted].' Law Commission of India, 'Thirteenth Report (Contract Act, 1872)', 26 September 1958, 7.

[97] This line of thought speaks to one of the key differences that sets apart Kennedy's idea of a 'will theory' (which he argues was at work in classical legal thought in general) from Atiyah's (which he suggests was at work only/mainly within the new field of the law of contract, in particular). In the former's usage, the idea is not simply equivalent to the emergence to primacy of the mutual intention to be bound through nothing more than the expression of reciprocal promises. For Atiyah, it is the latter idea of mutual intention that signalled the start of the rise of the freedom of contract because of the way it enabled the emergence of a more full-bodied notion of the wholly executory contract. For example, contrast Kennedy's discussion of the shift from the

nineteenth-century imaginary that structured the law as an arrangement of constituent domains of rightful interest and the wills that were to be respectively sovereign therein, there was little point in drawing strict lines around obligations that were supposed to be genuinely contractual, on the one hand, and those that were not, on the other. In this respect, rather than being a predecessor to quasi-contract, implied promising was simply part of a different juristic episteme.[98]

Ultimately, then, the shift from implied promising to quasi-contract portended a transformation of the key question understood to be raised by the types of disputes to which the doctrines were both otherwise potentially relevant. In the earlier historical period that question was whether, under the circumstances, doing justice required one party to be held responsible to the other. By the second half of the nineteenth century, however, the paramount question had become one of who—as in which juridical person—was to be understood as willing the obligation

---

term 'intention' to 'will' after 1870. Although it once again is a point Kennedy is making especially with reference to the context of the United States, it seems to be more broadly relevant to the English common law of contract that is Atiyah's main concern (not to mention, to the Indian Contract Act as well). As Kennedy thus notes,

> [early 19th-century contract theorists] almost never referred to the 'will' of the parties or even of the state ... For them, the crucial category had been 'intention.' The change in the dominant word after 1870 was more than formal. It signified a new preoccupation with locating a legal actor whose wishes would control the judge. 'Will' suggested that controlling actor's dominance; it suggested that he was empowered by the legal order to determine the outcome, and acted with that power in mind. The category of intention, by contrast, suggested the whole pre-Classical apparatus based on the process of judicial implication, stereotyped social relationships, and the norm of reasonable behavior. The pre-Classical approach blurred the distinctions between parties and judge, actual intent and moral duty, privately desired outcomes and socially desired outcomes. The essence of will was that it was an uncompromisingly *positive* concept. It represented a self-conscious decision to avoid fuzzing policy, morality and actual intention, and to avoid ambiguity about *whose* will was involved in any particular situation. Will was also *positivist*, in the sense that those who used it were insisting that the judge was always at the beck of some lawmaker, the sovereign or the holder of a legal right derived from the Constitution. The judge's task was to do that actor's bidding, not to twist or interpret his bidding into something compatible with the judge's view of policy or morality.

Kennedy, *The Rise and Fall of Classical Legal Thought*, 176–77.

[98] Here again we come to an important difference between Atiyah and Kennedy with respect to questions about doctrinal change, in general, and the role of the will theory in nineteenth-century legal history in particular. Consider the essential continuity that links the period from 1770 to 1890 as the era of contract's titular rise for Atiyah with Kennedy's division of this same era at roughly the mid-point of the nineteenth century to separate it into periods of pre-classical and classical legal thought. Compare e.g. Atiyah, *The Rise and Fall of Freedom of Contract*, chs. 14–15 and 21 with Kennedy, *The Rise and Fall of Classical Legal Thought*, chs. 3–4.

into being. Was it the parties, themselves, as private juridical individuals who meant to govern their mutual affairs through a regime of 'free' contract even if they did not properly memorialize their agreement? Or was it the state in its capacity as a public juridical individual capable of governing such situations by imposing its will from the outside in, so to speak? According to classical legal thought's new episteme, the belief in the law as aspiring without compromise towards creating a society based on autonomous self-determining agency could be preserved only if both possible answers to the second question were viable ones.

Of course, even if a contractual relationship—and the requisite intention to be bound—was to be implied on the basis of the facts of the parties dealing, it was hardly the case that the will of the state would fail to be at play in any manner at all. Clearly, the very context of adjudication meant, of necessity, that the organ of state settling the dispute was, in a sense, intervening into private affairs. Yet whatever act of state this involved, it was still imaginably different from the state substituting its will as a juridical person for (one of) the parties' own, as per the key feature that was meant to define quasi-contract as a doctrine. As Henry Maine explained, for example,

> [i]t has been usual with English critics to identify the quasi-contract with implied contracts, but this is an error, for implied contracts are true contracts, which quasi-contracts are not. In implied contracts, act and circumstances are the symbols of the same ingredients which are symbolized, in express contracts, by words; and whether a man employs one set of symbols or the other must be a matter of indifference so far as concerns the theory of agreement. But a Quasi-Contract is not a contract at all. The commonest sample of the class is the relation subsisting between two persons, one of whom has paid money to the other through mistake. The law, consulting the interests of morality, imposes an obligation on the receiver to refund, but the very nature of the transaction indicates that it is not a contract.[99]

---

[99] Henry Maine, *Ancient Law: its Connection with the Early History of Society, and its Relation to Modern Ideas* (London: J. Murray, 1861), 343–44. Maine goes on to further develop the point in its relation to the idea that quasi-contract was rooted in the imposition of political obligation. See ibid., 344–45.

Although an exceptional basis on which to foot binding obligation, quasi-contract was no less consonant than contract proper with the ontologizing impulse of classical legal thought. Accordingly, whether binding obligation was implied into being based on what the parties could be said, themselves, to have *really* intended or based on the state's taking the lead in implying such obligation into being by stepping in for the parties whatever exactly their own intentions, in either case the law would still be grounded in ultimately the same stuff of the will.

In the subcontinental context, this new outlook on implication doctrine in classical legal thought was made most vividly manifest through Justices Cunningham and Shephard's introductory comments to the Contract Act. 'Before quitting the subject of the obligations created by contracts', as they maintained, it was necessary

> to deal with certain duties which, though not really arising out of contract, and though consequently, strictly speaking, out of place in a law of contract, have, for convenience sake, been provided for in the present enactment. These duties are sometimes spoken of as arising *quasi ex contractu*, and the English law deals with them generally on the theory of an assumed contract, which, though the parties have not made it for themselves, the law, under the circumstances makes for them. They may be generally described as cases in which, on account of something or other done by one person, it is equitable that money should be paid to him by another. No contract has been entered into, no wrong has been committed, but a state of things has come about which requires an adjustment between the parties.[100]

Even as they concurred, in good classical fashion, with the ultimate enforceability of such agreements *quasi ex contractu*, Cunningham and Shephard also made haste to applaud the Indian Act for giving the doctrine what looked like something of a peripheral place. On their reading, chapter five did not really provide for any generalized phenomenon of quasi-contract based on an elaboration of first principles. Rather, it simply specified—through 'direct legal enactment'—a discrete list of example situations that could be said to give rise to binding obligation

---

[100] Cunningham and Shephard, 'Introduction'. In *The Indian Contract Act*, xxxvi.

owing to the way they resembled, even without truly being, contractual ones.[101]

Yet, as we saw earlier, it hardly goes without saying that chapter five's 'direct legal enactments' were exhaustive rather than illustrative, much less meant to be indicative of no broader principle.[102] Clearly, the situations detailed here were drawn from ones typically subsumed under quasi-contract. Cunningham and Shephard's inclination to peripheralize implied obligation in the Act, then, just as readily testifies to its significance relative to the law's new ontology.[103] Regardless of how terse the chapter's treatment, the large output of commentary on the 'certain relations resembling contract' the Act did discuss could not but, therefore, amplify their visibility; as other forms of doctrinal discourse assembled around chapter five, then, its dimensions simply expanded. In the end, this meant that whatever the small number of 'direct legal enactments' the Act did touch on, quasi-contract came to occupy much the same space as it generally did within the classical ontology of the law more generally—ensconcing the public will at the very heart of the law of private legal relations.

7.4.5 Infants' Contracts for Necessaries

To further clarify how the 1872 Act's version of quasi-contract carved out a place for the public will at the very core of the new ontology of the private

---

[101] Ibid. (noting that '[u]nder the present Act this notion of an implied contract is wholly got rid of, and the duty of paying is based in each instance on a direct legal enactment').
[102] The illustrative examples had to do with the imposition of liability in cases of claims for necessaries supplied to individuals generally deemed incapable of contracting, such as minors and those with different kinds of mental ability (section 68), cases involving the reimbursement of moneys paid by a third party but owed by someone else in the timely repayment of whose debts the third party had some sort of interest (section 69), cases involving acts done without the intention of their being undertaken for some other party gratuitously and which conferred some benefit upon that other party (section 70), cases in which one individual found goods belonging to another and took them into their custody (so as to become, in effect, a bailee under section 71), and cases involving money paid or goods delivered to a party mistakenly or under coercion (section 72). See *The Indian Contract Act, 1872*, ch. 5.
[103] As Pollock noted for his wider audience in his general treatise on contract '[t]he Indian Act provides for matters of this kind more simply in form and more comprehensively in substance than our present law, by a separate chapter'. See Frederick Pollock, *Principles of Contract at Law and in Equity: Being a Treatise on the General Principles Concerning the Validity of Agreements in the Law of England*, 4th Edition (London: Stevens, 1885), 12.

law it is worth considering in more detail how classical legal thinkers explained some of the particular situations that chapter five contemplated. The first such example had to do with agreements for 'necessaries' made by/on behalf of those lacking in capacity, such as minors and those of different mental ability. As William Anson explained in his canonical late-nineteenth-century treatise on the law of contract, in the common law's past, so-called infants' agreements were traditionally treated as voidable.[104] As such, they were further divided into two subcategories: those that were considered invalid until ratified by the minor upon reaching the age of majority and those presumed valid so long as not explicitly rescinded/avoided by the minor. As for agreements made by minors for so-called necessaries, they fell under neither subcategory, instead traditionally making for an exception to the general rule of voidability.

Importantly, however, in the cases of both the rule and the exception, the logic underlying the norm commenced from the same rationale of prioritizing a concern with doing justice by preventing unfairness more than any perceived place or lack thereof for the will within such agreements.[105] In contrast, by the late nineteenth century, this basic arrangement was turned on its head, with the move towards generally recasting infants' agreements as outright void rather than merely voidable coinciding with the new ontology of the law in classical legal thought. The change was made official in the English Infants Relief Act of 1874, the very first clause of which mandated that

> [a]ll contracts whether by speciality or by simple contract henceforth entered into by infants for the repayment of money lent or to be lent, or for goods supplied or to be supplied (other than contracts for necessaries), and all accounts stated with infants, shall be absolutely

---

[104] William Reynell Anson, *Principles of the English Law of Contract* (Oxford: Macmillan and Co., 1879), 98. As Anson further elaborated,
> [i]t would seem that where an infant acquires an interest in permanent property to which obligations attach, or enters into a contract which involves continuous rights and duties, benefits and liabilities, and has taken benefit under the contract, he would be bound unless he expressly disclaimed the contract. On the other hand, a promise to perform some isolated act, or a contract wholly executory, would not be binding upon the infant unless he expressly ratified it upon coming of age. Ibid., 99.

[105] This is reflected, still, in Joseph Chitty's discussion of voidness. See Joseph Chitty, *A Practical Treatise on the Law of Contracts, and Defences to Actions thereon* (London: S. Sweet, 1826), 215–28.

void: provided always that this enactment shall not invalidate any contract into which an infant may by any existing or future statute, or by the rules of Common Law or Equity enter, except such as now by law are voidable.[106]

In a sense, then, relative to the law's shifting ontology contracts by/on behalf of minors were bound to appear like less than the genuine article if, by definition, they could not be grounded in the ostensibly irreducible stuff of party will.

Of course, from the standpoint of outcomes in society, the changes emerging from this transition may have been minor: just as agreements for necessaries continued to be lawful on an exceptional basis, those made by/on behalf of minors more generally remained dubious. However, it is precisely because the difference between coding such agreements as void and coding them as voidable seems minor that it is also so telling, serving as a reminder that the law's new ontology was a function of the imaginary its rules and their rationalizations comprised in addition to their material effects. For what *was* at stake in the shift from counting such agreements as void rather than voidable was the possibility of giving proper pride of place to the will as the doctrinal foundation of binding obligation between parties. No matter how seemingly trivial in reality, subtly recasting the way infants' agreements were normed was still a way of using doctrine to inscribe upon the law's discursive sites a new assertion about its essence and true nature.

Anson's further discussion of cases in which 'an infant pays for goods [other than necessaries] which have not been delivered' is especially noteworthy in this regard. For as he recounted, prior to the English Infants Relief Act the minor would have been able to recover any amount paid 'by [simply] avoiding the contract', but after the 1874 Act the outcome became more uncertain. On the one hand, as Anson noted, '[i]t is difficult to suppose that no remedy would be available to the infant under such circumstances'. On the other, he went on to puzzle,

> it is hard to see how any remedy is available *ex contractu*. If a contract had ever been in existence the infant could avoid it while still executory,

[106] English Infants Relief Act of 1874, 37 and 35 Vict. *c.* 62.

and recover back money which he had paid under it; or he might recover the money as paid on a consideration which had wholly failed. But, since the Act, the contract is void; it never had an existence; and it would seem as though the money paid under it was paid voluntarily, and could only be recovered if paid upon fraudulent representation, or possibly by an application of the equitable machinery of trusts.[107]

Under the old approach, then, the idea of voidability rationalized the exception and general rule alike: whereas agreements for necessaries could remain unavoided, infants' agreements more generally could not. Under the new approach, if there could be no true contract that ever 'had an existence' in the first place, it was only on the basis of the will of the state that proper sense could be made of both rule and exception. The public will was, thus, generally to be conceived as pre-empting any purported act of private will by/on behalf of a minor from the get-go (with any sums already paid, as Anson suggests above, to be returned in accord with the state's equitable impulse). In the case of the exception, though, it was now on the basis of substituting the juridical will of the state for the void of will on the part of the minor that agreements for necessaries were to be conceived as legitimate.

Ultimately, for the domain of quasi-contract to be devoid of true contractuality in this manner was a mark both of the will's absence and its presence. In virtue of the absence of its private incarnation, quasi-contractual agreements were generally excluded from that innermost core of the law's system, comprising its rules for governing market relations. However, in virtue of its public incarnation, quasi-contractual agreements remained positioned just at the periphery of the law's core—governed not by mere whim or discretion but its rules of legal capacitation, which marked the internal boundary within the private law between the law of the market and the law of status.

* * *

To reiterate a point made earlier, then, despite the best efforts of those like Cunningham and Shephard to read chapter five of the Indian Contract Act so as to minimize its examples to a discrete list of 'direct legal

[107] Anson, *Principles of the English Law of Contract*, 102.

enactments', the symbolic import of those examples was hard to contain. Not surprisingly, section 68's narrow allowance for agreements by the otherwise incapacitated for necessaries quickly became tied up with a wider controversy over the contrary force attributed to section 11 of the Act, which read

> [e]very person is competent to contract who is of the age of majority according to the law to which he is subject, and who is of sound mind, and is not disqualified from contracting by any law to which he is subject.[108]

With its focus on those above the age of majority, section 11 was regarded by many as a blanket prohibition on contracting by anyone below that age. Yet, now by ostensibly negating chapter five's supposedly circumscribed allowance to the contrary for infants to contract for necessaries, in the end section 11, too, only amplified its symbolic importance.

Indeed, by 1903 the question of how to reconcile section 11 and section 68 came to a head as it moved from the Indian High Courts to the Privy Council in *Mohori Bibee v. Dhurmodas Ghose*,[109] which upheld the broad view of section 11 by making *all* agreements by/on behalf of minors absolutely void. However, in reaching this view the Council did not simply reason that it was appropriate to dispense with section 68's seeming exception for infants' contracts for necessaries but also that it was necessary to more fully dispense with the old lens of voidability, which, in the context of the subcontinent, it said was especially compelled by the norms of Hindu law. Perhaps inevitably, this aspect of the justification for its decision elicited significant criticism. In his well-known treatise on the Contract Act, for example, Frederick Pollock struck out at the Privy Council's interpretation of section 11, arguing that the provision arose largely as an accident, having been drafted at a time when a spurious view of the common law's approach to agreements by minors was on the momentary ascent. Citing to Anson, Pollock elaborated on the point as follows:

---

[108] *The Indian Contract Act, 1872*, ch. 2, §11.
[109] *Mohori Bibee v. Dhurmodas Ghose* (1903) L. R. 30 I. A. 114.

> [t]here was formerly ... a current opinion, countenanced by the lax forms in which some of the decisions were expressed, that infants' agreements were of three kinds: Namely, that some were wholly void as being obviously not for the infant's benefit, some valid as being obviously for his benefit, and all others voidable. This opinion is now quite exploded, but it was to be found in text-books at the time when the Indian Contract Act was framed. Still there was never any authority for saying that infants were absolutely incompetent to contract.[110]

Notwithstanding the misleading way Pollock was drawing on Anson, his squabble with the Privy Council remains striking.[111] For even if the Act was structured so as to try to remove quasi-contract from the spotlight in the way we saw Cunningham and Shephard suggesting it should be removed, true to form the opposite quickly happened here once more. That is, infants' contracts became a wedge prying chapter five of the Act open for all to see, revealing a discursive field with much the same breadth as quasi-contract more generally commanded within the space of classical legal consciousness. As the thicket of competing assertions about a matter even so hair-splitting as the voidness versus voidability of agreements by/on behalf of minors grew more tangled it only more insistently embedded the law's new ontology.

As should be apparent, one cannot assess the import of the Contract Act solely or even mainly through asking about the extent to which its rules were enforced in society. Just as fundamental was the way it furnished a collection of sites at which the discourse *of* the law could ontologize its object at the very same time that it inscribed upon even the most minutely technical of rule choices an increasingly standardized pattern of equivocation associated with liberal legalism—moving back and forth over the values of freedom and coercion, individualism and collectivism, and, at bottom, the private and the public will. In turn, from these sites the Act went on to become additionally networked into society through the communicative lines of the colonial public sphere, wherein discourse

---

[110] Pollock and Mulla, *The Indian Contract Act*, 49 (citing the 1903 edition of Anson's *Principles of the English Law of Contract*).

[111] As we saw earlier, Anson viewed voidability—not voidness—to be the organizing motif of the common law's approach to agreements by minors in the past. Moreover, his focus on that view came not by way of advocating for its superiority but of highlighting its abandonment.

about the law both pressed ontologization further and generated additional resources for equivocation, albeit here over the structural contradictions of the idealized liberal order as a whole. For in the public sphere, talk of the law's rule continuously promoted the norm of liberal freedom as exceptional in history; yet at the very same time, it continuously served as an apologia for liberal freedom-in-history's more pervasively embarrassing features: whether in the form of its evident passion for imperialist subjugation on a global scale, its commitment to neo-feudal (so to speak) capitalist class inequality, its opportunistic and anti-rationalist tendency to recast reality as mere derogation from theory, and so on.

7.5 Contractual Collectivism and the Expansion of the Public Law

As this chapter has sought to demonstrate, as it emerged in the subcontinent the imaginary of classical legal thought made for a delicate arrangement. Through the piecemeal pre-1850 enactments relating mostly to labour contracts and all the more through Act IX of 1872, a notion of the will came to ground the private law's rules for governing relations in the market in a way that proved emblematic of more than just a theoretical commitment to atomistic individualism. Of course, this is partly because once contract was organized as a distinct subdomain of the law in the nineteenth century, legal thinkers saw that it would be too onerous to conduct judicial business if the subjective intent of the parties demanded absolute deference. However, more important than this so-called 'objective theory' of bilateral agreement in breaking any equivalence between contractualism and atomistic individualism was the will's inherent duality as a doctrinal concept.[112]

In fact, as much is further borne out by the role of the law of tort, considered as the other key component of the law's rules for covering private relations beyond the home/domestic kin group, within the classical

---

[112] On the objective theory of contract (and for a view claiming it can be traced to 'time immemorial' rather than the late nineteenth century, as prevailing experts have mainly concurred) see Joseph M. Perillo, 'The Origins of the Objective Theory of Contract Formation and Interpretation', *Fordham Law Review* 69, no. 2: 427–77 (2000).

imaginary.[113] As the Third Indian Law Commission suggested, by providing for liability for non-criminal wrongs, codified tort law would complete the private law, comprising—together with contract—'two classes of personal obligations' united by a common instrument of remediation through money payment.[114] Of course, those in the colonial subcontinent for whom standardizing the approach to tort was next on the agenda would see their goal frustrated, once enthusiasm for the laborious task of comprehensive codification started lagging by the beginning of the twentieth century.[115] Regardless, relative to the law's new ontology as an infinitely generative system of rational ordering according to norms, the way tort rules were supposed to complement those of contract was highly revealing. If in the context of contract, as we have seen, there was a clear desire to minimize the visibility of the doctrine of quasi-contract and even consideration, given the way they enshrined a place for the public will within the core of the private law's all-important rules for rationalizing market relations, this was much less the case for tort doctrine. For the law of tort more readily appeared like a periphery within the rule system's core of norms for covering private relations and, hence, at least at first glance, more as if it was grounded in a regulatory rather than a voluntarist impulse and, in turn, an element of public rather than private will. (Here, the parallel between tort and criminal law—as a realm of outright publicity that comprised the law's main subsystem for covering wrongs—was also helpful.)

The implicit and explicit ways in which the duality of the will structured the law's ontology in classical legal thought meant that it was no mere instrument for instantiating a society based on any strict commitment to laissez faire, utility maximizing rationality, or Gesellschaft. As a result, it would be misleading to see the passage of the Contract Act in 1872 as merely a belated attempt by law reformers to keep British

---

[113] On the emergence of torts as a distinct field see Kennedy, *The Rise and Fall of Classical Legal Thought*, 181–86.
[114] As the Commission noted, both types of obligation could be 'satisfied by a money payment—liquidated and unliquidated damages' or, failing this, 'by some stipulated or compensatory act enforceable in a like way, from whichever source the obligation ... sprung'. *Report of the Indian Law Commission, 1879*, IOR v/26/100/12, 15 at par. 31.
[115] Among the most prominent supporters were Fitzjames Stephen (including while Law Member of the Council), Whitley Stokes, and Henry Maine. See generally Ilbert, 'Indian Codification'. See also Richard Dundas Alexander, *The Indian Case-Law of Torts* (Calcutta: Thacker and Spink, 1891). For his own part, Ilbert disagreed, arguing that 'it was doubtful whether the subject had sufficiently defined boundaries to admit of its forming a chapter in a theoretically complete Code'. Ilbert, 'Indian Codification', 363.

imperialism's founding ideal of the privity of property current with a state of the economic art in which land was losing its status as the unquestionably archetypical possession over which guaranteeing ostensibly absolute entitlement seemed necessary for the sake of the subcontinent's so-called improvement.

Of course, just because at the level of doctrinal discourse there was no simple equivalence between contract and private individualism this does not mean that ordinary-language discourse in the public sphere had to register as much, as I emphasized in chapter three in the first part of the book. To the contrary, the force of naked assertion and rhetorical reflex made public-sphere communication—whether against the backdrop of a highly industrialized political economy like Britain's or that of a still largely agrarian one like colonial South Asia's—well-equipped to function as a relatively independent means for embedding a strict correspondence between contractualism, individualism, and the principle of privity. Therefore, as with the different discursive registers at which property talk took place, the gap between public-sphere discourse about contract and the doctrinal discourse of contract was noticeable, especially given that contractualism's collectivist ethos ran deeper than its localization within the technical rules of consideration or quasi-contract alone.

Indeed, even in contract law's most rudimentary functioning, it was oriented towards a kind of collectivism. Consider, for example, the generalized ideal in public-sphere discourse of confining the law to the neutral enforcement of what the parties had themselves already autonomously agreed upon. At the point when any actual dispute necessitating judgement arose this ideal obviously offered cold comfort, proving little more than a rhetorical tautology. If there really was a mutually willed governance regime based on the special law set up by contractual agreement, there would obviously have not been any need to invoke 'the law' over that regime in the first place. This is because in reality only one party's respective will could, at best, prevail, even absent a case specifically turning on questions about quasi-contract or consideration; for cases (of dispute) *in general* involved the substitution of the public will for that of the losing party's own. Even this, moreover, could always be on either of two potential bases for making good on contract law's collectivist ethos.

On the one hand, actualizing the one party's will over the other's could be staked on some implicitly collectivist grounds of how doing so would bring to society at large increasing utility. That is, without facilitating the prevailing party's 'rights' under the contract by guaranteeing the bargain which that party was alleging to have been made, the very form of private economic planning for which that contract supposedly was the prerequisite would become impossible and, along with it, the general social utility it was supposed to bring. (Importantly, this argument from collectivism was compatible with the prevailing party's contractual rights conceived either as a freedom of action on that party's part or, conversely, as a security from having the *other party's* freedom of action destabilize their settled expectations.)

On the other hand, where the state intervened to substitute the public will for one party's private will by way of endorsing the will of the counterparty, if not on the basis of simply inverting the argument from social welfare, it would generally be on grounds of some implicit appeal to the moral impropriety of letting the individualist ethos of the market go too far. That is, the alternative basis of decision generally involved giving implicit sanction to the idea that the defeated party's will had superseded the limits of communitarian reciprocity, equitable burden-sharing, or the like. Of course, these two alternatives from collectivism were not necessarily unrelated. If the argument from communitarian reciprocity meant that the law could go only so far in allowing parties to realign the borders of their respective 'realms' of proprietary interest, doing so could always, itself, be seen as implicitly necessary to prevent an excessively short-term version of the drive to maximize social utility from threatening the very possibility of community that was its deeper precondition.

Be the latter a fine point as it may, from the standpoint of the adverse party the actualization of the prevailing party's will was always ultimately thus a form of the law standing for some one variety or another of collectivism. In this respect, the doctrinal logic of contract—and, more fundamentally, the logically operative character of the will as a doctrinal concept—was not once but twice removed from being inherently individualist, facilitative of private autonomy, committed to voluntarist self-determination, and so on. That is, in its collectivist guise, contract could just as well be seen as inherently paternalist, regulatory, and antithetical to the notional ethic of a purely 'free' market. Indeed, the inherent collectivism of the law of contract was arguably more consistent with the era after the mid-nineteenth century during which classical legal thought developed, which witnessed a general expansion of administrative power notwithstanding the oft-proclaimed laissez faire temper of the time. In the context of a general form of the state—including the colonial state—that was increasingly bureaucratic, disciplinary, and charged as it was the world over with the task of effectively managing the (incipient) capitalist economy, embedding the potential for the state's own justification in even the most arcane of considerations of 'mere' doctrine was of no small importance.

At the same time, the doctrinal discourse of contract's inherent equivocality did not mean it acted in isolation as a force for licensing the expansion of administrative power. After all, the rise of the will theory—and in the subcontinent, contract's associated codification—functioned synergistically with the larger ontologization of 'the law' writ large. In this respect, classical legal thought licensed the expansion of the market, as the supposed antithesis of the state, in an even more fundamental way. Through its most basic of commitments—to abstracting the law by abstracting property and contract—classical legal thought attitudinally insisted on an ever-present parallelism between the private and the public as the norm system's two halves.

The supposed paradigm case in which the law facilitated private social transactions through contract thus served as a model for when the state undertook its own public transactions. Indeed, the parallelism between the two served to legitimize the latter in the same proportion in which it normativized the former. Had this not been so, reconciling all the many ways in which institutional action in the name of the state was increasingly putting it into contact with society would have been impossible. Here, moreover, it was discourse about the law that once again proved critical to smoothing over any contradiction. It is little wonder, then, that even as the state was increasingly encroaching—both politically and economically—on society, in the culture of public-sphere communication the law was ever more vocally being saluted for its supposed raison d'être of putting limits on state power.

Insofar as the classical ideal of the private law licensed the expansion of the state, including in its colonial form, as this chapter started out by noting it was the will of the right-holder more than whatever realm the right-holder held that would increasingly come to the fore. As the most basic element in the law's new ontology, the will could be imagined as conserved across the divide between its private and public halves. In the process, the law's core subdomain for ruling contractual interaction among private actors in the market became a beachhead for juridifying administrative action, imparting to it a formal appearance as more than just politics or executive governance by another name. In the reflection of the rights that private juridical persons were supposed to command over the respective realms of their proprietary interest, the state's expanding portfolio of endeavours appeared as if it, too, was simply a function of a counterpart set of entitlements; these were, namely, the rightful legal *powers* the state could be said to command over its realm of sovereign interest as a public juridical individual in its own right. In turn, juridical relations with the state could be seen as being just as authentically 'legal' (and decidedly not 'political') as those connecting private actors through kinship and market commerce.

In historical ontological terms, the result of the parallelism between the private and the public law that contract (and the will) so crucially underpinned meant that the more administration was juridified the more, so too, was 'the law' objectified. For as the law was invoked to cover the state's ever-expanding array of transactions, it also came to seem like an infinitely generative system of norms for ruling not only the administration of justice but also administration in general. In this respect, the horizon beyond the law's ongoing birth over the course of the long nineteenth century was already visible, including in those places like the Crown's India in which the birth process was, in a sense, only still beginning near that long century's end. As the bureaucratized version of the territorial national state increasingly grabbed hold of the law, the law's seemingly concrete existence increasingly appeared as if it was a function of more than just its discursive objectification as a norm 'system' or, for that matter, of just the administrability of that system's norms. That is, over and above these baseline aspects of ontologization, insofar as 'the law' was the name under which the state acted as an entitlement-bearing juridical individual in its own right, so too did the law take on concrete existence as the supposed instrument through which group life in general was made possible, even absent the existence of a state.

I will resume this point directly in the next chapter, which turns to the law's ongoing ontologization—and universalization—through early sociologico-anthropological discourse about status in the subcontinent.

However, for now it is appropriate to conclude the present chapter by noting how the process of turning the law into a trans-historical universal clearly became a key force behind its coming ever more to be discoursed *about* by the late nineteenth century as if it was irreducible and unquestionably real, even separate and apart from whatever way in which it was also intimately tied up with the subjective experience of being normatively bound. In the final analysis, then, legal ontologization proved a mutually self-reinforcing process in the extreme, with all of its various aspects feeding relentlessly upon one another. If 'the law' became increasingly at large within the spheres of economy, society, and polity during the latter nineteenth century, this was inseparable from the way 'the will', itself, became increasingly at large within 'the law' during the same period.

8
From Contract to the Nascent Anthropological Discourse about Status

8.1 Introduction

If after the transfer of power, the subcontinent found an idea of the property right—in classical legal thought's relative, disaggregable, and immaterial vision of the same—that could finally serve as a model for a notion of legal right in general, with the passage of the *Indian Contract Act* it acquired the other bedrock piece of juristic machinery needed to formalize a distinct law of the market. As the end of the last chapter emphasized though, given its underlying duality the law of contract was oriented towards market action in a way that proved both intrinsically 'freeing' and intrinsically 'regulatory'. As a result, to the extent that contractualism was private *and* public, individualist *and* collectivist in its doctrinal incarnation, it was not always easy to draw a sharp line around where the law of the market ended and where that which lay beyond began. Whether at the external limit, where the law of the market marked the border between the private and the public law, or at the internal limit where, within the private law, it marked the border beyond which the law of the status community of the family/domestic kin group began, there was a bleeding edge rather than an unyielding boundary.

If there was some truth to Henry Maine's famed observation that so-called progressive societies moved from status to contract, then, it was not a truth of doctrinal discourse, which was an exceedingly ill-equipped basis for asserting that the latter evolved out of the former. To the contrary, 'the law of contract' and 'the law of status' came into being only side by side, both being products not only of classical legal modernity but also of mutual self-constitution, each of the other. Once across the law of contract's bleeding edges—as would eventually become the case with traversing from contract to tort within the law of private market relations—one thing that is undoubtedly clear is how it generally became more acceptable to openly identify the rule system's underlying purposes with the values of collectivism and regulation. Of course, this is not to say, as a corollary, that the ostensibly opposing values—of individualism and self-determination—were automatically deemed foreign to domains beyond the law of the market. Rather, the point is only that within the respective domains of the public law and the law of (personal) status (relations), there was generally less of a need than there was in the context of market law to assume a necessary alignment between doctrinal discourse and the proclamations of ordinary-language discourse in the public sphere about self-determination and individualism as the rule system's ostensibly most sacrosanct commitments.

In effect, then, there were actually two distinct sources from which variation could be introduced into classical legal thought's globalizing object. On the one hand, the supposed elemental values of freedom/individualism/self-determination and paternalism/collectivism/regulation remained free to mix in different proportions across the porous boundaries that were supposed to define the law's constituent taxonomic-cum-ontic subdomains. On the other, there was a standing possibility that in predicating its own independent existence, 'the law' would make the inevitable gap between the doctrinal and the ordinary-discursive meanings of its constituent terms diverge.

If the last observation is especially worth making up front, it is because in now shifting focus to the remaining non-market subdomains of the new ideal of the private law, the last two chapters of the book will address the question of variability within classical legal thought's globalizing object more explicitly than I have previously. In the final chapter, I will return to the implications of the porous boundary between the law of the market and the law of status relations within the domestic community of the family/kin group by using one specific doctrine—of the restitution of conjugal rights—as a case study. There, I look at conjugal restitution's evolution in the late-colonial subcontinent over the more than half-century leading into the first decades of the 1900s, and I focus, in particular, on its role as one highly localized sub-site for discursively constituting the law of status, in general, and the subsystems of the Hindu and Muslim religious personal law as its main subcontinental proxies, in particular.[1]

Before turning to conjugal restitution in chapter nine, however, in the present chapter I prepare the way by looking at the other key source of variation within classical legal thought's globalizing object. Turning to the realm of ordinary-language discourse in the colonial public sphere, the present chapter focuses on how ethnological and social evolutionist ideas about status were taken up by a broader array of scholar–administrators, especially in the Punjab after it was annexed to British India in 1849. Here, Maine's ideas were crucial in creating a larger context in which wrestling with the province's so-called customary law quickly became a matter of intense concern; and in the end, 'custom' became the Punjab's own special place-holder for the classical law of status, taking up the same space that was otherwise allotted to a subcontinent-specific Hindu and Muslim personal law elsewhere in British India.

After first discussing how non-market private relations were conventionally understood within classical legal thought, I continue in the vein of the book's general method of oscillating back and forth between the two overarching sites of the law's discursive constitution. Therefore, the present chapter focuses on the relatively autonomous life that 'status' lived within the ordinary-language discourse of nascent sociologico-anthropological speculation most commonly associated with Maine.

No less crucial to ontologizing the law, this discourse *about* status diverged noticeably from classical legal thought's discourse *of* status in the meaning it assigned to the concept. At the same time, especially in the subcontinent, it also redirected the concept's meaning in ways that could then feed back into doctrinal discourse. Accordingly, in the final section of the chapter I consider the relationship between the several ways status was intellectually construed and the various taxonomic-cum-ontic headings to which it was tied in classical legal thought—including 'the law of domestic relations', 'family law', and 'the law of persons'. More specifically,

---

[1] While the focus of this chapter is restricted to the Hindu and Muslim personal law, Christians and Parsis were also, at different points, effectively recognized as having their own distinct versions. Other religious/sectarian communities were generally assimilated by the Raj under one of these other main communal forms—as, most famously, with Sikhs being included under the Hindu law. For a more comprehensive discussion of the Christian and Parsi case, see Nandini Chatterjee, *The Making of Indian Secularism: Empire, Law and Christianity, 1830–1960* (New York: Palgrave Macmillan, 2011) and Sharafi, *Law and Identity in Colonial South Asia*.

in this final section of the chapter the focus turns to how the related notion of 'the personal law' that became so important in late-colonial times connected with the 'Anglo-Hindu', the 'Anglo-Muhammedan', and (in places like the Punjab) the 'customary' law as its special avatars in the subcontinent.

8.2 Status and the Law of Domestic Relations

That individualism and collectivism were principles along a continuum inextricably connecting the law of contract to the law of status was borne out well beyond the Indian Contract Act. For exponents of classical legal thought like Sir Thomas Holland, it was an important point of departure for arriving at a more systematic variety of analytical jurisprudence. In his famed *The Elements of Jurisprudence*,[2] for example, Holland explicitly affirmed a broad vision of quasi-contract grounded in several subtypes of 'antecedent rights in personam'.[3] Identifying a first subcategory in terms of 'domestic' rights proper, he contrasted these with antecedent rights that only appeared to be domestic but that were really rights that family members held vis-à-vis one another *in rem*. Even if of 'a somewhat undefined character', he maintained, the truly 'domestic' antecedent rights were 'clearly distinguishable' on the basis of their 'corresponding duties'. For those duties were unique insofar as they

> consist often in lifelong courses of conduct rather than in lists of acts capable of accurate enumeration. In advanced systems such rights are only to a limited extent enforced by law, and that rather by permitted self-help than by judicial process.[4]

---

[2] See Kennedy, *The Rise and Fall of Classical Legal Thought*, 190–91.
[3] Holland, *The Elements of Jurisprudence*. Holland's notion of 'antecedent' rights was meant to distinguish these from 'remedial' ones. Together, they comprised the two basic categories according to which he analysed substantive private law (as distinct from his other major branch of private law, the adjective, having to do with matters procedural and evidentiary). Whereas, for Holland, antecedent rights of substantive private law existed 'irrespectively of any wrong having been committed', remedial ones were 'given by way of compensation' for the violation of an antecedent right. Ibid.,107–08.
[4] Ibid., 165. The remainder of the passage, which Kennedy also quotes—particularly in the context of his discussion about the problem of whether marriage, itself, was to be considered a contract or a status—reads as follows:

On a view like Holland's, the law was seen as touching down on the realm of domesticity in two main ways. On the one hand, there were some legal entitlements that were held against the world at large—like those making for the husband's totalizing right over his wife's 'society'—and that 'ar[o]se from family relations' in only an incidental way. On the other hand, there were those entitlements that were more strictly creatures of domesticity insofar as they were held by individuals vis-à-vis one another only in virtue of their common *status* as members of particular kin groups. As per the above passage, moreover, here the law did not so much appear in the guise of individual rights that such members commanded relative to one another as it did in the form of indefinitely extended 'duties' defining their respective subject positions within the kin group.[5]

According to the classical schematization that Holland was channelling, then, domestic relations could be fully subsumed under the law even as they were actively distanced from the reach of legal administration. Of course, this is not to say that subsuming the domestic sphere under the sway of juridical formalism was unimportant. Relative to the transformation that was taking place in the colonial subcontinent—from a historical ontology of the laws (factoring into the administration of justice) of the kind the Company propagated to a historical ontology of the law of the kind that emerged under the Crown—it was crucial. To whatever extent Holland's arrangement might nonetheless appear contradictory, it is important to see that any dissonance it created within classical legal consciousness was dissipated by the implicit equation between

> It may appear questionable whether the rights of husband and wife can be reckoned among those which arise by operation of law rather than out of contract. It is however submitted that this is the true view. The matrimonial status is indeed entered upon, in modern times, in pursuance of an agreement between the parties, accompanied by certain religious or civil formalities; but its personal incidents are wholly attached to it by uniform rules of law, in no sense depending on the agreement of the parties, either at the time of the marriage or subsequently. The effect of the contract, coupled with the other acts required by law, in producing a status, to which rights of definite kinds are incident, closely resembles that of a sale of property. In the one case, as in the other, the contractual act is complete, so far as its direct effects are concerned, when the status has been produced or the ownership changed. The necessarily resulting rights of the person newly invested with the status, or who newly becomes owner of the property respectively, are the creatures not of the will of the parties but of fixed rules of law.
> For Kennedy's discussion of the problem of marriage as a contract or status see Kennedy, *The Rise and Fall of Classical Legal Thought*, 195–98.

---

[5] Holland, *The Elements of Jurisprudence*, 165.

patriarchal dominion over the family and the founding understanding of legal right that was extrapolated from property in the central domains of the common law world already by the end of the eighteenth century. Subsuming the family under 'the law' thus did not turn on the kin group's being a realm the internal relations of which were actively administered according to legalized rules of decision at the *ex-post* point after disputes broke out between its members. Rather, it turned on the family's being a realm of valued interest, and as such, an object of sorts that could be assigned *ex ante* to the exclusive command of him who could be deemed its rightful holder.

At the same time, just because the classical ideal did not entail actively administering domestic relations through the adjudicatory institutions of the state, this did not mean 'the law' simply disappeared once the threshold of juridification was reached through formally subsuming the family as the household head's realm of proprietary interest. Even absent greater administrative reach, the law was still immanent within the space of domestic relations in the form of Holland's other category of antecedent domestic entitlements. That is, it was still immanent in the form of the 'lifelong courses of conduct' defining status in doctrinal discourse as a temporally extended kind of duty-boundedness. In the imaginary of classical legal thought this meant that the juridification of relations *within* domestic space—as distinct from the relation between the head of the domestic kin group and society at large—turned on the core image of legal entitlement as a vehicle for not the contractual values of privity and party autonomy but the quasi-contractual ones of communitarianism and reciprocity.

From the vantage point internal to the norm order, therefore, Holland's schema was not a way of doctrinally codifying a Maineian view of status. Rather, it was a reminder that not all forms of non-market private interaction could be permitted to be left to voluntarist rearrangement, even if one might like to claim that doing so would be otherwise utility-maximizing. As a doctrinal category explicitly affirming the law's commitment to collectivism, then, status was even less an undisturbed vestige of social evolution's past than was consideration or quasi-contract. On the contrary, to imagine the individual kin group member's experience of law as being mediated through temporally extended chains of duty-boundedness (viz. Holland's 'lifelong courses of conduct') was to insist that so-called *in personam* contractual entitlements that could be made and unmade at will and those more durable ones of status were part of a functional rather than evolutionary continuum.

As I discuss in greater detail when turning to Maine and his disciples in the Punjab, the above role of status in the doctrinal imaginary of classical legal thought contrasts sharply with its appearance in the ordinary-language discourse of the public sphere. For there, the concept was used to point to an altogether pre-legal form of normativity more than any doctrinal subsegment of 'the law' writ large the existence of which was supposed to be logically necessary to norm, on the basis of the public will, the residuum of private relations involving non-market interaction. Indeed, in the nascent sociologico-anthropological discourse associated with figures like Maine and the late-nineteenth-century scholar-officials in the Punjab that he influenced, the preoccupation with status followed, above all, from the way it served as a sign of the law's absence, not the universality of its/its doctrinal subsegments' presence. In this sense, the doctrinal discourse of status in the Crown's India was at sharp odds with a public-sphere discourse that spoke in nominally similar terms but while assiduously avoiding connecting status to the law's inherently modern commitment to statist collectivism.

8.3 The Two Faces of Status in Maine's *Ancient Law*

Prior to the second half of the nineteenth century status had little essential role as a concept in either doctrinal or ordinary-language discourse under the Company's raj. Its rise to prominence instead took place only in a broader context informed by the publication of Maine's *Ancient Law* in 1861 and the approximate decade of effort to that point of building a neo-romanticist system of administration in the Punjab after it was annexed in 1849.[6] As per Lord Dalhousie's directive, with so-called native

---

[6] The term 'neo-romanticist' here evokes Eric Stokes' characterization of the 'Romantic'—rather than utilitarian—side in his 'Battle of the Two philosophies'. See ch. 7 at note 31. The neo-romanticism of administration in the Punjab can, thus, be said partly to follow from the fact that efforts at colonial state-building there did not begin until more than a half-century after Stokes' battle of the two philosophies had been largely settled in the areas the Company had taken over earlier. In part, it also follows from the fact that the Punjab was marked as being especially linked to a collectivist/non-individualist past.

institutions to be preserved in the province after its annexation in 1849 to the extent they were deemed just,[7] colonial officialdom in the Punjab enshrined a rule of ostensibly immemorial customary law in a way that could not but prove evocative of Maine's evolutionist perspective in which status and custom were fused as a conceptual pair.

Yet even as status emerged as a staple category within discussion of the Punjab, as noted earlier its meaning in public-sphere discourse diverged sharply from its meaning as a doctrinal concept within classical legal thought. A sense of equivocality thus marked Maine's way of using the concept, which picked up on aspects of Holland's use at the same time as it generally deviated from it. Consider, for example, Maine's baseline contention that law appeared in pre-state forms of social organization only within the space of inter-familial relations among patriarchs. In part, here he was echoing the idea that some 'antecedent domestic rights' were like those of property—held, that is, absolutely and exclusively like realms of valued interest belonging *in rem* to their patriarchal holders. At the same time, he was also suggesting that within the spaces of pre-modern domesticity law extended no further, leaving relations internal to the kin group's members outside its grasp. This was the basis of the analogy he drew between ancient law and the still emerging field of international law.[8] '[I]f a perhaps deceptive comparison may be employed', as he noted, both involved 'nothing as it were, except [to fill] the interstices between the great groups which are the atoms of society'.[9]

Maine drove home the same point about law's pre-modern limits even more markedly when observing that '[i]n a community so situated [as under conditions of ancient law], the legislation of assemblies and the jurisdiction of Courts reach only to the heads of families'. In going on to state that 'to every other individual the rule of conduct is *the law of his home*, of which his Parent is the legislator', Maine was indulging in a manner of speech more than he was allowing that legal normativity did, indeed,

---

[7] Alan Gledhill, 'The Compilation of Customary Law in the Punjab in the Nineteenth Century', in *La Redaction des Coutumes dans le Passe et dans le Present*, ed. John Gilissen (Brussels: University Libre de Bruxelles, 1962),131–64.

[8] In this vein, Maine focused especially on 'the size of the corporate associations [who he contrasted with natural individuals] whose rights and duties' ancient law settled and how those associations were analogous to the nation states the rights and duties of which international law settled. Maine, *Ancient Law*, 271.

[9] Ibid., 167.

breach the barrier of the domestic kin group.[10] Accordingly, he hastened to add that any such 'law' of the home would ultimately have to give way before the 'sphere of civil law' rather than come to constitute part of it. In Maine's view, then, the law of status and the civil law were generally antithetical forces, with the historical evolution of the latter being the logical undoing of the extra-legal normative order of the former. From here the further contours of his depiction of status can be inferred directly. For prior to being undone by the civil law, the immemorial era of status was one during which the members of the domestic kin group did not simply bear individualized duties for extended courses of time, as per Holland's view. Rather, it was one during which they bore complexes of responsibilities comprising totalizing social roles that had to be donned in whole cloth and that could not be disaggregated into individuated rights and duties.[11]

Of course, none of this is to say that the Maineian concept of status never converged with its doctrinal counterpart within classic legal thought. Indeed, it would have been difficult to avoid at least some overlap, given that it was not really possible for the idea of status, conceived as a totalizing social role, to function as an administrable concept. Even the canonical statuses—reflecting limitations on the legal personas of their bearers due to gender, illegitimacy, minority, sanity, and so on—could only be administered, ultimately, as some collection of individuatable rights and duties. Therefore, like those who were fully capable of actuating their juridical entitlements, those with only a more limited ability to do so had to hold what status they did on the basis of the operation of the public will and hardly in virtue of some primordial sociological necessity. In short, if the concept of status was to underpin any actually administrable claim, it could not but mean a state-recognized capacitation and this only in some appropriately delimited and disaggregated sense. Consider, for example, how Bombay High Court judge Raymond West used the concept while asserting that both the Hindu caste/*varna* divisions—of *brahmin*, *ksatriya*, *vaisya*, and

---

[10] Ibid. (emphasis added).
[11] To this end, Maine equated the expansion of the civil law with the progress of what he called 'the agents of legal change' (which he further identified as legal fictions, equity, and legislation) in removing such personal rights and property 'from the domestic forum to the cognizance of the public tribunals'. Ibid.

sudra—as well as the *ashrama* ranks—of 'householder', 'ascetic', and so on—into which members of the first three *varna*s could be divided were equally 'varieties of status'.[12] Here West was clearly not proposing these as auto-administering juridical identities cut from whole normative cloth. Rather, the 'status' of one, say, who was a 'Brahmachari' at best comprised only whatever individuated entitlement(s) it was that the colonial state sanctioned such a party to treat as actionable in the first place.[13]

For his own part, then—as when using 'the law of status' synonymously with 'the law of persons'—Maine was not invoking any altogether pre-legal normativity inhering in the individual's totalizing social role so much as he was standing in the shadow of the idea of legal capacitation. '[T]he child before years of discretion, the orphan under guardianship, [and] the adjudged lunatic', as he remarked, their 'capacities and incapacities' are all 'regulated by the Law of Persons', this being ultimately because theirs was each a type of juridical personhood 'subjected to extrinsic control'.[14] While Maine did not specify what precise source of 'extrinsic control' he had in mind here, his impulse seems to have been to try to have it both ways by distinguishing the determining force of the state's will from that of the despotic patriarch's. In joining ordinary-language and doctrinal discourse on such occasions, it would appear that Maine was navigating the quite different meaning of status in classical legal thought, which at its most narrow meant a set of rules for determining what level of legal capacitation those of 'infirm' age, gender, or mental state—that is, those who stood out most vividly as domestic dependants—could enjoy.

Against the backdrop of his equivocal approach to status, Maine's famed dichotomy about the movement of progressive societies also takes on a different complexion. In the first of the two main passages in *Ancient Law* where we find him developing the contrast between status and contract he tellingly begins as follows:

---

[12] Raymond West and Johann Georg Buhler, eds., *A Digest of the Hindu Law of Inheritance and Partition: From the Replies of the Sâstris in the Several Courts of the Bombay Presidency, with Introductions, Notes, and an Appendix*, 2nd edn. (Bombay: Printed at the Education Society's Pres, Byculla, 1878), 36–37.
[13] Ibid.
[14] Maine, *Ancient Law*, 170.

> [t]he movement of the progressive societies has been uniform in one respect. Through all its course it has been distinguished by the gradual dissolution of family dependency, and the growth of individual obligation in its place ... Nor is it difficult to see what is the tie between man and man which replaces by degrees those forms of reciprocity in rights and duties which have their origin in the Family. It is Contract. Starting, as from one terminus of history, from a condition of society in which all the relations of Persons are summed up in the relations of Family, we seem to have steadily moved towards a phase of social order in which all these relations arise from the free agreement of Individuals. In Western Europe the progress achieved in this direction has been considerable.[15]

In arriving at his explicit declaration of the contrast, Maine then goes on to explain why, on the grounds just stated in the last passage, status recommended itself as a conceptual frame in the first place. As he here noted:

> [t]he word Status may be usefully employed to construct a formula expressing the law of progress thus indicated, which, whatever be its value, seems to me to be sufficiently ascertained. All the forms of Status taken notice of in the Law of Persons were derived from, and to some extent are still coloured by, the powers and privileges anciently residing in the Family. If then we employ Status, agreeably with the usage of the best writers, to signify these personal conditions only, and avoid applying the term to such conditions as are the immediate or remote result of agreement, we may say that the movement of the progressive societies has hitherto been a movement *from Status to Contract*.[16]

As should be apparent, by the various 'forms of Status taken notice of' Maine was here denoting the canonical incapacitations based on age, gender, and mental fitness. At the same time, he casts these as historical remnants of an earlier sociological epoch. In other words, the 'Law of Persons' is portrayed not simply as a set of rules about who had what level of juridical personhood but a normative halfway house where the social roles of old still lived on.

---

[15] Ibid., 169.
[16] Ibid., 170 (emphasis in the original).

This social evolutionist view was even more forcefully reinstated in the second of the main passages in *Ancient Law* in which Maine can be found elaborating on the status/contract distinction. Here he provides a differently accented description of the 'Law of Persons':

> [n]ine-tenths of the civil part of the law practised by civilised societies are made up of the Law of Persons, of the Law of Property and of Inheritance, and of the Law of Contract. But it is plain that all these provinces of jurisprudence must shrink within narrower boundaries, the nearer we make our approaches to the infancy of social brotherhood. The Law of Persons, which is nothing else than the Law of Status, will be restricted to the scantiest limits as long as all forms of status are merged in common subjection to Paternal Power, as long as the Wife has no rights against her Husband, the Son none against his Father, and the infant ward none against the Agnates who are his Guardians. Similarly, the rules relating to Property and Succession can never be plentiful, so long as land and goods devolve within the family, and, if distributed at all, are distributed inside its circle.[17]

Reverting more strictly to the idea of status as a form of pre-legal normativity corresponding to a mode of social organization in which supra-individual corporate kin groups were the dominant units, Maine now more vociferously silences the echoes of its doctrinal conception. Accordingly, capacitation retreats as the lynchpin for striking an equivalence between 'the Law of Persons' and 'the Law of Status'. Instead, in this passage the emphasis is on the 'Law of Persons' as a wholesale supersession of the normative order of totalistic social roles, this being why it is said to be 'nothing else than' the 'law of status' for the age of sociological modernity.

Amidst the equivocality of Maine's way of invoking status, if the doctrinal conception came only flickeringly into view its role as a stand-in for the more generalized possibility of state intervention into the space of domestic relations was even more occluded. This contrasts sharply with Holland's formulation, which made the law of status about more than just capacitation based on age, gender, and mental fitness by giving

[17] Ibid., 369.

it a broader sense as well. In the colonial subcontinent, for example, we can consider the way Punjab High Court judge and later British parliamentarian William Henry Rattigan elaborated on status' doctrinal significance. In a text on general jurisprudence he authored specifically for audiences in South Asia he thus remarks on how

> when we speak of Persons and Things as being the Objects of Rights, we are obliged to use the terms in a natural as well as in an artificial sense. In a legal sense a Person, as the subject of a Right or of a Duty, may either be a 'natural person', i.e., a living human being, whether actually born or still in *ventre sa mere*, provided he is regarded by Law as capable of Rights or Duties; or he may be an artificial or 'juristical person' upon whom the law has conferred a legal 'status', and who is thus capable of sustaining the mask of personality, having the same capacity for Rights and liability to Duties as a natural person.[18]

Rattigan's broader doctrinal conception of status altogether bypassed Maine's vision. For it involved precisely what in the earlier quoted passage Maine denies to the 'Law of Persons' in its capacity as the replacement for the 'Law of Status': namely, a role as a mechanism for the operation of the public will to enable the members of the domestic kin community to abbreviate their 'lifelong courses of conduct' and, vis-à-vis one another, to individuate any normative totalities those courses of conduct entailed into disaggregated and actionable legal entitlements.

8.4 Legal Ontologization and the Gap between the Ordinary-Language and Doctrinal Discourse of Status

While equivocal, Maine's approach to conceptualizing status was hardly inexplicable. In fact, the ambiguity it harboured was demonstrative of how the ontologization of the law depended less on any perfect consistency between ordinary-language and doctrinal discourse than it did on

---

[18] W. H. Rattigan, *The Science of Jurisprudence: Chiefly Intended for Indian Students*, 2nd edn. (London: Wildy and Sons, 1892), 30.

a nominally overlapping lexicon. In this respect, status was a notable but hardly atypical example, with the two different versions of the concept being native to two different sites of discourse. If it was only within the discursive venues of ordinary language that status proved to be contract's categorically opposite rival, in its doctrinal incarnation—whether understood in the narrower or the broader sense of capacitation—it appeared more like contract's close cousin, this being not unlike what was the case for quasi-contract. Accordingly, rather than a pointer to the distant (sociological) past, within the venues of doctrinal discourse status was a means for legitimizing the values of regulation and collectivism that were so vital to the burgeoning of the modern territorial-bureaucratic national state, in both its liberal and its colonial manifestations.

At the same time, whether in the narrower or broader sense of capacitation, status was never a very high-level doctrinal abstraction, its operative power thus being limited. The exceedingly mundane profile this gave the concept as a source of binding deduction in the context of legal reasoning contrasted sharply with the visibility it enjoyed as an abstraction within nascent sociologico-anthropological theorizing. While in the latter context status served as something of an organizing principle, in the former it played no analogous role, much less to any effect of transforming the Maineian contrast with contract into the basis for an actually administrable norm.

Clearly, this deviation between status' two different discursive incarnations during the late-colonial period was reminiscent of the gap between discourse of and discourse about property under the Company's rule. Yet there were important differences as well, for as time went by property only became more and more abstracted as a doctrinal category under the colonial state's administration of justice. Accordingly, its most noticeable contribution to the ontologization of a distinctly legal kind of normativity came via its increasingly operative character within legal reason. In contrast, status' growing importance was largely a function of the way it fitted into ordinary-language discourse's wholesale generalizations about 'the law' in the course of social-evolutionist speculation. Just because status was destined to remain something between a minimally operative abstraction and a loose categorical tag within doctrinal discourse, then, this needed not to impose any constraint on the concept's ability to lead an autonomous life in the venues of ordinary-language discourse.

Ultimately, discourse about status made its chief contribution to the law's ontologization by dint of the sheer repetition of its central concept more than by the transformation of that concept into any first principle of legal reason. Importantly, among the ways such repetition occurred was through modes of reference to status that were implicit more than explicit—as through ubiquitous talk about the cellular, village-based, and essentially pre-legal foundation of social organization in the subcontinent and the way it allegedly forestalled the emergence of a deontic culture based on individual rights. As I will turn to directly, nowhere was this more apparent than in the newly annexed Punjab, where discourse about customary law circulated to the relentlessly ontologizing effect it did even when the concept of status, itself, remained in the background and even as its use by colonial officialdom was mired in much the same equivocality as it was in Maine's writings.

8.5 The Status of the Post-Annexation Punjab

Like the other major regions of the subcontinent absorbed under direct British rule, the Punjab witnessed a process of legal change driven by the need to elaborate a basic structure of colonial administration. While annexation took place only in 1849, subsequent events followed a pattern that was similar in important ways to that which had played out earlier in the Company's Presidencies of Bengal, Madras, and Bombay—even if in a more hurried manner. Of course, there were well-known particularities that obtained in the Punjab given its status as a non-regulation territory.[19]

---

[19] From 1793 to 1834—when the English Charter Act of 1833 again restructured the legislative process in colonial South Asia—some 676 regulations were passed in Bengal. As discussed in earlier chapters, these were variously extended to much of the rest of Britain's India, and especially the northern areas of the subcontinent, as well. While the Bengal Governor General and Council had some supervisory powers over the other Presidencies, the ability to pass regulations in those areas became largely independent after an initial period when it remained unclear as to whether any body outside Bengal had such a power. In Madras this took place in 1799 when Parliament empowered the Governor and Council to issue regulations in certain areas; and in Bombay the same happened later, in 1807. Up through the time of the English Charter Act of 1833 the Madras Governor and Council passed some 251 Regulations and its counterpart in Bombay some 259. After 1833 efforts were increasingly made to unify the respective regulations issued by the three Presidencies. Throughout this period, various published accounts and commentaries on the regulations—especially of Bengal—emerged, partly in hopes of bringing about a greater synthesis. See generally A. C. Banerjee, *English Law in India* (Delhi: Abhinav Publications, 1984), 92–139.

This meant that as in the North-Western provinces, in the Punjab, too, even the fluctuating commitment to separating the executive from the judiciary that characterized the Company's early Presidencies was formally eschewed from the very outset of British rule. Instead, to preside over the province's affairs the new Governor General, the Marquis of Dalhousie, established a Board of Control that quickly came under the influence of its president, Henry Lawrence, and his brother John, one of its members. Like other non-regulation territories, the Punjab was supposed to be free from procedural requirements that might hinder the role of discretionary decision-making in the administration of justice and revenue affairs, including through an institutional structure separating these functions rather than consolidating them.[20]

8.5.1 Situating Legal and Administrative Change in the Punjab

Even so, it would be misleading to make too much of these structural features of administration in the Punjab or, for that matter, of the anti-utilitarian resurgence that supposedly undergirded them.[21] Of course, this is not to say that the so-called Punjab school of administration may not have favoured 'direct and personal rule' through 'local customary law, rather than the Bengal regulations', with 'their Sanskritic uniformities,

---

[20] At the district level of administration in non-regulation territories the labour of government fell to covenanted civil servants proper (whose equivalents in the regulation territories were known as 'Collector-Magistrates') and also uncovenanted personnel who were known as 'Deputy Commissioners' (whose own counterparts in the regulation territories were also the Collector-Magistrates). At the top level of administration there was also a difference in terminology, with a 'Chief Commissioner' rather than a 'Lieutenant-Governor'. Of course, this terminology was subject to near constant change, especially as the constitutional structure of British India continued to be revised in the years after the transfer of power to the Crown. The stark opposition that often has been supposed to exist between a rule of/by law in the regulation territories and a deference to discretion in the non-regulation territories rests in no small part on the fact that the Deputy Commissioners of the non-regulation territories had to prove themselves jacks of all trades in a way the Collector-Magistrates of the regulation territories are said not to have, given the way their functions tended to be balanced to a greater or lesser extent by some separate individual assigned as a Civil Judge proper. However, as I suggested earlier, this distinction is clearly overstated. In both the regulation and non-regulation territories the executive office of Commissioner/Collector-Magistrate always carried with it some degree of 'judicial' responsibility—for example, in the areas of handling penal sanctions and administering revenue disputes.
[21] See Stokes, *The English Utilitarians and India*, 243–86.

for the adjudication of disputes'.[22] However, it is to say that as elsewhere in the subcontinent, in the Punjab as well justifying conquest inexorably dovetailed with a process of law reform staged as a call for increasing the supposed rationality of administration through finding ostensibly more reliable rules of decision. Consequently, the province's initial classification as a non-regulation territory can tell us only so much about whether its incorporation under the Raj really created reasons for it to diverge from the path travelled by other parts of the subcontinent subject to British rule.

Indeed, the idealization of man-on-the-spot administration and the general feeling that rough and ready rule was most appropriate for a place like the Punjab, with its supposedly martial tradition and tribal organization, had to contend with a quickening pace of bureaucratization throughout British India. Notwithstanding official indifference to separating institutional powers, therefore, already soon after annexation an office of Judicial Commissioner—essentially a chief judge for the province—was set up and granted exclusive jurisdiction over a range of matters. Likewise, it did not take long for the idea that the Punjab needed greater latitude for discretion in its ruling order to become its own reason for purportedly rationalizing administration through a tried and true search for more certain rules of decision, and this happened in much the same way as had been the case in the original regulation territories. That is, if discretion demanded a wide berth and obviated the need for a formal distinction between judiciary and executive then it was all the easier to argue that within its ambit some source of constraint was necessary.

Already by 1854 a so-called 'civil code' was being circulated in the province to help guide decision-making by executive officers charged with administering justice.[23] More a practical manual than proper code, the document ushered in fervent debate about whether it had binding legal force. An at least partially definitive answer in the affirmative came

---

[22] Metcalf, *Ideologies of the Raj*, 127–28.
[23] The 'code' was primarily the work of Richard Temple and was compiled at the order of John Lawrence and Robert Montgomery. At the time, prior to eventually becoming the Punjab's Lieutenant-Governor, Temple was the Judicial Commissioner of the province. After being completed in Lahore in 1854 the so-called code was published under the title of *Abstract Principles of Law, a Manual for the use of Judicial Officers in the Punjab*. A version published in London emerged a decade later in 1865. See generally Gledhill. 'The Compilation of Customary Law in the Punjab'.

through the Indian Councils Act of 1861, which also put to rest related controversies about the Punjab Board of Control's decrees by giving them much the same status as the enactments of the ordinary legislative councils.[24] Over the next several decades the Punjab also did not prove immune to the upsurge in legislation that more generally took place after the transfer of power from Company to Crown. A year after the Government of India Act of 1858, the Raj's new Code of Civil Procedure (Act VIII of 1859) replaced the first section of the 1854 Punjab civil code and significantly fortified the independence with which justice was administered in the province. Another half-decade later, the Punjab Courts Act (XIX of 1865) explicitly refined the hierarchy of provincial judicial institutions, creating seven different levels of courts. Through Act IV of 1866, the latter process was deepened by officially transforming the highest chamber of the Judicial Commissioner into a separate provincial Chief Court and making a number of other changes that continued to increase the de facto separation of functions. Another decade later, the Punjab Courts Act (XVII of 1877) continued to restructure what was, by then, clearly a distinct provincial judiciary by bolstering the ability of litigants to appeal lower court decisions. In 1884, through Act XVIII of that year, the Secretary of State for India again overhauled the appeals process while also pruning back many of the remaining adjudicatory functions that were still in the hands of the Punjab's revenue officers.

The overall effect of these various measures was to steadily but surely make the function of the commissioner a more squarely 'executive' one that was institutionally separated from that which was carried out by the personnel who administered civil and penal justice. More specifically, as in the regulation territories, by the 1880s in the Punjab, too, jurisdiction over revenue administration had become reasonably distinct from the jurisdiction of the courts proper that were focused on administering justice. Of course, most matters concerning land relations did still fall mainly within the purview of the deputy commissioners—thus scrambling the traditional boundary between the executive and judiciary to the extent that 'property' was positioned outside of 'judicial' reach. However, even this feature of the Punjab's administrative architecture was not unique to its non-regulation character. In those provinces considered

---

[24] A legislative council was established in the Punjab only in 1898.

regulation territories it was often equally the case that the collector-magistrates of the executive held sway over land-related affairs.[25]

If it was not so much by virtue of its non-regulation classification that the Punjab differed from the major Presidency territories that had begun their colonial careers under Company domination more than a half-century earlier, this does not mean that it differed in no way at all. For the present purposes, most notable was the larger context in which the Punjab's recapitulation of earlier administrative history was playing itself out, amidst the overall shift taking place in the ontology of the legal after mid-century and especially in the wake of the transfer of power. By the time efforts at colonial state-building in the Punjab were fully in effect, the discursive regime of old, which was the focus of part II of this book, was far along the path to giving way.

As prefaced in earlier chapters, then, by the 1860s the Company's founding focus on the 'laws' factoring into the administration of justice—considered as one of the defining constitutional tasks of sovereignty as a practical endeavour—was being displaced by new discourses of and about the law. The nascent sociologico-anthropological discourse that is the focus of the present chapter, of course, is a central example, being part of a new way to talk about 'the law' corresponding to what Kaius Tuori has usefully called 'legal primitivism'.[26] Whatever appearances might have been to the contrary, in its ontologizing function the neo-traditionalizing commitment to championing custom in the Punjab was, thus, of a kind with rather than mutually exclusive with the codifying and systematizing temperament of classical legal thought, as would be consistently borne out elsewhere in high imperial Afro-Asia as well.[27]

All told, these new specificities of context meant that parallel with the emergence of a greater separation of institutional functions, in the years after annexation the ontologization of 'the law' made for a second key arc along which the legal history of the colonial Punjab unfolded. In championing a regime ostensibly based on tradition, the so-called Punjab school of administration may have liked to imagine it was erecting a

---

[25] See Rothermund, *Government, Landlord, and Peasant in India*, 45.
[26] See generally Tuori, *Lawyers and Savages*. Among those Tuori draws on, Adam Kuper deserves particular mention. See Kuper, *The Invention of Primitive Society*.
[27] See e.g. Tuori's discussion of Keith Berriedale's 1924 report on native customary law in the British Empire. Tuori, *Lawyers and Savages*, 7.

'giant dam … [to] stav[e] off the flood of case-law and book-law' that would otherwise subject 'tribal custom' to 'obliteration'.[28] However, the customary law it purported to preserve was no less novel than the 'Anglo-Hindu' and 'Anglo-Mohammedan' personal law that were its analogues in other parts of British India. All three comprised a similar taxonomic-cum-ontic subsegment of the larger norm system devoted to the governance of non-market private legal relations in their subcontinental form. Indeed, as much was made official in the Punjab Laws Act (IV) of 1872, which pitted the customary and the religious personal laws against one another as alternative bases for normatively covering similar domains of fact, while further endorsing a preference for the former over the latter in the Punjab.[29]

8.5.2 'Systematizing' Custom in the Punjab

As both cause and consequence of the shifting of the target of ontologization in the later nineteenth century, the systematization of custom made for not only a second track along which legal change in the colonial Punjab played out but also one that was independent of the first. Moreover, being common to those involved in both the administration of justice and revenue affairs, custom's valorization spanned the newly annexed province's emergent divide between judicial and executive. Indeed, it was as part of the basic endeavour of revenue settlement in the Punjab that the colonial state first ordered the compilation of a record of rights, which took shape in the form of a *wajib-ul-arz* document for each district. Meant primarily to facilitate the Deputy Commissioner in arriving at more accurate tax assessments, the *wajib-ul-arz* was initially made to include a recording of custom within its four corners as well. After the first settlement period, covering the twenty years from 1845 to 1865, came to an end and while a revised settlement was being readied,

---

[28] Charles Lewis Tupper, 'Early Institutions and Punjab Tribal Law', *The Imperial and Asiatic Quarterly Review and Oriental and Colonial Record*, 3rd Series 5, nos. 9 and 10 (January 1898): 14.

[29] The specific areas enumerated for such treatment under Section Five of the Act were succession, the special property of females, betrothal, marriage, divorce, dower, adoption, guardianship, minority, bastardy, family relations, wills, legacies, gifts, partitions, and any religious usage or institution.

officers in the Punjab began channelling their recording efforts into the creation of a separate document known as the *rivaj-i-am*. Together, these two documents—the *wajib-ul-arz* and the *rivaj-i*-am, which started to be compiled in the vernacular at the direction of Settlement Commissioner Edward Prinsep in 1873[30]—were further consolidated into a new series of *Customary Law* reports published by Lahore's Civil and Military Press from 1865 onwards.

As these efforts to compile a new customary law from information about what was ostensibly happening on the ground went forward, the two arcs along which the story of legal change in the post-annexation Punjab played out also began to intersect. Given the familiar demand that the province's courts should base their work on rules of decision that were certain, already by 1867 the copious documentation relating to custom that Prinsep's staff was producing stoked calls to extend the spirit of systematization to the output of the judiciary as well. Only a decade after the data from the *wajib-ul-arz* and *rivaj-i-am* had started to be re-presented through the *Customary Law* reports, therefore, in 1878 W. H. Rattigan, then still a prominent advocate at the bar, and Charles Boulnois, a former judge at the High Court, jointly authored a treatise-like volume meant to begin elucidating the inner logic of cases that had been adjudicated in the Punjab according to custom to that point in time.[31] By 1880, their *Notes* on how the province's courts were 'administer[ing]' the 'customary law' were updated and expanded with the publication of the first volume of Rattigan's own more comprehensive treatise, entitled *A Digest of Civil Law for the Panjab*.[32]

A year later, another prominent Punjab official, Charles Lewis Tupper, added to this growing literature with his own three-volume *Punjab*

---

[30] Tupper, 'Early Institutions and Punjab Tribal Law', 15. This instruction was made good on only to the extent made possible by the settlement officer's capability of posing questions in a way that was intelligible to the group of village notables assembled in order that the officer might enquire into their customary practices and only to the extent that the answers of the notables could further be recorded in the same medium as that in which they were given.

[31] Charles Boulnois and W. H. Rattigan, *Notes on Customary Law as Administered in the Courts of the Punjab*, 2nd edn. (Lahore: Published at the Civil and Military Gazette, 1878).

[32] William Henry Rattigan, *A Digest of Civil Law for the Punjab, Chiefly Based on the Customary Law as at Present Judicially Ascertained* (Allahabad: The University Book Agency, 1880). Rattigan edited the subsequent editions that expanded on this volume until the seventh, which witnessed his son, H. A. B. Rattigan, taking over editorial duties in 1909. Further editions up through a thirteenth continued to emerge through the mid-1950s.

Customary Law.[33] Something of a supplement to Rattigan's *Digest*, the opening volumes of Tupper's work were partly devoted to offering a documentary history of the years leading up to the triumph of custom through reprinting important records of the provincial government. With the third volume the work then turned to providing settlement officers assistance in the process of preparing 'tribal' records. As Tupper explained, the larger aim of the work was to 'serve as an outline for a Code of Tribal Custom in the form of rules made by the Local Government, should it ever be determined to frame one'.[34]

In the decades after Tupper's text was published, attention to refining what was now generally referred to as the customary law of the Punjab continued. While this peaked with the Punjab Codification of Customary Law Conference in 1915,[35] in the preceding three decades there was a steady stream of other systematizing commentary and related literature published as well. In addition to new editions of existing works like Rattigan's *Digest*, there was also the continuation of the ground-level work of the settlement officers that focused on putting out data from districts where recording was yet to be done. (By the last decade of the nineteenth century, the process was being conducted through standardized questionnaires.) At the same time, there were also prominent new synthetic works, like Sir Charles Roe's *Tribal Law in the Punjab*,[36] which was produced in tandem with Henry A. B. Rattigan, the son of W. H. Rattigan. Like his father, the younger Rattigan had served as a judge on the Punjab's Chief Court (which was later restyled as a High Court); his own expertise thus complemented Roe's experience in settlement operations. In essence, *Tribal Law in the Punjab* was a compilation of unreported decisions, mostly concerning land-related matters that were settled according to the *rivaj-i-am* records, which, as the authors tellingly put it, 'formed so

---

[33] Charles Lewis Tupper, *Punjab Customary Law* (Calcutta: Office of the Superintendent of Government Printing, 1881). Further volumes and revisions were released on an ongoing basis well into the twentieth century.

[34] Charles Lewis Tupper, *Punjab Customary Law: Volume III. Questions on Tribal and Local Custom* (Calcutta: Office of the Superintendent of Government Printing, 1881).

[35] See Government of the Punjab, *Report on the Punjab Codification of Customary Law Conference* (Lahore, 1915).

[36] Charles A. Roe and H. A. B. Rattigan, *Tribal Law in the Punjab: so far as it relates to right in ancestral land* (Lahore: Civil and Military Gazette Press, 1895).

much of the base of the "case law"' that the colonial state had to offer up to that point in time.[37]

8.6 Status in Discourse about the Customary Law in the Punjab

Given the relatively limited importance of status as a doctrinally operative category, it was the Maineian version of the concept that most clearly found fertile ground in the growing textual space that collected around the customary law's systematization in the Punjab. In Tupper's three-volume work, for example, status appeared in neither the broad nor the narrow sense of capacitation. However, the Maineian dichotomy with contract was invoked in *Punjab Customary Law* to summon the idea of the past as an age of pre-legal normativity based on the binding force of totalistic social roles.

Warning against resorting to 'political economy, considered as a science', as the preferred basis for understanding Punjabi life, Tupper cited the limits of the assumption this involved making of a 'society' of 'contract and competition' that 'has outgrown *status and custom*'. Being 'in no way applicable to the townships which form the homes of the rural population of the Punjab', he continued, political economy was necessarily blind to 'the very existence of the village community, with its strong sense of the brotherhood of the proprietary body, its hereditary weavers and sweepers, its hereditary carpenter, blacksmith, barber and priest'. For these were 'proof that status is still a living fact' in the Punjab, making it unwise for 'inferences to be drawn from the existence of untrammeled competition amongst individuals whose mutual relations depend merely on the opposition or coincidence of commercial interests, not on habit or birth'.[38]

As the last remark suggests, if it was through its ordinary linguistic meaning that status cast as long a shadow as it did over speculation about the law in the Punjab, that meaning was mobilized for more than just theorizing the past. In another example in which the concept's present

---

[37] Roe and Rattigan, *Tribal Law in the Punjab*, i (emphasis added).
[38] Tupper, *Punjab Customary Law: Vol. III*, 201.

implications were up front, while contemplating a prevalent variety of Punjabi 'agricultural mortgages' Tupper found himself pondering the 'status' of the *niawadar*, a type of middleman who would obtain management rights over lands in exchange for advancing funds known as *niawi* and gain immunity from ouster until repayment of the advance.[39] Trying to make sense of this brand of authority, he concluded that it was wrong to see the *niawadar* simply for their role within a network of credit relations. More than being a financial functionary, to be a *niawadar* was to instead bear a role as a social notable that came closer to exhausting one's very identity. Maintaining that advancing credit was not, itself, critical to holding such a status, Tupper emphasized that

> [t]he *niawadar* might be manager for the whole clan, or a branch, a section, or a single family. He would often hold a number of adjacent plots acquired from different sets of proprietors under separate agreements. In this way he would sometimes get hold of large tracts, and perhaps found a village of his own. The advance of money as *niawi* is not a necessary concomitant to the status, many *niawadars* having obtained lands without any preliminary advance; and though the word *niawa* is never now applied except to mortgages, yet the original meaning of the word is [to] grasp, actual possession of the land.[40]

At other times, commentary on contemporary affairs tended towards more of a conceptual mixing, combining the idea of status as a social role with certain elements of the doctrinal notion of a publicly willed capacitation to hold individuated rights. For example, contemplating the effects of the Punjab Tenancy Act on those who formerly held '*ta kaim-i-chah*' tenures, Tupper observed how 'numerous tenants were recorded as having rights for fixed terms in lieu of occupancy rights', thereby giving them a new 'status so settled' that is 'now generally upheld as an agreement'.[41] Here it was as though Tupper was trying to credit colonial legislative intervention with forcibly bringing society in the Punjab into the

---

[39] For more on *niawi* advances see Shadi Lal, *The Punjab Alienation of Land Act, XIII of 1900 (as Amended by Punjab Act, I of 1907), with Comments and Notes of Cases* (Lahore: Addison Press, 1907), xxvi.

[40] Tupper, *Punjab Customary Law: Vol. III*, 223.

[41] Ibid., 187.

present by instituting fixed and individuated rights, even though there was a plain inconsistency in the way he characterized '*ta kaim-i-chah*' holders as moving from a proprietary tenure in the past to a statutorily-determined 'status' in the present.

Mixing discursive registers in this way in the course of holding forth on status was not uncommon. In his settlement report on the northern area of Bannu, S. S. Thorburn deployed the concept in a similar way. Discussing the territory's southern districts, Thorburn variously touched on how 'the status of land owner and canal owner' could be 'combined' in certain villages,[42] on how certain Khatak refugees held status as 'Crown tenants' on no rent land,[43] on how vernacular categories such as '*butamar asami* and *malguzar*' were vague with respect to the status of the respective parties they designated,[44] and on how certain consequences were likely to result from being endowed by the colonial state with the 'status of the occupancy tenant'.[45]

Even apart from occasions when it was fitting to explicitly equate custom with status as the mark of the sociological past or a normativity based on totalistic social roles in the present, its synonymity with either could still be asserted implicitly. Indeed, the very enterprise of investigating and documenting the so-called customary law was a means of doing so, depending as it did on a tacit assertion about the 'traditional' deontic culture of the Punjab. Consider, for instance, how by the 1890s efforts at further investigating the province's normative landscape had shifted from looking for its customary to looking for its *tribal* law—as for Roe and Rattigan. Of more than just terminological significance, this shift involved staking out a larger position in the ongoing debates that Maine had kicked off about the origins of property, law, and society, in which an equivalence between status and a pre-modern age of custom was taken for granted. Judged against such a backdrop, as Roe explained, to highlight the move from 'customary' to 'tribal' law was a way of building on Tupper's reasons for rejecting Maine's view 'that the order of development has been the Family, the House, the Tribe'.[46] In this Maineian sequence

---

[42] Septimus Smet Thorburn, *Report on the First Regular Land Revenue Settlement of the Bannu District in the Derajat Division of the Punjab* (Lahore: Printed at the Central Jail Press, 1879), 115.
[43] Ibid., 129.
[44] Ibid., 139.
[45] Ibid., 157.
[46] Roe and Rattigan, *Tribal Law in the Punjab*, 6.

the tribe was the culmination of custom's sway over the past of status-based society, being indicative of the rise of a new kind of village-based community. As such, it carried within itself the germ of its own undoing through the territorial polity, as epochs of previous generational diffusion dispersed what were the most primitive sociological units—taking shape in the form of the ancient family—into more extended joint proprietary corporations of kin, real or imagined, headed by 'sovereign' patriarchs whose mutual interactions were—as we saw maintained earlier—like then contemporary international law, just short of being truly legal.

Roe, on the other hand, pointed to a contrary view rooted in what he called the by then 'decided opinion that the order should be reversed, and that, at least as regards proprietary right, it has been the Tribe, the House, the Family'.[47] Professing 'no doubt whatever' in the indisputability of this alternative sequence, Roe was drawing on competing strands of ethnological thought as well as the views of fellow Punjab officials like Baden-Powell and Denzil Ibbetson. They had both broken with Maine based on their encounters with the evident diversity, rather than supposed uniformity, of land-control arrangements in the subcontinent.[48] Indeed, even simply with Baden-Powell's twofold division of Indian village types—into one variety originally descending from land reclamation by a group of cultivators and another from reclamation by an individual or single family founder[49]—one could contest

[47] Ibid.
[48] Ibbetson was Revenue Secretary to the Government of India from 1894 to 1898 and then later Governor of the Central Provinces from 1900 to 1902. He played a crucial role in garnering support among colonial officialdom for the Punjab Alienation of Land Act. He also authored two prominent works on tribalism: *A Glossary of The Tribes and Castes of the Punjab and North-West Frontier Province. Based on the census report for the Punjab, 1883* (Lahore: The Superintendent of Government Printing, 1911–1919) and *Panjab Castes, being a reprint of the chapter on 'The Races, Castes, and Tribes of the People' in the Report on The Census of The Panjab published in 1883* (Lahore: Printed by the Superintendent, Government Printing, 1916).
[49] In the case of the first village type, the idea was that the assemblage of cultivators from whom the village descended lacked any original claim as a joint body to the whole estate. Therefore, they were thought never to have been in the position—in the fashion of a sovereign overlord—afterwards of being able to divide that estate among themselves on their own principles or of remaining jointly responsible for making exactions from the wealth it produced. Nor, therefore, were they thought capable of coming to hold more than what each individual respectively could inherit, purchase, or clear, with the so-called waste then being seen necessarily as a commons. In the case of the second village type, being based on an original individual or family founder, Baden-Powell saw it as enabling claims to caste privilege, with the founder being able to assert rank over those later brought on to the estate as cultivating tenants. From here the idea was that the founder's descent group could go on to maintain superior rights over common village landmarks like graveyards, tanks, cattle stands, and the like. Over time the 'tenants', on the other hand, were said to come to be seen as using these facilities only on the basis of the founding

the question of custom's centrality to the evolution of the pre-legal past without having to put the notion of status, itself, into explicit consideration, much less contest.[50]

In the end, then, even Roe and Rattigan's emphasis on *tribal* law functioned as a mode of abbreviated reference to a whole chain of complicated evolutionist assertion about how to understand the way that custom and status were intertwined in the sociological past. In this respect, as much as it was a way of disagreeing with Maine, it was also necessarily a way of giving the Maineian discourse about status greater credence through making it more ubiquitous.

8.6.1 Status and Property

Tupper embraced a similar tendency in his 'Note on some Punjab Customs Resembling Easements', in which he considered the advisability of a bill proposing to recognize common-law-style easements in the province. His answer was a clear no, with '[t]he reason why this is so' being 'plain'. For, as he explained,

> [n]o man can have an easement in his own property. No primitive tribes or strongly constituted *zamindari* villages, would ordinarily admit outsiders. What rights they enjoy, they enjoy within their own *mark*; and as that is common property easements do not and cannot exist. Even if you have irrigation rights extending over a tract of country made up of numerous villages of different tribes, the shares in water are not easements. They are a mode of joint-enjoyment, probably based on common labour and the common expenditure of capital.[51]

---

lineage's permission or, alternatively, for a fee. With a superior right in hand, the founding lineage thus was thought to have acquired a 'natural' claim to jointly retaining village land, whether cultivated or waste, for itself. If land was released from the joint control of the founder's descent group, Baden-Powell further argued, it was natural to see it as being done so only on the basis of 'rent' from a tenant. See Baden-Powell, *The Land Systems of British India*, Vol. I, 107.

[50] Maine, *Ancient Law*, 126.
[51] Charles Lewis Tupper, 'Note on some Punjab Customs Resembling Easements', reprinted as 'Appendix' in *Punjab Customary Law: Vol. III*, 245–55 at 245.

For Tupper the problem with recognizing easement-style rights in the Punjab was that it contravened the province's ostensibly traditional order of collectivism based on the movement from the tribe to the house to the family, in which 'every owner of immoveable property has an exclusive right to enjoy and dispose of the same'. Accordingly, in the Punjab, there could be 'no such conception as that of a right residing in a plot of land or in a building', as per the idea in the common-law tradition of an easement-holder's claim inhering in the dominant character of their own estate (relative to the servient character of the counterpart estate over which the easement was claimed). Rather, lacking as the Punjab was in 'individual property', '[a]ll rights were conceived as residing in persons by virtue of their descent'.[52] (Of course, if consistency was a concern, on this logic Tupper also would have probably had to explain how easement rights could have existed in England, given that there could not really be any individually 'owned' property in its soil either, save by the king as the holder of the whole realm going back, at least, to the outset of post-Norman times.)

In elaborating the above line of thought, Tupper eventually found himself wrestling with rights of way of the kind that *pattidars* in the Punjab enjoyed over the fields of their fellow 'joint' holders. Dismissing any possibility that the Punjabi *patti* might be as much a 'real' interest as any traditional so-called non-possessory common-law tenement giving its holder an appurtenant right of way across a neighbour's land in England, here Tupper simply directed attention back to status, in the Maineian sense. Any entitlement the *pattidar* enjoyed vis-à-vis other joint tenants, therefore, was inseparable from the holistic matrix of prerogatives comprising their identity as a *pattidar* in the first place. Consequently, as he explained, whatever broader rights the *pattidar* enjoyed vis-à-vis their fellow holders, these did not inhere in the 'defined area called a "*patti*"' comprising their own immediate domain. Rather, they merely had to be personal rights that the *pattidar* enjoyed as a 'a member of the brotherhood' since it must have been the case that 'when they partially divided their possessions, they had no intention of depriving the several groups of this immemorial previous enjoyment'.[53]

[52] Ibid.
[53] Ibid., 245–46.

Continuing down the same path of analysis, Tupper eventually reached the soon-to-be Lieutenant-Governor of the Punjab J. B. Lyall's settlement report for the Kangra district.[54] In particular, here he found himself stopping on Lyall's discussion of certain *ikrarnama* tenures, which were devoted to assigning control over tracts of so-called waste that were situated between their respective holders' villages and neighbouring areas.[55] Yet rather than using the example to bolster the previous assertion about the impossibility of common-law-style easements in the Punjab, Tupper was now left confronting its arbitrary character. Accordingly, when forced to consider whether 'the rights of the inhabitants of the outside village to pasture, grass, &c.' may not really be varieties of genuine 'easement' interests, his initial conclusion was that 'it is difficult to say'. After all, he provisionally explained, if '[n]o single owner of the village whose waste is referred to has any exclusive right over it', who is to say whether 'the outsiders enjoy the rights because they are a specific class, or because they own or occupy specific lands, i.e. those of their own village'.[56]

The problem only deepened when Tupper conjured the hypothetical of a 'right of the landholders of the village to cut small timber for agricultural implements in forests [that are] the property of government'. With the hypothetical again calling into question the idea that in the Punjab there could be no such thing as true easements, once more Tupper could only fall back on the Maineian concept of status. Accordingly, after granting a concession with one hand by allowing that '[p]erhaps' a right over government forest 'is' a true easement if the 'land' of the respective holders 'will benefit, and they enjoy the right as being landholders of a particular

---

[54] Lyall was Lieutenant-Governor of the Punjab from 1887 to 1892, being appointed after holding previous posts as the Secretary to the Home Department of the Government of India and Chief Commissioner of Assam. After first making his way to the subcontinent as part of the Bengal Civil Service in 1867, before holding these higher-level posts he was undersecretary in the Punjab Revenue, Agriculture and Commerce Department between 1873 and 1880. Though he ended his career in London in the Judicial and Public Department of the India Office, it was through his expertise in Arabic poetry more than his career in the civil service that he gained wider notice. See Charles E. Buckland, *Dictionary of Indian Biography* (London: Swan, Sonnenschein & Co., 1906), 257.
[55] James Broadwood Lyall, *Report of the Land Revenue Settlement of the Kangra District, Panjab, 1865–72* (Lahore: Printed at Central Jail Press, 1874).
[56] Tupper, 'Note on some Punjab Customs Resembling Easements', 247.

village', he then immediately took it away with the other. Reiterating a version of his earlier argument, Tupper thus continued,

> [but] if you deny this, and say they enjoy all such rights, not in virtue of their possessing land, but in consequence of their descent; that the right is a *warisi*—an inheritance, a part of the status with which a man is invested by his birth in a particular family—there would be much in the circumstances of the Kangra District to support such a view; and perhaps the Courts might accept it as a reason for not considering any of these rights easements.[57]

Even while this passage makes it seem that the problem Tupper was addressing derived simply from the refusal of the facts of society in the subcontinent to conform to culturally alien conceptual schemas, as we saw in the discussion of Baden-Powell and the rise of the discourse of proprietary right in chapter six, here as well at issue was just as much a problem internal to legal discourse itself.

Whether it was possible for the Punjab to play host to 'true' easements was a question that could have a determinate answer only if the two relatively distinct registers in which the law was discursively constituted could be fully reduced, one to the other. However, not only were nascent sociologico-anthropological and doctrinal discourse not reducible in such a way, but it was also readily possible for them to be at odds. Indeed, the different meanings status could take on in each of these discursive registers made for a clear case in point given how it was only in the former rather than the latter that the concept proved the antithesis of contract, not to mention, also therefore, property. As a result, by invoking status as a basis for denying that rights to so-called waste in a place like Kangra were true common-law-style easements, Tupper was restating more than he was resolving the problem he faced. For if status was conceivable along classical doctrinal lines as a publicly willed capacitation to hold individuated (proprietary) rights, appealing to the idea that rights in the Punjab were inseparable from personalized social roles was simply question-begging.

[57] Ibid.

8.7 From Discourse about Status as (Social) Role/Identity to (Ascriptive) Identity as Status

Just because concepts could have distinct and even inconsistent meanings in different registers of discourse, this did not mean they were destined for obsolescence, as if bound to be annihilated by a tension between opposing semantic forces. On the contrary, the relative autonomy of ordinary-language discourse in respect of doctrinal discourse not only encouraged multiple meanings to develop around the nominally same juridical concept but also in so doing actually facilitated legal ontologization by rendering those concepts more pervasive, and, thus, seemingly more like the foundational building blocks of the law. Indeed, if in the venues of doctrinal discourse the law's appearance as an object in its own right depended on its key concepts having ostensibly singular basic meanings—so as to reinforce the sense that they were fonts of operativeness/deductive necessity, in the public sphere and other venues of ordinary-language discourse the opposite was the case. For there, what mattered was a concept's nominal recurrence, which was enhanced not only by the existence of something more than its technical meaning alone but also by the proliferation of multiple extra-doctrinal meanings under one heading.

Status was a case in point, with it being only a short step from the concept's core extra-doctrinal meaning of a holistic normativity embedded within the very identity of the individual to identity, itself, coming to signify a kind of 'status'. In fact, the vanishing point between these two meanings was already evident in the way those like Thorburn and Tupper envisioned anything from statutory tenure to voluntarist participation in contractual relations as grounds for speaking of new statuses made possible by the law's rule under Crown Raj. Of course, the drift from the first to the second of these extra-doctrinal meanings—from status understood as social role to status understood as an ascriptive basis for inclusion in a group—was not entirely random. The underlying connection between them was that if one bore a status because it was supposedly like a quality inhering in and exhaustive of one's very identity as an individual within the kinship collective, then it was obviously possible for that quality, itself, to be regarded as a further basis for classifying those sharing in it into another socially-defined group. In this respect, there was some logical confluence between, on the one hand, bearing a status inside the sociological unit (of the kinship group) within which that status was supposed to totalistically norm one's behaviour and to the ongoing existence of which one's regimented behaviour was then supposed to be essentially functional and, on the other, being ascribed, on that status' basis, to some other group definable in terms of all similarly situated individuals within society.

At the same time, the confluence between these extra-doctrinal meanings of status was still limited. Most importantly, in the move from status as (personal) identity to (ascriptive) identity as a kind of status the concept's Maineian valence as a form of ancient law was lost. For membership within the further group to which one could be ascribed on the basis of bearing what normatively totalizing status one supposedly did within the sociologically atomic kinship unit was not, itself, contingent on bearing some normatively binding role within that ascriptive group, nor, hardly, one that was connected to any organic existence it necessarily had to have. In other words, the status on the basis of which one could be ascribed to a larger group of other similarly situated holders of that status was not functional to that group's real social existence (if it even really existed at all) in the way it was supposed to be for the kinship group. In relation to those who merely shared an analogous role within their own respective kinship communities—whether communities of nuclear familial connection, manorial allegiance, or based on whatever other link—one simply did not bear rights and duties, much less ones that were amalgamated into complexes that could never be disaggregated into individual entitlements.

Yet, as per the larger point at hand, it was because of rather than despite its various meanings that the concept of status increased in ubiquity. Indeed, the more connotative senses of 'status' there were to underwrite the concept's recurrence in public-sphere discourse, the more the subcontinent could be made out to appear as if it played host to facts of 'traditional' sociological structure of precisely the kind that required the law's rule if they were to be fully normed out of existence. It is little surprise, then, that the short step from status being like an identity to shared identification being like a status was made as easily as it was in the late-colonial public sphere. For example, in his text on general jurisprudence the elder Rattigan contrasted the way 'early writers' developed the meaning of status through the doctrinal distinction between 'Status Civilis' and 'Status Naturales' and the way 'it is now employed' so as 'to mean any aggregate of Rights and Duties which are attached to a person either as a member of the community or as one of a class'. As if to put too fine a point on the matter, he then further explained that this made status all the more contract's clear antithesis, for

> [i]nasmuch, however, as there is a tendency to bring all Rights and Duties attached to individuals as members of a class more and more under the control of those upon whose assent they come into existence, it is usual to call those Rights and Duties which are capable of being altered, terminated, or otherwise affected at the desire of the persons entitled or subject to them, 'mere matters of contract.'[58]

Exemplifying the adage that if only a hammer is available everything will look like a nail, status ultimately became more and more a conceptual implement for cataloguing the various forms of social segmentation that were seen as making the subcontinent's such a caste-, tribe- and religion-ridden society. In this respect, it was also very much a tool of the so-called ethnographic state of late-colonial times as it pursued its mission of fixing and classifying all that passed before its gaze and growing administrative reach.

In his *Musalmans and Money-lenders in the Punjab*, for instance, when Thorburn turned to providing a thumbnail ethnological survey of the western areas of the province of his titular focus, he remarked on how even within the general category of 'Musalmans'—who 'form[ed] the entire rural population'—there were

> divi[sions] into tribes and sections, each settled in its own domain and each with a recognized status, all [being] bound together by devotion to a common creed and by a contemptuous impatience against the yoke of the common enemy—the Hindu usurer.[59]

---

[58] Rattigan, *The Science of Jurisprudence*, 31 (quoting the well-known 1871 text by William Markby, *Elements of Law*. Notably, Markby's *Elements*, like Rattigan's own, was originally intended for Indian students).

[59] Thorburn, *Musalmans and Money-Lenders in the Punjab*, 6.

From here he unpacked the above line of reasoning with more specific regard to the Muslim *jats* who formed the bulk of the peasantry in the southwestern Punjab. Insisting that they 'have no distinctive ethnology of their own' because they 'failed to make good a claim to Rajput descent', he explained how such Muslim *jats* nevertheless had a common 'social and political status' as a proprietary collective. Accordingly, for Thorburn the Muslim *jats* were similar to other communities like the 'Pathans and Biluches' on the 'Cis-Indus side' and relative to whom their own importance was being 'reduced',[60] since one and all were status groups of a similar kind.

The connotative promiscuity of status as a term of ordinary-language discourse became all the more apparent when Thorburn dispensed with restricting its use to quasi-ethno-national bases for ascribing individuals to groups. So was it that he predicted that 'Bunniahs' would leave behind the occupational basis—as village accountants—for ascribing individuals within their ranks to such a group once they respectively transitioned out of moneylending and fully took on the 'status of mortgagee or proprietor'. Their doing so, he continued, was only a matter of time given the 'leveling effect of the railway now open to Peshawar and the Swat River canal flowing through Yusafzai'. For this would inevitably 'encourage the Bunniah to cast aside his timidity, and invest freely in land throughout the Peshawar valley',[61] thereby shifting the basis of any such collective identity in virtue of a new occupationally shared affiliation.

For his own part, Tupper, too, showed how easy it was to transition from status as personal identity—in the sense of a social role functional to the organic existence of a larger kinship group—to all forms of identification to a group as purportedly real sociological statuses. Like Thorburn, he too was given to holding forth on how statuses of old could give way to new forms of collective identification. In 1893's *Our Indian Protectorate*, a work devoted to examining the larger relationship between 'the British government and the Indian feudatory states',[62] he did so while considering the ebb and flow of *zamindari* identity. The latter status, he thus

---

[60] Ibid., 24.
[61] Ibid., 90.
[62] Charles Lewis Tupper, *Our Indian Protectorate: An Introduction to the Study of the Relations between the British Government and its Indian Feudatories* (London: Longmans, Green, and Co., 1893).

argued, could only be understood as originating from—among other factors—the transformation of 'Hindu *chaudaris*' into 'Muhammadan officials' once a new basis of ascription arose with the ongoing emergence of 'Muhammadan government'.[63]

Elsewhere, Tupper could be found drawing on the same elision from status as individual social role/identity to group identity as status in more subtle ways. It was key, for example, to the way he sought to address the complicated problem of reconciling Maine's view about 'progressive societies' being uniquely modern in their shift to contract with the counterpart view he also gave voice to that it was the feudal age that marked the real passage to contractual society in the West.[64] Even apart from squaring these views with one another for the purposes of determining the point at which Maine placed the true origins of contractualism, the second view remains confounding on its own terms. For even if Maine simply meant that feudalism was contractualism's first phase in the West, this is plainly in tension with its diametrically opposed defining feature of mixing property and sovereignty.[65] Rather than marking the end of a

---

[63] Ibid., 193.

[64] Alan Macfarlane, 'Some Contributions of Maine to History and Anthropology'. In *The Victorian Achievement of Sir Henry Maine*, ed. Alan Diamond, 111–42 at 129–30 (explaining that for Maine '[t]he great transformation, and the one to be explained was the emergence of private property in land. This was inextricably linked to the development of the "feu" or indivisible estate ... [T]he collapse of feudalism set the individual free to dispose of all objects on the market as his own ... Maine saw a number of threads coming together to endow feudalism with this new arrangement. Partly it was the unrestrained power of manorial lords over their own demesne land. The "emancipation of the lord ... from ... custom" suggested "a plausible conjecture that our absolute form of property is really descended from the proprietorship of the lord in the domain"' (quoting Maine, *Village-Communities in the East and West: Six Lectures Delivered at Oxford*)).

[65] A sampling of Maine's reasoning to this effect was given in his lecture on 'The Early History of Contract' in *Ancient Law*. It is worth quoting in full:

> A Fief was an organically complete brotherhood of associates whose proprietary and personal rights were inextricably blended together. It had much in common with an Indian Village Community and much in common with a Highland clan. But still it presents some phenomena which we never find in the associations which are spontaneously formed by beginners in civilisation. True archaic communities are held together not by express rules, but by sentiment ... [N]ew-comers into the brotherhood are brought within the range of this instinct by falsely pretending to share in ... blood-relationships ... But the earliest feudal communities were neither bound together by mere sentiment nor recruited by a fiction. The tie which united them was Contract, and they obtained new associates by contracting with them. The relation of the lord to the vassals had originally been settled by express engagement, and a person wishing to engraft himself on the brotherhood by *commendation* or *infatuation* came to a distinct understanding as to the conditions on which he was to be admitted. It is therefore the sphere occupied in them by Contract which principally distinguishes the feudal institutions from the unadulterated usages of primitive

status-based order (in Maine's sense of the term), then, the feudal conflation of economic and political power would seem to have been the very embodiment of it. After all, whether as between the sovereign and the manorial lord, the lord and some higher tenant, or that higher tenant and the further sub-infeudated, at each level of the feudal pyramid the parties were supposed to be joined together by holistic complexes of reciprocal rights and duties.

With Maine's own attempt at resolving this tension being fleeting, at best,[66] Tupper's solution favoured the idea that contract was born with feudalism, albeit only if of the right kind. On his view, a status order of the supposedly traditional subcontinental variety simply failed to qualify. Even more tellingly, according to Tupper, the subcontinental order's inability to usher in an age of pre-modern contract in the way that Western feudalism supposedly did was not due to its being built on a sociology of individuals inscribed within totalizing social roles but rather on its overabundance of ascriptive social groups, which made for an inherent anti-individualism. In *Our Indian Protectorate*, Tupper made this point explicitly in a chapter entitled 'Feudal Tendencies in India', where he explained the point by way of the following example:

> [o]ut of the claims, conquests, and military assignments of the Marhattas arose their loose though complex military confederacy; and, in the end, a still surviving group of territorial despotisms. In its origin the Marhatta *chauth* was a payment to obtain protection as well as exemption from pillage. And in this case the difference between East and West is striking and characteristic. In Europe, an individual, by voluntary compact, assumes a new personal status; he takes upon himself a new legal clothing of German make and Roman materials. In India, a community agrees to pay to a new master a part of that share of the

---

races. The lord had many of the characteristics of a patriarchal chieftain, but his prerogative was limited by a variety of settled customs traceable to the express conditions which had been agreed upon when the infeudation took place. Maine, *Ancient Law*, 365–66.

[66] Highlighting the voluntarily willed nature of the lord/superior and vassal/inferior's assumption of their respective status roles, Maine's solution resembled Max Weber's effort to split a similar difference through the idea of 'status contracts'. See Max Weber, *Economy and Society*, vol. II, 668–80.

crop, or its cash equivalent, which by immemorial custom had been taken by the ruler of the day.[67]

Here Tupper was not just equivocating between two meanings of status in ordinary-language discourse. He was also, in effect, asserting that the second—of social group identity as status—was a unique feature distinguishing South Asian from Western civilization in kind. The key characteristic of 'feudalism' in the subcontinent was, thus, not the way subordinates, whether voluntarily by contract or otherwise, took on status roles that reciprocally normed their behaviour vis-à-vis superiors in an agrarian order resembling an extended (even if fictive) kinship network. Rather, it was that what Max Weber might call status groups as a whole entered into normative arrangements of subordination and superordination vis-à-vis one another so as to make for an agrarian order resembling a barely contained clash of sociopolitical factions. In this respect, Tupper mobilized the ordinary-language discourse of status towards an end that its doctrinal counterpart in classical legal thought was doubly incapable of reaching, so as not only to once more proclaim but also to extend the idea that society in the subcontinent was predicated on joint rather than individual juridical personhood.[68]

8.8 The Status of the Personal Law (Part I): The Emergence of 'the Personal Law' and the Muslim and Hindu Law as its Main Subsystems

By amplifying the sense that the subcontinent was a land of factionalized collectives, the proliferation of status' plural meanings across

---

[67] Tupper, *Our Indian Protectorate*, 224.
[68] Adam Kuper has emphasized that this was already latent in Maine's ideas about the basic legal unit of ancient law being the family, which 'figure[d] especially as one of the sources of a "jural" model of social structure'. As further developed in later British anthropology by Meyer Fortes, A. R. Radcliffe-Browne, and E. E. Evans-Pritchard, according to Kuper, such a model envisioned society 'as being made up not of individuals but of right-bearing entities, persons'. Actually underlying these units might be corporations, offices, or even 'roles in a domestic structure'; regardless, the important point was that, whether actually collectivities or real natural individuals, such 'jural' persons were 'linked to each other by reciprocal rights and duties' that 'outlived individuals and lent continuity and stability to a community'. Adam Kuper, 'The Rise and Fall of Maine's Patriarchal Society'. In *The Victorian Achievement of Sir Henry Maine*, ed. Alan Diamond (New York: Cambridge University Press, 1991, 99–110) at 109.

ordinary-language discourse came full circle by the outset of the twentieth century. Indeed, as I just indicated, Tupper's comments on the 'Marhatta *chauth*' were already suggestive of the way that status conceived as group identity could be fed back into thinking about jural relations in the subcontinent more broadly. His comments, therefore, also serve to remind how the impulse to systematize custom was hardly confined in its resonance to the Punjab alone, being clearly connected to related calls elsewhere in British India to systematize so-called Anglo-Muhammadan and Anglo-Hindu law—not to mention, the explicit constitutionalization of ascriptive difference through the introduction of separate electorates (for Muslims and Hindus in 1909 and for other religious communities in 1919).[69]

Moreover, as I began to discuss earlier in the chapter, whether in the Punjab or beyond this systematizing impulse reflected a still wider push to elaborate what within classical legal thought went more generally by the name of the law of (personal) status (relations) or simply the law of domestic relations. As touched on there, we saw that on one level the law of status was simply the set of rules for determining the degree of juridical personhood or capacitation natural individuals were to be enabled to enjoy. On another level, however, it was tied up with what Janet Halley forcefully argues was the 'nineteenth century invention' of 'family law'.[70] Echoing a notion of *Familienrecht* that Pandectist jurists had articulated already in the early part of the century in Germany, the emergence of its analogue under the preferred heading of the law of domestic relations in the central domains of the common-law world during the later part of the century would have to await the rise of Austinian analytical jurisprudence and a more thoroughgoing shift away from the early-modern household to the conjugal family as the most visible unit of kinship in society. For, as Halley puts it, there was only reason for the law of domestic relations

---

[69] See e.g. Jalal, *Self and Sovereignty*, 139–86. To be more exact, in 1919 separate electorates were extended to the Sikh and Indian Christian religious communities. There was, thus, not complete overlap between those religious communities to whom the principle of separate electorates was applied and those which, at some point, were recognized as having distinct systems of personal law.

[70] Janet Halley, 'What is Family Law?: A Genealogy, Part I', *Yale Journal of Law & the Humanities* 23 (2011): 1–109 at 66. See generally, also, Janet Halley, 'What is Family Law?: A Genealogy, Part II', *Yale Journal of Law & the Humanities*, 23 (2011): 189–293 and Janet Halley and Kerry Rittich, 'Critical Directions in Comparative Family Law: Genealogies and Contemporary Studies in Family Law Exceptionalism', *The American Journal of Comparative Law* 58, no. 4 (2010): 753–75.

to become its own distinct field once the 'social order' of old—'in which cohabitation, legitimate sexual relations, reproduction, and productive labor' intermingled and reciprocally united multiple kinds of biological and economic dependents—more fully gave way to one that could be represented as the entirely non-economic counterpart of the market.[71] If the contents of the law of domestic relations in the Anglo-common-law mainstream was thus restricted mainly to rules for capacitating husbands and their wives, on the one hand, and parents and their children, on the other, it was because it was assumed to go without saying—reality notwithstanding—that non-market society in the modern West rested on one main kind of ascriptive group affiliation.

At the same time, in the late-colonial subcontinent—and, partly based on its example, also in other parts of high imperial Afro-Asia that were similarly cast as rife with segmentary division—capacitation was rendered operative in a second key way as well. This was, namely, at the higher, supra-individual level of the communal religious group, the tribe, and so on. All told, then, legal technicians under Crown rule melded the basic doctrinal meaning of status with the additional sense it was given in the discourse of the colonial public sphere so as to make the concept further stand for the publicly willed capacitation of confessional groups, in virtue of their members sharing in an ostensibly uniform overriding identity that merited them being normed according to holistic complexes (viz. 'systems') of religio-legal normativity.

As the more specific mechanism through which the ordinary-language discourse of status-as-ascriptive identity ultimately fed back into doctrinal discourse under the Raj, through this melding 'the personal law' became an equivalent in the subcontinent not only of the law of status and what in the West was left at family law/the law of domestic relations but also for what Maine was particularly fond of identifying as the law of persons. As such, it, too, was a product of the same transformation in

---

[71] Halley, 'What is Family Law?: A Genealogy, Part I', 2 (further noting that within the household of old, 'the wife, the child and the servant were not just subordinate' but subordinate all in a similar way). It goes without saying, then, that even as the modern conjugal family and the market were represented as entirely distinct, the former clearly harboured a deep 'conceptual dependency' on the idea of contract that underpinned the latter. See Halley and Rittich, 'Critical Directions in Comparative Family Law', 757.

imagination that undergirded what Halley[72] calls 'the invention of family law'.[73] That is, none of these loose terminological equivalents was any way of merely restating the distinction between *personae, res*, and *actiones* that one can trace all the way back to the second-century Roman jurist Gaius. In fact, in the central domains of the common-law world any line going back to the ancient Roman law formula had already been disrupted twice over, not only by the long passage of time (whether since Gaius or even just since the so-called rediscovery of Roman law in late medieval times) but also the sizable influence of seventeenth-century jurist William Blackstone.[74] For Blackstone had explicitly reformulated Gaius' distinction into his own foundational tripartite division between 'rights of persons', 'rights of things', and 'wrongs'—pointing under the first heading to the mixed public-private relations of the early-modern household/ *oikos* that were inclusive of the ties of both the (extended) family and also those binding masters and servants as well as guardians and wards.[75] It is little wonder, then, that the factors preventing common-law jurists from adopting the German notion of *Familienrecht* before the second half of the nineteenth century also extended to the notion of *les lois personelles*

---

[72] It is not just Halley who has made such a point. See e.g. Wolfram Müller-Freienfels, 'The Emergence of Droit De Famille and Familienrecht in Continental Europe and the Introduction of Family Law in England', *Journal of Family History* 28 (2003): 31–51 at 32–33.

[73] It is worth noting that my emphasis is intended to be on the position of the conjugal family in the imagination more than in reality. This goes some way towards levelling the clear differences in its prevalence in the subcontinent as compared to the Anglo-common-law mainstream, especially to the extent that even in the latter context it had hardly fully displaced more extended kinds of household community by the late nineteenth century. Suffice to say, historians of the late-colonial subcontinent have hardly failed to document the increasing idealization of the conjugal family. See e.g. Indrani Chatterjee, 'Introduction', in *Unfamiliar Relations: Family and History in South Asia*, ed. Indrani Chatterjee (New Brunswick, NJ: Rutgers University Press, 2004), 3–45 at 3–4 and Partha Chatterjee, 'Colonialism, Nationalism and Colonialized Women: The Contest in India', *American Ethnologist* 16, no. 4 (1989): 622–33 at 623–24. I discuss the implications of the relative size of the gap between the ideal and the reality of the conjugal family in late-nineteenth-century British India versus Britain in greater detail elsewhere. See Chaudhry, 'Rethinking the Nineteenth-Century Domestication of the Sharī'a', 857–59.

[74] Alan Watson, 'The Structure of Blackstone's Commentaries', *The Yale Law Journal* 97, no. 5 (1988): 795–821 at 808. For a competing account of Blackstone's attempt at organizing the common law—and one that Watson's own contribution is staged as, if not necessarily successful as, a direct refutation of—see Duncan Kennedy, 'The Structure of Blackstone's Commentaries', *Buffalo Law Review* 28, no. 2 (1978–79): 205–382.

[75] Halley, 'What is Family Law? A Genealogy, Part I', 8. In Blackstone's schema the rules for governing the household thus stood alongside the discourses relating to its proper management, which, as per the original meaning of our own notion of economics, continued to be tied to a knowhow about the 'proper husbanding of resources' and the 'intelligent management of their circulation'. Timothy Mitchell, *Rule of Experts: Egypt, Techno-Politics, Modernity* (Los Angeles, CA: University of California Press, 2002), 4.

that appeared in the Napoleonic Code in 1804, to say nothing of its even more direct French counterpart, *le droit famille*.[76] (Of course, even *les lois personelles* differed markedly from the late-nineteenth-century idea of 'the law of persons', given how it was generally defined in the Code by way of contrast with the notion of *matière réelle*.)[77] Ultimately, in the Anglo-common-law mainstream it was really only from the 1870s that even Blackstone's seventeenth-century 'rights of persons' truly gave way to a 'law of persons' in the classical sense, amidst the dawning of a self-styled scientific search for the residuum of private-law rules thought necessary for covering non-market relations.[78]

To the perceptive onlooker, then, it should seem more curious than it evidently has that the notion of the personal law has acquired such a purchase on our understanding of the early colonial legal encounter with the subcontinent's Hindu and Muslim communities.[79] Especially in the light of the dual nature of the Company's judiciary—divided as it was over chartered Crown courts in the major Presidency capitals and its own *mofussil* courts in the countryside—reading the history of legal change back through the lens of personalization (or what we also might call domestication)[80] leaves the impression that the colonial state produced a uniquely bifurcated rule of/by law from its very outset.[81] With so-called codification also frequently seen as having begun at the same time—when what is really meant is that certain religious texts were translated to source ostensibly certain rules of decision for resolving a select range

---

[76] Halley, 'What is Family Law? A Genealogy, Part I', 46.
[77] Ibid., 37.
[78] Ibid., 64, 72. See also Janet Halley, 'What is Family Law? A Genealogy, Part II', 206–09.
[79] See e.g. Washbrook, 'Law, State and Agrarian Society in Colonial India', Cohn, 'Law and the Colonial State in India', Mani, 'Contentious Traditions', Kunal Parker, 'Observations on the Historical Destruction of Separate Legal Regimes'. In *Religion and Personal Law in Secular India: A Call to Judgment*, ed. Gerald James Larson (Bloomington, IN: Indiana University Press, 2001), 184–99 at 184–85, Sturman, *The Government of Social Life in Colonial India*, and Eleanor Newbigin, *The Hindu Family and the Emergence of Modern India: Law, Citizenship and Community* (New York: Cambridge University Press, 2013), 4–5. See also the articles in Eleanor Newbigin, Leigh Denault, and Rohit De, eds., *Indian Economic and Social History Review: Special Issue on Personal Law, Identity Politics, and Civil Society in Colonial South Asia* 46, No. 1 (2009): 1–130, and Elizabeth Kolsky, ed., *Law & History Review, Forum: Maneuvering the Personal Law System in Colonial India* 28, No. 4 (2010): 973–1065.
[80] See generally Chaudhry, 'Rethinking the Nineteenth-Century Domestication of the Sharīʿa'.
[81] The view from bifurcation is evident both in older work (see e.g. Michael R. Anderson, 'Classifications and Coercions') and more recent (see e.g. Chandra Mallampalli, 'Escaping the Grip of Personal Law in Colonial India: Proving Custom, Negotiating Hindu-ness', *Law & History Review* 28, no. 4 (Nov. 2010): 1043–65 at 1044).

of disputes—it has become all too easy to further envision legal development as underpinning an 'ethnographic' version of the colonial state, with its impulse to classify and reify, that was perpetually in the making.

Among the problems encountered when narrating legal change in such a manner is that it obscures how more than any culturally alien obliviousness to the downside of fixing otherwise fluid native norms, it was a clear-eyed—and decidedly high nineteenth-century—will to fetishize 'the law' at play, under which the effective priority was to fashion a more truly 'legal' norm 'system' for various kinds of reasons, not the least of which was the ideological utility of doing so.[82] In turn, narrating legal change by reading its history back through the lens of personalization also obscures the deep commonality—undergirded by classical legal thought—between not only British and Indian officials but also reformist South Asian jurists in the employ of the state and their so-called revivalist neo-traditionalizing counterparts who tended to remain distant from it. For each in their own way increasingly came to see the inheritance of the native juristic past in terms of its actual or potential ability to serve as both implement and emblem for 'ruling' the nation.[83]

On closer inspection, then, it should become clear that there was no idea of the personal law as such that was necessarily at the centre of colonial law reform discourse in the years immediately after 1757. Nor was it the case that the Company's raj was founded on confining native juristic tradition to matters of 'personal status'. Neither the latter nor the former concept served as any explicit point of reference in Governor General Warren Hastings' oft-mentioned 1772 regulation mandating that '[i]n all suits regarding inheritance, marriage, caste, and other religious institutions or usages the laws of the Koran with respect to the Mahomedans and those of the Shaster with respect to the Gentoos shall invariably be

---

[82] For a recent study that draws on this idea, see e.g. Stephens, *Governing Islam*, 11, 84 (arguing, overall, against the idea that rigidification predominated over 'fluidity and dynamism'—as sustained by Muslim litigants—in practice, while also seeing 'stasis and fixity' as the system's underlying 'normative commitments'.) See also Kugle, 'Framed, Blamed and Renamed'.

[83] A similar point is made in a different connection by Stephens, *Governing Islam*, 84–85. On the division between reformers and neotraditionalists/revivalists see generally Kugle, 'Framed, Blamed, and Renamed'. For Kugle, the dichotomy maps more specifically to what he envisions as a split between 'loyalist Muslim lawyers' and 'practitioners of "traditional fiqh"'. See also Barbara D. Metcalf, *Islamic Revival in British India: Deoband, 1860–1900* (Princeton, NJ: Princeton University Press, 1982), 144–45.

adhered to'.[84] In fact, Hastings' judicial reforms did not really single out such 'laws' for some kind of exclusive confinement to the administration of any jurally distinct set of relations involving familial/domestic conjugality at all. Rather, 'all matters of contract and dealing between party and party' were placed alongside 'inheritance and succession to land rent and goods' as matters that were to be administered 'in the case of Hindus', for example, 'by their own laws'.[85]

Neither heading—whether of the personal law or (the law of) personal status—even featured prominently in the subsequent building up of the Hastings system, which began with the early project of translating Hindu and Muslim texts that was spearheaded by figures like William Jones, Nathaniel Halhed, Charles Hamilton, and John Baillie.[86] As is well-known, under the rubric of the judicial regulations of the 1770s, Hastings' system was intended to provide the early colonial state's judges access to native 'laws' through assessors drawn from the ranks of Hindu *pandits* and Muslim *maulawis*.[87] However, the discontent that very quickly emerged with the performance of the assessors meant that criticism of Hastings' system had already begun culminating by the 1820s, leading to the first significant compilations of the early colonial judiciary's previous several decades of decision-making. Although ostensibly meant to remedy the much-bemoaned lack of certainty in the rules the assessors proffered for dispute settlement, this new wave of texts still did not reflect any self-conceived effort by their respective compilers to fill in the norm content of some target domain of 'the personal law'/'the law of (personal) status'.

In contrast, by the end of the century matters had become quite different. After 1860 the personal law became an increasingly recurrent

---

[84] Under clause 23, 'Questions concerning Inheritance, Marriage, Caste' were to be 'settled agreeably to the dictates of the Koran or Shaster'—a formula later adjusted to also include all 'other religious usages, or institutions'. See Warren Hastings, 'Plan for the Administration of Justice', August 15, 1772, reprinted in Jones, *Warren Hastings in Bengal*, 324–26.

[85] This was stipulated in section 17 of Lord North's famed Regulating Act of 1781 (21 Geo. III c. 70). See Rankin, *Background to Indian Law*, 9–10.

[86] See e.g. John Baillie, *A Digest of Mohummudan Law According to the Tenets of the Twelve Imams*, 4 vols. (Calcutta: Printed at the Hon. Company's Press, 1805) and Charles Hamilton, trans. *The Hedaya or Guide: A Commentary of the Mussalman Laws* (London: T. Bensley, 1791).

[87] Macnaghten the younger's companion text to his *Principles and Precedents of Hindu Law* (Calcutta: Baptist Mission Press, 1828) was the best example as more specifically relating to the administration of Muslim laws. See his *Principles and Precedents of Moohummudan Law* (Mirzapore: Printed at the Church Mission Press, 1825).

category of concern. This, moreover, proved as true for the exponents of a more systematized version of its Anglo-Hindu incarnation[88]—like advocate general of Madras, J. D. Mayne, in his well-known *Treatise on Hindu Law and Usage*[89]—as for those of a more systematized version of its so-called Anglo-Muhammadan incarnation.[90] In Sir Roland Wilson's 1895 *Digest of Anglo-Muhammadan Law*, for example, the idea that a system of modern Muslim personal law could be seamlessly sourced from Islamic *sharī'* norms was a constant theme.[91] The same idea also saturated Aligarh intellectual and Calcutta High Court judge Syed Ameer Ali's thinking, most obviously in 1880's *The Personal Law of the Mahommedans*.[92] Common to such texts was the tendency to invest the concept (of the personal law) with a special metaphysical heft through the melding of what I earlier called the Maineian public-sphere discourse about status

---

[88] Much of this literature was geared towards highlighting the colonial state's failure to grasp the customary foundations of the Hindu law. J. H. Nelson put the critique most polemically, arguing in the late 1870s and 1880s that if Hindu law existed it was confined to Brahmans alone and should not be applied to others in Madras. See his *A View of the Hindu Law as Administered by the High Court of Judicature at Madras* (Madras: Higginbotham, 1877) and his *Prospectus of the Scientific Study of the Hindu Law* (London: C. Kegan Paul & Co., 1881). The concern with customary 'usage' was also front and centre for the figure who was among the most illustrious scholars of Hindu law in the late nineteenth century, the German Julius Jolly. See his contribution to 1896's *Grundriss der Indo-arischen Philologie und Altertumskunde* ('Encyclopedia of Indo-Aryan Research'), which was translated (in 1928) under the title *Hindu Law and Custom* (Calcutta) and his Tagore Law Lectures of 1883, published under the title of *Outlines of an History of the Hindu Law of Partition, Inheritance and Adoption* (Calcutta: Thacker, Spink and Co., 1885).

[89] John D. Mayne, *A Treatise on Hindu Law and Usage* (Madras: Higginbotham, 1878).

[90] See e.g. Almaric Rumsey, *Moohummudan Law of Inheritance and Rights and Relations Affecting it: Sunni Doctrine* (London: W. H. Allen, 1880), Roland Knyvet Wilson, *An Introduction to the Study of Anglo-Muhammadan Law* (London: W. Thacker and Co., 1894), Dinshah Fardunji Mulla, *Principles of Mahomedan Law* (Bombay: Thacker & Company, 1905), A. F. M. Abdur Rahman, *Institutes of Mussalman Law: A Treatise on Personal Law* (Calcutta: Thacker, Spink, & Co., 1907), Syed Karamat Husein, *A Treatise on Right and Duty: Their Evolution, Definition, Analysis and Classification According to the Principles of Jurisprudence Being a Portion of the Muhammadan Law of Gifts* (Allahabad: Indian Press, 1899), Abdur Rahim, *The Principles of Muhammadan Jurisprudence According to the Hanafi, Maliki, Shafi'i, and Hanbali Schools* (London: Luzac Company, 1911), A. J. Robertson, *The Principles of Mahomedan Law, with an Appendix Tracing the Growth of Personal Law* (Rangoon: Myles Standish, 1911), Faiz Badruddin Tyabji, *Principles of Muhammadan Law* (Bombay: D. B. Taraporevala Sons, 1913), and the works of Syed H. R. Abdul Majid.

[91] Sir Roland Knyvet Wilson, A *Digest of Anglo-Muhammadan Law, setting forth in the form of a code ... with full reference to ... the rules now applicable to Muhammadans* (London: W. Thacker, 1895).

[92] Ameer Ali, *The Personal Law of the Mahommedans, According to All the Schools. Together with a comparative sketch of the law of inheritance among the Sunnis and the Shiahs* (London: W. H. Allen & Co., 1880).

as ascriptive identity (here, through ascription to the confessional group) and the doctrinal idea of capacitation in classical legal thought.

Mayne's work is instructive in this regard, maintaining as it did that Hindu 'law is not merely a local law'. Instead, as Mayne explained, '[i]t becomes the personal law, and part of the *status* of every family which is governed by it. Consequently, where any such family migrates to another province, governed by another law, it carries its own law with it'. Subsequently, Mayne proceeded to elaborate on the point by way of an example:

> [f]or instance, a family migrating from a part of India where the Mitakshara or the Mithila system prevailed, to Bengal, would not come under the Bengal law from the mere fact of their having taken Bengal as their domicile. And this rule would apply as much to matters of succession to land as to their purely personal relations. In this respect it seems an exception to the usual principles, that the *lex loci* governs personal relations. The reason is, that in India there is no *lex loci*, every person being governed by the law of his personal status.[93]

Here Mayne was drawing on the key logical difference upon which the category of the personal law is often said to rest—that is, the difference between a law that travels with one's (national) identity and a territorial law that follows from one's (domiciled) situatedness. At the same time, he was also inadvertently demonstrating the limits of that distinction's cogency; for where the notion of domicile could be rendered indistinct from that of nationality—as, for example, with British personnel living in the subcontinent—it was little guide.[94] That is, in such a situation was it a latent version of the 'personal law' of the British subject relocating into the subcontinent—like the family whose migration into Bengal Mayne was charting—that travelled or a territorial law that governed that subject

---

[93] Mayne, *A Treatise on Hindu Law and Usage*, 37.
[94] See e.g. Adair Dyer, 'The Internationalization of Family Law', *University of California Davis Law Review* 30 (1996–97): 625–45 at 625–29. As Dyer explains, '[i]n practice, English domicile came closer to the European concept of nationality, since upon departing from an acquired domicile the person automatically reacquired her or his original domicile'. Ibid.: 626. It can hardly be surprising, then, that it never became conventional to describe British personnel in the subcontinent as being subject to their own 'personal law' in the way that was the case for the colonized.

in virtue of their original domicile somehow extending from the metropole into the colonial space of *British* India? In his rush to spotlight the idea of a normativity inhering in one's very ascriptive group identity Mayne was obviously not inclined to ask such a question.

Nor was Ameer Ali, whose view of the Islamic juristic past as furnishing the basis for a Muslim subsystem of the personal law rested on a similar train of thought. Thus, he too firmly inveighed against portraying the subcontinent's history as a time when any *lex loci* predominated. Upon coming to 'the personal law of the Mussulmans properly so called', Ali instead noted that it is 'the law in fact which regulates the *status* of individuals subject to the Islamic system'. Further clarifying why 'the Mussulman law generally is a personal law', Ali went on to explain that

> its incidents remain attached to the individual Moslem whatever the domicil, so long as he continues even outwardly faithful to the commonwealth of Islam … According to the Mahommedan law, therefore, a mere change of domicil, when unaccompanied by a change of system, effects no alteration in the status or legal capacity of Moslems. It will be observed that this claim to exclusive jurisdiction is not peculiar to Islam. At least, analogous principles are to be found in several Western systems of law … Under the Italian and the French law it is the same,— allegiance instead of domicil furnishing the test of civil rights.[95]

Tellingly, it was the Fourth Law Commission that most clearly articulated the idea of the personal law as a law of status—understood in the particular sense of a normativity inhering in ascriptive group identity. In its report of 1879, the Commission sought to distinguish what it saw as the evolutionary level to which the subcontinent's pre-colonial forms of juristic development had brought it from that to which it saw British law-reform efforts as challenged with delivering it. As the report stated,

> [t]he law of personal capacity lies rather collateral to, than in any relation of logical antecedence or sequence to, the other great branches of the law. We may regard the impersonated State as addressing its commands only to persons of particular conditions, as alone conceived able

[95] Ali, *The Personal Law of the Mahommedans*, 124–25.

to obey them, or to the whole body of citizens, with following clauses of exception in favour of those deemed incapable of performing the duties imposed on each man in general. *In a Code recognizing caste or the distinctions of race or birth, as stamping an immutable legal character on every subject from the first, the law of status in this sense and the legislation determining it, might properly take precedence [over] other private laws. It would define certain dominant capabilities by which the whole operation of the laws of property, family, and obligations would be pervaded and modified at every step.* But in a system accepting as a principle the possibility of indefinite changes of personal condition a different set of considerations prevail. We are not met at every turn by an enlarged capacity attending a high caste or a *deminutio capitis* caused by a low caste: capacity for rights and duties presents itself as generally uniform, subject only to particular exceptions requiring special discussion. Thus, physical imbecility due to age or sex, mental, as in the case of lunacy, and disabilities arising from a foreign nationality or domicile, give rise to qualifications for their subjects of the commands and permissions that bear on others. A special extension of personal rights, as in the case of a British-born subject, is anomalous, and, like the exemption of a Native notability from attendance in Court, is best treated perhaps only as a singular provision of the particular law which in each case gives the privilege.[96]

The insistence on the notion that the Hindu and Muslim juristic traditions comprised so many forms of the personal law—rather than simply just instances of a 'sacred' or 'religious' law—was indicative of an implicit commitment to situating them within classical legal thought's taxonomic structure as place-holders for the law of status. In virtue of the ontic claims that structure made on the world of social facts, what those juristic traditions gained in return was an affirmation of their genuine legality, as they could now more easily be seen as naturalized constituents of the

---

[96] *Report of the Fourth Law Commission, 1879*, V/26/100/12, par. 32 (emphasis added). Of course, whether an anomalous 'special exception' was really needed—or used—to explain the 'case of a British-born subject' is questionable, given the alternative suggested by Dyer (see note 94) that starts from understanding the concept of domicile, itself, in a way that would make it not unlike nationality.

private law, subject as it was to the logical necessity of having immanent within it some source of rules for covering non-market relations.

Against the backdrop of this bargain, the Fourth Law Commission's aspiration of setting out the rule content of a 'complete future Code' of the law in the subcontinent in a way that would make room for what it called the 'great divisions' on either side of the 'personal law' (and its close cousin 'family law') made perfect sense. On the one hand, these divisions included what the Commission identified as 'Public' (and 'Political') law. On the other, it included what it described as the remaining areas of the private law involving 'Absolute Rights and Duties', 'Obligations', and 'Property'—with these being, by and large, what comprised the celebrated rules of 'modern' market society outside of the subcontinent, in all its supposed evolutionist stasis.[97]

The Commmission's schema being a clear break from the past, in its report it made a point of distinguishing its proposed vision of where 'the indigenous law' was to fit from the focus of the Hastings system on the so-called laws and usages of Hindus and Muslims. Accordingly, the Commission lamented how British India's inheritance from the Company's era was even more defective than what the past had left to legal reformers in late-nineteenth-century Britain. Notwithstanding the parallel efforts taking place there to cure the common law of its own supposedly anti-systematic legacy of casuistry, the Commission maintained that the Company had created a far worse problem for the Raj by deepening the reasons there were to suspect that the subcontinent's 'indigenous law' was totally irredeemable, as if not quite genuinely legal. For this reason, in its report the Commission argued that only the 'complete future Code' it was proposing would be capable of bypassing the limitations imposed by the subcontinent's immemorial legal past, which already long ago, as it further alleged, had witnessed the 'capacity for a spontaneous development of law in the people wane[] as the facts to be regulated' in society became more complex. As the commissioners went on to explain in the report, this was because, generally

[i]n the subordinate aggregations which form towns and villages, as in those divisions of the people which compose different classes, a unity

[97] *Report of the Fourth Law Commission*, par. 39.

of feeling springing from local neighborhood, similar pursuits or identity of moral tendency still gives birth from a contact with new circumstances to usages whose fitness is recognized, and causes their reception as rules of custom. [However, i]n the wider sphere of general law the requisite developments have to be effected by scientific evolution from the earlier established principles insensibly modified by the medium in which Courts and jurists work, or by positive legislation on the part of the sovereign authority.'

Absent such an ability to 'scientific[ally] evol[ve]' the 'general law', according to the Commission, it was only natural that in the face of an increasing complexity of facts in society a 'sense of comparative imbecility in the presence of the more definite and palpable embodiment of the public force [must] deprive[] its law-creative faculty of liveliness and vigour'.[98] As if to put too fine a point on things, it added, 'this, which is true of communities in general, is in a peculiar degree true of the great community of British India', since '[t]he apposition at almost every conceivable point of all that is oldest with all that is newest in civilization has produced groupings of fact and jural necessities with which it was impossible that the indigenous law should be able to cope'. From here, the Commission concluded the above line of reasoning with a flourish, coming full circle back to the outsized mess the Company had left for it to clean up and remarking that 'the legal consciousness of a people bound in the chains of caste and tradition could not develop itself concurrently with the new physical and moral changes brought in by the masterful foreigner.'[99]

8.9 Status as an Operative/Administrable Concept versus Taxonomic Heading

Given the role of the personal law in remapping the subcontinent's juristic traditions onto the hierarchy of classical legal thought's conceptual taxonomy, it is hardly surprising that an observer like Wilson should have so

---

[98] Ibid., par. 11.
[99] Ibid., par. 12.

quickly reached the conclusion that 'the hard fact to be reckoned with is, that the so-called Muhammadan Law of British India has come to be very largely a special branch of Anglo-Indian case-law'. Similar—and similarly oxymoronic—observations were made about 'the Hindu Law' as well.[100] Taken together, they are indicative of how, as I suggested earlier, what the subcontinent's normative traditions stood to gain in being confirmed as genuinely legal, they stood to lose by being made peripheral within the ontological structure of the law writ large as it globalized. For as a way of naming the subsystem of rules for governing non-market status relations, the very purpose of the category of the personal law was to prepare the normative contents falling under its heading to be cut down to the size demanded by classical legal thought's preferred imaginary.

In this respect, it is vital to see that from the standpoint internal to the law's own logic, as its doctrinal subdomain for norming non-market 'status relations' in the subcontinent the personal law remained an arena organized around the basic element of the will. Yet with the 'Anglo-Muhammadan' and 'Anglo-Hindu' law as its main subsystems, in some ways this was even more obscured than it was otherwise liable to be, as the intervening sovereignty of the religious community functioned as an additional screen for rendering the operation of the public will opaque. At a broader constitutional level, Queen Victoria's famed proclamation of 1 November 1858 on the occasion of the transfer of power from the Company to the Crown was perfectly emblematic of this situation. On the one hand, it quietly reserved ample latitude for the public will to operate within the arena of domestic (and, more generally, private) relations—in something very much like the way Holland did—through its reference to 'the equitable demands of the state'; on the other, it was its famed avowal against 'interference with the Religious Belief or Worship of any of [its] subjects' that was most audible, imbued as it was with the righteousness of the Crown's ostensibly sacrosanct recognition of communal authority.[101]

Likewise, the heightened importance of the role that status played in facilitating legal ontologization in the subcontinent was also, in ways, destined to remain obscured. For even as the notion of the personal law

---

[100] Wilson, *A Digest of Anglo-Muhammadan Law*, v.
[101] Reprinted in V. A. Smith, *The Oxford Student's History of India* (Princeton, NJ: Clarendon Press, 1921), 367–69.

made Hindu and Muslim juristic tradition things of a kind with 'the law' under which they were increasingly being subsumed, Maineian discourse about status continuously represented them as evolutionary vestiges of the ancient past and, as such, only a poor imitation that South Asian society could offer for the genuine legal article. Moreover, as I have already argued, in its most basic meaning in ordinary-language discourse—connoting a totalizing normativity borne in virtue of the individual's role within the kinship community—status necessarily remained a dead letter in the venues of legal administration. Finally, there is also the fact that in its doctrinal meaning as a publicly willed capacitation for private legal persons to individuate their rights and duties vis-à-vis one another, the concept of status was still no more highly operative or administrable in the subcontinent than it was in classical legal thought more generally.

At the same time, it also could not but be evident that status played a role of heightened importance in precipitating legal ontologization in the subcontinent to the extent that the concept's other meaning in ordinary-language discourse—connoting ascriptive group identity—migrated back into doctrinal discourse. After all, as this chapter has sought to demonstrate, the Crown's subcontinent was exemplary in transforming 'the law of status' into more than just the bare taxonomic heading—essentially overlapping with 'the law of domestic relations'—that it was within what are conventionally seen as the main centres of classical legal thought. As relating to this or that ascriptive religious or tribal/village affiliation, categories like the Muslim, the Hindu, and the Punjabi customary law had a clearly greater deductive potency than 'the law of status' did when simply functioning as a label for referring to the private law's rules for covering non-market relations (or, as the Fourth Law Commission put it while waxing philosophical on the theme of systematizing jurisprudential abstraction, as part of a mere 'grouping' of the kind used to create an 'arrangement of laws' on the model of a 'Linnaean system' of classification[102]). To the degree that these headings seemed to logically necessitate their contents, not only were they reminiscent of individually operative concepts like contract or the right to property, but, as I suggested earlier, they also served as a way to administer their 'indigenous' rule content into genuinely real 'legal' being. Accordingly, for jurists to 'systematize'

---

[102] *Report of the Fourth Law Commission*, par. 28.

what fell under the heading of the Muslim, Hindu, or Punjabi customary law in the subcontinent was not unlike the way scientizing adjudicators overlaid the law more generally with barely concealed metaphysical trappings in purporting to norm the facts of a case according to one of its individual rules (or, equally, when faced with an incompleteness in the norm system, the way they purported to deduce an unspecified lower-level rule of decision from some already specified higher-level rule or principle).

Contrary to what is likely to be surmised based on the assumption that the so-called gap between law and society must have been wider in a place like the subcontinent than in Britain, the unique role of the personal law within the structure of the Raj's rule system actually gave it a greater potential ontic purchase, not lesser. Of course, this was a double-edged sword. For if the taxonomic subheadings of the personal law were semi-operative, thereby increasing the logical interconnectedness of the system, this made the whole arrangement more fragile overall—on account of at least two reasons.

First, as an intellectual-conceptual construct, the law by which the late-colonial state purported to rule remained subject to all the same internal contradictions and objections to claims of deductive necessity that would eventually lead classical legal thought more generally to crumble under its own weight in the wider Anglo-common-law world.[103] More uniquely, second, insofar as the various subsystems of the personal law functioned as semi-operative taxonomic place-holders for the law of (personal) status (relations) in the subcontinent, the domain of rules for covering non-market relations was shot through with a much greater potential to become embroiled in the ideological politics of identity symbols. (As controversies about a uniform civil code in today's Republic of India as well as the trials and tribulations of legal Islamization in Pakistan and, even if to a lesser extent, Bangladesh continue to attest, that embroilment has obviously been lasting.)

Within the central domains of the common-law world, in contrast, the ontology of family law/the law of domestic relations made 'the law of status' only a much more limited field on which to play out any such politics. There, moreover, at least over the long haul the struggle was mainly confined to Liberalism's standard ideological conflict over the choice

---

[103] See generally, Kennedy, 'Three Globalizations of Law and Legal Thought'.

between liberal versus conservative symbols of *political* identity, given the tension stirred by a deep conceptual structure within doctrinal discourse that, contrary to political philosophical discourse's preferred way of dichotomizing civic life, clearly assigned the *public* will a standing place within the most intimate of *private* relations. Under the Raj, however, the law of (personal) status instead became a standing arena for symbolic struggle over all-India Muslim and Hindu *sectarian/'communal'* identity, as it was made into a proving ground for such communities to demonstrate how truly legal their respective juristic traditions were (and, hence, how truly 'modern' their respective 'religions' were).

It is not by accident, then, that the law of (personal) status (relations) should have become as contentious or simply as overloaded with symbolism and importance as it did. Being cast as instruments less for the free play of the will of the state than for 'Hinduism' and 'Islam' to assert their respective sovereignty, the subsystems of the personal law were ventriloquized by social actors in a way that mapped the general maldistribution of power in society. Indeed, this meant that arguments based on the notion of private will that usually seemed more at home inside the law of the market in the world of classical legal thought had a way of diffusing across doctrinal space's porous discursive boundaries in unpredictable ways in the late-colonial subcontinent.

Looking ahead to the next and final chapter, for example, it was no coincidence that twice within six years the esteemed Tagore Law Lectures focused on the more specific rule regime for governing marriage and the status therein of Hindu and Muslim wives relative to the private will of their husbands. In 1878 Gooroodass Banerjee went a long way toward recapitulating the whole of the 'Hindu law of marriage and *stridhan*' as a law of the dependent wife's status,[104] with the oft-expressed additional belief in Hindu marriage's fundamentally 'sacramental' nature further functioning to put men's power over women ostensibly beyond the will of the state. Likewise, six years later, in his own Tagore Law Lectures, so too did Ameer Ali discuss a woman's role within the 'status of marriage' in Islam

---

[104] Banerjee spoke interchangeably of the woman's role as wife and her having the status of wife. At the same time, even outside the law concerning a female spouse's status the law relating to her separate property was, itself, portrayed as 'depending' both on 'the nature of the property' and the 'status' she acquired 'in relation to marriage'. Gooroodass Banerjee, *The Hindu Law of Marriage and Stridhan* (Madras: Higginbotham & Co., 1879), 323.

at length,[105] insisting that the 'Mussulman law' vests an 'absolute and unlimited' power in the father to 'impos[e]' his will in such matters on his daughters.[106]

In both cases, of course, the politics of patriarchal assertion that was being played out is difficult to miss. At the same time, with all the surplus importance of the personal law as a field of ideological contest in the subcontinent, to propose to cognize the jural character of the marital relation was, of necessity, also to court complex strains of ontologizing assertion. Completing the book's reckoning with this ontologizing fetishization of the new ideal of the law writ large, by completing its picture of the emergence of a classical imaginary of the private law as that ideal's core, writ smaller, in chapter nine I thus turn directly to these twin aspects of contest that suffused the doctrinal discourse of domestic relations by looking more carefully at one specific area of controversy within its rules on marriage.

---

[105] Ali adopts this terminology in both volumes of his *Mahommedan Law*. The first volume of this work, based on lectures given in 1884, appeared under the full title of *The Law Relating to Gifts, Trusts, and Testamentary Dispositions among the Mahommedans: According to the Hanafi, Maliki, Shâfeï, and Shiah Schools* (Calcutta: Thacker, Spink, and Co. 1885). The second volume appeared under the title of *Mahommedan Law: The Law Relating to Succession and Status* (Calcutta: Thacker, Spink, and Co., 1885). The topic of 'The Status of Marriage' was also covered in the sixth chapter of Ali's *The Personal Law of the Mahommedans*.

[106] Ibid., 181.

9
The Restitution of Conjugal Rights and the Nature of Marriage

Constituting the Subsystems of the (Religious) Personal Law as a Law of Status

9.1 Introduction

In the second half of the nineteenth century in Britain's India, an uncertainty surrounding whether the marital relation between husbands and wives was to be viewed as one of status or contract played out within the subsystems of the personal law through cases concerning the restitution of conjugal rights. While rendered most visible in the famed *Rukhmabai* dispute of 1886, which involved a suit by a Hindu husband for the return of a wife whom he had wed as a minor, the doctrine was four decades in the making by that point in time. In the interim, the commitment to juridically redirecting restitution doctrine to the end of enforcing the ideal of the conjugal family had matured through a long period of judicial grappling with marital disputes between members not only of the subcontinent's Hindu communities, but its Muslim and Parsi ones as well.

In this chapter, I focus on the evolution of the case law on conjugal restitution from its origins in the mid-nineteenth century in Bombay to the early twentieth century, by which time suits under the doctrine were being tried across British India. Before doing so, however, I start with the larger legal and discursive context in which the doctrine of conjugal restitution was set as part of the non-market component of the private law in classical legal thought. Accordingly, in the next section I commence with an extended caveat on the significance of the norm of the conjugal family in a setting like the late-colonial subcontinent's before turning to elaborate on some of the points made in the final sections of the previous chapter. More specifically, in section three of the present chapter I return to the issue of how the newly emergent category of 'the personal law' functioned as a peculiarly colonial place-holder for the general taxonomic heading of 'the law of status' in classical legal thought. As suggested by the fact that under the Raj the category of the personal law was itself intermediated by the additional place-holders of the 'the Hindu law' and 'the Muslim law', the doctrinal discourse of status became an especially contentious site on which conflicts about ideology and communitarian identity played out. In short, during the late nineteenth and early twentieth centuries, in the subcontinent the law of status relations functioned as a much more visible arena for doing battle about the politics of identity symbols than it was in the central domains of the Anglo-common-law mainstream. Of particular importance in this regard was the way South Asian litigants enlisted the law of status to demonstrate the modernity of their respective religious traditions by trying to prove that they, too, were every bit as 'legal' as was the 'private law' core of 'the law' writ large.

Therefore, remaining true to the method for a historical ontological approach to jurisprudence outlined in part I and in the wake of the last chapter's focus on discourse about (the law of) status, in the main body of the present chapter I resume focus on the venues of doctrinal discourse. The lion's share of the chapter is devoted to the more than half-century of case law through which the doctrine of conjugal restitution developed. In particular, I highlight the growing prominence that the contractual theory of marriage took on within the law of conjugal restitution, and, by extension, the law of status relations more generally. As I argue, this contractual theory of marriage formed the common basis on which conjugal restitution doctrine rested, whether in the context of suits between Parsi, Muslim, or Hindu spouses. The doctrine's underlying rationale thus remained constant even as its instrumental function shifted, having originated as a means for wives to assert power over their estranged husbands only to become the opposite, as men increasingly sought control over women through bringing suits for the restitution of their own conjugal rights. Interestingly, this shared basis of conjugal restitution doctrine in the idea of marriage-as-contract persisted even when public-sphere discourse about marriage began to emphasize its 'sacramental' nature, a view that became especially recurrent as part of received wisdom on Hindu law.

One important lesson worth highlighting up front that reimpresses itself through closely scrutinizing the case law surrounding conjugal restitution is about the porous boundary between the different subdomains of the law. Accordingly, my overarching aim in this final chapter is to show how even a single and relatively arcane area of doctrine could become a highly localized discursive site for constituting 'the law' writ large, as an object in its own right (to once again borrow Hacking's borrowing from Foucault). At the same time, as I also mean to show, in contrast to the Indian Contract Act of 1872 conjugal restitution doctrine made for a more uniquely colonial site of classical legal thought's rise in the subcontinent. This is because its evolution did not simply reflect the unfolding process by which legal globalization was carving out a place within doctrinal space for the law of status relations or, as it came to be called in the late-colonial subcontinent, the personal law. On the contrary, the development of conjugal restitution doctrine also reflected tendencies that were peculiar to the Indian form that the law of status took under the Crown's raj.

9.2 The Conjugal Family in Late-Colonial South Asia

To whatever extent the transition from the household to the (conjugal) family was incomplete in the Anglo-common-law mainstream when the law of domestic relations began emerging, it was that much more likely to have been so in a less juridified context like British India's.[1] Even so, as Indrani Chatterjee has observed, since the late 1970s historians of South Asia have found ample grounds for investigating the 'ideological deployment of the family' during the colonial era. Focusing on Bengali Hindu milieus, for example, some like Partha Chatterjee have argued that nationalists envisioned the family as 'the last unconquered space under colonialism',[2] an inner 'spiritual' realm for asserting a sovereignty otherwise

---

[1] It is Durkheim who was the most visible early figure highlighting—albeit on evolutionist grounds—the emergence of the 'conjugal family'. See Emile Durkheim, 'The Conjugal Family', reprinted in *Emile Durkheim on Institutional Analysis*, ed. Mark Traugott (Chicago, IL: University of Chicago Press, 1978), 229.

[2] Chatterjee, 'Introduction', in *Unfamiliar Relations*, 3–4.

denied over the 'outer' realm of polity and economy.[3] Others, like Tanika Sarkar, have argued in contrary fashion that the ideal of domesticity was reimagined as 'an enterprise to be administered, an army to be led, a state to be governed'.[4]

Of course, even aside from such differences in how to construe the contours of the imagined family, the transposition of Halley's narrative of the invention of family law onto the Indian context must also contend with the well-known fact that the Hindu family was legally considered a 'joint' or 'undivided' coparcenary.[5] Yet even so, there remains ample reason why the colonial context must not be seen as more exceptional than it actually was. First, whatever the precise ideological valence of the 'imagined family', as in late Victorian Britain, in British India during late-colonial times as well there was an increasing insistence on conjugality as an ideal. Whether in the emergence of a 'new patriarchy' among middle-class Bengalis,[6] the tendency within the latter community to accuse Western marriage of being 'loveless' compared to the Hindu version,[7] the ethic favouring the transformation from matrilineal kinship and hypergamous sexual practices to 'proper' marital unions among *nair* caste reformers on the Malabar coast,[8] or the drive to discipline 'concubinage' as an illicit institution in Tamil country,[9] the 'simple conjugal family of nationalist male aspiration' was a 'site of desire' throughout British India during the final decades of the nineteenth century, even if—as in the West—not any fully 'accomplished fact'.[10] Therefore, no more than the Muslim family

---

[3] Partha Chatterjee, 'Colonialism, Nationalism and Colonialized Women', 623–24.

[4] Chatterjee, 'Introduction', in *Unfamiliar Relations*, 4 (quoting Tanika Sarkar, *Hindu Wife, Hindu Nation: Community, Religion, and Cultural Transformation* (New Delhi: Permanent Black, 2001), 197). For a different critique of Partha Chatterjee's inner/outer distinction see Himani Bannerji, 'Pygmalion Nation: Towards a Critique of Subaltern Studies and the "Resolution of the Women's Question"'. In *Of Property and Propriety: The Role of Gender and Class in Imperialism and Nationalism*, eds. Himani Bannerji, Shahrzad Mojab, and Judith Whitehead (Toronto: University of Toronto Press, 2001), 34–84.

[5] See generally Sturman, *The Government of Social Life in Colonial India*. On the post-colonial complications surrounding the 'jointness' of the Hindu family, its 'undivided' nature, and its identity as a 'coparcenary' see generally Newbigin, *The Hindu Family and the Emergence of Modern India*.

[6] Chatterjee, 'Colonialism, Nationalism and the Colonialized Women'.

[7] See Sarkar, *Hindu Wife, Hindu Nation*, ch. 2, especially at 39–45.

[8] Praveena Kodoth, 'Courting Legitimacy or Delegitimizing Custom? Sexuality, Sambandham, and Marriage Reform in Late Nineteenth-Century Malabar', *Modern Asian Studies* 35, no. 2 (2001): 349–84.

[9] Mytheli Sreenivas, *Wives, Widows, and Concubines: The Conjugal Family Ideal in Colonial India* (Bloomington, IN: Indiana University Press, 2008).

[10] Chatterjee, 'Introduction'. In *Unfamiliar Relations*, 17.

was its joint Hindu counterpart any exception to the growing 'heuristic' separation of the economic from the non-economic in the public-sphere imaginary of late-colonial times.[11]

Second, even purely in relation to the legal sphere, the ideal of conjugality was hardly without impact on the juridical construction of kinship, including among Hindus and, thus, notwithstanding the well-known idea of the so-called Hindu joint family. Indeed, '[f]rom the 1870s onward' it was the marital relationship of the husband and wife rather than that of either with their extended relations that became the centre of the joint family as a juridical construct.[12] To the degree that there was reason under Company rule to shy away from refashioning the Hindu family into a purely 'cultural' formation—given the way the judiciary used the notion of jointness as a means of advancing the early colonial state's extractive aims[13]—this was much less the case following the transfer of power. After the 1860s, while the role of jointness remained notionally important to Hindu 'inheritance law', the same was less and less true for its role in keeping movable assets within families so as to create more readily targeted amalgams of unmarketed wealth for servicing liability chains and debt-based interests of the kind the Company's rule depended on.[14] Even the expressly economic features of the Hindu coparcenary as a so-called household firm were being curtailed after 1870. Here we need look no further than the concerted legislative effort to quarantine 'vernacular capitalists' to the realm of the domestic by recoding the joint family as an exclusively cultural institution.[15]

Finally—and most importantly—contrary to what is usually suggested about Hindu and Muslim personal law alike, just because their norm content may have been important for inheritance and succession

---

[11] Ibid., 8.
[12] Newbigin, *The Hindu Family and the Emergence of Modern India*, 94. On the 'nuclearization' of the 'joint' family, see Leigh Denault, 'Partition and the Politics of the Joint Family in Nineteenth-century North India', *Indian Economic and Social History Review* 46, no. 1 (2009): 27–55.
[13] Washbrook, 'Law, State and Agrarian Society in Colonial India', 669. See also Sturman, *The Government of Social Life*, which, while accented differently, is largely in line with Washbrook's view on this matter and others about the law's political economic imperatives.
[14] Washbrook, 'Law, State and Agrarian Society in Colonial India', 670–73, 698, 712 and Sturman, *The Government of Social Life*, ch. 3, especially at 113–35.
[15] See generally Birla, *Stages of Capital*.

matters this, itself, does not sum to any attempted prying apart of the economic from the non-economic or even the private from the public. Indeed, echoing a point made in the previous chapter and as I discuss further in the next section, it is misleading to portray the early appeal to Islamic and Hindu juristic tradition for the purposes of the Company's administration of justice as tantamount to the advent of a system based on 'personal' versus 'public' law already from 1772. That after 1860 the principle of 'jointness' may have remained salient—even if diminishingly so—to questions about succession within the Hindu family does not make the Raj's legal regime any exception to the generalized decline of the household as a juridical construct. In the subcontinent, no more than in eighteenth- or nineteenth-century Britain was it a need to norm questions about the intergenerational transfer of wealth that coded jural relations within the kin group as more or less 'œconomic' in character. Rather, what made family law an instrument of the ostensibly non-economic was the preoccupation in classical legal thought with deciphering those rules that were to govern the two key relations mentioned in the previous chapter: between parent and child, on the one hand, and husband and wife, on the other. It was for this reason that the notion of the 'law of domestic relations' in the Anglo-common-law mainstream excluded all but the rules for governing these two key sets of—inter-spousal and filial—ties.

9.3 The Status of the Personal Law (Part II): Anglo-Muslim and Anglo-Hindu Law as Place-Holders for the Law of Status

The development of the law of conjugal restitution in the second half of the nineteenth century can be understood only against the backdrop of the ongoing evolution of Hastings' original plan for administering disputes involving religion, caste, inheritance, and several other matters according to the laws of the 'Koran', 'the Shaster', and additional native usages. The most noticeable aspect of this evolution involved the ever-stricter isolation of these laws from the earlier living intellectual traditions of which they were a part. Of course, the definitive step in this direction after the transfer of power from Company to Crown came in 1864 when the Raj terminated the Hindu *pandits* and Muslim *qazis*, whose institutional role under British rule stretched back to Hastings' retention of such individuals after 1773 to act as legal assessors charged with expounding the rules of decision that the colonial courts were supposed to administer. In the wake of the abolition of the assessors, the normativity of native laws would rest only on the institutional memory and records of the colonial administration of justice itself. At the same time, with the general upsurge in 'codifying' legislation from 1860 to 1890 there also came a renewed effort to curtail the subject-matter jurisdiction of ostensibly Hindu and Islamic rules of decision and to situate those that remained applicable upon new footings of statutory authority.

While these developments intensified what scholars of South Asia have typically seen as the 'domestication' or 'privatization' of the normative contents of religious tradition, there was more to the process than just this. If the so-called laws of the subcontinent's sacred traditions were being further beaten back in the second half of the nineteenth century, it is only an incomplete picture we get by imagining that they were being deprived of a fuller sway over an otherwise clearly delimited space within doctrinal discourse, much less one that they had always previously been sovereign over, whether as dating to the origins of the Company's administration or to the more remote pre-colonial past.

As I began to discuss at the end of the last chapter, the late-nineteenth-century reconstitution of Hindu and Islamic juristic tradition as a law of status did not simply involve their further circumscription to a single sector within some pre-eternal doctrinal field they once ranged more freely over. Rather, the emergence of (Anglo-)Hindu and (Anglo-)Muslim law as doctrinal subsystems of the personal law came only in tandem with the emergence in Britain's India of classical legal thought's overall object. Seen in such a manner, the Hindu and Muslim personal law came into being under Crown Raj as a periphery within the classical private law. They occupied a place that classical legal thinkers had only fully carved out within doctrinal discursive space during the latter half of the nineteenth century, as they molded the law of status relations into the non-commercial complement of the law of the market.

9.3.1 Marriage as a Status or a Contract? Situating Conjugal Restitution within the Law of Domestic Relations

If the previous observation can be borne out anywhere, it is within the venues of day-to-day colonial legal administration. For it was in actual disputes between kith and kin that the rhetorical politics of communitarian identity symbols that attached to the field of personal law was distilled and refined into more discrete and manipulable form. Only in such venues were ideological inclinations fully commingled with operative doctrinal concepts as well as the arguments through which those concepts were set in motion by litigants/their representatives and adjudicators alike. In these settings, moreover, conflict was not overtly driven by attempts to shutter native tradition into an 'inner' realm of culture or patriarchy that was symbolized by the absence of the legal order of the state, as is so routinely intimated by scholars of the colonial subcontinent. On the contrary, in the venues of dispute administration whatever triumph that might be secured by the party representing patriarchal dominance also had to be translated into more precise doctrinal terms in a way that would fit the classical structure of the law of status relations.

Importantly, as the passage from Holland that I excerpted in the previous chapter indicated, there were two different forms of operative legal right that could be imagined to fall under the taxonomic heading of 'the law of status'. On the one hand, there was the right *in rem* through which he suggested the family was 'held' by the private will of its dominant member against the outside world at large, as if by unitary and absolute legal entitlement. On the other hand, there were what he called 'the rights of one member of a family against another' that were correlative with the 'corresponding duties consist[ing] often in lifelong courses of conduct' with which other family members were burdened.[16] As we saw, it was through these two varieties of legal right—more than in its capacity as a constituent of a taxonomic heading—that status held what primary significance it did in doctrinal discourse. That is, it was only through the individuation and administration of such rights (and the duties that were correlative with them) through the publicly willed capacitation of

---

[16] Holland, *The Elements of Jurisprudence*, 165 (cited in full, ch. 8 at note 4).

the members of the family to make them actionable vis-à-vis one another that status was made a legally operative element of doctrine. Conversely, it was only as part of the law of status that such rights could be confirmed in their essential legality as realms of interest (and, hence, as ostensibly real *things* like property/'proprietary' entitlements) capable of being held by the subordinate members of the family, including, in principle, in opposition to its patriarchal head.

In theory, only one of the ways in which status could be made operative involved the head of the domestic unit equating the domestic community with a realm in which Holland's first type of legal right alone was implicated. More specifically, this would involve arguing that the family was an arena in which non-market private relations transpired and over which the patriarch had a right of absolute dominion. Running counter to this was the second stance by which subordinates, in theory, might legalize status through equating the domestic community with a realm in which Holland's other type of legal right was implicated. This would involve arguing that the status community of the family made for an internally juridified arena as well, and that as such, its further legalization required the 'lifelong courses' of rights and duties upon which it was built to be individuated and rendered administrable by the public will of the state in the name of equity, fairness, communitarian reciprocity, or the like.

As may be apparent, then, if the legalization of status became complicated in the actual context of disputes between husbands and wives, it was because of the ambiguity within classical legal thought about whether marriage was to be considered a relation of status or one of contract. The complexity, in other words, came from the difficulty surrounding how to determine whether marriage involved an ongoing state of relations characterized by 'lifelong courses' of rights and duties that could be individuated only by state intervention or whether it was more like a voluntarist agreement into which spouses entered, from the start, like autonomous individuals. In principle, this complexity should have opened the way for counter-patriarchal assertion in marital disputes to appeal to the private will in addition to the interventionist public will of the state; and in point of actual fact the origins of the doctrine of conjugal restitution in the colonial subcontinent during the middle of the nineteenth century can be traced to arguments of roughly this kind. For it was on the basis of a *contractual* vision of marriage that Parsi wives were the first to make use of conjugal restitution suits to hold their estranged husbands to obligations of maintenance and alimony.

Yet as I have described in the previous section, the law of marriage in the Crown's subcontinent did not just occupy some corner of doctrinal discursive space that classical legal thought normally assigned to the law of the domestic status group/family law. As part of the subsystems of the Hindu and the Muslim personal law, in their own capacity as place-holders for the law of the family, the doctrinal discourse of marriage could not cast the relation between husband and wife as one of contract (or inversely, one of status) without coming to be invested with various other shades of ideological significance besides just those that were obviously connected to conflicting visions of gender roles. Especially important in this regard was how arguments for and against construing marriage as a contract resonated with the tumultuous late-nineteenth-century politics of communitarian identity symbols; as one of the most active sites upon which the law of marriage was being discursively constituted, therefore, conjugal restitution overflowed with tensions. It is little wonder, then, that the doctrine became a litmus test used by the subcontinent's ascriptive communities to authenticate the purported legality of their respective forms of the personal law and, by extension, the purported modernity of their normative traditions, especially in hopes of substantiating larger claims to nationhood. (As the idea went: every 'nation' had to be governed by and govern through its own 'law'; and without such a thing, it could have little real hope of proving itself a real nation in the first place.)

Keeping this inherent complexity of the law of status in mind, I turn directly to the case law surrounding conjugal restitution. In the next section of the chapter, then, I start by examining the doctrine's effective origins during the mid-point of the century and in the context of Parsi marital disputes involving wives contractually asserting rights over their husbands. In the subsequent subsection of the chapter I continue to trace the path that conjugal restitution doctrine took over the course of the next fifty years. Here, the chapter turns to the way the doctrine was increasingly taken up in disputes between Hindu, and especially, Muslim husbands and wives. In so doing, it also considers the way conjugal restitution law increasingly became a tool for male assertion, all the while with its doctrinal basis in a contractual vision of marriage remaining largely intact. Finally, I close the chapter by considering what the history of conjugal restitution doctrine reveals about the instrumental function of the law in late-colonial South Asia (and, by implication, possibly beyond as well).

9.4 Conjugal Restitution and Parsi Spouses in the *Perozeboye* Case and its Aftermath

The beginnings of the articulation of a clear doctrine of the restitution of conjugal rights in Britain's India were rooted in events that transpired just prior to the rebellion of 1857, in a dispute between a Parsi husband and his wife that reached the Privy Council in April 1856. On appeal from the High Court of Bombay, *Ardaseer Cursetjee v. Perozeboye* involved a claim by the defendant on appeal for the restitution of her conjugal rights as well as maintenance.[17] Both descending from members of the Bombay merchant community, the parties in dispute had been married in 1830. However, on account of the 'tender age' of the adolescent wife at the time, she remained in her familial home for three years until reaching puberty. After the first several years of residency with her husband and upon taking ill, Perozeboye, the wife, returned to her father's home temporarily in 1836 to recuperate. Following a second period of temporary stay by his wife in her parental home later that same year, Cursetjee, the husband, refused to allow her to return to the marital home. When Perozeboye attempted once more to do so in 1843 her estranged husband forcibly expelled her.

It was at this point in the sequence of events leading up to the Privy Council's decision in 1856 that Perozeboye made her earliest attempt to seek legal redress. She did so by filing a complaint in 1843 against Cursetjee in request of a judicial decree that he 'take back his lawful wife' and 'treat her with conjugal kindness'.[18] At this earliest stage in the litigation the main issue was whether Perozeboye's claim should be dismissed because it seemed to require that the court take ecclesiastical

---

[17] *Ardaseer Cursetjee v. Perozeboye*, (1856) 6 M. I. A. 348.
[18] Ibid., 377. A report of the 1843 case is also given in Erskine Perry, *Cases Illustrative of Oriental Life, Decided in H.M. Supreme Court at Bombay and the Application of English Law to India*, 1853 (Reprint, Asian Educational Services, 1988), 57–72.

jurisdiction over a member of the Parsi religious community when, as Cursetjee maintained, it was not authorized to do so. Though the court rejected Cursetjee's argument, little came of Justice Erskine Perry's decision for Perozeboye given her inability to pursue its enforcement. Instead, for the next seven years Perozeboye resumed full-time residence in her father's home. Meanwhile, with the parties never having divorced, during their separation Cursetjee took a second wife with whom he had several children by the early 1850s. During this period Cursetjee refused to provide material support to his first wife, and with her father's death in 1851 Perozeboye's circumstances deteriorated precipitously. It was, thus, against the backdrop of these later developments that she filed a second complaint in 1853, again for the restitution of her conjugal rights and an award of maintenance. It was this second case that proceeded all the way up the chain of appeal, reaching the Privy Council in London in 1856, after a final decision by the Bombay Supreme Court that largely endorsed Perry's 1843 decision in favour of Perozeboye.

As in the 1843 case, on the surface the most visible issue in the 1853 case concerned whether the Court had adequate jurisdiction over the wife's restitution claim. This was because Perozeboye had again staked her position on the Bombay Supreme Court's 'ecclesiastical jurisdiction' over 'British subjects' under the Bombay Charter of Justice of 1823. Also as in 1843, a decade later Cursetjee again contended that the Court could not claim such jurisdiction over members of the Parsi community. As for the lingering controversy around this question, it derived from an ongoing uncertainty about the laws and usages that should be applied to Parsis in the absence of any explicit provision of the type by which Hastings' regulations specified that Hindus and Muslims should be governed by the laws of the 'Koran and Shaster'. Therefore, before the Bombay Supreme Court the real issue was whether Parsis should be considered 'British subjects' under the provisions of the Charter that were the basis for any ecclesiastical jurisdiction the Court might claim over the parties.

While in the 1853 case the Bombay Supreme Court again found in favor of Perozeboye, the controlling decision was marked by a clash of opinions that found Chief Justice William Yardley's view opposed by Puisne Judge Charles Jackson's dissent. For Yardley's part, he endorsed Perry's ultimate conclusion in the earlier case, warning that it was only with hesitance that the court was even considering Cursetjee's arguments, which were essentially unchanged from those that already had been rejected a decade earlier. Jackson, however, was of the opposite mind, insisting that the Bombay Supreme Court could not take ecclesiastical jurisdiction over the matter, especially in order to force a non-Christian husband to take back a non-Christian wife. Moreover, as he further opined, Perozeboye had more than adequate alternative remedies she could pursue—for example, on the plea or equity side of the court to seek maintenance or to have a third party sue on her behalf for the cost of any 'necessaries' she required.

On appeal, at the Privy Council a thoroughly mixed result ensued, with the decision of the Bombay Supreme Court being upheld only in part. The Council thus did ultimately accept that the Court had ecclesiastical jurisdiction over the marriage, emphasizing that conjugal restitution was, indeed, a remedy that 'the Supreme Court on the civil side might administer' and that Perozeboye could perfectly well pursue.[19] As a result, Cursetjee's main legal argument—that the Supreme Court did not have authority over a marriage between members of the Parsi community—was effectively rejected once more. At the same time, the Council also endorsed much of Jackson's dissent—favouring Cursetjee— and its underlying views about the nature of marriage, thereby effectively discarding significant parts of Chief Justice Yardley's opinion. I clarify these clashing outcomes further directly.

* * *

The path of litigation Perozeboye set out on in 1843 followed from a previous context in which there was no clear doctrine of conjugal restitution in the colonial subcontinent. In fact, even after the Privy Council's 1856 decision the doctrine remained on a tenuous footing, staked as it was on trading the traditional ecclesiastical basis for the remedy in English law for a foundation resting on the rather vague idea that Perozeboye's suit could just as well—and even more aptly—have been taken up on the Bombay Supreme Court's civil side. Tellingly, any prior cases Yardley found to support the Supreme Court's decision once more favouring Perozeboye in 1853 were all the progeny—direct or indirect—of the earlier decision. Each one involved Parsi wives seeking to make good on

---

[19] *Ardaseer Cursetjee v. Perozeboye*, 391.

Perry's 1843 decision by pleading to be 'taken back' by their husbands and 'treat[ed] with marital affection' and 'render[ed] conjugal kindness'.[20]

As to how conjugal restitution doctrine evolved between 1843 and 1856, perhaps most notable is how in the progression from Perry's initial decision to the decisions issued by the Bombay Supreme Court and the Privy Council the question that became ever more central was how best to understand marriage as a doctrinal phenomenon. More specifically, this involved asking whether marriage should be considered more like a relationship of contract or one of status. In Perry's 1843 decision the focus was squarely on the long-term historical 'course' that was adopted by 'the Crown and Legislature of England' in establishing the authority of the Bombay Presidency's 'laws and judicial establishments'. While Perry called attention to the 'contract of marriage' or the 'marriage contracted' on several occasions, it would be a mistake to see these mentions as allusions to a classical idea of contract. Perry was not, in other words, analogizing marriage to a general form of binding agreement meant to facilitate the autonomy of the voluntarist will in establishing the boundaries of the realms of legal interest that private individuals held vis-à-vis one another.

This last point can be clarified if we consider another of the early conjugal restitution cases that Perry handled and in which his reasoning was recorded in somewhat greater detail. Also involving a Parsi wife bringing suit against her husband, *Buchaboye v. Merwangee Nasserwangee* found Perry drawing on his own decision in the 1843 *Perozeboye* case. Here once more, then, he backed the wife in the dispute, approving her request for the restoration of 'conjugal kindness' and maintenance. In an important passage from the decision, Perry explained his reasoning as follows:

[h]aving decided that the Court is open to natives for the settlement of disputes arising out of the marriage contract, and Parsis being subject to the English law generally, it follows that as a Parsi husband is liable for the debts of his wife, and absorbs her property, a Parsi wife is entitled to

---

[20] The cases are detailed in ibid., 375–76 as *Buchooboye v. Merwanjee Nasserwanjee*, which was filed in February 1844 and decided in April of 1846 (see Perry, *Cases Illustrative of Oriental Life*, 73–75); *Perozeboye v. Nanabhoy Framjee*, which was filed in February 1844 and decided in January 1846; and *Awaboye v. Nasserwanjee Merwanjee*, which was filed in November 1853.

alimony on exactly the same principles as an English wife would be if she claimed it in this Court.[21]

Perry's tangential reference here to the 'marriage contract' is telling for the way it eschews alluding to any hard and fast distinction between the formation of the marriage and the state of affairs following therefrom. Consistent with the 'English law' to which he had decided that Parsi unions should be subject in 1843, in *Buchaboye* Perry did not puzzle over whether marriage was a contract or a status. For neither in the English law of the time nor, evidently, in Perry's own reasoning was there a need to focus on doctrinally distinguishing between the voluntarist dimension of marriage as a privately willed agreement and its non-voluntarist dimension as a lifelong course of amalgamated duties and rights that could only be individuated by the publicly willed capacitation of the parties to bring suit against one another. In his reference to the 'marriage contracted' in the above passage, then, Perry was not invoking the idea of an autonomously arranged instance of private dealing through mutual assent. Instead, he was attributing assent retroactively to the fact of the party's *marrying* in much the same way that ongoing assent could be attributed to the factual state of *being married* that came afterwards. This idea of assent was not, in other words, the same as the idea of 'will' that became so central to the classical image of contract (and to the classical image of the law, both private and public, more generally).

However, traces of the way in which this earlier doctrinal concept of assent was changing were detectable in the Bombay Supreme Court's 1853 decision. While it was still generally an idea of contract in the preclassical sense that Jackson was backing in his dissent, he did so by distinguishing it from the very much classical idea of status that Yardley was invoking in his controlling opinion. Of course, to reach his own ultimate position endorsing the 1843 decision, Yardley had reimagined the line of reasoning by which Perry concluded that the duties owed to Perozeboye arose by implication from the 'marriage contracted'. Instead, Yardley justified the court's ecclesiastical jurisdiction over a marriage between Parsi spouses by arguing that it was warranted on grounds of the marital relation's being one of status, thus making state intervention therein all

---

[21] *Buchooboye v. Merwanjee Nasserwanjee* in Perry, *Cases Illustrative of Oriental Life*, 74.

the more acceptable. For this reason, as Yardley suggested, in order to allow Perozeboye to lay claim to the amalgam of rights that went with the factual state of being married it was up to the court to capacitate her to pursue them individually, maintenance being only one of the several such legal entitlements that were hers to pursue. The following passage from Yardley's opinion, which comes in the course of his reviewing Perry's support for Parsi wives in the several conjugal restitution cases from the 1840s and early 1850s he handled, is the crucial one:

> [i]t has been pointed out, too, that Sir Erskine Perry's judgment proceeds on the assumption, that unless the Court exercise an Ecclesiastical jurisdiction, natives of Bombay would have no means of enforcing the rights and obligations springing from the married state, and would be altogether without remedy; and in reply to this argument, it is suggested that the wife, in a case like the present, might sue her husband, either on the equity or plea side of the Court, and that at all events persons supplying her with necessaries might sue him. That is quite true, and it might constitute some argument against the existence of an Ecclesiastical jurisdiction in such cases, if the only 'conjugal rights' acquired by marriage by a Parsee female were a right to be maintained at the expense of her husband; but though it is true that marriage is a contract, it is something more than a contract. It is the most important of all social institutions, and under it a female acquires a *status*, rights, and privileges which would be very inadequately vindicated by an action for necessaries; and I am not aware of any authority for the position that she could enforce those rights and privileges by a suit against her husband on the equity side of the Court.[22]

Yardley's view here represents a clear contrast with Jackson's, which saw the dissent insisting that Perozeboye's proper remedy was for 'breach of contract' and not for any claim that would—in Jackson's view—allow her to force herself upon an unwilling husband.[23] Yardley, thus, disagreed that marriage should be seen primarily as a species of contract (even of whatever more pre-classical kind that Jackson generally thought

---

[22] Quoted in *Ardaseer Cursetjee v. Perozeboye*, 362–63.
[23] Ibid., 369, 372, 373.

it to be). Instead, for Yardley marriage was primarily a relation of status that followed from the ongoing state of being a husband to one's wife and vice versa.

At the same time, if Yardley's reasoning in 1853 was indicative of the transitional moment the Bombay Supreme Court found itself in, it was not only because conceptualizing marriage as a status was the inverse of conceptualizing it as a relation of contract. Rather, the transition was also signalled by the equivocal nature of Jackson's own view of contract. On the one hand, we thus find him generally eschewing Yardley's view that marriage was a relation of status by affirming something more like the *pre-classical* image of the 'marital contract' as an implied agreement that Perry set out in the 1843 decision. (Indeed, in this respect, it was Jackson who was the clearest partisan of Perry's reasoning despite its being Yardley who was the one who endorsed the ultimate decision in the 1843 case.)

On the other hand, at times we do also find Jackson lending support to something more like a *classical* image of contract—for example, insofar as he invoked the ideal of the ostensible voluntarism of the market to reach the conclusion that Perozeboye was really seeking a remedy through conjugal restitution that simply could not lie. In this connection, he started by observing that '[t]he jurisdiction to compel cohabitation seems to flow peculiarly from the Canonist's notions of indissolubility of a Christian marriage, and the obligation, under dread of spiritual censure, to perform all conjugal duties'. He then proceeded to further declare that such a remedy was 'inapplicable to natives, who are not bound by any law that I know of to live with their wives'.[24] Whereas Yardley emphasized the inequity of denying Perozeboye the remedy she sought and leaving her only with some alternative like a third-party suit for necessaries or a bare claim to maintenance on the plea side of the Court's jurisdiction, Jackson was recasting her other potential options as more consistent with a contractual vision of marriage. This, more specifically, he did through offering what might at first glance seem the unexpected argument that the eminently modern ideal of contractualism proved more consonant with marriage in the major religious traditions of the subcontinent than their counterpart Christian traditions in the West, albeit on the Raj's tried

---

[24] Ibid., 370.

and true grounds of the latter's categorical difference from the former. As he stated,

> I cannot see why [Perozeboye] should not have a right of action against her husband for damages, or a suit in equity for a maintenance. Marriage, whatever the form of the contract may be, constitutes, if not an express, at all events an implied contract between the parties that the husband shall maintain his wife. In Christian countries a breach of this contract cannot be enforced by the wife in a Civil Court directly against the husband, because the law considers a man and his wife as one person, and will not permit an action by the wife against her husband; but no such principle is known to the Mahomedan, Hindoo, or Parsee law; and the Supreme Courts at Calcutta and here have always treated native married women as *femes sole,* and indeed it is quite impossible, upon any *a priori* or natural reasoning, to treat them as anything else. There being, then, as alleged in this case, a breach of contract, the husband having refused to receive his wife, having forcibly expelled her from his house, and having failed to maintain her, what is there to prevent this Parsee *femme sole* from bringing an action against her husband for damages, or a suit in equity for a maintenance past and future, to be secured from his estate? A great wrong has been done her, and there must be some remedy. The mere fact that such an action is novel, and unknown to the English law, would be no answer to her claim, for the reasons already stated; and she seems to have just the same right to sue in respect of this breach as any other person has to sue for any other breach of contract.[25]

Even while generally seeing marriage to be only an implied agreement of whatever limited kind that Perry believed, Jackson elaborated his opposition to the court's ecclesiastical jurisdiction by arguing it would be more appropriate for Perozeboye to pursue a purely monetary remedy for contractual breach, whether for damages or through a claim for maintenance. On Jackson's view, then, the implication was that monetary recompense would better approximate something like Perozeboye's forward-looking expectation about the value of the marital bargain at the

[25] Ibid., 372–73.

time of its formation.[26] Indeed, true to the vision of contract that was still emerging in nascent classical legal thought during the 1850s, this part of Jackson's reasoning found him taking a stance in favour of what looked very much like what was soon to become the law's canonical market-price rule of expectation damages.

* * *

As if to verify the shifting nature of the doctrinal conception of marriage that was reflected in the Supreme Court's decision of 1853, as I noted earlier the Privy Council fully endorsed neither Yardley nor Jackson's view. Instead, the Council found that a suit for conjugal restitution under ecclesiastical jurisdiction could not be permitted for Parsi disputants without violating the substance of the ecclesiastical law. Consequently, it reversed Chief Judge Yardley's controlling decision. However, it also by-passed the restrictive character of Jackson's view that would have confined Perozeboye to a purely monetary remedy for breach of contract. Instead, the Privy Councillors gave the contractual view of marriage a much wider berth than had Jackson. Their view was that conjugal restitution, no less than maintenance, should be considered a remedy for a routine variety of contractual breach. The point was elaborated on in the following noteworthy passage from the decision:

> [w]e do not pretend to know what may be the duties and obligations attending upon the matrimonial union between Farsees, nor what remedies may exist for the violation of them, but we conceive that there must be some laws, or some customs having the effect of laws ... It may be that such laws and customs do not afford what we should deem, as between Christians, an adequate relief; but it must be recollected that the parties themselves could have contracted for the discharge of no other duties and obligations than such as, from time out of mind, were incident to their own caste; nor could they reasonably have expected

---

[26] Thus, Jackson noted that

> [t]here is certainly nothing impolitic or *contra bonos mores*, in her recovering damages for the wrong done her, or obtaining that maintenance, past and future, to which she is justly entitled; and I must say, I think that this lady would have a remedy directly against her husband. But even if this were not so, under the circumstances he alleged it is clear that the parties who supply her with necessaries will be entitled to recover against her husband, and this Court has already so decided. Ibid., 373.

more extensive remedies, if aggrieved, than were customarily afforded by their own usages. Such remedies we conceive that the Supreme Court on the civil side might administer, or at least remedies as nearly approaching to them as circumstances would allow.[27]

In the notion of an inability to contract for other than the duties incidental to one's own ascriptive 'caste' group we find the Councillors doing something decidedly different from Perry's wholesale elision in *Buchaboye* of any distinction between the formation of a marriage and the state of being married. On the contrary, here the Councillors were splitting the difference between Yardley's view of marriage as a status and Jackson's view of marriage as a contract through the notion of voluntarist entry into a state that entailed an attendant amalgam of rights and duties 'from time out of mind'. In grasping at the still-emerging distinction in classical legal thought between the contract-like rules of marital formation and the status-like nature of the ongoing set of relations that followed, the key idea the Councillors were missing had to do with the necessity of publicly willed capacitation for a party to such an arrangement to prove capable of individuating their package of immemorial rights and duties into separately actionable and, hence, realignable entitlements. In this respect, the Privy Council's 1856 decision was pointing the way to a conception of marriage resting on an element of the will that was simply missing from the notion of the marital contract that Perry could be found alluding to in the 1840s.

* * *

Further bearing out the last observation, one finds a rapid growth of conjugal restitution as a remedy pursued by members of the subcontinent's major religious communities following the Privy Council's decision in *Perozeboye*. With the doctrine having been transformed from an ecclesiastical remedy (drawn from English law) into an ordinary civil remedy in British India, it was the contractual conception of marriage that would ultimately prove most important. At the same time, there was a marked reversal in the identity of the plaintiffs pursuing suits for conjugal restitution during the next several decades. No longer was it mainly female

---

[27] *Ardaseer Cursetjee v. Perozeboye*, 390–91.

litigants who were invoking the doctrine against their husbands but men who were doing so to restore control over their wives.[28] Along the way, the contractual view of marriage came to be embedded within the subsystems of the personal law as a means of facilitating the autonomy of the private will of husbands so that marital bargains once made (and ostensibly assented to on the basis of mutuality by wives) should not be allowed to go unmet.

At the same time, it was not simply because conjugal restitution became a means of patriarchal assertion that the contractual view of marriage rose to prominence as the remedy's doctrinal basis. Rather, conjugal restitution doctrine also took on what importance it did because such an underpinning put the contractual entitlement that had taken over from property as the law's most characteristic form at the very centre of the personal law. In other words, if spousal relations were, at least in part, relations of contract, then there was no denying the essential legality of the subsystems of the personal law from which the normative contour of those relations derived.

As I will examine in the next section of the chapter, this undercurrent became especially prominent in the context of the Muslim personal law. Undoubtedly, here as well conjugal restitution was a means of patriarchal assertion by litigious Muslim husbands seeking control over their wives. However, it is not insignificant that the remedy also created a sub-site of doctrinal discourse that certain Muslim actors could use to constitute the Islamic juridical tradition as part of the law writ large. Of course, one must not see these different instrumental functions of the contractual

---

[28] As Padma Anagol shows, the two lines of cases that were emerging into a full-fledged doctrine of conjugal restitution by the time of *Perozeboye* were later split in two by Articles 34 and 35 of Schedule II of Act XV of 1877. These measures laid the basis for a distinction between suits for the 'restitution of conjugal rights' available to both husbands and wives and those available only to husbands for the 'recovery' of a wife who was being harboured with 'ill-intent' by some third party. It was in relation to this statutory regime that Sections 259 and 260 of the Code of Civil Procedure of 1882 further mandated the creation of regulations for executing decrees in both restitution and recovery cases and by which defendants could be imprisoned and/or their property attached as a remedy. As Anagol explains based on her own survey of some 150 cases from the mid- to the late nineteenth century, as was so in *Perozeboye*, early on women litigants had tended to 'resort[] to the first form of suit, restitution of conjugal rights, knowing full well that husbands would rather agree to a maintenance grant than give up the privilege of making polygamous arrangements'. After the early cases up through 1856 had witnessed a strong trend towards upholding the rights of wives for maintenance grants as an effective remedy for such failed marriages, the trend began reversing. See Padma Anagol, *The Emergence of Feminism In India, 1850–1920* (Burlington, VT: Ashgate, 2005), 185.

theory of marriage that conjugal restitution doctrine was built upon as mutually exclusive; they clearly were not. Rather, more to the point is that patriarchal assertion and proving the modernity of South Asian juridical tradition turned out to be complementary and, hence, mutually reinforcing aims.

9.5 Purely a Civil Contract? The Nature of Marriage among 'Muhammadans'

9.5.1 *Moonshee Buzloor Ruheem v. Shumsoonnissa Begum*

The first important conjugal restitution case involving Muslim spouses also made for the next step in the progression of the doctrine in the wake of *Perozeboye*. In *Moonshee Buzloor Ruheem v. Shumsoonnissa Begum*[29] the Privy Council consolidated four earlier conjugal restitution suits filed with the Calcutta High Court while considering the case of Shumsoonnissa Begum. A Muslim woman observing *parda*, Shumsoonnissa Begum was seeking to recover both personal and real property passed down to her from a previous marriage in 1837, which had ended with the death of her first husband and the father of her five children. Remarrying in 1847, Shumsoonnissa Begum claimed to have granted control over her property to her second husband, a Bengali zamindar named Moonshee Ruheem, only for the purposes of its management and the collection of interest income. When discord began emerging between the spouses in 1855, especially over Moonshee Ruheem's handling of his wife's inheritance, Shumsoonnissa Begum entered a petition with the magistrate of the *zilla* court alleging abuse and seeking protection from him on grounds of mistreatment. In response, the magistrate ordered that Shumsoonnissa Begum be permitted to live where she chose, though without mandating that the spouses thereby be considered legally separated or undertaking to change any other aspect of their relationship as husband and wife.

It was at this point that Shumsoonnissa Begum filed further suit (in April of 1856) at the *zilla* court for recovery of the assorted elements of her inheritance, which she alleged were valued at more than 500 thousand

---

[29] *Moonshee Buzloor Ruheem v. Shumsoonnissa Begum*, (1867) 11 M. I. A. 551.

rupees. In response, her estranged husband maintained he had purchased what his wife was claiming as hers from her outright and that it was his to do with as he pleased. However, the *zilla* court rejected Moonshee Ruheem's claim, instead decreeing that Shumsoonnissa Begum be awarded some 250 thousand rupees. Still claiming to hold an interest in what the *zilla* court recognized as belonging to Shumsoonnissa Begum, Moonshee Ruheem and an associate appealed the case to the Calcutta High Court, which affirmed the previous decision in 1862, save for some minor modifications. It was through Moonshee Ruheem's further appeal from the latter decision that the path to the Privy Council commenced.

Simultaneously with all of this, Moonshee Ruheem had initiated a separate suit before the *zilla* court for conjugal restitution, asking for a determination of his right as a Muslim husband to recover his wife's person in light of their 'marriage contract being still in force'.[30] In response, Shumsoonnissa Begum officially registered her opposition, alleging that her husband had perpetrated cruelty and abuse upon her in contravention to the dictates of Islamic norms. Here, before the *zilla* court, in Moonshee Ruheem's action a number of issues arose that would remain central points of consideration for the Privy Council on the consolidated appeal. First, there was the baseline issue of whether the original decree allowing Shumsoonnissa Begum to live where she wished precluded her husband's suit for conjugal restitution. Second, there was the issue of whether Moonshee Ruheem's alleged abuse violated the norms of Islam and whether he was guilty of 'oppression on his Wife'. Third, there was the question of whether Moonshee Ruheem could be awarded the kind of restitution he sought absent the assent of his estranged wife if he was proved guilty of cruelty and oppression. Lastly, in the event that he not be found guilty of those offences, the court asked whether it was authorized to take active possession of Shumsoonnissa Begum to return her to Moonshee Ruheem/the marital home.[31]

As for the *zilla* court's handling of these issues, in relevant part, the law officer found that a Muslim husband remained entitled to his wife's person, notwithstanding whether he was guilty of 'tyranny and oppression';[32] that Moonshee Ruheem was, in fact, guilty of cruelty and

[30] Ibid., 556.
[31] Ibid., 557.
[32] Ibid.

oppression towards his wife; and that she was in genuine danger for her life. Against this rather confounding backdrop of conclusions, the *zilla* court's ultimate ruling was that Moonshee Ruheem was not entitled to its aid in recovering actual possession over his wife's person, whether on grounds of Islamic juristic dictates or even simply those of 'natural justice'.[33] Upon Moonshee Ruheem's subsequent appeal of the decision—here once more to the Calcutta High Court—the Court arrived at its own mix of rather misaligned conclusions. On the one hand, it held that the case should be decided 'in conformity to the principles of the Mahomedan Law', which, furthermore, it saw as 'g[iving] no relief' to a wife seeking to separate from her husband without his consent. On the other hand, it opted to uphold the decree's overall directive, claiming that even notwithstanding the first conclusion the court had no choice but to refuse the forcible return of Shumsoonnissa Begum to her husband on grounds of 'equity, and good conscience'.[34]

* * *

At the Privy Council, then, multiple lines of earlier dispute converged. After addressing the long and complex procedural history of the cases to that point and disposing of the issues surrounding the disputed elements of what Shumsoonnissa Begum had inherited, the Councillors reached the 'novel and difficult questions raised by the appeal in the "Restitution suit"'.[35] Here their focus picked up closely from where matters were left in the *Perozeboye* case; the main question that was framed for consideration was, thus, whether a suit by a Muslim husband for restoring the conjugal relation would lie under the Calcutta High Court's civil jurisdiction. However, in actuality the Council's decision was less about the jurisdictional question than it was about Moonshee Ruheem's claim that the High Court had erred in its assertion that to follow 'the Mahomedan law' would have been 'repugnant to natural justice'.[36] More specifically, Moonshee Ruheem argued that the High Court should have 'decided the case according to the Mahomedan law' rather than 'exercis[ing] a fanciful

---

[33] Ibid., 558.
[34] Ibid., 613–14.
[35] Ibid., 618.
[36] Ibid., 614.

discretion in refusing a just right' of the type he was claiming over his estranged wife 'by that law'.[37]

While the Privy Council ultimately did find the Calcutta High Court to have erred in its conclusion, it did not take issue with its view that Islamic marriage norms afforded no latitude to a wife trying to separate from her husband without his consent. Yet in so doing, the Privy Council was doing more than just following the High Court's own view of the substantive content of Islamic marriage norms. Rather, the Councillors made a special point of emphasizing that in their estimation marriage between Muslim spouses was contractual in nature. Finding the High Court's real act of 'fanciful discretion' to be its decision to adopt equity and good conscience rather than the 'Mahomedan law' as its ultimate rule of decision, the Councillors charged the Court with ignoring the clear terms of the marriage 'contract' in Islam.

To be sure, in the Privy Council's decision in *Moonshee Ruheem* there remained signs of much the same ambiguity that characterized its view of contract in the *Perozeboye* case. For example, the decision left it fundamentally unclear whether the Council was attributing the ongoing obligations generated by marriage to the will of the spousal parties. On the one hand, the Councillors could be found asserting that the High Court should have been 'prepared to enforce all the obligations, however minute', which not only 'flow[ed] from the contract' but which did so at the compulsion of 'the Mahomedan law' as opposed to the parties' own determination.[38] On the other hand, elsewhere they could be found more intently firming up the contractual view of marriage—most obviously through the vehemence with which they repeatedly asserted that in 'Mahomedan law' marriage was no different from any other ordinary 'civil contract'.

The ambiguity was most visibly on display in the ultimate outcome of the appeal, which found the Privy Councillors stopping short of holding that the restitution of Moonshee Ruheem's rights for the breach of the marital contract under the 'Mahomedan law' demanded that he be given

---

[37] Ibid., 570.
[38] Ibid., 607 (noting that 'being founded on the contract of marriage, which the Mahomedan law regards as a civil contract, the Court entertaining the suit must be prepared to enforce all the obligations, however minute, which, according to that law, flow from the contract, whichever party has a right to insist upon them'.)

outright 'custody of his wife'.[39] Of course, there was no dearth of reasons for wanting to avoid involving the colonial state in such an enforcement regime, not to mention for being concerned with the genuine danger Shumsoonnissa Begum might face if forcibly returned to the marital home. Even so, in remanding the case back to the High Court for retrial and a more adequate finding of facts about whether Moonshee Ruheem really did pose a threat to his wife, the Council was hardly working against the grain of the contractual view of marriage that it seemed to be so keen on attributing to Islamic juristic tradition. In fact, in expressing their reticence about forcing Shumsoonnissa Begum back to the marital home, the Councillors found themselves once again appealing to the argument from contract. More specifically, they did so by inverting the logic of contractual breach upon which Moonshee Ruheem's own restitution claim was based. In explaining the Council's order to send the case back to the High Court, the Councillors explicitly linked the need for further fact-finding about Moonshee Ruheem's possibly abusive behaviour to the question of whether it was not really the husband who was the party in breach of the marital contract in the first place:

> [their Lordships] do not mean to lay down ... that there was no answer to [the husband's] suit unless it could be shown that the wife had been separated from him either by *Talak* or *Kolah*, either of which would dissolve the *vinculum*. This assumption, which seems to have been made by the Judges of the High Court, is, their Lordships think, erroneous. It seems to them clear, that if cruelty in a degree rendering it unsafe for the Wife to return to her Husband's dominion were established, the Court might refuse to send her back. It may be, too, that gross failure by the Husband of the performance of the obligations which the marriage contract imposes on him for the benefit of the Wife, might, if properly proved, afford good grounds for refusing to him the assistance of the Court. And, as their Lordships have already intimated, there may be cases in which the Court would qualify its interference by imposing terms on the Husband.[40]

[39] Ibid., 615.
[40] Ibid., 615–16.

9.5.2 Justice Syed Mahmood and the *Abdul Kadir v. Salima* Decision

Any hesitance in the Privy Council's view of the contractual nature of Muslim marriage after the *Moonshee Ruheem* case was all but eliminated by the time the High Court of Allahabad made its landmark decision in *Abdul Kadir v. Salima* nearly twenty years later.[41] Another in the line of prominent cases involving the doctrine of the restitution of conjugal rights, *Abdul Kadir* was perhaps most noteworthy because of the even more assertive tone with which the Allahabad High Court insisted that contractualism was at the heart of the law of the Muslim family. It should come as little surprise, then, that the controlling decision was handed down by Justice Syed Mahmood, one of the most prominent reformist Muslim lawyer-intellectuals of the late nineteenth century.[42]

Involving *Sunni* Muslims who were wed in March 1883, the *Abdul Kadir* case originated through a suit the husband, Abdul Kadir, brought for the restitution of his conjugal rights at the end of June 1883, shortly after his wife, Salima, left the marital home to take up residence with her father. Unlike the situation in *Moonshee Ruheem*, the focus on the contractual nature of Muslim marriage in *Abdul Kadir* was not joined to any question about the Court's jurisdiction. Rather, the primary issue before the Allahabad High Court involved determining whether a husband who had failed to meet his dower obligation could still bring suit under the conjugal restitution doctrine. As a result, the case turned on the sceptical

---

[41] *Abdul Kadir v. Salima*, (1886) 8 All. 149.
[42] Mahmood was the son of the famed Muslim modernist Syed Ahmed Khan, alongside whom he, too, played a pivotal role in the founding of the Muhammadan Anglo-Oriental College at Aligarh. The most oft-cited features of Aligarh modernism were on clear display in decisions like *Abdul Kadir*, which was one of more than three hundred that Mahmood authored in his time on the Allahabad High Court. Though his period of full appointment on the High Court bench extended only from 1887 to 1893, Mahmood had been appointed in temporary capacities on four separate occasions starting from 1882. For the best account of these and other biographical details of his life see Alan M. Guenther, *Syed Mahmood and the Transformation of Muslim Law in British India* (Unpublished Ph.D. dissertation, McGill University, 2004), 80–82. The canonical account of the Aligarh school's thought can be found in David Lelyveld, *Aligarh's First Generation: Muslim Solidarity in British India* (Princeton, NJ: Princeton University Press, 1978). On the vexed question of whether dichotomizing between Muslim 'modernists'/reformists and traditionalists/'revivalists' is misleading, see e.g. Jalal, *Self and Sovereignty* and Muhammad Qasim Zaman, *The Ulama in Contemporary Islam: Custodians of Change* (Princeton, NJ: Princeton University Press, 2002).

stance Salima staked out on this issue in her answer to the initial complaint Abdul Kadir filed with the *munsif* court at Mirzapur.[43]

At that initial stage of the proceedings the case had started out favourably for Abdul Kadir. The *munsif* court found that at the time of the marriage the parties had failed to specify whether the dower was to be paid immediately ('a prompt dower', according to Islamic juristic categories) or only by a later date. It thus followed what it claimed to be the default rule, requiring that it assume that 'only a part of [the dower] becomes, under the Muhammadan law, payable on demand'. Because the *munsif* court also held that Salima had failed to make such a demand prior to answering Abdul Kadir's initial complaint, it refused to find any of the several points she raised in defence persuasive.[44] However, on appeal the district judge at Mirzapur overruled the *munsif* court's decision and dismissed Abdul Kadir's claim, holding, in relevant part, that 'the whole of the dower was to be considered as "prompt" under the Muhammadan law'.[45] Accordingly, the payment Abdul Kadir entered with the *munsif* court in August 1883 after commencing suit was deemed inadequate on appeal, and the district court maintained that he had no justifiable cause of action for conjugal restitution. It was in the wake of this adverse outcome at the intermediate appeal stage that Abdul Kadir further pursued the matter up to the High Court of Allahabad in March 1885. There, at the final level of appeal, the sole question Justices Oldfield and Mahmood referred for the full bench's consideration concerned whether Abdul Kadir had the right to maintain his claim for the restitution of his conjugal rights.[46]

* * *

While at each previous point in the path of litigation, the question of how the dower was to be classified under Islamic juridical categories stood on its own, in his decision for the full bench of the High Court Justice

---

[43] While it is not important to dwell on for the present purposes, it is worth noting that the facts of the case were actually more complicated than what I have just set out, given that Abdul Kadir did actually deposit the full amount of the dower he owed with the Mirzapur court by August 1883, after Salima's answer to his complaint.
[44] *Abdul Kadir v. Salima*, 151.
[45] Ibid.
[46] Justice Mahmood had been temporarily assigned to the Court during this period, filling in for Justice William Tyrrell.

Mahmood treated the matter as an incident to the larger question of the nature of marriage between Muslims. Through his larger framing of the dower issue, therefore, Mahmood created an in-built presumption that among Muslims there was a particularly intense attachment to the contractual idea of marriage upon which the doctrine of conjugal restitution had come to rest in British India. Towards this end, he commenced his consideration of the issue by quoting from the opening remarks on the doctrinal nature of marriage among Muslims that Shama Sircar set out in his 1873 Tagore Law Lectures:

> [m]arriage among Muhammadans is not a sacrament but purely a civil contract. And though it is solemnized generally with recitation of certain verses from the Quran yet the Muhammadan law does not positively prescribe any service peculiar to the occasion. That it is a civil contract is manifest from the various ways and circumstances in and under which marriages are contracted or presumed to have been contracted. And though a civil contract, it is not positively prescribed to be reduced to writing, but the validity and operation of the whole are made to depend upon the declaration or proposal of the one, and the acceptance or consent of the other, of the contracting parties, or of their natural and legal guardians before competent and sufficient witnesses; as also upon the restrictions imposed, and certain of the conditions required to be abided by according to the peculiarity of the case.[47]

Reinforcing the point, Mahmood made further reference to Neil Baillie's 1869 *Digest of Moohummudan Law*, which also pronounced that

> [m]arriage is a contract which has for its design or object the right of enjoyment and the procreation of children. But it was also instituted for the solace of life, and is one of the prime or original necessities of man. It is therefore lawful in extreme old age after hope of offspring has ceased, and even in the last or death illness. The pillars of marriage, as of other contracts, are *Eejab-o-kubool*, or declaration and acceptance. The

---

[47] *Abdul Kadir v. Salima*, 154–55 (quoting Shama Churun Sircar, *The Muhammadan Law: Being a Digest of the Law Applicable Especially to the Sunnis of India* (Calcutta: Thacker, Spink, and Co., 1873), 291).

first speech, from whichever side it may proceed, is the declaration, and the other the acceptance.[48]

What was notable about the attempt here to invoke 'eejab' and 'kubool' in the Islamic concept of *'aqd* (lit. to tie or join together) was not only the analogy it was being used to suggest with offer/proposal and acceptance in the classical theory of contract, but how it served as Mahmood's starting rather than ending point. In the works he was drawing upon, and especially in Baillie's text, the analogy between contract and Islamic marriage tended to extend only as far as the act of marrying. In contrast, Mahmood effectively pressed the analogy beyond the bare act of marrying and instead used 'eejab' and 'kubool' as indicators of the contractual nature of the ongoing state of being married that obtained between spouses. This is why he put such keen emphasis on the marital relation in Islam being one of 'purely civil contract' and even more emphatically on discounting the status-like character of marriage, especially as compared to the reasoning of the Privy Council in *Moonshee Buzloor Ruheem*.

On Mahmood's view, the ongoing marital relation was no different from the aftermath of any ordinary contract, during the period when the rights and duties the bargain prospectively set out for its parties to take on were actually taken on. This, he argued, was the case even if the obligations accompanying the marital relation were made manifest not only through a mutuality of will between the spousal parties but also by the external normative compulsion of the personal law. In this respect, for Mahmood the contractual obligations that characterized the marital relation among Muslim spouses inhered in their very (ascriptive) identity as Muslims. As he observed,

> [t]hese authorities leave no doubt as to what constitutes marriage in law, and it follows that, the moment the legal contract is established,

---

[48] *Abdul Kadir v. Salima,* 155 (quoting Neil B. E. Baillie, *Digest of Moohummudan Law on the Subjects to which it is Usually Applied by British Courts of Justice in India / Compiled and Translated from Authorities in the Original Arabic, with an Introduction and Explanatory notes,* 2nd edn. (London: Smith, Elder & co., 1875), 4. The first edition of the text was published in 1869. (Baillie the younger's *Digest* should not be confused with the text his father, John Baillie, published in 1805 under a similar title. See ch. 8 at note 86.)

consequences flow from it naturally and imperatively as provided by the Muhammadan law.[49]

According to the way Mahmood pressed the analogy between Muslim marriage and contract beyond the mere act of marrying, then, the relevant legal effects that followed became more or less the same as willed contractual terms. In expounding the argument, he cited to sections from Baillie's translation of the *Fatawa-i-Alamgiri*,[50] contending that according to Islamic jurists such obligation-generating 'legal effects' 'come into operation as soon as the contract of marriage is completed by proposal and acceptance', with 'their initiation [being] simultaneous'.[51]

With the analogy having been extended this far, the rest of the path of decision favouring Abdul Kadir in his claim for the restitution of his conjugal rights was clear. Mahmood's insistence that marriage in the Muslim personal law must be understood as an ongoing state of relations involving the contractual obligations that both parties had assented to at the time of entering the agreement allowed him to suggest that each party had an expectation interest against the other's breach. On this view, the further implication readily followed that Abdul Kadir should be protected against the realignment of the terms of the original bargain, including through the public will of the state intervening into private dealings between his wife and him.

In reasoning towards the desired outcome, Mahmood was ultimately making a significant trade-off to guarantee a certain symbolic stature for the Muslim personal law (and, really, in the larger argument the Islamic *shari'a*). By insisting that marriage between Muslims was contractual, he was making the law of the family the central foundation on which the category of the Muslim personal law should rest. In exchange for doing so, he secured a path to show that the ostensibly Islamic norms at work in the domain of the family were every bit as legal as those of classical legal thought's genuine article. Simply put, where the norms of Islam ruled, they did so—for Mahmood—by virtue of partaking in the rule of the law.

---

[49] *Abdul Kadir v. Salima*, 155.
[50] This translation and paraphrasing effort constituted the first volume of Baillie's 1869 *Digest of Moohummudan Law*. Its second volume consisted of selective translations of the writings of some other Islamic juristic thinkers.
[51] *Abdul Kadir v. Salima*, 157.

Even more significantly, insofar as these norms were at least partly contractual (as in the case of the law of marriage), the Muslim personal law could then be imagined to be animated by much the same principle as the law of the market, in its capacity as the innermost core of the private-law core of the law writ large. Indeed, the appeal of Mahmood's sequence of suggestions probably extended still further insofar as the insistence on the contractual nature of the Muslim law of marriage was liable to make it appear more authentically 'legal' than its counterpart rule regime within the Hindu personal law.

In securing the gains from the trade-off Mahmood was opting for, it became all the more important—than it generally was in classical legal thought—to secure the law of the family, itself, from the intercession of the public juridical will of the state. Moreover, barring the state from this domain was important regardless of whether doing so proved consistent with liberal imperial rhetoric professing a desire to alleviate the condition of the beleaguered South Asian woman. In disputes between spouses for conjugal restitution, therefore, patriarchal dominance over the domain of marriage was not staked solely on the rhetorical grounds of the 'sovereignty' of Indian men over the 'traditional' realm of culture and domesticity that became the consolation prize for their exclusion from the halls of power. Rather, the doctrinal grounds on which the inhabitants of the domain of the personal law staked their communitarian right against regulatory interference with privately willed arrangements was also critical to energizing the patriarchal impulse.

* * *

The last observation notwithstanding, that the contractual image of marriage was consonant with the process by which the colonial courts facilitated what Padma Anagol has called the 'rearguard action by Indian men' to seize control over the doctrine of conjugal restitution for their own purposes cannot be doubted.[52] The eventual limit Justice Mahmood

---

[52] Anagol, *The Emergence of Feminism in India*, 183. It is worth mentioning once more that, as Anagol shows, statutorily speaking this dynamic was embodied in what were, by mid-century, two distinct kinds of suits for enforcing conjugal rights. The first came eventually to be embodied in Article 35 of the second Schedule of Act XV of 1877. Such suits—for the restitution of conjugal rights, proper—were available to both husbands and wives. However, those of the second variety—for the recovery of conjugal rights—were available only to husbands. In the latter type of case, suit would be brought for the recovery of a wife who, according to Article 34 of

reached, beyond which he would not try to extend the analogy between Muslim marriage and contract, suggests no less. Not by accident, his abrupt halt came in the face of Salima's efforts to redirect the analogy to her own ends, by arguing that her estranged husband's suit should be rejected given his failure to fulfil the preceding obligation relating to the dower, which she claimed was necessary to set any larger chain of ongoing contractual reciprocity in motion. Without being able to demonstrate that he had done so, according to Salima, Abdul Kadir could not show there was any binding contract between them that had been properly entered into in the first place. Nor, in turn, could he establish that his estranged wife had actually breached any contractual duty that she, for her own part, owed to him.

To Justice Mahmood, Salima's argument simply could not stand. After granting that it could, in principle, mean that a husband was the one who violated the spirit of contractualism at the heart of Muslim marriage, he immediately proceeded to discount this possibility in the actual case at hand. As he noted,

[n]ow the legal effects of marriage, as enumerated in the *Fatawa-i-Alamgiri*, come into operation as soon as the contract of marriage is completed by proposal and acceptance; their initiation is simultaneous, and there is no authority in the Muhammadan law for the proposition that any or all of them are dependent upon any condition precedent as to the payment of dower by the husband to the wife.[53]

Setting aside Salima's straightforward notion—commensurate as it was with standard ideas about conditionality within classical contract law—that the voluntarism of the binding agreement at hand depended on the proper fulfilment of the relevant contingency,[54] Mahmood went to the lengths of suggesting that the dower obligation instead might just as

---

the same legislation, would have to be claimed as being harboured by another with ill intent for the action to prove successful.

[53] *Abdul Kadir v. Salima*, 157.
[54] As Mahmood clarified, though non-payment of dower 'cannot be pleaded in defence of an action for restitution of conjugal rights; the rule so laid down [had], of course, no effect upon the right of the wife to claim her dower in a separate action'. Ibid., 167.

well be seen as akin to an independent covenant.⁵⁵ Harkening back to common-law thinking from early-modern times—before the emergence even of any general field of *contracts*, let alone one of *contract*—Mahmood thus directed Salima to the possibility of bringing a separate action on the dower. As he made clear, however, her doing so would be neither here nor there with respect to any potential right on her husband's part to enforce the benefit of the bargain he was claiming via conjugal restitution.

At the same time, rejecting the possibility that Abdul Kadir's dower-related obligation was a condition precedent to the formation of a binding marital contract was only one of the ways Mahmood opposed Salima's underlying effort to redirect the ethos of contractual voluntarism in her own favour. Perhaps even more fundamental was his objection from what he contended was the proper methodology for choosing between competing Islamic juristic authorities, which Mahmood came to in the course of considering 'the second point, upon which the greatest stress has been laid in the argument at the bar'. This involved Salima's further claim that 'under the Muhammadan law, [her] dower is regarded as nothing more or less than price for connubial intercourse, and that the right of cohabitation does not therefore accrue to the husband till he has paid the dower to the wife'.⁵⁶

Without addressing the point directly, Mahmood began his response by simply reiterating that Abdul Kadir's failure to properly fulfil his obligations relating to the dower at the time the parties were wed did not render the marital contract suspect. In so doing, he acknowledged that at least based on past case law—like that from the North-Western provinces—it might appear that a suit for conjugal restitution could not lie in the context of a husband who failed to pay a prompt dower.⁵⁷

---

⁵⁵ It is possible to argue that Mahmood was not so much abandoning his commitment to the contractual view of Muslim marriage as he was availing himself of an argument from contractual collectivism that was not unlike that which Lieutenant-Governor Campbell had made in support of the amendment he proposed to the final draft of the Contract Act. (As the reader will recall from chapter seven, Campbell had argued that there was a collectivist ethos that was as inherent within the law of contract as the ethos of individualism. On such a basis, he insisted that provision should be made in the Contract Act for mitigating 'hard and one-sided bargains'—a suggestion that Fitzjames-Stephen decried as tantamount to basing the law on no more than discretion and a vague sense of equity. See ch. 7 at note 48.)

⁵⁶ *Abdul Kadir v. Salima*, 157.

⁵⁷ This was the outcome of *Sheikh Abdool Shukkoar v. Raheem-oon-nissa* (NWP HCR 1874), with the rule it established then being followed in two other cases cited by the defendant. The first was *Wilayat Husain v. Allah Rakhi* (ILR 2 All. 831) and *Nasrat Husain v. Hamidan* (ILR 4 All. 205).

He even cited another decision by the Allahabad High Court, itself upholding a lower court's dismissal of a husband's conjugal restitution claim in which the division bench held that it did not matter that the plaintiff tried to make good on his unmet dower obligation by trying to pay at a later date.[58]

Needing to distinguish the case before the court from these troubling earlier counterparts, Mahmood resorted to insisting that it differed in its essential facts. For special emphasis he singled out how the dispute between Abdul Kadir and Salima involved a wife who had already consummated her marriage refusing ongoing cohabitation with her husband; it did not involve a wife who was alleging that her husband had failed to pay a so-called prompt dower, the conveyance of which could not generally be deferred past the moment it was demanded, according to what Mahmood further argued was the dominant consensus among Muslim jurists.

In seizing upon this factual distinction—and the need that doing so created to make it look dispositive to the differing result he would ultimately reach in *Abdul Kadir v. Salima*—Mahmood was compelled to consider the prior question of how to reconcile divergent opinions among the exponents of Islamic *fiqh*. If consummation had already occurred, he thus noted, there was a 'conflict of authority ... too great to render it an undoubted proposition of the Muhammadan law' that a wife could oppose a husband's suit for conjugal restitution simply on the basis of his failure to meet a dower obligation. Here as well Mahmood worked to reframe matters, arguing that any seeming precedent to the contrary was simply decided by an incorrect methodology. According to Mahmood, in assessing whether a suit for conjugal restitution remained viable in the face of a husband's past failure to properly fulfil his dower obligation, colonial adjudicators had wrongly assumed they should follow the opinion of Abu Hanifa, the namesake of the relevant 'school' of *fiqh*.

However, as he asserted to the contrary, it was really the opposing view of Abu Hanifa's 'two eminent disciples, Qazi Abu Yusuf and Imam Muhammad' that should have been followed.[59] He explained himself as follows:

---

[58] *Nazir Khan v. Umrao*, Allahabad Weekly Notes, 1882, 96.
[59] *Abdul Kadir v. Salima*, 162.

Imam Abu Hanifa and his two disciples are known in the Hanafi school of Muhammadan law as 'the three Masters,' and I take it as a general rule of interpreting that law, that whenever there is a difference of opinion, the opinion of the two will prevail against the opinion of the third. Now, bearing this in mind, it is clear the two disciples of Imam Abu Hanifa regarding the surrender of the wife to her husband as bearing analogy to delivery of goods in sale, held that the lien of the wife for her dower, as a plea for resisting cohabitation, ceased to exist after consummation. According to the ordinary rule of interpreting Muhammadan law, I adopt the opinion of the two disciples as representing the majority of 'the three Masters,' and hold that, after consummation of marriage, non-payment of dower, even though exigible cannot be pleaded in defence of an action for restitution of conjugal rights.[60]

If there was an illusory quality to Mahmood's reasoning, it was because he made little attempt to justify what he claimed was the 'general rule' necessitating the choice of the one rather than the other view from within Hanafi juristic opinion on how to resolve the question before the court. The intuitive appeal of following the more widely supported rule notwithstanding, Mahmood was hardly offering any exhaustive basis on which to accept that the 'the opinion of the two' was more prevalent than that of 'the third' among Hanafi jurists overall. Even less was he demonstrating that concurring with the one rather than the other either followed from or was the only way of implementing the general recognition of the authority of consensus (*ijmaʿ*) in the *usul al-fiqh*. Instead, in borrowing the opinion of Hanafi jurisprudence's later 'two masters', Mahmood seems to have simply found a source of guidance that tracked with his own preferred way of delimiting the contractual nature of the marital relation in Islam so as to deprive Salima of its use.

This is thrown into particularly sharp relief by the evident persistence with which Salima nonetheless sought to press the court's emphasis on the contractual nature of Muslim marriage in her favour. With Mahmood having opened the door to analogizing the dower to a sales price for goods exchanged in order to reject Salima's first argument from the voluntarism of contract, she sought to make virtue of vice by introducing a second. As

[60] Ibid., 166–67.

a further point, she thus argued that even on Qazi Abu Yusuf and Imam Muhammad's logic there was little reason why the dower-cum-sales-price could not be likened to contractual consideration more generally. With Mahmood now again being painted into a corner, he once more opted to abruptly cut short a logic of contract that he, himself, had introduced with his own brush. Re-invoking the 'opinion of the two' Hanafi masters, his reasoning makes the following passage from the decision the crucial one:

> [d]ower, under the Muhammadan law, is a sum of money or other property promised by the husband to be paid or delivered to the wife in consideration of the marriage, and even where no dower is expressly fixed or mentioned at the marriage ceremony, the law confers the right of dower upon the wife as a necessary effect of marriage ... Even after marriage the amount of dower may be increased by the husband during coverture ... and indeed in this, as in some other respects, the dower of the Muhammadan law bears a strong resemblance to the *donatio propter nuptias* of the Romans which has subsisted in the English law under the name of marriage settlement. In this sense and in no other can dower under the Muhammadan law be regarded as the consideration for the connubial intercourse, and if the authors of the Arabic text-books of Muhammadan law have compared it to price in the contract of sale, it is simply because marriage is a civil contract under that law, and sale is the typical contract which Muhammadan jurists are accustomed to refer to in illustrating the incidents of other contracts by analogy.[61]

As the passage makes apparent, Mahmood had little choice other than to argue that the parallel between dower and consideration that Salima was arguing for was simply a contractualist step too far. Read in tandem with the previous passage excerpted from the decision, here we find Mahmood indirectly reasserting that the real equivalence licensed by the analogy to the sales price had to be understood in terms of an identity between dower and a vendor's provisional lien on goods once sold if some part of their price remained unpaid. On this preferred way of seeing things, then, the idea of a lien 'essentially presumes the right of ownership

[61] Ibid., 157–58.

in the vendee, and terminates as soon as delivery has taken place'.[62] As a result, even if 'pushing the analogy to the law of sale to its fullest extent, the right of a Muhammadan wife to her dower is at best a lien upon [the husband's] right to claim cohabitation'. In turn, this meant that for Salima the contractualist analogy was simply to no avail because there was no rule that 'would render such lien capable of being pleaded so as to defeat altogether the suit for restitution of conjugal rights'.[63]

In order both to ensure that his own appeal to contractualism on Abdul Kadir's behalf trumped Salima's and to summarize what he saw as the real symbolic importance of the analogy between the Muslim law of marriage and the classical law of contract, Mahmood concluded his decision with the following telling observation:

> [t]here is one more consideration which I wish to add to the reasons which I have already given at such length in support of my view. The Muhammadan law of marriage recognizes nothing except right, in its legal sense, as the basis of legal relations and of those consequences which flow from them. And if the husband did not before payment of dower possess the right of cohabitation with his wife, it would follow as a necessary consequence in Muhammadan jurisprudence that, where the dower is prompt and cohabitation has taken place before the payment of such dower, the issue of such cohabitation would be illegitimate. It would be easy to show that such would be the logical consequence in Muhammadan law of the reasoning pressed on behalf of the respondents; but I need not go further in considering this matter, as I have referred to it only because in the course of the argument it was said that, before payment of prompt dower, the cohabitation of a Muhammadan wife with her husband was simply a matter of concession and not of right as understood in that law ... And I may add that I have considered it my duty to go so fully into this question out of respect for the rulings which were cited on behalf of the respondents, but in which I have been unable to concur, and also because such questions, which usually arise only among the poorer classes of the Muhammadan population,

---

[62] Ibid., 166.
[63] Ibid., 171.

seldom come up to this court for adjudication, but of course affect domestic relations of the Muhammadan community at large.[64]

9.6 The Contractual Nature of (Muslim) Marriage and Law in the Politics of Communitarian Identity Symbols

If, as Justice Mahmood suggested, the law of marriage in Islam was about 'nothing except right, in its legal sense', there was clearly an additional importance to conjugal restitution doctrine beyond simply its role as a tool for the assertion of gendered dominance within 'the Muhammadan community at large'. As much can be gleaned from the reluctance of the colonial judiciary to transform the remedy into a full-fledged means of forcibly restoring women to their marital homes, which was not generally the outcome of such suits when won by men from any religious community. Instead, as Mahmood's concluding remarks in the *Abdul Kadir* decision make so clear, the law of conjugal restitution also became an important site for discursively articulating the Muslim personal law's claim to full legality as part of the law writ large. His assertion that 'the Muhammadan law' gives rise to a 'basis ... of relations and of those consequences which flow from them' that is irreducibly legal in nature is particularly instructive in this regard. For it was clearly meant to hold even if the compass of 'Muhammadan law' was confined to norming the facts relating to interactions between the members of the (Muslim) family alone.

Ultimately, if the insistence on contractual right as the heart of the law of marriage among Muslims was more emphatic than was really warranted, there was good reason for this to be so. After all, Islamic juristic tradition did not make available the same type of general theory of voluntarist agreement[65] that was becoming so important to the evolving historical ontology of the law in classical legal thought.[66] Furthermore,

---

[64] Ibid.

[65] See e.g. M. E. Hamid, 'Islamic Law of Contract or Contracts', *Journal of Islamic and Comparative Law* 3 (1969): 1–11. The point is one Joseph Schacht also insisted on in his *Introduction to Islamic Law* (New York: Clarendon Press, 1964), 144.

[66] While marriage was, indeed, seen by the canonical 'schools' of Islamic jurisprudence to be one subspecies of *'aqd*, the point is that the latter corresponded much more clearly only to pre-classical ideas of binding obligation in the common-law mainstream. Therefore, the analogy between conjugal restitution and remediating breach of contract pushed this idea of *'aqd*

notwithstanding public-sphere discourse to the contrary, there was also the clear indeterminacy in the classical doctrinal logic of contract that we earlier saw exemplified in Act IX of 1872, which always made appeals to voluntarist individualism unstable at best as a general matter. In *Abdul Kadir* the same indeterminacy could not but be evident—especially insofar as each major conclusion Mahmood sought to draw based on the principle of contractual individualism proved just as capable of being reached by treating marriage as a status relation instead. Indeed, much the same was true even for the various contractualist counter-conclusions Salima sought to put forth for her own part.

That is, from the standpoint of the doctrinal treatment of marriage as a status the result that followed from facilitating the autonomous contractual will of the husband instead could always just as well be made to follow from what Holland called the rights *in rem* that the head of the household enjoyed over the family, considered as an ascriptive status community. Conversely, the same held true for whatever counterpart result a party like Salima might advocate for on the basis of the facilitation of her own autonomous will (for example, through arguing that Abdul Kadir's failure to meet his dower obligation was tantamount to a missing consideration that invalidated the marital contract). It would have been just as easy to reach the latter conclusion by arguing that there was a need for the public juridical will of the state to capacitate a party like Salima to individuate and enforce what Holland would have called 'the lifelong courses' of rights/duties that she enjoyed in virtue of her *status* of being a wife—whether those that entitled her to separate marital property, bodily security, or whatever else.

---

in a direction noticeably more towards the understanding of contract in classical legal thought. See e.g. Hussein Hassan, 'Contracts in Islamic Law: The Principles of Commutative Justice and Liberality', *Journal of Islamic Studies* 13, no. 3 (2002): 257–97. As Hassan points out, '[i]t would seem that *'aqd* [was] used ... in its etymological sense ... rather than as a technical term' by jurists of the so-called classical and post-classical eras of Islamic legal history. Whether it corresponded to any general technical notion of legal obligation in the Islamic tradition is, itself, questionable. As Hassan further observes, while *'aqd* did appear most commonly in manuals from Islamic legal history's classical era as the term for denoting two-party transactions, it was also used to refer to one-sided obligations such as bequests and gifts. Still further, it was used for 'acts merely juristic in nature' such as divorce and the manumission of debts. Ultimately, this was because the term 'cover[ed] obligation in every field: one's religious obligations to God, the interpersonal obligations of marriage, the political obligations expressed in treaties, and the commercial obligations of the involved parties in a range of particular contracts'. Ibid., 257.

Similarly, towards the end of the last chapter, it is hardly by accident that the equivalence we saw Ameer Ali drawing between the personal law and the law of status went hand in hand with his recurrent reference to marriage, itself, as a status. (Indeed, in *The Personal Law of the Mahommedans* we *also* find him explicitly comparing marriage to the other main special types of status in classical legal thought like legitimacy, mental incapacity, and the like.)[67] Of course, to make such an observation is not to say that in a systematizing text like Ameer Ali's the idea of Muslim marriage as a contract was missing. In fact, in his treatise overall there were nearly twice as many references to the contractual nature of marriage as there were to its supposed nature as a status.

However, what Ali's inability not to at least sometimes equate marriage with a status *does* signify is that arguments from the premise that spousal relations in Islam entailed no more than an ordinary civil contract were always only one side of a coin. For as we saw earlier, even in the central domains of classical legal thought exactly how to parse the connection between spouses was a supremely equivocal affair; channelling that logic for the sake of 'systematizing' the Muslim law could not change this, try as those like Ali or Mahmood might to make good on whatever separate attraction they had towards wanting to represent marriage in Islam as being contractual to its core.

* * *

Even more than the *Moonshee Buzloor Ruheem* decision before it, *Abdul Kadir* came at a time when emphasizing the essentially legal nature of the rights underlying the law of Muslim marriage can hardly be regarded as surprising. The emphasis was clearly consistent with the larger politics of communitarian identity symbols into which the *shariʿa* was being drawn as Islamic 'reform and revival' met the new age of nationalist anti-colonialism in the subcontinent.[68] As Michael Anderson has

---

[67] See Ali, *The Personal Law of the Mahommedans*, 140, 148, 215, 343, 374, 401, 411. For the previous discussion see ch. 7 at note 95.

[68] As concerning the emergence of the split between so-called *shariʿa*-minded, scripturally oriented Muslim 'revivalists' and modernizing Muslim 'reformers' that is conventionally thought to have arisen over the course of the nineteenth century as the old class of Muslim notables

stressed, while there was a long-standing history of Islamic idioms being used to 'translate economic discontent into focused political action' before the late nineteenth century, after 1857 there was nonetheless a 'new approach to Islam' that was taking root. This saw various groups 'mobilizing around Muslim identity in opposition to colonial rule' through 'a particular version of Islamic law [that] came to be juxtaposed with colonial attacks upon it'.[69]

Among the more noticeable forms that such mobilization took was through the retrenchment of traditionally learned Islamic scholars, who tended to 'reject[] British law as a profession' and instead turned their energies towards keeping *fiqh*-centred knowledge practices alive—even if, as Scott Kugle observes, primarily within 'the private realm of community ritual, family sanctity, and local politics'. Even more telling for the present purposes, however, is the form of mobilization around Muslim identity that I have been considering here, in the context of what Kugle calls the 'Anglo-Muhammadan fusion' that was being developed by jurists such as Syed Mahmood, Ameer Ali, and others like them. For it was this emergent class of Muslim lawyer-intellectuals who 'turned to the shari'ah that had been framed by Anglo-Muhammadan court activity as "Muslim personal law"' to fashion it into an instrument for defining an all-India Muslim community.[70]

---

tied to state patronage was displaced into society with the rise of British rule, see e.g. Metcalf, *Islamic Revival in British India* and Francis Robinson, *The 'Ulama of Farangi Mahall and Islamic Culture in South Asia* (London: C. Hurst, 2001). Of course, as noted earlier, the dichotomization of Islamic modernism into reform and revivalist camps has aroused its own sort of attention and critique. See also note 42.

[69] Michael R. Anderson, 'Legal Scholarship and the Politics of Islam in British India'. In *Perspectives on Islamic Law, Justice and Society*, ed. R. S. Khare (New York: Rowman & Littlefield, 1999), 65–92 at 82. In a similar vein, Kugle has described the ongoing consequence of the pruning away of Islamic norms through measures like the Penal Code and the Indian Evidence Act between 1860 and 1890 as one that left Muslims in the subcontinent seeking 'to regain political power through rhetoric justified by ... [a] "colonized" shari'ah'. As he further puts it, this was the mark of a 'paradox' in which the *shari'a* came to be captured under British rule. Thus, through 'the juridical operation of [British colonial] courts, the shari'ah became a reified and static entity', being 'largely codified by the British act of wrestling political power away from Muslims' only to have later Muslim politics increasingly expressed through rallying around this same increasingly static entity. See Kugle, 'Framed, Blamed and Renamed', 258–59.

[70] Ibid., 302, 303.

Yet even if the exponents of the so-called Anglo-Muhammadan fusion helped transform 'Islamic law [into] a form of political rhetoric' that was clearly 'Orientalized' in its contours,[71] this was not attributable to the Muslim lawyer class alone. Rather, it was also a function of the increasing pace and volume with which discourse about the law proliferated during the second half of the nineteenth century—not only in the subcontinent but throughout the world. In the ordinary-language discourse of the public sphere—whether in Britain's India or elsewhere—having a specifically legal variety of normativity in hand was simply too important to go without if a 'national' group was to seriously aspire to meeting the governance challenge its would-be claim to co-extensivity with the modern nation state implied. In this respect, both the exponents of the Anglo-Muslim personal law and those who continued their learning in the traditional Islamic *fiqh* 'sciences' shared what was, in fact, a widely held view—that conditions of modernity were clearly incentivizing—about the importance of a normativity that could be imagined to be essentially legal.

Nor, for their own part, were the various stripes of reformers and revivalists from within the subcontinent's Hindu community insulated from the same tendency, as they too seized upon conflicts between co-religionist spouses to try to demonstrate the modernity of what was also quite audibly proclaimed to be their own religio-national group's unimpeachably legal tradition. At the same time, given the increasing importance of discourse about both Muslim and Hindu law as demarcators of communitarian identity, its apprehensibility as a form of 'political rhetoric' did not simply depend on the public sphere. Instead, as I have been seeking to demonstrate in this chapter through tracing the evolution of the doctrine of conjugal restitution, the politics of communitarian identity symbols was also played out within the arenas of doctrinal discourse, including for the sake of trying to prove that whatever given 'non-Western' normative tradition had a legitimate place within the new ontology of the law writ large. Whatever ideological agendas impelled the exponents of the personal law under Crown Raj, therefore, they were bound to be pursued both through the rhetoric of the public sphere that

---

[71] Ibid., 303.

was native to the realm of extra-administrative affairs and also the discourse of the law itself.

9.7 Making Doctrinal Sense of the 'Sacramental' Nature of (Hindu) Marriage

While the contractual view of marriage became most visible in the context of spousal relations between Muslims in the subcontinent, it remained the foundation of the remedy of conjugal restitution more generally. As a result, it was all but destined to be an important feature of the other confessional subsystems of the personal law as well. Of course, this is not to deny that discourse about the 'sacramental' nature of Hindu marriage took on increasing importance during the years in and around the famed *Rukhmabai* controversy of the 1880s. However, equally must it not be forgotten that the conjugal restitution suit at the heart of that controversy still rested on an underlying notion of the marital relation between Hindu spouses as a contract the breach of which demanded vindication through restoring the parties to their ostensibly original expectations, as I explore in more detail directly.

9.7.1 Conjugal Restitution and the Suspect Contractualism of Hindu Marriage in *Rukhmabai*

Beginning from a petition filed with the Bombay High Court in 1884 and involving a complaint by a husband who was seeking the return of a wife who was still a minor, the *Dadaji Bhikaji vs. Rukhmabai*[72] case became best-known for the swirl of publicity surrounding it. Even after litigation came to an end the outcry over the case would not subside until the passage of the Age of Consent Act of 1891, which raised the age at which marriage with a minor could be lawfully consummated from ten to twelve.[73] Having married in 1873 when Dadaji was nineteen and

---

[72] *Dadaji Bhikaji vs Rukhmabai*, (1885) ILR 9 Bom. 529. Of course, there was a series of other cases that constituted the overall controversy that I am omitting from the present citation.

[73] The legal contests, together with the highly public controversy the *Rukhmabai* cases gave rise to, have been the subject of significant scholarly attention. Sudhir Chandra's monograph is the

Rukhmabai only eleven, husband and wife lived apart after they wed, with Rukhmabai remaining in her parental home. This otherwise commonplace arrangement persisted for more than a decade, during which the parties' marriage remained unconsummated. With Dadaji being economically dependent on his maternal uncle, largely uneducated, and of allegedly ill temper, his in-laws remained hesitant in the face of his demands for them to turn their daughter over to his custody.

Against the backdrop of their refusal to do so, Dadaji eventually turned to the courts. There, at the initial stage of proceedings, Justice Robert Hill Pinhey presided over the case and held that because the parties had never cohabited with one another, Dadaji could not properly ask for the reinstatement of conjugal rights that he had never fully laid claim to in the first place. On Pinhey's understanding, then, Dadaji was improperly demanding an order for the 'institution' rather than restitution of his conjugal rights and, thus, asking the court to 'complete his contract' with Rukhmabai by forcing her to consummate a previously unconsummated union.[74] With the institution-versus-restitution distinction in hand, Pinhey ultimately dismissed the suit, declaring that it was lacking in any basis in the Hindu personal law. The next stage of proceedings took place in March 1886, when the case was reheard before a two-member appellate bench of the Bombay High Court. Reversing the earlier ruling, the High Court held that Pinhey's distinction between the institution and restitution of conjugal rights was specious and remanded the case for further rehearing before the court of first instance.[75] The ensuing retrial was

---

most extended and detailed factual account of the context of and the immediate events behind these events. See her *Enslaved Daughters: Colonialism, Law and Women's Rights* (Delhi: Oxford University Press, 1998). Chandra's focus on the opposing forces in the controversy beyond the courtroom—as they played themselves out more specifically in the print media of orthodox Hindu reformers and the Anglo-Indian press—is complemented by Antoinette Burton's concern with the attention the case garnered within the late Victorian metropolitan press. See generally, Antoinette Burton, 'From Child Bride to "Hindoo Lady": Rukhmabai and the Debate on Sexual Respectability in Imperial Britain', *The American Historical Review* 103, no. 4 (Oct. 1998), 1119–46. Perhaps the most illuminating examination of the doctrinal aspects of the case—albeit giving a view from which that presented here differs in significant ways—is Anagol's. See her *The Emergence of Feminism in India*, 187–95.

[74] *Dadaji Bhikaji v. Rukhmabai*, 533–34.
[75] See T. N. Madan, 'Of the Social Categories "Private" and "Public": Considerations of Cultural Context'. In *The Public and the Private: Issues of Democratic Citizenship*, eds. Gurpreet Mahajan and Helmut Reifeld (New Delhi: Sage Publications, 2003), 88–102 at 94.

completed a year later in March 1887, with one Justice Farran deciding in Dadaji's favor and ordering Rukhmabai either to take up residence in his home or to face a six-month term in prison.

Though Rukhmabai appealed Farran's decision, by 1887 events in the courtroom had been overtaken by the enormous controversy that built up around the case, which had become visible starting already from the outset with the filing of Dadaji's original suit three years earlier. This was partly because Rukhmabai forced the case into the public sphere, authoring pseudonymous letters in protest of her situation that were prominently published in *The Times of India*. With the letters making the case into a cause célèbre, there ensued a heated response from the forces of orthodox Hindu reaction, which generally painted anything short of a victory for Dadaji as a threat to the entire Hindu communitarian order. As a result, even before Pinhey issued his initial decision, the case was being tried in the court of public opinion, conducted in both the English and vernacular-language press in the most prominent cities of North India (to say nothing of the British metropolitan world);[76] this gave orthodox discontent ample lead time to coalesce around the view that the colonial state was encroaching upon the Hindu religion. The Bombay High Court's impending reversal of Pinhey's decision would only add fuel to the fire, especially given the increasing renown Rukhmabai achieved in certain corners as her public declarations found her vowing to resist cohabitation with Dadaji, no matter what the consequence.

With outside pressures building as the different stages of complaint and appeal progressed, the case's path of litigation ended in somewhat anticlimactic fashion when Dadaji was ultimately persuaded to accept a settlement for two thousand rupees in July 1888. Yet, because the Bombay High Court's compromise decree emerged only after the case had already become such a lightning rod for controversy the contest over the legal age of consent that it reopened did not abate. Only a few months later, in 1889, another prominent case involving child marriage—of an eleven-year-old girl in Bengal who died after forcible intercourse with a 35-year-old husband—burst into the spotlight. Because the victim was over ten years of age, the husband could only be prosecuted for negligence in her death, which further stoked the fires the case fanned.

[76] See ibid.

Together with the still unfolding aftermath of *Rukhmabai*, the Bengal case paved the way for the beginning of serious talks aimed at passing reform legislation to raise the age of consent. Recommendations were submitted to the Government of India to expand its statutory definition of rape by two years, effectively raising the age of lawful intercourse with a female child from ten to twelve.[77] By 1891 the proposals for reform were officially enacted into law, though not without the larger outcry on all sides that the above events ignited persisting well into the future.[78]

* * *

Without detracting from the issues of grave social import the *Rukhmabai* case involved, relative to the concerns of the present chapter what may be most noticeable is that public-sphere discourse in the vernacular, Anglo-Indian, and metropolitan press did not fundamentally alter the overall doctrinal framework within which the basic legal battle was fought. For example, reaction articulated in the pages of the Bombay-based English-language bi-weekly, *Native Opinion*—founded in 1864 by the lawyer, Marathi man of letters, and expert on Hindu law Vishvanath Narayan Mandiik—may have concentrated on the idea that Hindu marriage was not a 'contract' but a 'sacrament'; but the larger point that ideologues of orthodox opinion were making was still that the duties associated with such a sacrament were ones the colonial state had no business cancelling on a wife's behalf. Nor did the actual decisions of the colonial judiciary, at various stages, turn on elaborating the special doctrinal structure of any concept of marriage-as-sacrament.[79] On the contrary, the doctrinal logic according to which the cases were parsed remained the contractualist one that underpinned conjugal restitution more generally. This was why

---

[77] Of course, even the existing rule setting the age at ten was a provision of colonial law rather than one directly corresponding to any consensus from Hindu juridical authorities. It was for this reason, of course, that the issue, along with the related matter of specifying a minimum age for marriage, had already long previously proved contentious. (The 1872 Marriage Act, for example, had sought to set a general minimum age of marriage for girls at fourteen and boys at eighteen.)

[78] On the case of the eleven-year-old girl, Phulmonee, see generally Tanika Sarkar, 'A Pre-History of Rights: The Age of Consent Bill in Colonial Bengal', *Feminist Studies* 26, no. 3 (Autumn 2000): 601–22.

[79] Anagol, *The Emergence of Feminism in India*, 187. Relative to my own account, Anagol would seem to overestimate the degree to which mid-century conjugal restitution doctrine envisioned 'Indian marriages [to be] more contractual rather than sacramental in character'. As we saw earlier, the view in *Perozeboye* was decidedly more mixed. For this was stated not just

Pinhey's decision at the first stage of proceedings focused on whether a wife who was a minor had the ability to consent to the marital contract.

As Sudhir Chandra can be read to suggest, the persistence of conjugal restitution's underlying contractualist framework also accounts for much of the back and forth that took place after the case was remanded back to Justice Farran's court. Indeed, the central question Farran's decision focused on concerned the extent to which the marital relation was to be regarded as an ordinary civil contract.[80] Accordingly, Dadaji's estranged wife claimed that the Specific Relief Act (I of 1877) distinguished marital from ordinary contracts by arguing that the particular duties they entailed were generally unenforceable. In a slightly different vein, Rukhmabai argued, in the alternative, that the remedy of conjugal restitution implied that if specific performance was appropriate it was 'not of the marriage contract, but of the obligations arising out of that contract'.[81]

However, it was the reversal of Pinhey's decision on appeal by the Bombay High Court's two-judge panel that best corroborates the determining importance of the contractual theory of marriage in the *Rukhmabai* case.[82] This is because it was hardly on grounds of the 'sacramental' nature of the union between Hindu spouses that the panel reversed Pinhey's decision in favour of Rukhmabai. Rather, the two-judge

through drawing on an explicit dichotomy between the contractual and sacramental character of marriage but also through distinguishing its character as a set of contractual versus *status* relations. Anagol's point that 'Indian legal experts' took this supposed early contractual image of marriage and 'turned [it] on its head' through transforming it into a 'sacramental' one seems to be less true as a function of doctrinal discourse than it was as a function of the fulminations of the public sphere. That 'orthodox' Hindu assertion may, indeed, have been insistent on contrasting the sacramental nature of Hindu marriage with the contractual nature of its Christian or Muslim counterparts should not be assumed constitutive of such a distinction in the doctrinal discourse of conjugal restitution. In this respect, the Hindu law of marriage was neither categorically distinct in the questions of doctrinal construction it faced nor completely different from the subsystem of the Muslim personal law with respect to the ontologizing pressures it was subject to on the basis of what I have been calling the symbolic politics of communitarian identity symbols.

[80] See Chandra, *Enslaved Daughters*, 86–89.
[81] Quoted in ibid., 87–88. The related argument that was made by Rukhmabai to the effect that marital rights and duties were merely forms of 'imperfect' (that is to say, moral) obligation emphasized much the same point.
[82] The further argument that Rukhmabai pressed concerning the absence of any contractual state of relations between her estranged husband and her was rejected outright by Chief Justice Charles Sargent, who emphasized that in the '[c]ontractual relation according to Hindoo Law [t]he parents or guardians may contract for' minors. Quoted in ibid., 88.

panel simply dismissed Pinhey's institution-versus-restitution distinction as irrelevant to the availability of a remedy for the breach of what it saw, ultimately, as a clearly binding voluntarist agreement between Dadaji and Rukhmabai.

* * *

If the notion of marriage as a sacrament made for any operative doctrinal concept in constituting the subsystem of the Hindu personal law, it did so only to the extent that it was a synonym for the doctrinal concept of status. Looking beyond the *Rukhmabai* case, it is precisely in such a manner that we find Gooroodass Banerjee treating the concept in his 1878 Tagore Law Lectures. While Banerjee echoed the oft-repeated claim that '[m]arriage in [Hindu] law is not merely a contract but also a sacrament', he expounded on this assertion by noting how 'the rights and duties of the married parties are determined solely by *the law*, and are incapable of being varied by their agreement'.[83] In fact, Banerjee elaborated much the same point earlier in his lectures as well when he insisted that

> it ought to be observed that the legal consequences of marriage depend in almost every civilized country, not upon the will of the parties to it, but upon the law which governs them … For this reason, it has been sometimes doubted whether marriage is, properly speaking, a contract. 'It is rather', says Story, 'to be deemed an institution of society, founded upon the consent and contract of the parties; and in this view it has some peculiarities in its nature, character, operation, and extent of obligation, different from what belong to ordinary contracts'. No doubt it is not a contract in the sense in which any other agreement, such as betrothal, is a contract. In one sense, however, marriage is a true contract; for the parties when they marry, in fact enter into an agreement to perform certain duties towards each other for the rest of their lives: it is a contract to be followed by a whole life of specific performance. 'But', as a distinguished Scottish judge observes, 'it differs from other contracts in this, that the rights, obligations or duties arising from it are not left

---

[83] Banerjee, *The Hindu Law of Marriage and Stridhan*, 113 (emphasis added). Such references to 'the law' or 'the operation of law' were, of course, fairly standard ways of distinguishing facts that were to be normed by a will other than the parties' own.

entirely to be regulated by the agreements of parties, but are, to a certain extent, matters of municipal regulation, over which the parties have no control by any declaration of their will'. The object of this interference of law with the freedom of parties in their mutual dealings, is to guard against the consequences of individual caprice and want of foresight, in a transaction which is of the most serious importance not only to themselves, but to society in general.[84]

Banerjee's comments here are clearly reminiscent of Holland's view that the law of status was to be found partly in the 'lifelong courses' of rights and duties obtaining between the members of the family. Yet even more notable is how he went beyond Holland. For what Banerjee was doing in this part of his lectures was to doctrinally translate public-sphere discourse about the sacramental nature of Hindu marriage into the language of classical legal thought. (Indeed, his references, alone, suggest as much.)[85] In order to do so, he adopts the tried-and-true formula that so many late-nineteenth-century thinkers used to reckon with the problem of marriage's contract-versus status-like nature, splitting the doctrinal conceptualization of Hindu marriage down the middle. On the one hand, there would be certain contract-like rules that applied to the 'formation' of the marital agreement. These, it turned out, were based on the private will or what Banerjee called the 'freedom' of the parties, the mutuality between them, and the like. On the other hand, marriage's oft-proclaimed 'sacramental' quality would be found in 'the whole life of specific performance' that followed the formation of the agreement. If Hindu marriage was a sacrament, then, it was because the ongoing state of being married was, doctrinally speaking, a non-market private relation of status.

In keeping with this solution to the problem of doctrinally parsing marriage, it was no less important a consequence of Banerjee's view that the sacramental aspect of the union demonstrated the essentially legal nature of Hindu normative tradition than it was of Justice Mahmood's view in *Abdul Kadir* that the contractual nature of marriage between

---

[84] Ibid., 111–12 (citing Joseph Story's 1834 text *Commentaries on the Conflict of Laws, Foreign and Domestic*).
[85] See Kennedy, *The Rise and Fall of Classical Legal Thought*, 201.

Muslims demonstrated the same for Islamic normative tradition. At the same time, Banerjee's doctrinal reconstruction of the public-sphere discourse about Hindu marriage as a sacrament also plainly paralleled the concept of Muslim marriage as a status that subsisted side by side with Justice Mahmood's contractualist view. For on Banerjee's depiction, if need be, the parties to the status relation of Hindu marriage could always be endowed with the capacity to individuate their 'lives of specific performance' into specifically *legal* rights and duties; this they would do by what in the above passage Banerjee called the 'interference of law' and 'municipal regulation'.

Whether in the Hindu—or, for that matter, any other communitarian—context above all it is important to see that the public-sphere idea of marriage as a sacrament could only be translated into doctrinal discursive form through the concept of status. Insofar as this was the case, moreover, translating the concept into a doctrinally operative category was bound to reverse the goal that orthodox Hindu opinion sought to secure through invoking the discourse about Hindu marriage as a sacrament in the first place. For in appealing to the sacramental nature of such unions the point was to warn the colonial state to keep its distance from the 'inner' spaces of Hindu domesticity. However, any such warning could only be instituted as a form of administrable doctrine through rules that would invariably result in the opposite.

That is, for discourse about Hindu marriage-as-sacrament to be made administrable (as part of 'the law of the family') there were only two basic routes for a non-contractual logic to take. Yet both of these two routes were bound to involve 'the interference of' the state—at least in its formal role as the individual bearer of the public juridical will. On the one hand, barring an appeal to the discourse of contract, Dadaji, or some equivalent, might try to push for his desired outcome on the basis of a doctrinal conceptualization of the specifically legal normativity of the 'sacrament' of marriage by invoking the right *in rem* that the 'law of status' gave to the head of the household over the family, considered as a realm of his own unitary and exclusive entitlement. On the other hand, again barring an appeal to the discourse of contract, Dadaji, or some equivalent, might try to push for his desired outcome by conceptualizing the specifically legal normativity of the 'sacrament' of marriage in the same way that Banerjee did by rendering it synonymous with the 'status' of marriage in his Tagore

Law Lectures. In this second scenario, Dadaji, or some equivalent, would be articulating the need for the public will to intervene into the space of domestic relations in order to capacitate him to individuate the 'lifelong courses' of duty his wife was subject to by making actionable his own correlative rights to have those obligations be performed. This would include his individuatable right to expect his wife to meet the specific duty to cohabit.

As just noted, in neither scenario would translating the public-sphere discourse about the sacramental nature of marriage into doctrinal terms really exclude the state from the realm of native domesticity. In the second scenario, this is openly conceded insofar as Dadaji, or some equivalent, would be affirmatively summoning the interventionist will of the state to give him the capacity to individuate his wife's duties in order to make them actionable as his own rights. Even in the first scenario, the state would obviously not really be excluded. It is true, of course, that in the first scenario Dadaji, or some equivalent, would be claiming that he had sovereignty over the status community of the family and, hence, that the state should be barred from interfering in the sacramental union between husband and wife. Yet such a claim would only be the other side of the wife's own, as the adverse party. In this respect, it would now simply be the adverse party who was the one openly calling for the intervention of the public will into the status community of the family in order to capacitate her to make good on her own opposing rights.

9.7.2 Meaning-Making in the Ordinary Language versus Doctrinal Discourse of (the Law of) Marriage

The gap between the public-sphere outcry about Hindu marriage as a sacrament and the doctrinal idea of status to which it was, at best, referring serves as another reminder that there were reasonably distinct planes on which discourse of and about the law appeared. Likewise, it is also suggestive of the distinct ways in which the verbalizable concepts and propositional content that circulated at these different levels of discourse could be given meaning, including when they revolved around the nominally selfsame terms. This is because doctrinal concepts, like status, that had a relatively low degree of operativeness, were less likely to be appropriated by public-sphere discourse as is—that is, through the same terminology in which they were articulated in the discourse of the public sphere. Conversely, where it was some more highly operative doctrinal abstraction that was at issue—whether one like 'contract' or even one like 'the Hindu law' itself—these were all the more likely to be picked up *as is* when appropriated as wider means for communitarian self-assertion in the public sphere.[86] The more highly operative some bit of doctrinal discourse was, in other words, the greater was its chance to find a nominally equivalent counterpart term in ordinary-language discourse.

Here a second point of note is worth highlighting as well. For in either case—whether the propositional content of ordinary-language discourse was or was not verbalized through the nominally selfsame terms as that of doctrinal discourse—there was still reason for the respective meanings of concepts articulated through these two registers of discourse to remain distinct. This followed from the fact that the concepts of doctrinal discourse were self-consciously deployed with the sense that they were generally more tightly bound to a whole array of other concepts through relations of inferential logical necessity (whether of a deductive or inductive variety). After all, so is what it meant for doctrinal discourse to be operative in the first place and, thus, what it meant for it to be distinct from the ordinary-language discourse of the public sphere. If the meanings of its concepts and the wider propositional content built therefrom were not interlinked through ostensible relations of logical necessity, there would be no basis for the widely held image of the legal administrator as a figure driven by compulsion, a discretionless conduit of the norms they were tasked with applying.

Lastly, there is a third and final point worth making about the standing possibility of divergence between doctrinal and ordinary-language discourse with respect to the terminology through which they were articulated and the meanings of the underlying concepts and propositions they trafficked in. This is, namely, that the elements of the law's propositional content could easily persist in the public sphere past the point when the components to which they were deductively linked in their doctrinal

---

[86] This remained the case, whether such assertion was elite-led or more popularly based, as well as whether it came in opposition to the colonial state or through the making of some plea, implicit or explicit, to it.

instantiation had, themselves, started to retreat or even come to be redefined. Within doctrinal discourse, even if a concept became less operative and thus part of only a much shorter chain of deductive necessity, this did not mean it had to simultaneously fall into desuetude in its capacity as a constituent of public-sphere discourse. Rather, the opposite could just as well be true, given the generally greater promiscuity of connotative meaning-making in the venues of ordinary-language discourse.

The last observation can be corroborated by the tendency in public-sphere discourse for new terms to be substituted for those of doctrinal discourse's own—as is evident in the case of 'sacrament' and 'status' in discourse about the Hindu law of marriage. In such cases, even in the wake of the full-fledged emergence during the late nineteenth century of a new ontology of the law—which placed such great emphasis on the logical unity of the norm system's doctrinal contents—the burden of legal ontologization could still be thrown back upon processes of meaning-making in the venues of ordinary-language discourse. Therefore, even if a doctrine like conjugal restitution was untethered from its basis in 'the law of contract,' it could yet persist as part of 'the law of status', given the active tendency within the discourse of the public sphere to point in that same direction through its own way of idiomizing marriage as sacrament.

9.7.3 From Contract to Sacrament: Muslim Marriage and the *Anis Begum* Case of 1933

This last point can be further illustrated by looking more closely at a final important case between Muslim spouses involving the law of conjugal restitution, 1933's *Anis Begum v. Muhammad Istafa*.[87] This is because in *Anis Begum* the contractual view of Muslim marriage was finally subjected to critical scrutiny by the Allahabad High Court, near a half-century after the *Abdul Kadir* decision. Coming when it did, the case was decided in a context in which conjugal restitution remained intact as a doctrine not because it was still understood to follow as a necessary

---

[87] *Anis Begum v. Muhammad Istafa* (1933) 55 ILR All. 743, reprinted in Asaf A. A. Fyzee, ed., *Cases in the Muhammadan Law of India, Pakistan, and Bangladesh*, 2nd edn. (New York: Oxford University Press, 2005), 15–35.

logical implication—and hence inherent part—of 'the law of contract' so much as because of the general import the notion of restoring inherently legal rights belonging to husbands had taken on within the public sphere. Considered for this symbolic import, the restitution of conjugal rights continued not only to stand for the power of husbands over their wives, but also as a testament to the supposed law-like essence of the Muslim personal law.

In fact, these symbolic valences came to extend back over the Allahabad High Court's own reasoning in *Anis Begum* in a noticeable, even if ultimately cosmetic way. Most immediately, the Court's decision was simply about affirming the lower court's ruling in favour of the plaintiff, Muhammad Istafa, in his demand for the restoration of his rights over his estranged wife, Anis Begum.[88] However, even as it professed to have its hands tied by past precedent, the Court used its decision to cast a sceptical eye over the very foundation on which conjugal restitution doctrine had come to rest. This is why still today *Anis Begum* remains most memorable for the way the Allahabad High Court urged that time had come for the older view of Muslim marriage 'as a mere civil contract' to be abandoned; instead, as the Court declared, marriage between Muslims was 'a religious sacrament'.[89] In drawing on the discourse about marriage-as-sacrament, the Court also famously charged Justice Mahmood with being the chief culprit in 'carr[ying] the analogy' to contract—especially to the contract for sale—'too far' through his decision for the full bench in *Abdul Kadir*.[90]

For reasons we saw earlier in the chapter, of course, this was clearly a skewed way of describing *Abdul Kadir*; for it was not Mahmood (nor even

---

[88] The court thus declared itself unable on *stare decisis* grounds to do anything but to leave intact Mahmood's conclusion in *Abdul Kadir* that it was the position of Abu Hanifa's disciples that was the definitive one. (At the same time, it did question/deny Mahmood's assertion that the proper method for choosing between Abu Hanifa's position and that of his disciples was based on a supposed general rule of Islamic jurisprudence under which one would have to defer to the latter as a majority opinion rather than the former as a mere minority one.) Ironically, perhaps the most notable way in which the *Anis Begum* court softened the doctrinal logic of conjugal restitution involved making use of something very much like one of Mahmood's own observations. Even if cohabitation—in its capacity as the most basic 'performance' to which a spouse agreed under the marital contract—could not be counted as a condition precedent, the court held, this did not mean that non-payment of dower could not, itself, still be pled as a condition precedent—in its case, to the execution of any decree a husband might secure for the return of an estranged wife.
[89] Ibid., 24.
[90] Ibid., 23.

Abdul Kadir) who introduced the analogy to the contract for sale. Rather, it was Salima who had done so in the course of proffering the argument that her estranged husband was the first to have failed in fulfilling the relevant conditions required for the marital contract to remain valid or, in the alternative, that he had failed to even properly form the contract in the first place by paying the dower-cum-contractual consideration promptly. As the reader will recall, it was only in the face of the second of these arguments that Mahmood was prompted to compare Salima's dower right to a lien held by a vendor on goods still in their possession. Likewise, it was only in response that Mahmood found himself rushing to avail himself of the private law's underlying principle of collectivism to abruptly check Salima's attempt to further extend the voluntarist ethos of the market into the law of the Muslim family.

If Mahmood was not, therefore, wholly on his own initiative pushing the voluntarist ethos to its limit, why was the Allahabad High Court so keen on chastising him for 'grotesque[ly]' extending contractualism into the sphere of Muslim family law? The answer would seem to be that the Court was really expressing its opposition to the view that Muslim marriage should be counted as any kind of contract at all. In this respect, the purpose of the *Anis Begum* court's dictum questioning the analogy between marriage and the contract for sale was very different from Mahmood's own discussion of the same matter, as if the point was now to express embarrassment at the very outcome of his decision in *Abdul Kadir*, recognizing as it did a husband's right to conjugal services.

Along with summoning the discourse about marriage-as-sacrament to call for the true nature of the relationship between Muslim spouses to finally be recognized, in *Anis Begum* the Allahabad High Court thus went so far as to directly dispute Mahmood's treatment of consideration doctrine in order to clarify its clear feeling that Abdul Kadir's suit should have simply been rejected more than a half-century earlier. More specifically, it highlighted the inconsistency in Mahmood's use of consideration doctrine—for if the dower was not 'consideration' for the act of consummation, the *Anis Begum* court maintained, nor could it be so for the purposes of answering the prior question of whether any contract had been legitimately entered into in the first place. Instead, according to the *Anis Begum* court, the dower could only be called consideration in a figurative, shorthand sense, and this not for conjugal services but rather only 'the society of the life during the married life' that followed from the ongoing community of relations between spouses.[91] Not surprisingly, then, in calling for the true nature of the relationship between Muslim spouses finally to be recognized, the *Anis Begum* court was questioning Mahmood's reasoning in *Abdul Kadir* by reconstructing the discourse about marriage-as-sacrament in terms of the doctrinal discourse of status in precisely the same way that we saw Banerjee doing earlier.

9.8 A Conclusion: A Note on the Instrumental Function of the Law (of Conjugal Restitution)

As the evolving case law I have examined in this chapter suggests, the distinction between the law of the market and the law of the family in classical legal thought—including in the particular form it was taking in its rise under Crown rule in South Asia—did not turn on any contrast between the norming of the behaviour of the legal subject in the economy versus domestic space. Even less did it turn on the differing purposes behind the rules that did the norming. It was not, in other words, as if with respect to the law of the market, its rules were ones that were—in some pure 'in theory' sense—meant to advance laissez faire individualism alone, whereas with respect to the law of the family its rules were ones meant to exclusively nourish forms of collectivism that lingered from epochs past within the now extra-economic social spaces of (still private, but somehow more interior and less worldly) interaction. Rather, the distinction within the private law between the law of the market and the law of the family, much like the distinction between the private and the public law themselves, was inherently vanishing.

The more relevant distinction, instead, was between principles of voluntarist individualism and communitarian collectivism that were simultaneously at play within the rule regimes of both domains (as too were they across the divide between the private and the public law). Therefore, the distinction between the law of the family and the law of the market did not turn on believing, much less demonstrating, that only one rather than the other of these organizing principles underpinned the historical

[91] Ibid.

ontology of these respective subdomains of the private law. On the contrary, the distinction depended mainly on a selectivity of emphasis that emerged in the course of characterizing these domains—whether as part of the rhetorical politics of ordinary-language discourse in the public sphere and the standard puffery it entailed about the civilizational uniqueness of 'the rule of law' in the West and its centrality to modernity or the rhetoric of justification within doctrinal discourse itself, especially when handling what Ronald Dworkin would call 'easy' cases.[92]

Indeed, within the venues of doctrinal discourse, even when more complicated questions (making for what Dworkin would call 'hard cases') were involved—like those that were raised in the course of fashioning novel rules, as for conjugal restitution—the classical view about where the law of the market ended and where the law of the family began became extremely confusing. This is because the simultaneity with which the principles of individualism and collectivism became manifest made doctrinally conceptualizing the normativity through which the law ruled relations of domestic community a highly manipulable affair.

As we have seen, even on the most straightforward understanding, considered as a law of status relations, the law of the domestic community/family could be rationalized through two very different modes of imagining. On the one hand, at its external border, the family's legalization could be imagined to be the product of a 'law of status' that ruled the domestic community by virtue of that community's being doctrinally conceived as held by the private juridical will of its dominant member, as per a right *in rem* that the patriarch commanded against the world at large. On the other hand, within the borders of the family, domestic relations could be imagined as being ruled by a doctrinally operative concept of status that was liable to make the normativity at play within the family seem not so very different from that which was at play within the law of the market. For here the family's legalization could be conceived as a product of the will, albeit in its public incarnation as that which belonged to the individual juridical person of the state. It was, thus, the public will that could capacitate the family's members vis-à-vis one another where necessary, thereby enabling them to individuate their correlative rights

---

[92] See generally Ronald Dworkin, 'Hard Cases', *Harvard Law Review* 88, no. 6 (1975): 1057–1109.

and duties in a way that would make explicit the basis of these rights and duties in an inherently legal kind of normativity called by the name of 'the law'.

Still more confounding is that even where only the second image of the law of the family as a law of status was at hand, these twin principles could still reiterate themselves within the doctrinal schema that obtained between the members of the family just as they did within the law of contract. As we saw in the context of contract, this followed from the way in which the principle of party autonomy privileging voluntarist individualism stood always alongside either of two other bases for asserting collectivism's justificatory appeal. For surveyed from the adverse party's perspective the facilitation by the adjudicator of the triumphant individual's will in cases of dispute could always be imagined as an endorsement of a collectivist ethos rooted in privileging the (purported) maximization of general social utility over the adverse party's own conception of where the equities of the dispute should have lain. Conversely, if it was the adverse party's will that was to be actualized, if this did not occur on the basis of a simple reversal of the direction of the counterparty's argument from maximizing general social utility, it could always also be rooted in some alternative way of cashing out collectivism's significance. For example, one routine way of doing so involved appealing to the need to prevent the individualist ethos of the market that was being advocated by the counterparty from going too far and thereby threatening the very possibility of social and moral community, rooted as it was in the values of equity and reciprocity that were its prerequisites.

In contrast to the above possible manifestations of individualism and collectivism in contract, in the context of the law of the domestic community—conceived as a law of publicly willed status capacitations of family members vis-à-vis one another—the confounding potential with which these dual principles could reiterate themselves appeared through the mediumship of a prior question. For in the context of the law of the domestic community there was a need to first consider whether relations of voluntarist agreement between family members should be allowed at all. The questions of how such agreements could be validly formed and whether their terms should be strictly enforced came only next. Consequently, if instead of being just a law based on the right *in rem* by which the family was to be held by its dominant member the normativity that ruled the domestic community was conceived as a law based on the way that inside its borders there were inter-subjective relations that were themselves governed legally, then a new question presented itself. For now it became necessary to ask whether 'the law' operating inside of the domestic kin community could be staked ultimately on the publicly willed status capacitation to individuate the lifelong courses of rights and duties that otherwise bound its members to one another: whether as wives to husbands or husbands to wives, as fathers to sons and daughters or sons and daughters to fathers, as dependent domestic labourers to the members of the genetic family or as members of the genetic family to their dependent domestic labourers, and so on. The new question that presented itself, in other words, had to do with whether the legal entitlements that underlay such domestic relations of reciprocity be left—in the way that relations in the market ostensibly were—to the possibility of full or partial realignment through privately willed and formally mutual agreement.

In principle, the answer to this prior question could involve either of the same two potential bases of collectivism we saw above, notwithstanding whatever 'individualist' answers might also be given. On the one hand, if the privately willed realignment of the individuated rights and duties of family members was to be sanctioned—that is to say, were such parties to be granted so-called negative rights against the intercession of the will of the state into the enforceable terms of their agreements to such an effect—this would have to always remain open to being understood as a means of promoting some larger collective interest of the domestic group. (Of course, in whatever specific case of dispute, doing so would always also mean that some one member's individual interest was being privileged over some other's.) For the idea here would be that allowing voluntarist realignment of relations between family members would encourage the transformation of the society of the domestic community according to the image of civil society at large; the echoes of some form of argument from increasing social utility would, thus, always be audible from somewhere in the not-too-distant background, waiting to be brought to the fore.

On the other hand, if this prior question was instead answered in the negative—by disallowing voluntarist agreement between the private individuals who constituted the domestic community—then there was an alternative principle of collectivism to which such an answer could just as readily be attributed. For at hand in the negative answer would be nothing other than a reaffirmation of the default circumstance of the law of the family in classical legal thought. That is, prohibiting voluntarist agreement between the members of the domestic community would have to derive from some version of the argument for repelling the advance of the illegitimate ethos of private individualism into the shared sanctum of the domestic group, with its should-be ethic of extra-economic communitarian reciprocity.

Of course, in reality it was the negative answer that tended to carry greater appeal; hence, more often than not, the irreducibly legal character of the law of the family was staked on the absence within the domestic sphere of the types of negative rights against the intercession of the state that were the hallmark of the sphere of the market. Consequently—and also more often than not—the domestic sphere was symbolized as one in which the public will could be freely substituted for some individual family member's own, at least where the larger ethic behind doing so was to ensure that domestic relations remained ostensibly reciprocal.

At the same time, any such effort at maintaining reciprocity was always contingent on the varying ways there were for construing the collectivist ethic of communitarian reciprocity, itself. Since doing so could range, in principle, from doing equity to the less well-off to preserving the family's 'stability' by shoring up its hierarchy, the intercession of the public will into the domestic realm could correspond just as easily to a support for the weaker members of the family as it could to a support for the stronger. Capacitation, thus, could just as easily mean individuating the duties of some subordinate member of the family that were correlative to whatever the opposing rights that would then be getting claimed by the patriarch as it could individuating the subordinate's rights relative to the patriarch's own correlative duties.

* * *

All told, then, it was only against the backdrop of a highly unwieldy, even if simultaneously quite regimented, set of permutations of individualism and collectivism that construing the nature of marriage within classical legal thought could proceed, including in the Crown's subcontinent. To the extent that marriage contained elements that made it look both like a form of voluntarist agreement between autonomous private parties and like an ongoing state of reciprocal relations between members of a community, then, it precipitated the maximally confounding situation in which the principles of individualism and collectivism were free to function in almost every possible way within the law of the family at once. Marriage, then, very clearly did raise what above I called the prior question of whether privately willed voluntarist agreement should be allowed in the context of domestic relations in the first place.

Accordingly, a final point that bears mentioning is that even if the prior question did tend, overall, to be answered in the negative, there was nothing in the doctrinal nature of things that required there to be more rather than less state action where marriage was deemed a status (viz., the characterization that followed from the negative answer). For, as noted earlier, capacitating members of the domestic community with the status to bear individuated legal rights was an equivocal affair, given that doing so could just as easily render other of their duties more distinctly actionable. In fact, even within the central domains of the Anglo-common-law world amidst classical legal thought's rise, one reason why the view of marriage as a set of status relations seems to have recommended itself is because that view obviated the need for state action that would have resulted if marriage was instead viewed primarily as a form of contract. As the story of conjugal restitution as a civil remedy for breach of contract in late-colonial South Asia so well suggests, there were many thorny, costly, and administratively difficult questions involved in judicially refereeing—on any widespread scale—the inevitable conflicts over the terms of spousal duties that were attendant with the conception of marriage as a contract.

When measured in terms of the minimization of state action, it was a moot point as to exactly which treatment of marriage—whether as a contract or status—should have proved most consistent with a commitment of the type the colonial state in the subcontinent professed against so-called interference in the inner sphere of native culture, domesticity, and religion. At the same time, the more confounding the doctrinal conception of marriage was made by the standing presence of the animating principles of individualism and collectivism, the more revealing it proved with respect to the larger impact of legal ontologization; and this is just as true whether we are thinking about the ontologization of the law of conjugal restitution as one subsegment of the law of marriage, the law of marriage as one subsegment of the law of status, the law of status as one subsegment of the private law, or the private law as one subsegment of the law writ large. For in all of these cases, ontologization could just as easily have proceeded on the basis of the ostensibly opposite animating principle for justifying the supposedly 'correct' conception of 'what' the law was to be seen as being, in its essence.

All the more clearly, therefore, should we now be able to see how indirect the instrumental function of the ontologized components of the law could be. Where what was supposed to be *the* legal outcome could be aligned with the preferences of actual or imaginable disputants by paths of deductive logic that radiated from so many different directions at once as the arrangement of the various permutations of argument I have outlined here suggests, all the more could contests over material domination, patriarchal assertion, and communitarian identification come to be conducted within doctrinal discourse in quite subtle ways. In fact, this was especially the case where even the more direct incarnations of such interests—whether material or gendered—could be translated into positions that purported to 'systematically' align with 'the law' through such varied configurations of its underlying doctrinal elements. Given the variety of these configurations, it can be little surprise that assertions about the genuine legality of the forms of the personal law—meaning, assertions of the very type that factored so heavily into claims of communitarian identity in a context like the late-colonial subcontinent's—were being made from so many direction at once.

Conclusion

In this book I have taken the long view of the development of the law's rule in colonial South Asia, arguing for a significantly different image than what historians of modern South Asia have heretofore tended to see. This has come not only through the explanatory approach—of historical ontology—I have sought to develop and adopt, but also through the multi-stage substantive argument the book has made. While I will not attempt to summarize all of the particularities of the argument here, I will close by highlighting three main levels at which it has unfolded.

At the first such level, though periodization is always an imperfect enterprise, in the book I have sought to show that with respect to legal change there was a considerably different character to what came before and after the transfer of power from Company to Crown in 1858 than what is most often suggested. In this connection, the book has resisted the idea that the transition across these periods can adequately be understood in terms of the intensification of a commitment to 'codifying' the law that had been the mark of colonial rule from its inception. Neither, relatedly, can the period after the transfer of power adequately be distinguished as involving a more pronounced resort to lawmaking through 'positivist' legislation, nor even a quickening pace to the 'transplantation' of existing English legal rules into the subcontinent.

Whether implicitly or explicitly, in the book I have also expressed scepticism about reading legal change after the transfer of power as simply an extension of a growing utilitarian tendency within colonial rule that had started several decades earlier, going back to the 1820s or, for that matter, that had arisen from tendencies that can be traced back all the way to the first years after the East India Company had achieved supremacy in Bengal. All told, then, neither eventualities that materialized before 1800—like Hastings' judicial and administrative reforms or the mushrooming of interest in the subcontinent's own so-called 'native' laws and usages—nor ones that materialized by the end of the 1830s—like the Governor Generalship of Bentinck, Macaulay's selection as the first Law Member on the Governor General's Council, or the start of work on the Indian Penal Code—can unproblematically be taken as antecedents more proximal than the transfer of power itself to some true point of transition to a subsequent era of intensified codification, legislation, and/or transplantation as the key supposed aspect(s) of legal change.

Beyond the role of codification/legislation/transplantation as specific mechanisms of legal change, the book has also resisted one of the key consequences the attention they have commanded has tended to create—namely, a skewed image of the intellectual currents circulating in and around the law during the era of British rule. On the more standard view of legal change under colonialism that scholars of South Asia have developed or (implicitly) adopted, at the level of the history of ideas the above mechanisms have been understood as set in motion by wholesale political philosophies, ideologies, or disciplinary discourses. Moreover, these macro-intellectual forces have too often been seen as tantamount to schools of administrative and political thought or means, like any other, of the ethnographic state's classificatory and reifying impulses alone. On such views, the law's rule is too easily seen as being architected chiefly from outside the law itself, leading all the more seamlessly to the latter's naturalization. In the process, the intellectual tradition of classical legal thought has gone entirely unnoticed; indeed, the fact that it came into being as any coherent, much less transnational, formation only after the middle of the nineteenth century has left its developmental history too easily mistaken for the very intensification of codification/legislation/transplantation after the transfer of power that has obscured its importance in the first place.

Of course, this is not to say that either the study of law and history in South Asia or the study of its history of ideas—or, if one prefers, its intellectual history[1]—has remained stuck on what Eric Stokes famously identified as 'the battle' of the main 'philosophies'[2] of the 'official mind'.[3]

---

[1] Beyond references given earlier (see e.g. ch. 1 at note 97) see also e.g. Shruti Kapila, ed., *An Intellectual History for India* (New York: Cambridge University Press, 2010) and Francesca Orsini, 'Where to Find Indian Menocchios?' *Journal of South Asian Intellectual History* 1, no. 1 (2019): 1–12.

[2] Stokes, *The English Utilitarians and India*, 1–24.

[3] As noted in the first chapter, this specific turn of phrase comes from one of Stokes' essays. See generally Stokes, 'The Land Revenue Systems of the North-Western Provinces and Bombay Deccan'.

Indeed, as I have indicated at several different points in the presentation, even attention to the seemingly most official of philosophies—of liberalism—that was connected to the Raj's supposedly exceptional rule of law has undergone various transformations at the hands of historians in the time since Stokes was writing. Nor does the book's effort to look at the law's rule from the inside out, so to speak, proceed in blindness to the fact that grounding legal change in deeper currents of polity, society, and economy—in the way those adopting a law and history frame have been wont to do—has been meant, in its own right, as a correction to the insularity of the narrow and de-contextualized tradition of legal history as 'law-office history'.[4] Even so, by demanding that we revisit the question of periodization through calling attention to classical legal thought the book has sought to work against the grain of the paradoxical tendency such correction has produced to regard the law, in effect, as secondary to the story of legal change. It would not be wrong, then, to read the book as an attempt to correct for an overcorrection—namely, that by which the law has too often been left to reside somewhere on the purportedly less important (first) side of the historiographical divide between colonial rule's ideology and actuality, its theory and practice, its ostensibly hegemonic discourse and invariably negotiated reality, and so on.

In this last respect, the historical ontological approach to legal change that I have pursued in the book has comprised a further aspect of the first level of its substantive argument. For the conceptual vocabulary formulated in part I—and especially the distinction between the ordinary linguistic and the doctrinal as two different discursive sites or registers on/through which the ontology of the legal was (re)constituted—points to the polyphonic nature of 'the theoretical' in the type of historical change the book has been seeking to understand. Moreover, the express point of tracing how, as Hacking would put it, words 'occur' in different types of sentences or styles of reasoning[5] at these two different sites, even while often being articulated in terms that are nominally the same, has really been a way of tracing how the constitution of new objects of thought was simultaneously a way of constituting new kinds of real objects in the

---

[4] For the origins of the phrase see Alfred H. Kelly, 'Clio and the Court: An Illicit Love Affair', *Supreme Court Review* 1965 (1965): 119–58 at 122, n. 13.
[5] Hacking, *Historical Ontology*, 174–75.

(social) world. By treating historical ontology as a method for addressing the great question of jurisprudence and by outlining the details of such a method, then, the book's express aim has been to disperse the dichotomy between ideology and actuality, discourse and practice, law and society, and so on.

Beyond the first level of argument, on the second the book has sought to complicate received wisdom about the more specific features of law's rule in the colonial subcontinent that are commonly understood to have persisted across the dividing line between Company rule and Crown Raj. In this vein, one major focus of the preceding chapters has been to question the notion that the native personal law was quarantined within a realm of the inner and the cultural already from the time of Hastings' judicial reforms of the 1770s. More specifically, this point was at the centre of the book's final two chapters, in which I contended that it was only after the middle of the next century that the category of 'the personal law' really emerged in the first place, including in its capacity as a place-holder for 'the law of status' and the subcontinent's own ostensibly unique subsystems thereof. As I tried to demonstrate in those chapters, the emergence of the personal law occurred only in tandem with the amalgamation of what, by dint of another element of the conceptual vocabulary developed in part I, we can call these several quasi-'operative' (as well as quasi-'administrable') categories into a uniquely colonial version of classical legal thought's schematization (and concretization) of the very object that it was, at the same time, universalizing.

Even more concertedly, at this second level of argument I have sought to revisit the long-standing but still absolutely critical question of property's rule in the subcontinent—especially across the lengthy span of the book that extends from the two chapters of part II through the first chapter of part III. Of course, summarizing these chapters primarily through reference to the book's overarching goal of complicating received wisdom about legal development under colonial rule probably underplays the nature of the intervention they seek to make into the history of property. This is not the least because of the larger implications of that intervention beyond just the history of modern South Asia, given the (perceived) magnitude of the importance of law and landed entitlement to the emergence and dynamics of capitalist modernity more generally.

Considered on its own terms, then, the book's intervention into the question of land control and its reconstitution in colonial South Asia has involved demonstrating how under the Company's rule property was left extrinsic to what I have called the ontology of the legal. Set against the persistence of an early-modern discourse of 'constitutionism', defining sovereignty as a practical endeavour based on the two key tasks of administering taxation and administering justice, the subcontinent's ontology of 'the laws'—more than any of 'the law', considered as a systematic logical unicity infinite in its normative reach—was never premised on extrapolating an idea of legal right in general from that of the property right in particular in the same way as was afoot in the metropolitan world by the late eighteenth century.

In contrast, in the colonial subcontinent property's internalization into the ontology of the legal would take place in earnest only after the middle of the next century and only side by side with the rise and globalization of classical legal thought. In this last respect, as far as doctrinal ideas go, of particular note was the notion of legal right as a realm of 'proprietary' interest, which was articulated in the subcontinent through the varied genres of legal scientism and new forms of so-called agrarian special legislation that became prominent after 1860. Complementing this new idea of 'proprietary' right, which generally corresponded to the similarly disaggregated, relativized, and de-physicalized idea of property in classical legal thought, was also a second key idea—of 'the will'—that even more directly corresponded to classical legal thought's express analytic. Together, as the two foundational elements of the law in classical legal thought, these twin ideas—of rights as realms of proprietary interest, on the one hand, and the will of the juridical person, on the other—became key points within a new doctrinal discourse of contract under the Crown. At the same time, this new doctrinal field itself would host an ongoing shift away from the element of the right-holder's realm and towards that of their ability to realign its boundaries according to the will as the key atom of irreducible legality.

Ultimately, through the whole sequence of discussion of property and contract that extends from chapters four to seven, the book seeks to clarify how, more specifically, the subcontinent's path of legal modernization unfolded in a way that was unique when compared to the Anglo-common-law mainstream, given its status as a colonial dependency. This is even notwithstanding the growing role classical legal thought would play as a common influence in both Britain's India and the West. For on the account presented in the foregoing pages, what rendered the colonial path unique was not that the proverbial gap between law and society was necessarily greater in a place like the subcontinent compared to the fast-industrializing (and supposedly rationalizing) spaces of Anglo-America. Nor was it even just because of any so-called rule of colonial difference by which Britain's South Asian subjects were denied a genuine rule of law and instead saddled with only the same non-parliamentary rule by law that was in place already from the time of the Company's ascent to power. Simultaneously, the book's accounting for what made the subcontinent's path of legal modernization unique has also avoided too directly equating the key factor with the Company's 'bastardized' version of the pre-colonial state and the inconsistency between its overriding extractive aims and any real interest in fashioning a 'true' capitalist regime of private property 'freed' into the market.[6]

Without underplaying the importance of such differentiating factors, especially the last, in the book I have instead drawn attention to how the doctrinal discourse of property in early colonial South Asia departed from its counterpart in the Anglo-common-law mainstream. As I have already begun to describe, this partly followed from the relative failure of such discourse to furnish a doctrinal concept of the property right in particular that could serve as much of a template for any highly operative or administrable notion of legal right in general. More than this, it was also a product of the way that an equally unique brand of talk about rendering property 'absolute' in the early-colonial public sphere—focusing as it did on creating a fully certain security of expectation regarding control over land's rent—had to be translated into doctrinal terms. In this respect, then, the middle several chapters of the book spanning the discussions of property and contract in parts II and III have offered a comparative history of sorts—of British India versus the wider Anglo-common-law world—in which the focus has been on the developmental trajectory of the core entitlements of the private law, in its capacity as a twofold discursive phenomenon.

---

[6] Washbrook, 'Law, State and Agrarian Society in Colonial India', 661.

If at the first two levels of the argument that I have been summarizing so far there is justification beyond simple reasons of manageability for the book to have excluded consideration of the public law, it is that from the standpoint of charting the emergence of 'the law', writ large, it was the schematization of the private law that was most important. For as I discussed at some length in the conclusion to chapter seven, it was the private law that served as the model for the further schematization of the other main 'public' half of classical legal thought's object, more than vice versa. (As the reader will recall, it was also the conclusion of chapter seven that made for the bridge to chapters eight and nine and their discussion of classical legal thought's most explicit way of reserving a place within the space of private legal relations for the public juridical will—that is, through discourse of and about the law of status.)

With the last observation, we now arrive full circle back at the concern with ontologization that was the book's point of departure. Therefore, it is appropriate to close with a few words about the third and final level at which the book's argument has unfolded over the course of the previous nine chapters. For to prioritize ontologization in the understanding of legal change in Britain's India has been to attempt to say something of note about legal theory and jurisprudence as well. It has, in other words, been a way of bringing the book's reach beyond not only the history of modern South Asia but also the field of history, as such. It is, thus, worth reminding ourselves that at this final level of the argument, the fashioning and deployment of a historical ontological approach to the law, in specific, has been a way of keeping the great question of jurisprudence—as central as it was to the colonial encounter with native juridical tradition the world over—at hand.

Of course, here it may be important to note that especially insofar as I have privileged the term *jurisprudence* over *legal theory* (or even *legal thought*), it is likely that many a philosopher of law would object to the claim I am making on behalf of the book with respect to its third level of argument—at least given a field of the philosophy of law that is often cast as co-extensive with anything that can properly be called by the name of jurisprudence. Likewise, from the other side, the book has obviously also not much engaged with distinctions—often cogent—that can be made between doing legal theory or investigating legal thought and engaging in philosophical jurisprudence/the philosophy of law, proper. (David

Kennedy and William Fisher's way of dividing up these lines of enquiry especially comes to mind here.)[7]

Yet, to the extent that the book has been silent with respect to providing a more elaborate defence of why it *should* be taken to hold implications for jurisprudence and, for that matter, legal theory, this is hardly because of indifference to or a lack of awareness of the way boundaries can be constructed between such fields—let alone, between either of them and that of history. On the contrary, it is because existing ways of erecting borders hardly seem foolproof, much less based on some kind of unimpeachable logic rather than strictures born of professionalization and its tendency to incentivize status-seeking through asserting exclusive ownership over certain kinds of questions on the part of certain kinds of experts. Here, therefore, it should suffice to simply reiterate that trying to capture the way 'the law' emerged as an object in its own right in the colonial subcontinent is to ask how its nature has been cognized. Consequently, it is also necessarily a way of engaging the question posed by H. L. A. Hart that was quoted in the last of the three epigraphs with which the introduction to the book opened. Stark and simple, as the reader will recall, that question asked: '[w]hat *is* law?'[8]

Indeed, over the course of its nine main chapters the book has offered a running attempt to offer one kind of answer to this question. In a sense, then, at its third level of argument the book's historical ontological approach to jurisprudence has involved formulating what we can alternatively call a discourse theory of the law. Of course, the attentive reader may here be picking up echoes—including from part I—of Habermas' extension of his own so-called discourse theory of ethics to law, but if so, they are merely nominal (and inadvertent).[9] In fact, whatever implications I have tried to draw out from the book's own discourse theory of/

---

[7] David Kennedy and William W. Fisher, III, 'Introduction'. In *The Canon of American Legal Thought*, eds. David Kennedy and William W. Fisher (Princeton, NJ: Princeton University Press, 2006), 2 (distinguishing the investigation of legal thought as a field concerned with how scholars/analysts have sought 'to clarify and reform the way legal professionals think about the law' from that of jurisprudence/the philosophy of law/legal theory which 'asks questions about the nature of "law"—as an institution, as a social or political form, even as a form of speech' but which is not 'first and foremost concerned to describe or reform the modes of reasoning legal professionals use in their everyday work').

[8] Hart, *The Concept of Law*, 1 (emphasis added).

[9] See generally Habermas, *Between Facts and Norms*.

historical ontological approach to the law are likely to be more at odds with Habermas' approach than in consonance with it.

At the same time, if echoes of Habermas' discourse theory of law nevertheless prove audible to the reader, it is not wholly unwelcome, especially if they are heard to sound in some tone of critique. This is because notwithstanding the obvious differences between focusing on colonial rule in the South Asian subcontinent and on civic and political life in the 'modern' states of the liberal democratic West, the empirical case to which the book's own jurisprudential theory has been applied has hardly been accidental. Rather, as I made clear in part I, the choice of focus has been very much intentional—with that intention being for the focus on South Asia to run directly at odds with the backdrop against which scholars of jurisprudence have typically scaled their theories. For even when ostensibly silent on the matter, jurisprudential theorizing almost always involves abstracting over a story about legal development in the West, whether that story functions more precisely as explanandum or explanans. Of course, this is little surprise, given the mutually constitutive relationship between the categories of our modern understanding and the forms of (social/institutional) fact like 'law', 'the law', 'the legal', 'the legal system', and so on, which they have named as part of the historical making and remaking of the modern West—rather than which they were just used to explain after the fact, as if as part of some pure enterprise in scientific discernment.

Accordingly, in whatever way the book's more specific empirical-historical case has been meant to juxtapose its approach to explaining the law's nature with more conventional varieties of jurisprudence and legal theory, it hopefully at least partially serves to justify the other major omission from the preceding pages. For that omission has involved the choice I have had to make to simply leave aside the obviously critical question of how the subcontinent's various pre-colonial juristic traditions continued to develop beyond the purview of the colonial state and its rule of/by the law. If there are defensible reasons for doing so, here again among them are considerations of manageability that have made it necessary to engage with the colonial subcontinent in its capacity more as an arena of legal modernity than as one of legal plurality, as one might imperfectly put it.

That said, I believe the omission is also justifiable for other reasons as well—especially on grounds of the confluence between framework and fact, given the seemingly undeniable reality that almost everywhere in the world juridical life was remapped in terms of a notion of 'the law' that cannot simply be regarded as a world-historical universal existing outside time and circumstance. Therefore, the question of the historicity of 'the law', itself, is no less pressing or in need of attention than any that should be asked about the histories of the forms of native juristic tradition that I have either had to ignore or illuminated only insofar as they came under the law's own ambit. In this respect, it would not be wrong to say that the emergence of 'the law' as a common object of concern over the last 150-plus years has meant that long nineteenth-century legal modernization took an obviously similar course almost everywhere around the world. For this transpired not only under the globalizing influence of classical legal thought, but also amidst the rise of the territorial-bureaucratic state, the attendant national society it could be imagined as subsuming while still standing separate from, and an increasingly marketized economy that could be envisioned as ostensibly disembedded from both without ever having actually been so much as even formally freed from either.

Bibliography

Archives

British Library, India Office Records (IOR), London
  Bengal Regulations

Indian Legislative Consultations
Public and Judicial Department Records
Political and Secret Department RecordsNational Archives of India, New Delhi
  Proceedings of the Home Department:
  Judicial Branch
  Political Branch
  Public Branch
  Proceedings of the Legislative Department:
  General Branch
  Legislative Branch

Published Primary Sources

Government Publications

Government of India. *The Indian Contract Act, 1872* (Act No. IX of 1872).
Government of the Punjab. *Report on the Punjab Codification of Customary Law Conference*. Lahore: Superintendent, Government Printing, 1915.
House of Commons. *The Fifth Report from the Select Committee on the Affairs of the East India Company, 1812. Vol. I: Bengal Presidency*. Madras: J. Higginbotham, 1866.
House of Commons. *The Fifth Report from the Select Committee on the Affairs of the East India Company, 1812. Vol. II: Madras Presidency*. Madras: J. Higginbotham, 1866.
House of Commons. *Minutes of Evidence taken before the Select Committee on the Affairs of the East India Company, III—Revenue, Parliamentary Papers*, 1831–32. Vol. XI.
Law Commission of India, *Report of the Fourth Law Commission*, 1879.
Law Commission of India. 'Thirteenth Report (Contract Act, 1872)', 26 September 1958.

Case Law Reports
Allahabad Weekly Notes

Calcutta Weekly Law Notes
Calcutta Law Journal
Fyzee, Asaf A. A. ed. *Cases in the Muhammadan Law of India, Pakistan, and Bangladesh*. 2nd edn. New York: Oxford University Press, 2005.
English Reports
Indian Law Reports
Allahabad Series
Bombay Series
Calcutta Series
Patna Series
Madras Law Journal
Madras Law Times
Moore, Edmund F. *Reports of Cases Heard and Determined by the Judicial Committee and the Lords of His Majesty's Most Honourable Privy Council, on Appeal from the Supreme and Sudder Dewany Courts in the East Indies* (Moore's Indian Appeals [M. I. A.]). London: J. and H. Clark, 1838–1873.
Perry, Erskine. *Cases Illustrative of Oriental Life, Decided in H. M. Supreme Court at Bombay and the Application of English Law to India*. London: S. Sweet, 1853 (Reprint, Asian Educational Services, 1988).
Punjab Law Reporter

Other Published Primary Sources

Abdur Rahman, A. F. M. *Institutes of Mussalman Law: A Treatise on Personal Law*. Calcutta: Thacker, Spink & Co., 1907.
Addison, Charles, Greenstreat. *A Treatise on the Law of Contract*. London: W. Benning, 1847.
Alexander, Richard Dundas. *The Indian Case-Law on Torts*. Calcutta: Thacker, Spink, 1891.
Ali, Ameer. *The Personal Law of the Mahommedans, According to All the Schools. Together with a comparative sketch of the law of inheritance among the Sunnis and the Shiahs*. London: W. H. Allen & Co., 1880.
Ali, Ameer. *The Law Relating to Gifts, Trusts, and Testamentary Dispositions among the Mahommedans: According to the Hanafi, Maliki, Shâfeï, and Shiah Schools*. Calcutta: Thacker, Spink, 1885.
Ali, Ameer. *Mahommedan Law: The Law Relating to Succession and Status*, Calcutta: Thacker, Spink, 1885.
Anson, William Reynell. *Principles of the English Law of Contract*. Oxford: Macmillan and Co., 1879.
Arbuthnot, A. J. *Major General Sir Thomas Munro, Governor of Madras: Selections from His Minutes and Other Official Writings*, vol. I. London: Kegan Paul, 1881.
Ardaseer Cursetjee v. Perozeboye, 1856. 6 M. I. A. 348.
Austin, John. *The Province of Jurisprudence Determined*. London: John Murray, 1861 [1832].Austin, John. *Lectures on Jurisprudence, or, the Philosophy of Positive Law*. London, J. Murray, 1869 (1863).
Baden-Powell, Baden Henry. *A Manual of Jurisprudence for Forest Officers: Being a Treatise on the Forest Law and Those Branches of the General Civil and Criminal Law*

with a Comparative Notice of the Chief Continental Laws. Calcutta: Superintendent of Government Printing, 1882.

Baden-Powell, Baden Henry. *A Manual of the Land Revenue Systems and Land Tenures of British India*. Calcutta: Office of the Superintendent of Government Printing, 1882.

Baden-Powell, Baden Henry. *The Land Systems of British India: Being a Manual of the Land-tenures and of the Systems of Land-revenue Administration Prevalent in the Several Provinces*, 3 vols. Oxford: Clarendon Press, 1892.

Baden-Powell, Baden Henry. *Forest Law. A Course of Lectures on the Principles of Civil and Criminal Law and on the Law of the Forest (Chiefly Based on the Laws in Force in British India)*. London: Bradbury, Agnew, & Co., 1893.

Baden-Powell, Baden Henry. 'The Permanent Settlement of Bengal', *English Historical Review* X, no. 38 (Apr. 1895): 276–93.

Baden-Powell, Baden Henry. *A Short Account of the Land Revenue and its Administration in British India: with a Sketch of the Land Tenures*. Oxford: Clarendon Press, 1907.

Baillie, John. *A Digest of Mohummudan Law According to the Tenets of the Twelve Imams*, 4 vols. Calcutta: Printed at the Hon. Company's Press, 1805.

Baillie, Neil B. E. *Digest of Moohummudan Law on the Subjects to which it is Usually Applied by British Courts of Justice in India / Compiled and Translated from Authorities in the Original Arabic, with an Introduction and Explanatory notes*, 2nd edn London: Smith, Elder, & co., 1875.

Banerjee, Gooroodass. *The Hindu Law of Marriage and Stridhan*. Madras: Higginbotham & Co., 1879.

Bentham, Jeremy. *Principles of the Civil Code (N.D.)*, reprinted in *Theory of Legislation*. R. Hildreth, trans. London: Trübner & Co., 1908.

Bernard, William Leigh. *The Irish Land Question: Suggestions for the Extended Establishment of a Peasant Proprietary in Ireland*. Dublin: Hodges, Foster, & Figgis, 1880.

Bernier, François, *Travels in the Mogul empire*, 2 vols. Irving Brock, trans. London: W. Pickering, 1826 (1670).

Blackstone, William. *Commentaries on the Law of England, Book the First*, Oxford: Clarendon Press, 1765.

Blackstone, William. *Commentaries on the Law of England, Book the Second*, 9th edN. London: W. Strathan, 1783 (1765).

Bolts, William. *Considerations on Indian Affairs; Particularly Respecting the Present State of Bengal and its Dependencies*, 2nd edn. London: J. Almon, 1772.

Boulnois, Charles and William Henry Rattigan. *Notes on Customary Law as Administered in the Courts of the Punjab*, 2nd edn. Lahore: Published at the Civil and Military Gazette, 1878.

Campbell, George. *The Irish Land*. Dublin: Hodges, Foster, and Co., 1869.

Chitty, Joseph. *A Practical Treatise on the Law of Contracts, and Defences to Actions thereon*. London: S. Sweet, 1826.

Coke, Edward. *The First Part of the Institutes of the Laws of England or a Commentary Upon Littleton*, 10th edn. London, 1703 (1628).

Colebrooke, Henry Thomas. *Treatise on Obligations and Contracts*. London: C. Roworth, 1818.Comyn, Samuel. *Treatise of the Law Relative to Contracts and Agreements Not Under Seal*. London: J. Butterworth,1807.

Connell, Arthur Knatchbull. *Discontent and Danger in India*. London: C. Kegan Paul, 1880.

Connell, Arthur Knatchbull. *The Economic Revolution of India and the Public Works Policy*. London: Kegan Paul, Trench, & Co., 1883.

Cowell, Herbert. *The Hindu Law: A Treatise on the Laws Administered Exclusively to Hindus by the British Courts in India (The Tagore Law Lectures of 1870)*. London: W. Thacker & Co., 1870.

Cunningham, Henry and H. H. Shephard. *The Indian Contract Act: No. IX of 1872, together with an Introduction and Explanatory Notes, Table of Contents, Appendix and Index*, 7th edn. Madras: Printed at the Lawrence Asylum Press, 1894.

Dicey, A. V. *An Introduction to the Study of the Law of the Constitution*. London: Macmillan, 1885.

Dow, Alexander. *The History of Hindostan; Translated from the Persian. To which are Prefixed Two Dissertations*, 3 vols. London: J. Walker, 1812.

Dutt, Romesh Chunder. *The Economic History of India in the Victorian Age. From the Accession of Queen Victoria in 1837 to the Commencement of the Twentieth Century*, vol. II. London: Kegan Paul, 1906.

Dyer, Adair. 'The Internationalization of Family Law', *University of California Davis Law Review* 30 (1996–97): 625–45.

Elliot, Henry Miers. *Supplement to the Glossary of Indian Terms*. Agra: Printed at the Secundra Orphan Press, 1845.

Elliot, Henry Miers. *Memoirs on the History, Folk-lore, and Distribution of the Races of the North Western Provinces of India: Being an Amplified Edition of the Original Supplemental Glossary of Indian Terms*, vol. 2. London: Trubner, 1869.

Field, C. D. ed. *The Regulations of the Bengal Code: With a Chronological Table of Repeals and Amendments, an Introduction, Notes and an Index*. Calcutta: Thacker, Spink and Co., 1875.

Field, C. D. ed, *A Digest of the Law of Landlord and Tenant in the Provinces Subject to the Lieutenant Governor of Bengal*. Calcutta, 1879.

Forrest, George, ed. *Historical Documents of British India: Warren Hastings*, 2 vols. Delhi: Anmol, 1985.

Fox, William. *A Treatise on Simple Contracts and the Action of Assumpsit*. London: V. & R, Stevens and G. S. Norton, 1842.

Francis, Philip. *Original minutes of the Governor-General and Council of Fort William on the settlement and collection of the revenues of Bengal: with a plan of settlement, recommended to the Court of Directors in January, 1776*. London: J. Debrett, 1782.

Grant, James. *An Inquiry into the Nature of Zemindary Tenures in the Landed Property of Bengal, &c: in two parts: with an appendix, including a discussion of the great national question; whether, by the grant and condition of such tenures, the Zemindar, or the sovereign-representative-government, is to be considered the legal real proprietor of the soil*. London: J. Debrett, 1791.

Halhed, Nathaniel Brassey. *Code of Gentoo Laws: or, Ordinations of the Pundits from a Persian Translation, made from the Original, written in the Shanscrit Language*. London, 1776.

Hamilton, Charles, trans. *The Hedaya or Guide: A Commentary of the Mussalman Laws*. London: T. Bensley, 1791.
Holland, Thomas Erskine, *The Elements of Jurisprudence*. Oxford: Clarendon Press, 1882 (1880).
Holwell, J. Z. *Interesting Historical Events, Relative to the Provinces of Bengal, and the Empire of Indostan*, vol. I. London: T. Becket and P. A. De Hondt, 1765.
Hunter, W. W. ed., *A Life of the Earl of Mayo, Fourth Viceroy of India*, vol. II, London: Smith, Elder & Co., 1876.
Husein, Syed Karamat. *A Treatise on Right and Duty: Their Evolution, Definition, Analysis and Classification According to the Principles of Jurisprudence Being a Portion of the Muhammadan Law of Gifts*. Allahabad: Indian Press, 1899.
Ibbetson, Denzil. *A Glossary of The Tribes and Castes of the Punjab and North-West Frontier Province. Based on the census report for the Punjab, 1883*. Lahore: The Superintendent of Government Printing, 1911–19.
Ibbetson, Denzil. *Panjab Castes, being a reprint of the chapter on 'The Races, Castes, and Tribes of the People' in the* Report on The Census of The Panjab, *published in 1883*. Lahore: Printed by the Superintendent, Government Printing, 1916.
Ilbert, Courtenay. 'Indian Codification', *Modern Law Review* V, no. 20 (Oct. 1889): 347–69.
Jolly, Julius. *Outlines of an History of the Hindu Law of Partition, Inheritance and Adoption*. Calcutta: Thacker, Spink, 1885.
Jolly, Julius. *Hindu Law and Custom*. Calcutta, 1928.
Jones, Mary Evelyn Monckton. *Warren Hastings in Bengal, 1772–1774*. Oxford: Clarendon Press, 1918.
Jones, Robert Alun. *The Development of Durkheim's Social Realism*. New York: Cambridge University Press, 1999.
Jones, William. *Institutes Of Hindu Law: or, the Ordinances of Menu, according to the Gloss of Cullúca. Comprising the Indian System of Duties, Religious and Civil*. Calcutta: Printed by the Order of the Government, 1796.
Kaye, John William. *The Administration of the East India Company: A History of Indian Progress*. London: Richard Bentley, 1853.
Keene, H. G. 'Art. I.—India in 1880', *The Calcutta Review* 73, no. 145 (1881): 1–15.
Lal, Shadi. *The Punjab Alienation of Land Act, XIII of 1900 (as Amended by Punjab Act, I of 1907), with Comments and Notes of Cases*. Lahore: Addison Press, 1907.
Lawes, Edward Hobson Vitruvios. *A Practical Treatise on Pleading in Assumpsit*. London: W. Reed, 1810.
Leake, Steven Martin. *The Elements of the Law of Contract*. London: Stevens, 1867.
Lyall, James Broadwood. *Report of the Land Revenue Settlement of the Kangra District, Panjab, 1865–72*. Lahore: Printed at Central Jail Press, 1874.
MacDevitt, E. O. *A Manual of the Irish Land Acts of 1870 & 1881*. Dublin: Thom, 1881.
MacDevitt, E. O. *The Land Act of 1881: Rent, Peasant Proprietary, and Some Observations on the Congested Districts Board, and on the Departments of Agriculture and Industry*. Dublin: John Falconer, 1903.
Macnaghten, Francis Workman. *Considerations on the Hindoo Law as it is Current in Bengal*. Serampore: Printed at the Mission Press, 1824.
Macnaghten, William Hay. *Principles and Precedents of Hindu Law: Being a Compilation of Primary Rules relative to the Doctrine of Inheritance, Contracts and Miscellaneous Subjects*, 2 vols. Calcutta: Printed at the Baptist Mission Press, 1828.

Macnaghten, William Hay. *Principles and Precedents of Moohummudan Law: Being a Compilation of Primary Rules Relative to the Doctrine of Inheritance, Contracts and Miscellaneous Subjects.* Mirzapore: Printed at the Church Mission Press, 1825.

Maine, Henry Sumner. *Ancient Law: its Connection with the Early History of Society, and its Relation to Modern Ideas.* London: John Murray, 1861.

Maine, Henry Sumner. *Village-Communities in the East and West: Six Lectures Delivered at Oxford*, 2nd edn. London: John Murray, 1872.

Maine, Henry Sumner. *Dissertations on Early Law and Custom.* London: John Murray, 1883.

Malthus, Thomas. *An Inquiry into the Nature and Progress of Rent.* London: John Murray, 1815.

Markby, William. *Lectures on Indian Law.* Calcutta: Thacker, Spink, 1873.

Markby, William. *Elements of Law: Considered with Reference to the General Principles of Jurisprudence.* Oxford: Clarendon Press, 1871.

Marx, Karl. *Capital: A Critique of Political Economy,* vol. 3. New York: Penguin, 1993.

Mayne, John D. *A Treatise on Hindu Law and Usage.* Madras: Higginbotham, 1878.

Mill, James. *The History of British India.* London: Baldwin, Cradock, and Joy, 1817.

Mill, James. *A History of British India, in six volumes.* 3rd edn. London: 1826 (1817).

Mill, John Stuart. P*rinciples of Political Economy with Some of Their Applications to Social Philosophy.* W. J. Ashley ed., London: Longmans, Green and Co, 1909 (1848).

Miller, William Galbraith. *Lectures on the Philosophy of Law.* London: Charles Griffin and Company, 1884.

Montesquieu, Charles de Secondat (baron de) et al., *The Spirit of the Laws.* New York: Cambridge University Press, 1989 (1748).

Morris, William O'Connor. *The Irish Land Act: 33 and 34 Vict. Cap. 46: with a Full Commentary and Notes.* Dublin: E. Ponsonby, 1870.

Mulla, Dinshah Fardunji. *Principles of Mahomedan Law.* Bombay: Thacker & Company, 1905.

Naoroji, Dadabhai. *Poverty an Un-British Rule in India.* London: Swan Sonnenschein & Co., 1901.

Nelson, J. H. *A View of the Hindu Law as Administered by the High Court of Judicature at Madras.* Madras: Higginbotham, 1877.

Nelson, J. H. *Prospectus of the Scientific Study of the Hindu Law.* London: C. Kegan Paul & Co., 1881.

Orme, Robert. *A History of the Military Transactions of the British Nation in Indostan from 1745. To which is prefixed a Dissertation on the Establishments Made by Mahomedan Conquerors in Indostan.* London: Printed for John Nourse, 1763.

Petty, William. *A Treatise of Taxes and Contributions.* (Reprinted) in Charles Henry Hull ed., *The Economic Writings of Sir William Petty,* vol. I, 1–97. New York: Augustus M. Kelly Booksellers, 1963 (1662).

Phillips, Arthur. *The Law Relating to the Land Tenures of Lower Bengal.* Calcutta: Thacker, Spink, 1876.

Pollock, Frederick. *Principles of Contract at Law and in Equity: Being a Treatise on the General Principles Concerning the Validity of Agreements, with a Special View to the Comparison of Law and Equity, and with References to the Indian Contract Act, and Occasionally to Roman, American, and Continental Law.* London: Stevens, 1876.

Pollock, Frederick. *Principles of Contract: Being a Treatise on the General Principles Concerning the Validity of Agreements in the Law of England.* 4th edn. London: Stevens, 1885.
Pollock, Frederick. *The Law of Fraud, Misrepresentation and Mistake in British India.* Calcutta: Thacker & Spink, 1894.
Pollock, Frederick and Dinshah Fardunji Mulla. *The Indian Contract Act, with a Commentary, Critical and Explanatory.* Bombay: Thacker & Company, 1905.
Pollock, Frederick and Dinshah Fardunji Mulla. *The Indian Partnership Act: with a Commentary, Critical and Explanatory.* Calcutta: Eastern Law House, 1934.
Pollock, Frederick and Robert Samuel Wright. *An Essay on Possession in the Common Law.* Oxford: Clarendon Press, 1888.
Pound, Roscoe. *Outlines of Lectures on Jurisprudence: Chiefly from the Analytical Standpoint*, 2nd edn. Cambridge, MA: Harvard University Press, 1920 (1903).
Powell, John Joseph. *Essay Upon the Law of Contracts and Agreements*, 2 vols. London: J. Johnson and T. Whieldon, 1790.
Rahim, Abdur. *The Principles of Muhammadan Jurisprudence According to the Hanafi, Maliki, Shafi'i, and Hanbali Schools.* London: Luzac Company, 1911.
Ranade, Mahadev Govind, *Essays on Indian Economics: A Collection of Essays and Speeches.* Madras: G. A. Natesan and Co., 1906.
Rattigan, William Henry. *A Digest of Civil Law for the Punjab, Chiefly Based on the Customary Law as at Present Judicially Ascertained.* Allahabad: The University Book Agency, 1880.
Rattigan, William Henry. *The Science of Jurisprudence: Chiefly Intended for Indian Students*, 2nd edn. London, Wildy and Sons, 1892.
Reinsch, Paul Samuel. *Colonial Administration.* New York: Macmillan, 1905.
Ricardo, David. *On the Principles of Political Economy and Taxation.* London: John Murray, 1817.
Robertson, A. J. *The Principles of Mahomedan Law, with an Appendix Tracing the Growth of Personal Law.* Rangoon: Myles Standish, 1911.
Roe, Charles A. and H. A. B. Rattigan. *Tribal Law in the Punjab: so far as it relates to right in ancestral land.* Lahore: Civil and Military Gazette Press, 1895.
Rumsey, Almaric. *Moohummudan Law of Inheritance and Rights and Relations Affecting it: Sunni Doctrine.* London: W. H. Allen, 1880.
Savigny, Friedrich Karl von. *Von Savigny's Treatise on Possession: or, the Jus Possessionis of the Civil Law.* Erskine Perry, trans. London: R. Sweet, 1848.
Savigny, Friedrich Karl von. *System of the Modern Roman Law.* William Holloway, trans. Madras: J. Higginbotham, 1867.
Savigny, Friedrich Karl von. *Jural Relations: or The Roman law of Persons as Subjects of Jural Relations, Being a Translation of the Second Book of Savigny's System of Modern Roman Law.* William Henry Rattigan, trans. London: Wildy & Sons, 1884.
Savigny, Friedrich Karl von. *Possession in the Civil Law. Abridged from the Treatise of von Savigny, to which is added the text of the title on possession from the digest with notes.* J. Kelleher, trans. Calcutta: Thacker, Spink, 1888.
Scrafton, Luke. *Reflections on the Government of Indostan: With a Short Sketch of the History of Bengal, from 1739 to 1765; and an Account of the English Affairs to 1758.* London: W. Richardson and S. Clark, 1763.

Sircar, Shama Churun. *The Muhammadan Law: Being a Digest of the Law Applicable Especially to the Sunnís of India.* Calcutta: Thacker, Spink, 1873.

Smith, V. A. *The Oxford Student's History of India.* Princeton, NJ: Clarendon Press, 1921.

Story, Joseph. *Commentaries on the Conflict of Laws, Foreign and Domestic.* Boston, MA: Hilliard, Gray, and Company, 1834.

Strange, Thomas. *Elements of Hindu Law: Referable to British Judicature in India,* 2 vols. London: Butterworth and Son, 1825.

Tarkapanchanana, Jagannatha. *A Digest of Hindu Law, on Contracts and Successions.* H. T. Colebrooke, trans. Calcutta: East India Company Press, 1801.

Temple, Richard. *India in 1880,* 3rd edn. London: John Murray, 1881.

Temple, Richard. *Men and Events of My Time in India,* 1882. Reprint, Delhi: B. R. Publication Corporation, 1985.

Thorburn, Septimus Smet. *Report on the First Regular Land Revenue Settlement of the Bannu District in the Derajat Division of the Punjab.* Lahore: Printed at the Central Jail Press, 1879.

Thorburn, Septimus Smet. *Musalman and Money-lender in the Punjab.* Edinburgh: W. Blackwood and Sons, 1886.

Thorburn, Septimus Smet. *The Punjab in Peace and War.* London: W. Blackwood and Sons, 1904.

Tupper, Charles Lewis. *Punjab Customary Law.* Calcutta: Office of the Superintendent of Government Printing, 1881.

Tupper, Charles Lewis. *Punjab Customary Law: Volume III. Questions on Tribal and Local Custom.* Calcutta: Office of the Superintendent of Government Printing, 1881.

Tupper, Charles Lewis. *Our Indian Protectorate: An Introduction to the Study of the Relations between the British Government and its Indian Feudatories.* London: Longmans, Green, and Co., 1893.

Tupper, Charles Lewis. 'Early Institutions and Punjab Tribal Law', *The Imperial and Asiatic Quarterly Review and Oriental and Colonial Record* 5, 3rd series, nos. 9 and 10 (Jan. 1898): 12–27.

Tupper, Charles Lewis. 'English Jurisprudence and Indian Studies in Law', *Journal of the Society of Comparative Legislation* New Series 3, no. 1 (1901): 84–94.

Tyabji, Faiz Badruddin. *Principles of Muhammadan Law.* Bombay: D. B. Taraporevala Sons, 1913.

Vansittart, Henry. *A Narrative of the Transactions in Bengal, from the year 1760, to the year 1764.* London: J. Newberry, 1766.

Watts, William. *Memoirs of the revolution in Bengal, Anno Dom. 1757. By which Meer Jaffeir was raised to the government of that province, together with those of Bahar and Orixa.* London: A. Millar, 1760.

West, Raymond and Johann Georg Buhler, eds. *A Digest of the Hindu Law of Inheritance and Partition: from the Replies of the Sâstris in the Several Courts of the Bombay Presidency, with Introductions, Notes, and an Appendix,* 2nd edn. Bombay: Printed at the Education Society's Pres, Byculla, 1878.

Wilson, Lee B. 'A "Manifest Violation" of the Rights of Englishmen: Rights Talk and the Law of Property in Early Eighteenth-Century Jamaica', *Law and History Review* 33, no. 3 (2015): 543–75.

Wilson, Roland Knyvet. *An Introduction to the Study of Anglo-Muhammadan Law.* London: W. Thacker and Co., 1894.

Wilson, Roland Knyvet. *A Digest of Anglo-Muhammadan Law, setting forth in the form of a code... with full reference to... the rules now applicable to Muhammadans.* London: W. Thacker, 1895.

Wingfield, Charles. *Observations on Land Tenure and Tenant Right in India* (London: W. H. Allen & Co., 1869.

Secondary Sources

Agamben, Giorgio. *Homo Sacer: Sovereign Power and Bare Life.* Daniel Heller-Roazan, trans. Stanford, CA: Stanford University Press, 1998.

Ágel, Vilmos and Klaus Fischer. 'Dependency Grammar and Valence Theory.' In *The Oxford Handbook of Linguistic Analysis*, edited by Bernd Hein and Heiko Narrog. Oxford: Oxford University Press, 2009, 223–56.

Ahmed, Aijaz. *In Theory: Classes, Nations, Literatures.* New York: Verso, 1992.

Ahuja, Ravi. 'The Origins of Colonial Labour Policy in Late Eighteenth-Century Madras', *International Review of Social History* 44, no. 2 (Aug. 1999): 159–95.

Aitchison, Jean. *Language Change: Progress or Decay.* New York: Cambridge University Press, 2004.

Aitchison, Jean. *Words in the Mind: An Introduction to the Mental Lexicon.* West Sussex, UK: Wiley Blackwell, 2012.

Alchian, A. A. and H. Demsetz. 'The Property Right Paradigm', *Journal of Economic History* 33, no. 1 (Mar. 1973): 16–27.

Alexander, Gregory. 'The Dead Hand and the Law of Trusts in the Nineteenth Century', *Stanford Law Review* 37, no. 5 (1985): 1189–266.

Alexander, Gregory. *Commodity and Propriety: Competing Visions of Property in American Legal Thought, 1776–1970.* Chicago, IL: University of Chicago Press, 2008.

Ali, Amir. 'Evolution of the Public Sphere in India', *Economic and Political Weekly* 36, no. 26 (Jun. 30–Jul. 6, 2001): 2419–25.

Ali, M. Athar. 'The Mughal Polity—A Critique of Revisionist Approaches', *Modern Asian Studies* 27, no. 3 (1993): 699–710.

Ambirajan, S. *Classical Political Economy and British Policy in India.* New York: Cambridge University Press, 1978.

Anagol, Padma. *The Emergence of Feminism in India, 1850–1920.* Burlington, VT: Ashgate, 2005.

Anderson, Michael R. 'Classifications and Coercions: Themes in South Asian Legal Studies in the 1980s', *South Asia Research* 10, no. 2 (November 1990): 158–77.

Anderson, Michael R. 'Legal Scholarship and the Politics of Islam in British India.' In *Perspectives on Islamic Law, Justice and Society*, edited by R. S. Khare. New York: Rowman & Littlefield, 1999, 65–92.

Anderson, Michael R. 'India, 1858–1930: The Illusion of Free Labor.' In *Masters, Servants, and Magistrates in Britain and the Empire, 1562–1955*, edited by D. Hay and P. Craven, Chapel Hill, NC: University of North Carolina Press: 2004, 422–54.

Anderson, Perry. *Lineages of the Absolutist State.* New York: Verso, 1979.

Anghie, Antony. *Imperialism, Sovereignty, and the Making of International Law.* New York: Cambridge University Press, 2005.

Anscombe, G. E. *Intention.* Oxford: Blackwell, 1957.

Arnold, David. 'Agriculture and "Improvement" in Early Colonial India: A Pre-History of Development', *Journal of Agrarian Change* 5, no. 4 (Oct. 2005): 505–25.

Atiyah, Patrick. *The Rise and Fall of Freedom of Contract*. New York: Oxford University Press, 1979.

Austin, J. L. *How to Do Things with Words: The William James Lectures delivered at Harvard University in 1955*. Oxford: Clarendon Press, 1962.

Baak, Paul E. 'About Enslaved Ex-Slaves, Uncaptured Contract Coolies and Unfreed Freedmen: Some Notes about "Free" and "Unfree" Labour in the Context of Plantation Development in Southwest India, Early Sixteenth Century–Mid 1990s', *Modern Asian Studies* 33, no. 1 (Feb. 1999): 121–57.

Bagchi, Amiya Kumar. 'Land Tax, Property Rights and Peasant Insecurity in Colonial India', *The Journal of Peasant Studies* 20, no. 1 (1992): 1–49.

Banerjee, A. C. *English Law in India*. Delhi: Abhinav Publications, 1984.

Banerjee, Sumanta. *Crime And Urbanization: Calcutta in the Nineteenth Century*. New Delhi: Tulika Books, 2006.

Bannerji, Himani, Shahrzad Mojab, and Judith Whitehead, eds. *Of Property and Propriety: The Role of Gender and Class in Imperialism and Nationalism*. Toronto: University of Toronto Press, 2001.

Baxi, Upendra. *Towards a Sociology of Indian Law*. New Delhi: Satvahan, 1986.

Bayly, C. A. *Rulers, Townsmen and Bazaars: North Indian Society in the Age of British Expansion, 1770–1870*. New York: Cambridge University Press, 1983.

Bayly, C. A. *Indian Society and the Making of the British Empire*. Cambridge: Cambridge University Press, 2008 (1988).

Bayly, C. A. *Empire and Information: Intelligence Gathering and Social Communication in India, 1780–1870*. New York: Cambridge University Press, 1996.

Bayly, C. A. *Recovering Liberties: Indian Thought in the Age of Liberalism and Empire*. New York: Cambridge University Press, 2011.

Bayly, Susan. *Caste, Society and Politics in India from the Eighteenth Century to the Modern Age*. New York: Cambridge University Press, 2001.

Baz, Avner. *When Words Are Called For: A Defense of Ordinary Language Philosophy*. Cambridge, MA: Harvard University Press, 2012.

Benton, Lauren. *Law and Colonial Cultures: Legal Regimes in World History, 1400–1900*. New York: Cambridge University Press, 2002.

Benton, Lauren and Richard J. Ross. 'Empires and Legal Pluralism: Jurisdiction, Sovereignty, and Political Imagination in the Early Modern World.' In *Legal Pluralism and Empires, 1500–1850*, edited by Lauren Benton and Richard J. Ross. New York: New York University Press, 2013, 1–20.

Berger, Peter. 'Theory and Ethnography in the Modern Anthropology of India', *HAU: Journal of Ethnographic Theory* 2, no. 2 (2012): 325–57.

Berger, Peter L. and Thomas Luckmann. *The Social Construction of Reality: A Treatise in the Sociology of Knowledge*. Garden City, NY: Doubleday, 1966.

Bhabha, Homi. *The Location of Culture*. New York: Routledge, 1994.

Bhandar, Brenna. *Colonial Lives of Property: Law, Land, and Racial Regimes of Ownership*. Durham, NC: Duke University Press, 2018.

Bhat, M. Mohsin Alam, Mayur Suresh, and Deepa Das Acevedo. 'Authoritarianism in Indian State, Law, and Society', *Verfassung und Recht in Übersee (VRÜ) / World Comparative Law* 55 (2022): 459–77.

Bhattacharya, Neeladri. 'Remaking Custom: The Discourse and Practice of Colonial Codification.' In *Tradition, Dissent and Ideology: Essays in Honour of Romila Thapar*, edited by R. Champakalakshmi and S. Gopal. Delhi: Oxford University Press, 1996, 20–51.

Bhattacharya, Neeladri. 'Notes Towards a Conception of the Colonial Public.' In *Civil Society, Public Sphere, and Citizenship: Dialogues and Perceptions*, edited by Rajeev Bhargava and Helmut Reifeld. Thousand Oaks, CA: Sage Publications, 2005, 130–58.

Bhattachayya-Panda, Nandini. *Appropriation and Invention of Tradition: The East India Company and Hindu Law in Early Colonial Bengal*. New York: Oxford University Press, 2008.

Bilgrami, Akeel. *Belief and Meaning: The Unity and Locality of Mental Content*. Cambridge, MA: Basil Blackwell, 1992.

Birla, Ritu. *Stages of Capital: Law, Culture, and Market Governance in Late Colonial India*. Durham, NC: Duke University Press, 2009.

Blaug, Mark. *The Methodology of Economics: Or How Economists Explain*. New York: Cambridge University Press, 1992.

Boghossian, Paul. *Fear of Knowledge: Against Relativism and Constructivism*. New York: Clarendon Press, 2006.

Bohman, James and William Rehg. 'Jürgen Habermas', *The Stanford Encyclopedia of Philosophy* (Fall 2017 Edition), Edward N. Zalta (ed.), https://plato.stanford.edu/archives/fall2017/entries/habermas.

Bose, Sugata. *Peasant Labour and Colonial Capital: Rural Bengal Since 1770* New York: Cambridge University Press, 1993.

Bose, Sugata and Ayesha Jalal. *Modern South Asia: History, Culture, Political Economy*. 2nd ed. New York: Routledge, 2004.

Bourdieu, Pierre. *The Logic of Practice*. Richard Nice, trans. Palo Alto, CA: Stanford University Press, 1990.

Bratman, Michael E. *Shared Agency: A Planning Theory of Acting Together*. New York: Oxford University Press, 2014.

Brett, Annabel S. *Liberty, Right and Nature: Individual Rights in Later Scholastic Thought*. New York: Cambridge University Press, 2003.

Brewer, John and Susan Staves, eds. *Early Modern Conceptions of Property*. New York: Routledge, 1995.

Broome, John. 'Normative Requirements', *Ratio: An International Journal of Analytical Philosophy* 12, no. 4 (1999): 389–419.

Brown, Ian. *A Colonial Economy in Crisis: Burma's Rice Cultivators and the World Depression of the 1930s*. New York: Routledge, 2005.

Buckland, Charles E. *Dictionary of Indian Biography*. London: Swan, Sonnenschein & Co., 1906.

Burchell, Graham, Colin Gordon, and Peter Miller, *The Foucault Effect: Studies in Governmentality: with Two Lectures by and an Interview with Michel Foucault*. Chicago, IL: University of Chicago Press, 1991.

Burton, Antoinette. 'From Child Bride to "Hindoo Lady": Rukhmabai and the Debate on Sexual Respectability in Imperial Britain', *The American Historical Review* 103, no. 4 (Oct. 1998): 1119–46.

Caldwell, Peter. *Popular Sovereignty and the Crisis of German Constitutional Law: The Theory and Practice of Weimar Constitutionalism.* Durham, NC: Duke University Press, 1997.

Campbell, Joseph Keim, Michael O'Rourke, and Matthew H. Slater, eds. *Carving Nature at its Joints: Natural Kinds in Metaphysics and Science.* Cambridge, MA: MIT Press, 2011.

Candlish, Stewart and George Wrisley. 'Private Language.' *The Stanford Encyclopedia of Philosophy* (Fall 2019 Edition), Edward N. Zalta (ed.), https://plato.stanford.edu/archives/fall2019/entries/private-language/

Chakrabarti, Upal. 'The Problem of Property: Local Histories and Political-Economic Categories in British India,' *Journal of the Economic and Social History of the Orient* 61, nos. 5–6 (2018): 1003–33.

Chakrabarti, Upal. *Assembling the Local: Political Economy and Agrarian Governance in British India.* Philadelphia, PA: University of Pennsylvania Press, 2021.

Chakraborty, Titas. 'Controlling Labor Mobility as a State Building Process: The Ascendancy of the English East India Company State in Bengal 1700–1819.' Paper presented for 'New Directions in South Asian Labor History' session of the 48th Annual Conference on South Asia, University of Wisconsin-Madison, October 18, 2019.

Chakraborty, Titas. 'Desertion of European Sailors and Soldiers in Early Eighteenth-Century Bengal.' In *A Global History of Runaways: Workers, Mobility, and Capitalism, 1600–1850*, edited by Marcus Rediker, Titas Chakraborty, and Matthias van Rossum. Oakland, CA: University of California Press, 2019, 77–95.

Chakravarty-Kaul, Minoti. *Common Lands and Customary Law: Institutional Change in North India over the Past Two Centuries.* Delhi: Oxford University Press, 1996.

Chandra, Bipin. *The Rise and Growth of Economic Nationalism in India: Economic Policies of Indian National Leadership, 1880–1905.* New Delhi: Har-Anand Publications, 2010.

Chandra, Sudhir. *Enslaved Daughters: Colonialism, Law and Women's Rights.* Delhi: Oxford University Press, 1998.

Charlesworth, Neil. *Peasants and Imperial Rule: Agriculture and Agrarian Society in the Bombay Presidency, 1850–1935.* New York: Cambridge University Press, 1985.

Chatterjee, Indrani. *Gender, Slavery, and Law in Colonial India.* New York: Oxford University Press, 1999.

Chatterjee, Indrani, ed. *Unfamiliar Relations: Family and History in South Asia.* New Brunswick, NJ: Rutgers University Press, 2004.

Chatterjee, Nandini. *The Making of Indian Secularism: Empire, Law and Christianity, 1830–1960.* New York: Palgrave Macmillan, 2011.

Chatterjee, Nandini. *Negotiating Mughal Law: A Family of Landlords cross Three Indian Empires.* New York: Cambridge University Press, 2020.

Chatterjee, Partha. 'Colonialism, Nationalism and Colonialized Women: The Contest in India,' *American Ethnologist* 16, no. 4 (1989): 622–33.

Chatterjee, Partha. *The Nation and its Fragments.* Princeton, NJ: Princeton University Press, 1993.Chaudhary, Latika, Bishnupriya Gupta, Tirthankar Roy, and Anand Swamy, eds. *A New Economic History of Colonial India.* New York: Routledge, 2016.

Chaudhry, Faisal. 'The Promise and Paradox of Max Weber's Legal Sociology: The "Categories Of Legal Thought" as Types of Meaningful Action and the Persistence of the Problem of Judicial Legislation', *Southern California Interdisciplinary Law Journal*, 20 (2011): 249–88.

Chaudhry, Faisal. 'Rethinking the Nineteenth-Century Domestication of the Sharīʿa: Marriage and Family in the Imaginary of Classical Legal Thought and the Genealogy of (Muslim) Personal Law in Late Colonial India', *Law and History Review* 35, no. 4 (2017): 841–79.

Chaudhry, Faisal. 'Property and its Rule (in Late Indo-Islamicate and Early Colonial) South Asia: What's in a Name?', *Journal of the Economic and Social History of the Orient* 61, nos. 5–6 (2018): 920–975, 944–47.

Chaudhry, Faisal. 'Property as Rent', *St. John's Law Review* 94, no. 2 (2021): 363–438.

Chaudhuri, Binay Bhushan. 'Land Market in Eastern India, 1793–1940 Part II: The Changing Composition of the Landed Society', *Indian Economic & Social History Review* 12, no. 2 (1975): 133–67.

Chaudhuri, Binay Bhushan. *Peasant History of Late Pre-Colonial and Colonial India*. New Delhi: Pearson Longman, 2008.

Chevalier, Jacques. 'Public Administration in Statist France.' In *Comparative Public Administration: The Essential Readings*, edited by Eric E. Otenyo and Nancy S. Lind. Oxford: Elsevier, 2006, 741–59.

Chibber, Vivek. *Postcolonial Theory and the Specter of Capital*. New York: Verso, 2013.

Chomsky, Noam. *New Horizons in the Study of Language and Mind*. Cambridge: Cambridge University Press, 2000.

Coase, Ronald. 'The Problem of Social Cost', *Journal of Law and Economics* 3 (Oct. 1960): 1–44.

Cohn, Bernard S. 'Structural Change in Indian Rural Society, 1596–1885.' In *Land Control and Social Structure in Indian History*, edited by Robert Frykenberg. Madison, WI: University of Wisconsin Press, 1969, 53–121.

Cohn, Bernard S. 'The Command of Language and the Language of Command', *Subaltern Studies, IV: Writings on South Asian History and Society*, (edited by Guha), 1985: 276–329.

Cohn, Bernard S. 'Law and the Colonial State in India.' In *History and Power in the Study of Law: New Directions in Legal Anthropology*, edited by June Starr and Jane F. Collier. Ithaca, NY: Cornell University Press, 1989, 131–52.

Conrad, Dieter. 'Administrative Jurisdiction and the Civil Courts in the Regime of Land-Law in India.' In *Our Laws, Their Lands: Land Laws and Land Use in Modern Colonial Societies*, edited by Jap de Moor and Dieter Rothermund. Münster: LIT, 1994, 134–54.

Constable, Marianne. *Just Silences: The Limits and Possibilities of Modern Law*. Princeton, NJ: Princeton University Press, 2005.

Constable, Marianne. *Our Word is Our Bond: How Legal Speech Acts*. Stanford, CA: Stanford University Press, 2014.

Costa, Luiz and Carlos Fausto, 'The Return of the Animists: Recent Studies of Amazonian Ontologies', *Religion and Society* 1, no. 1 (2010): 89–109.

Davis, Kathleen. *Periodization and Sovereignty: How Ideas of Feudalism and Secularization Govern the Politics of Time*. Philadelphia, PA: University of Pennsylvania Press, 2008.

Davis, Mike. *Late Victorian Holocausts: El Niño Famines and the Making of the Third World*. New York: Verso, 2001.

de Castro, Eduardo Viveiros. 'Exchanging Perspectives: The Transformation of Objects into Subjects in Amerindian Ontologies', *Common Knowledge* 10, no. 3 (2004): 463-84.
Delacroix, Sylvie. *Legal Norms and Normativity: An Essay in Genealogy*. Portland, OR: Oxford University Press, 2006.
Del Mar, Maksymilian. 'Legal Norms and Normativity', *Oxford Journal of Legal Studies* 27, no. 2 (2007): 355-72.
Denault, Leigh. 'Partition and the Politics of the Joint Family in Nineteenth-century North India', *Indian Economic and Social History Review* 46, no. 1 (2009): 27-55.
den Otter, Sandra. 'Freedom of Contract, the Market and Imperial Law-Making.' In *Critiques of Capital in Modern Britain and America: Transatlantic Exchanges 1800 to the Present Day*, edited by Mark Bevir and Frank Trentmann. New York: Palgrave Macmillan, 2002, 49-72.
den Otter, Sandra. 'The Political Economy of Empire: Freedom of Contract and "Commercial Civilization" in Colonial India.' In *Worlds of Political Economy: Knowledge and Power in the Nineteenth and Twentieth Centuries*, edited by Martin Daunton and Frank Trentmann. New York: Palgrave Macmillan, 2004, 69-94.
den Otter, Sandra. 'A Legislating Empire: Victorian Political Theorists, Codes of Law, and Empire.' In *Victorian Visions of Global Order: Empire and International Relations in Nineteenth-Century Political Thought*, edited by Duncan Bell. New York: Cambridge University Press, 2007, 89-113.
Descola, Philippe. *Beyond Nature and Culture*. Chicago, IL: University of Chicago Press, 2013.
Devitt, Michael and Kim Stereiny. *Language and Reality: An Introduction to the Philosophy of Language*, 2nd edn. Cambridge, MA: MIT Press, 1999.
Devji, Faisal. *Muslim Zion: Pakistan as a Political Idea*. Cambridge: Harvard University Press, 2013.
Dewey, Clive. 'Images of the Indian Village Community: A Study in Anglo-Indian Ideology', *Modern Asian Studies* 6, no. 3 (1972): 291-328.
Dewey, Clive. 'The Influence of Sir Henry Maine on Agrarian Policy in India.' In *The Victorian Achievement of Sir Henry Maine*, edited by Alan Diamond, New York: Cambridge University Press, 1991, 353-75.
Diamond, Alan, ed. *The Victorian Achievement of Sir Henry Maine: A Centennial Reappraisal*. New York: Cambridge University Press, 1991.
Dirks, Nicholas B. 'From Little King to Landlord', *Comparative Studies in Society and History* 28, no. 2 (Apr. 1986): 307-33.
Dirks, Nicholas B. *The Hollow Crown: Ethnohistory of an Indian Kingdom*. Ann Arbor, MI: University of Michigan Press, 1993.
Dirks, Nicholas B. *Castes of Mind: Colonialism and the Making of Modern India*. Princeton, NJ: Princeton University Press, 2001.
di Robilant, Anna. 'Property: A Bundle of Sticks or a Tree', *Vanderbilt Law Review* 66 (2013): 869-932.
di Robilant, Anna. *The Making of Modern Property: Reinventing Roman Law in Europe and its Peripheries 1789-1950*. Cambridge: Cambridge University Press, 2023.
Dodson, Michael. *Orientalism, Empire, and National Culture: India, 1770-1880*. New York: Palgrave Macmillan, 2007.

Dowell, H. S. *The Cambridge History of the British Empire*, vol. 4, *British India 1497–1858*, edited by H. H. Dowell. Cambridge: Cambridge University Press, 1940.

Dube, Ishita Banerjee. *Religion, Law and Power: Tales of Time in Eastern India, 1860–2000*. London: Anthem Press, 2009.

Durkheim, Émile. *The Division of Labor in Society*. New York: The Free Press, 2014 (1893).

Durkheim, Émile. *The Rules of Sociological Method*, W. D. Halls, trans. New York: Free Press, 1982 (1895).

Dworkin, Ronald. 'Hard Cases', *Harvard Law Review* 88, no. 6 (1975): 1057–1109.

Dworkin, Ronald. *Law's Empire*. Cambridge, MA: Harvard University Press, 1986.

Dyzenhause, David. *Legality and Legitimacy: Carl Schmitt, Hans Kelsen and Hermann Heller in Weimar*. New York: Clarendon Press, 1997.

Edney, Matthew. *Mapping an Empire: The Geographical Construction of British India, 1765–1843*. Chicago, IL: University of Chicago Press, 1997.

Egan, David. *The Pursuit of an Authentic Philosophy: Wittgenstein, Heidegger, and the Everyday*. New York: Oxford University Press, 2019.

Egan, David. 'Can you step in the same river twice? Wittgenstein v Heraclitus', *Aeon*, August 9, 2019. https://aeon.co/ideas/can-you-step-in-the-same-river-twice-wittgenstein-v-heraclitus

Ehrlich, Eugen. *Fundamental Principles of the Sociology of Law*. Walter L. Moll, trans. New Brunswick, NJ: Transaction Publishers, 2002 (1936).

Endicott, Timothy. 'Law and Language', *The Stanford Encyclopedia of Philosophy* (Summer 2016 Edition), Edward N. Zalta (ed.), https://plato.stanford.edu/archives/sum2016/entries/law-language/.

Falk-Moore, Sally. 'Law and Social Change: The Semi-Autonomous Social Field as an Appropriate Subject of Study.' Reprinted in Sally Falk-Moore, *Law as Process: An Anthropological Approach*. Reprint, Hamburg: LIT, 2000 (1978), 54–81.

Falk-Moore, Sally. *Law as Process: An Anthropological Approach*. Reprint, Hamburg: LIT, 2000.

Falk-Moore, Sally, ed. *Law and Anthropology: A Reader*. Malden, MA: Blackwell, 2005.

Feaver, George. *From Status to Contract: A Biography of Sir Henry Maine, 1822–1888*. London: Longmans, 1969.

Ferguson, Niall. *The Ascent of Money: A Financial History of the World*. New York: The Penguin Press, 2008.

Feteres, Eveline. *Fundamentals of Legal Argumentation A Survey of Theories on the Justification of Judicial Decisions*. Amsterdam: Springer, 2017.

Figdor, Carrie. *Pieces of Mind: The Proper Domain of Psychological Predicates*. New York: Oxford University Press, 2018.

Finnis, John. *Natural Law and Natural Rights*. 2nd edn. New York: Oxford University Press, 2011.

Fisch, Jörg. *Cheap Lives and Dear Limbs: The British Transformation of the Bengal Criminal Law, 1769–1817*. Wiesbaden: F. Steiner, 1983.

Fitzmaurice, Andrew. *Sovereignty, Property and Empire: 1500–2000*. Cambridge: Cambridge University Press, 2014.

Fox, Richard G. *Lions of the Punjab: Culture in the Making*. Berkeley, CA: University of California, 1985.

Freitag, Sandria. *Collective Action and Community: Public Arenas and the Emergence of Communalism in North India*. Berkeley, CA: University of California Press, 1989.

Frykenberg, Robert Eric, ed. *Land Control and Social Structure in Indian History*. Madison, WI: University of Wisconsin Press, 1969.

Frykenberg, Robert Eric. *Land Tenure and Peasant in South Asia*. New Delhi: Orient Longman, 1977.

Furber, Holden. *John Company at Work: A Study of European Expansion in India in the late Eighteenth Century*. Cambridge, MA: Harvard University Press, 1948.

Galanter, Marc. *Law and Society in Modern India*. Oxford: Oxford University Press, 1989.

Ganshof, F. L. *Feudalism*. Philip Grierson, trans. Toronto: University of Toronto Press, 1964.

Ghosh, Durba. *Sex and the Family in Colonial India: The Making of Empire*. New York: Cambridge University Press, 2006.

Gledhill, Alan. 'The Compilation of Customary Law in the Punjab in the nineteenth century.' In *La rédaction des coutumes dans le passé et dans le présent*, edited by John Gilissen. Brussels: Université Libre de Bruxelles, 1962, 131-64.

Golder, Ben and Peter Fitzpatrick. *Foucault's Law*. New York: Routledge 2009.

Goodrich, Peter. 'Law and Language: An Historical and Critical Introduction', *Journal of Law and Society* 11, no. 2 (1984): 173-206.

Gordon, Robert W. 'Paradoxical Property.' In *Early Modern Conceptions of Property*, edited by John Brewer and Susan Staves, New York: Routledge, 1995, 95-110.

Goswami, Manu. *Producing India: from Colonial Economy to National Space*. Chicago, IL: University of Chicago Press, 2004.Gooderson, R. N. 'English Contract Problems in Indian Code and Case Law', *The Cambridge Law Journal* 16, no. 1 (1958): 67-84.

Gordley, James. *The Philosophical Origins of Modern Contract Doctrine*. New York: Oxford University Press, 1991.

Gordley, James. 'The Common Law in the Twentieth Century: Some Unfinished Business', *California Law Review* 88, no. 6 (Dec. 2000): 1815-75

Graeber, David. *Debt: The First 5,000 Years*. New York: Melville House, 2011.

Graeber, David. 'Radical Alterity is Just Another Way of Saying "Reality": A reply to Eduardo Viveiros de Castro', *HAU: Journal of Ethnographic Theory* 5, no. 2 (2015): 1-41.

Gray, Kevin and Susan Gray. *Land Law*, 5th edn. New York: Oxford University Press, 2007.

Greene, Christopher D. and John Vervaeke, 'The Experience of Objects and the Objects of Experience', *Metaphor and Symbol* 12, no. 1 (1997): 3-17.

Grey, Thomas C. 'The Disintegration of Property.' In *NOMOS: XXII: Property*, edited by J. Roland Pennock and John W. Chapman. New York: New York University Press, 1980, 69-85.

Gross, Neil. 'Comment on Searle', *Anthropological Theory* 6, no. 1 (2006): 45-56.

Guenther, Alan M. *Syed Mahmood and the Transformation of Muslim Law in British India*. Unpublished Ph.D. dissertation, McGill University, 2004.

Guest, Anthony Gordon, ed. *Oxford Essays in Jurisprudence: A Collaborative Work*. Oxford: Clarendon Press, 1961.

Guha, Ranajit. *A Rule of Property for Bengal: An Essay on the Idea of Permanent Settlement*. New Delhi: Orient Blackswan, 2016 (1963).

BIBLIOGRAPHY 515

Guha, Ranajit, ed. *Subaltern Studies, No. 4*. Delhi: Oxford University Press, 1985.
Guha, Ranajit, ed. *Subaltern Studies No 5*. Delhi: Oxford University Press, 1987.
Guha, Sumit. *The Agrarian Economy of the Bombay Deccan, 1818-1941*. New York: Oxford University Press, 1985.
Guildi, Jo. *The Long Land War: The Global Struggle for Occupancy Rights*. New Haven,CT: Yale University Press, 2021.
Habermas, Jürgen. *The Theory of Communicative Action, vol. 1: Reason and the Rationalization of Society*. Thomas McCarthy, trans. Boston, MA: Beacon Press, 1985.
Habermas, Jürgen. *The Theory of Communicative Action, vol. 2: Lifeworld and System—A Critique of Functionalist Reason*. Thomas McCarthy, trans. Boston, MA: Beacon Press, 1987.
Habermas, Jürgen. *The Structural Transformation of the Public Sphere: An Inquiry into a Category of Bourgeois Society*. Thomas Burger, trans. Cambridge, MA: MIT Press, 1989.
Habermas, Jürgen. *Between Facts and Norms: Contributions to a Discourse Theory of Law and Democracy*. Cambridge, MA: MIT Press, 1996.
Habermas, Jürgen. *Inclusion of the Other: Studies in Political Theory*. Cambridge, MA: MIT Press, 1998.
Habib, Irfan. 'Studying a Colonial Economy without Perceiving Colonialism', *Modern Asian Studies* 19, no. 3 (1985): 355-81.
Habib, Irfan. *The Agrarian System of Mughal India, 1556-1707*. New York: Oxford University Press, 1999.
Hacking, Ian. *The Social Construction of What*. Cambridge, MA: Harvard University Press, 1999.
Hacking, Ian. *Historical Ontology*. Cambridge, MA: Harvard University Press, 2002.
Halder, Tamoghna. 'Colonialism and the Indian Famines: A Response to Tirthankar Roy'. *Developing Economics: A Critical Perspective on Development Economics*. Feb. 20, 2023. https://developingeconomics.org/2023/02/20/colonialism-and-the-indian-famines-a-response-to-tirthankar-roy/.
Hallaq, Wael. *The Impossible State: Islam, Politics, and Modernity's Moral Predicament*. New York: Columbia University Press, 2014.
Halley, Janet. 'What is Family Law?: A Genealogy, Part I', *Yale Journal of Law & the Humanities* 23 (2011): 1-109.
Halley, Janet. 'What is Family Law?: A Genealogy, Part II', *Yale Journal of Law & the Humanities* 23 (2011): 189-293.
Halley, Janet and Kerry Rittich. 'Critical Directions in Comparative Family Law: Genealogies and Contemporary Studies in Family Law Exceptionalism', *The American Journal of Comparative Law* 58 (2010): 753-75.
Hamid, M. E. 'Islamic Law of Contract or Contracts', *Journal of Islamic and Comparative Law* 3 (1969): 1-11.
Hanfling, Oswald. *Ordinary Language Philosophy and Ordinary Language: The Bent and Genius of Our Tongue*. New York: Routledge, 2000.
Hann, C. M. ed. *Property Relations: Renewing the Anthropological Tradition*. Cambridge: Cambridge University Press, 1998.
Hardiman, David. 'From Custom to Crime: The Politics of Drinking in Colonial South Gujarat'. In *Subaltern Studies, no. 4*, edited by Guha, 1985, 165-228.

Harding, Sandra. *Objectivity and Diversity: Another Logic of Scientific Research*. Chicago, IL: University of Chicago Press, 2015.
Harman, Graham. *Object-Oriented Ontology: A New Theory of Everything*. London: Penguin, 2018.
Hart, H. L. A. *The Concept of Law*. New York: Oxford University Press, 1961.
Hasan, Farhat. *Paper, Performance, and the State: Social Change and Political Culture in Mughal India*. New York: Cambridge University Press, 2021.
Hassan, Hussein. 'Contracts in Islamic Law: The Principles of Commutative Justice and Liberality', *Journal of Islamic Studies* 13, no. 3 (2002): 257–97.
Hatekar, Neeraj. 'Information and Incentives: Pringle's Ricardian Experiment in the Nineteenth-Century Deccan Countryside', *Indian Economic and Social History Review* 33, no. 4 (1996): 437–57.
Hauser, Gerard. 'Vernacular Dialogue and the Rhetoricality of Public Opinion', *Communication Monographs* 65, no. 2 (June 1998): 83–107.
Hay, Douglas and Paul Craven, eds. *Masters, Servants, and Magistrates in Britain and the Empire, 1562-1955*. Chapel Hill, NC: The University of North Carolina Press, 2004.
Haynes, Douglas E. *Rhetoric and Ritual in Colonial India: The Shaping of a Public Culture in Surat City, 1852-1928*. Berkeley, CA: University of California Press, 1991.
Hexter, J. H. ed. *Parliament and Liberty from the Reign of Elizabeth to the English Civil War*. Palo Alto, CA: Stanford University Press, 1992.
Heywood, Paolo. 'Ontological Turn, The.' In *The Cambridge Encyclopedia of Anthropology*, edited by F. Stein et al. (2017), http://doi.org/10.29164/17ontology.
Hoeflich, Michael H. 'John Austin and Joseph Story: Two Nineteenth Century Perspectives on the Utility of Civil Law for the Common Lawyer', *American Journal of Legal History* 29, no. 1 (Jan. 1985): 36–77.
Hoeflich, Michael H. 'Savigny and His Anglo-American Disciples', *The American Journal of Comparative Law* 37, no. 1 (Winter 1989): 17–37.
Holdsworth, William. *An Historical Introduction to Land Law*. Oxford: Clarendon Press, 1927.
Holmes, Oliver Wendell. 'The Path of the Law', *Harvard Law Review* 10 (1897): 457–78.
Honoré, A. M. 'Ownership.' In *Oxford Essays in Jurisprudence: A Collaborative Work*, edited by Anthony Gordon Guest. Oxford: Clarendon Press, 1961, 107–47.
Hooker, M. B. *Legal Pluralism: An Introduction to Colonial and Neo-Colonial Laws*. New York: Oxford University Press, 1975.
Horwitz, Morton J. *The Transformation of American Law, 1870-1960*. New York: Oxford University Press, 1992.
Hovenkamp, Herbert. 'Law and Morals in Classical Legal Thought', *Iowa Law Review* 82 (1997): 1427–65.
Hovenkamp, Herbert. 'The Historical Foundations of Modern Contract Law', *Harvard Law Review* 87, no. 5 (1974): 917–56.
Howell, Martha C. 'The Language of Property in Early Modern Europe.' In *The Culture of Capital: Property, Cities, and Knowledge in Early Modern England*, edited by Henry S. Turner. New York: Routledge, 2002, 17–27.
Hudson, Michael and Cornelia Wunsch, eds. *Creating Economic Order: Record-Keeping, Standardization, and the Development of Accounting in the Ancient Near East*. Bethesda, MD: CDL Press, 2004.

Hulliung, Mark. *Citizens and Citoyens: Republicans and Liberals in America and France*. Cambridge, MA: Harvard University Press, 2002.
Hussain, Nasser. *A Jurisprudence of Emergency: Colonialism and the Rule of Law*. Ann Arbor, MI: University of Michigan Press, 2003.
Ihalainen, Pasi. *Agents of the People: Democracy and Popular Sovereignty in British and Swedish Parliamentary and Public Debates, 1734–1800*. Leiden: Brill, 2010.
Ikegame, Aye. *Princely India Re-imagined: A Historical Anthropology of Mysore from 1799 to the Present*. New York: Routledge, 2013.
Inden, Ronald. *Imagining India*. Cambridge, MA: Basil Blackwell, 1990.
Islam, M. S. *The Permanent Settlement in Bengal: A Study of its Operation 1790–1819*. Dacca: Bangla Academy, 1979.
Jaffrelot, Chrostophe. *Modi's India: Hindu Nationalism and the Rise of Ethnic Democracy*. Princeton, NJ: Princeton University Press, 2021.
Jalal, Ayesha. *Self and Sovereignty: Individual and Community in South Asian Islam since 1850*. New York: Routledge, 2000.
Kalpagam, U. 'Colonial Governmentality and the Public Sphere in India', *Journal of Historical Sociology* 14, no. 4 (Dec. 2001): 418–40.
Kapila, Shruti and C. A. Bayly, eds. *An Intellectual History for India*. New York: Cambridge University Press, 2010.
Kearns, Thomas R. 'Legal Normativity and Morality', *Western Ontario Law Review* 14 (1974): 71–104.
Keil, Frank C. *Concepts, Kinds, and Cognitive Development*. Cambridge, MA: MIT Press, 1989.
Kelly, Alfred H. 'Clio and the Court: An Illicit Love Affair', *Supreme Court Review* 1965 (1965): 119–58.
Kelsen, Hans. The *Pure Theory of Law*. Max Knight, trans. Berkeley, CA: University of California Press, 1967.
Kelsen, Hans. *General Theory of Law and State*. Cambridge, MA: Harvard University Press, 1945.
Kennedy, David and William W. Fisher, eds. *The Canon of American Legal Thought*. Princeton, NJ: Princeton University Press, 2006.
Kennedy, Duncan. 'Legal Formality', *The Journal of Legal Studies* 2, no. 2 (1973): 351–98.
Kennedy, Duncan. 'The Structure of Blackstone's Commentaries', *Buffalo Law Review* 28, no. 2 (1978–79): 205–382.
Kennedy, Duncan. 'Three Globalizations of Law and Legal Thought.' In *The New Law and Economic Development. A Critical Appraisal*, edited by David Trubek and Alvaro Santos. New York: Cambridge University Press, 2006, 19–73.
Kennedy, Duncan. *The Rise & Fall of Classical Legal Thought*. Washington, DC: Beard Books, 2006.
Kerr, Ian J. 'Labour Control and Labour Legislation in Colonial India: A Tale of Two Mid-Nineteenth Century Acts', *South Asia: Journal of South Asian Studies* XXVII, no. 1 (Apr. 2004): 7–25.
King, Michael and Chris Thornhill. *Niklas Luhmann's Theory of Politics and Law*. New York: Palgrave Macmillan, 2003.
Klein, Daniel B. and John Robinson. 'Property: A Bundle of Rights? Prologue to the Property Symposium', *Econ Journal Watch* 8, no. 3 (Sep. 2011): 193–204.

Knapp, George Friedreich. *The State Theory of Money*. London: Macmillan, 1924.
Kodoth, Praveena. 'Courting Legitimacy or Delegitimizing Custom? Sexuality, Sambandham, and Marriage Reform in Late Nineteenth-Century Malabar', *Modern Asian Studies* 35, no. 2 (2001): 349–84.
Kolff, D. H. A. 'The Indian and British Law Machines: Some Remarks on Law and Society in British India.' In *European Expansion and Law: The Encounter of European and Indigenous Law in 19th- and 20th-Century Africa and Asia*, edited by W. J. Mommsen and J. A. de Moor. New York: Oxford University Press, 1992, 201–35.
Korsgaard, Christine M. *The Sources of Normativity: The Tanner Lectures on Human Values*. New York: Cambridge University Press, 1996.
Koskenniemi, Martti. *The Gentle Civilizer of Nations: The Rise and Fall of International Law, 1870–1960*. New York: Cambridge University Press, 2002.
Kosselick, Reinhart. 'Social History and Conceptual History', *International Journal of Politics, Culture, and Society* 2, no. 3 (1989): 308–25.
Kozlowski, Gregory C. *Muslim Endowments and Society in British India*. New York: Cambridge University Press, 1985.
Kramer, Larry D. *The People Themselves: Popular Constitutionalism and Judicial Review*. New York: Oxford, 2004.
Kroeze, Irma. J. 'Legal Positivism.' In *Jurisprudence*, edited by Christopher Roederer and Darrell Moellendorf. Lansdowne, South Africa: Juta & Company, Ltd., 2004, 62–83.
Kugle, Scott Alan. 'Framed, Blamed and Renamed: The Recasting of Islamic Jurisprudence in Colonial South Asia', *Modern Asian Studies* 35, no. 2 (May 2001): 257–313.
Kumar, Dharma and Tapan Raychaudhuri, eds. *The Cambridge Economic History of India, volume 2: c. 1757–c. 1970*. New York: Cambridge University Press, 1983.
Kumar, Ravinder. *Western India in the Nineteenth Century: A Study in the Social History of Maharashtra*. Toronto: University of Toronto Press, 1968.
Kuper, Adam. *The Invention of Primitive Society: Transformations of an Illusion*. New York: Routledge, 1988.
Kuper, Adam. 'The Rise and Fall of Maine's Patriarchal Society.' In *The Victorian Achievement of Sir Henry Maine*, edited by Alan Diamond. New York: Cambridge University Press, 1991, 99–110.
Lakoff, George. *Women, Fire and Dangerous Things: What Categories Reveal about the Mind*. Chicago, IL: University of Chicago Press, 1987.
Lakoff, George and Mark Johnson, *Philosophy in the Flesh: The Embodied Mind and its Challenge to Western Thought*. New York: Basic Books, 1999.
Lapidus, Ira M. *A History of Islamic Societies*, 2nd edn. New York: Cambridge University Press, 2002.
Larson, Gerald James, ed. *Religion and Personal Law in Secular India: A Call to Judgment*. Bloomington, IN: Indiana University Press, 2001.
Leach, Edmund. *Pul Eliya: A Village in Ceylon, A Study of Land Tenure and Kinship*. Cambridge: Cambridge University Press, 1961.
Lefebvre, Henri. *The Production of Space*. D. Nicholson-Smith, trans. Oxford: Blackwell, 1991 (1974).
Legg, Stephen. *Spaces of Colonialism: Delhi's Urban Governmentalities*. Malden, MA: Wiley-Blackwell, 2007.

Leiter, Brian. 'Legal Realism and Legal Positivism Reconsidered', *Ethics*. vol. 111, no. 2 (2001): 278–301.
Leiter, Brian. 'Legal Formalism and Legal Realism: What Is the Issue?' *Legal Theory* 16 (2010): 111–33.
Lelyveld, David. *Aligarh's First Generation: Muslim Solidarity in British India*. Princeton, NJ: Princeton University Press, 1978.
Lemke, Thomas. 'Foucault, Governmentality, and Critique', *Rethinking Marxism* 14, no. 3 (Sep. 2002): 49–64.
Letwin, William. *The Origins of Scientific Economics*. London: Methuen and Co., 1963.
Lewis, Oliver. 'John Broome on Rationality', *Interviews with Philosophers*, 2008, available at http://podcasts.ox.ac.uk/john-broome-rationality
Lhost, Elizabeth. *Everyday Islamic Law and the Making of Modern South Asia*. Chapel Hill, NC: University of North Carolina Press, 2022.
Libecap, Gary. *Contracting for Property Rights*. New York: Cambridge University Press, 1989.
Litowitz, Douglas. 'Reification in Law and Legal Theory', *Southern California Interdisciplinary Law Journal* 9 (1999–2000): 401–28.
Livesey, James. *Making Democracy in the French Revolution*. Cambridge, MA: Harvard University Press, 2001.
Lobban, Michael. 'Austin and the Germans.' In *The Legacy of John Austin's Jurisprudence*, edited by Michael Freeman and Patricia Mundus. New York: Springer, 2012, 255–70.
Loux, Michael. *Metaphysics: A Contemporary Introduction*, 3rd edn. New York: Routledge, 2006.
Ludden, David. *Peasant History in South India*. Princeton, NJ: Princeton University Press, 1985.
Luhmann, Niklas. 'The World Society as a Social System', *International Journal of General Systems* 8, no. 8 (1982): 131–38.
Luhmann, Niklas. *Law as a Social System*. New York: Oxford University Press, 2004.
Lukes, Stephen. *Emile Durkheim: His Life and Work, a Historical and Critical Study*. New York: Harper and Row, 1973.
Ma, Debin and Jan Luiten van Zanden, eds. *Law and Long-Term Economic Change: A Eurasian Perspective*. Stanford, CA: Stanford University Press, 2011.
Macfarlane, Alan. 'Some Contributions of Maine to History and Anthropology.' In *The Victorian Achievement of Sir Henry Maine*, edited by Alan Diamond, New York: Cambridge University Press, 1991, 111–42.
Macpherson, C. B. *The Political Theory of Possessive Individualism*. Oxford: Clarendon Press, 1962.
Madan, T. N. 'Of the Social Categories "Private" and "Public": Considerations of Cultural Context.' In *The Public and the Private: Issues of Democratic Citizenship*, edited by Gurpreet Mahajan and Helmut Reifeld. New Delhi: Sage Publications, 2003, 88–102.
Maitland, F. W. *Equity, Also, the Forms of Action at Common Law: Two Courses of Lectures*. Cambridge: Cambridge University Press, 1909.
Malinowski, Bronislaw. *Crime and Custom in Savage Society*. New York: Harcourt, 1926.
Mallampalli, Chandra. 'Escaping the Grip of Personal Law in Colonial India: Proving Custom, Negotiating Hindu-ness', *Law & History Review, Forum: Maneuvering the Personal Law System in Colonial India* 28, no. 4 (2010): 1043–65.

Mamdani, Mahmood. *Citizen and Subject: Contemporary Africa and the Legacy of Late Colonialism*. Princeton, NJ: Princeton University Press, 1996.

Mani, Lata. 'Contentious Traditions: The Debate on Sati in Colonial India', *Cultural Critique* 7 (1987): 119–56.

Mani, Lata. *Contentious Traditions: The Debate on Sati in Colonial India*. Berkeley, CA: University of California Press, 1998.

Manikumar, K. A. *A Colonial Economy in the Great Depression. Madras (1929–1937)*. Chennai: Orient Longman, 2003.

Manjapra, Kris. *Age of Entanglement: German and Indian Intellectuals across Empire*. Cambridge, MA: Harvard University Press, 2014.

Mantena, Karuna. *Alibis of Empire: Henry Maine and the Ends of Liberal Imperialism*. Princeton, NJ: Princeton University Press, 2010.

Marmour, Andrei. 'The Nature of Law', *The Stanford Encyclopedia of Philosophy* (Fall 2008 Edition). Edward N. Zalta (ed.), https://plato.stanford.edu/entries/lawphil-nature/.

Marshall, P. J. *Bengal: The British Bridgehead: Eastern India, 1740–1828*. Cambridge, 1987.

Marshall, P. J. *The Making and Unmaking of Empires. Britain, India, and America, c. 1750–1783*. New York: Oxford University Press, 2005. Marx, Karl. *The Poverty of Philosophy*. Marx/Engels Internet Archive, 1999 (1847).

McLane, J. R. 'Revenue Farming and the Zamindari System in Eighteenth-century Bengal.' In *Land Tenure and Peasant in South Asia*, edited by Robert Frykenberg. New Delhi: Orient Longman, 1977, 19–36.

McNally, David. *Political Economy and the Rise of Capitalism: A Reinterpretation*. Berkeley, CA: University of California Press, 1988.

Mehta, Uday Singh. *Liberalism and Empire: A Study in Nineteenth-Century British Liberal Thought*. Chicago, IL: University of Chicago Press, 1999.

Meier, Gerald M. *Biography of a Subject: An Evolution of Development Economics*. New York: Oxford University Press, 2005.

Merry, Sally Engle. 'Review: Law and Colonialism', *Law & Society Review* 25, no. 4 (1991): 889–922.

Merry, Sally Engle. *Colonizing Hawai'i: the Cultural Power of Law*. Princeton, NJ: Princeton University Press, 2000.

Mertz, Elizabeth. 'Language, Law, and Social Meanings: Linguistic/Anthropological Contributions to the Study of Law', *Law and Society Review* 26, no. 2 (1992): 413–46.

Metcalf, Barbara D. *Islamic Revival in British India: Deoband, 1860–1900*. Princeton, NJ: Princeton University Press, 1982.

Metcalf, Barbara D. and Thomas R. Metcalf. *A Concise History of Modern India*. New York: Cambridge University Press, 2006.

Metcalf, Thomas R. 'The British and the Moneylender in Nineteenth-Century India', *The Journal of Modern History* 34, no. 4 (Dec. 1962): 390–97.

Metcalf, Thomas R. 'Laissez-Faire and Tenant Right in Mid-Nineteenth Century India', *Indian Economic and Social History Review* 1, no. 74 (Jan. 1964): 74–81.

Metcalf, Thomas R. *Ideologies of the Raj*. New York: Cambridge University Press, 1995.

Mitchell, Timothy. *Rule of Experts: Egypt, Techno-Politics, Modernity*. Los Angeles, CA: University of California Press, 2002.

Mizushima, Tsukasa. 'From Mirasidar to Pattadar: South India in the Late Nineteenth Century', *Indian Economic Social History Review* 39, nos. 2 & 3 (2002): 259–84.

Mohapatra, Prabhu. 'From Contract to Status? Or How Law Shaped Labour Relations in Colonial India, 1780–1880.' In *India's Workforce: of Bondage Old and New*, edited by Jan Breman, Isabelle Guérin, and Aseem Prakash. New York: Oxford University Press, 2009, 96–125.

Mootham, Orby. *The East India Company's Sadar Courts, 1801–1834*. London: Sweet and Maxwell, 1983.

Moreland, W. H. *The Agrarian System of Moslem India*. Delhi: Oriental Books, 1968 (1929).

Morris, Morris D. *The Emergence of an Industrial Labour Force in India: A Study of the Bombay Cotton Mills, 1854–1947*. Berkeley, CA: University of California Press, 1965.

Morrison, W. L. *John Austin*. Palo Alto, CA: Stanford University Press, 1982.

Moyn, Samuel and Andrew Sartori, eds. *Global Intellectual History*. New York: Columbia University Press, 2013.

Mukharji, Projit Bihari. *Doctoring Traditions: Ayurveda, Small Technologies, and Braided Sciences*. Chicago, IL: University of Chicago Press, 2016.

Mukherjee, Aditya. 'The Return of the Colonial in Indian Economic History: The Last Phase of Colonialism in India', *Social Scientist* 36, nos. 3/4 (2007): 3–44.

Mukherjee, Nilmani. *The Ryotwari System in Madras, 1792–1827*. Calcutta, 1962.

Mukhopadhyay, Anindita. *Behind the Mask: The Cultural Definition of the Legal Subject in Colonial Bengal (1715–1911)*. New Delhi: Oxford University Press, 2006.

Müller-Freienfels, Wolfram. 'The Emergence of Droit De Famille and Familienrecht in Continental Europe and the Introduction of Family Law in England', *Journal of Family History* 28 (2003): 31–51.

Nader, Laura. *The Life of the Law: Anthropological Projects*. Berkeley, CA: University of California Press, 2002.

Nair, Janaki. *Women and Law in Colonial India: A Social History*. New Delhi: Kali for Women in collaboration with the National Law School of India, 1996.

Naregal, Veena. *Language Politics, Elites, and the Public Sphere*. London: Anthem, 2002.

Neale, Walter. 'Land is to Rule.' In *Land Control and Social Structure in Indian History*, edited by Robert Frykenberg. Madison, WI: University of Wisconsin Press, 1969, 3–15.

Newbigin, Eleanor. *The Hindu Family and the Emergence of Modern India: Law, Citizenship and Community*. New York: Cambridge University Press, 2013.

Newbigin, Eleanor, Leigh Denault, and Rohit De, eds. *Indian Economic and Social History Review: Special Issue on Personal Law, Identity Politics, and Civil Society in Colonial South Asia* 46, No. 1 (2009): 1–130.

Newton, Arthur Percival, ed. *The Cambridge History of the British Empire*, vol. 2, Cambridge: Cambridge University Press, 1940.

Nichols, Robert. *Theft is Property! Dispossession and Critical Theory*. Durham, NC: Duke University Press, 2020.

North, Douglass C. *Institutions, Institutional Change and Economic Performance*. New York: Cambridge University Press, 1990.

O'Hanlon, Rosalind and David Washbrook. 'Culture, Criticism, and Politics in the Third World', *Comparative Studies in Society and History* 34, no. 1 (1992): 141–67.

Orsini, Francesca. *The Hindi Public Sphere, 1920–1940: Language and Literature in the Age of Nationalism*. Oxford: Oxford University Press, 2009.

Orsini, Francesca. 'Where to Find Indian Menocchios?', *Journal of South Asian Intellectual History* 1, no. 1 (2019): 1–12.

Parker, Kunal. 'Observations on the Historical Destruction of Separate Legal Regimes'. In *Religion and Personal Law in Secular India: A Call to Judgment*, edited by Gerald James Larson. Bloomington, IN: Indiana University Press, 2001, 184–99.

Pashukanis, Evgeny B. *Law and Marxism: A General Theory*, trans. Barbara Einhorn and C.J. Arthur, ed. London: Pluto Press, 1989.

Patterson, Dennis. *A Companion to Philosophy of Law and Legal Theory*. Cambridge, MA: Wiley Blackwell, 1999.

Peers, Douglas M. 'Gunpowder Empires and the Garrison State: Modernity, Hybridity, and the Political Economy of Colonial India, circa 1750–1860', *Comparative Studies of South Asia, Africa and the Middle East* 27, no. 2 (2007): 245–58.

Penner, J. E. 'The "Bundle of Rights" Picture of Property', *UCLA Law Review* 43 (1996): 711–820.

Pennington, Brian K. *Was Hinduism Invented? Britons, Indians, and the Colonial Construction of Religion*. New York: Oxford University Press, 2005.

Pennington, Kenneth. *The Prince and the Law: Sovereignty and Rights in the Western Legal Tradition*. Berkeley, CA: University of California Press, 1993.

Pennock, J. Roland and John W. Chapman, eds. *NOMOS: XXII: Property*. New York: New York University Press, 1980.

Perillo, Joseph M. 'The Origins of the Objective Theory of Contract Formation and Interpretation', *Fordham Law Review* 69, no. 2 (2000): 427–77.

Pernau, Margrit. *Emotions and Modernity in Colonial India: From Balance to Fervor*. New York: Oxford University Press, 2019.

Pernau, Margrit, Helge Jordheim, and Orit Bashkin, eds. *Civilizing Emotions: Concepts in Nineteenth Century Asia and Europe*. New York: Oxford University Press, 2015.

Pildes, Richard. 'Forms of Formalism', *The University of Chicago Law Review* 66, no. 3 (Summer 1999): 607–21.

Plato. *Plato in Twelve Volumes, vol. 9*. Harold N. Fowler, trans. Cambridge, MA: Harvard University Press, 1925.

Pocock, J. G. A. *Virtue, Commerce, and History: Essays on Political Thought and History, Chiefly in the Eighteenth Century*. Cambridge: Cambridge University Press, 1985.

Poovey, Mary. *Genres of the Credit Economy: Mediating Value in Eighteenth- and Nineteenth-Century Britain*. Chicago, IL: University of Chicago Press, 2008.

Posthumus, David. *All My Relatives: Exploring Lakota Ontology, Belief, and Ritual*. Lincoln, NE: University of Nebraska Press, 2018.

Pound, Roscoe. 'Mechanical Jurisprudence', *Columbia Law Review* 8 (1908): 605–23.

Prakash, Gyan. *Bonded Histories: Genealogies of Labor and Servitude in Colonial India*. New York: Cambridge University Press, 1990.

Prakash, Gyan. 'Writing Post-Orientalist Histories of the Third World: Perspectives from Indian Historiography', *Comparative Studies in Society and History* 32, no. 2 (1990): 384–408.

Prakash, Gyan. *Another Reason: Science and the Imagination of Modern India*. Princeton, NJ: Princeton University Press, 1999.

Prichard, H. A. 'Does Moral Philosophy Rest on a Mistake?', *Mind* 21, no. 81 (1912): 21–37.
Priest, Claire. *Credit Nation: Property Laws and Institutions in Early America*. Princeton, NJ: Princeton University Press, 2021.
Prinz, Jess J. *The Conscious Brain: How Attention Engenders Experience*. New York: Oxford University Press, 2012.
Putnam, Hilary. *Reality and Representation*. Cambridge, MA: MIT Press, 1988.
Rabinow, Paul, ed. *The Foucault Reader*. New York: Pantheon, 1984.
Raman, Bhavani. *Document Raj: Writing and Scribes in Early Colonial South India*. Chicago, IL: University of Chicago Press, 2012.
Rankin, George. *Background to Indian Law*. Cambridge: Cambridge University Press, 1946.
Ray, Ratnalekha. *Change in Bengal Agrarian Society, 1760–1850*. Delhi: Manohar, 1980.
Ray, Ratnalekha and Rajat K. Ray. 'Zamindars and Jotedars: A Study in Rural Politics in Bengal', *Modern Asian Studies* 9, no. 1 (1975): 81–102.
Raz, Joseph. *The Authority of Law: Essays on Law and Morality*. New York: Oxford University Press, 1979.
Raz, Joseph. *The Concept of a Legal System: An Introduction to the Theory of Legal System*. New York: Clarendon Press 1980 (1970).
Raz, Joseph. *Practical Reason and Norms*. New York: Oxford University Press, 1990 (1975).
Rediker, Marcus, Titas Chakraborty, and Matthias van Rossum, eds. *A Global History of Runaways: Workers, Mobility, and Capitalism,1600–1850*. Oakland, CA: University of California Press, 2019.
Reetz, Dietrich. *Islam in the Public Sphere: Religious Groups in India, 1900–1947*. New Delhi: Oxford University Press, 2006.
Roach, John. 'James Fitzjames Stephen (1829–94)', *Journal of the Royal Asiatic Society of Great Britain and Ireland*, no. 1/2 (Apr. 1956): 1–16.
Robb, Peter. 'Bihar, the Colonial State and Agricultural Development in India, 1880–1920', *The Indian Economic and Social History Review* 25, no. 2 (1988): 205–35.
Robb, Peter. 'Law and Agrarian Society in India: The Case of Bihar and the Nineteenth-Century Tenancy Debate', *Modern Asian Studies* 22, no. 2 (1988): 319–54.
Robb, Peter. *Ancient Rights and Future Comfort: Bihar, the Bengal Tenancy Act of 1885 and British Rule in India*. Richmond, Surrey: Curzon Press, 1997.
Robb, Peter. *A History of India*. New York: Palgrave, 2002.
Robb, Peter. *Liberalism, Modernity and the Nation*. New York: Oxford University Press, 2007.
Robinson, Francis. *The 'Ulama of Farangi Mahall and Islamic Culture in South Asia*. London: C. Hurst, 2001.
Rorabacher, John Albert. *Property, Land, Revenue, and Policy: The East India Company, c.1757–1825*. New York: Routledge, 2017.
Rosen, F. 'Eric Stokes, British Utilitarianism, and India.' In *J. S. Mill's Encounter with India*, edited by Martin I. Moir, Douglas M. Peers, and Lynn Zastoupil. Toronto: University of Toronto Press, 1999, 18–33.
Rothermund, Dietmar. 'Freedom of Contract and the Problem of Land Alienation in British India', *South Asia* 3, no. 1 (1973), 57–78.

Rothermund, Dietmar. *Government, Landlord, and Peasant in India: Agrarian Relations Under British Rule, 1865–1930*. Wiesbaden: Steiner, 1978.
Rothermund, Dietmar. *An Economic History of India: From Pre-Colonial Times To 1991*, 2nd edn. New York: Routledge, 1993.
Rothermund, Dietmar and Hermann Kulke. *A History of India*. 4th edn. New York: Routledge, 2004.
Roy, Tirthankar. 'Economic History and Modern India: Redefining the Link', *The Journal of Economic Perspectives* 16, no. 3 (2002): 109–30.
Roy, Tirthankar. *India in the World Economy: From Antiquity to the Present*. New York: Cambridge University Press, 2012.
Roy, Tirthankar. *Natural Disasters and Indian History*. Oxford: Oxford University Press, 2012.
Roy, Tirthankar. 'Rethinking the Origins of British India: State Formation and Military-fiscal Undertakings in an Eighteenth Century World Region', *Modern Asian Studies* 47, no. 4 (2013): 1125–56.
Roy, Tirthankar. *A Business History of India: Enterprise and the Emergence of Capitalism from 1700*. New York: Cambridge University Press, 2018.
Rubiés, Joan-Pau. 'Oriental Despotism and European Orientalism: Botero to Montesquieu', *Journal of Early Modern History* 9, nos. 1–2 (2005): 109–80.
Rudolph, Susan. 'Presidential Address: State Formation in Asia—Prolegomenon to a Comparative Study', *The Journal of Asian Studies* 46, no. 4 (Nov. 1987): 731–46.
Rumble, Wilfrid. *Doing Austin Justice: The Reception of John Austin's Philosophy of Law in Nineteenth-Century England*. New York: Continuum, 2004.
Rungta, Syam. *The Rise of Business Corporations in India, 1851–1900*. London: Cambridge University Press, 1970.
Ruskola, Teemu. *Legal Orientalism: China, the United States and Modern Law*. Cambridge, MA: Harvard University Press, 2013.
Said, Edward. *Orientalism*. New York: Pantheon Books, 1978.
Sangari, Kumkum and Sudesh Vaid, eds. *Recasting Women: Essays in Colonial History* New Delhi: Kali for Women, 1989.
Saradamoni, Kunjulekshmi. *Matriliny Transformed: Family, Law, and Ideology in Twentieth Century Travancore*. Walnut Creek, CA: Alta Mira Press, 1999.
Sarkar, Tanika. 'A Pre-History of Rights: The Age of Consent Bill in Colonial Bengal', *Feminist Studies* 26, no. 3 (Autumn 2000): 601–22.
Sarkar, Tanika. *Hindu Wife, Hindu Nation: Community, Religion, and Cultural Transformation*. New Delhi: Permanent Black, 2001.
Sartori, Andrew. *Bengal in Global Concept History: Culturalism in the Age of Capital*. Chicago, IL: University of Chicago Press, 2008.
Sartori, Andrew. 'A Liberal Discourse of Custom in Colonial Bengal', *Past and Present* 212, no. 1 (Aug. 2011): 163–97.
Sartori, Andrew. *Liberalism in Empire: An Alternative History*. Oakland, CA: University of California Press, 2014.
Saumarez-Smith, Richard. *Rule by Records: Land Registration and Village Custom in Early British Panjab*. New York: Oxford University Press, 1996.
Schacht, Joseph. *Introduction to Islamic Law*. New York: Clarendon Press, 1964.
Schepple, Kim Lane. 'Autocratic Legalism', *The University of Chicago Law Review* 85, no. 2 (2018): 545–83.

Schmitt, Carl. *The Nomos of the Earth in the International Law of the Jus Publicum Europaeum*. New York: Telos Press, 2003 (1950).
Scott, David. 'Colonial Governmentality', *Social Text* 43 (Autumn 1995): 191–220.
Scott, James. *Seeing Like a State: How Certain Schemes to Improve the Human Condition Have Failed*. New Haven, CT: Yale University Press, 1998.
Searle, John. *Intentionality: An Essay in the Philosophy of Mind*. New York: Cambridge University Press, 1983.
Searle, John. *The Construction of Social Reality*. New York: The Free Press, 1995.
Searle, John. *Making the Social World: The Structure of Human Civilization*. New York: Oxford University Press, 2010.
Sen, Sudipta. *Empire of Free Trade: The East India Company and the Making of the Colonial Marketplace*. Philadelphia, PA: University of Pennsylvania Press, 1998.
Shapiro, Scott J. *Legality*. Cambridge, MA: The Belknap Press of Harvard University, 2011.
Sharafi, Mitra. *Law and Identity in Colonial South Asia: Parsi Legal Culture, 1772–1947*. New York: Cambridge University Press, 2014.
Sheth, Sudev J. 'Revenue Farming Reconsidered: Tenurial Rights and Tenurial Duties in Early Modern India, ca. 1556–1818', *Journal of the Economic and Social History of the Orient* 61, nos. 5–6 (2018): 878–919.
Simpson, Alfred W. B. 'The Horwitz Thesis and the History of Contracts', *The University of Chicago Law Review* 46, no. 3 (1978): 533–601.
Singha, Radhika. 'The Thuggee Campaign of the 1830s and Legal Innovation', *Modern Asian Studies* 27, no. 1 (Feb. 1993): 83–146.
Singha, Radhika. *A Despotism of Law: Crime and Justice in Early Colonial India*. Delhi: Oxford University Press, 1996.
Skyttner, Lars. *General Systems Theory: Problems, Perspectives, Practice*. Singapore: World Scientific Publishing, 2005.
Smith, K. J. M. *James Fitzjames Stephen: Portrait of a Victorian Rationalist*. New York: Cambridge University Press, 1988.
Snyder, Francis. 'Anthropology, Dispute Processes and Law: A Critical Introduction', *British Journal of Law and Society* 8, no. 2 (Winter 1981): 141–80.
Sohn-Rethel, Alfred. *Intellectual and Manual Labour: A Critique of Epistemology*. Boston: Brill, 2021 (1978).
Spaak, Torben. 'Legal Positivism, Law's Normativity, and the Normative Force of Legal Justification', *Ratio Juris* 16, no. 4 (Dec. 2003): 469–85.
Sreenivas, Mytheli. *Wives, Widows, and Concubines: The Conjugal Family Ideal in Colonial India*. Bloomington, IN: Indiana University Press, 2008.
Srivastava, Dharma Bhanu. *The Province of Agra: its History and* Administration. Delhi: Concept Publishing, 1979 (1959).
Stanek, Lukasz. 'Space as Concrete Abstraction: Hegel, Marx, and Modern Urbanism in Henri Lefebvre.' In *Space, Difference, Everyday Life: Reading Henri Lefebvre*, edited by Kanishka Goonewardena, Stefan Kipfer, Richard Milgrom, and Christian Schmidet. New York, Routledge, 2008, 62–80.
Stapleford, Thomas A. 'Historical Epistemology and the History of Economics: Views Through the Lens of Practice.' In *Including a Symposium on the Historical Epistemology of Economics* (*Research in the History of Economic*

Thought and Methodology), *vol. 35*, edited by Luca Fiorito, Scott Scheall, and Carlos Eduardo Suprinyak. Bingley, UK: Emerald Publishing Limited, 2017, 113–48.

Stein, Burton. *Thomas Munro: The Origins of the Colonial State and His Vision of Empire*. New York: Oxford University Press, 1989.

Stein, Burton. *A History of India*, 2nd edn. Malden, MA: Wiley Blackwell, 2010.

Steinfeld, Robert. *Coercion, Contract, and Free Labour in the Nineteenth Century*. New York: Cambridge University Press, 2001.

Stephens, Julia. *Governing Islam: Law, Empire, and Secularism in Modern South Asia*. New York: Cambridge University Press, 2018.

Stern, Philip J. *The Company-State: Corporate Sovereignty and the Early Modern Foundations of the British Empire in India*. New York: Oxford University Press, 2011.

Stevens, Robert. *Law and Politics: The House of Lords as a Judicial Body, 1800–1976*. Chapel Hill, NC: University of North Carolina Press, 1979.

Stokes, Eric. *The English Utilitarians in India*. New York: Clarendon Press, 1959.

Stokes, Eric. *The Peasant and the Raj: Studies in Agrarian Society and Peasant Rebellion in Colonial India*. New York: Cambridge University Press, 1978.

Stokes, Michael. 'Formalism, Realism and the Concept of Law', *Law and Philosophy* 13, no. 2 (1994): 115–59.

Stolleis, Michael. *Public Law in Germany: 1800–1914*. New York: Berghahn Books, 2001.

Sturman, Rachel. *The Government of Social Life in Colonial India: Liberalism, Religious Law, and Women's Rights*. New York: Cambridge University Press, 2012.

Sugarman, David. '"A Hatred of Disorder": Legal Science, Liberalism and Imperialism.' In *Dangerous Supplements: Resistance and Renewal in Jurisprudence*, edited by Peter Fitzpatrick. Durham, NC: Duke University Press, 1991, 34–67.

Sugarman, David and G. R. Rubin, eds. *Law, Economy and Society, Essays in the History of English Law, 1759–1914*. Abingdon, UK: Professional Books, 1984.

Sugarman, David and G. R. Rubin. 'Towards a New History of Law and Material Society in England, 1750–1914.' In *Law, Economy and Society*, edited by David Sugarman and G. R. Rubin, Abingdon, UK: Professional Books, 1984, 1–123.

Sugarman, David and Ronnie Warrington. 'Land Law, Citizenship, and the Invention of "Englishness": The Strange World of the Equity of Redemption.' In *Early Modern Conceptions of Property*, edited by John Brewer and Susan Staves, New York: Routledge, 1995, 111–43.

Swaminathan, Shivprasad. 'Eclipsed by Orthodoxy: The Vanishing Point of Consideration and the Forgotten Ingenuity of the Indian Contract Act 1872', *Asian Journal of Comparative Law* 12, no. 1 (Jul. 2017): 141–65.

Sweetser, Eve. *From Etymology to Pragmatics: Metaphorical and Cultural Aspects of Semantic Structure*. New York: Cambridge University Press, 1990.

Sylvest, Casper. '"Our Passion for Legality": International Law and Imperialism in Late-Nineteenth Century Britain.' *Review of International Studies* 34, no. 3 (2000): 403–23.

Tadros, Victor. 'Between Governance and Discipline: The Law and Michel Foucault', *Oxford Journal of Legal Studies* 18, no. 1 (Spring 1998): 75–103.

Taggart, Michael. 'Prolegomenon to an Intellectual History of Administrative Law in the Twentieth Century: The Case of John Willis ad Canadian Administrative Law', *Osgoode Hall Law Journal* 43, no. 3 (2005): 223–67.

Tamanaha, Brian. *A General Jurisprudence of Law and Society*. New York: Oxford University Press, 2001.
Thompson, E. P. *Whigs and Hunters: The Origin of the Black Acts*. New York: Penguin, 1975.
Tomlinson, B. R. *The Economy of Modern India, 1860-1970*. New York: Cambridge University Press, 1993.
Tönnies, Ferdinand. *Gemeinschaft und Gesellschaft*. Jose Harris and Margaret Hollis, trans. New York: Cambridge University Press, 2001 (1887).
Traugott, Mark, ed. *Emile Durkheim on Institutional Analysis*. Chicago, IL: The University of Chicago Press, 1978.
Travers, Robert. '"The Real Value of the Lands": The Nawabs, the British and the Land Tax in Eighteenth-Century Bengal.' *Modern Asian Studies* 38, no. 3 (July 2004): 517-58.
Travers, Robert. 'Ideology and British expansion in Bengal, 1757-72', *The Journal of Imperial and Commonwealth History* 33, no. 1 (2005): 7-27.
Travers, Robert. *Ideology and Empire in Eighteenth-century India: The British in Bengal*. Cambridge: Cambridge University Press, 2007.
Travers, Robert. *Empires of Complaints: Mughal Law and the Making of British India, 1765-1793*. New York: Cambridge University Press, 2022.
Trubek, David, Favio Sa e Silva, Marta Machado, Conveners. 'Comparative Perspectives on Autocratic Legalism: Brazil, India, and South Africa.' *Law & Society Association*: International Research Collaborative, 2021 www.lawandsociety.org/lsairc27/
Tuck, Richard. *Natural Rights Theories: Their Origin and Development*. New York: Cambridge University Press, 1979.
Tuori, Kaius. *Lawyers and Savages: Ancient History and Legal Realism in the Making of Legal Anthropology*. New York: Routledge, 2014.
Twining, William, ed. *Legal Theory and Common Law*. New York: Basil Blackwell, 1986.
Twining, William. *Globalisation and Legal Theory*. London: Butterworths, 2000.
Umbrello, Steven. 'Book Review: A Theory of Everything?', *Cultural Studies Review* 24, no. 2 (2018): 150-53.
Vaggi, Gianni. *The Economics of François Quesnay*. Durham, NC: Duke University Press, 1987.
Vandevelde, Kenneth J. 'The New Property of the Nineteenth Century: The Development of the Modern Concept of Property', *Buffalo Law Review* 29 (1980): 325-67.
Varzi, Achille C. 'From Language to Ontology: Beware the Traps.' In *The Categorization of Spatial Entities in Language and Cognition*, edited by M. Aurnague, M. Hickmann, and L. Vieu. Amsterdam: John Benjamin, 2007, 269-84.
Vinogradoff, Paul. *The Teachings of Sir Henry Maine: An Inaugural Lecture Delivered in Corpus Christi College Hall on March 1, 1904*. London: Henry Frowde, 1904.
Vinx, Lars, ed. *The Guardian of the Constitution: Hans Kelsen and Carl Schmitt on the Limits of Constitutional Law* Cambridge: Cambridge University Press, 2015.
Washbrook, David. 'Law, State and Agrarian Society in Colonial India', *Modern Asian Studies* 15, no. 3 (1981): 649-721.

Washbrook, David. 'Economic Depression and the Making of "Traditional" Society in Colonial India 1820-1855', *Transactions of the Royal Historical Society* 6th Ser., 3 (1993): 237-63.

Washbrook, David. 'India, 1818-1860: The Two Faces of Colonialism.' In *The Oxford History of the British Empire, Vol. III, The Nineteenth Century*, edited by Andrew Porter. Oxford: Oxford University Press, 1999, 395-421.

Washbrook, David. 'Sovereignty, Property, Land and Labour in Colonial South India.' In *Constituting Modernity: Private Property in the East and West*, edited by Huri İslamoğıu-İnan. New York: I. B. Tauris, 2004, 69-99.

Watson, Alan. 'The Structure of Blackstone's Commentaries', *The Yale Law Journal* 97, no. 5 (1988): 795-821.

Weber, Max. *Economy and Society: An Outline of Interpretive Sociology*, 2 vols. Guenther Roth and Claus Wittich eds., Ephraim Fischoff et al., trans. Berkeley, CA: The University of California Press, 1978 (1921-1922).

Wieacker, Franz. *A History of Private Law (with particular reference to Germany)*. Tony Weir, trans. New York: Oxford University Press, 1995.

Wiecek, William. *The Lost World of Classical Legal Thought: Law and Ideology in America, 1886-1937*. New York: Oxford University Press, 1998.

Williams, Robert A. *The American Indian in Western Legal Thought: The Discourses of Conquest*. New York: Oxford University Press, 1992.

Williams, Robert A. *Savage Anxieties: The Invention of Western Civilization*. New York: Palgrave Macmillan, 2012.

Wilmarth, Arthur. 'Elusive Foundation: John Marshall, James Wilson, and the Problem of Reconciling Popular Sovereignty and Natural Law Jurisprudence in the New Federal Republic', *George Washington Law Review* 72 (Dec. 2003): 113-93.

Wilson, Jon E. 'Anxieties of Distance: Codification in Early Colonial Bengal', *Modern Intellectual History* 4, no. 1 (2007): 7-23.

Wilson, Jon E. *The Domination of Strangers: Modern Governance in Eastern India, 1780-1835*. Basingstoke: Palgrave Macmillan, 2008.

Winch, Donald and Patrick K. O'Brien. *The Political Economy of British Historical Experience, 1688-1914*. New York: Oxford University Press, 2002.

Wittgenstein, Ludwig. *Philosophical Investigations*. G. E. M. Anscombe, P. M. S. Hacker, and Joachim Schulte, trans. West Sussex, UK: Wiley-Blackwell, 2009.

Yang, Anand, ed. *Crime and Criminality in British India*. Tucson, AZ: University of Arizona Press, 1985.

Zalta, Edward, N., ed. *The Stanford Encyclopedia of Philosophy*. Fall 2008 Edition. http://plato.stanford.edu/archives/fall2008/entries/lawphil-nature/.

Zaman, Muhammad Qasim. *The Ulama in Contemporary Islam: Custodians of Change*. Princeton, NJ: Princeton University Press, 2010.

Index

For the benefit of digital users, indexed terms that span two pages (e.g., 52–53) may, on occasion, appear on only one of those pages.

Act in Bengal 1885 284–85
Act IX of 1872 319–30, 463–64
administrable quality of doctrinal discourse 140, 144–46, 155–56
  implicit quality 146
  meaning-making 144–45
  propositional content 146
administration of justice 172–73, 275–78
  institutional architecture for 275–76, 277
  magistrate-level decision-making 276–77
Age of Consent Act of 1891 468–69
Alam II, Shah 174–76
Ali, Syed Ameer 413–15, 465, 466
altamgha grants 239–46
  in'am gifts 244
  irrevocable rights 243–44
Anagol, Padma 456–57
analytical jurisprudence 51
Ancient Law 1861 20–21
Anderson, Michael 65–66, 465–66
Anglo-common-law 13, 16–17, 18–19, 25, 56–57, 60, 155–56, 157, 162, 193, 215, 235–36, 246–47, 259, 301–2, 493–94
  absolute, unitary, and physicalist conception of rights 199–200
  conception of property right 267–68, 270–71
  contract 321–22
  land's rent in 166, 168
  law of domestic relations in 408–9, 427–28
Anglo-Maratha War of 1817–18 254–55
Anson, William 358–59, 360

antecedent rights in personam 374
appellate or '*adalat* courts 275–76
Ardaseer Cursetjee v. Perozeboye decisions 21–22
Asiatic despotism 16–17, 179–88
Austin, John 47–48, 126–27
authoritarian legalism 24–25

Baden-Powell, Baden Henry 264, 273–74, 396–97
  as Conservator of Forests 288–89
  disaggregability of property 294–95
  early years 288–89
  Land Systems 288, 289, 291–93
  mahalwari revenue system 298
  Manual of Jurisprudence for Forest Officers 294–95
  proprietary nature of land rights 289–90
  tenets of forest law 293–94
  under-/sub-proprietary tenures 295
Baden-Powell, Robert Stephenson 288–89
Bagchi, Amiya 164–65
Baillie, John 413
Baillie, Neil 453
  Digest of Moohummudan Law 453
  Fatawa-i-Alamgiri 455
Banerjee, Gooroodass 423–24, 473
  1878 Tagore Law Lectures 473
Battle of Buxar in 1764 174–75
Battle of Plassey in 1757 173–74, 319–20
Bayly, C. A., 255
Baz, Avram 123–24, 146
  representational theory of language 124–25

530 INDEX

Bengal Regulation VII of 1819 320
Bengal Rent Act of 1859 18, 273, 284–85, 296–97, 305
Bengal Tenancy Act of 1885,C6P29
Bentham, Jeremy 111–12, 196–97
Bentinck, General William 46–47
Benton, Lauren 91–92
Bernier, Francois 190–91
Bird, R. M., 258–59
Birla, Ritu 70, 316
Blackstone, William 409–11
Blue Mutiny of 1860 327
Bolts, William 200–1, 204–5
Bombay Charter of Justice of 1823 436
Bombay Khoti Leases Act of 1865 284–85
Bose, Sugata 282–83
Boulnois, Charles 391
Buchaboye v. Merwangee Nasserwangee 438
Burke, Edmund 178

Calcutta Trade Association 323–24
Campbell, George 299–300, 332
  equivocality of contractualism 332–33
  The Irish Land 299–300
capitalist farmers 166
Central Provinces Tenancy Act of 1883 284–85
Chakraborty, Titas 320
Chandra, Sudhir 469–70
Charter Act of 1813 254–55
Chatterjee, Indrani 427–28
Chatterjee, Partha 427–28
classical legal thoughts 53–60, 287, 292–93, 302, 312, 314, 328–29, 349–50
  conception of private rights and public powers 57
  connection to ideological functions 154
  contract 321–22
  discourse of status 373, 379–80
  family law 59–60
  individualism 54–56
  individualism in 308

law of domestic relations 421–22
motive force 152–53
municipal and international law, distinction between 58–59
normative force 152–53
parallelism between rights and powers 56, 59
private and public law, distinction between 57–58
property right 272–73
right to property 56–57
status 373, 379–80, 425–26
will theory in 57–58
classical private-law theory 22
Clive, Colonel Robert 174–75
Code of Civil Procedure (Act VIII of 1859) 387–88
Code of Tribal Custom 391–92
codification 5, 411–12, 490
  all-purpose ethic of 67–68
  contract's associated 318–19, 364–65, 368
Cohn, Bernard 68–69
Colebrooke, Henry 320–21
collective intentionality 73–74
Colonial Bengal
  governance by Company 174–78, 221
  relationship between constitutionism and property's discourses 219
  under Scrafton 188–95
  Tax Farming Scheme of 1772 200–5
communitarian identity 23–24
comparative jurisprudence 51
confirmation bias 105–6
conjugal family 427–30
  inheritance and succession 429–30
  law of domestic relations 429–30
  marital unions among *nair* caste 428–29
  in Muslim family 428–29
  notion of jointness 429–30
  in Tamil country 428–29
conjugal restitution doctrine 21–22, 23, 425–26, 434–46, 481–87
  as a civil remedy for breach of contract 486

evolution 438
Jackson's view 442–43
Perry's 1843 decision 435–36, 437–38, 439–40
principles of individualism and collectivism 481–82, 483–84, 485–86
Connell, Arthur 337
conscience collective 63
Contract Act of 1872 330
contracts 19–20
  before Act IX of 1872 319–30
  agreement forms 320–21
  contractual collectivism 364–70
  doctrinal discourse of 344–45
  fixed, abstract, rational and universal rules of 329–30
  Indian Contract Act of 1872 322–23, 327, 330–39
  of Indigo Production, Bihar 327–30
  infants' agreements 358–64
  inherent equivocality 368
  parallelism between private and public law 368–69
  private individualism 366
  quasi 353–58, 364–65
  role of law of tort 364–65
  Second Indian Law Commission 322–23
  standard of 'fairness' and 'equity,' 328–30
  Workman's Breach of Contract Act of 1859 323–27, 328–29
contractual freedom 306–7, 311–12, 316
contractual individualism 19–20, 308
Cornwallis, Governor Charles 16, 173–74, 195, 201, 211, 285–86, 303, 305
  'absolute' security 217–18
  approach to revenue settlement in Bengal 229, 230–31
  Permanent Settlement 217–18, 221
counterfactual stabilization 115–17
Criminal Breach of Contract Act of 1865 323–24
Crown Raj 6–7
Crown rule 13–14, 46–47
  administration of justice 275–78

agriculture economy 280–81, 282–83
legal modernization 313–14
mode of surplus appropriation 282–83
new forms of 'proprietary' right 278–88
occupancy rights 285–86
shifting economy 278–88
Cunningham, Sir Henry 343–44, 361–62, 363
quasi ex contractu 357–58
customary law 49–50

Dalhousie, Lord 377–78
Deccan Agriculturists' Relief Act of 1879 284–85, 306–7, 311–12
denaturalization 123, 126–27
'detail-to-aggregate' method 258–59
Dicey, A. V., 44–45
direct legal enactments 357–58
Dirks, Nicholas 237
discourse of law *vs.* discourse about law 136–39
  as complementary 149–50
  constitutive effect 138
  of contract 148–49
  notions of publicity/collectivity 151–52
  role in mediating juristic reason 139
  role of public sphere 150–52
dispute-settlement practices 90
duality of law and state 29–33, 61
  jurisprudential problem 31–32
  Kelsen's approach to 30–31, 32–33
Durkheim, Emile 63
  conscience collective 73–74
  direct inheritors in social theory 63–65
  social facts 63, 65–66
Dutt, Romesh Chunder 281–82
Dworkin, Ronald 481–82
  theory of rights 109–10

East India Company 33–35, 489–90
  administration of justice 40
  administration of property 167–68, 170–72
  arrangements for financing commercial and sovereign affairs 176–77

East India Company (*cont.*)
  as a chartered corporation 34–35
  dual judiciary 35
  land revenue 176
  land-revenue extraction 267
  laws of native tradition/society 39
  Permanent Settlement regulations of 1793 174–75, 179, 187–88, 195, 208–9
  Police Regulations 324–25
  revenue collection from *diwani* territories 177
  role in Bengal's internal governance 174–78
  rule of property 17–18, 121–22, 156–57, 167–68, 248, 273–74, 288–89, 291, 301, 304
  sovereignty of 33–35
Ehrlich, Eugen 87–88
Elphinstone, Mountstuart 257–58
'English' concept of property 273
English Infants Relief Act of 1874 359, 360
equity law 335–36

fair shares 164–65
family law 59–60
Field, C. D., 303–4
  Digest of the Law of Landlord and Tenant in Bengal 303–4
Fifth Report 225–26
first globalization of law 7–8
formalism 97–99
formal law 85–88
  vs. living law distinction 86–87, 88–89
Foucault, Michel 9, 10, 65–66, 70, 76–77, 128–29
Francis, Phillip 179
  notion of possession 209–10
  Permanent Settlement in 1776 201–2, 205–11
Frykenberg, Robert 237–38
Furber, Holden 176

Gaius 409–11
German legal thought 54
German Pandecticism 54–55

globalization of law and legal thought 53, 55–56, 57, 81–82, 152–56, 287–88, 314, 493
  ontologization and 152–55
Gordon, Robert 161–62
Goswami, Manu 70, 132
Grant, James 211–13, 236–37
  Shore's disagreement with 213–14
  sovereign's control over rent 211–13, 215–16
  zamindar proprietorship 213
Greene, Christopher 62–63
Grey, Peter 299–300
Guha, Ranajit 68–69
  A Rule of Property for Bengal 179

Habermas, Jurgen 106, 150–51, 496–97
  communicative rationality 106–7, 109, 113–14
  conception of systematicity 111–12
  dialogical principle of universalization 107–8
  discourse theory of ethics to law 496–97
  Dworkinian interpretivism 109–10
  Between Facts and Norms 107–8
  jurisprudential thinking 110–11
  legal system 111–12
  rationality problem 109–10
  self-application of law 110–11
  The Structural Transformation of the Public Sphere 106–7
  view of law 108
Hacking, Ian 9, 11, 12–13, 76–77, 150–51
  historical ontology 128–29
Halhed, Nathaniel 413
Halley, Janet 408–11, 428–29
Hamilton, Charles 413
Hart, H. L. A., 8, 93, 100, 105, 496
  The Concept of Law 96–97
  rule of recognition 93–94, 118
Hastings, Warren 173–74, 177–78, 206–8, 319–20, 430–31, 489–90
  accusation and exoneration 178
  judicial reforms 412–13, 492
  Tax Farming Scheme of 1772 200–5, 412–13

INDEX 533

Hay, William 320–21
Heidegger, Martin 75–76
Hempel, Carl 137–38
Hindu marriages
   Dadaji Bhikaji vs. Rukhmabai 468–76
   Hindu personal law 456, 469–70, 473
   idea of status in 476–78
   remedy of conjugal restitution 472
   sacrament nature of 468–81
historical jurisprudence 51
historical ontology 9, 10, 16
   as a method of jurisprudential accounting 132
historical ontology of law 76–78
Holland, Thomas Erskine 300–1, 432–33
   antecedent domestic entitlements 374, 376
   domestic relations 375–76
   The Elements of Jurisprudence 374
   'lifelong courses' of rights and duties 474
   types of legal rights 433
Holmes, Oliver Wendall 111–12
Holwell, John Z., 191–93, 204
   Interesting Historical Events, Relative to the Provinces of Bengal, and the Empire of Indostan 193–94
   right to property 193–94
Horwitz, Morton 349
Howell, Martha 267–68
   property discourse 269–70
Hugo, Gustav 54
Hunter, W. W., 304
hypostatization of state 30–33, 45–46, 61, 81, 83–84, 121–22

Ibbetson, Denzil 396–97
in'am
   category of 222–23
   privileges 236–39
in'am based-rights 246–54
   adjudicatory processing 252–54
   monetizable value of land's produce 252
Indian Companies Act 316–17

Indian Contract Act of 1872 19–20, 322–23, 327, 330–39, 365–66, 427
   Campbell's proposal 332–36
   chapter five 353–54, 361–62
   communication of intentions 347
   critique 337–39
   discursive contents 340
   distinction between contractual and non-contractual agreement 341
   doctrinal discourse of consideration 351–52
   interpretation clause 341–42
   organization of 341–43
   presumption of 'undue influence' 338
   Privy Council's interpretation of section 11 361–62
   rule of discretion 339–40
   self-determination and regulation 340–41
   Thorburn's remarks 337–39
   unilateral agreements 345–47
The Indian Contract Act (IX) of 1872 317–18
Indian Councils Act of 1861 387–88
indigo production in Bihar 327–30, 332–33, 334–35
individualism 54–56
   in municipal law 59
   rights of private person 55–56
Indo-Islamic juristic tradition in North India 2
   Chatterjee's *Negotiating Mughal Law* 3–4
infants' agreements 358–64
   voidability of 361, 363
institutional facts 62–66, 68–69, 70, 73–74
intellectual history of South Asia 71–72
Irish Land Act of 1870 299–300
Irish Land Act of 1881 299–300
Islamization 23–24

Jones, William 8, 413
   Digest of Hindu Law 320–21
judicial interpretation 52
juridical discourse 140

juridical individualism 57–58
jurisdictional pluralism 92
jurisprudential enquiry 79–80

Kadir, Abdul 455, 456–57, 464
Kedar Nath v. Gorie Mahomed 352–54
Kelsen, Hans 14, 61–62, 93, 118
  approach to duality problem 30–31
  basic norm 93–94, 118
Kennedy, Duncan 53
  concept of operativeness 141
  formulation of classical legal thought 55–56, 57–58
  idea of will theory 354–55
Khan, Muhammad Assim 240–42, 248
Khoti Settlement Act of 1880 284–85
King, Michael 119
Kosseleck, Reinhart 72–73
Kozlowski, Gregory 277
Kugle, Scott 466

Lakoff, George 62–63
Land Alienation Act of 1901 284–85, 306–7
The Land Systems of British India (Baden-Powell) 18
language problem in law 122–31
  denaturalizing perspective 126–27
  expert modes of discursive production 130
  idiomizations 128–29
  ordinary-language philosophy 126–27
  representational theory of language 124–25
  sociality of language 129
  verbalizable rule content of law 125–26, 127–28, 137
Law, Thomas 201–2
law as a validity-claiming system 89–90
Lawrence, Henry 385–86
Lawrence, John 309–10
law's ontologization 15–16
Lefebvre, Henri 136–37
legal historical enquiry 67
legal history, colonial rule 33–40
  Acts 42
  administration of justice 39–40

centralization of judiciary 42
'direct' *vs.* 'indirect' rule 34–35
dual judiciary 35
under East India Company 33–35
executive *vs.* judiciary rift 36
Hastings-Cornwallis system 37–39
Hastings' 'Plan for the Administration of Justice,' 36–37
legislative power 44–45
rise of legislative state 40–42, 45–46
Supreme Court of Judicature at Calcutta 35
legal pluralism 90–92
legal positivism 93–106
  connection between formalism and 99–100
legal primitivism 389
legal realism 97
legal scientism 46–48
legislative state, rise of 40–42, 45–46
Leiter, Brian 97–99
  notion of formalist determinacy 99
linguistic turn 8–9
Litowitz, Douglas 133
Lord North's Regulating Act of 1773 34–35
Ludden, David 234
Luhmann, Niklas 106
  concept of autopoiesis 118–19
  positivism 119–20
  social systemic 'coding' of actions 115–16
  socio-legal theory 112–18, 120
  temporal dimension 114–15
  tenable principles 118
Lukacs, Georg 134–35
Lyall, J. B., 399

Mackenzie, Holt 257, 260
Macnaghten, Francis 320–21
Madras Estates Land Act of 1908 284–85
Maine, Henry 8, 47–48, 264, 328–29, 334–35, 371–72, 395–96
  about 'progressive societies,' 405–6
  Ancient Law 377–78, 380, 382
  feudalism 405–6

INDEX

inter-familial relations 378
quasi-contract 356
standard of fairness 329–30
status 376–83
status/ contract distinction 382
view of status 376–83, 399–400, 405–6, 420–21
Malabar Tenancy Act of 1887 284–85
Malinowski, Bronislaw 88–89
Malthus, Thomas 258
Manual of Jurisprudence for Forest Officers 1882 291–92
marital relation
among Muslims 446–63
Ardaseer Cursetjee v. Perozeboye 435–46
Bombay Supreme Court's decision of 1853 439–40, 441
conjugal restitution doctrine 426–27
contractual theory 426
marital unions among *nair* caste 428–29
marriage as a status 432–35
in Muslim family 428–29
in Parsi religious community 435–46
politics of communitarian identity symbols 463–68
Rukhmabai case of 1886 425
in Tamil country 428–29
Markby, William 300–1
Marquis of Dalhousie 385–86
Marshall, Alfred 299–300
Marx, Karl
commodity fetishism 134–35
identity of land as rent 163–64
Massey, W. N., 330–31
Mayne, J. D., 413–16
Mazzolini, Sylvester 196–97
McNally, David 198
Mill, James 46–47, 255–56, 260
notion of rent 162–63
Mill, John Stuart 299–300
Mitchell, Timothy 70
Mohori Bibee v. Dhurmodas Ghose 362
monetizable value 163
Muhammadan Law of British India 419–20
Mulla, Dinshah 347

municipal law 58–59, 117
Munro, Thomas 197, 224–26, 227, 234
disagreement between Supreme Court and 246–47
distinction between property (in rent) and public revenue 245–46
distinction between small proprietors and small farmers 227–28
English Treasure by Foreign Trade 197
granting of *in'am-i altamgha* 239–46
'Minute on Altamgha Inams,' 222–23, 248–49
shadow concept of property 242–43
Muslim marriages 446–63
Abdul Kadir v. Salima Decision 451–63
Anis Begum v. Muhammad Istafa 478–81
Islamic concept of *'aqd* 454
Moonshee Buzloor Ruheem v. Shumsoonnissa Begum 446–50, 465–66
Muslim personal law and 445–46, 455–56, 466
politics of communitarian identity symbols 463–68
Muslim personal law 23–24

Naoroji, Dadabhai 281–82
naturalization of law 14–15, 79–85, 121–22
ought (or ought not) measurement 83–84
problems of 122–31
Neale, Walter 164–65
Negotiable Instruments Act 316–17
normative pluralism 92
normativity principle 2, 5–6, 14–15, 44–45
North, Lord 177–78, 195
North-Western Provinces Tenancy Act of 1901 284–85

'objective theory' of bilateral agreement 364
object-oriented ontology 75–76
occupancy property 303–4

ontologization of legal concepts 132–36, 246–54, 301–2, 313–14, 349–50, 369–70, 389–90, 420–21
  administrable quality of doctrinal discourse and 144–46
  of conjugal restitution 486–87
  discourse about law 147–52
  globalization of law and legal thought 152–55
  operative quality of doctrinal discourse and 141
operative quality of doctrinal discourse 140
  as binary 141–42
  connection between ontologization and 141
  continuum of operativeness 142–43
  vertical and horizontal dimensions 142–44
Oppenheim, Peter 137–38
oriental despotism 188, 190, 204–5
Orme, Robert 191–93
Oudh Tenancy Act of 1868 284–85
ownership 166, 303–4

Peasant Indebtedness Inquiry of 1895–96 337–38
peasantization 166
Peers, Douglas 176
permanent system
  Kanara coast 226–27
  Permanent Settlement in 1776 201–2, 205–11
  Permanent Settlement in 1793 174–75, 179, 187–88, 195, 208–9, 303
  value of permanency 217–18
Perry, Thomas Erskine 49–50, 435–36
personal law 22–23
personal law in British India 20–21
Petty, William 197
  depiction of economic value 198–99
  formulation of rent 198–99
Phillips, Arthur 305
Pinhey, Robert Hill 469–70, 472–73
Pitt the Younger, William 201
  India Act of 1784 34–35
plan positivism 103, 105–6

Plato 125–26
Pollock, Sir Frederick 8, 47–48, 264, 300–1, 347, 362
  English contract law 342
Polyani, Karl 70
positivism 14–15
positivist philosophy of law 82–83
post-modernism 71–72
post-structuralism 71–72, 73, 75–76, 123–24
premodern gemeinschaft 316–17
Pringle, Robert 258
private law 13–14
property rights 161–62, 262–64, 371
  Anglo-common-law 267–68, 270–71
  as a basis of legal right 302–14
  as bundle of sticks 271–72
  classical view 272–73
  colonial rule of property 164–65
  under Company's regime 269–70
  doctrinalizing the *zamindari* right 173–74
  legalization of 268–69
  legal *vs.* economic thought 170–72
  public-sphere discourse about 173–74
  as a unitary 170–72
proprietary right 18
  status and 400
proprietary rights 278–88
  agrarian rights 286–87
  degrees of 300–1
  of land rights 273–75, 289
  operativeness and administrability of 300–2
  revisionist view 289–90, 291
  subordinate rights 286–87, 291–92
  sub-proprietary tenures 296–97, 298–99
  of *taluqdars* 296
Proudhon, Pierre-Joseph 163–64
public law 14
Punjab, status in 385–93
  agricultural mortgages and 393–94
  ikrarnama tenures 398
  legal and administrative changes, role of 386–90
  of *niawadar* 393–94

as a non-regulation territory 385–86
of *pattidars* 398
political economy and 393
social role 394–95
systematization of custom 390–93
wajib-ul-arz document 390–91
Punjab civil code of 1854 387–88
Punjab Codification of Customary Law Conference in 1915 392–93
Punjab Courts Act (XIX of 1865) 387–88
Punjab Courts Act (XVII of 1877) 387–88
Punjab Laws Act (IV) of 1872 389–90
Punjab Tenancy Act of 1868 284–85

Qasim, Mir 174–75
quasi-contractual agreements 353–58, 361, 363, 364–65

racial regimes of ownership 7
Radcliffe-Brown, A. R. 88–89
raiyatwari system in Madras 221–22, 223–26, 257–58, 285–86, 303
 auctioning of *raiyatwari* rights 236
 in Chingleput 224–25, 234–35
 cultivator settlement 225–26
 differences between *zamindari* system and 233–34, 236
 distinction between small proprietors and small farmers 227–28
 in'am holdings of individuals 236–39
 as lease right 230–36
 method of *putcut* assessment 234–35
 notion of property as entitlement 228–29
 notion of property in rent 235–36
 patta document under 235
raiyatwari system of settlement 17–18
Ranade, Mahadev Govind 281–82
Rattigan, Henry A. B. 20–21, 49–50, 392–93
Rattigan, Sir William Henry 20–21, 49–50, 391, 392–93, 395–96
 A Digest of Civil Law for the Panjab 391
 doctrinal conception of status 382–83
Raz, Joseph 100–1

The Concept of a Legal System 96–97
 formal unity 101–2
 notion of legal system 96–97
 role of discretion in administrative decision-making 101
 rule scepticism 97
Read, Captain Alexander 224–25
 settlement in Baramahal 224–25
rebellion of 1857 5, 40–41, 270–71, 275, 323–24
Regulating Act of 1773 177–78, 195
Regulating Act of 1781 319–20
Regulation IX of 1833 258–59
Regulation VII of 1822 257–59, 260
Regulation XXXVII of the Bengal Code 239
reification of law 132–36
 role of linguistic resources 135
 as a subjective process 135
 use in socio-legal theory 133–34
religious pluralism 108
rent 162–64, 168
 as definitive form of Indian property in land 211–16
 differential 162–63
 dominion over 167–69, 195–96, 218
 Petty's formulation 197
 private property in 205–11
 property in land's rent 195–200
 Ricardian rent doctrine 254–64
'revenue jurisdiction' of civil courts 173
revisionism 288–300
Ricardo, David 162–63
 The Poverty of Philosophy 163–64
rights, definition 1
*rivaj-i-*am 390–91
Robb, Peter 302–3
Robinson, Sir William 334–35
Roe, Charles 20–21, 395–97
Roe, Sir Charles 392–93
 Tribal Law in the Punjab 392–93
Ross, Richard 91–92
rule of property 16
Ryle, Gilbert 126–27

Said, Edward 65–66
Sarkar, Tanika 427–28

538 INDEX

Sartori, Andrew 255, 303, 306-7
Savigny, Friedrich Carl von 48-49, 54, 294-95
Schmitt, Carl 196-97
Scott, James 6-7, 67-68, 152-53
Scrafton, Luke 188
  Bengal's governance by Company 174-78
  'Gentoo laws,' 190
  Reflections on the Government of Indostan 188, 191-92
Searle, John 73, 74
  account of institutional facts 74
  philosophy of society 73-75, 128-29
sedantarization 166
self-containment of law 82-83
self-limiting approaches to law 78
self-reflexivity of law 65-70
Shahjahan, Emperor 239
Shapiro, Scott 103, 104
  plan positivism 103, 105-6
Shephard, H. H., 343-44, 361-62, 363
  quasi ex contractu 357-58
Shore, John 211, 236-37
  identity between property and rent 215-16
  value of permanency 217-18
  zamindari settlement 214-16
Sircar, Shama 452-53
Smith, Adam 163, 210
  The Wealth of Nations 163, 205
social action 63-65
social construction 12, 70-71, 73, 123-24
  of woman refugee 11
social constructionism 76
social facts 63, 65-66, 68-69, 70, 73-74
social rationalization 301-2
sociological tradition of legal enquiry 88
sole proprietorship 204-5
South Asian legalities, self-reflexive difficulty in 65-69
Specific Relief Act (I of 1877) 472
State
  basic constitutional powers of 29-30, 31-32
  legal decision-making 45-46
  rights 44-45
state and non-state law 88-92
  territorial-bureaucratic national state 92
status
  Anglo-Muslim and Anglo-Hindu Law 430-35
  as an operative/ administrable concept 419-24
  classical law of 373, 379-80, 425-26
  connotative promiscuity of 404
  contrast between contract and 380-81
  distinction between 'Status Civilis' and 'Status Naturales,' 402-3
  doctrinal discourse of 383-85
  as doctrinally operative category 393-400
  in domestic relations 374-77
  Familienrecht, notion of 409-11
  Hindu caste/*varna* divisions 379-80
  les lois personelles, notion of 409-11
  'lifelong courses' of rights and duties 433-34
  Maineian view of 376-83, 399-400, 405-6, 420-21
  marriage as 432-35
  of marriage in Islam 423-24
  of mortgagee or proprietor 404
  in ordinary-language discourse 407
  ordinary-language discourse of 407
  as personal identity and ascriptive identity 402, 404-5, 413-15
  in personal law 407-19
  plural meanings 407-8
  property and 397-400
  in Punjab 385-93
  social group identity as 407
  as social role 394-95, 401-7
  status-as-ascriptive identity 409-11
  taxonomic heading of 432-33
Stephen, James Fitzjames 8, 47-48, 331-32, 333-34, 337, 341-42, 343
  interpretation clause 341-42
Stokes, Eric 490-91
  The English Utilitarians and India 162-63
  utilitarian ideology 255

Stokes, Whitley 337
Strange, Thomas 320–21

Tamanaha, Brian 87–88
Tax Farming Scheme of 1772 200–5, 412–13
Temple, Richard 335
　agrarian tenant's occupancy 312–13
　The Calcutta Review 309–10
　contractual freedom 311–12
　on Deccan Agriculturists' Relief Act 311
　India in 1880 309–10
　notion of will 312–13
Tenancy Act of 1885 302–3
territorial-bureaucratic national state 92
Thackeray, William 226–27
Thibaut, Anton 54
Third Anglo-Mysore war 224–25
Thompson, E. P., 134–35
Thorburn, Septimus 337–39, 395, 401–2
　Musalmans and Money-lenders in the Punjab 337–38
Thornhill, Chris 119
Transfer of Property Act of 1882 322–23
Travers, Robert 179–80
Treaty of Seringapatnam 224–25
Tuori, Kaius 389
Tupper, Charles 49–50, 391–92, 398, 401–2
　agricultural mortgages 393–94
　ikrarnama tenures 398
　Marhatta *chauth* 407–8
　Musalmans and Money-lenders in the Punjab 403
　Our Indian Protectorate 406
　Punjab Codification of Customary Law Conference in 1915 392–93
　Punjab Customary Law 391–92
　subcontinental order's inability 406
　'*ta kaim-i-chah*' tenures 394–95
Tupper, Charles Lewis 20–21

ud-Daulah, Siraj 174–75, 192–93
uniform civil code 23–24
utilitarianism 47–48, 254–64

Vansittart, Henry 191–93
verbalizable rule content of law 125–26, 127–28, 137
Vervaeke, John 62–63
vulgar formalism 98–99

Wallajah, Muhammad Ali Khan 240–41, 245–47
Wallajah, Nawab Ali Khan 242
Washbrook, David 237, 262
Watts, William 191–93
　Memoirs of the Revolution in Bengal 192–93
　notion of property 193
Weber, Max 63–65, 87, 101, 301–2, 407
West, Raymond 379–80
Wiener, Norbert 112–13
will, notion of 312–13, 316, 493
　duality of 348–54, 365–66
　juristic ideas 315–16
　as law of contract 318–19
　logically operative character 367–68
　mutuality of 343–47
　public 354–58
Wilson, Sir Roland 413–15
Wingfield, Sir Charles 305
　occupancy tenants in 305–6
Workman's Breach of Contract Act of 1859 323–27, 328–30, 332–33
　core values of collectivism 326–27
　criminal penalties 325–26
　punishments 324–25

Yardley, William 436–37

zamindari identity 404–5
zamindari system 17–18

www.ingramcontent.com/pod-product-compliance
Lightning Source LLC
Chambersburg PA
CBHW050832130125
20240CB00016B/20